CHINESE POLESTAR ASTROLOGY

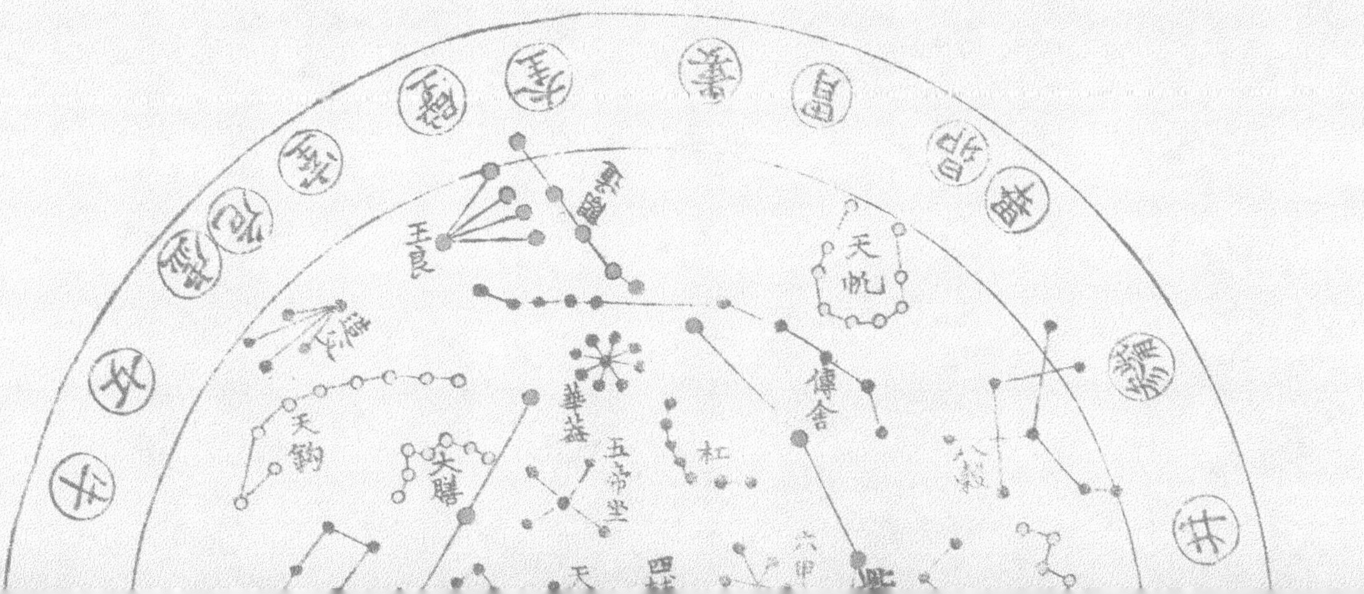

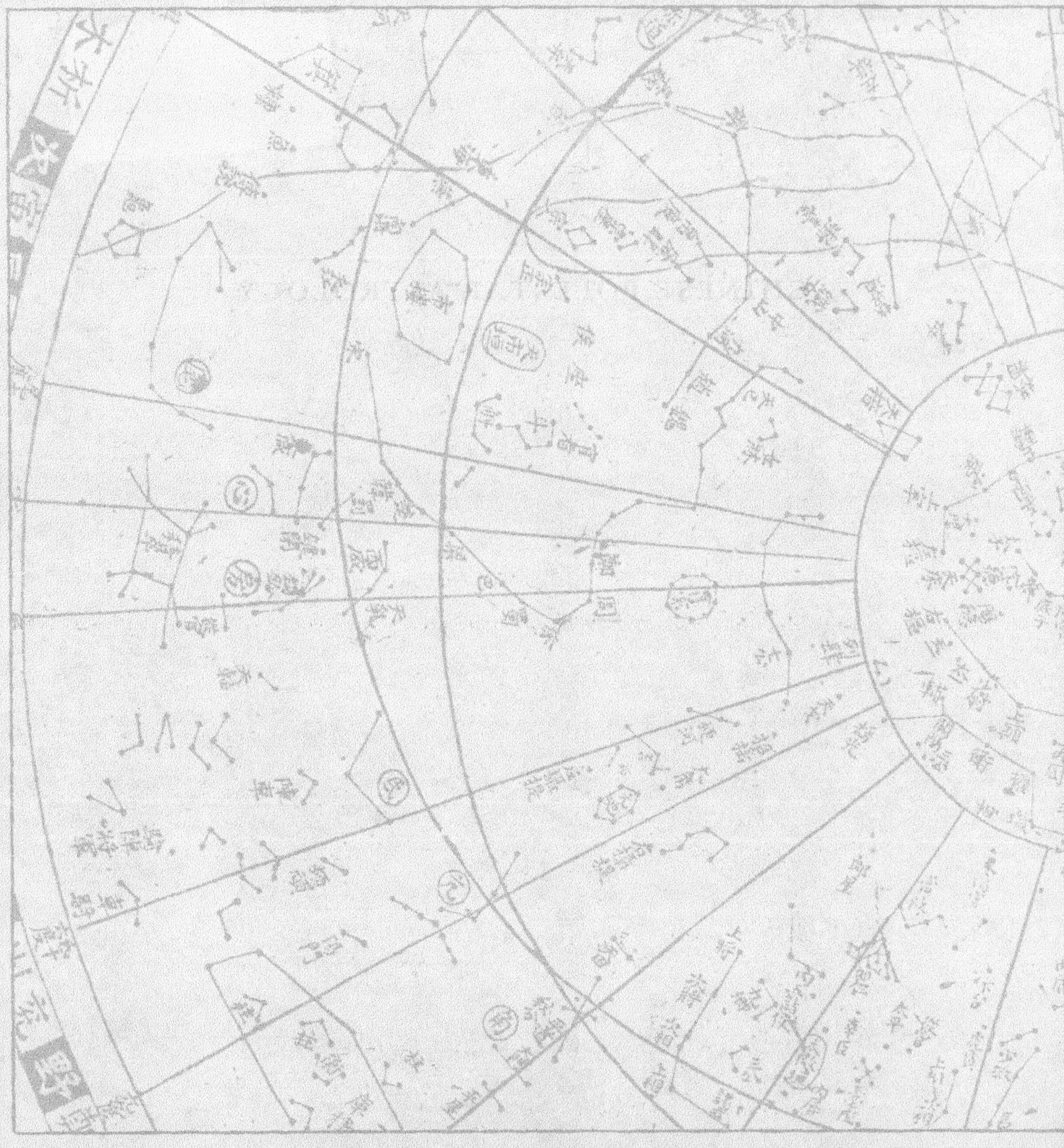

CHINESE POLESTAR ASTROLOGY

A PRACTICAL GUIDE TO DECODING THE SECRETS OF YOUR CHARACTER, INNER NATURE, AND FATE

GREGORY DAVID DONE

SHAMBHALA

SHAMBHALA PUBLICATIONS, INC.
2129 13th Street
Boulder, Colorado 80302
www.shambhala.com

Illustrations of the Twelve Animals by Bryan Chan

Cover art: from the collection Japanese Maps of the Tokugawa Era, Rare Books and Special Collections, University of British Columbia Library, G3190.1802 I8
Cover design: Daniel Urban-Brown
Interior design: Anna Becker

9 8 7 6 5 4 3 2 1

First Edition
Printed in the United States of America

Shambhala Publications makes every effort to print on acid-free, recycled paper.
Shambhala Publications is distributed worldwide by Penguin Random House, Inc., and its subsidiaries.

LIBRARY OF CONGRESS CATALOGING-IN-PUBLICATION DATA
Names: Done, Gregory David author
Title: Chinese polestar astrology: a practical guide to decoding the secrets of your character, inner nature, and fate / Gregory David Done.
Description: Boulder, Colorado: Shambhala, [2026] |
Includes bibliographical references. |
Identifiers: LCCN 2025049191 | ISBN 9781645473404 trade paperback
Subjects: LCSH: Astrology, Chinese
Classification: LCC BF1714.C5 D664 2026 | DDC 133.5—dc23/eng/20260105
LC record available at https://lccn.loc.gov/2025049191

The authorized representative in the EU for product safety and compliance is eucomply OÜ, Pärnu mnt 139b-14, 11317 Tallinn, Estonia, hello@eucompliancepartner.com.

Dedicated to all my teachers and to all the practitioners
who have kept the flame of knowledge alive

Thank you—may the teachings flourish!

To all my Ancestors, my parents, and the memory of my mother, Carol—
thank you for this precious human birth.
May we all be free of suffering and remain in boundless love!

To my beautiful, loving wife, Amber—
for your clarity, wisdom, and unbelievable integrity.
You are my inspiration, and I love you more than words can say!

CONTENTS

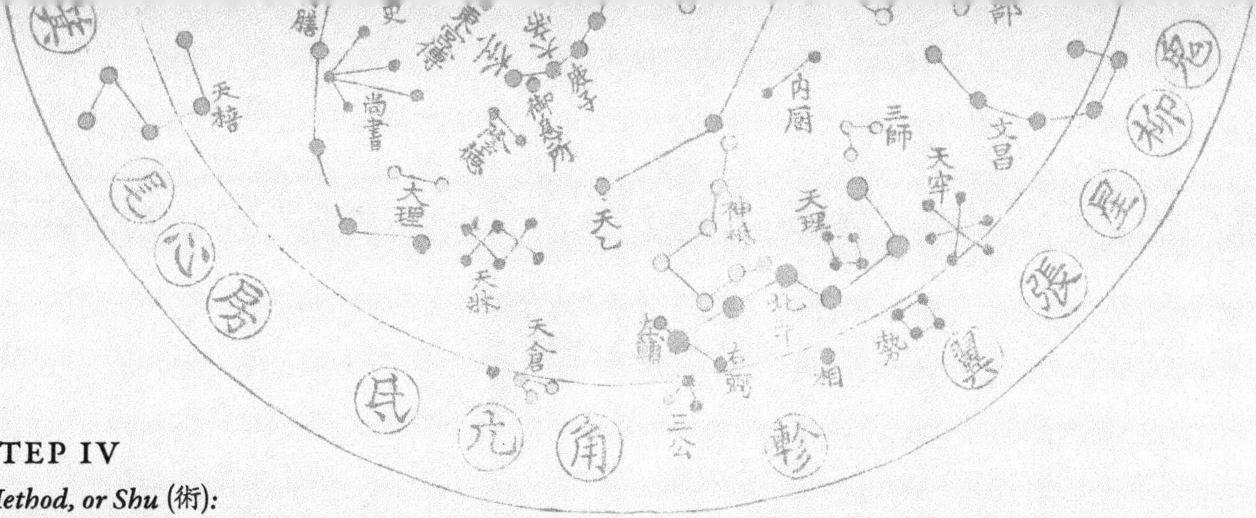

STEP IV

Method, or Shu (術): *Part Two–Fate, or Ming* (命)

STEP V

Fruition, or Guo (果)

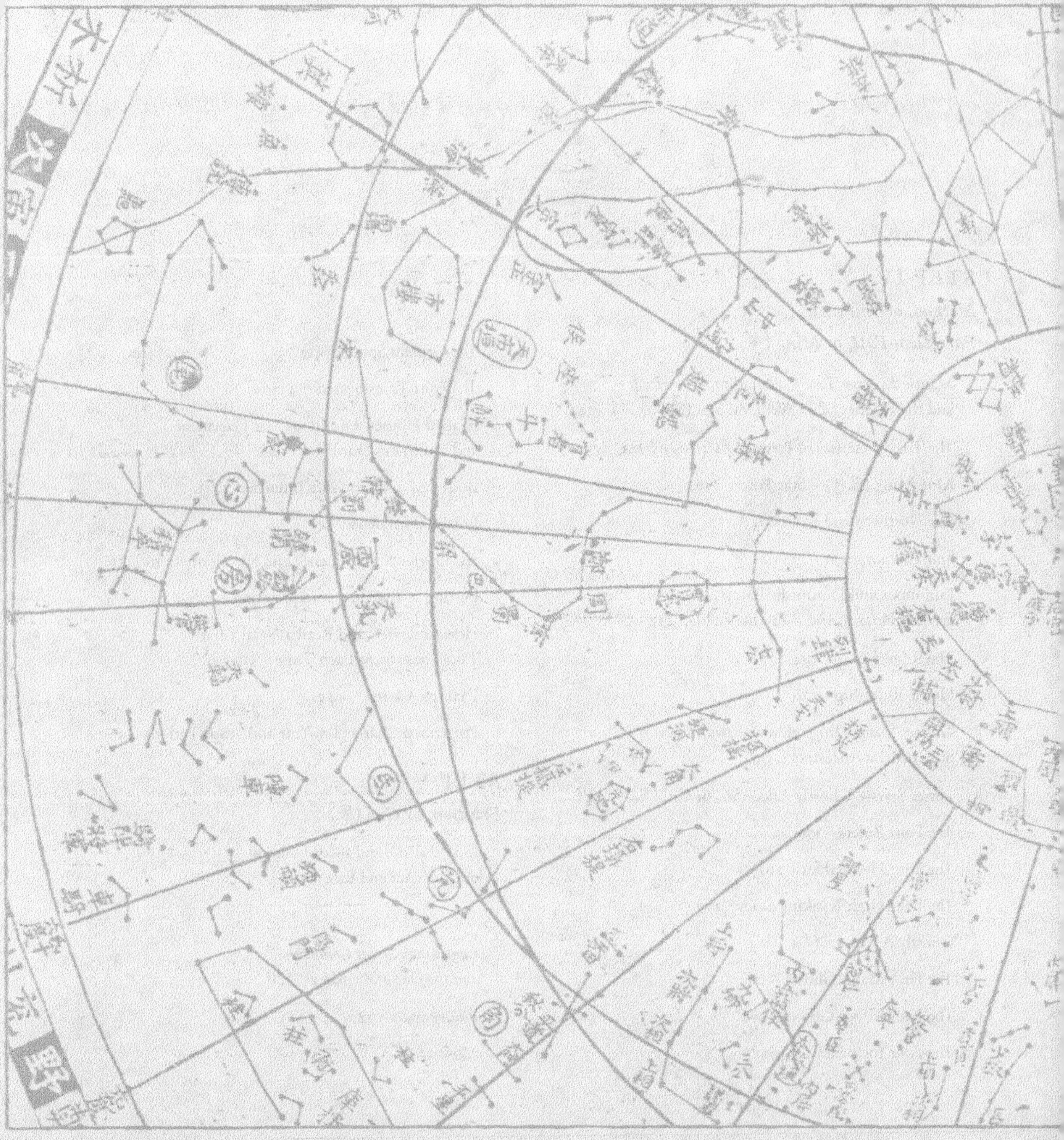

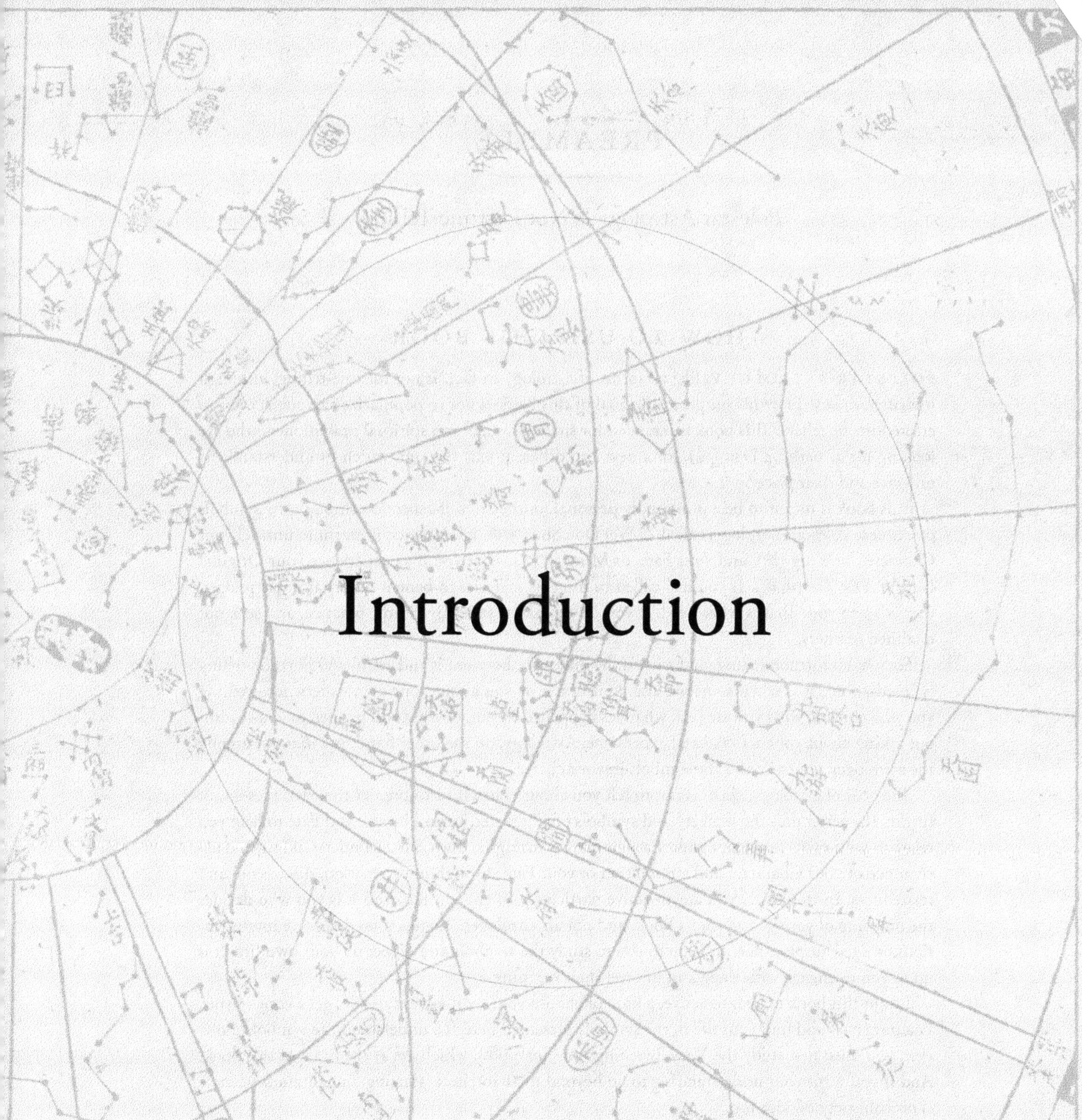

Introduction

PREAMBLE

Polestar Astrology Is Not Fortune-Telling!

HOW TO USE THIS BOOK

POLESTAR ASTROLOGY, like all forms of astrology in fact, is not fortune-telling, although it is often misused for this purpose. The goal of this book is not to popularize this subject nor to create fortune tellers. This book is intended for sincere seekers and spiritual practitioners who are looking for a "path," a Dao (道), for a new and different lens through which to understand the universe and their place in it.

This book is meant to be a profoundly personal journey of self-reflection through the symbols of Chinese Polestar Astrology, called Zi Wei Dou Shu (紫微斗數), which is meant to unravel your Character, or Xing (性), and your Fate, or Ming (命), so that you may experience your Original Nature, Dao De (道德). If you feel called to use this material to benefit others as an astrologer, that is up to you. That is what I did. If you do so, take it seriously. Study, practice, and seek out qualified teachers.

So, what is fortune-telling, and what is the difference between it and astrology? Fortune-telling is "prediction"; it is when someone else pontificates at you about your own experience—telling you who you are, what you are like, what has happened to you, or what will happen to you—without asking about your actual, lived experience. Astrology, on the other hand, is a *dialogue* among the astrologer, yourself, and the symbols in your chart.

The goal of astrology, then, is not to tell you about yourself or to predict the past, present, or future. Rather, it uses the imagery and symbols of Character, Inner Nature, and Fate to help you relate to your own experience and, through playful dialogue, draw out an understanding and acceptance of your Character and a resolution of your Fate through interpretation, discussion, and relatedness. In this sense, you are an active participant in the journey, and it is you who decides the meaning of your chart—not a book, and not an astrologer. There are no definitive interpretations or fixed auspices here. It is up to you to study the symbols and reflect on your own life. It is up to you to engage with them and unravel their meaning.

I want this book to be interactive, a kind of choose-your-own-adventure. So, get a copy of your Polestar chart and find your life in the symbols presented here. To understand the symbols, however, you must first study the View Teachings, or Guan (觀), which are at the heart of this book. And if you want your understanding to go beyond mere intellect, starting a meditation practice is probably a good idea too.

LIU MING AND THE CHINESE TRADITION

Fate is not actually created (has no beginning) but is the predisposition to recreate and solidify Fated patterns. The ever-present option/disposition to openly express our true nature is freedom. Together, Fate and freedom constitute the naturally dynamic dimension we are in.

—Liu Ming[1]

IN THIS BOOK, I will teach you everything I have learned about how to follow Chinese Polestar Astrology (Zi Wei Dou Shu) as a spiritual path. And, if you're interested, this book will teach you something about how to be an astrologer. First and foremost, though, this is a book about what Confucianism calls self-cultivation, or Xiu Shen (修身), meditation, and the development of wisdom through the study of astrological symbols concerning what the Chinese call Yuanfen (缘分), or the feeling of Fated affinity. With proper study and this book as a companion, you should be able to sit down with friends and family, and perhaps one day with clients, and read their Natal Charts. However, you must first have a deep understanding of your own, so this book is, first and foremost, about how to read and study your own Natal Chart and relate to the symbols found within.

The style of this book is called Fu (賦) in Chinese literature, which means "to compose or rhapsodize." Throughout the Han dynasty, court officials and poets composed special "Fu on things," called Yongwu Fu (詠物賦), in which they extensively described and cataloged new and unusual things. These "Fu on things" became a significant genre that covered many instruments, objects, and phenomena. So, this book is my Zi Wei Dou Shu Fu, my contribution to what Liu Ming called the "Chinese Tradition." As such, it is profoundly personal and represents my own take on the subject.

This is not a how-to book per se, nor is it meant to be a complete or comprehensive guide to the whole tradition, which would be impossible to produce. Instead, I mean this to be a kind of practice text meant to communicate the heart of these symbols as I have come to understand them. This could be called the Path, or "Dao," of Astrology. Indeed, the study of astrology is a path and a lifelong practice, and its true meaning comes to fruition only when you integrate these symbols into your life and let them speak through your direct experience. With consistent practice, you will eventually see life through these symbols and, in so doing, rediscover everything as an expression of the rhythms of cyclical time. You will discover that these symbols are endlessly revelatory and universal in their application to human life.

This book is an amalgamation—the result of thousands of hours spent studying the recorded lectures and notes on Polestar Astrology left behind by the enigmatic Daoist teacher Liu Ming, among other sources, merged with my own experience and understanding, which I have developed by practicing these teachings and offering Polestar Astrology readings for over ten years.

However, I want to be clear that I am not a "lineage holder" or "inheritor" of this tradition, nor do I represent the school Liu Ming established[2] or presume to represent him or his teachings in any definitive way. In fact, I never met the man! But I'll get to that later. The concept of the teacher–guru relationship and lineage is a minefield in modern times, for American culture now lacks the framework for traditional religious communities, and Westerners are not equipped to handle the feudalism inherent in traditional South, Central, and East Asian religions. Most attempts to construct and maintain such lineages in the West have been rife with sexual and political scandals, full of abuse and power dynamics that undermine the whole point of lineage in the first place.

Ming himself began training priests in an Orthodox Daoist lineage, but later in his life he abandoned this mission for a more personal, "animist" approach with a more egalitarian and universal outlook. He often joked that he never intended to create a "church." He never wanted to be the leader, the guru, the lama, the daoshi, or anything like that. He was affectionately known to many of his students simply as Lao Ge (老哥), which means "older brother." He did, however, speak in the role of teacher—often ad nauseam, and frequently digressing into long-winded profundities, and his students adored him for it.

The teachings here do not belong to Liu Ming or to me; they belong to what Ming called the "Chinese Tradition," which is eclectic and syncretic, a blend of Daoism, Confucianism, Buddhism, and the animist pre-Chinese traditions. The word *Chinese* in this case does not refer to one religion, ethnicity, language, or place. Daoism, for example, predates "China." Buddhism came from India but disappeared there following the Islamic invasions and colonialism of the twelfth century; it took five hundred-plus years for Buddhism to become Chinese after it was first introduced. Classical Chinese Medicine digested medical traditions from all over the Middle East and Central and South Asia and has since spread all over East Asia. Confucianism is the only tradition that can be called uniquely Chinese, but it too has spread all over East Asia to become culturally diverse. The point is that there are no pure original teachings anywhere.

Polestar Astrology developed relatively late, during the Tang and Song dynasties, as a response to the Indian astrology brought to China by Buddhist monks. It synthesizes many elements from Persian and Indian astrology. That said, it is important to state that these teachings come from Asia, and their cultural origins should be respected. I have done my best to do so.

The tradition has an unspoken agreement that no one should ever write a how-to book on this subject, lest they be cursed, and Liu Ming did seem to be of two minds about sharing these teachings. On the one hand, he was deeply reluctant to share anything, especially on the internet. On the other hand, I believe he shared the attitude of many modern Tibetan spiritual teachers who openly share "secret" teachings—an attitude that amounts to "screw it." Ancient traditions are dying, and few seem to care. We can no longer count on the tradition of lineage to preserve inner and secret teachings. So, many who hold these teachings have been sharing them freely over the past century, like throwing a handful of seeds into the wind, hoping that perhaps one will take root somewhere and grow.

The traditional fear of secret teachings being taught publicly is mitigated by making them an "open secret." In other words, either you get it or you don't. A great master may impart the most profound teaching on the nature of reality to you, but if you are not prepared and do not study and practice diligently, it amounts to nothing more than beautiful nonsense. And while many people need the reins of a traditional lineage to keep them from going off the rails, it is simply impossible to police all the charlatans, of which there will always be many.

So, I am putting everything I know in this book. To the best of my ability, I intend to give you a map, a vehicle, and keys to explore your life and the nature of reality through this unique wisdom tradition. This is traditionally called the Threefold Logic—View Teachings, or Guan (觀); Method, or Shu (術); and Fruition, or Guo (果)—which we will explore in the following chapters. If you have the capacity, or

Character—Xing (性)—and the Fate—Ming (命)—then perhaps you can follow this path and experience Da Yuan (大圓), or Great Completion—the resolution of Fate and the experience of human freedom.

LIU MING

As this book will expound on the View Teachings, Method, and Fruition of Chinese Polestar Astrology as I learned them from the recorded lectures and writings of the late Liu Ming, naturally, to honor him, I should begin this book by saying something about Liu Ming, about myself, and about how I came to learn this form of astrology.

When asked about his life story, Liu Ming said, "The thing is: nobody should really be too interested in anybody else's biography. It's hard enough trying to find value in our own experience; finding value or meaning in someone else's story is absurd."[3]

With that in mind, I'll keep his story to a minimum. Liu Ming was a Euro-American, born Charles Edmund Belyea on September 17 in the Year of the Yin Fire Pig, 1947, in Waltham, Massachusetts. In the late seventies he lived as a Buddhist monk in Taiwan, where he met a Daoist teacher who legally adopted him and gave him lineage transmission from the Liu family and the name Liu Ming. He became the first American to identify as a Daoist priest and to teach religious Daoism.[4]

In 1984, Ming helped to found Five Branches, a college of Traditional Chinese Medicine in Santa Cruz, California, and served on its faculty for twelve years. Before his death in 2015, Ming cofounded and taught through many organizations and newsletters, including Five Branches; Orthodox Daoism in America (renamed Da Yuan Circle, or DYC); the *Frost Bell Newsletter*, which presented his teachings to an academic audience; the Daoist Studies Institute; and the Golden Gate Feng Shui School, among others. In his last thirty years, he served as a beloved and often enigmatic teacher, offering instruction in Buddhist and Daoist meditation, ritual, contemplative and practical alchemy,[5] Chinese Polestar Astrology, Chinese Medicine, and traditional Chinese dietetics.

When Liu Ming changed the name of the Orthodox Daoism in America organization to Da Yuan Circle, Ming was deemphasizing the importance of lineage in order to draw on a broader Daoist-Buddhist vision[6] and beginning to emphasize a more "animist" approach to the spiritual path. This later approach is the one I found in his recorded lectures and the one that inspires this book. While I did not study directly under Ming, and I do not claim any official connection to him or his lineage, I do feel that, in some way, I have found the same inspiration that Ming found through his teachers.

DHARMA BODHI

There is a timeline from Liu Ming's life that is also worth noting here, which intersects with the life of my primary spiritual teacher, Dharma Bodhi, and therefore segues into my story of how I came to these teachings.

Legally named Kolbjörn Martens, Dharma Bodhi is a Euro-American who lived in Australia from the early eighties until the late nineties. During that time, he traveled extensively to India, where he studied with Indian gurus. He formally received a lineage of Shaiva Tantric Yoga in 1996, when he was given the name Dharmanidhi. In the mid-nineties, soon after he began formally teaching Tantra Yoga, Dharma Bodhi discovered Liu Ming's teachings and began using Ming's book *Dragon's Play* as a textbook with his students. The Twelve-Stage View of human life presented in that book would correspond with a similar Twelve-Stage View that Dharma Bodhi would then receive from his Indian teachers. (Liu Ming later gave Dharma the twelve paintings commissioned for *Dragon's Play*, which he still has today.)

Dharma Bodhi was given a mandate by his gurus to return to the United States to teach for at least seven years, so he moved his teaching operation from Australia to Berkeley, California, where he founded the Tantric College of America, later renamed Yoga Mandala.[7] Dharma lived in the Bay Area for seven years before moving to Thailand to found Kailash Akhara, a permaculture farm and yoga retreat center. During these seven years, Dharma studied closely with Liu Ming, and they became good friends. Da Yuan Circle and Yoga Mandala would interact for many years, and they shared many students. Dharma and Ming lived as neighbors in Oakland during that time (three years of which Mayor Jerry Brown lived in the same building as the famed loft where Ming lived and taught until he died).

From 2004 to 2005, Dharma Bodhi studied Daoist meditation with Liu Ming using Ming's excellent translation of the Daode Jing.[8] Concurrently, he participated in Ming's first two-year Daoist Polestar Astrology course and was able to sit in on some of Ming's private client readings. Dharma also completed training in the Zhou Yi (Book of Changes) as translated by Liu Ming and received transmission of many other Liu family texts, as well as pith instructions on alchemical practices, Dream Yoga, Tomb Affairs, and Zuo Wang. Liu Ming and Dharma Bodhi also cotaught a summer retreat on the Twelve-Stage View Teachings at Pema Ösel Ling Dzogchen retreat center in 2005.[9]

MY STORY

This brings me to my part of the story. Who am I, and how did I come to these teachings?

I was born with a deep, insatiable desire for wisdom, God, awakening, enlightenment—whatever you want to call it. For as long as I can remember, I have wanted to know and experience directly some "ultimate" nature of reality, and have been drawn to meditation practice to understand the nature of the mind, suffering, human nature, and so on.

Although I grew up in America, I was not raised Christian and therefore escaped some of the burdens of that worldview. My father presented me with a somewhat secular worldview and said it was up to me to study everything the world offers and decide what is true for myself. He did, however, study many spiritual traditions, both Eastern and Western, and had an extensive library filled with the work of poets, philosophers, and mystics from all over the world.

As a child, I read extensively from these books, and my father and I would talk about them regularly. I was most interested in the philosophies of India, Hinduism, and Sufism, most notably the life and teachings of Meher Baba. My father was deeply interested in the works of a Western mystic named Walter Russell, and my father and I spoke of these two often. Together, they formed the basis of my worldview as a child.

My paternal grandfather, Clark, was a Western astrologer deeply interested in ancient wisdom traditions. He studied with an astrologer named Marc Edmund Jones and, in his lifetime, did over 10,000 astrology readings. I only met him once, and in that meeting he read my astrology chart, which profoundly impacted me. He trained my father in astrology as well, and although my father never did readings professionally, he was deeply influenced by astrology and raised me with an appreciation for it as a symbol science. In this sense, I am a third-generation astrologer, and you could say the practice runs in my blood.[10]

My childhood was more or less stable, as my father worked hard to make sure I had a roof over my head and went to good schools. Emotionally, it was rough, as my mother had a lot of undiagnosed mental health challenges due to her abusive childhood, and my father often had to work two jobs to make ends meet. They argued a lot, and as an only child, I was alone most of the time. Because of this, I developed a powerful sense of self-reliance and searching for meaning, as well as a rich inner world where I read, studied, wrote, and of course, goofed off.

Around the age of fourteen, while I was riding my bike around my neighborhood in Lafayette, California, I stumbled upon the Chan Buddha Gate Monastery, which had just been established by Master Wei-Chueh in the lineage of the Great Master Xuyun (虛雲) to serve the growing Taiwanese population in the area. I recalled having seen a minivan full of monks in brown robes with shaved heads driving around my neighborhood and wanting to know where they came from.

I soon began to attend meditation classes and Dharma talks given by the head monk at Buddha Gate Monastery. Other students and I learned the practice of Zuochan (Jap. *zazen*), and we would sit for an hour in nonconceptual meditation, followed by walking meditation that would get faster and faster following the rhythm of a drum, then stop suddenly. The meditation instruction was remarkably simple, primarily focusing on posture and on being aware of awareness. We would then go to the teaching hall, where the head monk taught lessons on the basics of Buddhism. Although I have now studied and practiced many forms of Buddhism, this tradition has remained my primary practice for over twenty-three years, and I visit this monastery whenever I go home.

After graduating from high school, I moved out of my parents' house and worked menial retail jobs for three years before deciding that college was the only way for me to have a future. Over the next fifteen years, I would earn an associate's degree in architecture, a bachelor's degree in English education, a master's in Indo-Tibetan Buddhist studies with an emphasis in Buddhist history, and a doctorate in Classical Chinese Medicine. I never had a clue what to "do" with my life in the traditional sense, so I just kept studying my passions and hoped it would work out.

A severe bout of anxiety and depression at the age of twenty set me on a serious meditation path, and I began attending ten-day Vipassana courses led by S. N. Goenka and sought out as many Buddhist teachings as I could find. I was deeply influenced by the teacher Shinzen Young and would eventually begin to study Tibetan Buddhism through teachers like Alan Wallace and Reggie Ray at Naropa University.

This is where Liu Ming and Dharma Bodhi come into the picture. In 2010, at the age of twenty-three, while studying at San Francisco State and living in Oakland, I met Dharma Bodhi. He had recently moved to Thailand to establish the teaching center Kailash Akhara, but he regularly returned to the Bay Area to teach at Yoga Mandala.

At first, Dharma Bodhi deeply bewildered me, as I was heavily identified as a Buddhist at the time. He was teaching Shaiva Tantric Yoga and challenging the narrative of Tibetan Tantric Buddhism—namely, the myth that Tantra came from Buddhism, when in fact it originated from the Shaiva religion.[11] He was also unlike any other spiritual teacher that I had ever encountered: He was a trash-talking, weight-lifting, catch-wrestling meat eater who taught a "householder" path that was radically different from the Buddhism I was practicing.

Despite my objections, he rattled my world, and I would study his teachings intensely over the next three years and take formal Tantric initiation in 2013, just after moving to Boulder to study at Naropa University. At Naropa, I completed my degree in Indo-Tibetan Buddhist studies, learning Sanskrit and Tibetan language and studying intensely with many Buddhist teachers from the Shambhala Institute, the Nithartha Institute, and the Dharma Ocean Foundation in the lineage of Trungpa Rinpoche, including Judith Simmer-Brown (for whom I served as a teacher's assistant), Reggie Ray, Acharya Lama Tenpa Gyaltsen, Phil Stanley, and Lama Sarah Harding, among others. During this time, I also continued to study with Dharma Bodhi as my primary teacher, and I went through a kind of identity crisis, as I was studying both Tantric Shaivism and Buddhism, which seemed historically at odds. I wrote my master's thesis on this very subject.

During that time, I also began to study Liu Ming's teachings, which Dharma Bodhi referenced frequently. The first lecture I heard from Ming would change my world forever. At the time, however, I was too deep into my Tantric studies to make his teachings a priority. Ming would float on my periphery, intriguing me deeply, until eventually I developed a deep desire to meet him.

After graduating from Naropa, I wrote Dharma Bodhi a letter formally requesting to become an *acharya*, or lineage holder, of his tradition. He accepted, and I soon moved to Thailand to live and study with him as a formal acharya in training. During this time, I lived in the jungles of Phu Ruea on a permaculture farm called Kailash Akhara, an intentional community founded by Dharma Bodhi for the study and practice of Tantric Shaivism and Bönpo Dzogchen. Kailash Akhara was home to one of the largest outdoor yoga temples in Asia—one of only two dedicated to Macchanda Natha—and to an official Bönpo Dzogchen temple officiated by His Holiness the 33rd Menri Trizin.

Living there was one of the most transformational and challenging times of my life. During this time, I deepened my study of Jyotish, Indian astrology, and discovered that astrology is an integral part of my path. Here, at the suggestion of Dharma Bodhi, I pursued and became deeply interested in Liu Ming's teachings on Polestar Astrology, revitalizing my interest in him as a teacher, and became dedicated to meeting him and studying with him. I downloaded every one of Ming's recorded lectures from his website and began to dedicate all my time to his teachings.

However, although I greatly hoped to meet and study with him in person, I soon learned that Liu Ming had been diagnosed with late-stage stomach cancer. He passed away within a month. I remember the day after he died: I was at Dharma Bodhi's house, and Dharma told me he had felt Ming go during the night. Dharma's then wife, Ajama, then received a message confirming that Ming had passed. I was distraught to learn that I would never have the chance to meet someone who was impacting my life so deeply. I resolved to study his legacy and receive as many teachings as possible from Dharma and Ajama, who were close to him. Ajama had many journals of notes from his lectures that she let me study.

Unfortunately, the yoga center was struggling to stay open due to financial difficulties and was in the beginning stages of what would be a long process of closing. I was working full-time as a volunteer to help keep the doors open, but with no income, I was burning through my savings. After nearly a year in Thailand, I realized I had to return home. I made the decision to leave, but I had no idea what I would do next.

Around this time, I met my primary Chinese Medicine teacher, Bryan McMahon. Bryan had been living, studying, and working in China for the past ten years. Despite being a Westerner, Bryan had completed his degree in Chinese and had worked as a doctor of Classical Chinese Medicine in Shanghai. He studied herbalism deeply with a profound teacher named Li Xin and acupuncture with Jacques Pialoux, a key figure in the transmission of the French–Indochina lineage of acupuncture. Bryan had met Dharma Bodhi in Shanghai the previous year and begun studying with him. After this, Bryan started coming to Thailand.

Bryan presented a vision of Chinese medicine that inspired me deeply. Bryan and I became good friends and traveled together on a pilgrimage to India. Soon he would return to the United States to teach at the National University of Natural Medicine (NUNM).

Ming's presentation of the Chinese Tradition, too, included Classical Chinese Medicine, Polestar Astrology, and Daoism as an integrated worldview. All this would sow the seeds of the next ten years of my life. Before returning to the United States, I did a monthlong solitary retreat in Thailand in a secluded beach bungalow. During this retreat, I studied Ming's teachings on Polestar Astrology, day and night, and studied my own chart intensively while practicing nonconceptual meditation, or Zuo Wang.

Upon returning home, I was again at a loss about what to do with my life, so I kept studying Ming's teachings (while applying for jobs I did not want). It was then, in 2015, that I began to write my blog on Chinese astrology, titled *Tiger's Play*, which is a nod to Ming's book *Dragon's Play*[12] and to the year I was born, the Year of the Fire Tiger.

I never intended to do astrology readings, but one day I casually mentioned to a friend that I had been studying Chinese Polestar Astrology, and she asked me to give her a reading. I was reluctant, but agreed, as I thought it would be good practice. It went so well that she paid me despite my offering it for free, and I enjoyed it too. I figured I was onto something, so I started offering readings on my website. I continued to do readings and amused myself by writing the blog on Chinese astrology, both of which came naturally, as I loved the teachings.

At this point, I had three college degrees with no value in today's economy, yet I had amassed hundreds of thousands of dollars in student loan debt. No career made any sense to me, so after a lot of soul searching, I found myself at a crossroads with all signs pointing toward Chinese medicine. So, I applied to the doctoral program in Classical Chinese Medicine at the school where my friend Bryan McMahon was about to begin teaching: NUNM in Portland, Oregon. I was accepted, so I moved there and spent the next five years closely apprenticing with him and with many other fine teachers, including Heiner Fruehauf, Brandt Stickley, and Joon Hee Lee.

During my five years at NUNM, I continued to study Ming's teachings day and night, and I continued to do astrology readings all over the world. Since 2015, I have done hundreds of readings with people in many countries, including Australia, India, China, Germany, Taiwan, and Thailand. Since then, I have also continued to write my blog and, since 2017, do public talks on the Chinese New Year. My blog became the basis for this book.

I graduated with a doctorate in Classical Chinese Medicine and have been in clinical practice in Washington state ever since. I am now devoted to the full-time practice of Chinese medicine and have little time to do astrology readings. However, Chinese astrology deeply informs my medical practice, and Polestar Astrology is, and always will be, a central part of my spiritual path. I hope to impart the wisdom I have gained from these practices over the past decade and from the many hundreds of astrology readings I have done.

At this point, I should point out that my trajectory over the past ten years has been driven by the teachings of Liu Ming. It is odd that a man I never met should influence my life so powerfully that I would write a book about it, but without Ming, I would never have pursued Chinese astrology or medicine, and I would not be where I am today. Clearly I am Fated to practice these subjects; I cannot imagine things having gone any other way. I must also thank my root teacher, Dharma Bodhi, for introducing me to Ming and for continuing to inspire and guide me.

In many ways, I am glad that Ming and I never met. Of course, I admire him deeply and have tremendous gratitude for the teachings he left behind. I adore the personality I found in his recordings, especially his profound wisdom and his humor. His was an odd mix of silliness and intensity with a wry and almost wrathful wisdom. I have studied with many spiritual teachers, but Ming's knowledge, insight, and eloquence are singular, and his teachings changed my life and opened my perspective in ways that no others have.

The Buddhist term *prajna*, penetrating insight, certainly applies to Liu Ming. He had an unmatched ability to express the heart of things, often called the "pith" instruction, in direct and accessible language designed to point directly at the foibles of Westerners. His wisdom had a lightness and sense of relaxation that revealed how nuts we all are, as he would say, "pressing our faces against the windshield to get there faster." He seemed to embody the much-lauded Chinese ideal of Wuwei (無為), which we can translate as "no effort" or, in plain English, "relax."

Part of me is deeply pained that we never met in person. I have spent thousands of hours listening to Liu Ming's talks, so in a way I feel like I know the man, but I do not. I suppose this is no odder than someone today studying the works of Carl Jung or any other deceased historical figure. However, I have spoken to many people who did know Ming, and many of them agree that, in the end, it is probably best that we never met. If I had, then who knows what kinds of emotions, hang-ups, entitlements, resentments, and so on about our relationship I might have had. Not knowing him has allowed me to approach the teachings purely, in a sense, without personalities getting in the way. Of course, I can never ask him questions or thank him, but I think it all happened the way it was supposed to.

THE TEACHINGS IN A NUTSHELL

If I were to summarize the core of Liu Ming's teachings as I have come to understand them, it would be this: Do what you need to do to die well. Whatever you do not finish is the Ghost you will become. Ming's teachings and Polestar Astrology often center on the Chinese term Gui (鬼), or Ghost, which we will define in detail later.

In short, the whole subject of Polestar Astrology is to understand how we are possessed by the dead. We are the warm, wiggling end of a long line of dead people. Life is immortal. We do not stop. Nothing stops, for nothing is ever created or destroyed. Everything is a pattern in flux, Yi (易)—in the process of changing into something else. At birth, we inherit everything unfinished from the bodies of our Ancestors. The Polestar Pantheon of Stars and the Currents of Fate, or Mingyun (命運), represent images and symbols, called Tian Xiang (天象), of our Ancestral inheritance from both our Beneficial Ancestors and the other ones (Ghosts). Polestar Astrology, then, offers us a map of our Ancestral Fate so that we can resolve our inheritance and die well, without "unfinished business."

We can summarize Ming's teaching in one word: *Relax*. Relax, because no "self" possesses Fate. Self and world are a strenuous mirage generated by fantasy. By rushing around trying to maintain a self, we become living Ghosts, and we die as a Ghost when we fail to realize the selflessness of our situation before we die. The following book will offer a path to understanding the complex dynamics of Character, Inner Nature, and Fate so that we can liberate our Ghosts and be free of both self-hatred and self-cherishing, so that we can live and die well, freeing our Ancestors and descendants of burden. This is again called Da Yuan (大圓), or "Great Completion," which is the resolution of Fate and the experience of our natural state of Freedom.

Completion or resolution is different for everyone. There is no one-size-fits-all on the spiritual path, and often we are our own worst enemy. Sometimes, our capacity and opportunity do not align the way we want, and sometimes, we squander our energy pursuing a life we are not fated for. Sometimes, we feel lost and without purpose, like a bag blown around in the wind. And, as an old saying goes, if a man knows not to which port he sails, no wind is favorable. Sometimes, it helps to have a map to guide your sails, and Polestar Astrology offers us a powerful, personalized one.

A word of warning, though: This map is not geared toward happiness per se but, again, toward completion and resolution. Completion has little to do with getting what you want, but is perhaps about getting what you need. Astrology does not provide "answers" so that we can stop looking; it only offers us questions for self-reflection and symbols for contemplation. These symbols act as guides, connecting us to the wisdom of our Beneficial Ancestors. Astrology can be bewildering if you get too attached, so relax. If you find yourself obsessed with or looking for answers, I offer the best advice a teacher ever gave me: Live your life, and look at the chart after.

Ultimately, everything is self-resolving, Ziran (自然), but with some practice, we can perhaps experience freedom and resolution before we die or at least relax the bitter edges of Fate enough that we do not pass on our burdens to future generations.

This practice has immensely benefited my life, and I hope you greatly benefit from this work!

A NOTE ON TRANSLATION AND SYMBOLS

ALTHOUGH THIS BOOK IS INSPIRED BY ANCIENT CHINA, I insist that its core teachings are universal and transcend time and culture. In this book, I hope to reveal the secular nature of Chinese cosmology as universal and unlimited in its applications to human life.

However, I cannot separate these teachings from their traditional and cultural origins. In my experience, modern culture and the English language do not have the same depth and profundity, and many of these ideas cannot be translated. Although the English language has the most extensive vocabulary on Earth, it has no equivalent for Chinese ideas such as Dao (道), Qi (氣), Yinyang (陰陽), Huntun (餛飩), and so on. Therefore, I will leave these terms in their original language and in Pinyin and define them experientially to help bring them further into the modern English lexicon. When it comes to the names of the stars, like Zi Wei (紫微), I will include the dictionary definition of each character and explain how and why we translate the names as we do, in the hope that this clarifies the teachings.

Chinese is a symbolic language, and its written system is based on pictograms. Each character is a picture, a symbol, with layers of meaning and depth that English words do not have. We study these symbols' cultural, spiritual, and historical associations to get at something nonconceptual that lies beneath them.

The ultimate unknowable Dao (道), which is beyond form, manifests into form through pure symbols, called Xiang (象), which then express dynamic patterns of movement called Qi (氣), which then appear or manifest as the myriad forms called Xing (形), and from here these forms have function, or application, called Qi (器). The Chinese sciences are symbol sciences, and therefore focus on first understanding Xiang (象), symbol, for this is the first manifestation of duality from the non-dual Dao, and everything that we can perceive flows from 象. Symbols are the bridge between the dual and non-dual.

This book is, therefore, focused on understanding symbols through associative thinking. Done with a light touch, everything flows through association from the symbolic to the practical. Symbol study is a playful act; everything presented here is playful. There are no definitive translations or interpretations. I invite you to play in the symbols that follow, for as Ming said, it is all Dragon's play, or in my case, Tiger's play.

AN INTRODUCTION TO THE SYSTEM AND PRACTICE OF ZI WEI DOU SHU (紫微斗數), OR POLESTAR ASTROLOGY

POLESTAR ASTROLOGY TEACHES THAT LIFE IS A DANCE, a reciprocity, or Ganying (感應), among three factors: Character, Inner Nature, and Fate, which will be explored in this book.

Here is a step-by-step guide on how to use this book.

STEP 1

Study and Contemplate the View Teachings, and Develop a Consistent Meditation Practice

The first section of this book will introduce the View Teachings, or Guan (觀), that inform this tradition and the meditation practice that supports them, called Zuo Wang (坐忘) or nonconceptual meditation, also known as "Sitting and Forgetting." Step one, before delving into the details of astrology, is to study this View, contemplate its meaning, and begin a meditation practice of some kind. You must digest the View and perhaps even let it change your life. If you do not consider the View, you will ultimately turn Polestar Astrology into something else—either a weak form of Western astrology or a way to substantiate an ignorance that perpetuates an abiding self and world.

STEP 2

Calculate Your Natal Chart to Determine Your Character, Inner Nature, and Fate

Before you can study your own Natal Chart, you must, of course, calculate your Natal Chart. Although there is a tedious way to calculate a chart by hand, and there is certainly something valuable to be learned in this process, in today's technological, internet society, it is easy to produce a chart online, where this information is already readily available. I highly recommend downloading the DYC Polestar astrology app produced by Darren Gibbs, which is available for purchase on an iPad. This program contains many of Liu Ming's notes and is a great companion to this book. If you do not wish to purchase this app, many websites can produce a chart for free, such as Destiny and Luck.[1] If you want to make charts by hand, I suggest buying *The Complete Book of Chinese Horoscopes* by Kwok Man-Ho, which contains everything you need.[2] *The Empyrean Matrix: A Guide to Purple Star Astrology (Zi Wei Dou Shu)* by Y. M. Lim is almost useless as a guide but full of technical information that is difficult to find elsewhere.[3] Once you have your chart, make sure you have your Four Pillars, your complete Twelve Houses with the appropriate Stars, and your Inner Nature. Once this is all in place, you are ready to study this tradition.

STEP 3

Contemplate the Character (the Heavenly Stem and Earthly Branch) of Your Year and Hour

The second part of the book will introduce and explore the idea of Qi Character, or Xing (性)—the notion that Qi is Time and that Time itself is characterized and we can use the symbols of the zodiac to describe that Character and, therefore, ourselves, because we are living, embodied expressions of Time. This part will explore the famous Twelve Animals of the Chinese zodiac, with the understanding that what is called your Qi Character is a synthesis of the year and the hour in which you were born. You must first study your year and hour separately and then learn to synthesize them. It is important, then, to understand the immutable nature of Character, for your Character is with you until death and determines the auspiciousness of your Fate.

STEP 4

Review the Twelve Houses of Your Natal Chart While Being Mindful of Character

The third part of this book will introduce the idea of Ming (命), or Fate. It will introduce and explain the Twelve Houses of a Natal Chart and give an in-depth discussion of the Thirty-Six Stars of the Polestar Pantheon, with an emphasis on the Twelve Ruling Stars. It will walk you through each Star in the Twelve Houses and give examples of how to interpret them, synthesize them with other Stars, and reflect on them through the lens of Character. Here, it becomes essential to contemplate the relationship dynamics between your Character and Fate to understand the resolution of Fate so you can experience your Inner Nature.

STEP 5

Understand the Fruition through the Contemplation of Your Inner Nature

This book will conclude with an exploration of the Five Inner Elements, or Wu Neixing (五内行), which is perhaps the most important and yet most difficult subject to discuss. This will cover the concept of Original Nature or Inner Nature, and the resolution of Character and Fate through these Five Inner Elements of Polestar Astrology. Each of us expresses one of the Five Inner Elements calculated from the Natal Chart, and this guides the kind of meditation practice we should pursue (like the Five Buddha Families in Vajrayana) and determines the nature of our spiritual or religious experience.

STEP 6 (OPTIONAL)

Study and Follow the Tong Shu, or *Farmer's Almanac and Calendrical Astrology*, and the Wu Yun Liu Qi, or the "Five Movements and Six Climates" Theory

The optional sixth step is to study and follow the *Farmer's Almanac and Calendrical Astrology*, which is called the Tong Shu (通書), and the Wu Yun Liu Qi (五雲六七), or the "Five Movements and Six Climates." These are not generally a part of Polestar Astrology and will not be covered in this book. However, they are important to mention, as they are integral to the Chinese Tradition.

The Tong Shu is the Chinese farmer's almanac and calendar that combines various solar and lunar cycles and is used as a method for selecting dates and times for farming tasks and for important events like marriages, funerals, opening ceremonies, house moving, contract signings, renovations, and travel. It is the most widely printed book in human history (even over the Bible), and it has been published and used without interruption for thousands of years. The Tong Shu includes the Ten Heavenly Stems and Twelve Earthly Branches, which are covered in this book, the Twenty-Eight Lunar Mansions, the Twenty-Four Qi Nodes/Seasons, and the Ten-Day Solar Index, among others.

The Wu Yun Liu Qi comes from the canonical source text of Classical Chinese Medicine, the Huangdi Neijing (黃帝內經), and is said to govern the distribution of the annual Qi as weather patterns and to produce resultant effects on living beings, such as illnesses. It has been used in Chinese medicine for thousands of years to predict weather and navigate diseases and epidemics.

These subjects are enormous. Although they are related to Polestar Astrology and highly informative to its practice, they are separate subjects and not required for understanding Zi Wei Dou Shu and our individual natal astrology.

In short, they describe the various cycles of Qi/Time that we all go through, regardless of our natal astrology. They are like Western and Indian notions of planetary transits. As such, we can study these to know the cycles that we all traverse together. And, in a sense, our Natal Chart is flowing within these cycles. We can either flow with them or against them, and our Natal Chart can be read in relation to these cycles. So, to be a complete astrologer, you must eventually study these subjects, but they will have to be the subjects of another book.

ZI WEI DOU SHU (紫微斗數)

SO, WHAT IS ZI WEI DOU SHU? In short, divination. Beyond that, it is not entirely clear, for its origins are shrouded in mystery. Polestar Astrology appeared in China in the Tang dynasty (618–907 C.E.) and was further developed in the Song dynasty (960–1280 C.E.) as a response to the influx of Indian astrology being brought to China by Buddhist monks. Before this period, China was primarily concerned with the *Farmer's Almanac and Calendrical Astrology*, the Tong Shu, and had no well-developed form of natal astrology, despite the many thousands of years of astrological calculation that preceded Zi Wei Dou Shu.

It never occurred to the Chinese that the Fate of any individual was significant, not even of the emperor, so they never bothered with natal astrology to understand one's personal Fate. However, with the influx of Indian medicine, astrology, and religion during the medieval period came the idea of a "self/soul" with a story, and it became popular to get natal readings. So, the Chinese decided to create their own version of natal astrology that expressed Chinese values and synthesized Daoism, Buddhism, and Confucianism. I will draw upon all three for our understanding and connect them to modern life.

The Polestar tradition has a largely Daoist pedigree, and the primary teachers credited with its creation are Luchunyang (呂純陽), during the Tang dynasty; Chenxiyi (陳希夷), during the Song dynasty; and Luohongxian (羅洪先), during the Ming dynasty.[1] There is also an oral tradition that attributes Zi Wei Dou Shu to the immortal Daoist Chen Tuan (陳摶), who is the progenitor of Yun Gong (雲功), or Dream Yoga (literally translated Cloud Yoga) in the Liu family tradition.

The system is named after Zi Wei, the Polestar or North Star, the only star in the sky that does not appear to move, which every culture on Earth has used since time immemorial to guide themselves home. It is the pivot point of Chinese astrological and astronomical calculations. The Polestar changes every few thousand years due to the axial movement of the Earth, and in this age the Polestar is Polaris, which the ladle of the Big Dipper, or Beidou (北斗), points to year-round.

The Chinese observed that everything in the heavens moves except for this one star, which felt quite significant to them. The Chinese, therefore, called it the Emperor, and Zi Wei Dou Shu teaches that all Fate is recorded and distributed from this heavenly pivot. Every culture on Earth has worshipped planets and stars, and the Chinese were no different. The Stars in this system were often deified and worshipped, and many Daoist practices involve visualizing, connecting with, and invoking these Stars as deities and symbols of higher spiritual principles.

The Daoist tradition of Polestar Astrology talks of Nine Heavenly Realms that we traverse on our way back to the Source upon completing our human Fate. The Polestar is a symbolic representation of the Yang light emanating from the Ninth Heaven, disseminating the celestial currents of Ancestral Fate resolution throughout our world system. These currents are sometimes called the Empyrean Matrix.

The term Zi Wei literally refers to a kind of flower, which some believe to be the purple myrtle flower. Zi (紫) means "purple," and Wei (微), in this case, means something delicate, fragile, subtle, and profound—a metaphor for Fate. Dou (斗), refers to the Big Dipper, and Shu (數) here means "calculation."

The system is also called Purple Star or Flying Star Astrology, and it is associated with a transmission from Shang Qing (上清) Daoism, associated with teachings that are said to manifest from noncorporeal realms of purple light. In Daoism, the color purple is associated with the depths of heaven, astral divinities, celestial phenomena, spectral visitations, cosmic totality, and wholeness.[2] The tradition was said to have been downloaded to Earth through trance mediums or shamans called Wu (巫), from beings called the Jade Ladies (玉女) and the Golden Lads (金童), from the Purple Library, an immortal realm that serves as an intermediary between Heaven and Earth.

All the teachings from this period are called the Purple Teachings. Earlier transmissions in China were called the Yellow Teachings, associated with the Yellow Emperor, Huangdi (黄帝).

Jade Ladies are like dakinis in Tantra or angels in Western mythology, enlightened feminine beings who hold and transmit Dharma teachings. Chögyam Trungpa called them inspiration beings and said that inspiration is the body of the dakini. When you feel alive and inspired and wisdom or insight pours through you, the Jade Ladies are said to be giggling around you in clouds of purple light.

Jade Ladies are depicted as teenage girls made of purple light who appear in dreams and visions. Wherever they gather, amethyst crystal is said to form. Xiwangmu (西王母), the Queen Mother of the West, is the Daoist female immortal who presides over this tradition with Zhenwu (真武), the True Warrior and a patron deity of the Liu family. Xiwangmu is said to fly around the world touching those who will become immortal. Jade Ladies gather around whomever Xiwangmu touches and transmit teachings from the Purple Library. Many poems from the Shang Qing period describe the Jade Ladies as muses who come and go, often creating despair in their absence. Shang Qing Daoism is a highly detailed and complex spiritual path that views the Stars of the Polestar system as deities. It is like Tantra, which developed around the same time, also from deities through trance mediumship.

While the focus of this book is Polestar Astrology, it is important to understand that the living Chinese Tradition is syncretic and utilizes many forms of Chinese astrology, including the Four Pillars, the Tong Shu almanac, and many others, that will be referenced throughout this book. The deeper history and context of these other systems are important but can be found elsewhere, and I recommend the work of Derek Walters for such an overview.[3] It is important to know that none of these systems is truly separate; in practical application, they all blend. Polestar Astrology draws wisdom from all the Chinese sciences, for they are all helpful in understanding our Character, Inner Nature, and Fate.

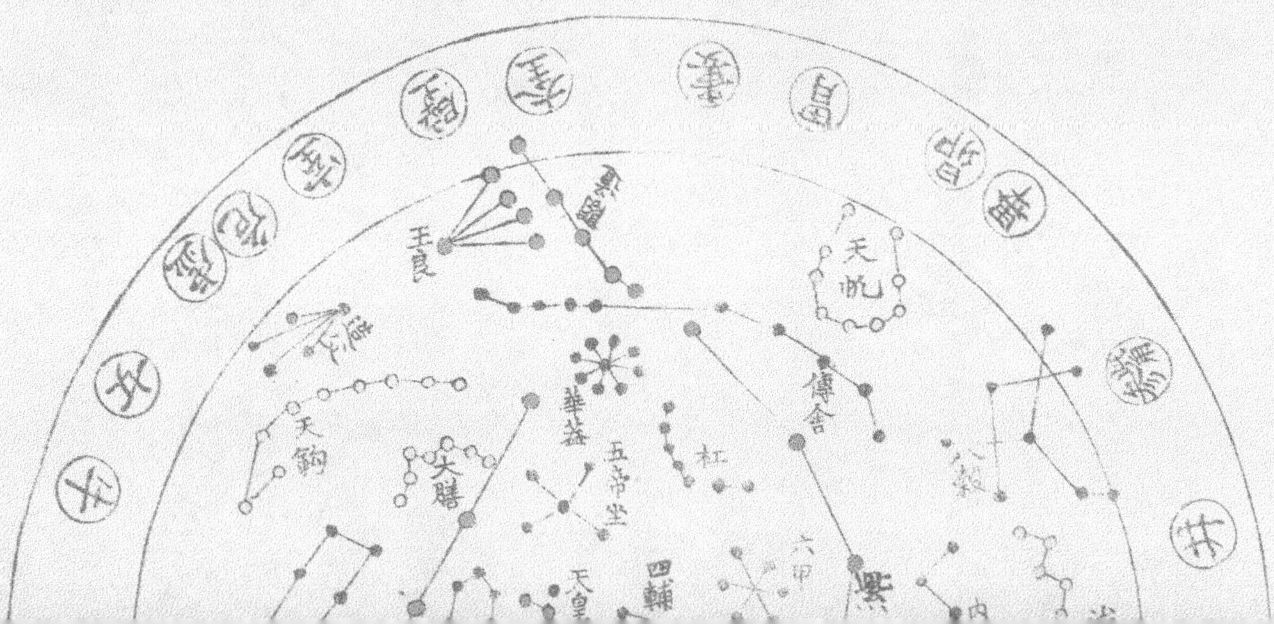

女
虛
危
室
壁
奎
婁
胃
昴
畢
觜
井
王良
天鉤
華蓋
五帝坐
杠
傳舍
天帆
大膳
四輔
六甲
八穀

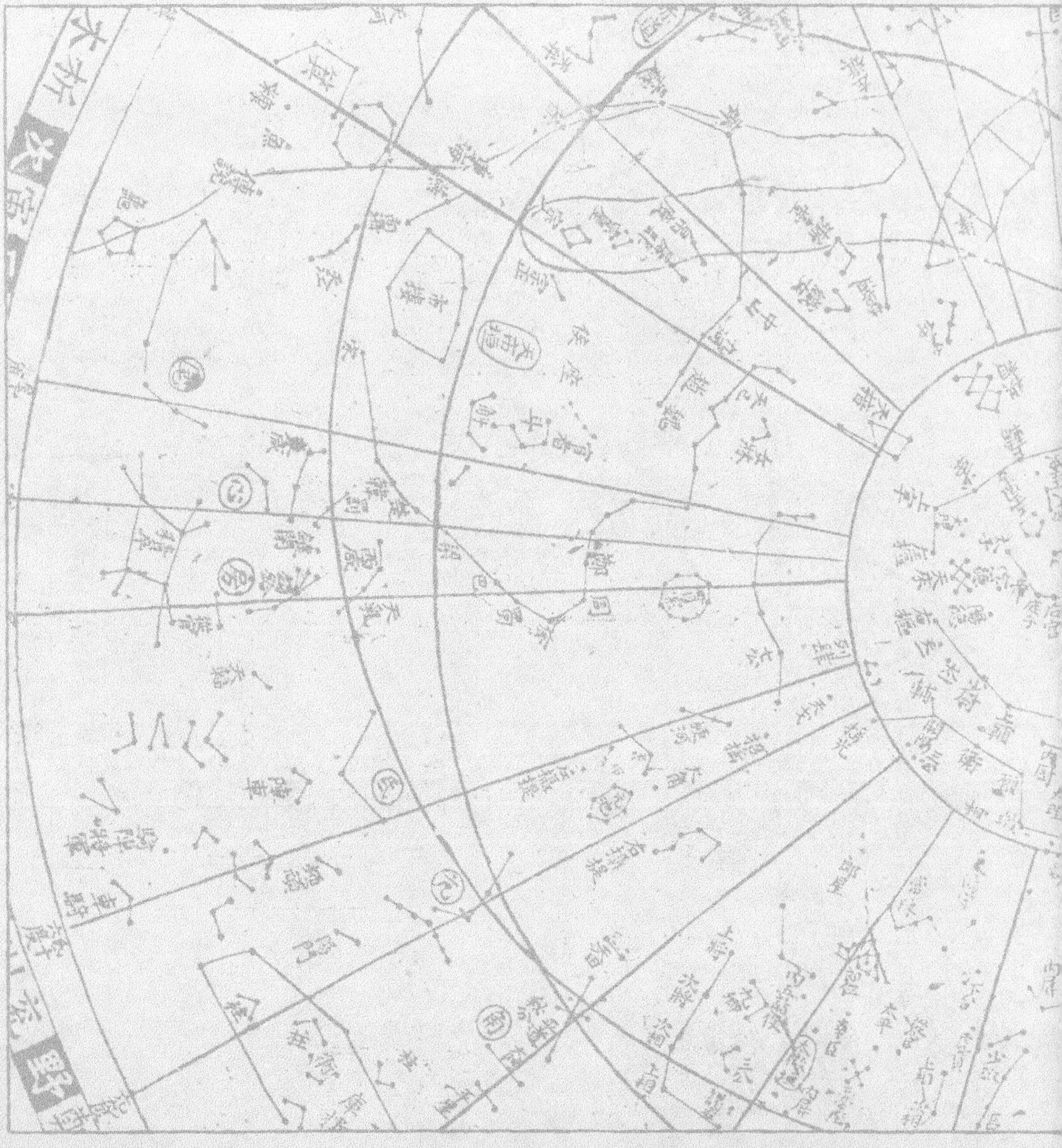

STEP I

View Teachings, or Guan (觀)

Establishing a Base

THE THREEFOLD TRAINING, OR SAN HUI (三慧)

BUDDHIST TRADITIONS OFFER A THREEFOLD TRAINING, or San Hui (三慧), of learning, contemplation, and meditation, or Wen Si Xiu (文思秀; Skt. *sruta cinta bhavana*). These Three Trainings inform and reinforce each other in a cyclical feedback loop that eventually transforms our experience.

Dzogchen Ponlop states:

> In the Buddhist path, we accumulate knowledge in three ways: through study, contemplation, and meditation. First, we gain intellectual knowledge, then we personalize it through reflecting on it, and then we go beyond that to a whole new state of knowing—one that's free from reliance on reference points. That's the nature of our journey. First, we're handed a map and learn to read it; next, we're on the road but still relying on our map for directions; finally, we realize we don't need to look at the map anymore—we know it by heart. Our confidence doesn't waver, whether we're looking at the map or the road ahead; the map has dissolved into the landscape. That's higher knowledge, or one way of looking at it.[1]

This is the key to making astrology a living reality, and it is my most heartfelt recommendation for practitioners of this or any wisdom tradition. There is a tremendous amount of detailed information available, but we must start by learning and contemplating the View, or outlook on reality; this establishes a base. We must correctly understand the View intellectually to have a basis for contemplation. We then hold the View in our hearts and live our lives, reflecting on our experience through the lens of the View. Slowly, we start to see these teachings come alive. If we rush into the details of the Method without letting the View transform us, we will ultimately get overwhelmed and confused, and we will have shallow Fruition. Astrology will not work for us.

Once we have intellectual understanding and begin contemplating the teachings in our lived experience, we must start a meditation practice so that our intellect and lived experience have a place to digest and integrate. Meditation allows the mind to rest while it wrestles with itself. We give our mind space and our body stillness, and in this space/stillness, our study and contemplation trickle down, and we begin to embody the teachings. We then study more, learn new concepts, and keep sitting. This is the way.

Daoism, Buddhism, and Confucianism deeply inform the View, or Guan (觀), presented here; it is all these, an amalgamation. Yet, it becomes its own tradition through the application of astrology. Before we can dive into that, it is essential for you to pause and examine your motivation. Why do this? Why are you interested? Why do you want to study astrology or be an astrologer?

THE THREE MOTIVES OF THE MANTIC ARTS

THIS TRADITION IS A "MANTIC" ART, meaning a form of divination. Chinese language has many terms for divination: Bushi (卜筮), Jiao (珓), Shi (筮), Zhan (占), Gua (卦), Yujian (預見), Fang (方), Shu (術), and more. Astrology is often called Mingli Xue (命理學), which we can playfully translate as "studying the textures of Fate."

Whatever the name, humans have always had a deep curiosity and a fundamental instinct for survival; we've been divining the ways of Heaven and Earth for as long as we've been around. Divination, as related to what is commonly called "shamanism," is the "old religion." In a way, it lies behind all the world's religions and, in the broadest sense, all human culture.

Divination is the curiosity about and attempt to shape the direction of time and experience. You may create philosophies, teachings, stories, and so on, but as soon as you try to make these practical and apply them to experience, you are attempting to shape the future—you are divining—and your teachings, or "View," will determine the fruition of your methods.

The future is unformed and empty, but the "present moment" has a momentum called the past; it has expectations and direction that can be read and shaped. Every spiritual tradition is trying to do this in one way or another. Every culture has divination systems, such as tarot, astrology, the Yi-Jing, birdsong, tortoise shells, and so on. This tradition takes this premise and turns it into a deliberate path that we call "resolving Fate," which is the purpose and fruition of Zi Wei Dou Shu.

So, why practice the mantic arts? Liu Ming taught three "motivations" for practicing divination: fear, advantage, and wisdom.[1] Before we get started, it is important to examine which of these motivates you. These motives can apply to anything you do in life. It is important to be honest. This tradition emphasizes wisdom as the path, but we may unconsciously be operating from all three. Sit with this. No judgment. Above all, self-honesty is the key to arriving, eventually, at wisdom.

FEAR

Simply put, humans are freaked out about the future and want to feel better; we want to feel in control in a world out of control. Divination is most often used to "predict" calamity and provide safety from the fear of the unknown. This is fine. Used in this way, divination provides knowledge of possible futures to avoid "punishment" for our misdeeds, evil Fate, Ancestral Ghosts, and so on. Divination from the motivation of fear often seeks "answers" as to why life is so difficult: *Why does this keep happening to me? I can't believe I did that again!* Fear is not bad, for it often gets us started on the path. However, it is limited, emotionally painful, and will only take us so far. If used out of fear only, these teachings will ultimately have no ultimate Fruition.

ADVANTAGE

The second motive is to gain an advantage. We learn and practice astrology to get one-up on the universe. Although fear is often still an underlying motive, astrology, when used for advantage, is usually a lot more fun. We use astrology to become better people and to learn more about our patterns so that we can do better in life. This kind of astrology is often about timing—knowing when to advance and retreat. It can be used to predict the stock market, when to invest, when to start a business, when to get married, whom to marry, when to buy a house, when to have children, and so on. This motive is also acceptable, but it often stays superficial, and we end up creating more and more Fate in the process of trying to control our Fate, rather than becoming free of it altogether. The clear majority of astrology I see out there is done with this motive. It often looks spiritual, but beneath the surface, many use astrology as a tool to gain an advantage in a scary world. I have tried to use astrology to my advantage, but I'm not very good at it. If used for advantage, these teachings will have mixed fruitions: You can benefit yourself and others, but in the end, you will likely not have a deep experience of your Original Nature.

WISDOM

Cultivating the Dao (道)

The following is a meditation on the View Teachings, or Guan (觀), of this tradition used to cultivate wisdom. I have adapted and paraphrased this from the various teachings of Liu Ming mixed with my own understanding of Chinese philosophy. You should read this section slowly and return to it repeatedly. If you take this to heart, then your practice may have Fruition.

Time and Space are an irresolvable chaos called Huntun (餛飩). Great sages tell us the ultimate nature of reality is Taiji (太極), a supreme unity, but good luck finding this. The Dao (道) that can be conceptualized is not the pristine Dao, so to the mind and its world, Taiji is Wuji (無極), an unknowable emptiness full of light displays happening everywhere all at once.

When we look closely, we find no concrete time, place, or self; however, the patterned appearance of these factors bewilders us for lifetimes. Reality appears to be ordered or patterned, but close analysis brings no certainty, and the illusion or assumption of knowledge becomes big trouble when things fall apart.

Analysis or scrutiny brings with it an irresolvable confusion that humans have debated since time immemorial. Religion, philosophy, science—all these are myths trying to make sense of Huntun. When we look closely, chaos appears to be the source of all things, and this is the paradox that lies at the heart of our experience: Strands of Time (Yang) and Space (Yin) weave together to form an unreadable but observable, constantly changing, astro-geomantic pattern that the Chinese call "Dao."

The Dao constantly displays itself as the dualistic, ephemeral, impermanent, and dreamlike phenomena we call a self and world, and the microcosm of our personal Fate mirrors the macrocosm of the nameless Dao. Through relaxed observation, this becomes apparent.

The spiritual path of the mantic arts, and the true purpose of Polestar Astrology, comes through embracing this irresolvable paradox at the heart of all experience. Relaxing our need to know and understand becomes our direct path to wisdom. The dual world we are divining through our astrology chart and the calendar, which appears to be comprehensible, reveals patterns within chaos and patterns as chaos. Astrology becomes a mirror that reflects our Original Nature, which goes beyond concepts. This is the very meaning of chaos.

Our practice is to observe the matrix of patterns in our experience through the symbols of astrology without strict meaning-making or naming. Without the compulsion to predict, fix, or improve any particular part of our experience, our false notions of an abiding self and world unravel through playful observation. Chaos is never vanquished; samsara and the dual world are never fixed or improved. They are revealed as Dao—an ever-flowing stream of experience in the natural state of presence.

The mantic arts are a non-dual revelation of things as they are. Life is revealed as an ever-flowing phantasm of light that cannot be named or known, and we accept our "Fate," agreeing to be swept up in whatever has been inherited and "preordained" by our Ancestors. It would be helpful to have answers and generate a story of great meaning and purpose, a "reason" why everything happens, but perhaps there isn't one; perhaps this is all Dao.

However, the Chinese Tradition teaches that we are not alone in the chaos. The teachings of Kong Fu Zi, or Confucius, beat at the heart of Polestar Astrology and reveal the complex nature of our relatedness. Are we isolated individuals? Or do we live as the center of interpersonal relationships? These are the fundamental questions of the Confucian tradition and of Polestar Astrology.

Confucius established a secular, nontheistic society in which the Dao is unknowable and all gods and spirits are equally unimportant in light of our primary goal: learning to be human, or Ren (仁). In the Confucian tradition, the self is a dynamic center of creative transformation defined by relationship. We possess no abiding self that is separate from our relationships with nature or our Ancestors, family, community, country, world, and universe.

In contrast to Western notions of "basic brokenness" (original sin), in the Confucian tradition, human beings and nature are intrinsically good, and there is no salvation or enlightenment required of us. Our Original Nature is complete and self-existing, already within.

The starting point of the Confucian path is self-worth, which is derived from education and self-cultivation for its own sake. The impetus for and commitment to changing the world must come from within. Therefore, self-cultivation and the mantic arts that support it are not done for social improvement; they are an end, rather than a means to an end.

However, the central teaching of Confucianism is human relatedness, where community is the most necessary vehicle for human flourishing. Personal development is expressed within an open-ended series of concentric circles of relatedness, which we divine in our Natal Chart.

Confucian spirituality and Polestar Astrology aim to create a society where everyone is cared for, has a place, and has the freedom to cultivate themselves and actualize their full potential. Human fellowship does not undermine our individuality, and each person's dignity, autonomy, and independence need not be based on individualism. Therefore, we should not choose to be loners. Rather, each human being can reach their highest potential through communication and communal participation with other human beings.

This worldliness is, then, both the core Confucian value and what Polestar Astrology is concerned with, first and foremost.

In the Confucian tradition, people may worship whatever gods or spirits they choose, if those beliefs do not interfere with the responsibilities of human relatedness. However, its non-theism states that knowledge of an Ultimate or the existence of a one true God is not required to return to Dao. We need only to cultivate our humanity with other humans. No gods or spirits need be supplicated.

In the Unknowable Dao, everything is Ziran (自然), "self-resolving." Everything born dies. Everything compound dissolves. Everything that struggles will eventually exhaust itself. Human beings, then, cannot be "perfected." We do not evolve toward any ideal state; instead, we are cyclical, and our life is a dynamic rhythm (Yinyang)—sometimes wonderful, sometimes painful. Since we cannot be perfected, we are relieved of any permanent notion of progress or self-improvement.

Without a creator or an event of creation, sin or salvation, beginning or end, or any notion of perfection, we simply respond naturally to the ever-changing present, the immortal procession of Time in the here and now. Transcendence is found in immanence. The ordinary world is the unknowable Dao, manifesting in and as the cycles of Time. Natural morality is, then, defined by our relationship to spring, summer, fall, and winter, and this defines our conduct accordingly.

The Confucian paradox states that all human beings are inherently and inevitably a sage, or Sheng Ren (聖人), but no human being can ever become one. Education in our humanity never ends, and it begins with studying cyclical time, which is understood by many traditional cultures around the world. Unlike modern people, who are frantic and plagued by the anxiety of linear time, traditional folk possess a deep calm that lives in their hearts. This deep, abiding calm is a kind of memory that comes from the continuity of life, a confidence that comes from knowing who you are and where you come from, a relaxation that comes from knowing there is neither a perfect future nor a sullied past. It comes from the immortal cycles of life, called birth and death, in the natural world, and from generations who survived countless winters only to witness the renewals of spring. It is hard to say what is remembered, so traditional folk call this memory the Ancestors . . .

This dream, this memory, is the temporary, compound condition of our many lifetimes and Ancestors inherited at birth. It appears as a "world" and as a "self"; it appears as our compulsion to do, make an effort, reproduce, and survive. This memory, this dream, appears in our stories, intelligence, wisdom, ignorance, patterns of pain, and unfinished business.

Traditional cultures understood that substance is relative Time. Nothing is solid; things only appear solid in Time: Mountains flow like waves, and gold eventually turns to dust. Time, as such, is not a straight line but rather a series of spirals that appear to repeat only because they are constantly renewed. In Chinese Polestar Astrology, we call this Jieqi (解氣). In this sense, humans have no history; we have memory. We've all been here before, yet it feels like the first time.

Why? Because birth is the cause of death, and therefore, death must be the cause of birth. Everyone ages and falls ill from time to time and eventually dies. Old age and illness, however, are not the cause of death but simply a natural unwinding of the polarity, or Yinyang (陰陽) that temporarily holds together human Jing (精), or substance, and Qi (氣), or energy, as Shen (神), experience.[2]

Ming once said that death is a fish returning to the water after a leap into the air—a natural return home.[3] It is neither tragic nor mistaken. For, although death can appear gradual or sudden, no one has ever died from illness or injury; they died because they were born. The experience of our "life" is, in fact, a constant alternation of birth and death, like inhaling and exhaling, like waking and sleeping.

Everything that comes together comes apart, and all rivers return to the sea. And just as the sea again becomes the rivers, death is not permanent or even a "stop." How could it be?

As such, life and death alternate in an endless circle. Everything flows, carrying momentum from start to finish and from finish back to start. To hear this story of endlessness may sound like a punishing wheel (samsara), full of ignorance and suffering, but it is also a nameless and incomprehensibly permissive Reality, animated with endless presence.[4] In Polestar Astrology, the "story" of this endlessness—the immortality of our presence, the complex interaction between life and death—is called "Fate," or Ming (命), and Fate is a state of possession. We are all possessed.

What possesses us? Our *ancestors*—the disembodied human impulse or memory called Gui (鬼), "Ghosts," specifically the "unsettled" dead. A Ghost is the uncomfortable, painful "story" or conflicted mental-emotional state of an Ancestor who died physically but was unable to emotionally complete the process of death. These unresolved emotions and thought patterns are called Ghosts and do not "stop" in death. Rather, Ghosts lose the body-mind-Qi context that generated them, and without the reference point of human embodiment, they cannot resolve, so they seek embodiment to "finish."

An Ancestral Ghost can "possess" or "visit" a descendant and take them through the Ghost's incomplete life and death by attempting to relive, complete, and heal their unresolved negative emotions that are stuck outside time through repeating negative or unhealthy behavioral patterns. This may cause illness, or it may cause temporary or chronic, compulsive, self-destructive, or addictive behavior that is not ordinary for the living person.

Humans possessed by Ghosts may abuse themselves and other humans. In this case, a person's disintegration is not "physical" but is expressed through "locked" and inappropriate emotional states. These emotional states often do not respond to logic or ordinary changes in circumstances but follow conditioned patterns of emotional attachment and aversion.

In other words, we inherit what has not been finished, and whatever you do not finish is the Ghost you will become and pass on to your descendants.

So, what possesses you? Do you have the courage to let go?

Liu Ming once asked his teacher what could be done to exorcise the ocean of illness and injury caused by possession. Ming's teacher looked sly and answered, "Kindness." We can all take responsibility for the unevenness of life by being as kind and gentle as we can. And we can all call on the ocean of wisdom and compassion that comes from our Beneficial Ancestors, for although we inherit and are charged with resolving the Ghosts of the past, we are each blessed with a pantheon of accomplished Ancestors who completed their human Fate and are now working for the resolution of everyone's Fate. These Ancestors form the primary image of Fate in our Natal Chart, and their beneficial radiance is the actual subject of this book.

The big picture here reminds us that creating and maintaining an orderly society and avoiding selfishness and aggression in our relationships are good for our health.[5] But how do we do this? Polestar Astrology offers a path, a method to understanding the dynamics of our relatedness through our own compound nature.

According to Polestar Astrology, human beings are a compound of Character, or Xing (性), Inner Nature, or Dao De (道德), and Fate, or Ming (命). Nature, the world, and human beings are a single interconnected, ongoing cyclical pattern of self-arising and self-resolving movement called "Time." Due to Time's cyclical and repetitive nature, like the changing of day to night and night to day and the alternation of the four seasons, it becomes possible to name and characterize. In Polestar Astrology, the patterned movement of Time is called Qi (氣).[6]

We characterize Qi, or Time, by Yinyang, the Five Phases or Elements, and the Twelve Animals of the zodiac, a metaphoric language describing the facets and flavors of change itself. The real nature of our experience is a constantly unfolding, unsolidified, un-abiding movement of Qi.[7] The profundity of Chinese astrology is found in the direct experience that everything is compound and in a constant process of change, or Yi (易).

In human beings, these qualities compound during birth to create what we call "Qi Character." In each moment, the universe exudes a certain pattern, and when you are born, you emerge as a living, embodied expression of that pattern. The pattern of the universe patterns you. Our Qi Character does not dissolve until death, and therefore constitutes our basic "capacity" to resolve Fate in this lifetime.

Fate is the predispositions we inherit from our many past lives and Ancestors (宗), to re-create and solidify patterns. As Liu Ming once said, "Fate's most bitter edge is the apparently 'un-learnable' lesson—repeated inauspicious conduct. We have all probably said: 'I can't believe I did that again!' Freedom's worthless edge is sloth. Squandering freedom is common. Most of us spend most of our time in the vagaries in between."[8]

Because we are a compound of patterns in flux, we have no permanent or abiding self, for a permanent self could not interact with an impermanent flux. Our Original Nature is neither fixed nor unchanging. Our Original Nature is Freedom, the freedom of light to move within space unimpeded, creating the temporary appearance of solidity. Our Nature is Pristine Awareness, fundamentally empty, or Kong (空), and therefore free to manifest or project an apparent "world."

This Freedom, what Buddhists call emptiness, Sunyata (舜若多), does not manifest chaotically. To the conceptual mind, freedom is chaos, Huntun (餛飩), but because it is chaos, it manifests order, for chaos without order would be meaningless. It does so through rhythms of Time, Space, and Light. The movement quality of Time, Space, and Light create the "appearance" of an abiding "world" and "self," of subject and object, but upon investigation, these appearances are empty projections. Their appearance is nothing other than movement, a dream, a vision, a film, a mirage, an apparition of light that plays out in open space.

Fate and Freedom interact and alternate. Using our Freedom can untangle our Fate or harden it into tighter knots. According to Chinese astrology, this untangling process is imminent. All knots are predisposed to untangle. This is the Dao of Wuwei. The story we imagine to be a "self" is Nature's predisposition to manifest in limits that resolve back into Nature without a trace. In this way, all animate beings are unborn. Human beings are not in Nature. We are Nature. This is the principle of Original Nature, or Dao De (道德).

The resolution of Fate, the return to Source, comes through the realization of the perfect completion of things as they already are. Everything that has ever happened or will ever happen is a perfect demonstration of your Original Nature, no matter how you feel about it. You have always been light having an experience of light.

This resolution of Fate is called Da Yuan (大圓), Great Completion, completing the Circle, returning to Source. This is symbolized in Polestar Astrology by the Dragon and the Rainbow Body, or Hong Shen (虹身). The ultimate Fruition of the Path is the primordial and inherent union of Yinyang, represented by the Cosmic Egg, realized as the essence and Original Nature of all experience as light in space-awareness. The process of life unfolding since beginningless time seeks to complete all human possibilities through the dual dance of Yinyang: birth–death, awake–asleep, and pain–joy. Eventually, this dance of opposites exhausts itself, and the endless stream of Ancestors is finished; all past lives, past, present, and future, are resolved, and all facets of humanness are gathered back to the center of our being.

The practitioner of the Way draws all creation into their heart or navel Dantian (丹田), creating a "Cosmic Egg" or "Immortal Fetus," an expression of the Ultimate Yin, the return to Source. The result of Ultimate Yin turns to Ultimate Yang, which is the Dragon, the ultimate freedom of primordial energy, bursting from the Egg, light flowing freely and consciously into all dimensions, consciously becoming the universe that it has always been, which other people witness as the body dissolving in rainbow light. The Dragon's flight is the primordial gesture of the Dao itself, the demonstration of Source's power to become everything, which all humans are destined for.

SITTING AND FORGETTING, OR ZUO WANG (坐忘)

ONCE WE TAKE THE VIEW TO HEART, starting a sitting meditation practice is important. Any practice from the Chinese Tradition will do, if you get proper instruction from an experienced teacher. Meditation techniques are a dime a dozen, and while they each lead to specific fruitions, anyone who has practiced for decades will likely agree that the specifics are not as important as the consistency of practice. Sit every day, and keep sitting. Conceptual practice will eventually break down, as most conceptual practices eventually deconstruct concepts intentionally or as a by-product of the insight gained in practice.

So, if you have a conceptual Daoist, Buddhist, or Confucian practice, stick with it. If your primary practice comes from another tradition with a different View, this will likely lead to confusion if you attempt to mix it with Polestar Astrology. So, for the purpose of this book, if you wish to take the practice seriously, it is best to leave other practices aside and give this a fair try.

Liu Ming taught "Sitting and Forgetting," or Zuo Wang (坐忘), also called nonconceptual meditation, as a primary base practice for studying the Chinese Tradition. It is an excellent foundation for all training and cultivation, for it is nonspecific and can be practiced by anyone at any time. While it is the most basic and straightforward of practices, it can carry you from beginner to complete Fruition. This practice embodies the popular notion of "beginner's mind." The idea is to express our enlightened nature rather than trying to attain it. Suzuki Roshi once said, "Express Buddha first, become Buddha later."

Instruction should ideally be received in person from someone who has done the practice every day for at least two years without missing a day, and who received it from someone who received it from someone, and so on. However, idealism here is unimportant. Zuo Wang defies such gatekeeping because there isn't a way to do it wrong if you can sit in the proper posture and maintain a consistent practice.

Liu Ming said, "The basic View of Zuo Wang is that all truth is self-evident. There is no universally patterned path outside of our own experience . . . the practice of Zuo Wang is not the search for or production of mental states. The method of Zuo Wang is primarily a seated posture, and it is important to receive correct instruction. There is no specific instruction on how to 'forget.' 'Forgetting' naturally occurs when the posture is assumed."[1]

Here is the Liu family lineage transmission poem for Zuo Wang practice:

Gather up your legs.
Pin your gaze.
No effort—relax.
Let go of preciousness, and
You will see and know without obscurity![2]

This practice must be done every day for at least an hour. The pith instruction on the View and Method should be received in person, but anyone can sit and forget. This practice cannot really be discussed, which is why it is called "nonconceptual." There are no instructions on what to "do" with your mind, and thinking is no problem. It's just sitting. We do not know what our Original Nature is, so we don't do anything. We "just sit."

But how do you sit? The traditional seven-point posture of Vairochana (Skt. *saptadharma-vairocana*) has been offered in many Buddhist traditions:

Sit with legs crossed in whatever way is comfortable. The hands sit in the lap or on the knees, and the back and spine are straight with the crown rising to the sky. The shoulders spread like a vulture's wings, chest open. The head, neck, and chin are straight, slightly tucked in and lowered. The mouth is gently closed and the tip of the tongue touches the palate. The eyes gaze past the tip of the nose.[3]

In this tradition, the gaze is of central importance. We sit with eyes open, relaxed, and the gaze is fixed or "pinned" at a point in space a few feet before us. You focus on space itself, but with the eyes relaxed so that the visual field softens, and nothing particular is in focus. This may reveal squiggly floating specks or tadpoles in your field of vision, called myodesopsias; these can be watched playfully or not. We then leave the mind alone. You are free to think or not. You may follow the breath, but this is not important. Just let go of preciousness. The body is to remain relaxed and still, the gaze still, so that the "wind" in the mind, channels, and body dissipates. A pith instruction attributed to Machig Labdrön goes, alert, alert, yet relax, relax. This is a crucial point for the view in meditation.

It is recommended that you sit for about forty-five minutes to an hour each sitting at least once per day, preferably in the early morning. Anything shorter than forty-five minutes does not allow enough time for the wind in the channels to dissipate or the body and mind to fully relax.

With the daily practice of Zuo Wang and the ongoing study of the View as the base for understanding the symbols in your Natal Chart, Polestar Astrology becomes a wisdom path. As we will later discuss in-depth, we contemplate our Qi Character as our "personality display": our behavior as patterned by Time. We contemplate our Fate as an opportunity in the form of life experience as it appears to "happen to us" through the symbols of Stars in our chart. We contemplate how our Character manages and resolves our good and bad opportunities. And the daily practice of Zuo Wang becomes the container where these contemplations integrate nonconceptually. This is the path of Polestar Astrology. As we continue, our Character and Fate resolve, and we get glimpses of our Original Nature.

Now that we have introduced the View and the practice of nonconceptual meditation, let's revisit Fate and unpack some important aspects of the View that make them relevant to modern life.

WHAT IS FATE?
THE POLESTAR AND LIFE PURPOSE

BEFORE DELVING INTO THE METHODS OF POLESTAR ASTROLOGY, we need to backtrack and define why it is relevant to modern life. To do this, we must explore the question: What is Fate?

Disassociation and purposelessness are perhaps the most troubling epidemics of modern technological culture. Now more than ever, human beings dissociate from their natural environment, from one another, from history, from culture, and from their own embodied human experience. Disassociated from natural cycles, we throw everything out of balance. We have become a society of floating heads.

Our culture, especially in America, has lost any sense of coherent or cohesive values. As a culture, we are inundated with confusing, ever-changing ideas from the shrine of Scientism, which changes its mind every few hours, presenting us with contradictory and often conflicting views about everything. Many of us have rejected our religious heritage, and if we haven't, we tend to proselytize others or judge them silently. As a culture, we argue over just about everything, confusing each other with bad ideas, and unfortunately, the most coherent value structures in American society are being provided by corporatism, consumerism, and biased media.

Our hard-won individualism has given us freedom, privilege, and comfort, but we have no idea about what to do with our freedom. Because of this, many people lack "life purpose." We're not quite sure why we were born, and we spend a great deal of time wasting our energy in pursuit of an outdated and unsustainable model of success. Most of us exhaust ourselves just trying to survive our own life.

The American Dream seems to have died (probably sometime in the eighties), and yet the whole world tries to achieve it. I have lived in Asia, I have been to over twenty countries, and I have seen the whole world struggling to have "everything." We all want a career, kids, family, money, two cars, a house, money in the bank, and so on. Failing to achieve this, many become despondent and lost, and many blame themselves or a vague bogeyman like "capitalism," which, ironically, is the only economic system to successfully lift people out of poverty. Who's to blame us for feeling this way?

The view of modern culture (or lack thereof) lags far behind the reality of our actual situation. We cannot have it all. And we are not supposed to have it all. In the Chinese Tradition, we are supposed to have what we are Fated for. We're supposed to work together and support one another to balance and create social harmony. What one lacks, another has in abundance, and through social order and voluntary exchange without coercion we keep the balance. We have enough resources to feed, clothe, and shelter everyone in the world, and yet we do not, because we are disassociated from this natural wisdom.

According to the Chinese Tradition, we waste tremendous energy and life force trying to achieve things we are not Fated for. So first, according to Polestar Astrology, you have something called "Fate," or Ming (命). This may be news to you; you may even have some objections to the idea, which is quite normal. So, I will say again up front that Fate is not determinism.

Fate means opportunity. Obviously, we all have different opportunities in life based on where, when, and to whom we were born, meaning our opportunity is astrological. Furthermore, the circumstances surrounding our opportunities are much bigger than we can grasp. Our actual situation is enormous.

Some people seem lucky—always in the right place at the right time. Some people are phenomenally talented and yet live lives of quiet desperation with little to no opportunity. The American Dream tells us we can "pull ourselves up by our own bootstraps," and yet we all know this is nonsense. Through no amount of hard work will I be a center in the NBA. The Chinese Tradition's answer to this paradox is Fate. We are each Fated to have a certain potential for experience and certain opportunities in life, and these potentials manifest or unfold based on the time and place of our birth.

According to the Chinese Tradition, Fate is rhythmic, cyclical, and mathematical. For thousands of years, the ancients observed the cycles of time, space, and nature and discovered many different patterns within them. One of these cycles generates what the Chinese call Character, and another generates what we call "Currents of Fate," or Mingyun (命運), which we will discuss in more detail later.

The Currents of Fate are related to mathematical calculations based on the Polestar, or Emperor Star, the only star in the night sky that does not appear to move. If you visit the homepage of my website, you will see the Emperor Star in time-lapse photography, with the heavens swirling around it. Every few thousand years, the Polestar changes; it was Vega, and now it is Polaris. Every culture on Earth since time immemorial has used the Polestar for navigation and, more important, for astrology.

After thousands of years of observation, the Chinese noticed that the constellations in the night sky swirled in patterns around the Emperor Star and that these patterns were cyclical, rhythmic, and mathematical. Furthermore, they noticed that the circumstances or opportunities of human life are intimately related to these patterns in a predictable way. These patterns are energetic expressions of vibrating light, and so are we.

Imagine that the energy or light of the entire universe flows in big cyclical patterns according to the relative position of heavenly bodies within space. From our position on Earth, we are connected mathematically to one of many intertwined and interrelated swirling patterns of energy within the galaxy and greater universe. Every planet, then, would determine different but related patterns. From Earth, our patterns are determined by the fixed position of the Polestar. The patterns that we can observe shift every hour, every year, generating and concluding different phases in the cycles of time and energy. This flow shifts from one pattern to another in a predictable way, like sunrise and sunset.

Imagine now that the energy of the universe is not disconnected, cold, insentient energy, but rather that the whole universe is an intimate web of living, breathing, cycling energy. Finally, consider the possibility that you are also an expression of this basic living energy and that you are fundamentally interconnected to greater cycles and patterns beyond the grasp of your conscious mind. No definable point of separation between yourself and the universe can be found; you are a breathing pulsation of the entire matrix of life.

According to Polestar Astrology, when you were born, you emerged as a living, embodied expression of the same energy pattern the universe was exuding at that moment. Imagine that the universe is exuding or "doing" a certain pattern in each moment. At the time of your birth, the pattern of the universe, to which you are fundamentally connected, patterns you. In other words, you become a living expression of that pattern. Everything that "began" in that moment also expresses that pattern. These patterns radiate outward, containing and relating to one another like a Russian doll, and they express a continuum from microcosm to macrocosm.

Imagine that in the moment of birth, you are plugged into one of these streams, these currents of cycling time. Imagine that this stream is already in motion, set to unfold as a rhythmic pattern, and it will carry you along in it like a flowing river. As you flow through life, this pattern of Time will unwind and create the potential for certain kinds of experiences to manifest. This potential for experience, based on these patterns of energy, is what the Chinese Tradition calls Fate. These Currents of Fate are finite in number but infinite in their potential, variety, and multiplicity of expression.

Have I confused you? Not to worry. To simplify, you have something called "Fate," which is determined by the time of your birth—whatever pattern of Time you "dropped" into. So, how is this related to life's purpose? Polestar Astrology is also called "Fate calculation." A Polestar Astrology session reads the "pattern" of your birth and can tell you how this pattern may unfold. Remember, it is not fortune-telling; it cannot predict the future, but it can tell you about the possibilities within the container of your "pattern." The value of Polestar Astrology comes through dialogue, meaning the astrologer provides interpretations of Fate, but it is up to you to define that meaning in terms of your own experience. In this book, you will learn how to interpret this for yourself.

The Chinese Tradition is very practical, as it comes from Confucian worldly values. Fate, then, is read in relation to practical human life. In a Natal Chart reading, we examine Fate through the Twelve Houses and through the lens of family, marriage and romantic partners, children, money, career and work in the world, and pleasure. In the Chinese view, your Fate lies within these basic categories. While Fate is spread throughout these categories, our major Fate, what we are here to "do," lies within one of them, and we see this through the placement of the Polestar, or "Emperor." Some people, then, are Fated to be parents, and that is the most important thing they are Fated to do. The rest is unimportant in the big picture and may even constellate around parenthood. Some are Fated for careers, but not everyone, which can terrify Americans. Some are just Fated to enjoy themselves.

Knowing this, Polestar Astrology can take immense pressure off the confusion of modern technological life. First, if we lack direction, it can give it to us. Polestar Astrology can tell us, quite plainly, what we were born to do, with something as simple as locating the Polestar in our chart. Polestar Astrology provides the big picture, the context for our entire life. Sometimes Fate is clear (Yang), and sometimes it is mysterious (Yin). Knowing that our life is Fated to be unclear may relieve us of trying to "figure it out." In that space, we may even relax and experience deeper insights. Knowing that our Fate lies in family life, we can relax and not waste our energy trying to build a "successful" career. In other words, knowing that we can't "have it all," we can stop wasting our energy trying to have it all, and we can put our energy into what we are Fated for.

Sometimes we are Fated for difficulties. Polestar Astrology can tell us where those difficulties may manifest, which provides us with a tool for navigating them. Some people are Fated for freedom; knowing this, we can use our freedom to experience our Original Nature and benefit others. Modern life tells us we are supposed to do and have everything, but perhaps this need not be the case. Maybe we can relax and let go of this madness.

A central goal of Polestar Astrology is to relax because everything is self-resolving. This means that in the cycles of time everything resolves of its own accord. Birth always resolves in death, which resolves in birth, both of which express the continuum of Life.

FREE WILL AND RECIPROCITY

How does free will factor into the discussion of Fate? Unlike the West, China has not argued much about fatalism and free will. It has long been understood that one cannot exist without the other. They alternate, blend, and define each other; they are Yinyang.

Our Original Nature is a free, open space that is the context of all experience. But our experience is conditioned by our Character and Fate. Therefore, our astrology chart's auspices are defined by our choices and how we use our freedom to manage our Character in response to our Fate. In this sense, we have "free-ish" will, and because our Original Nature is inherently free and unconditioned, we can ultimately be liberated from the conditioning of Fate and Character. In this sense, the Chinese notion of Fate is very similar to the Indian concept of karma. As far as I am concerned, they are interchangeable, although historically they are quite different, which is all I will say about that.

So, there is no inherently auspicious chart. The auspice of any chart is made by what the Chinese call Ganying (感應), or reciprocity: The relationship among Character, Inner Nature, and Fate is a reciprocity determined by choice. We find our life in the play and dance of these factors, and astrology is found in the dialogue between them.

WHAT IS THE UNIVERSE? THE RESOLUTION OF FATE

NOW THAT WE UNDERSTAND FATE, we must address the question, "What is the universe?" And "How do we resolve Fate?" using Polestar Astrology. In doing so, I would like to present the "big picture" of Polestar Astrology and how this view helps us to follow astrology as a wisdom path.

The "universe" is ***unknowable***. The Chinese Tradition refers to the unknowable universe as Dao, although that is not a direct translation, as Dao has no English equivalent. The first and most famous line of the Dao De Jing goes something like, "That which can be known or named is not the Dao." For those suffering from expertise, this may be disconcerting. Expertise is probably the biggest troublemaker in the world, as assumed knowledge, especially of other people's experience, is far more dangerous than conscious ignorance. One of my all-time favorite quotes comes from a Christian mystic, Bernadette Roberts: "When you have learned it all and lived it thoroughly, then you had better get ready to have it all collapse when you discover the highest wisdom is that you know nothing."[1]

When we examine our experience, Time and Space appear to be an incomprehensible chaos, which the Chinese call Huntun. When we examine our experience closely, we are confronted with irresolvable, unending confusion brought about by analysis, what we now call *analysis paralysis* (or paralysis by analysis). In other words, the universe, the world, and our "self" appear to exist, but this appearance is dubious. When we try to find the objects referred to by these big universal terms, we cannot. We find no particular time, place, or self. Rather, we find an infinite number of temporarily compounded "things," each made up of bigger or smaller things, ad infinitum, in the flow of ordinary experience, which is processional. And the universe, or Dao, as some "ultimate reality," is beyond conceptual elaboration, beyond the grasp of human thought. It is far too "big" to understand, which is the same as saying the universe is made up of things too small to understand.

Paradoxically, this Huntun, this irresolvable chaos, is the source of everything and every being. When we relax our need to know, our need to "figure everything out," we open the door to wisdom and direct experience. When we embrace reality as incomprehensible, our experience opens to what we can actually observe, which is temporary patterns of energy or light called Qi. Our actual experience tells us that we are a weaving of "Qi strands," or light waves. We are like a candle flame, a stream of energy that appears temporarily to display a certain pattern, which we call "I/me/mine."

The world, too, appears to be solid and stable. But under relaxed examination, the world is revealed as nothing but an appearance of cycling energy. What we know as the world is merely the tendency of Qi to look like "stuff," crystallized by the conceptual process of labeling the unknowable.

I often make fun of Western science because it seeks to "prove" through objective observation, and in trying to do so, it proves itself wrong every five minutes. Furthermore, it has eternally embarrassed itself with its own greatest discovery, the Uncertainty Principle: Everything you observe, you change. In other words, objectivity is a myth. In the Chinese Tradition, everything is seen as fundamentally empty and ultimately unknowable, and therefore, saying anything "conclusive" based on objective statistical data is seen as foolishness. Wisdom Science does not operate from the assumption that anything reliable can be said about anything. The only reliable constant is change; the patterns of change are what we seek to describe, and even these are not reliable as concepts. You may get cancer, but this will resolve in death. You may die, but this will resolve in birth. All we can say about health is "for whom and when."

The view of Polestar Astrology, then, has two dimensions: the dual and the non-dual. Buddhism calls these the Two Truths: the ultimate and the relative.

In the non-dual view, we practice divination, or "Fate calculation," to observe things "as they are," to investigate the fundamental nature of things, and to break down our compulsion to predict, fix, or improve particular aspects of the limitless sea of Dao. We observe these patterns as compound and processional in order to recognize that we are too. The constant observation of flowing patterns, then, undermines our notions of a solid world and of an abiding self. When these notions fall away, what remains is the ever-flowing nameless cosmos.

In this revelation, we experience ourselves and the world as a phantasm of light (Qi). This revelation, however, comes from the dual view of Polestar Astrology. In other words, what we divine through astrology is a dual or relative vision of the world, called Yinyang, which we see in the dance of microcosm and macrocosm. As soon as we begin to name the patterns of Qi, we separate them from the chaos of Huntun and from the nameless Dao.

In the view of Chinese astrology, the dual and the non-dual are not opposed; in fact, the non-dual contains the dual, and by investigating the weaving of the cosmic matrix we find ourselves in, we unravel our Fate. Huntun is not vanquished; it is embraced, and we agree to be swept along by the cycles in which we are already flowing. In other words, our experience is already flowing, and by naming the patterns we find ourselves in, we define a sense of personal Fate within the greater cycles. Through identifying our personal Fate, we define a path composed of smaller cycles regarding our health and happiness.

By studying the dual vision of the universe and by creating a personal sense of Fate and freedom, we learn how to disentangle our Qi from Fated debts (repeating patterns of depletion) and aggression (false views of a solid world and an abiding self). This disentanglement is called the resolution of Fate. In the resolution of Fate, we experience what the universe, the Dao, actually is: freedom with no agenda.

This freedom appears to the conceptual mind as the irresolvable chaos I mentioned in the beginning. Because of our anxiety, we try to pin down and describe everything to get "control" of the chaos, which is exemplified in modern science. But when we are resolved of Fate, this chaos relates openly with order, and the dual and non-dual are no longer experienced as two. In this, we experience our Original Nature, devoid of self and other yet freely generating Character and Fate. We find ourselves perfectly situated in the magnificent matrix of Dao: no self, no problem.

The resolution of Fate is called "Great Completion," or Da Yuan (大圓), the realization that everything is already harmonious. In Tibetan, it is called Dzogchen, the "Great Perfection." The universe (Dao) consists of cycles of Fate moving from apparent chaos to Great Completion and back again. As I have mentioned, these cycles are self-resolving, which means that the universe is characterized by a kind of balance, Yinyang, which is self-correcting. Yin is always moving in the direction of Yang, and Yang is hurling in the direction of Yin. Hence, the famous Yinyang symbol is depicted as one circle. Even when our life appears chaotic, it is moving toward order. Completion comes when we recognize that perfection includes both chaos and order.

From the non-dual perspective, the universe is an open space full of dancing light. From the dual perspective, this light vibrates in cycles and "appears" as patterns, which we call "things": people, places, planets, kittens, flowers, and so on. This experience of light, however, is unknowable. Great Completion is demonstrated when we become what we are: light having an experience of light. As Liu Ming's teacher demonstrated, those who experience Great Completion leave behind no corpse. The Rainbow Body, however, is not a special experience; it is what everything in the universe eventually does in the cycle of time.

Astrology as a wisdom path begins from the view that reality is an unknowable experience. We practice divination and study the cycles of change, time, space, Character, and Fate to undermine our notions of a solid world and an abiding, separate self. So, to answer the original question, "What is the universe?" Polestar Astrology replies, "Unknowable." What we can "know" is only what we can observe, which is nothing but temporary patterns of appearance.

THE NATURAL WISDOM OF YINYANG

CERTAIN ASPECTS OF DAOIST AND CHINESE COSMOLOGY have become popular. When I mention Yin and Yang, Qi, or Fengshui, most people nod their heads. However, many students, including myself, are too eager to abandon these basic notions and get to the "details," the important part where we know stuff.

The engineering or mechanistic view of reality tells us that the universe is some kind of Swiss watch and that its significance is in the details. If we can examine all the details and measure everything, somehow, this is supposed to produce insight. In the Chinese view, this is nonsense, like taking a watch apart to find the time. According to this View, basic teachings are the key to wisdom. If we rush to expertise, we become hysterical maniacs. Master the basics, and you will flourish.

The following two chapters will zoom out again and continue to examine the big picture, through the cosmology of Yinyang, and the Five Elements. To understand anything Chinese, we must understand these teachings in cosmological terms, meaning we must understand how they relate to our lived experience of the cosmos.

But first, I must say something more about View Teachings and Polestar Astrology. We, as modern, post-religious, secularized, industrial-engineer merchants, are far too eager to adopt techniques and methods from Asian wisdom traditions, as if the methods, the "doing stuff" part, hold the key to "evolution" or "progress." Expertise without wisdom is bankrupt and will fail. We must ask basic questions again and again. If we do not start from a basic understanding of our humanity, our expertise will lead us to aggression.

What the Chinese call "the Ten Thousand Things," or Wan Wu (萬物), all fall into two categories: Yin and Yang (陰陽). Forget the Ten Thousand; learn the two.

I have been studying and attempting to practice Asian religions for more than twenty-five years now, and I have almost nothing to report. However, I have learned that all methods—mindfulness, for example—come from a particular "View" about reality. Furthermore, all methods are intended to have inevitable Fruition based on that View. Without View, methods are meaningless and will, at best, produce a kind of neutral effect. If I have learned anything quantifiable, I have learned that methods are a dime a dozen. There are literally thousands of techniques of meditation, yoga, and divination. In short, if we practice a method without adopting its View, that method will not give its intended Fruition; it may even be harmful.

I once asked a friend interested in learning Daoist practice what he thought a human being was, and he replied, "A piece of shit." And he is not to blame; our culture tells us that human beings are basically bad, and our popular media and religions certainly reflect this view. However, the fundamental View of the Chinese Tradition states that humans are flawed but basically good, or Ren (仁). If you believe that humans are basically sinful, bad, broken, greedy, and so on, then you can practice meditation for a million years and never experience liberation, because your View and your method are mismatched. When we study View Teachings, we fundamentally alter our way of relating to experience, opening the space for transformation from the inside out.

If we adopt a method without adopting its view, then we supply the method with the view we already have, conscious or unconscious. In the case of Americans, this often places the individual and their problems (psychology) at the center of the universe. In this case, astrology and meditation become a new vocabulary for our own self-importance. Polestar Astrology should make us gentle people and free us from the hysteria of self-hatred and self-cherishing. In the Chinese Tradition, no individual is significant, and the goal of astrology is to discover what we have in common, not what makes us different.

In the Chinese Tradition, astrology should never be used as a form of aggression, smashing our afflictions and murdering our obstructions to get a one-up on the universe. Neither should the information be used to condescend to and exalt us over others. Nor should it be used to obsess over details, as if the exact position of the stars will give us "answers."

The View Teachings of Polestar Astrology, then, are of central importance to the practice and to receiving and giving a Natal Chart reading. To make use of it, we must understand the Chinese cosmological view. It is easy to learn technical vocabulary and techniques; it is not so easy to change our view. To be clear, View is not philosophy; we consider View as if it were describing reality as it actually is. Philosophy is an option, and it is very easy to break with: "People should be kind." View is not an option: "All that is compound is impermanent."

So far, I have discussed these View Teachings by exploring the questions, "What is a human being?" and "What is the universe?" Within these basic questions, I have begun to explore fundamental View Teachings on Character, Freedom, and Fate. I have also been hinting at the "big picture" by discussing Huntun, the view that reality is an unknowable chaos, and that all we can observe is cyclical patterns of movement. But how do these View Teachings relate to our actual experience?

Take a moment right now and ask yourself, what is experience? The Chinese would answer, Qi.

What is Qi? Qi is not a substance; it is a non-abiding movement. We experience movement, and all movement has direction and duration, which is why we also equate it to time.

Modern New Age spirituality often talks about "oneness" and "non-duality." The term ***non-dual*** often implies a kind of pretentious sophistication, the idea that non-duality is the "highest" teaching. However, "oneness" and "non-duality" in the Chinese View are meaningless and say nothing about our actual experience. What we experience is dual movement alternating in polarity. Like the poles of a magnet, this duality is inextricable yet defined by two-ness.

Life is splendidly dualistic, but in most traditions, dualism is problematic. Duality is somehow a kind of evil, a misunderstanding, a delusion, rather than something that defines the natural world. Duality is our closest image to the natural world, and it is not mistaken.

This alternating image of the natural world is known as Yin (陰) and Yang (陽), or Yinyang, which is probably the most famous Chinese idea. To understand anything Chinese we must understand Yin and Yang. As I mentioned in the beginning, our tendency to obsess over details often causes us to overlook the big picture. However, I assure you, if you study Yinyang theory, it will irreversibly change your life. It describes the whole of our experience, not through details but through the understanding that everything, absolutely everything, is in an alternating process of change.

The Yinyang symbol is plastered on everything from surfboards to sauerkraut labels, so the idea is at least familiar. The popular understanding, however, tends to miss the point. Popular literature often splits Yin and Yang into two lists. On the Yin side you see words like ***negative, dark, contracting, descending, cold, heavy***, and ***substantive***. On the Yang side you see opposite terms, like ***positive, light, expanding, ascending, hot, light***, and ***active***. And this is all true. But that is not the point.

I once mentioned Yinyang in conversation, and a friend asked, "Which one is push, and which one is pull?" The Chinese answer is, yes! In other words, it depends. We describe Yin and Yang only to get a basic understanding of their qualities, but they are a continuum. Our experience flows along an alternating continuum. This continuum is circular:

We can identify something as Yin, which means it is turning into Yang. We can describe something as Yang, which means it is turning into Yin. They constantly transform into one another as a kind of cyclical wave pattern. Traditionally, six Yinyang relationships describe this pattern:

1. Yin–Yang coexist in opposition (陰陽對立)—they are always juxtaposed.
2. Yin–Yang are interdependent (陰陽互根)—they are mutually rooted; you can't have one without the other.
3. Yin–Yang can be further subdivided into Yin–Yang (陰陽可分).
4. Yin–Yang consume and support each other (陰陽制約).
5. Yin–Yang can transform into one another (陰陽轉化).
6. Yin contains Yang (陰中有陽), and Yang contains Yin (陽中有陰).

Let's take "cold" as an example of these complex relationships. We can generically identify cold as Yin. But no temperature is static. A refrigerator can maintain a cold temperature, but this is strenuous, which is Yang, requiring energy. In this case, cold is in a tenuous state of Yang produced through effort. If the refrigerator breaks down, cold disperses, and temperature warms. In this case, the heating process is Yin because it is the natural release of strenuous energy. In other words, Yin and Yang cannot be pinned down in absolute terms like hot or cold; nothing can. Nothing is established in the way that it appears. Each appearance can only be temporarily described as Yin or Yang on the Yin–Yang continuum.

Our actual moment-to-moment experience also alternates along the same wave pattern. Any experience you can identify is turning into another kind of experience. Identifying confusion, for example, is clarity. Our emotions are never static.

We experience suffering, discontent, and disease when we believe our experience is static. But our experience is never stable; nothing is stable. We exhaust ourselves trying to make things stable and secure, when their natural state constantly alternates. This is the true wisdom of Yin and Yang. If we are upset, we are moving in the direction of contentment, only sometimes we must go a little further down before we start moving up again. We may be elated in the thralls of a peak experience, but this means we are moving toward depression, because you can only go "up" for so long. Experiences like happy and sad are identifiable through their contrasting opposite, and we vacillate through emotions all the time. The more we understand our experience as naturally alternating, the more we can relax. Knowing that sadness is already moving in the direction of happiness, we can learn to enjoy both, for they are each natural and tell us something about our experience. We develop equanimity only when we accept that nothing is static and that all movement is circular; we then begin to relax and let our awareness host the whole process.

In the Chinese Tradition, this movement is called self-resolving, or Ziran (自然). Yinyang is the basic pattern of movement, and it is a self-resolving pattern. This means there are no problems to fix. Everything coming apart is also coming together. If we have this big View, then we do not need to panic when our life falls apart (panicking a little is okay). Something needs to fall apart for other things to come together. This is the natural cycle of everything, from the vastness of galaxies to our very breath.

We do not try to inhale; exhalation naturally resolves with inhalation—this is Yinyang. You cannot find a distinct point when inhalation becomes exhalation (go ahead, try!), because they are a continuum.

That said, we still have Freedom, meaning we can resist the natural cycles. Our culture operates on the notion that progress is infinite, and our culture has an immense prejudice toward Yang in the form of activity and productivity. This prejudice, I think, comes from a kind of general, unnamed anxiety stemming from many diverse factors and concepts: Christian linear time, judgment day, and original sin, the notion that God is dead and that religious belief and authority has lost its power in the modern world, rugged mercantile individualism and the survival of the fittest, two hundred-plus years of modern war and atrocity—fear and anxiety lurk beneath the surface of modern culture. Our culture is losing cohesion, and we rarely support one another (how are your neighbors?).

I don't know about you, but I am exhausted just being an American. We are constantly trying to "improve" everything, and we are expected to be "productive" all the time, reflected in the standard forty-hour work week, which depletes us and leaves little-to-no time for anything but recovering from our exhaustion. I don't believe anyone can work forty or more hours a week and be healthy. And everything we do is work: We work at our relationships, work on our bodies, work on spiritual practice. Work hard and play hard. All this is excessive Yang, and it's exhausting.

Our excessive productivity depletes us and causes all kinds of illness and disease. Our standard of health is often, "Just get me back to work." We see Yin as weakness, and we hate weakness. Trying to be strong, strong, strong all the time is like a bridge with no sway; it will crumble in an earthquake. Because we have Freedom, we can resist Yinyang through Yang force, and we can resist our Fate, but not for long.

According to Classical Yinyang theory, the two are not equal, but they are in balance. Americans want everything to be equal, so we exalt Yang. The universe, however, is about 98 percent Yin and 2 percent Yang, which is just enough Yang to make it move. Most of what we do requires no effort: digesting, circulating blood, breathing, thinking, hearing, seeing, and so on. Very little actually requires effort. The planets revolve around the sun with no effort. The Chinese call these natural processes self-resolving, or Ziran (自然), which literally means "of itself so"—in other words, Yin. We barely need to "do" anything; we are already flowing in a spontaneously arising, self-resolving universe. And everything that we identify with is a complete mystery of spontaneity.

I have no idea how I form thoughts, how I speak, or how I remember. It would take a thousand years to describe the complexity of digesting a sandwich in technical language, and yet I do it without effort. Yang is the tiny push of a ball at the top of a hill that sends it rolling. The key to balance is learning when to apply just a little effort, enough to set things in motion. But if we are constantly applying effort, we deplete Yang, which is limited, and we become ill, sometimes so ill that death is the only Yin resolution.

Yinyang is both movement and rhythm, and movement implies that nothing abides. That is, there is no "thing" that moves. How could there be? Qi is not a substance, a thing that moves; it is movement itself. Movement creates the illusion of solidity and substance. Yin tends toward the substantive, and in the process of this tendency, it is already alternating toward dispersal. The constantly alternating quality of movement is cyclic and rhythmic, and this rhythm has no end.

Our culture has a linear view of time, and therefore, we are terrified of death. Anything that has a beginning has an end. We imagine that, in death, we somehow "stop." But nothing stops. And there was never a first movement, because there would have had to be something before that to generate it, ad infinitum. No amount of time deregulates the movement from Yin to Yang: The sun may be ancient, but its energy will eventually disperse.

So, how does all this apply to Polestar Astrology? First, our Character tends toward Yin or Yang. I am a Yang Fire Tiger, for example. Meaning, I tend toward the generative impulse. Second, our Fate has Yin and Yang aspects. Meaning, some things we are Fated to "do," and some things are Fated to happen by themselves. In general, our Fate cycles according to Yinyang. But these are the details. Without first understanding the basic View that *everything* is Yinyang, trying to understand our Character and Fate is infuriating. We must ask ourselves these basic questions again and again.

Every possible detail falls into either Yin or Yang, and the two always turn into one another. We cannot use astrology and Fate calculation if we are hysterical over details. We study astrology to see the cyclic pattern of our life, and Yinyang is the fundamental dynamic of all patterns. Without Yinyang, we get lost in the details and miss out on true wisdom.

NON-THEISM, NON-MATERIALISM, AND THE FIVE ELEMENTS

FROM COMPLETE "I DON'T KNOW," called Dao, our experience alternates in a Yinyang pattern. This cosmology provides a view of our experience so we can work with it directly rather than conceptually.

We explored the concepts of Dao and Yin-Yang as a basis for cosmology, addressing the questions, "What is the universe?" and "What is a human being?" Delving further into fundamental cosmology, the Chinese Tradition describes the movement of Qi in a cycle of Five Phases, or Five Elements, which we will explore next.

First, however, we need to address two views central to Western thought that are antithetical to the Chinese Tradition: theism and materialism. In ancient China, these would have been nonissues. In American culture, however, they are central. In short, Chinese astrology operates from a non-theistic and non-materialist view. If we operate from a theistic or materialist view of reality, our use of Chinese astrology won't work.

Theism is central to the cosmology of India and the West. Although broad and diverse, theism is simple. Here, I define theism not only as the belief that god(s), goddess(es), or deities exist but as the belief that they are essential and spiritually necessary. For example, God created the universe in Genesis. Or, from the countless examples of India, we are penetrated by Śiva (called *samaveśa*), and our limited being merges with cosmic or divine Being. China heard many forms of theism and said it was not interested. In response to the Bible, the Chinese replied that all the deities who live in the mountains say they created the universe, and they are all wrathful; why would you get involved with them?

Polestar Astrology is not atheistic; it is non-theistic. In other words, Chinese cosmology recognizes the existence of many kinds of beings (64,000 types of Ghosts, for example), all of which fall into six broad categories or Realms shared with most Asian traditions: the Demon or Hell Realm, Ghost Realm, Animal Realm, Human Realm, Demigod Realm, and God Realm. While beings are not all "equal," no one is more significant than another. There are teachings for Ghosts, teachings for gods, teachings for humans, and so on. We all move in different rhythms, have various kinds of bodies, and experience the universe quite differently. Deities are just other kinds of beings with a different, more holy, more ethereal type of experience. While many deities are prayed to in China, they are often seen as part of a celestial bureaucracy rather than a single deity. In terms of a universal or primordial Being or Cosmic Consciousness as often described in India, the Chinese Tradition would say: very clever, but "unknowable"; don't bother. And the Dao is certainly not God in the Western sense.

Many wisdom traditions say that we are really God in disguise. Many people want to discover who they truly are, find their passion, find God and great meaning behind everything, or that they possess great power or purpose. Many seek a big, heavenly enlightenment experience where everything is revealed and we get to have a big birthday party—the big Enlightenment doughnut in the sky, as one of my teachers called it. If you study Chinese astrology and come out the other side of Fate, you find out your non-existence rather than the "real you." The "real you" is something like space—very disappointing to the ego, and not very satisfying to big spiritual appetites. In the study of Polestar Astrology, we are not looking for God's plan or design, and we are not looking to find our true purpose or passion. We are looking to find our ordinary human experience in our actual situation, which is an enormous thing.

Theism is not denied in the Chinese Tradition; it is just seen as irrelevant to our ordinary human experience. In Chinese astrology, we aspire to follow the human spiritual path, not the path of deities. The experience of deities is not given a special significance, nor is the idea of a one true God. Confucius refused to talk about God, but rather taught that you actually have a father, and this is significant; you don't need to make a bearded daddy in the sky. The human spiritual path is about how humans relate to other humans, not to gods.

Chinese Tradition begins from the view that our ordinary human condition is complete and perfectly harmonious with the Dao. The only thing preventing this experience is false views about reality based on our belief in an abiding world and self. We do not need help from God or deities to realize our Original Nature; we need only to be in our actual human experience, which is already a perfect expression of the Dao. The human path of spirituality is based on ordinary human life, which consists of ordinary rhythms such as waking, dreaming, sleeping, eating, digesting, inhaling, exhaling, and circulating blood, all in relation to our human experience on Earth.

Chinese astrology is also non-materialist, which brings us to the discussion of the so-called Five Elements. Element theory in Europe and India is often materialist: When we say, "Earth Element," people often visualize dirt, or when we say, "Fire Element," they see flames.

While modern physics is slowly offering us a vision of reality that has been known in Asia for thousands of years, we are still a decidedly materialist culture. In other words, we believe in a solid, abiding world and that we are solid, abiding beings. I might say the proof that I "exist" is that I cannot pass my hand through the table. I know that my cat exists because he looks the same as he did yesterday and two weeks ago, and so on. We believe in material, in stuff, in things. Since things appear to be stable and consistent, we think they are solid entities existing from their own side.

We entertain the notion that we are compounds (made of parts, pieces, components) because we have common sense, but as a culture, we still believe that these components are reliable. We searched for, and apparently "found," the "God particle." We examine things in the hope that we will finally find something "undividable" (the meaning of the word ***atom***), whether it be particles or light waves—there must be building blocks, something that makes up or accounts for everything. This was the impetus for ancient element theory in Europe. Well, the Chinese Tradition, and especially Buddhism, says no. It says there is no ultimate stuff, and if there were, it would be unfindable, ungraspable, and indefinable by concept; this is one meaning of the word ***emptiness***. The fact that everything escapes investigation and description means there is nothing solid or abiding to ultimately find; everything is infinitely divisible. What you're looking at is what you think you're looking at. In other words, your world is a projection, a mental construct, the mind crystallizing a display of light and mirrors.

Holding the view of an abiding self and world is painful, and nothing will ever be more exhausting than trying to maintain a self, so just let it go—that's Buddhism in a nutshell. Reality is an unimpeded, unbounded, dynamic flux, so as soon as we fixate our view and hold on to stability and permanence, reality begins to grind us down—this is the meaning of the word ***dukkha*** in Buddhism. Suffering occurs when our view is misaligned with reality. The ancient meaning of the word ***dukkha*** is of an axle that does not fit properly into its spoke; you can force it, but the wheel rolls funny, and the axle grinds away.

If people actually exist, then they actually die. If there was a creation, then there would be annihilation, and all of this is a nightmare. At this moment, we are hurtling toward the grave. However, there is no real "you" anywhere in this hurtling; there is just the hurtling—a compound in procession.

Everything is compound, period. And everything is in procession, meaning in a flow or flux. And actually, what we observe is the movement, but there is no "thing" moving.

This is what is meant by "non-materialist." What moves is Qi, but Qi is not a "thing"; it is just movement itself. Again, we describe movement as Yinyang, which further differentiates into a cycle of the Five Elements. Two—Yin and Yang—times five makes ten. In Polestar Astrology, these combinations of two and five are called the Ten Heavenly Stems: Yang Wood, Yin Wood, Yang Fire, Yin Fire, and so on.

This view is in direct opposition to theistic creationism and scientific materialism. Our culture tends to fixate on an either-or situation regarding religion and science. You believe in either science or religion, or you compromise between the two while secretly believing that one is "real." When push comes to shove, most of us believe in Scientism; when sick, we turn to science and Western medicine to save us (especially when the machines go "ping!").[1]

We cannot approach Chinese astrology from this perspective; it won't work. Yinyang and Five Element cosmology does not involve creation or destruction. We speak of the procession as generating and concluding, but this does not imply a beginning or end. There was no beginning, first movement, or Big Bang that started everything (because what would have come before that?). Things resolve, but resolution is the mother of generation; death is the mother of birth. There is never an end to this continuity. Life is an eternal rhythm that goes birth–death–birth–death–birth–death . . .

In the Chinese Tradition, there is nothing outside Yin and Yang and the Five Elements; there is nothing—no one, no creator—watching and judging. If instead you use Polestar Astrology as a replacement view—if you replace God the Father or Jesus with Shiva, Dao, or Buddha—this is almost as stressful as the view of a permanent soul or self. All you have done is find a new language to substantiate a misunderstanding.

In Polestar Astrology, we describe our Character and Fate in terms of Yinyang and the Five Elements, but to make sense of this, we must understand these Elements as fundamental principles. Remember, these Five Phases describe the procession of all movement, all change, and all experience—your experience! Wisdom comes from your own living experience.

This cosmology is not religious; it is a vocabulary to help us feel into our experience, nothing more. And, again, it is not materialist: Wood Element is not lumber, Fire Element is not flames, Earth Element is not dirt, Metal Element is not gold, and Water Element is not H_2O. These literal associations are symbolic and used only as metaphors to help us learn. The Five Elements are principles describing the cyclical procession of Qi. And while they are processional, they can appear simultaneously. They can be big, describing the movement of galaxies, or small, describing the movement of thought. We begin with Wood; we start with starting.

MU (木): WOOD ELEMENT

Although we start with Wood, we must remember that Water is the mother of Wood, meaning that, when things end and resolve, they have nowhere to go and nothing to do except start over again. Wood Element is the starting-over part of our experience—the Qi experience of "start," or birth, made possible by death.

Wood Element is the fundamental impulse or whim to manifest, generate, grow, and move. However, it does not manifest; manifestation does not happen until Earth. Wood is eternal freshness, eternal beginning, naive and new—before everything, before thought. Everything is about to happen; Wood Element is a potential that never demonstrates itself. You cannot paint freshness and hang it on a wall, nor can you see Wood Element.

The first two of the Five Elements cycle are "unmanifest," meaning they do not actually appear. They are the process that must occur before anything can appear. Wood is associated with the juicy, young, fresh quality of experience. The image of Wood comes from the sapling, the sprouting seed, associated with spring, and the color green or turquoise, the color of new life starting again. Even within the oldest tree, there is still something juicy sucking up rain. While we use this imagery to describe Wood Element, the actual experience of Wood is this impulse, this prompting before things manifest. When spiritual people talk about the Eternal Now, they describe a Wood Element experience. Wood is also the mother of Fire.

Here are some of the traditional associations of Wood Element:

AGE: Birth, youth

WEATHER/ENVIRONMENTAL FACTOR: The wind, subtle and gentle movement

COLOR: Green, turquoise, the color of plant life

DIRECTION: The East, the rising sun, outward expansion

POSITIVE EMOTIONS: Gentleness, acceptance, modesty, naivety

NEGATIVE EMOTIONS: Anger, frustration

SEASON: Spring

HOURS AND ORGANS: 11 p.m. to 1 a.m. (gallbladder) and 1 a.m. to 3 a.m. (liver)

EARTHLY BRANCHES: Tiger, Rabbit

CONTROLS/DESTROYS: Earth Element

APPLIED TO CHARACTER: When applied to any natal astrology Character, the Wood Element adds a naive element of Peter Pan–like innocence, simplicity, and youthful responsiveness with a never-grow-up quality, as Wood is the Element of birth and youth. It adds ambition, an appetite for growth, artistic creativity, knowledge, and resilience, which makes people apt to start over and bend like a supple reed. When depleted, it has little depth and tends toward explosive anger and frustration.

HUO (火): FIRE ELEMENT

As soon as Wood's prompting, its impulse to manifest, moves, this movement generates a kind of friction or heat that we call the Fire Element. This heat gives direction toward appearance. Fire Element is not flames. Fire is still "unmanifest." In other words, we do not actually see heat or fire. What we call "fire"—that is, the color of flames—comes from the combustion of wood, but heat itself is invisible; it is just temperature. The image of Fire Element, associated with summer and the color red/orange, does come from flame, but this is only an image. Fire Element is the warming, heating up, directional part of our experience. For example, the end (Water)—being satiated—prompts the beginning of a new cycle (Wood), which begins to heat up (Fire), generating hunger. As soon as any impulse happens, it gains momentum and a direction: The Now, for example, has a direction; it flows. Fire is the quality of vigor and energy, the impulse of Wood Element to get excited and want to manifest and appear. So, Fire is the mother of Earth, giving birth to appearance.

Here are some of the traditional associations of Fire Element:

AGE: Teenagerhood, young adulthood

WEATHER/ENVIRONMENTAL FACTOR: Heat/fire

COLOR: Red, orange, the color of fire

DIRECTION: South, the path of the sun through the sky, rising upward

POSITIVE EMOTIONS: Joy, vigor, inspiration, celebration, laughter

NEGATIVE EMOTIONS: Hysteria, mania, consumption, violence

SEASON: Summer

HOURS AND ORGANS: 11 a.m. to 1 p.m. (heart), 1 p.m. to 3 p.m. (small intestine), 7 p.m. to 9 p.m. (pericardium), and 9 p.m. to 11 p.m. (Triple Burner)

EARTHLY BRANCHES: Snake, Horse

CONTROLS/DESTROYS: Metal Element

APPLIED TO CHARACTER: When applied to any natal astrology Character, the Fire Element adds force, vigor, passion, strength, sensuality, and courage. Fire consumes and makes a character more active, aggressive, engaged, and energized. The forceful burning and consumptive quality makes it difficult for Fire Characters to stay still and rest; it makes it difficult for them to be confined and for them to see and stay within boundaries. When depleted, Fire Characters are restless and more impatient. As Fire represents the bluster of teenagerhood, Fire Characters are like eternally angsty teenagers.

DI (地): EARTH ELEMENT

The heating, stirring, and frictional quality of fire makes sparks, and what "began" as an impulse with the Wood Element, and generated momentum and friction with Fire, now manifests with the Earth Element. Earth Element is the tendency of Qi to appear and manifest temporarily as form. Earth Element describes the continuity and stabilizing of Qi in the cycle of change. Earth Element constitutes a great deal of what we consciously experience. Earth and Metal are the qualities of our experience that present form (Earth) and names (Metal).

Looking in front of me, I see a form which, in and of itself, is nonconceptual. I may call it "table," and the table appears to be solid and to exist. The continuity of the "table" may last a while, but in a few thousand years, it will decay and be gone. The Five Element cycle of change, which is largely invisible, does not actually produce anything that lasts. It creates temporary appearances; Earth defines the temporary (however long) aspect of form. The table appears to exist for a while, but it will disappear. Just because titanium lasts for a really long time (relatively speaking) does not mean it is permanent; titanium is still in a process of movement and change.

Earth is heaviness, the experience of continuity and solidity. My body, for example, feels solid and heavy, and so I become attached to its existence. However, I shed my cells every seven to eight years; my body is not the same body I had at sixteen. Nothing about it is stable, and I may die tomorrow. The image of Earth Element, associated with the continuity of the seasons and the color yellow, comes from the ground, the mountains—from things that appear to endure but, in fact, flow like water in the cycles of time. Alone, Earth Element is mere appearance. As soon as appearance manifests, it immediately begins to transform and change, giving birth to Metal Element. Earth is the mother of Metal.

Here are some of the traditional associations of Earth Element:

AGE: Adulthood

WEATHER: Dampness, thunder

COLOR: Yellow, gold, earthen tones

DIRECTION: The Center, central unmoving pivot, stillness

POSITIVE EMOTIONS: Loving, caring, supportive, nurturing, sympathy

NEGATIVE EMOTIONS: Worry, greed, avarice, materialism, possessiveness

SEASON: Seasonal transition, the ground beneath all seasons

HOURS AND ORGANS: 7 a.m. to 9 a.m. (stomach) and 9 a.m. to 11 a.m. (spleen)

EARTHLY BRANCHES: Ox, Goat, Dragon, Dog

CONTROLS/DESTROYS: Water Element

APPLIED TO CHARACTER: When applied to any natal astrology Character, the Earth Element adds grounded emotional stability and maturity. It represents the still center of the moving seasons and the age of adulthood. The Earth Element is solid, adding confidence, power, and a strong sense of sympathy, caring, and nurturing. As Earth is the Element of manifestation, it adds worldliness and a desire for material acquisition, wealth, and development.

JIN (金): METAL ELEMENT

As soon as appearance stabilizes, Earth begins to become differentiated and variegated. Nothing is what it appears to be. Metal is the maturation of Earth; it is appearance crystallizing into "things"—form taking on names and, therefore, qualities—but it is always changing in its particularity. The form in front of me is a mere form, but as soon as I recognize and distinguish its qualities, I label it a "table," and it becomes a "thing." I can now describe the table, and this refinement is the Metal Element. Metal Element is the conceptual and refined quality of our experience.

Associated with fall and the color white or silver, the image of Metal Element comes from alchemy, the refinement of precious metals from raw ore. Practically, Metal Element is refinement—our organs refining and extracting nutrients from food and air, for example. Together, Earth and Metal constitute most of what we call "stuff": appearance and conceptual designation.

Qi tends to appear as stable stuff, but this stability is merely a momentary aspect in the cycle of Qi. Soon, we forget; we have moments, perhaps when spacing out, when we forget about who we are and where we are going. Metal Element is tenuous and strenuous, and refinement cannot be maintained. Our concepts about reality are limited and must fall apart. It is exhausting to maintain appearances, so Metal gives birth to Water, collapsing into oblivion.

Here are some of the traditional associations of Metal Element:

AGE: Middle age, late adulthood

WEATHER/ENVIRONMENTAL FACTOR: Dryness, cold

COLOR: White, silver, clear crystal

DIRECTION: West, downward, the setting sun

POSITIVE EMOTIONS: Sensitivity, intelligence, analysis, clarity

NEGATIVE EMOTIONS: Grief, worry, anxiety

SEASON: Autumn

HOURS AND ORGANS: 3 a.m. to 5 a.m. (lungs), 5 a.m. to 7 a.m. (large intestine)

EARTHLY BRANCHES: Monkey, Rooster

CONTROLS/DESTROYS: Wood Element

APPLIED TO NATAL ASTROLOGY CHARACTER: When applied to any natal astrology Character, the Metal Element adds discretion, reluctance, refinement, and fastidiousness. Metal is the Element of autumn, when leaves fall and nature is stripped of inessentials and we prepare for winter, and of middle age, when we mature and begin to prepare for old age. Metal is more withdrawn and self-reflective, enhancing intellectual, political, and spiritual matters. This adds a kind of maturity, wisdom, and insight that creates inward self-confidence.

SHUI (水): WATER ELEMENT

The peak of manifestation and appearance has nowhere to go, nothing to do, except collapse and fall apart. Water Element is the falling-apart aspect of our experience. Water is the "end" of the cycle, so it is also the beginning, the mother of Wood. Water is associated with death and dissolution.

Our experience of life is full of death. We experience so many endings, it is amazing we fear death. Every inhalation ends; every thought passes away; every sensation dissolves. Every night, we die when we fall asleep. Water Element is the collapsing of particulars into undifferentiated soup.

Nothing would move if things didn't end; there would be no room for anything new. The constant dissolution of our experience constantly makes way for Wood's impulse for newness. Associated with winter and the color blue or black, the image of the Water Element is like water itself, describing life's flowing, liquid, malleable, interconnected, fluid nature. Water Element is the recognizable, dramatic experience of change.

Usually, we don't notice change until things collapse and dissolve. Water Element is therefore associated with drama, with Big Yin. But nothing can end permanently; dissolution naturally generates the impulse to manifest. Nature abhors a vacuum. So, Water is the mother of Wood, and the cycle begins again.

Here are some of the traditional associations of Water Element:

AGE: Old age, death

WEATHER/ENVIRONMENTAL FACTOR: Cold, rain, snow

COLOR: Blue, black, the color of the sea and night sky

DIRECTION: North, inward contraction, sinking

POSITIVE EMOTIONS: Wisdom, empathy, acceptance

NEGATIVE EMOTIONS: Fear, anxiety

SEASON: Winter

HOURS AND ORGANS: 3 p.m. to 5 p.m. (bladder) and 5 p.m. to 7 p.m. (kidneys)

EARTHLY BRANCHES: Pig, Rat

CONTROLS/DESTROYS: Fire Element

APPLIED TO CHARACTER: When applied to any natal astrology Character, the Water Element adds a sense of profundity, wisdom, depth, and scale. It creates drama, emotionality, generosity, fluidity, and acceptance, as Water is the Element of dissolution and death. Water creates a deep pull inward, greatly enhancing spiritual matters, but the fluidity enhances the sense of interconnectedness and political and social matters. Water Element adds empathy and sensitivity to the feelings of others.

I have just described the "generating" cycle of the Five Elements. Naturally, there is a "concluding" or controlling cycle, which is sometimes called "Destructive." Water extinguishes Fire, meaning dissolution contains excitement. Wood eats Earth, meaning freshness lightens heaviness. Fire melts Metal, meaning inspiration softens rigid thinking. Earth absorbs and contains Water, meaning continuity and stability uphold the fear of death. And Metal cuts Wood, meaning logic and reason edit naivety.

The wisdom of the Five Elements of Qi is meaningless until we recognize it in our own experience. The Chinese Tradition is relative. It does not come from God; it must be examined over and over again. Do not accept it until you examine it. If you can identify part of your experience that does not fall into these five categories, then we can add a sixth. However, since millions of people have not been able to do so over thousands of years of this tradition, and neither have I, I find it comprehensive.

Yinyang and Five Element cosmology is quite profound. Here, I have attempted to describe only the basic qualities of each Element as a basis for your own inquiry, and as we go through the various symbols of Character and Fate in this book, you should keep these qualities in mind and apply them as you go.

WHERE DOES FATE COME FROM?

Ancestors, Immortality, and the Spirit World

BELIEVE IT OR NOT, THE EARTH IS ALIVE. In fact, the Earth and universe are Life itself. There is nothing but sentient, living awareness. And yet so few of us feel this. Modern life has hardened our senses, and in many minds, modern materialistic science has made the Earth into a mere unconscious process of chemistry, biology, and physics. Those with salvational views may believe the Earth to be God's creation, but this makes it little more than an artifact, albeit a magnificent one. These are both, of course, myths (myths not meaning false but simply different stories explaining reality). And while these myths can seem outdated in the modern technological age, they still greatly influence our culture.

The Chinese Tradition has a different myth. If we call the Scientific myth "mechanical/chemical" and the Creationist myth "ceramic" (implying the universe was made by an outside agent, like a potter who shapes clay), then we can call the Chinese myth "organic." In other words, the Chinese see the universe as an organism, growing from the inside out in a living, flowing process of eternal cyclical movement (Qi). Their view of the living world is vast and incomprehensible to modern minds. Daoists say that we share this space with 64,000 kinds of 64,000 categories of birth ("animal," for example, being one category), most of which we cannot "see."

In the Chinese organic view, the Earth is populated by a vast network of "realms" and "spirits," governed or "managed" by the blessings and unresolved patterns and issues of everything that came before, and we call these precedents "Ancestors." These realms share the same space, and while we experience only one space, the Chinese conceive of many spaces that all "vibrate," or move, at different frequencies. When other beings in other realms are happy and being themselves, they are invisible to us, and we are invisible to them. We do not "possess" one another. When beings in other realms are not happy or their space is disturbed by human activity, they can cross over into our space, and we can get possessed by spirits.

Although this may sound "conveniently unprovable" by modern scientific standards, modern science does state that our eyes cannot see heat, nor most of the spectrum of light, for example. In the same way, the Chinese Tradition sees Earth as "multidimensional," with the many simultaneous, unseen dimensions intertwining, blurring, and flowing into one another. The deep ocean and dense wilderness, for example, are considered hell and spirit realms. The Chinese Tradition says that we should not disturb these places, for they are full of beings we cannot see, and their exile, say, through deforestation, has powerful consequences, for they are set loose elsewhere. Some of these "other" beings we can see, such as animals. But we can all agree that your dog does not see the same Earth you do, because they do not see most colors, and their sense of smell creates a much different world for them.

You may say that we cannot see heat like a snake can, but we can detect it with instruments and "prove" its existence. And so you may say that, on the other hand, we cannot see Ghosts or detect them with machines, so they don't exist. In response, I would ask you, What color is your mind? Obviously, your mind, like a mirror, has no color—you cannot "see" your mind or "prove" to another person you had a thought—but I doubt you would say your mind does not exist, which itself would be a thought and proof of mental activity.

Perhaps one day we will develop a solution to the "hard problem" of consciousness, but Eastern spirituality has always said that the brain is not the source of the mind; it is only a conduit. The mind has a different kind of reality, a mental one, and materialistic science will always be at a loss so long as it considers the mind as an emergent property of the brain. It is not. Until this difference is acknowledged and reconciled, Western science and Eastern wisdom will never actually meet.

Like your mind, many types of beings in the universe have a different, nonphysical, unmeasurable existence, and the Daoist and Tantric traditions teach many ways to "see" them with "other" eyes. Daoism teaches that we have five inner eyes, like the famous third eye depicted in New Age literature. So, I will unequivocally say that, as human beings, we can cultivate the ability to "see" other realms and open our wisdom eyes, but to do so, we need first to acknowledge that subjective reality is, in fact, a reality, and second, we need to practice meditation. Many modern meditation teachers liken meditation to developing an internal microscope, which is an excellent place to start.

All kinds of birth (womb, egg, moisture, mental/miraculous/light—how deities are born, etc.) are Life. In the Chinese View, rocks, trees, rivers, and everything on Earth is alive, and everything has Qi. Everything expresses an immortal continuity—a web with no weaver and no beginning. Buddhism calls this interconnected web Indra's Net, which is sometimes likened to infinite drops of dew in a vast spider's web, each reflecting every other drop, ad infinitum. Indra's Net represents dependent origination, interpenetration, and emptiness.

Central to this organic view is the continuity of Life, called immortality. I will explore the notion of immortality later, but to begin with, we must understand the fundamental notion that we express an ongoing continuity; in other words, we all came from somewhere. We express and come from a past rhythm, like the ripple of waves on water.

Where did you come from? Have you ever seriously thought about it? Chances are you have probably thought about it a little but dismissed it as unimportant or just unknowable.

So, where *do* we come from? The short answer is, we come from parents who came from parents who came from parents, and so on. We come from life and can generate life. As long as humans keep getting horny, we can keep the life going forever. You are a link in an unbroken chain of countless beings who reproduced. The very fact that you're here means that life has come to you, unbroken, from the beginning of the universe. I'll give you a minute on that one.

The proper term for this is ancestry. Your Ancestors are your precedent; you inherited everything you are from them. If you dismiss your Ancestors as unimportant, you are an anomaly among the human species. Most humans all over the Earth, in most civilizations throughout human history, have considered ancestry extremely important. And our culture today does not. Some may argue that this disconnection from our roots, history, and Ancestors in all their forms is the reason for our confusion and discontent.

We do not seek to liberate the negativity of our past, and so we are ruled by it. The saying goes, those who do not study history are doomed to repeat it. One only needs to study history to see that humans have repeated the same patterns throughout time. One only needs to examine the politics, rhetoric, and cultures of our time to know that we are now repeating history—only this time, we're doing it on the internet with giz-widgets, at an exponential rate.

In the study of astrology, we study our history—what preceded our birth. A Natal Chart is a map of your Fate at the time of birth and a map of your Ancestors, which are one and the same. Your "past lives" are also your Ancestors in the Buddhist interpretation of astrology. Your body, too, is a map of your Ancestors. To honor the past, we begin with our Ancestors, because they gave us our body, they gave us life, and they gave us our Fate.

In the Chinese View, you have many "bodies." You have a family body, a social body, a friendship body, a cultural body, a religious body, a Fated body, a dream body, a universal body, an energy body, an Ancestral body, and so on. Your life is lived in all these bodies simultaneously, and your Fate is related to each in turn.

These bodies are like a Russian doll, and some are so big that you cannot really work with them, at least not without straining yourself. So, in spiritual practice, we work from the inside out, with the view that the subtle affects the gross more than the gross affects the subtle. Our Ancestral body is at the core of our Fate and is the easiest to work with. As our bodies radiate outward, they open into our "shared" Fate, and our Ancestral body lies at the core of this shared Fate. There is a reason we are born into our family.

We share Fate with our family—why else should our lives be so intimately connected? In the Chinese Tradition, we don't really have personal Fate. In other words, our Fate is not isolated in a box for us to work with as a private experience. Our actions ripple throughout the universe, spiraling in and out of our many bodies. The fact that you were born to your parents means you are connected to them, and everyone in your family is linked throughout time, playing many roles in many lifetimes.

This Ancestral body includes about seven generations of humans and is likened to a stream. There are many streams of Fate in the universe; some flow into each other, and all are heading toward the sea, which in turn becomes rivers again in the cycles of time. Some rivers come from different mountains and take different paths to return home. The time of our birth, our birth chart, tells us which river we were born into and where this river runs. In Polestar Astrology, we call these "Currents of Fate," or Mingyun (命運).

When we are born, we enter, or reenter, the stream heading to the Ocean and returning to the Source. Not all currents are the same; some are like lazy rivers, and some are like whitewater rapids. The nature of each stream is determined by all those in it, or in other words, by our Ancestors. Through birth, some are dumped in the rapids, and others ride in a yacht. This stream is a stream of human heart-minds connected by Fate in the cyclical flow of time. Again, each cycle spans about seven generations, forward and backward from each person.

These streams connect most strongly through blood, but some connect in other ways. You may have "Wisdom Ancestors," or past life spiritual connections, and be Fated to reconnect to your Ancestral Stream through a teacher, tradition, or lineage. Your best friends or co-workers may be your spiritual Ancestors from another life, and your Fate may be to reconnect with them in this lifetime to work in the world together. Whether this is the case or not, your Fate is connected to your family at least a little, and this is what Polestar Astrology tells us: where and how your Ancestors appear in your life.

In the cycles of Fate, some humans resolve their Ancestral Fate through spiritual practice, good luck, tremendous sacrifice, or great generosity, and exit their stream at the time of death. At this moment, a human who has lived a complete life, who has resolved their Fate, can choose to "return" into the cycles (also called samsara) and take birth in a new stream or in the same stream, or they can leave the Six Realms altogether and experience Great Completion, becoming a "pure/light being."

In Buddhism, a returning being is called a bodhisattva, and we assume that if someone returns to the Six Realms, they do so to help out in the flesh. If they leave the Realms, they can become a "Beneficial Ancestor" and benefit beings from "behind the scenes." If, say, your great-grandmother chooses this role, then she may appear in your natal astrology as the Empress, Moon, or Oracle Star, a guiding force in your Fate and in the resolution of the Ancestral Stream through your conduct in the world. Your Beneficial Ancestors become both your drive and your calling: giving you your path in life, directing you, prompting you, and creating opportunities to liberate not only you, but the whole family. They work in the world to create positive circumstances to resolve your Ancestral Fate.

As an Ancestral body flows, Beneficial Ancestors come and go, holding "office," so to speak. Your great-grandmother may very well be the precedent for your career. If you powerfully resolve your Fate regarding career, she may release into what the Daoists call "Great Completion," or returning to Source. If we resolve all our Ancestors and Fate, we can experience Great Completion, or the Rainbow Body, in this life and leave behind no corpse, meaning that we resolve our birth.

That being said, not all your Ancestors are happy and resolved; some become Gui (鬼)—what we call Ghosts or Demons. This means they have an incomplete death, or get "stuck" in their transition, and you inherit their unfinished business, which I will discuss later with the Ghost Stars.

All your Ancestors together to form a "team," a pattern of Fate that you inherit at birth. In Polestar Astrology, we read the Fate you were given at birth as a pattern, determined by the Twelve Ruling Stars, which we again call your Currents of Fate or Fate stream. All the Stars we read in a Natal Chart represent Yin and Yang currents of Ancestral Fate.

Polestar Astrology, which is not astronomical but chronological, describes the flow of these currents in the universe as they are governed by the greater macrocosmic cycles, spiraling outward from the fixed point of the Polestar, or the Emperor of Fate, the place where Fate is recorded and dispersed. Heaven flows in a pattern, and it governs the flow of Ancestral Streams on Earth. A human being is where these two things, Heaven and Earth, life and death, meet.

In other words, your Ancestors are important. Of course, I'm sure your parents and grandparents are important to you; perhaps you are even in therapy because of this. And although modern psychology gives us a vocabulary for understanding our family relations, in my mind, it completely misses the mark. The influence of our Ancestors is far greater and far more significant than most of us realize. Indeed, it is far greater, albeit far less dramatic, than our "Mommy/Daddy issues."

Ancestry has been abstracted in being "psychologized," and so although many of us explore our family issues, few of us honor them. In other words, we exalt our issues but do not exalt our Ancestors. In Chinese astrology, we call the presence of the Ancestors in our life Yuan Qi (元氣), or Ancestral or Source Qi. In modern parlance, your Ancestors are your "issues," but they are also your talents, goals, aspirations, and health.

In the past century, terms such as *Ancestor worship* and *spirits* have been used to denigrate many old-world traditions, relegating them to superstitions. It was not only missionaries but anthropologists and modern scientists alike who brutalized the Animistic Traditions because they did not perceive that their own worldviews were also religious. In other words, we are plagued by hundreds of years of Western scientific materialism and salvational Christianity that have misinterpreted other cultures by perceiving them through their own biased lenses. It is only in the past few decades or so that scholarship has begun to rectify this.

Sadly, cultures (especially here in America) are losing touch with their ancestral roots, and as a whole we have certainly lost touch with the Spirit World. As a culture, Americans do not honor our elders, and we do not honor our Ancestors. As a result, the past few generations have become very "loose"; we have become a generation of Ghosts. We drift around like floating heads, and the quickness of our technological advancement has displaced us from the cycles of nature so fast that we have barely begun to realize the consequences. Furthermore, the popular myths of Creationism and Scientism have dominated our minds and made us insensitive to the vast networks of life on Earth, which is exemplified by our pollution of the environment.

This network, this flow of life, has many dimensions, names, and expressions that I have already mentioned, such as the Spirit World and the Ancestors. If we open our minds to the situation we are actually in, if we experience everything in the world as alive, and if we learn to honor and respect this life, then we have the opportunity to transform our experience and reconnect to our Original Nature.

I do not personally believe that science has "disproved" the old-world views; rather, I believe it never understood them in the first place. I do not advocate a "return to the jungle" (well, maybe a little), but I do believe there is great value in understanding what the Chinese and many other traditional cultures mean by "Ancestors." And I believe there is even greater value in honoring our Ancestors in the terms of these traditions.

Ancestral Fate is the main subject of Polestar Astrology, which is difficult for most people to understand. During astrology sessions, I introduce this idea to people, and while most are open to it, many look at me like I'm crazy. It never occurs to us that our neurotic, self-limiting tendencies are not actually ours but come from our Ancestors. Our human form hosts and expresses inherited patterns, and because our Inner Nature is inherently free, we can choose to work with them and resolve them.

So far, I have gone to great lengths to discuss foundational View Teachings on Yin and Yang, Huntun, and the Five Elements, but when it comes down to it, Polestar Astrology is about Ancestors. This is a vast topic, and once we understand the basic view on Ancestral Fate in a practical and accessible way, the entire tradition of Chinese astrology opens and becomes a powerful tool in the path to Human Freedom.

But before I explore the practical understanding of Ancestral Fate, I would like to return to the subject of immortality, an often-misunderstood idea from Chinese and Indian cosmology. Immortality is often interpreted as "not dying." The longevity cults and traditions of immortality in China have long been interpreted by the West as attempts to extend physical life forever. This is in line with Western myths about the Fountain of Youth, but in the Chinese Tradition it is nonsense.

In the Chinese Tradition, immortality has nothing to do with not dying. The purpose of studying Polestar Astrology, following a spiritual path, and resolving our Ancestors is to discover our Original Nature, which is immortal. In other words, when we have resolved and are free of the tangles of Fate, we touch our Source, which was never born, never dies, and yet flows forever in an immortal procession. Reproducing eternally in interdependent sex-paired opposites, Life has been flowing since beginningless time.

By realizing the dimension of our experience that is already immortal—realizing that what we are, in essence, does not die because it was never born—we become immortal. When we realize our immortality, our Fate and all our Ancestors are liberated. In the traditional Chinese and Indian view, a realized immortal is free to benefit beings in all the realms throughout time, no longer bound to the Fate of their Ancestors or to their karma.

So, how do we work with our Ancestors? How do our Ancestors influence our everyday life? Well, this is actually quite simple. First, we must get the fundamental view that we have no abiding self.

If we have no abiding self, what are we? In short, we are a compound of our Ancestors. In other words, we are a stream of the echoes of thousands of people flowing together into a single body-mind. We identify with this stream and call it "I/me" because our nature is reflexive, but actually, you are the flowing Fate of many other people, and they, too, were a compound of many other people, individual expressions in the flow of Ancestral Streams.

Let's first take your body; obviously, you received your body from your parents. When your parents kicked boots, Yin and Yang, red and white, came together and produced you, a combination of two Ancestral Streams. So, you may have your mom's eyes, your dad's jaw, your grandmother's butt, your granddad's poor circulation, your great-grandmother's hair, and your great-uncle's freckles. Our physical constitution and health are clearly an expression of many people. Our health and Fate for illness and disease are largely Ancestral, and otherwise produced by our freedom, or conduct.

But what about the rest of you? Our culture recognizes that talent "runs in the family," but we don't seem to acknowledge that everything else runs in the family. Your intelligence, talents, interests, and likes and dislikes are also inherited from your Ancestral Stream. Perhaps you inherited your grandmother's intellect or your great-great-aunt's musical abilities. In other words, in order to honor our Ancestors, we must realize that *everything* we are has a precedent; everything comes from an Ancestor, from past actions. We are simply a new and unique combination of all the people we come from, including our own past lives.

So, this obviously means that we inherit negativity as well. Our fear, neurosis, hatred, prejudice, dullness, allergies, illness, accidents, addictions, and so on also come from our Ancestral Stream. Since our culture is narcissistic and self-obsessed, we exalt our "specialness" and blame ourselves for our negative traits, creating all kinds of stories about how messed up we are. Or we blame our parents, which is the wrong interpretation of Ancestral Fate. If we are taught from an early age not to identify with the negativity we inherit, then we can work with it without blaming ourselves or our parents.

Of course, we must take responsibility for our actions, but we need not blame ourselves for, say, inheriting a long pattern of addiction. Then we can take action to break the cycles of negativity we inherited. If you take on this responsibility without blame, then you will realize that no one (no "self") was ever personally to blame, and all your Ancestors will become free. Unfortunately, many paths, such as psychology, exalt the notion of working with our negativity but don't teach us that it was never "ours" (or anyone's) to begin with. In this way, cycles of blame are perpetuated in endless "talk therapy" sessions digging through the past.

You may be addicted to chocolate. You can't stop eating it. Perhaps your great-aunt grew up poor and only tasted chocolate once at a rich person's house. Perhaps she died poor and never tasted chocolate again. So, she died with the taste of chocolate as a painful reminder of everything she could never have and always wanted. Now, you can't stop eating chocolate, and it is giving you problems. You must stop, but you can't because you identify with the problem and do not realize that it is not you but your great-aunt who wants the chocolate. Her desire was passed down to you energetically. In the Chinese Tradition all our patterns are like this—all our compulsions, addictions, and bad habits. We are just streams of Fate that get passed down through Ancestors.

Perhaps your grandmother died in World War II. She was sitting at home, heard the sirens, and a bomb was dropped on her in an air raid. Now you're thirty-five, have no stability, and move from place to place; every time you make a home, you feel unsafe, like something bad will happen, and you must get out.

Maybe your great-grandfather lost everything in the Great Depression and could not feed his family. He turned to drink and became very depressed. Disgraced, he hanged himself in the barn. The family survived but never spoke of him again. Now, you're a teenager and are haunted by an irrational depression; one day after school, you try to hang yourself in the garage.

Perhaps your grandfather was an immigrant. In a new land, he worked eighty hours a week to build a business from nothing. He succeeded through hard work but never spent time with his children or wife. Now you're forty and a workaholic. You have spent your whole adult life getting ahead and succeeding, making the best of what your grandfather created for you, but you, too, never see your family.

Here's a personal example. I had a relative who had a heart attack on a dance floor and died. If you ask me to dance, I feel like I will die. Or let's take the Buddhist perspective of Ancestors as past lives. Perhaps you have been a celibate monk for the past thirty lifetimes. Now, you're a modern American with a tremendous impetus toward the spiritual path and no idea how to date.

This can get very dark. Say you lived all your life as a good person. But your village was raided, and in your last moment before death, you watched a soldier murder your child. And in that last moment, you bit down and felt the most unbelievable rage, followed by the desire to kill the person who killed your child. In death, you forget all the goodness of your human life and can remember nothing but the rage and the feeling of biting down, and you get stuck in it, unable to release. In anger, after death you chase after the only beings you can "see," which are your Ancestors, and your great-nephew gets terminal cancer. This is an example of one of the Ghost Stars, called the Seven Killings Star, which turned Demonic. We will examine that later.

In the Chinese Tradition, this is called "possession." And these issues are called "Ghosts" and "Demons." This is a vast topic. In short, a Ghost is an Ancestor who had a very incomplete death, full of longing, desire, or dissatisfaction that you may inherit as anxiety and low self-esteem, for example. A Demon is an Ancestor who died full of anger and hate, which you may inherit as an incurable illness or irrational aggression or as a freak car accident. This may sound negative, and I don't want to spook you. I want to open your mind to the continuum of death experiences and the notion that, while your body may die, your energy, momentum, and Fate continue and become Fate in your Ancestral Stream.

But we are not bound to the Fate of our Ancestors. According to Polestar Astrology, every human is a compound of Character, Inner Nature, and Fate. Humans are, by nature, free. I'll say that again: *We are free by nature.* Our limitations and our Fate are inherited. We have no self. We are a swirling stream of past actions coming to fruition in a body-mind, and nowhere in this stream is there a solid you. What you call "I/me" is just the ability of this compound stream to self-reflect and create temporary self-images to manage conventional reality.

When we liberate our Ancestors, we are free to rest in our Inner Nature, which is clear, radiant, and calm but also dynamic and active. A human being free of their Ancestors is relaxed and has no compulsion to do anything other than respond appropriately to their natural appetites. The momentum of the pain and happiness behind them has vanished into light. The more we relax into our Inner Nature, the more we experience ourselves and the world as a phantasm of light (Qi).

So, how do we work with our Ancestors? Better yet, how do we honor them? First, get your astrology chart! As I mentioned, Polestar Astrology describes the nature of your Ancestral Qi in terms of your Fate and Freedom. A reading will tell you if your Fate is in family, career, children, money, and so on, and this tells you how all your Ancestors are crowded behind you.

All my Fate is out in the world, for example. It is not with marriage and children. Of course, I can have a family, but if I do so, they will demonstrate my Freedom rather than Fate. Knowing where our Ancestors are pushing us (and you should already be aware of this to a degree because it's your life) is helpful. We can deplete ourselves by wasting energy in the areas of life that are not Fated.

Honor yourself as an expression of everything and everyone that came before you. Recognize that all your talents, skills, fears, and neuroses come from others. This means letting go of self-hatred and blame as well as self-cherishing. When you do this, thousands of Ghosts disappear into the light. Letting go of self-blame does not mean blaming our Ancestors, for they, too, were in the same position. We want to liberate them, not blame them. And we do this by following a spiritual path.

By choosing to work with and release our limiting patterns, we release our Ancestors. Release self-blame and self-cherishing, and cultivate self-respect and self-love. Love yourself, love your Ancestors, for you are one and the same. Your Ancestors exist in you, as you; they do not float around in a heaven or hell. They are your living body-mind.

If we live a very thorough life, full of intent and generosity, and if we cultivate a spiritual path, then in the moment of death, we do not get "stuck." Our issues do not get passed down. If we do not have a complete experience of life, then we do not have a complete death; we get stuck in the "bardo" between birth and death, like a skipping record in a place outside time, and our momentum continues. So, most important, cultivate self-reflection and release your negative patterns through conduct and meditation.

Honor your literal Ancestors, which means your parents, grandparents, culture, and so on. You should thank your parents for life, honor their wisdom, and treat them with respect. You should love them no matter what, no matter what kind of childhood you had. Your enlightenment is theirs, too.

Ritual offering is one of the most powerful ways we can honor our Ancestors. Every Chinese home has an Ancestor altar. Create an Ancestor altar and make offerings to it every day. Put pictures of your family on the altar and offer them symbols such as food, flowers, incense, prayer, songs, or anything that comes from your heart. When you make an offering, cultivate the intent to free everyone in your family line from all their negative Fate and yours. You are thousands of people embodied, and everything you do, you do as them, for them.

Do prostrations in front of your Ancestor altar. In the Tantric and Daoist traditions, prostrations are the main practice for liberating your Ancestors. Visualize all your female Ancestors in an unbroken line behind your right shoulder and all your male Ancestors behind your left shoulder. Honor everything you come from, and bow (even better, get transmission on prostration practice, and do it as part of your spiritual path). Prostrations are embodied; your body is the living expression of your Ancestors, and to bow in full prostration with your body to the stream that generated it is very powerful.

Have proper funerals. Whatever your deceased Ancestor expected, do that. If your dad was an Irish Catholic and wanted you to get drunk at his funeral and tell stories about him, do it. You may say, "I'm a Buddhist; I don't drink." On that day, you get drunk like an Irishman. If your mother wanted to be cremated, do it. Never do what you want at their funeral; do what they wanted and expected. This helps their transition, especially if you have strong family traditions, which is why it is important to write a will. Do not chant Buddhist sutras at your Polish grandmother's funeral; you will probably confuse her. Tell their stories and allow yourself time to grieve. Say everything you want to say to them, and make sure that you keep speaking to them for at least seven weeks after their death. Visualize them resolving into light and love.

Also, if you have the honor to be around a family member in the dying process, do whatever you can to make their experience peaceful and full of resolution. Do not cry and sob and wail around a corpse. The dead can hear for a long time after death. If their last moments are of you crying, "Don't leave me!" They may feel guilty for leaving, and a part of them may stick around as a Ghost.

Research your genealogy. Find out who you come from and where you come from. Make a family tree. Get a DNA test. Find out all their names and stories. Go back as far as you can. Find out if and how they immigrated. Did they go to war? Were they farmers? What languages did they speak? What religious traditions did they follow? Has anyone in your family been forgotten? Are there sad stories waiting to be told? Sometimes, an Ancestor can linger for generations, just waiting to be remembered, for their name to be spoken. Sometimes this is enough.

Eat the food of your Ancestors, at least a little. If your Ancestors spent the past three hundred generations eating potatoes, pork, and cabbage—or yak butter and barley, or rice, beans, and squash, or bread, clams, and pasta—and now you're a gluten-free vegan, they may be unhappy. If your body came from pork and cabbage, and you're giving it tofu—unhappy Ancestors. Of course, eat what you want, but try to eat ancestral food mindfully at least occasionally.

And finally, contemplate the preciousness of human birth, the reality of impermanence and death, the difficulties of samsara, and the truth of Fate. These are called the Four Thoughts That Turn the Mind Toward the Dharma. While the Buddhist traditions are immensely complex, 98 percent of the Buddhist paths are in these preliminaries.

To be born human and to hear the Dharma is said to be a very rare pair of circumstances and, therefore, precious. Imagine a single sea turtle swimming alone in a vast, infinite ocean. This turtle comes up for air only once every million years. On the surface of this ocean floats a golden ring tossed about on the waves. The likelihood of being born human and hearing the precious Dharma is said to be as rare as this turtle coming up for air and poking his head through the golden ring. So, be thankful for being human, having human parents, and having the chance to have human babies. Out of all 64,000-times-64,000 kinds of birth, human beings are the freest and the most apt to become enlightened, even more so than deities—more reason to thank and honor your Ancestors.

Everything is compound, processional, and in a state of flux or flow, hurtling toward death. All compound phenomena are impermanent and subject to birth, old age, sickness, and death. *You will die.* And this is not morbid or depressing; it is natural. Death is as natural as birth. Birth is the cause of death. We live to learn how to live, and how to die well and be liberated in the moment of death. Contemplate this every day so that, when loved ones die and when you face death, you can relax and open into the experience. Death is the greatest opportunity to understand Life, but you do not have to wait until death to learn this lesson. Die before you die, and you are free.

Samsara means "to cycle." Everything cycles in time; this is the meaning of astrology. The cyclical procession of Time is immortal; we cannot get out of it. This was the realization of Daoism and Mahayana Buddhism. We're immortal, and we either cycle in ignorance or in enlightenment. So, if we're immortal and here forever, we might as well work for liberation so that we can help out. If we do not take up the Path and free our Ancestors and our Fate, then they and we continue to cycle in ignorance and suffering, repeating the same patterns of negativity forever. But if we follow the Path, liberate our Ghosts, and empty our hells, then can we realize that samsara and nirvana are the same place, the same Immortal Procession of Light. We are then free to relax, go with the flow, and benefit beings with our naturalness and generosity.

Every action has a cause, and every action is a cause. This is called Fate. In your every step, thought, and action, contemplate this. When our actions and our experiences are incomplete, they continue as fragments of our former self as unresolved emotions at the time of death, called Ghosts. When our actions liberate ourselves and others, they continue as virtue energy, and we call this the good Fate, which is shaped by the blessing of our Beneficial Ancestors.

Our Ancestral Stream is full of Ghosts and Beneficial Ancestors, and their blessings and issues create the tapestry of our lives. This tapestry is nothing other than past actions coming to fruition. If we truly understand the nature of this matrix, we can disentangle from it. Its nature is empty yet luminous; it is unrestricted and free to manifest as the appearance of cause and effect. If we identify with the cycles of cause and effect as truly existing, whether good or bad, we cycle in ignorance. Realizing the Emptiness of Fate, we experience the universe as an empty display of loving awareness-light, and we are complete.

Great Completion is not ours but belongs to our Ancestral Stream to benefit all beings. Our liberation liberates the countless beings who came before us, going back to beginningless time. Our Precious Human Birth and our opportunity for liberation were given to us by our Ancestors. So, honor them and honor yourself.

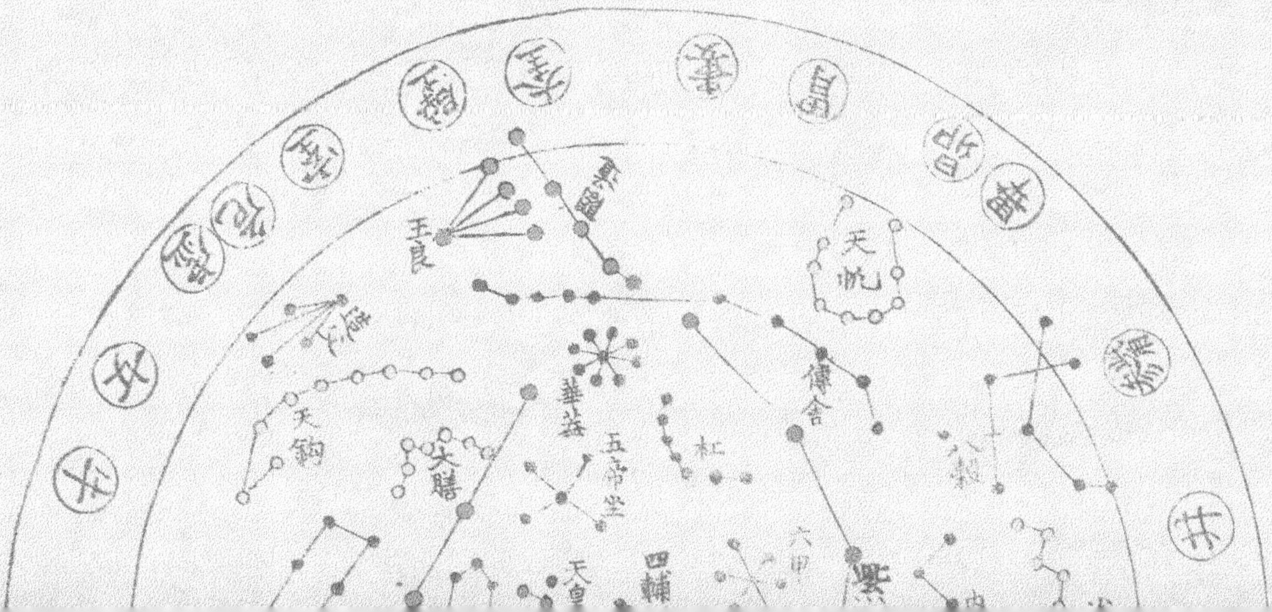
王良
傳舍
華蓋
五帝坐
杠
天鈎
八穀
六甲
四輔

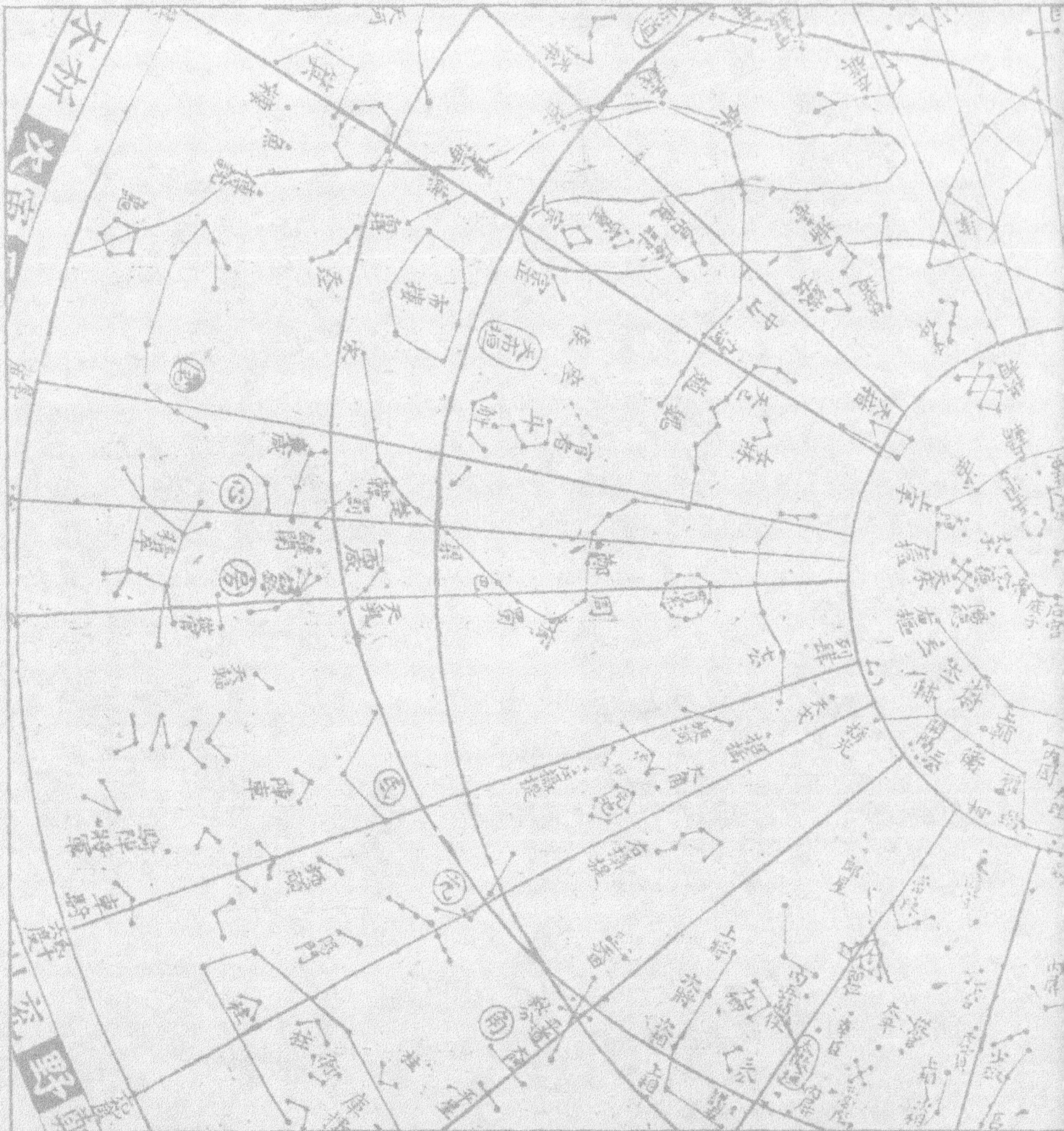

STEP II

Calculate Your Natal Chart

<table>
<tr>
<td>MING
TIAN FU (EMPRESS)
Lu Cun (Storehouse)
Huo Xing (Fire)

(2–11) Snake Palace</td>
<td>ANCESTORS
TIAN TONG (VASSAL)
TAI YIN (MOON)
WEN CHANG (MAGISTRATE)
Yang Ren (Goat Blade)
Hua Lu (Salary)
Hua Quan (Authority)
(12–21) Horse Palace</td>
<td>PLEASURE
WU QU (GENERAL)
Tan Lang (Greedy Wolf)
Ling Xing (Water)
Di Kong (Void)
Tian Xi (Happiness)

(22–31) Goat Palace</td>
<td>PROPERTY
TAI YANG (SUN)
JU MEN (GREAT GATE)
Hua Ji (Jealousy)
WEN QU (PRIEST)
Tian Yao (Beauty)

(32–41) Monkey Palace</td>
</tr>
<tr>
<td>YOUTH
Tuo Luo (Humpback)
Tian Xing (Punishment)

(112–121) Dragon Palace</td>
<td colspan="2" rowspan="2">GREGORY DAVID DONE
Zi Wei Dou Shu Chart
FOUR PILLARS:
YEAR: Yang Fire Tiger
MONTH: Yin Fire Rooster
DAY: Yang Metal Horse
HOUR: Yang Metal Dragon

SOLAR BIRTH INFORMATION
1986/9/23 7:00am to 8:59am (DST)

LUNAR BIRTH INFORMATION:
Bing Yin /8/20
Chen

Tiger, Yang Male

INNER NATURE: Water</td>
<td>SUPERIORS
TIAN XIANG (TUTOR)
Tian Yue (Halberd)

(42–51) Rooster Palace</td>
</tr>
<tr>
<td>PARTNERS
Lian Zhen (Concubine)
Po Jun (Rebel)
You Bi (Right Assistant)
De Jie (Loss)

(102–111) Rabbit Palace</td>
<td>ASSISTANTS
TIAN JI (ORACLE)
TIAN LIANG (ROOF BEAM)
Hua Ke (Examination)

(52–61) Dog Palace</td>
</tr>
<tr>
<td>OFFSPRING

(92–101) Tiger Palace</td>
<td>WEALTH
Hong Luan (Red Bird)

(82–91) Ox Palace</td>
<td>HEALTH

(72–81) Rat Palace</td>
<td>CAREER/TRAVEL
ZI WEI (EMPEROR)
Qi Sha (7 Killings)
Zuo Fu (Left Assistant)
Tian Kui (Leader)
Tian Ma (Travel)

(62–71) Pig Palace</td>
</tr>
</table>

CHART CALCULATION

IT IS NOW TIME TO STUDY YOUR NATAL CHART, but before you can do this, you must first calculate your own Natal Chart. I recommend that you produce a chart for yourself, and with permission, make a few charts of your family and friends and perhaps a few celebrities. Your chart should always be the foundation of your study, but it helps to have the charts of a few people you know intimately or whose lives are a public record. This will provide many examples of how these various astrological symbols manifest in real people. But you will never know anyone like you will know yourself. As the ancient philosophical maxim goes, *Temet nosce*, "Know thyself."

Your chart is a mirror. You are the one in the chart. The Houses, Stars, Animals, and so on are symbolic mirrors. But the map is not the territory; astrology charts pale in comparison to the complexity of our lives. Still, it is a profound experience to find your life in these symbols.

As we go through the "methods" of Character and Fate, remember that there are no definitive meanings. These are symbols; strive to understand how you and your life express these patterns rather than trying to force yourself to fit into a box. Everything here is malleable and playful. You create the meaning and choose the interpretation.

People often object, "Isn't this just a self-fulfilling prophecy? Isn't this just suggestion, susceptibility, and cognitive bias?" Yes! Remember, this is playful. This is divination. God does not hand down these symbols or your chart; no hammer of rational, materialistic science is coming down on you.

As I mentioned in the introduction, there is a slow and tedious way to produce charts by hand by referencing many tables and what are called ephemerides, but all this information has already by codified, and it is easy to make a chart online or with an app. I recommend downloading the DYC Polestar astrology app and the DYC TongShu app. These programs contain many of Liu Ming's notes and are a great companion to this book. If you do not wish to purchase these apps, many websites can produce a chart for free: Google it. Once you have your chart, make sure it contains your Four Pillars, a complete Twelve Houses with the appropriate Stars, and your Inner Elemental Nature. Once this is in place, you are ready to study this tradition.

I have included my own chart and the charts of my parents, which I will use as the main examples for this book. I consider my own life an open book, and I can think of no better way than to lead by example. So, I will include reflections from my own chart and that charts of my parents in the later chapters and use what I have learned from astrological readings that I have done over the years.

Now that we have charts, we can begin to study Character.

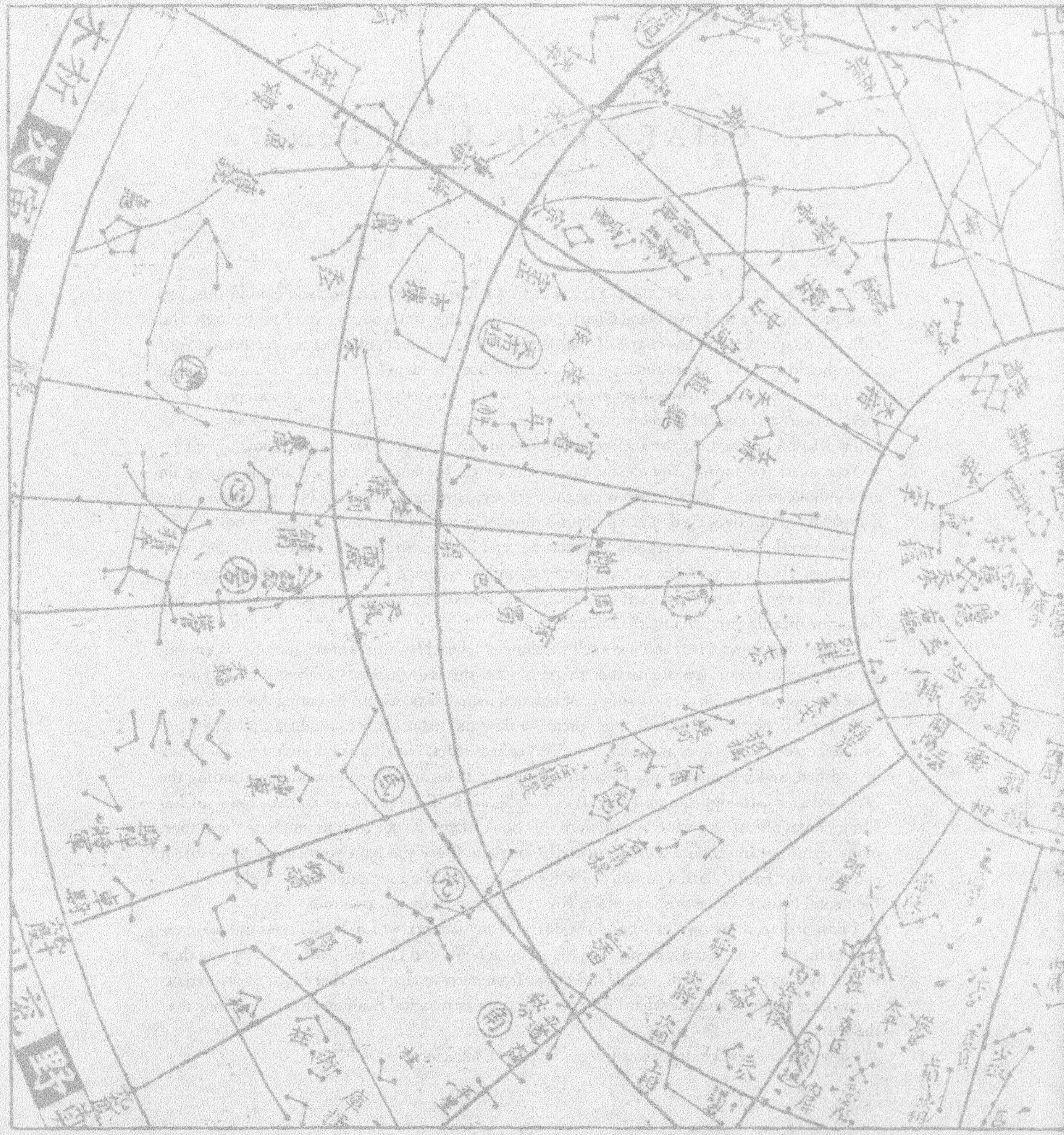

STEP III

Method, or Shu 術

Part One

Qi Character, or Xing (性)

STEMS, BRANCHES, AND THE MEANING OF QI CHARACTER IN POLESTAR ASTROLOGY

QI CHARACTER is one of the most essential teachings in Chinese astrology, yet it is often the most misunderstood. This is mainly due to the availability of vague information about the Twelve Animals on the back of Chinese restaurant menus. Qi Character is a big idea that includes any astrological influence that "characterizes" you, but in this tradition, we focus on the Ten Heavenly Stems and the Twelve Earthly Branches in the form of the Chinese zodiac and may use them synonymously. Most people have heard of their Qi Character in the Chinese zodiac, but very few grasp the profundity of what is meant by Goat, Monkey, or Rooster Qi. So, before we can understand our own Qi Character, we must understand the fundamental wisdom of what is meant by Qi Character.

I will begin by saying that one's Qi Character is a description of their Qi (hopefully this is obvious). In other words, the use of animals is clearly symbolic. If we get hung up on the symbol, we fail to look beyond "Monkey" into our own experience. Monkey is a description of a pattern or display of Qi, which is to say, a pattern of energy and movement, which we understand in astrology as a pattern of Time.

Qi is one of the true profundities of the Chinese Tradition. The Chinese mantic arts represent over 10,000 years of research into the questions, "What is a human being?" and "What is the universe?" In contemplating these questions, the Chinese never came up with God, an abiding self, or a substantial world. What they discovered was Qi.

What is Qi? Well, that is a difficult question to answer. As we have already discussed, Chinese cosmology describes the universe as a vast sea of unimpeded light moving within unbounded, limitless space; we call this vast, unknowable sea "Dao." We can see and experience the light of Dao because it moves or vibrates on a spectrum, like a rainbow. This movement quality of light is called Qi, and everything we call "stuff," "substance," or objects in space displays Qi patterning and moving in a particular way, both cyclic and rhythmic. An aspect of our fundamental nature is mirror-like Shen (神), sometimes translated as heart-mind, spirit, or awareness. Shen gives us self-reflexive experience. This heart-mind reflects the light of Dao and crystallizes it into a universe that appears to be somewhat stable due to the five-phase, or Five Element, cycle of Qi, which I described in a previous chapter. Of course, that is all philosophical and abstract. Big, fancy ideas aside, we need not look anywhere but our own experience to understand Qi.

What is a human being? A pattern of Qi. If you observe your own experience, you will find that what you are has a streaming quality to it, like the flame of a candle. All you experience is a movement made visible or apparent because of a still, spacious, transparent, and aware background. Everything alternates between motion and stillness, and even in the most profound state of meditative quiescence, a subtle undulation or pulsation always persists. Emptiness is pregnant with vitality and infinite potential, so Qi is also a kind of vitality, life, or sentience. Everything in the universe is alive and eating.

No stillness exists apart from movement, and no movement apart from stillness. We call this movement Qi. We can call Qi "energy," which aligns more with quantum physics, whatever that is, but it is essential to recognize that we experience energy because it is always in a state of flux. Qi Character, then, symbolically describes the character or quality of Qi depending on where and when it appears in the eternal flow or procession of time. Qi is movement, and all movement takes place in time; so, for astrologers, Qi is Time, which is compound and processional.

The View of Polestar Astrology states that this flux of Qi flows in a temporal and mathematical procession. Chinese astrology, strictly speaking, is not actually astrology but "chronology." This flow of Qi, like our clocks (which, ironically, are also a chronological circle), goes around and around. It does not go anywhere except "around." Suppose we have a linear view of time. In that case, we believe that time is "going somewhere"—that it is progressing or evolving toward a perfect future or some big catastrophic apocalypse, which goes hand in hand with saying that there was a Big Bang. Astrology cannot accept the notion of a beginning or end unless we state that they are the same point on a circle.

Through thousands of years of observation, the Chinese Tradition has been able to identify and name the mathematical steps, the tick marks, in this procession of Qi/Time, which flows in concentric circles, spiraling outward from our Shen (which is located symbolically in the chest) to Dao, or the big, non-dual "whatever."

Still with me? So, the Chinese Tradition states that Qi/Time in our solar system flows in basic numerical patterns of two, five, ten, twelve, and sixty. Yin and Yang are two. The Five Elements are five. These together form the Ten Heavenly Stems—Yin Wood, Yang Wood, Yin Fire, Yang Fire, and so on. There are twelve animals in the zodiac, called the Twelve Earthly Branches, and the Twelve Animals times the Fives Elements gives us a pattern of sixty. It is important to note here that the Ten Heavenly Stems and Twelve Earthly Branches do not overlap entirely. In other words, they do not create a cycle of one hundred twenty as in ten times twelve (10 x12) but rather as in two cycles of sixty times two, [(5 x 12) x 2]. This is because the Earthly Branches are fixed as either Yin or Yang in succession, starting with the Rat, which is always Yang, followed by the Ox, which is always Yin, and so on. For example, all Rats are always Yang, so therefore, there are no Yin Fire Rats. All Ox are always Yin, so there is no Yang Fire Ox. Each sexagenary cycle of sixty years is either Yin or Yang, which gives us sixty times two or one hundred twenty years.

One hundred twenty years is our basic life expectancy according to Classical Chinese Medicine. This is the total length of an individual cycle of Fate—what the Chinese Tradition calls our "allotted years," or Suifen (隨分), given to us by our Ancestors—which is what we read in a Natal Chart during an astrology session.

The cycle of sixty is derived from the cycle of Jupiter, which is also called "the Yearly Star," or Suixing (歲星). It takes Jupiter one year to traverse one of twelve 30-degree sections of the night's sky, which each equate to one Zodiac symbol. It takes twelve years in total to traverse the whole sky, but it does so in a kind of zig-zag pattern. It takes Jupiter sixty years to end up back in the exact same place that it started, and over the course of that time, we get five different elemental versions of Jupiter in each Zodiac sign over a sixty-year period. This cycle of sixty then creates sixty years, sixty months, sixty days, sixty hours, and sixty seconds. The year, month, day, and hour are called the "Four Pillars," and each has its own Heavenly Stem and Earthly Branch. This is the basic Chinese calendar in use since the Shang dynasty.

The Ten Heavenly Stems and Twelve Earthly Branches describe the flow of Qi in the universe from macrocosm to microcosm. In other words, this is one of the primary ways that Qi displays as patterns of Time on planet Earth in relation to the greater cycles of Yinyang and the Five Elements in Heaven.

To grasp the profundity of the Twelve Branches, we describe them with basic and relatable animal symbols, each connected to a myriad of details within Chinese culture, medicine (organs, for example), astrology, Fengshui, and so on.

After thousands of years of observing Qi in human beings, the natural world, and universe, the Chinese noticed that specific animals exemplified certain traits, which captured the essence of these patterns of Qi. Over time, these animals became iconic, and they settled on Twelve Animals, each with five elemental variations, which brings the types to sixty. The Stems and Branches are among the earliest time records in human history, discovered on oracle bones from the Shang dynasty (ca. 1200–1045 B.C.E.). This sexagenary cycle is now used throughout Asia to form the primary calendar. In China, this calendar is called the Tong Shu, and it is the longest printed book in human history.

In the big picture, this cycle of sixty describes epochs of sixty years, the last of which began in 1984 with the Year of the Yang Wood Rat. The cycle of Qi/Time spirals outward, infinitely marking the spiraling of galaxies, and it spirals inward, marking sixty months, sixty days, sixty hours, sixty seconds, and so on. This same cycle is reflected in our body, in our breathing, food digestion, and blood circulation. It is also in our waking, dreaming, and sleeping and in our reproductive system.

In famous folk astrology, our basic Qi Character is read according to the year, month, day, and hour, called the Bazi, the Eight Characters or Four Pillars. In this tradition, our Qi Character is derived primarily from a synthesis of the year and hour, which we will explore in more detail. But what does all this mean?

First, the View of Chinese astrology states that we are a Qi Character. We do not *have* a Qi Character so much as we *are* a Qi Character. In other words, our Qi Character has something to do with the time of our birth. We come into being in the procession of time when the Qi of the universe is patterning in a particular way, as a compounded flow of sixty types of Qi, according to the year, month, day, and hour.

For example, I was born during a Yang Metal Dragon hour on a Yang Metal Horse day during a Yin Fire Rooster month of a Yang Fire Tiger year. So, at my birth, the Qi on planet Earth synthesized these patterns. According to astrology, I emerged during Dragon Hour as a living, embodied expression of these patterns of Qi.

In a way, the pattern we are born out of and into patterns us; we are conditioned by this energy. Everything that comes into being at a particular moment in time expresses that moment in time—everything from people to cats, mold, tadpoles, countries, ideas, and so on. Anything that we can say "began," relatively speaking (nothing really begins in Chinese astrology), has a Qi Character and a Fate.

The timeliness of our birth generates a pattern of Qi that we display from birth to death. So, as I often explain to clients, the wisdom of understanding our Qi Character begins by understanding that it is with us until death. Our living embodiment comes together as a synthesis of these energies, and this basic pattern does not disperse until death, when our Five Spirits and Five Elements return to Dao, to "don't know."

So, I was born a Tiger and I will die a Tiger. My "Tigerness" does not change; it does not improve; it does not get educated. And I cannot choose to change into a Rabbit. Tiger represents a basic pattern of Qi that displays certain qualities and characteristics depending on my health, harmony, happiness, and so on. If I am in a state of ill health and disharmony, then I tend to display the more negative or constricted qualities of Tiger Qi. Likewise, I display its virtue qualities if I am healthy, happy, and harmonious. Tiger Qi is natural to me, and whatever Qi Character you display is natural for you.

We study our Qi Character in Chinese astrology to learn our natural pattern so that we do not resist or fight against it, trying to be something we are not. In turn, we learn about the Qi Character of others to understand what is natural for them, so we do not expect them to change in a way they never will. Knowing we cannot escape our Character, we can learn to "go with it," especially when it comes to our more complex patterns. Tiger Qi, for example, represents a basic impulse to "break free" and "start again" because our Native Element is Yang Wood, which often causes Tigers to disappear and abandon situations we find difficult or constraining. Monkeys do this too, but in a different way because it is the Tiger's opposite. Each Character has a specific energetic impulse that manifests as behavior based on how we relate to it.

In this tradition, the year is our primary Qi Character, and the hour is secondary. The year is like a noun, and the hour is like an adjective. The year represents the big picture of our behavioral patterns based on our deepest fundamental impulses, and the hour often describes more surface-level personality traits.

I am often asked, Why is the year the primary? Doesn't this mean everyone born in 1986 has the same Qi Character? Yes.

Character is not personality. Everyone born in 1986 has the same Qi Character but not the same personality. Character represents a pattern of Qi, an energetic impulse that can display many complex personalities depending on numerous conditions. According to the Chinese Tradition, everyone born in 1986 has a great deal in common. The wisdom of Chinese astrology is not individualistic. In studying astrology you aim to discover how much you have in common with everyone. We are all a cast of sixty Characters, repeatedly playing out the same stories of Fate with different details.

Chinese astrology says there are sixty basic types of people. If we multiply all Four Pillars, the year, month, day, and hour (60 x 60 x 60 x 60), we get 12,960,000 types of people. However, because the Year is the primary image of Character, basically, there are sixty types, and that sixty is actually five different elemental versions of the basic Twelve Animals, which I call the Twelve Characters of Destiny. In Chinese astrology, we first focus on learning the Five Elements and the Twelve Animals separately. We then synthesize them to understand the full sixty. In other words, if I really understand the Goat Character and the Five Elements, then I can imagine what a Wood Goat might be like in contrast to an Earth Goat, and so on.

Each Qi Character interacts with the other Qi Characters in a particular way, creating complex, dynamic relationships. Some are opposite; some are complementary; some are neutral. Studying these patterns reveals a great deal, not only about human relationships but also about history, politics, and human society.

Finally, we cannot understand the Twelve Characters of Destiny if we get hung up on them as personalities. They are more like a whirlwind in open space. Imagine dropping a leaf into this whirlwind; it falls fast at some points and slowly at other points. In other words, if we make them into personalities, then we want them to be equal, but they are not. Our calendar in the West is fixed, so Western astrology is off by almost a month, but nature is not fixed. Some months are longer than others; for that matter, so are some days. Time does not flow equally, and so the different Qi Characters are not "equal," but they are each capable in different and distinct ways.

So, why does this work? I have no idea, but it does. This knowledge has been known and tested for thousands of years in Asia. I have no interest in explaining why everyone born in 1986 (within the lunar year) is a Fire Tiger; we just are.

Many people are skeptical of their Qi Character. Many read the back of Chinese menus and say, "That's not me—I don't do that!" Yes, you do. If you have any self-reflection at all, your Qi Character will resonate with you. And often, the most fundamental statements are the most revealing. Tigers are impulsive. This wisdom changed my life.

Often, the basic descriptions are vague, and we can say, "Everyone does that!" Yes, that's the point: What we have in common, not what makes us unique snowflakes. Most of the personal stories that we cherish and that we think are special are as common as dirt.

Now that we understand the basics of Qi Character, we can delve more deeply into the animal symbols called the Twelve Characters of Destiny.

ANIMALS AS SYMBOLS

THE CHINESE TRADITION has used animal symbols to communicate complex ideas since the beginning of Chinese culture. Most tribal people associated a particular animal as their ancestral or tribal symbol, and the first important clan to take charge among the myriad tribes of East Asia was called the Bear Clan. Animals were a common part of everyday life; everyone was familiar with them, for certain animals have lived with humans forever.

The Ox, for example, has been happily domesticated for over 12,000 years. So, it is not a stretch to think of a person as an Ox. The Ox Clan, perhaps, came from the swampy regions of southern China and was the first to domesticate the ox, or water buffalo, so it was identified with them. The history of the Chinese animal zodiac is a connection to our human nomadic, tribal, shamanic, and agricultural history, which is far, far older than anything we practice today. Humans and animals go together because humans *are* animals.

The Chinese astrological vocabulary settled on twenty-eight animals to represent the constellations of their lunar cycle. For example, I am writing this on the day of the Stag constellation, and there was once a Stag Clan. Among these twenty-eight, the Chinese eventually settled on twelve as iconic. These Twelve Animals eventually became the Twelve Earthly Branches, which are well known throughout the world.

I have always been reluctant to write about these, because so much has already been written. Most books on Chinese astrology cover the Twelve Animals and not much else. While most of these books are fine, they are often too general to be helpful, and they usually focus on the Animals solely in terms of personality traits. I think I can do a little better.

I have already explained the meaning of Qi Character, so rather than repeat myself, I will jump in. Rather than focus too much on personality, my goal here is to describe the essential impulse that characterizes each of the Twelve Animals and explain them in terms of human characteristics. Of course, as a Fire Tiger, I interpret the Twelve Animals from a Tiger's lens. But to the best of my ability, I would like to describe these as I understand them.

I often describe Qi Character as a kind of impulse, a pattern, and a set of tendencies that can manifest as various personalities. Of course, not everyone born in an Ox Year has the same personality. But Chinese astrology says everyone born in an Ox Year has the same Qi Character, meaning they all share something in common.

Each of the Twelve Animals has five elemental flavors, which can make them quite different. The five Tigers, for example, are very different. Before we get to the sixty, though, first we must understand the Twelve's basic impulses and character traits.

Usually, the series begins with the Rat, but since that has been done to death, I would like to start from the "end" with the Pig, in honor of Liu Ming, who was a Fire Pig. But first, let's briefly look into the timing of our birth, which is what determines our Animal in the first place.

CONCEPTION AND BIRTH TIME IN CHINESE ASTROLOGY

BEFORE STARTING OUR JOURNEY THROUGH THE INDIVIDUAL TWELVE CHARACTERS OF DESTINY, I would like to back up and examine a fundamental question in the consideration of astrology: the moment of parturition, or birth. We cannot generate a birth chart without the time of birth. Why is this moment so important? And why does the chart of this moment represent the Fate cycles of an entire human life?

In the View of Chinese Polestar Astrology, our birth chart represents a cycle of Fate, given to us by our Ancestors, spanning 120 years. In the Chinese (and Indian) view, every human is allotted 120 years, give or take, and our ability to "live out our allotted years" is based on both Fate and conduct. Without adverse Fate for sickness and death, and with good conduct, every human should live about 120 years. Few do, which says something about our conduct.

A Polestar chart, based on the moment of birth, offers 12 ten-year cycles that tell us how our Fate will unravel. So, if someone lives to be 120, they will have naturally unraveled all their Fate and experience true Freedom. By studying our astrology, we can work with Fate and experience Human Freedom well before then.

The moment of birth opens into a new dimension of Time, different from Time in the womb, an entry into cycles our tradition of astrology calls Currents of Fate. A new window opens roughly every two hours, and those born in each opening are, in a sense, dropped into one of these Currents, which I liken to a flowing river. We're dropped in and carried along in a stream that's already flowing. The momentum of this Current, our precedent, comes from the thousands of people who came before us, our Ancestors. All the trials and tribulations, successes and failures, hopes and fears of our Ancestors create a momentum that we inherit to some degree. We are here to work out these hopes and fears and resolve them through our experience. We have no self. We are open, unconditioned awareness hosting the conditioned, incomplete experience of our Ancestors. And they, too, did the same. We inherit the moment of experience that is incomplete, fragmented, and emotional, and this momentum is passed on to us through our parents during the moment of conception. In theory, the more our parents have resolved their Fate before conceiving children, the less unfinished business the children will receive.

We are the result of a lot of sex. Our parents got it on, and so did their parents, and so on. You are the result of an unending chain of successfully reproducing life, coming to you unbroken since the beginning of Life itself. If you don't have children, you may end that stream, which is a powerful idea. Or you may keep it going. The Daoist and Tantric models of spiritual practice suggest that we can turn our reproductive capacity inward in order to birth what is called an immortal fetus, redirecting our fundamental desire to keep Life going, but that's another story.

Our parents' desire created us. Sorry for the graphic detail, but in the View of Classical Chinese Medicine and astrology, our parents' desire for each other, their desire to have a child, their arousal during sex, and the moment of conception itself all play a massive role in our Character and Fate, as does our time in the womb. Our astrology chart is, in a sense, a map leading back to our moment of conception. We can follow our Fate backward, unwind, and resolve our birth.

The modern spiritual scene makes a big fuss over Tantric and Daoist sex, but they generally miss the point. In the Chinese View, sexual practice is, in part, an art of producing good children. There are, of course, higher spiritual goals, but the general purpose of the sexual technique is to create complete arousal of our Jing (精), our reproductive "essence." Incomplete Jing makes incomplete children.

Jing is a fundamental predilection toward physicality and manifestation. It is the memory of the infinite number of beings that reproduced successfully to bring Life to us in an unbroken line since the beginning of Time. Our Jing contains the memory of our Ancestors, which contains the energetic blueprint for creating a human being. This memory carries the impulse to keep life going, which the Chinese call immortality. Life is immortal, and we are a rhythm that never stops.

Our Jing also re-creates us. When we cut ourselves, the Jing rides the blood to the wound and helps to re-create skin. A scar is a faulty Jing memory. Our Jing contains our blueprint, and we receive two sets of blueprints at birth: We may get our dad's jaw, our mother's eyes, and so on. But we may also be a reproduction of our great-great-grandfather. Why is this? According to Chinese astrology, this is decided at the time of conception.

Conception does not usually happen unless our parents have a more or less complete experience of arousal. Arousal is more than just genital. All twelve of our organ systems must be aroused for our arousal to be complete. The purpose of most Daoist sexual practices is to arouse our entire being, which is said to magnetize our Jing, refining it to an essential quality. If this complete arousal is met with the intention to generate a child, it acts as a kind of magnet, signaling to our Ancestors that a new Ancestor is about to come through. If this arousal is complete and full of love, then this generates a kind of queue, and all the Beneficial Ancestors show up and sort of hover around the bed (or wherever).

When Mom and Dad are all hot and sweaty and lose themselves in the moment, this is a signal that arousal is complete, and in the moment of orgasm, even before the sperm and ovum meet, conception occurs, and the Ancestors help guide the rest of the process. Your great-aunt may be present during the moment of orgasm, and so you end up getting her lips. Whatever Ancestors show up give us our appearance and Fate. The Beneficial Ancestors show up to demonstrate their completion and pass on their strength through the child. The Ghosts also show up to be resolved. If the moment of arousal is not complete—if Mom is checked out, or if Dad can't be present in the moment because he is in a state of chronic depletion—then a lesser tier of Ancestors shows up. You may get confused Uncle Harry and his gambling problem. If the conception is a rape, none of the Ancestors may be present due to shock, and only local Ghosts queue up. In the Chinese Tradition, giving birth to a stranger is possible. So, having good sex is essential, and intention is crucial in the generation of children.

What does this have to do with astrology? Well, that moment sets a pattern in Time that is roughly nine months. We do not spend a full twelve months in the womb, which is very significant in astrology. We miss one season. The seasons shape our development in the womb, and so we are incomplete in our development. I missed winter, for example. So, I'm chronically Yin deficient, but that's another story. In short, we spend our lives making up for those last three months.

Our elemental makeup or constitution, then, depends on this nine-month period beginning at conception and manifesting at the moment of parturition. Our birth time reflects everything leading up to that moment and is a map leading back to the presence of our Ancestors. As I try to communicate to clients, our Natal Chart is a map of our Ancestors, showing who was present from conception to birth and then from birth to death.

From the Chinese perspective, our development in the womb is quite significant. Per the Chinese View, what happens from birth to death is a flash of lightning compared to our experience in the womb.

THE TWELVE CHARACTERS OF DESTINY, PART 1: PIG QI

NATIVE ELEMENT: Yin Water

HOUR AND MONTH: 9 p.m. to 11 p.m., 10th Moon

ORGAN NETWORK: Triple Burner

COMPATIBILITY TRINE: Rabbit, Goat

MARRIAGE PAIR: Tiger

OPPOSITE: Snake

SYMBOLISM (象) AND QI (氣) DYNAMICS

THE "NATIVE ELEMENT" OF THE PIG IS YIN WATER—dissolution, death, collapse, return, resolve, completion, the end—and in my eyes, it makes sense to begin with the end, because there is no end in the Chinese View. No start makes sense without a stop. Liu Ming once described the Western notion of death as annihilation to his Daoist teacher, and he replied, "Stop? You stop. . . . Tell me, how do you stop?" In other words, the very meaning of cyclical time is that nothing stops; everything cycles. But things do appear to stop because they must appear to start. And Pig Qi is the expression and character associated with this dissolution into "don't know." For things to appear fresh and new, they must come from nothing, from "don't know."

Our fear of death could be alleviated if only we remembered our immortality. However, if we had to remember our countless past lives, this life would seem an insufferable bore. So, in the cycle of time, Yin Water, Pig Qi, is the dissolution that allows for wonder and newness.

What is the nature of things as they fall apart and dissolve? Turns out, it's a celebration! The Pig in the Chinese View, despite being characterized by Yin Water, by dissolution, is the party animal. Pig is the party at the end of the cycle, the warmth of homecoming, and the gathering around the hearth.

First, to understand the nature of the Pig, we must examine the Chinese character for family, Jia (家). The character contains the radical Mian (宀), which means "roof," and the radical Shi (豕), which means "pig or boar," so it's a pig under a roof, and it is the Chinese word for family, or blood relations. It also means household, home, and domestic, and it is also a term for a lineage, tradition, or school, as in Chanjia (禪家), meaning "Buddhist," and Daojia (道家), meaning "Daoist."

The character Jia and the symbol of the Pig are intimately related to the Chinese principles of family, continuity, immortality, and procession, which exemplify the nature of traditional culture itself. The Pig is at the heart of what it means to be Chinese, for "China" was the result of a decision by about eighty cultures to stop being nomads and to farm grain instead. That meant no more herds, and since there are no herds of pigs, the pig became their meat of choice.

There is an expression among Chinese farmers: "We only dig in our Ancestors." This means the family has been there so long the soil is made of their dead relatives. This is Pig Qi. Wealth in traditional Chinese culture was often measured by the number of pigs you owned, for pigs were, and still are, a mainstay of the Chinese diet: fatty pork, rice, and cabbage. Many other ancient traditions outlawed pork, but the Chinese made a different decision, in part because pigs don't need to be grazed like cows and sheep. Everyone in China eats pigs, and as any vegetarian who has traveled in China can attest, it is very common to order a vegetarian meal only to find big hunks of pork in it.

Of course, this sounds strange from our perspective, but take yourself back to an early agricultural person, transitioning from a nomadic to a domestic relationship with animals. Within a few generations, the wild boar transformed from a big, black, hairy tusked beast to a fat, pink pig that could give birth to and nurse up to one hundred piglets in a litter—this is the very meaning of family, reproductive essence, and motherhood. The pig is, therefore, the ultimate symbol of nourishment, nurturing, and generosity.

Furthermore, the Chinese were astounded to find that pigs ate everything; they were garbage disposals and were sometimes even kept under the outhouse. Yet, their flesh is white, cool, and sweet, with no toxicity. Lamb, in contrast, was the food of nomads, a lifestyle the Chinese were trying to distance themselves from. Lamb flesh was hot, and their marrow was bitter and hot, which made you want to ride into battle. The cool nature of the pig, however, makes you want to wallow, stay in the same place, and give up fighting. To the Chinese, the value of animals lies in their capacity to transform, and pigs are the "great transformers," able to digest anything! This capacity is at the heart of the Pig's Qi Character.

In Classical Chinese Medicine, the Pig is associated with the San Jiao, or Triple Burner, a mysterious and much-debated organ network with no physical reality (although many are trying to make it physical to appease materialists) that is associated with transformation. While the function of the Triple Burner is manifold, we can summarize it as "metabolism," divided into "upper, middle, and lower." The Triple Burner is the unseen Qi that governs the cohesive processes of transformation, the conversion of our intake to Qi and blood, and the harmonizing force that allows our organ networks to flow and work together as a whole.

The symbol of the Pig in China came from the wild mother boar, so like many Animals of the Chinese zodiac, the Pig has a dual image: domestic yet fierce. The wild mother boar was seen as a god of forest fecundity and a protector of forest spirits, for she is the most ferocious of protectors. Unlike many wild animals, she will die to protect her young. A mother boar will charge at a tiger three times her size without a second thought. Pigs, then, carry this element of ferocity despite their Yin nature.

Together, the Pig and Dog Years share the theme of protecting that which is most valuable. The Dog follows orders and is selective and tribal, but the Pig is not; to the Pig, everyone is family. As such, Pigs are considered the ultimate protectors, associated with the power and wrath of the Feminine—the energy of momma bear. Originally the Pig was related to the Bear in Chinese cosmology, associated with the Milky Way, the Big Dipper, and the House Constellation of the Northern Palace. The Pig and Bear are associated with the Daoist ritual dance of thunder magic called the Pace of Yu, which mirrors the cyclical creation and destruction of the universe.

In Chinese astrology, the Pig is the most "domestic" of symbols, exemplifying our most cherished notions of home. It shares this quality in a trine with the Rabbit and Goat. Pigs make family wherever they go. Of all the signs, the Pig is the most personable; they are "people" persons, and as such, they are the most humanitarian, accepting, and concerned with the welfare of others. This connection to people, to the home, and to reproduction is why the Pig is the most connected to the Chinese teachings on Ancestors.

Again, the Native Element of the Pig is Yin Water: release, sleep, dissolution, death, collapse, return, resolve, completion, "the end"—which in the Chinese Tradition is a cause for celebration because there is no end! The nature of Water offers us the possibility of relief, of being finished, and of feeling accomplished and relaxed because the work has been done.

For the Pig, Yin Water represents a strange paradox called extreme Yin. This paradox says that when things become extreme, they turn into their opposites. So, although the Pig's nature is the most Yin, the most connected to death and dissolution, it is also the most "manifest," the most embodied of all the signs. Pigs are deeply sensual; for them, the senses reveal the nature of reality through direct experience.

Yin Water is complete dissolution, which sounds mysterious, but in general, Pigs don't have a "hidden" nature; they might as well be naked. Therefore, they are the antithesis of the Snake, who is the most secretive, hidden, mysterious, and ineffable. Pigs can be intense, spiritual people, but they'll tell you all about it. They'll share everything about themselves, whether you ask or not.

Pig Qi itself, embodied in human individuals, is this impulse to let go, to release all conceptualization into direct experience through the senses. In one sense, Yin Water represents emptiness, but it does so in the Buddhist sense, as in the emptiness of our concepts, not our direct experience. The experience of Pig Qi, then, is the fullness of life beyond conceptualization, seeking fullness and completion through the senses. Our senses offer us the most direct experience of life; our body is how we know manifest reality.

Pig Qi sees the fullness of the manifest world as something to be devoured, savored, and enjoyed. Pig Qi revels in art, music, food, dance, clothing, painting, and the sensations they inspire. Pigs collect material items and derive great power and sustenance from them, for objects are not mere symbols but energy. Pigs, therefore, are sensuous characters who make great chefs, artists, musicians, lovers, parents, and nurturers.

Pigs, then, see and experience everything that is material and physical and manifest to the senses as the reason we come into being. If you were to ask a Pig, Why are people born? they may respond, Food! And this is not shallow. Perhaps the only reason there is a universe is so you can enjoy the taste of ice cream. Losing yourself in the moment is a Pig moment.

MANIFESTATION/CHARACTER (形)

Now that we have covered the symbolism and energetic dynamics, let's explore the key words for the Pig and discuss how this symbol manifests in and as people.

The first key words for the Pig's Qi Character are honesty and enjoyment. The direct experience of our senses beyond thinking is a kind of honesty. We all wish to enjoy ourselves without guilt, but many of us feel guilty when we indulge. We overthink, justify, and strategize when it comes to our senses. We "treat" ourselves for doing hard work as if enjoyment must be earned through suffering.

Pig Qi is enjoyment without guilt. If we're sincere, we all want to eat, sleep, and screw, and sometimes that's just fine. This honesty manifests itself as plain speaking, as confessing to deep sensual desire, and as seeking simplicity. Enjoyment is human honesty.

Pig Qi is blunt and to the point, yet it is also caring and compromising, like a grandmother who wants to see everyone happy. This grandmother energy of the Pig is associated with the family, and Pig Qi is, again, the very symbol of family life. As part of the "domestic trine," alongside the Goat and Rabbit, Pigs are often homebodies who would rather throw a barbecue and socialize than be alone and meditate. Pig Qi is gregarious; it enjoys people and relating to others, especially through enjoyment. So, Pigs are often fun-loving and fun-seeking.

Because Pigs want everyone to be happy and enjoy themselves, they are among the most tolerant and accepting of Characters. Pigs are often very humanitarian, unselfish, and interested in human rights and dignity. Yin Water, the end of the cycle, has seen it all and done it all, and so accepts everything in totality and wants to have fun before we all bite the dust.

This accepting quality of the Pig is a form of generosity. Pig generosity would give you the shirt off its back. At the end of the cycle, Pig Qi represents everything being let go of and given away. If a Pig had only one bowl of soup, they would most likely divide it up and give away spoonfuls so everyone could taste it—and they really want you to taste it, and enjoy it like they do.

When describing themselves, Pigs may very well describe their favorite food, let's say strawberries, and when tasting a strawberry, you taste them. Liu Ming once described a fellow Pig he met traveling who kept a journal of all the desserts he tried in each country; these tastes represented the quintessence of his experience.

However, the sensuous nature of the Pig is not stupid. Pig Qi is the height of eloquence, for they experience words, ideas, and symbols as food and art, and they revel in finding delicious ways to express and say things to evoke deep feelings. Liu Ming was like this; he was a gifted speaker, and his talks evoked deep experiential rather than mere conceptual understanding, as if his wisdom came directly from unmediated experience. Liu Ming was also a natural comedian who spent most of his life giggling. Pig Qi is naturally funny, and their humor comes from their honesty. Being honest about our selfish desires should make us laugh, because laughing at ourselves is the highest wisdom.

Pigs are naturally spiritual, for Pig Qi and Yin Water represent the fluidity, interconnectedness, emotion, and empathy associated with the profundity of chaos, death, and dissolution beyond reckoning. Pig Qi represents the headlong charge into letting go, giving everything away into direct experience.

Pigs are often unstoppable and have a unique kind of aggression. Their fierce and protective character lends them to a hardworking nature that stops at nothing to get what it wants. This struggle feels heroic to the Pig, because they share the rewards of their struggle with others and give everything away for the greater good. Pigs often start aggressive and end up heroes.

Pig's natural experience of the senses can lead to self-indulgence. The image of the Pig is often associated with overeating, and in our culture, calling someone a "pig" is very specific accusation. This revelation of the senses and the nature of Yin Water can lead to drugs, drinking, risky sex, and depletion through hedonism and self-destruction.

Their artistic and sensual nature can also become an addiction to comfort, luxury, and flamboyance, spending money thoughtlessly on material objects and finery. This comfort seeking can turn to lethargy, laziness, and aimless loafing, especially in the form of the Earth Pig, which is the most prone to stagnation. Pig Qi is well represented by the character Pig-Pen from *Peanuts*, a disheveled kind of dust cloud associated with a lack of care. The desire for material objects can turn greedy, toward a selfish secretiveness that strives to get what it wants so it can indulge.

The generous, accepting, and loving nature of the Pig can easily turn to gullibility. Pigs are the most likely to trust and can be easily duped, likely to give everything away to the first stranger with a sad story. Their honesty expects honesty, and so Pigs may believe everything you tell them. And they can be generous to a fault, giving you the shirt off their back.

Pig tolerance can turn to long-suffering abuse. Known as "great transformers," out of all the Characters, Pigs (and Oxen) can take the most abuse and are likely to stay in bad situations for a long time, especially in domestic situations, and especially because they love so deeply and want to help their abuser. Pig Qi can handle anything without trauma because Yin Water lets everything go. The great transformer can turn any difficulty into enjoyment and humor, and Pigs can laugh at the most challenging situations.

Finally, the eloquence of the Pig can turn to what is commonly known as pigheadedness. Pigs can be forceful, aggressive, and argumentative, and can hold very strong opinions. Their honesty in speech can also get them into trouble, for they are likely to say anything despite the consequences.

These qualities of the Pig are available to everyone during a Pig Year and will be heightened during a Pig Month, on Pig Days, and during Pig Hours. Pig Hour is between 9 p.m. and 11 p.m. and is the time for relaxation, sex, and falling sleep, all very "piggy" experiences. If you were born during this time of the day, you are also part Pig.

In terms of the Five Pigs, each has its unique characteristics that contribute to the overall understanding of the Pig zodiac sign. Wood or Traveling Pigs are the most naive, sweetest, and potentially the best-natured and kindest of all sixty signs. Fire or Mountain Pigs are the most intense, driven, and stubborn of all the Pigs, and they have the strongest "consumption" quality, with the Fire burning up the Water element. Earth or Monastery Pigs and Metal or Garden Pigs are the most stable, mature, and restrained, as they can contain and give shape to the fluidity of Water. And finally, Water or Forest Pigs are the most natural and quintessential of the Pigs. Understanding these different characteristics provides a comprehensive view of the Pig zodiac sign.

THE TWELVE CHARACTERS OF DESTINY, PART 2: RAT QI

NATIVE ELEMENT: Yang Water

HOUR AND MONTH: 11 p.m. to 1 a.m., 11th Moon

ORGAN NETWORK: Gallbladder

COMPATIBILITY TRINE: Dragon, Monkey

MARRIAGE PAIR: Ox

OPPOSITE: Horse

SYMBOLISM (象) AND QI (氣) DYNAMICS

A FAMOUS CHINESE STORY describes a contest set by the Buddha, or sometimes the Jade Emperor of Daoism: a race to determine who would be the first of the Twelve Animals. At the end of the race, there was a mighty river. The Ox was the only animal strong enough to cross. Rat, small yet clever, jumped on Ox's back. Undetected by Ox, clever Rat jumped off his nose just in time to cross the finish line first. Rat won the honor of being first in the cycle, and the Character of Rat, or Rat Qi, came to represent the wisdom, the virtue or De (德), and the resourcefulness of all things small.

Of the Twelve Animals of the zodiac, some are small, and some are large. The difference in size symbolizes the Chinese view that strength comes in all shapes and sizes. Every perspective is valuable and has a proper place.

As a cycle of View Teachings, the Twelve Qi Characters are a study in perspective and represent twelve (or really sixty) ways of viewing the world. We find wisdom by learning our perspective in contrast or relation to others. The tallest rat will never see the same world as a horse. Which perspective is correct? The question is meaningless; both are valid and describe different perspectives. Rat Qi represents the perspective of little creatures, the most "zoomed-in" quality of life. Most important, it represents the fact that all beings must make alliances to survive.

The Native Element of the Rat is Yang Water—the power of the weak, the yielding, the adaptable, the soft, the pliant to overcome all obstacles, like water carving the Grand Canyon. Water may be weak, but through diligent perseverance, it carves canyons, and in great mass, water can devastate. This is the Yang Water nature of Rat Qi, the paradoxical strength of weakness.

As the first Animal, the Rat represents "start," but it starts at the end, as its Native Element is Water. Rat Hour is from 11 p.m. to 1 a.m., when we are supposed to be asleep. Pig Hour, 9 p.m. to 11 p.m., is falling asleep, Yin Water. Yang Water is an active time of dreaming in which we disassemble and process the previous day. Rat, therefore, represents the active imagination of "backward" dreaming. If you were born during this time of the day, you are also part Rat. The Rat and this time of day are also associated with the Element of Yang Wood and the gallbladder in Chinese medicine, which catalyzes and rectifies the movement of Qi in the body. Rat Hours, Rat Days, Rat Months, and Rat Years, then, catalyze and initiate change.

Rat Qi is Yang, active and dynamic, and the power of the Rat is ambitious and unstoppable like water, so don't let the image of smallness fool you; Rat Qi is anything by "mousy." Yang Water also represents synthesis, sentiment, sensitivity, reflection, cooperation, persuasion, and effectiveness, among other virtues.

Of all the Twelve Animals, I find people most dismayed to find out they are Rats. This is mainly due to the image of the Rat as vermin and a disease carrier in Western culture. In Asian cultures, the Rat has a much different image that I would like to encourage.

The Rat of Chinese cosmology was well known to farmers as the "Grain Rat." Grain rats would appear with the harvest. So, in Asia, the Rat has always been associated with prosperity, wealth, resources, and the rewards of diligent hard work. In many forms of Asian lore, the Rat is the God of Wealth, and Rat Years in Asia are expected to be profitable in every sense of the word.

The symbol of wealth is essential and often glossed over. People are all too quick to associate wealth with money, especially Americans. Understanding wealth, however, is essential to understanding Rat Qi. What is wealth? In short, wealth is resources: material, food, energy, land, intelligence, labor, and so on. Money is an abstract symbol measuring these tangible and demonstrable realities.

But why are resources necessary to the Rat? Because they are tiny.

Individually, Rats are small and weak, so they always appear in groups and work together to manage resources. Together, Rats can undermine an entire building by gnawing and nibbling away at the foundations, piece by piece. For this reason, Rat Qi represents the Confucian teaching that all humans must make alliances to flourish. We can't do much alone, but together, we can accomplish anything.

In the Chinese View, individuals are redundant. It is only through alliances that we do anything. No person ever did anything great, period. American culture exalts heroes, saints, sports stars, and so on, forgetting that sports stars usually play on a team.

So, Rat Qi is the antithesis of American individualism and demonstrates the ideals of the Confucian tradition, for it views social life as central to existence and represents the human virtue of community. Sociability is required to survive, and no person is special. This is a Rat realization. Rat Qi, in a sense, stands for the little guy, the underdog, the meek, and the unacknowledged, and it hates the abuse of the strong over the weak. The character Piglet from *Winnie-the-Pooh* represents this Virtue of the Small, and there is a popular book on this very subject.

Rat Qi represents a fundamental insight into the nature and value of "things," appearances, and stuff—the resources that compose the world. And to work with resources, Rats must take them apart—not to analyze them (that's Rooster), but to make them small enough to carry.

Again, Rat Qi represents the most "zoomed-in" quality of life, like a magnifying glass or microscope; the Rat is very close to everything and, therefore, sees how everything works and is composed. The impulse to "zoom in" to understand is a Rat impulse. The impulse to take apart, dismantle, and dissect are also Rat impulses—again, not to analyze but to observe, look closely, and take in the details. Modern science is very "Rat," and I know many scientists born in the Year of the Rat.

Rat Qi probes, inquires, and studies to make sense of the overwhelming amount of data we perceive through the senses. Rat power breaks everything down into bite-sized, manageable pieces. This ability allows for incredible "productivity" in the Western sense, so Rats are very capable people.

Rats (the animals, not the people) tend to have big, bulging eyes and make short, quick, twitchy movements. Rat Qi has a nervous quality due to its constant observation, evaluation of safety, and taking stock of its surroundings.

Rat Qi is the wisdom of the compound nature of things: Everything is composed of pieces ad infinitum. This wisdom communicates that everything compound is impermanent, which is the source of the Rat's power and fear.

Rat Qi restarts the cycle emerging from the Pig. Suppose the Year of the Pig represents dissolution, everything falling apart. In that case, Rat Qi represents everything coming back into fragments, still dissolute but active—the dust cloud settling, coming back into focus, starting over. Pig is the final blowout, the party, the Big Bang, and Rat is left to pick up the pieces.

MANIFESTATION/CHARACTER (形)

Now that we have covered the symbolism and energetic dynamics, let's explore the key words for the Rat and discuss how this symbol manifests in and as people.

Embodied in individuals, Rat Qi is first and foremost charming. As astute social observers, Rats make fantastic actors and mimics, and they love being center stage, especially when they can play at being someone else. For Rats, other people are valuable resources, so Rat charm is a social power and often their best resource in life.

Rat Qi is fundamentally social, community-oriented, and cooperative, but more in the sense of making things happen than out of pure enjoyment. That being said, Rats are fun-loving and funny, and they often possess a wry kind of wit derived from their astute social observations.

Rat Qi is methodical and detail oriented. Many of the professions we value in our culture are very "Rat." Engineering, accounting, IT, consulting, what we can call information work, anything that requires manipulating data, money, or numbers, moving around bits and pieces, filling out spreadsheets and forms—all this is Rat work. It's busywork, and it goes to show that our culture actually exalts and highly values Rat intelligence. Math and the sciences—chemistry, physics, biology, and Western medicine, what we can call "reductionist disciplines"—are also very Rat-like.

Rat Qi revels in the details. And although I have mentioned science and math, Rat Qi can be wonderfully artistic. Rats can spend hours painting and penciling in detail, focusing on and fleshing out patterns, shades, and textures. A famous architect once said, "God is in the details"; this is a Rat-like sentiment. Shakespeare, in theory, was born in the Year of the Rat, and he invented thousands of words by taking apart existing words and putting them back together into new formations, words like ***auspicious, sanctimonious,*** and ***multitudinous.*** Shakespeare exemplified the poetic nature of Rat insight.

Rat Qi also exemplifies the Chinese virtues of industry, diligence, and perseverance. Imagine you're on a long journey and come across a mountain in your path. Some characters might go around; some might climb to the top heroically, overcoming obstacles; some might wax philosophical and never go anywhere. Rat Qi would probably get a shovel and carve a path through the mountain, one shovelful at a time. You may laugh at such an approach, but Rat Qi can move mountains in this fashion.

At its best, Rat Qi is diligent and patient. Perhaps a family lost everything in a war, exiled to a foreign land with nothing. So, the family bands together and starts a small dry-cleaning business. For three generations, the family perseveres and eventually builds back their fortune. This is the Rat's work ethic: Eventually, the little things pay off. Since Rats are famously discreet and frugal, they can manage resources and money and make a little go a long way.

As you can imagine, the virtues of Rat Qi have their opposites. Rat charm and social observation can turn to nervousness and complaining, seeing endless faults and problems in themselves and others. Rat Qi can be self-conscious, worried about appearance, nitpicky, and overly critical of details.

At its core, Rat Qi is very susceptible to the fear of impermanence, deficiency, and loss, which can turn into a panic over resources. This can turn to scheming and manipulating situations, people, things, money, and so on to create safety and security. It can also turn to emotional and material stinginess and selfishness, and Rats are often stereotyped as hoarders who live in clutter and develop strong attachments to material possessions.

Rats can turn cowardly, afraid to take risks. Rats can quickly become overwhelmed with details and paralyzed, overanalyzing and never acting. "But . . . wait!" is a very Rat-like response. Rat Qi can feel small in a big, scary world. Alone, Rat Qi is vulnerable. Without a nest, resources, friends, partners, family, or a support system, Rats are at their weakest and can wander, feeling lost and depressed.

Rat Qi, at its best, has an immense ability to focus. However, when depleted, the close-in quality of Rat Qi can become fidgety and restless. It can also lead to overconcentration and a racing mind, endlessly thinking, reevaluating, and second-guessing, a kind of mono-focus or tunnel vision that can be obsessive.

Because Rat Qi is fragmented, Rats can compartmentalize their experience. They can put memories, feelings, thoughts, and so on into categories and boxes and "think" their feelings. If traumatized, this compartmentalization can cause them to become detached, unemotional, and unable to connect.

The fundamental impulse of Rat Qi is to make sense of the world. Rat Qi represents active dissolution, characterized by Yang Water—what we can call "activated impermanence," a primal fear that can easily turn to the spiritual path, and I have met many Rats with a strong spiritual bent. Rat's spiritual insight awakens through deep observation, breaking down appearances.

This observant quality of the Rat is available to us all through a Rat Year. It is also especially available during the Rat Month, which is at the beginning of winter, every Rat Day, and every Rat Hour, between 11 p.m. and 1 a.m.

In terms of the Five Rats, each has its unique characteristics that contribute to the overall understanding of the Rat zodiac sign. Wood Rats, or Rats on the Roof, are the most nervous and precarious of the Rats. Fire or Field Rats are the most aggressive, excitable, and brave of the Rats. Earth or Storehouse Rats are the most clever and thrifty, as Earth is the Element of wealth. Metal or Rafter Rats are the most sensitive, meticulous, and resourceful, as the Metal Element gives them calculating moral and spiritual values. And finally, Water or Mountain Rats are the most natural and quintessential of the Rats, and they are the most cunning, changeable, and paranoid. Understanding these different characteristics provides a comprehensive view of the Rat zodiac sign.

THE TWELVE CHARACTERS OF DESTINY, PART 3: OX QI

NATIVE ELEMENT: Yin Earth

HOUR AND MONTH: 1 a.m.–3 a.m., 12th Moon

ORGAN NETWORK: Liver

COMPATIBILITY TRINE: Rooster, Snake

MARRIAGE PAIR: Rat

OPPOSITE: Goat

SYMBOLISM (象) AND QI (氣) DYNAMICS

LET ME BE HONEST: Of all the Twelve Qi Characters, I find Ox the most difficult to express. I often find myself stumbling when communicating the energetic experience of Ox to my clients, and often, it comes out sounding negative. Perhaps this is because I'm a Tiger, and as I will write about in my chapter, Tiger Qi is a rebellion against everything the Ox stands for, energetically speaking. Every astrologer, every person, is limited by the bias of their character; it is a primary lens through which we view the world. Naturally, with self-reflection, our Four Pillars are available to us, and so they are the easiest to understand. But a Tiger can never become an Ox.

I know many Oxen. My father is an Earth Ox, and one of my childhood best friends is a Wood Ox. I entered kindergarten a year early, so many of my peers at school were Wood Ox, which makes a lot of sense to me in hindsight, for I never fit in, and many of my friends were also weirdo Tigers who didn't fit in.

We herd children together, and schoolteachers (if they're paying attention) should recognize that every year's batch of kids is different, yet each group is similar. So, I was herded in with the Oxen, and although I find Ox Qi somewhat incomprehensible, I am intimate with it and will do my best to transmit the experience.

In many ways, the Ox is a symbol of China, for if China is anything, it is perseverant, and its traditions are enduring. Dynastic China was the longest continuous civilization of the modern era. China and the Ox represent the virtue of the heroic preserver and the continuity, stability, and convention of tradition. In the face of chaos, they represent a return to the wisdom of the Ancestors, who survived countless generations.

In the Ten Heavenly Stems scheme, this continuity of tradition is represented by the Ox and its Native Element, Yin Earth. The Chinese character for Earth, Tu (土), contains two horizontal lines, representing a surface and a deep sense of stability. There is no Earth season in Chinese astrology, but instead, Earth represents the continuity, or ground, beneath the changing seasons. While Earth suggests solidity, the Chinese Earth Element is like space, the indestructible openness in which everything happens.

The Ox symbol is related to the Yin (rather than Yang) aspect of Earth. It expresses the malleability or spacious quality of Nature represented by the strength of the plow animal, shaping the Earth beneath us. Medieval China was the old world's greatest agricultural society, and the Ox was the main event that made it possible to break away from tens of thousands of years of nomadic culture.

In the process of becoming agrarian, the Chinese attempted to domesticate the Mongolian horse, but even after hundreds of years, the horse's wild nature could not be made to plow. After the unification of tribes, the Ox Clans brought the Ox up from the swampy regions of southern China, and as soon as they attached reins to it, they were amazed to find that, without goading, the Ox plowed furrows in straight lines. Farmers could let go of the reins, and the Ox would plow forward, turn around, and come back on its own, making even furrows. Because of the Ox, China's agricultural productivity and population increased exponentially, and in a few centuries, China became the most successful and wealthy society on Earth. The Ox was ever after associated with the rewards of consistent hard work and the Confucian value of perseverance in what is right. It came to represent a new contract with Nature to shape the Earth and create a new human realm, free of the hardships and uncertainty of nomadic existence.

The Ox is a gentle giant, embodying a natural Yin strength achieved through gentleness rather than aggression. In Asia, it is common to see children running fearlessly side by side with these enormous animals. Oxen are strong and made of confidence, but they are not aggressive, and this is a valuable symbol for interpreting Ox Qi.

The Ox represents "the way things are done," exemplified in farming, craft, religion, and martial arts—systems of knowledge and custom passed on and preserved through the repetition of skill and experience. To preserve these systems, tradition must maintain an unchanged integrity, lest they be altered and lose their strength, becoming something altogether different. Animals like the Tiger, Monkey, and Goat represent innovation and revolution, but the Ox represents the integrity of conventions and customs unchanged by time.

In Classical Chinese Medicine, the Ox is associated with the liver and likened to a general. It is associated with work ethic, physical and mental endurance, and the strategizing and responsible decision-making related to the military. As such, it is a stern, disciplined, and rather serious symbol, representing the stable foundation that cultures need to maintain integrity.

However serious, Ox's strength is peaceful and gentle in nature. In Chinese spirituality and religion, the Ox is often associated with Guan Yin, the goddess of compassion and wisdom. Laozi is depicted riding an Ox, representing the natural wisdom of Wuwei. In Chan Buddhism, as illustrated in the Ten Ox-Herding Pictures, the taming of the wild Ox is an ancient simile for the discipline of meditation practice that leads to humility and service. Likewise, in India, the Cow is revered and worshipped as a symbol of abundance, nourishment, and nonviolence.

The Ox Year represents a natural return to convention and stability, and to understand Ox Qi, we must look to the Tong Shu, or Chinese calendar. The Ox rules the 12th Moon, the dead of winter (roughly January), and the hours from 1 a.m. to 3 a.m. Ox exemplifies the still, silent, calm, and slow power of winter. In the cycle of the day, Ox represents the middle of the night, the time of deep sleep, rest, and rejuvenation.

Everyone knows they should be asleep at 1 a.m. to 3 a.m. Qi-wise, this is the time of day when we are most able to get deep sleep. Ox Hour draws us deep into the dark silence of "don't know," where the unconscious, automated functions of the body are most efficient. During Ox Hour, you should be like a catfish, hidden in the murky depths of your unconscious. If you were born during this time of the day, you are also part Ox.

The Native Element of the Ox is Yin Earth, which is described as sedated, solid, nourishing, grounded, sleepy, calm, and stable. Ox is the wisdom of orthodoxy and establishment, of thoughtlessness, steadfastness, and automation. Yin Earth represents alliances, wealth, leadership, mothering, and balance. It is the center, Yin and Yang unified, associated with borders and boundaries defined by the empty space at the hub.

MANIFESTATION/CHARACTER (形)

Now that we have covered the symbolism and energetic dynamics, let's explore the key words for the Ox and discuss how this symbol manifests in and as people.

The first quality of Ox Qi is calm—in modern parlance, "chill." Ox is by nature easygoing and relaxed. This easygoing nature comes from the ox's size and strength; not much can kill an ox. They are not intimidated or scared easily. Their strength is unquestionable and, therefore, unhurried, unrushed, and natural. Left alone in the wild, oxen tend to stand around eating grass, but when put to work, they can do anything. Ox Qi, Yin Earth, is grounded and steady. Qi-wise, this comes out as a kind of natural dignity and confidence, at home in their self and skin.

The natural strength of the Ox demonstrates a kind of self-assured confidence. Oxen tend to believe resolutely (and often unconsciously) that their way of seeing the world and doing things is normal. "Doesn't everyone do that?" and "This is the way we've always done it," are very Ox statements. In the Chinese Tradition, this is again described as "conventional." Even the strangest Oxen I have known do their strangeness in a conventional, consistent, and dependable way. Most of them think their strangeness is normal and are often perplexed when others disagree.

This confidence is often demonstrated as being just and committed. The Ox symbolizes the Confucian values of family, society, and nature, which are fundamentally rooted in equality and the fair distribution of resources. Oxen often possess a strong sense of justice, and oxen are natural-born leaders, at their best when in charge and constantly challenged. Without challenge, work, or responsibility, they will create it to demonstrate their worth. Oxen need to work or be busy all the time, or else they feel useless.

Oxen are the most likely to receive criticism for being "stuck in their ways," for not growing, changing, or improving. The consistent and dependable nature of the Ox is natural, and it the Animal least apt toward innovation, which is not to say Oxen are not creative. Expecting an Ox to change based on abstract notions of self-improvement is detrimental. Their wisdom comes from their consistency, and it is harmful to force them to change.

The calm nature of the Ox often expresses itself as quiet and reserved, but this is not always the case. I have known plenty of extroverted Oxen. Ox Qi tends toward a kind of "sleepiness," which can be literal. Oxen are often champion sleepers and can cure most illnesses with deep sleep. They often possess strong physical constitutions by nature and are long lived, rarely taken out by illness or injury.

Ox Qi is unflappable (one of my favorite words in the English language) and "thick skinned." Of all the Characters, Ox is the least likely to be traumatized. Ox Qi has a tremendous capacity to undergo hardship and difficulties and come through unscathed, and Oxen can shrug off the most painful of circumstances.

Despite the calm nature of Ox Qi, it is tenacious and uncompromising. Again, it is in the Ox's nature to work, plow forward, lead, and take on responsibility. They need tasks, and they need to be constantly challenged; otherwise, their strength will be wasted and stagnate. Without something to do with their strength, their tenacity can be destructive to themselves, and without self-reflection, it can harm others. They can become slave drivers, dictators, tyrants, or an asshole boss who only cares about the bottom line.

Oxen often have a strong work ethic and lead lives of great accomplishment. By nature, they are dependable, reliable, consistent, punctual, and so on—all characteristics of Yin Earth, the manifestation of smooth, steady, even Qi. Although they are often materially successful, they usually lack attachment to material things, because they are self-sufficient and do not need much.

As a work animal, the Ox is independent and yet carries others. Oxen are not usually loners, however. They do not rely on other people but rather others tend to rely on them; they are protectors and providers. They take it upon themselves to do things for other people and rarely ask for anything in return. The Ox's independence, strength, and conventionality cause them to assume responsibility for everything. They can see it as their mission to carry others, and they often feel they carry the world on their shoulders.

Ox Qi is also loyal and supportive, sometimes to a fault. It is hard to get on the wrong side of an Ox, and if you act like a jerk, they probably will not notice. Once they accept others, they usually protect them until the end. Sometimes, they can stay in difficult situations or abusive or dysfunctional relationships for a long time out of misplaced feelings of duty and responsibility.

Oxen tend to be outdoorsy and at home in nature. The Native Element of Yin Earth lends them to a deep connection with nature and a desire to connect to the wilderness and seek refuge in solitude. I know many an Ox with a strong sense of adventure.

Ox is sincere, humble, and often sweet, and they are sometimes naive. The image of the Ox is of a gentle, doe-eyed cow. Generally, Ox is honest and straightforward and does not have mysterious or confusing intentions. They mean what they say and are always honest and sincere in their beliefs and efforts.

Ox Qi can tend toward a kind of seriousness, and Ox tends to grow up very fast. They often miss out on childhood and become children later in life, especially the Fire Ox. This seriousness can also turn sullen, depressed, and even humorless. Oxen are, perhaps, the most susceptible to "toxic seriousness," and their experience can become very heavy, with them feeling downtrodden (Wood Ox being the least susceptible).

The heavy and dense quality of Yin Earth can turn to insensitivity and thoughtlessness. Many of the Oxen I know have been accused of being oblivious, unaware, and clueless to the feelings of others. Oxen tend to "not notice" things, people, and situations, and they can hurt or offend others by becoming aloof and dull.

Ox's routine, conventional, and consistent qualities can quickly get "stuck in a rut." Oxen possess an immense capacity to do the same old thing, and they can become slaves to their own conventions—physically, mentally, and spiritually. Their confidence in their beliefs can be pretty convincing, and they are unwilling to entertain other ideas. Furthermore, they can be fearful of change and resist the messages of others for a long time.

Oxen can be ruthless if crossed. As I mentioned, it is hard to get on the bad side of an Ox, but when you do, they can become belligerent and hold grudges for a long time, fixated in their opinions about others and situations. They can have difficulty letting things go—bringing up the past, repeating patterns of negativity, and becoming stuck in a loop. Once drawn into confrontation, Ox Qi can be a scary and formidable adversary.

Finally, they can be too strong for their own good. If they are not challenged, Oxen can use their strength to deplete themselves without noticing, and break down in old age. Or they can generate problems and challenges where there are none and become their own worst enemies.

Ox Qi has a tremendous capacity for resolving Fate. I am always impressed by Ox characters, and I have been blessed to know many in my life.

In terms of the Five Oxen, each has its unique characteristics that contribute to the overall understanding of the Ox zodiac sign. Wood Ox or the Ox at Sea is the humblest, most naive, sweetest, and least characteristic of the Oxen. Fire Ox or the Ox at the Lake is the most assertive, focused, and oafish of all the Oxen, as the Fire Element gives their strength belligerence. Earth or Penned Ox is the most natural Ox, and as such, they are the most active, stubborn, and highly motivated. Metal or Traveling Ox are the most accommodating, strong, and reliable. And finally, the Water or Field Ox is the toughest, most ornery, and most solitary of the Oxen, as the Water and Earth result in more insensitivity. Understanding these different characteristics provides a comprehensive view of the Ox zodiac sign.

THE TWELVE CHARACTERS OF DESTINY, PART 4: TIGER QI

NATIVE ELEMENT: Yang Wood

HOUR AND MONTH: 3 a.m.–5 a.m., 1st Moon

ORGAN NETWORK: Lung

COMPATIBILITY TRINE: Horse, Dog

MARRIAGE PAIR: Pig

OPPOSITE: Monkey

SYMBOLISM (象) AND QI (氣) DYNAMICS

I HAVE READ SEVERAL POPULAR BOOKS on the Chinese zodiac, and I can usually tell the author's Character. However, I have never read an author who admits their Character up front, which is strange. Personal astrology is generally considered private, and people in traditional cultures are often discreet when discussing it, but not usually among family and friends, for it is regarded as an essential guide to relating. Most writing on the Chinese zodiac is, to me, impersonal, and descriptions are usually lopsided. Writers often exalt or diminish certain Animals based on their personal Character's bias.

Personally, I see astrology as a tool for self-reflection. Any astrological consideration begins with studying your own Character and Fate. I can only understand the Twelve Animals through my primary Character—the Yang Fire Tiger—and I will display this Character until death; it is my capacity to resolve Fate.

The Tiger relates differently with each animal. In other words, no description of the Twelve Animals can be fair or equal, for they do not relate equally. The Twelve Animals are patterns of Qi, and some match like a Phillips head screw and screwdriver. Others may relate to one another like dialing a cell phone with a sledgehammer or, as the saying goes, like a square peg in a round hole. So, I am up front about my astrology, as you will see in this book. To a Monkey (Tiger's opposite), my way of life may seem like the sledgehammer.

I am a Fire Tiger. Therefore, this exploration of Tiger Qi will fundamentally differ from my other expositions, because I know this one from the inside out. I cannot help that this description is personal, perhaps even emotional, for understanding the Tiger has been a tremendous source of personal revelation. The year is primary in a person's Qi Character, so I imagine that other Tigers will resonate with this, but perhaps not. Hopefully, my personal experience does not get in the way too much.

The Chinese love the Tiger, but it is in many ways the antithesis of China, for it represents revolution and change. Therefore, it holds a special place in Chinese cosmology, for despite their attachment to tradition, the Chinese have always welcomed change, because no healthy society can function without destruction and renewal. This is called passing the torch to the next generation.

In the chapter on the Ox, I mentioned that the Ox symbolizes China as it represents the virtue of the heroic preserver, the continuity, stability, and convention of Tradition. The Tiger is a symbol of rebellion against everything the Ox stands for, energetically speaking, just as youth constantly rebels against authority with each new generation. Suppose the Ox represents the stability, continuity, and consistency of Yin Earth. In that case, the Tiger, whose nature is Yang Wood, represents a forceful breaking away from all these qualities, for Wood eats, destroys, or controls Earth in the Five Element cycle.

Historically, the tiger has been the most successful predator of humans, and conversely, humans have been the only successful predator of the tiger. At one point, there were hundreds of thousands of tigers in Asia. Many of the earliest recorded human remains have been found with the bones of tigers, which has puzzled archaeologists for years. They're not sure who killed whom.

In the Han dynasty, the number one cause of death among peasants listed in medical records, besides war, was tigers. They roamed freely, wandering into villages at whim, eating anything in their path. In short, tigers disrupted the day-to-day functioning of an orderly society.

The Han government waged war on tigers, and over more than a century, they used the military to systematically hunt and kill thousands of them. This trend continued, which is why the tiger came close to extinction in Asia, although it has recently been coming back. Famous generals were depicted wearing tiger skins as a symbol of their fearlessness in battle, and killing a tiger earned you the title "Tiger." The image of the fearless general who rode into battle, inspiring the troops, and then went off into the mountains to live as a hermit and write the Art of War is a classic metaphor for Tiger Qi. The Tiger way is there and back again—to leave the world as a rebel and return with wisdom.

The Chinese character for Tiger's Earthly Branch Yin, (寅), depicts a bow drawn and about to fire, implying a long history of hunting tigers. Energetically, the drawn bow represents the tiger stalking its prey, waiting, crouching in the tall grass, ready to be unleashed. In Classical Chinese Medicine, the Tiger is associated with the Lung, representing their powerful roar and the Lung's connection to the hair and skin. This is demonstrated by their stunning color and markings, which became a symbol of power in ancient China. Chinese shamans often donned tiger skins and masks to perform exorcism, and warriors wore tiger skins on their shields, armor, or helmets to intimidate their enemies.

We can call the early religion of China "Animism," which later became Daoism. Rural and tribal religion was officiated by Animist priests, who were great arbiters of the Spirit World. Today, they are known as "Red Hat" Daoists. "Black Hat" Daoists are the later Orthodox priests who uphold the more official and orthodox lineages. In his early years, Liu Ming started as a Black Hat Daoist but later shifted toward a much more Animist, or Red Hat, View.

Alive, tigers presented a significant threat, but dead, they were considered the most powerful of spirit protectors. Part of the war on tigers was to "put them on the other side," so to speak. After the systematic hunting of tigers, Daoist priests would then work to command tiger spirits. Zhang Dao-Ling, the founder of Orthodox Daoism, is depicted riding a tiger, symbolizing this command of the Spirit World, his control of the uncontrollable. Similarly, the second Patriarch of Chan Buddhism is always depicted sleeping on a tiger.

This trend is also found in Tantra, for tigers were just as common in India, and great Tantric masters and deities are often depicted sitting on tigers or tiger skins, wearing tiger shawls, using tigers as pillows, and so on. This symbolizes that a practitioner has conquered their fear and impulsiveness. Tiger Qi is considered the wisdom of fearlessness and the victory over danger, and tigers have long been associated with the great yogis and yoginis of the non-dual meditation traditions. As a symbol of Wisdom, in contrast with the gentle Guan Yin image of the Ox, Tiger represents the fierce, cutting, and "crazy wisdom" of the great Mahasiddhas.

Still, to this day, it is common in China to write the Chinese symbol for tiger, Hu (虎), on doors or amulets to ward off fire, theft, illness, and possession. The Tiger symbolizes exorcism, dispossession, power, and warriorship. In many martial arts traditions, the Tiger is depicted with the Dragon in a Yinyang symbol in a push-pull battle for dominion of Heaven and Earth.

When we look at the actual animal, the first thing we see is that the tiger is striped, which is perhaps the key to understanding the symbol. Tigers wish they could be lions or panthers (i.e., one color), but they cannot; they have stripes. And as the saying goes, a tiger can't change their stripes, which symbolizes a fundamentally dual nature that Tigers seek their whole lives to reconcile. So, perhaps, the most important thing we can say about Tigers is that they're striped.

To understand Tiger Qi, we must understand its Native Element, Yang Wood. Yang Wood is the first Element in the cycle of the Ten Heavenly Stems, which is why the Tiger Moon coincides with the Chinese New Year, and the season of spring begins. The Tiger is, therefore, the symbol of spring, representing the impulse of birth arising out of death, the raw force of the sprout bursting through a seed or a chick breaking open an egg.

The force of Yang Wood is the fresh, dynamic, naive, innocent, pliant, new, unformed, spontaneous, impulsive, and forceful arising of movement from complete stillness. Yang Wood is invisible and pure; it represents birth, initiation, renewal, potentiality, creativity, and adaptation. Force arising from stillness—this is the Tiger. Imagine a cat, still and unmoving, then pouncing on their prey.

Tiger Hour is from 3 a.m. to 5 a.m. Here, we emerge from the dreamless state of Ox Hour to express wild, symbolic, creative, and fearless dreaming. This is when we can fly and visit other worlds; this is when we are most likely to have "weird" dreams that make no sense whatsoever. Tiger dreams are a pure expression of the creative impulse of the unconscious. If you were born during this time of the day, you are also part Tiger.

So, beneath this Qi Character is the primal impulse of movement, and the Tiger Year, like the Tiger Moon, is the first significant push forward in the twelve-year cycle. Although the Rat and Ox come before it, they are retrospective, evaluating the past and planning and working for the future. The Tiger, however, is done with all that and impulsively, impatiently, and unapologetically lurches forward.

MANIFESTATION/CHARACTER (形)

Now that we have covered the symbolism and energetic dynamics, let's explore the key words for the Tiger and discuss how this symbol manifests in and as people.

We must first understand that Tigers feel the full force of primal hunger-energy with startling intensity, creating the impulse to break free, innovate, create, destroy, or jump headfirst. This impulsive lurching often causes inconsistent and unreliable behavior, which confuses others. This impulse is always present, even when still, like a cat about to pounce, waiting for the right moment.

This behavior is often perceived as aggressive, because the Tiger is a predator that needs to hunt. But really, Tiger Qi is in constant intimate interaction with its surroundings, deeply sensitive, drawing all other energies into it, alert to minute changes, moods, and emotions, ready to pounce instantly. Even when resting, Tigers are like a loaded weapon. They can be champion loafers and lazy house cats without challenges, but they are always primed to jump and knock things over.

Tiger Qi is very physical and embodied. By nature, Tigers possess strong constitutions and boundless energy, which can express complete stillness and meditative equipoise alongside an immense physical capacity, vitality, and endurance. Tiger Qi is fully present, ready for action, but also naive; Wood element is always naive. Imagine a Tiger running through the jungle, leaping over obstacles—suddenly, the Tiger leaps off a cliff. Halfway down, the Tiger realizes, *Oh, I'm falling*! In other words, Tiger Qi lurches, jumps eagerly into danger, and often doesn't realize its mistakes until it's too late. It does this because it is king of the jungle and assumes it's on top of the game.

This stripiness and impulsiveness make Tigers difficult for others to understand. The stripes denote a powerful need to act, to connect, to be in the world, to love, and at the same time, to run away, to be still, and to hide alone in their cave, for tigers are solitary animals. They are independent and need huge territories in which to roam. In the wild, tigers mate and then go their separate ways. If too many cubs are born, the parents may kill a few so they don't encroach on their hunting territory.

Tigers are pillars of strength and capacity, but then they disappear. They can be the life of the party, and then you may not see them for months. They often jump full force into things and then abandon them before completion, and then they must abandon their abandonment, and so on.

Yang Wood is spontaneity, creativity, and innovation. Tiger Qi may not be reliable, but it can change things, break the mold, and think outside the box. Tiger Qi rebels against everything no matter what; it hates to be confined, hates expectations, and answers to no one. This rebellion is impossible to control and can only be handled with self-discipline. The Tiger finds its Qi power when fear becomes transparent, then its power turns to natural self-discipline and then fearless leadership.

With training, Tigers make tremendous warriors, soldiers, fighters, and shamans; they are heroic and noble defenders. Without training, however, the impulsive force of the Tiger can be disastrous. Violence is available in the Tiger (also in Dragon, Horse, Pig, Rabbit, and others), for some of the Characters must be willing to fight, and to be whole, all people born in the Year of the Tiger need to recognize this part of themselves and accept it.

The influence of Tiger Qi is undeniably potent; Tigers possess a magnetic, almost hypnotic allure. They often emerge as charismatic, dynamic, and innovative leaders, captivating their audience with their oratory skills. However, their inherent inconsistency and unreliability suggest that they are not suited for a leadership role. Tigers are designed to inspire, dazzle, and then fade away, serving as beacons of power, action, and creativity.

Of all the animals, Tigers, Goats, and Monkeys are considered the most creative and artistic (but, of course, everyone can be artistic). Yang Wood, as imagination, creates an immense appetite for knowledge, information, and expression, so Tigers constantly seek creative outlets. Tiger art is very "Jackson Pollock," very modern. The impulse to splatter paint on a wall and call it art to break convention is a Tiger impulse. And of course, once this becomes convention, the Tiger happily returns to the classics to break that convention.

With their stripes and impulsiveness, Tigers are perceived to have a high potential for self-destruction. The alternating nature of their stripes and their strong internal drive can lead to inner conflict and turmoil, making them their own worst adversaries. With their unpredictable, impulsive creativity and uniqueness, it's a challenge for Tigers to carve a niche in the world, to achieve something and maintain consistency. This contradicts the norms of a society that expects them to conform and be the same person all the time. Tigers rebel, and without the right environment and support, they can spiral into self-destruction.

Tigers need unconditional acceptance, love, and tolerance. Therefore, Pigs are a great support, for they are the most tolerant. Others need to know that Tigers will always "let you down" if you expect consistency from them. It may sound harsh, but Tigers can be in a relationship only if others manage not to need them. They will do their best, but they will most likely show you their stripes, and as the saying goes, a Tiger can't change those.

Because of the Tiger's dual nature and tendency toward inner conflict and self-destruction, they also tend toward great spiritual awakening. Many Tigers become mystics hell-bent on the spiritual path, seeking the reconciliation and union of their opposites. Many Tigers have become famous spiritual teachers, many of whom have inspired me. My favorites are Alan Watts, Thomas Merton, Walt Whitman, Namkhai Norbu, and my teacher Dharma Bodhi.

So, now we get to key words. The first are courageous, daring, and brave. Tiger Qi, again, represents fearlessness, a kind of samurai mentality, hurling into danger, charging into the unknown, and seeking adventure. This courage comes from a deep flirting with death in the core of their being, for Yang Wood emerges from death (Yin Water). This courage lends to being strong-willed, seeking to conquer the fear of death, and despite our impulsiveness, Tigers have famously terrifying willpower, usually to accomplish or study strange and unusual things.

Tiger Qi is energetic, passionate, and enthusiastic. Yang Wood's force is physically and mentally expressed in the Tiger. Physically active, even hyperactive, Tigers can be balls of energy, freely expressing themselves in all kinds of uncontrollable ways, which is why they need self-discipline early in life. Discipline forced upon them will most likely be rebelled against.

Mentally and energetically, this unstoppable energy bubbles forth as enthusiasm and dedication. Tigers usually get really, really into things and champion what they love. Once they love something or someone, they become incredibly dedicated. However, because of their inconsistency, this dedication rarely leads to mastery.

Tiger Qi is competitive. Tigers always seek opportunities to demonstrate their strength, primarily to themselves. The Tiger's motivation often derives from inner conflict; however, it is due to their dual nature, which is a need to prove something to themselves. So, usually, they compete with themselves and test this competition through others.

Tigers are honest due to their naivety. Yang Wood does not have maturity or discretion, so Tigers tend to wear their hearts on their sleeves. They usually don't make very good actors, due to an inability to be anything other than what they are (or, like Tom Cruise or Bill Murray, play the same character in every movie). Because of this they can be incredibly vulnerable. As kids, Tigers are very vulnerable, and if traumatized, they can get stuck in arrested development.

Tigers are often very dignified in their expression. Imagine a big, noble jungle cat. Or look at any house cat that spends all day cleaning itself. This dignity lends to what Ming called the "awesome deportment," and Tigers often find great value in cultivating and expressing a powerful or impressive image. Places, things, and skills all must have power, meaning, and significance to add to the Tiger expression. Otherwise, they're not interested. Tigers can treat people this way, too; they love everybody, but to get them interested, they must be mesmerized and impressed.

Finally, Tigers are considered lucky and generous. Luck is a very Chinese idea, and some Characters are considered to have it more than others. Luck is defined by being in the right place at the right time, which is usually a matter of Fate. At their best, Tigers are gregarious pleasure-seekers who love sharing their luck with others.

Of course, astrology is about self-reflection, so now we get to the flip side of all this and admit to the depleted qualities of Tiger Qi.

As I mentioned, their impulsiveness can become profound restlessness and rebellion. All Yang Characters are prone to be restless, but Tigers' restlessness is scary and goes hand in hand with feeling confined and stuck—in need of exploding out of their situation. If Tigers do not have problems or obstacles, they often create them to have something to rebel against, something to break out of, something to pounce on. Tigers are rebels without a cause, their own worst enemies. Tigers, especially Water and Fire Tigers, can be risk-taking land mines of passion and emotion. Uncontrolled drama and half-baked scheming can make their lives calamitous. Something usually becomes a "savior," whether a teacher, mentor, partner, or child. Tigers must be regulated, so if they can settle down, family is good for them. At their worst, Tigers are indecisive, constantly second-guessing, so having others take over, such as a strong partner, can be a blessing.

Often, Tigers are so busy generating problems that they are inconsiderate of others. At their best, Tigers are incredibly generous, and part of their path is to learn to give, let go, and see outside their problems to the bigger picture. Tiger's inconsiderateness can come from being self-involved, morose, negative, and moody. Tiger Qi can become very dark, but it always returns to the light.

Tiger restlessness can lead to a unique kind of stubborn egotism, thinking and being utterly convinced they are right (Ox, Horse, Dog, and Goat also do this famously). Tigers are unchallenged in the wild; they have no natural predators. Tigers get flustered, confused, and bewildered when challenged, for in the end, they are sure they're right and plan to do what they want. It isn't easy to convince Tigers otherwise, unless they can adopt something as their own idea. Because of their strength, Tigers usually want to dominate situations and be in charge, which can come across as aggressive, egotistical, and overbearing.

Finally, the Tiger's dignity and deportment can lead to tremendous vanity and pride. Tigers can be very concerned about their appearance and the opinions of others, although they'll never admit it. Tigers are very sensitive to criticism and rejection and can be wounded deeply by others if they do not possess a strong sense of self-love and self-possession.

In terms of the Five Tigers, each has unique characteristics that contribute to the overall understanding of the Tiger zodiac sign. Wood or Standing Still Tigers are the most natural and quintessential of the Five Tigers, and they are vicious, ferocious, and scrappy. Fire or Forest Tigers are the most emotional, passionate, and risk-taking of the Tigers, as the Fire Element empowers the force of the Wood Element. Earth or Mountain Tigers are the most grounded and regal, and as such, they have fantastic energy and strength but are obstinate and cavalier. Metal or Descending Tigers are the most demanding, candid, and vigorous, and the restraint of Metal makes them both aggressive and forgiving. Finally, the Water or Roaming Tiger is the proudest, stubbornest, and most vital, as the Water Element empowers Wood and makes them profoundly honest and restless. Understanding these different characteristics provides a comprehensive view of the Tiger zodiac sign.

THE TWELVE CHARACTERS OF DESTINY, PART 5: RABBIT QI

NATIVE ELEMENT: Yin Wood

HOUR AND MONTH: 5 a.m. to 7 a.m., 2nd Moon

ORGAN NETWORK: Large Intestine

COMPATIBILITY TRINE: Pig, Goat

MARRIAGE PAIR: Dog

OPPOSITE: Rooster

SYMBOLISM (象) AND QI (氣) DYNAMICS

THE RABBIT SYMBOL opens us into a dimension unique among the Twelve Animals: intuition.

When studying the cycle of the Twelve Animals, we must remember that each Animal transforms into the next in a meaningful, although nonlinear, way. The cycle is a whirlwind, centripetal and centrifugal, a tornado of energy that flows in a kind of lopsided pattern.

Suppose the Ox represents strength, tolerance, and continuity, and the Tiger represents an escape from continuity through rebellion, creativity, and change. In that case, the Rabbit represents the result of the Tiger's impulsive revolutionary bluster: a raw, open, and vulnerable sensitivity, represented by the Rabbit's Native Element, Yin Wood.

Yin Wood is innocence, spontaneity, flexibility, renewal, humility, gentleness, sensitivity, subordination, and potentiality. While Yang Wood represents a naive impulsive force to come into being, Yin Wood demonstrates the outcome of that force, which is exposed, raw, and tender but with great creative potential, like a sprout emerging from the earth, ready to grow into a mighty oak. The Tiger represents the sprout's brave and daring impulse to rise into the world's danger, and the Rabbit is the tender shoot needing protection and nurturing to thrive.

The Tiger represents a necessary rebellion against stagnation, and the insight of the Rabbit understands that rules, as defined by the Ox, must have intuition if they are to be free of stagnation. Revolution cannot be sustained (hence the Tiger's struggle) and should end with a refreshed look at things, and we call this the Rabbit. The Rabbit sees into and understands the Tiger's rebellion with empathy beyond the Tiger's grasp, which is why it is the natural outcome of Tiger Qi. The mystical state, Tiger, needs heart, Rabbit. When this succeeds, the result is the Dragon, which has unlimited potential.

In the Chinese View, the qualities of the Rabbit are best described by the term *lunar*, and the history of the Rabbit as a symbol comes from the moon. The Chinese call the moon Taiyin, which means Great Yin, so Rabbits are very Yin, and Water Rabbits are very, very Yin. When the Chinese look at the moon, they see a rabbit called Yuetu (月兔), Moon Rabbit. Americans see cheese or something, but the Chinese see a rabbit. In other words, rabbits are lunar creatures; they come from the moon and are seen as manifestations of moonlight.

Therefore, rabbits were revered, and harming or eating them was considered very bad luck. Surprisingly, although the ancient Chinese ate nearly everything else, rabbits were rarely eaten. This says something very important about the Rabbit—that they should be protected and revered for what they offer.

Daoist alchemists saw the Rabbit as producing an elixir of immortality, nectar from the "bardo" of night turning into day, from mist and moonlight. The Rabbit, therefore, became a symbol of the inner world, Nei (内), associated with Nei Dan or Nei Gong and the practices of Internal Alchemy.

The Rabbit rules the dawn, from 5 a.m. to 7 a.m., and these lunar creatures are most active during this crepuscular, or twilight, hour. To understand Rabbit Qi, take a walk in the woods at 6 a.m. The energy is gentle, vibrant, soft, and transparent. Dawn is a time of transition: Light emerges, and we wake, emerging from the subconscious and dreams to cross into our waking reality. Writers often use dusk and dawn as a literary device to denote shifts or changes in our perception of reality. If you were born during this time of the day, you are also part Rabbit.

The lunar image of the Rabbit represents their strong need to escape the light of day and their fear of confrontation, a symbol of the delicate, sensitive, and vulnerable nature of Rabbit Qi. While this may sound "weak" to some, the Chinese Tradition insists that weakness is significant. Some Characters are strong, and some are weak, but each contributes something essential to society.

Classical Chinese Medicine diverged from Roman medicine based on this very principle. Around the turn of the Common Era, the main form of medicine around the world was bleeding, which was a powerful treatment that often killed the weak. Romans responded, "Good, the weak are unworthy Roman citizens." On the other hand, the Chinese said, "Wait—perhaps weak people are sensitive and have something to offer society that strong people overlook." So, the bleeding needles became smaller, and the treatments became weaker. According to some, acupuncture developed as a natural outcome of these earlier, more forceful bleeding treatments. The instinct to preserve, protect, and listen to sensitive people is a Rabbit instinct, and Chinese medicine is "sensitive" or weak medicine—and proud of it.

Energetically, the Rabbit burrows, and is submerged, in the "subconscious" stream flowing beneath everything—a mumbling dialogue our energy has with itself, a constant flow of imagination, and a smooth flow of emotional responses going on all the time. Yin Wood represents the roots below the surface, tapping into a deep underground lake.

Rabbits are like exposed wires, picking up on signals invisible to the rest of us. This raw, exposed quality has many interesting manifestations in terms of Character, but before we discuss these in key terms, we must look deeper into the symbol of the actual animal itself: Think bunnies.

Rabbits are tiny and soft, and they're not predators capable of defending themselves, so they hide, a symbol of their fragility and justified paranoia. They are the prey, and everything wants to eat them. They often live in burrows or bushes, a symbol of being beneath, hidden, submerged in the subconscious stream, protected from the light. The burrow also represents the Rabbit's "nesting instinct," which manifests in their need for safety and security.

They have big, sensitive ears, like satellites picking up on frequencies all around them. They live in communal families, symbolizing their social nature and the importance of relationships to Rabbit Qi. Finally, despite their delicate appearance, they have powerful hind legs and can be vicious if backed into a corner. All these symbols will become clear as we go through the key terms.

To understand the Rabbit, we must understand its social instinct, which we call "dependent" and "domestic" in a trine with the Pig and Goat. Above all, Rabbit Qi is vulnerable yet profound in its intuitive capacity, so Rabbits seek safety, protection, alliance, and stability in the form of "home." When the Rabbit feels safe and secure and has a tribe or circle of close friends, a strong protector or partner, or their own home, they shine; they become the Dragon—powerful and dynamic leaders with insight and heart, capable and successful. If Rabbits have strong siblings or parental guardians, they can learn their power early in life. If they are hurt or alone, they close off and put up armor, and their intuitive gifts are often repressed and come out as defensive and vicious.

Not only do Rabbits need good protection as children, but they also need an environment that nurtures their intuition. The Rabbit Character is at odds with modern culture, which enjoys exploiting Rabbit characteristics but does not generally nurture them. In a culture jockeying for resources and status, sensitive, empathic people often struggle.

MANIFESTATION/CHARACTER (形)

Now that we have covered the symbolism and energetic dynamics, let's get into key words for the Rabbit and talk about how this symbol manifests in and as people.

The first key term for the Rabbit is gentle. The gentle quality of Rabbit people is not always apparent, especially with Fire Rabbits, and this has a lot to do with their childhoods, family circumstances, and current relationships. In their nature, though, Rabbits are sweet, kind, nice, and peace-loving. Most Rabbits I meet, and people born in Rabbit Hour, have a good-natured sweetness that I find immediately apparent, but sometimes this sweetness is lying under the surface and comes out only after they trust you.

Conversely, at their worst, Rabbits turn vicious. Energetically, they are like bunnies, so people think they can do anything they want to them or in front of them. They are often the victims of trauma and abuse. Because of their sweet and sometimes timid nature, Rabbits can remain frozen and scared and take abuse for a long time until it becomes intolerable, in which case they often lash out and end their abuse and suffering in vicious and violent ways. Hell hath no fury like a Rabbit scorned. Liu Ming used to say, "Watch out for those hind legs!" When they're hurt, Rabbits have a potential for darkness beyond the other signs.

Rabbits are usually quiet by nature, for they are always listening and can't help it, symbolized by the big ears. Rabbits feel at home being hidden, silent and listening to the ethers. Ming was once interpreting for a Tibetan lama when a student returned from retreat. The lama asked, "How was your meditation?" and the student replied, "It was amazing: By the second month, my mind was so quiet, I could hear the thinking of the people in the town below me!" This is a very Rabbit response: "Now I can hear everyone!"

On the flip side, being quiet and humble by nature can turn to being a gossipy chatterbox. Rabbits can have a profound capacity for talking shit, which comes from being slightly nervous all the time. In Classical Chinese Medicine, the Rabbit is associated with the large intestine, which is one of the more comical associations, as it is connected to their superficiality and ability to talk shit along with the fact that rabbits poop a lot more when they are stressed, nervous, or scared. Relaxed and in their power, Rabbits feel no need to speak and are natural listeners. Still, when out of their element and vulnerable, they may speak uncontrollably, trying to get a handle on the situation. Furthermore, since Rabbits are socially dependent, they can use speech and gossip as tools for manipulation, talking people up and down to gain an advantage. Rabbits hate confrontation, but when backed into a corner, they can retaliate with nasty, hurtful vitriol.

Rabbits can also be incredibly sweet, supportive, and loving. Rabbits, by nature, are supportive and caring friends, partners, lovers, and parents. The Rabbit is perhaps the most "domestic" of the Twelve Animals. Rabbit Qi seeks to nest, nurture, and create a loving and supportive environment in which they and others can thrive.

From birth, Rabbits possess a strong social drive to create family and friendship, to bond with others and create a tribe or clan, and to belong to and feel part of a small, close-knit group or community. In their hearts, they are not loners, although when in pain, they can hide from the world so as not to be seen or hurt again. When Rabbits find their home and their tribe, they thrive and become great leaders and successful entrepreneurs. Empowered, Rabbits are among the most authoritative and confident of the Twelve Animals, which is how the Rabbit turns into a Dragon.

Early in life, Rabbits often seek a stable base to get their "security" taken care of. They can often appear very independent to others, but as soon as they have a protector, a guardian, a home base, and something to rely on, they lose their independent nature and become dependent, so they can let their other gifts, which need support, come forward. To others, the Rabbit can appear deceptive and lazy, but this is a very lopsided "American" understanding: the idea that everyone needs to be a rugged, independent individual. Rabbits yearn to let go of their independence to merge with family, friends, lovers, and so on—to offer up their big, squishy hearts. Others often become dependent on them for nurturing and emotional support, which is part of the Rabbit gift.

Rabbits have a powerful, even mystical, connection to objects, especially objects related to the home: furniture, clothing, cookware, and so on. They love to "feather their nests" and often collect material possessions. They derive nourishment from stuff. Rabbits will make a home wherever they go.

This connection with objects is related to the Rabbit's heightened sense of aesthetics. Rabbits are creative designers with a natural sense of Fengshui, the auspice of placement. This aesthetic sensibility lends to a deep appreciation of the nature of beauty and offers artistic depth to the Rabbit sweetness.

Rabbits are naturally intuitive and empathetic. We can also call this subliminal or subconscious. Rabbits are like a radar dish; internally, they are open receivers. Rabbits can walk into a room and immediately feel everything going on, and for the Water Rabbit, this capacity is oceanic, like Guan Yin, who hears the cries of the whole world. Rabbits can sense everyone's mood and body language; they intuitively perceive all the unconscious signals people put out through their "energy." A Rabbit might see your aura.

This has positive and negative consequences. Positively speaking, Rabbits have an unusual capacity to feel and empathize, and their intuition, when properly trained, gives them tremendous emotional intelligence and insight into others and the world.

On the other hand, it is very easy to mistake intuition for wisdom; they are not the same thing. There is a lot of "static" in the universe, most of which is just psychic garbage floating around. The subconscious ethers, the invisible world of Ghosts and spirits, the hum of habitual emotional processing that people emit all the time without knowing it—that comes out as unconscious behaviors, and Rabbits feel all this more than the other signs. If their vulnerability is exposed to too many influences, their intuition can go haywire from so much "noise."

Rabbits cannot shut down their intuition. They could struggle to live in cities, places with a lot of activity, data, noise, pollution, people, and so on. If the apartment they live in has too much chaotic activity, they can feel crazy and not know why. This sensitivity is often embodied, which can lead to all kinds of allergies. They can also be affected by minute changes in the weather. In general, they should live somewhere dull, and being outside in nature should be selective, for that too is full of all kinds of noise.

It may seem unusual to channel a nature spirit, but really it isn't. A Rabbit may easily go into a trance and channel a nature spirit; others may think this is profound, and Rabbits may think so too. However, anyone who has seen into the Spirit World can tell you that actually it is full of useless, dumb, confused, greedy, and hungry spirits, milling around all over the place, that will appear as anything you like in order to feed on your kidney Qi. It may seem "special" to be a trance medium, but you might be lunch. It is, of course, possible to be a wise medium, but this takes a lot of training, which is the purpose of Daoism. Daoism is basically ritual training to manage the Spirit World. Rabbits are natural Daoists, and should receive this training early on, so they don't become the aforementioned lunch.

Practically speaking, Rabbits are often lunch, in fact, for other people. Just like most disembodied spirits are looking to feed on others, so are most people who are not self-possessed. Rabbits are easy prey to aggressive people looking to dominate and feed on others. Because Rabbits want to merge and depend, they can easily attach to the wrong people. Relationships of all kinds are crucial for the Rabbit. They need training to be self-possessed and careful about whom they choose to let in. If a healthy Rabbit lets you into their world, you should feel blessed, because they are the greatest support.

The receptivity of Rabbits makes them the most susceptible to paranoia, schizophrenia, anxiety, nervous disorders, and so on. Rabbits can be scattered and twitchy, and they can constantly feel threatened. This is another reason Rabbits need training in their emotional intelligence from an early age. Otherwise, they can become "weird" or develop neuroses and mental health problems. In traditional terms, they are among the most susceptible to possession, for they hear the voices of their Ancestors and can perceive Ghosts and Demons more than other signs, especially as children. If they have good training, they make amazing counselors, teachers, guides, and social workers, and they love serving and supporting others.

The Rabbit's health and well-being have everything to do with how they handle their emotional facilitation. An uneven flow of emotion compromises their immune system and is the ground of all their illness. If they undergo surgery, for example, and the nurse says something terrible before they go under, there will be complications in the surgery. If they feel that the surgeon "understands" them, the recovery from surgery will go well. It is important to understand that Rabbits do not "think" this way; it is the nature of their Qi. They're vulnerable.

Rabbits possess exceptional social charm. They can be incredibly seductive and sexy, mesmerizing and alluring, and appear as a kind of "prize" to others wanting to "catch" them. This skill comes from their social instinct, and at their best, Rabbits bring out the best in others, bringing people together and inspiring them. At their worst, this social skill is opportunistic, and they use their charm to gain an advantage over others socially.

They can manipulate and control others, especially with their sexuality. Rabbits (and Roosters) are by nature one of the most sexual signs (as rabbits can reproduce like crazy in the wild), and they can use their sexual power as a tool of leverage over others as another way to gain security. The need to be safe, if driven unconsciously by fear, can turn Rabbits into superficial snobs who will do anything to secure a partner or good social status, like marrying for money.

Rabbits are naturally diverse and accepting of everyone, a testament to their unique emotional intelligence and empathy. Their intuition is a beautiful gift, one that they share with anyone born during Rabbit Hour, fostering a sense of inclusivity and understanding.

Rabbits also teach us much about the central relationship between Character and Fate in Polestar Astrology. Rabbits have fantastic potential, and yet they're delicate and have no built-in "muscle," so their blooming in life is very dependent upon the circumstances of Fate. If a Rabbit has good-Fated relationships with partners, family, and Fengshui, they bloom. If their relationships are haunted, then they tend to be held back and can become very self-destructive. If Rabbits are hurt or feel unsafe, they will do anything, including taking their own life. Rabbits have the potential to go darker than any other sign, which most people do not want to talk about, but I will repeat it: Hell hath no fury like a Rabbit scorned. So, Fate for Rabbits is essential. Rabbits also bloom when they have a modest or gentle Fate. A Rabbit born with a big Fate to be a leader in the spotlight is most certainly an affliction.

When free from the constraints of Fate, Rabbits have the potential to transcend, for they possess a tremendous capacity for self-cultivation. This unique trait sets them apart, offering a path to personal growth and self-discovery.

In terms of the Five Rabbits, each has its unique characteristics that contribute to the overall understanding of the

Rabbit zodiac sign. Wood or Temple Rabbits are the most natural, vulnerable, and potentially the sweetest and most sensitive of all sixty signs. Fire or Moon Gazing Rabbits are the most independent, stubborn, and angsty—the teenage Rabbit. Earth or Emerging Rabbits and Metal or Burrow Rabbits are the most mature, secure, and stable—the least rabbity Rabbits. And finally, Water or Forest Rabbits are beyond profound and mystical, yet they are perhaps the most troubled and paranoid due to the darkness of Water. Understanding these different characteristics provides a comprehensive view of the Rabbit zodiac sign.

THE TWELVE CHARACTERS OF DESTINY, PART 6: DRAGON QI

NATIVE ELEMENT: Yang Earth

HOUR AND MONTH: 7 a.m. to 9 a.m., 3rd Moon

ORGAN NETWORK: Stomach

COMPATIBILITY TRINE: Rat, Monkey

MARRIAGE PAIR: Rooster

OPPOSITE: Dog

SYMBOLISM (象) AND QI (氣) DYNAMICS

CHINESE ASTROLOGY AND CULTURE have had a long-standing love affair with the Dragon, the mystical culmination of the Celestial Zodiac. During Dragon Years, everyone in China tries to get pregnant. In the Chinese mind, the promise of a male Dragon son has always represented a potential for greatness unmatched by the other signs. The Dragon has always been a symbol of the Emperor and the ruling power of Heaven. This has led to a long pattern of sex-based discrimination, and the imbalance of the one-child policy will lead to a massive population collapse in China, but that's another story.

I always dread exploring Dragon Qi, for the Dragon cannot be defined. However, I was born in a Metal Dragon Hour, so I am half Dragon, for the year and the hour form the primary image of someone's Qi Character. Like the Tiger, studying the Dragon has been a great source of personal revelation, and I hope I can offer some of the insight gained from my self-reflection.

Whenever I do readings for Dragons or Snakes, I throw my hands up and say, "¿¡!?" As the mystical Yinyang culmination at the center of the zodiac, the Dragon and Snake are ineffable, characterized by their unknowable quality, but in different ways. The Snake is Big Yin, emptiness and space, and the Dragon is Big Yang, fullness and light expanding into the Heavens. The Snake represents the inner, open capacity to become any of the other eleven Qi Characters without being them, but the Dragon is all eleven Qi Characters embodied.

The symbol of the Dragon is, then, a synthesis. If you look at depictions of the Chinese Dragon, you will see that it is a composite of every animal. According to tradition, it is said to have the whiskers of the Rat, the face and horns of the Ox, the claws and teeth of the Tiger, the belly of the Rabbit, the body of the Snake, the legs of the Horse, the goatee of the Goat, the wit (or brain) of the Monkey, the crest of the Rooster, the ears of the Dog, and the snout of the Pig.

The Dragon is the only animal of the twelve capable of flight, an essential part of the symbol. Yet, it is rarely depicted with wings, for its ability to fly is supernatural. It is the only supernatural animal in the group, so people question its existence. However, the Chinese never questioned the existence of dragons, because everyone knew they controlled the weather and water. Dragons were thought to be behind the clouds, causing storms, floods, and rain. If you could ride to the source of a great storm or flood, then maybe you would see one and earn the title "Dragon."

The synthesis of all eleven into the supernatural dragon represents infinite potential, which is the first and most important thing we can say about Dragons. Dragon Qi is said to have the qualities, capacities, and skills of all eleven Animals and the power to express all or none of them if it chooses, which is sort of like the nine on the Enneagram. The Dragon can choose to deny its potential, which is why Dragons need a path. Their infinite potential is meaningless to the Chinese unless it is turned away from selfishness and toward self-reflection, dedicated to the benefit of others.

Ming used to say that each Character is like a toolbox with a specific set of tools or skills, but that the Dragon toolbox just has a Dragon in it. In other words, we don't know what Dragons are for. They are a paradox outside the paradigm, and often they are an enigma to their friends and family. The Snake is an enigma even to themselves, but Dragons, while mysterious, are often very self-confident and assured, which is part of what baffles people about them.

Historically, the dragon is a symbol of the Emperor and the rising sun to the East, the ruling power of Heaven from an unknown mystical origin. Because of their potential, Dragons were considered great leaders, capable of the most inclusive view with the most compassion. So, it is easy to understand why the Chinese revere the Dragon as the Emperor.

There is a mountain of lore around the Dragon symbol. I will do my best to make this specific, but again, Dragons may be all or none of this, and the uncultivated Dragon may be a mess of everything all at once, unable to make sense of themselves.

The Dragon's Native Element is Yang Earth, also shared by the Dragon's opposite, the Dog. They each express the virtues of Yang Earth in different ways. For the Dragon, Yang Earth represents flight—the ability to break away from the Earth—symbolizing the Dragon's capacity to see and travel beyond. The Dog represents territory and the ability to intuit, cover, and protect the terrain. In Chinese medicine, Yang Earth and the Dragon represent the stomach and the fires of digestion, which is our desire to devour life and experience.

Yang Earth represents manifestation, confidence, alliance, leadership, wealth, abundance, balance, caring, and power—Yang expressions as opposed to the Yin aspects of Earth (nourishing, mothering, stabilizing, supporting). By nature, the Dragon has these capacities but often has difficulty expressing them without training. Yang Earth is also connected to Dragon Hour, from 7 a.m. to 9 a.m., when the Yang of the Sun emerges over the horizon to start the day. If you were born during this time of the day, you are also part Dragon.

If there is one thing we can say about Dragon Qi, it is that it's big, sometimes too big. Dragon Qi is pervasive and expansive. It is Big Yang exploding out into heaven and the sky, seeking to fly beyond and above all boundaries, exploring and playing and unaware of its own strength. Sometimes, it makes a mess; sometimes, it breaks and destroys, but not out of spite. The Dragon breaks things because it is exploring its boundaries through playful inquiry. I believe this bigness tends to give Dragon characteristics, which we can discuss, that they otherwise transcend.

The transcendent and fresh quality of the Dragon makes them natural mystics, and often, people with Dragon Qi are interested in spiritual occult traditions, especially those with extraordinary cosmologies. The way Dragons experience themselves and the universe is just too big for ordinary views. To me, Bruce Lee was the quintessential Dragon (he's a Metal Dragon born in Earth Dragon Hour), and his life demonstrated the mystical power of Dragon Qi.

Like the Snake, Dragons see through and beyond ordinary appearances, but unlike the Snake, their powerful, expansive Qi pushes them toward action and adventure. Dragons want to go beyond and actualize their potential and can go farther than any other sign. If a Dragon chooses to leave the world, they're never to be seen again; if they choose to embrace the world, they can go into it deeply and lose themselves in the service of greatness.

MANIFESTATION/CHARACTER (形)

Now that we have covered the symbolism and energetic dynamics, let's explore the key words for the Dragon and discuss how this symbol manifests in and as people.

The first key words are strong and powerful. The Yang Earth character of the Dragon has a strength unmatched by any of the other eleven Characters. Dragon strength is different from, say Ox or Horse strength. Ox strength represents the capacity to carry, maintain, and endure, and Horse strength represents the power to manifest, work, and accomplish, but Dragon strength is not related to any specific capacity and is better represented by the power of a great storm, the strength of nature unleashed. We marvel at the strength of nature, and we respect and fear its destructive side. The power of water, when harvested by a dam, can generate immense energy, yet uncontrolled, a tidal wave can demolish a town. We do not consider tidal waves evil, yet we mourn over and fear nature's destruction. In the same way, Dragon's strength is immense, raw, wild, and can be destructive, but as with the dam, it can be harnessed for good.

This strength, the explosive Yang, can turn to profound compulsiveness. Dragon Qi can be overwhelming, and Dragons can be a handful—bundles of energy that need channels to flow in, lest they flow everywhere. Like Tiger Qi, Dragon Qi has an explosive, outward-moving quality, in this case symbolized by flight, that can propel Dragons toward uncontrolled action and reaction. This compulsive strength can be physical, mental, or emotional. It can manifest as unruly behavior or speech patterns, especially Fire Dragons, who may speak freely and challenge everyone and every idea as a demonstration of power. In general, Dragons need an outlet to demonstrate their strength. Otherwise, they will destroy themselves.

The strength of the Dragon feels very natural and becomes a kind of confidence, not necessarily social confidence but self-assuredness and confidence in their view. Other Characters, such as Roosters, have this too, but the Rooster arrives at confidence through analysis. Dragons need no analysis; they're born assured and cannot be convinced otherwise.

The Dragon has a big, glorious vision. The problem is that nothing can live up to the Dragon's dreams, so it is hard for them to come back down to Earth. Dragons feel like they're the rulers of the universe, masters of destiny—the most capable, the smartest, the best, and so on.

With training, they can be that, but often, their self-assured confidence is overconfidence, all talk—what we call "delusions of grandeur." So, Dragons can be selfish and "egotistical" in the ordinary sense. Dragons often feel like royalty, like everything should be given to them, like they're already awesome and should be rewarded justly. They may even have low self-esteem, but that's because people don't get how awesome they are. They can be attention-hungry and expect others to acknowledge them, regardless of what they do.

The Dragon can be so confident in their abilities that they never actually work to do anything. Often, they need extensive reality checks to "eat humble pie" and put in the time and effort to master something. And when they do, this natural confidence in their abilities can be actualized and taken to great heights, like those of Bruce Lee.

Dragons, therefore, possess a natural charisma. Something about their power, confidence, and ineffability becomes enigmatic and impressive to others. Patrick Stewart, who played *Star Trek*'s Captain Jean-Luc Picard, and is a

Metal Dragon and a fantastic Shakespearean actor, is an excellent example of the Dragon's charisma. He exudes a natural confidence, and the Metal element gives his expression of the Dragon restrained power and stability.

Dragons are a mystery to others, and they defy labels. At their best, Dragons love showmanship and can be flamboyant and outgoing. Dragons often have prominent personalities, even when that personality is introverted. The outgoing nature of the Dragon is based on a kind of ambition and adventurous spirit. Grand is the only scale Dragons work with. They have a big, broad, expansive, and inclusive vision and the capacity to see a panoramic picture. Philosophically, the Dragon has a view or insight no other Character is capable of, that can fly out beyond the clouds. Dragons seek grand, Peter Pan–style adventure. Small goals and narrow ideas seem unimportant to the Dragon—like, why bother?

Dragons have a tremendous capacity for fantasy and envision themselves as great, magnanimous beings; they take the whole "I want to grow up to be an astronaut" to ridiculous proportions. They may even live in a fantasy world in which they are invincible and infallible. Even when a personal vision is not defined, Dragons feel destined for greatness, and many are, like Oprah Winfrey or Jeff Bezos. Living in the clouds, fantasizing about greatness, Dragons can therefore appear aloof and distant, difficult for others to connect with.

Dragons are unrealistic. Nothing can live up to the Dragon's scale. It is hard for Dragons to sweat the small stuff and to pay attention to details. Dragons are telescopes looking out to the stars, not microscopes. They can be unrealistic about everything: their abilities, plans, and expectations of life and of others.

Dragons are also dramatic. They can make a big deal out of small things, because big and expansive is how they roll. When things don't go their way and when things fall short of expectations, Dragons can be sarcastic drama queens. The feeling of bigness, too, can lead to being insensitive, blunt, and unconcerned with people's emotions, except for their own, and in this arena they "make mountains of molehills."

The power and self-assuredness of the Dragon can be assertive, willful, confident, dedicated, and demanding. Dragons demand the best from themselves and others and tend to assert and insist upon their opinion, which is both a virtue and a challenge. To be a leader, one must be assertive and able to make decisions, and the Dragon is the most skillful leader. Dragons should not be put in subordinate positions; they thrive in leadership roles, but without feet on the ground, they can fly over the little guy. Once the Dragon has developed their heart, their assertive willfulness can accomplish greatness for better or worse.

If turned toward the spiritual path, this capacity to assert willpower, to connect to the Yang expression of Heaven, can be unparalleled. A great example is the late teacher and Earth Dragon Swami Rudrananda, or Rudi. His book, *Spiritual Cannibalism*, is a fantastic exposition of Dragon Qi applied to the spiritual path. Rudi had titanic willpower and dedication, and he taught people to essentially "eat" and be nourished by everything as energy to become what Tantra calls a Viśvabhuj, a digester of the universe. Unfortunately, most people don't possess Rudi's willpower and fall short of his example. Not everyone can live up to a Dragon's vision, but he was inspiring, nonetheless.

The final positive Dragon virtue I will offer is generosity. It may sound like Dragons have a lot of potentially challenging qualities, but we must remember that they have unlimited potential. The Dragon can display all virtues to the grandest scale. Dragon Qi is big and overflows all boundaries, which naturally turns to generosity. The flip side we discussed is selfishness, but the Dragon can be giving and demonstrate tremendous sacrifice for others.

I must reiterate that Dragon Qi is a paradox that cannot be defined other than to say it has unlimited Yang creative potential. The qualities I have discussed are merely an attempt to discuss what happens when Dragon Qi is confined to human Character. Dragons can be anything or nothing if they choose, and they represent a culmination of the zodiac—everything rolled into one, exploding out.

Liu Ming wrote a book on the stages of human spiritual development called *Dragon's Play*. In the book, the Dragon represents the twelfth and final stage of human life, the most significant expression of Yang Qi and human potential: the

Rainbow Body, Ja lü in Tibetan, Prakaśakaya/Tejukaya in Sanskrit, and Hong Shen in Chinese. In Daoist and Tantric cultivation, a practitioner of the Way is said to draw all creation into their heart or navel, creating a Cosmic Egg, or "immortal fetus," an expression of ultimate Yin, the return to Source. The result of Ultimate Yin turns to Ultimate Yang, which is the Dragon—ultimate freedom bursting from the Egg, light flowing freely and consciously into all dimensions, consciously becoming the universe, which other people witness as a display of light. The Dragon is the primordial gesture of the Dao itself, demonstrating the power of Source Qi to become everything, which all humans are destined for.

This may sound fantastic, but of course, every Character has this potential too; it is not limited to Dragons. Dragons are just a symbol of our unlimited potential. Dragon Characters need a path; otherwise, this potential is meaningless. Above all, Dragons need training and a path, but they must never be controlled. Dragons must be left alone to follow their own way, or they will eat you.

Dragons, like Rabbits, exemplify the relationship between Character and Fate. An Earth Dragon born in a slum with no opportunity to demonstrate their leadership capacity might become a gang leader, go to prison, and be king of the inmates. A Dragon without significant obstacles and challenges, without training, help, and restraint, will most likely destroy themselves. The strength of the Dragon demands a "big" Fate.

In terms of the Five Dragons, each has its unique characteristics that contribute to the overall understanding of the Dragon zodiac sign. The Wood or Laughing Dragon is the most artistic, creative, and ingenious, and they are persuasive and humorous. The Fire or Sky Dragon is the most challenging and explosive, with Fire making them extremely resourceful, lovable, and attractive. The Earth or Yielding Dragon is the most grounded and regal as the most natural Dragon. The Metal or Angry Dragon is the most powerful, restrained, and articulate, and they have the most tremendous sense of morality and law. And the Water or Rain Dragon is the most nurturing, idealistic, and mystical. Understanding these different characteristics provides a comprehensive view of the Dragon zodiac sign.

THE TWELVE CHARACTERS OF DESTINY, PART 7: SNAKE QI

NATIVE ELEMENT: Yin Fire

HOUR AND MONTH: 9 a.m. to 11 a.m., 4th Moon

ORGAN NETWORK: Spleen

COMPATIBILITY TRINE: Ox, Rooster

MARRIAGE PAIR: Monkey

OPPOSITE: Pig

SYMBOLISM (象) AND QI (氣) DYNAMICS

IN THE LAST CHAPTER, I tried to communicate the ineffable nature of the Dragon, which may have been confusing, and I'm afraid the Snake may be worse. The Dragon is ineffable due to its unlimited potential, but still, it is the Yang version of potential, meaning it is the result of full manifestation, *extreme Yang*, and is therefore easier for us to understand in this Yang culture. As a culture, we know about doing, but being, on the other hand, is a mystery. The Snake represents this mystery, the Yin to the Dragon's Yang.

Yin is manifestation, the condensation of everything into apparent form, which turns into Yang, the expression of form through movement and dynamism. As Yin expresses into Yang, it opens, expands, and rises to Heaven, becoming more and more transparent, heading back toward the unmanifest. Dragon Qi symbolizes the height of this expression and movement—all manifestations integrated, directed, and flying free, Yin that went all the way to extreme Yang.

Yinyang theory teaches that Yin and Yang turn into one another; extreme Yang gives way and turns into extreme Yin, which is symbolized in the Chinese zodiac by the Snake. The Snake is extreme Yin, the flip side of the Dragon.

In the Dragon, the entire zodiac is manifest and expressed. In the Snake, the entire zodiac is in seed or potential form, having been expressed fully and then disappeared, leaving behind a complete, open, and transparent vacuum. Snake is the emptiness, potential, and openness that hosts all forms. Snake Qi is the empty spoke in the center of the turning wheel.

Pig Qi, where we began our exploration of the zodiac, while similar in some ways, is actually Snake's opposite. Pig Qi expresses Yin Water, the dissolution of everything at the end of the cycle. Snake is not a dissolution, for dissolution is a gradual process. Snake is not gradual. Snake is the sudden and extreme flip from Yang to Yin, like the popping of a bubble or a Snake striking its prey. Dragon Qi expands until . . . pop! This sudden flip from everything to nothing represents Yin Fire, the Native Element of the Snake.

Even in complete emptiness, total vacuity, there is Yang—a spark, an ember, a warmth pulsating, undulating in the Void. For all emptiness is pregnant with unlimited potential. Emptiness is said to contain all potential. Every possibility is inherent in emptiness; the entire universe resides in and emerges from space. In Tantra, space is called the Inexhaustible Treasury, the Dharmadhatu. Everything comes from space, yet space is never altered, stained, harmed, or destroyed. It is indestructible, or "Vajra," immaculate, and pristine. Of all the Twelve Animals, Snake is said to be closest to this pristine, open, spacious quality of life. Snake, Yin Fire, is the warm and radiant nature of life emerging from the womb of space.

Yin Fire also represents the nature of Snake Hour, from 9 a.m. to 11 a.m., the time of day after the sun has appeared and begins to warm the Earth slowly. Snake Hour is bright and transparent; it is the gap between the great manifestation of sunrise (the Dragon) and the productivity of midday (the Horse). Snake Hour is a time of revelation, transparency, and reflection, where we process and gather ourselves before being productive. If you were born during this time of the day, you are also part Snake.

Yin Fire is the slow, smoldering transformation of a simmering fire, like a Crock-Pot rather than a barbecue. It is the catalytic force of alchemy and cooking—stimulating, energizing, yet still, pulsating, warming, consuming, mesmerizing. It is internal, rather than external, vigor. The Snake symbolizes the Yin Fire of the Heart, the Shen—the still, warm, beating center of things, awake and alive yet passive and Yin, for the heart beats without effort. In Chinese Medicine, the Snake also symbolizes the spleen, associated with the power of snakes to swallow prey larger than their own body, to slowly digest and transform anything, and to resist decay while buried under cold damp earth.

The Snake symbol is immensely old, tracing back to China's shamanic roots. The Snake symbol is universal, and its expression is similar across cultures. Unlike the view of some cultures, the Chinese conception of the Snake is not evil or sinister; it is Yin. It represents the unknown and unknowable world—the subterranean, the submerged, the unconscious.

There is no "evil" in the Chinese Tradition, but Yin has a dark side, and the Snake can symbolize darkness. This darkness, however, is the basis for transformation. We cannot truly transform unless we consider all our dark places; we must turn over all the rocks and look at the creepy-crawlies beneath the surface. Snake is what lies beneath the surface.

In this sense, the Snake is like the Rabbit, but taken to another level. The Rabbit is submerged in the unconscious, subterranean world, but the Snake *is* that world; it sees through it unattached, where the Rabbit's innocence is potentially lost in the static of the ethers. Snake Qi sees through the nature of appearances, so Snake Characters are said to lead uniquely self-reflective and insightful lives. It is in the character of Snake to reflect, mirror, question, and peek behind the curtains.

Snake Qi, Big Yin's impulse, is sinking, gathering, descending, internalizing, and seeking stillness and silence. Like snakes in the wild, Snake Qi seeks to be hidden and unseen, to blend in with the environment. Therefore, Snakes have a natural inclination to "disappear"—to hide, to renounce, and to recede from the world by blending in with the surroundings. A snake might look like a vine on the tree, so it is there, present in the world, but it is not the vine, not what it appears to be.

Snake Qi is unknowable and ineffable. Big Yin defies all labels and definitions. Emptiness, by definition, is beyond conceptual elaboration, as the Buddhists say. As I mentioned in the last chapter, the Snake represents the inner, open capacity at the heart of the zodiac to become any of the other eleven Characters without being defined by them. In contrast, the Dragon embodies all eleven Characters.

This unknowable quality is said to be the source of Snake's unmatched charm. Snakes can become anything and anybody without being attached, representing all potential. They have all the capacities of all eleven Characters available, like the Dragon, but they are not defined by, nor do they take pride in, what they display. They are a mystery even to themselves.

Their instinct is to hide, but they can hide in a crowded room because they are inwardly unknowable. You can "know" a Snake for years and still not know who they are. And this is not deceptive, because they aren't anybody (no one is really), and this is their power.

Snakes are a mystery to themselves and other people. They cannot be known. Remember this as I get into the key words. We may use words to describe Snake Qi, but Snakes are not these words. The Snake symbolizes the reality that no one is what they think they are, nor are we how others perceive us. We are all a mystery. You can never really know another person, not really. We are all symbols to each other.

In China, the Snake is the sorcerer-philosopher and symbolizes the process of alchemy and inner transformation, for the Snake sheds its skin. It is always in the process of becoming something else. They also represent "striking force," like Muhammad Ali (born in the Year of the Snake), which is an aspect of the Fire Element—the ability to remain perfectly still and then strike, or act, seemingly out of nowhere, like a snake paralyzing its prey.

MANIFESTATION/CHARACTER (形)

Now that we have covered the symbolism and energetic dynamics, let's get into key words for the Snake and talk about how this symbol manifests in and as people.

The key terms for the Snake are, again, how they appear but not actually how they are. You may know or be a Snake and not identify with these labels, and that's fine. No person is really their Character; it is merely a pattern, a tendency of our Qi to display a certain way. Snake Qi symbolizes the idea that we can all transcend our limitations through detachment.

The first key term, then, is deeply reflective. In many ways, it is not easy to be a Snake. Snakes are natural mystics in a non-mystic world. Snake Qi can be called penetrating insight. Without trying, Snakes tend to see through things, through the nature of appearance, to essential qualities. Since Snake Qi is naturally open and empty, it is natural for Snakes to reflect on life and their situation, for their Qi display is in direct contrast with what society tells us. With training, this can lead to insight. But if Snakes are told from an early age that the world is solid, that people are real, that situations are concrete, and that they must "be somebody," then they will fake it and pretend, while internally, they may experience deep depression, resentment, and even fear.

As it turns out, reality can be frightening to glimpse. Imagine finding out that up and down are meaningless; this is called vertigo. My teacher calls this the "round world," as opposed to the "square world." In the round world, that is, in reality, we don't have a leg to stand on; all concepts are relative, and nothing has any inherent meaning. If you do not grasp at solidity, this realization liberates you, and emptiness becomes the source of much giggling. If you grasp at solidity, emptiness inspires terror, nihilism, and possibly suicidal tendencies. Snakes may feel that the world is meaningless, that everyone is a fake, that everything is nonsense. They may feel crazy because they see this and no one else does.

Depleted, Snake Qi can turn to paranoia. They can get into trouble if they are not taught to trust their insight and vision into what lies beneath the surface. Seeing signs, hearing voices—these are all very Snakey, like Rabbit Qi in this sense. The truth is that there are voices; the universe is full of psychic static, and people project their thoughts and emotions all over the place with little discretion. While Rabbits tend to feel the emotional, energetic, embodied quality of this static, Snakes tend to see into the more "psychic" mental dimension of things.

Snake Qi is transparent and clear, and Snakes are probably the most distant from the rich, direct experience of the senses that is embodied by Snake's opposite, the Pig. Snakes can easily be disembodied and live in a flat mental world, which can turn to nihilism. They may mistrust the display of the world. On the other hand, this transparency offers insight.

If Snakes go with their insight, they become wise. The Snake is synonymous with wisdom. On the surface, this wisdom comes from a natural observant quality, which comes from the Snake's impulse to lie still, wait, and watch. Snakes tend to observe and attend very closely to details, which lends them profound intelligence. On a deeper level, Snake's wisdom is both visionary and philosophical, which I'll get to later. In Buddhism, wisdom is identical to sunyata, emptiness; they are synonymous. Emptiness is a complex idea, but at the deepest level, Snake Qi represents this side of reality.

Snakes can be too smart for their own good and capable of immense calculation and planning. Of course, everyone can be intelligent, but Snake intelligence encapsulates the concept of genius. This kind of intelligence, however, often goes hand in hand with depression. Snakes have the opposite of "ignorance is bliss." Instead, Snake intelligence tends to obsess about how messed up the world is and about how messed up they are themselves. Their skepticism can lead to cynicism and, very often, depression. This depression does not need a cause, for Snake Qi is by nature depressed, sinking, and dark, energetically speaking. So, Snakes can appear moody and brooding.

The Snake's tendency toward depression can turn to self-loathing, however, especially if their intelligence is not put to more creative outlets. Intelligence can quickly turn to hatred either of the world or of themselves. When Snakes are unsuccessful and do not find an outlet for their vision, they can turn bitter and hostile, criticizing everything and everyone and picking apart their own faults.

Because of their visionary and creative qualities, Snakes make natural artists. Snakes want to leave the world behind, follow their vision, and lose themselves beyond the horizon. They want to disappear. Snake Qi is a vision quest, a spirit journey into the unknown, into the underworlds. In their imagination, Snakes see through this world to realms beyond. They may even have tangible visions in their waking lives.

So, Snakes can be a bit weird, although others may never know, for Snakes are the best at hiding. Snakes must find a way to express this weirdness, primarily through art or creativity. The challenge for the Snake is to go out beyond and come back. They must return their vision to the ordinary world and share it with others. Snakes are often inventive innovators, and Snake years usually produce societal breakthroughs. Without art, the Snake has no way of communicating reality as they experience it. Whether through painting, poetry, or film, Snakes communicate the dreamlike nature of reality, as in the work of Pablo Picasso or Edgar Allan Poe (both born in the Year of the Snake)

Snakes tend to be solitary and reclusive. All the Snakes I know, whether by year or hour, tend to seek and enjoy time alone (of course, everyone can), and some even dream of being hermits. Snakes take great pleasure when no one knows where they are or what they're up to. They tend to be somewhat evasive, which is both positive and negative; this tendency toward evasiveness can be a skill: knowing when to duck, avoid, or do nothing. This evasive quality can appear distant, aloof, avoidant, and secretive to others. You're never quite sure about them; think Snape from Harry Potter. Snake Qi is also very discreet, which again can appear positive and negative.

Spiritually, being discreet and humble is an excellent idea; showing off and making a big flap about yourself can create many challenges. Snakes tend to be quiet, never revealing their actual experience to anyone, even when that experience is profound. Being discreet is the Snake's form of camouflage, hiding in plain sight.

Since Snake Qi is Big Yin, and because its impulse is to disappear toward stillness and silence, Snakes are naturally calm, patient, and slow in their display. *Chill* is the word. Snake Qi is the opposite of scattered, and in its depleted state it can turn to laziness and lethargy. But in general, Snakes are relaxed and calm; they have a big, open capacity to host other people's craziness. This peaceful nature can be called meditative. Many Snakes I know have a natural inclination toward meditation as an expression of their Qi, which also has an immense capacity for trance.

The Yin Fire nature of the Snake is also hypnotizing and trance inducing. Think snake charmers. Snakes have an alluring charm because of their mysteriousness. People want to figure them out, and Snakes love this because they love avoiding and evading people's attempts to understand them and pin them down.

Snakes can play with all this, which gives them a specific social capacity. They make great actors and can become anyone, like in method acting. They can use this capacity for social advantage, which we call "Yin Power." Yin Power is essentially manipulation, which is not inherently wrong, although it can be used that way. It can be used for good, too; like many Snake qualities, even their manipulation evades judgment—we're just not sure about it.

Ming once told a story of a friend who learned to speak Chinese by simply "becoming" the teacher: imitating the teacher's mannerisms, dress, body language, and so on. Monkeys have this capacity, too. Rather than learn the language, this person just became someone who already knew it—very Snakey.

Snakes can embody a social role for years—at work, for example—even if it is not who they are. They can work for years as salespeople and then one day become carpenters. This changeability may sound bad, but it isn't for Snakes necessarily, for they are unattached. Snakes can love and be fascinated by material things and then sell everything they own without a second thought. Snake Qi loves to shed its skin, change appearances, transform, drop attachments, and move on. In the Chinese Tradition, the Snake, like the Rabbit, is associated with the practice of Inner Alchemy, refining our experience backward to the Source.

When depleted, the ability to become anything and take on any form can turn to helplessness. Depleted, Snakes can feel empty, without inner and outer resources and unable to manifest things in the world. The tendency to not take the "real world" seriously can appear to others as a lack of ambition, but Snakes don't have ordinary worldly ambition; their aspirations in life tend to reflect a more profound impulse: most often, to understand this strange world of appearances, this ephemeral dance we're all born into. Snakes are perplexed as to why everyone takes the life game so seriously.

I mean, why bother? Why bother constructing wealth and systems of value when everything falls apart? Of course, if a Fire Snake chooses to be successful, they can outdo everyone and make us all look like fools, but they would never believe in their actions.

Hopefully, this does not sound too negative. But negativity must be available in the cycle of time. We must remember that there is no absolute negativity or even evil in the Chinese Tradition, but there is Yin. And all Yin Characters represent the necessity of darkness in the cycle of time. Darkness, depression, destruction, and so on must be available in Time. Otherwise, everything would grind to a halt. Of course, not all Snakes are depressed, but they do represent that tendency.

The Snake symbol is rich and deep. In the collective imagination, snakes conjure up primal, primordial, shamanic images, like Ouroboros, the serpent eating its tail. If you want to understand Snake Qi, look at these images, for they all speak to the wisdom of the Snake.

In terms of the Five Snakes, each has unique characteristics that contribute to the understanding of the Snake zodiac sign. The Wood or Emerging Snake is the most honest, shy, and calm of the Snakes. The Fire or Fishpond Snake is the most natural of the Snakes, and they are the most mesmerizing, ambitious, and disciplined. The Earth or Golden Snake is the worldliest and, therefore, the most determined, fortunate, and often successful of the Snakes. The Metal or Hibernating Snake is the most bright, sensitive, and insightful, but the Metal Element makes them the most restrained and aloof. And the Water or Hidden Snake is the most mystical, secretive, and elusive of Snakes, and their potential for wisdom is excellent (the Buddha is said to have been a Water Snake). Understanding these different characteristics provides a comprehensive view of the Snake zodiac sign.

THE TWELVE CHARACTERS OF DESTINY, PART 8: HORSE QI

NATIVE ELEMENT: Yang Fire

HOUR AND MONTH: 11 a.m. to 1 p.m., 5th Moon

ORGAN NETWORK: Heart

COMPATIBILITY TRINE: Tiger, Dog

MARRIAGE PAIR: Goat

OPPOSITE: Rat

SYMBOLISM (象) AND QI (氣) DYNAMICS

WE'VE REACHED NUMBER EIGHT OF TWELVE as Snake Qi turns to Horse. Before we move on, however, I think we need to back up and look again, briefly, at the idea of Character, for it is too easy to get simplistic in studying these primary symbols.

The Animal, or Earthly Branch, of our year is in the primary image of our Qi Character, so these twelve animal symbols are essential to study and understand, especially at an energetic level. We want to understand the impulse that lies at the base of these patterns, and I hope I have communicated this so far. The impulse of each Qi Character is beyond words. These impulses generate identifiable patterns. But we must ask: patterns of what?

Time. Each Qi Character communicates a felt pattern in time; in astrology, Qi is time. Time or Qi is movement itself, rhythm—not a thing moving, just movement—and we know movement only because of duration. This duration is a spectrum we call light. Qi can be called light or energy, visible because it moves at different frequencies.

Time flows in a circular pattern. This pattern is very lopsided. The Twelve-Animal cycle of Time is like a whirlwind, a tornado. At some parts, it spins fast; at some, it spins slow. Some parts are big, messy gusts of wind; some parts are wind funneling into a point; and so on.

We are a swirling of many patterns of wind or movement; among the many others, the patterns of the year, month, day, and hour are primary. The Qi movement of the year is the most profound flow of Time relative to Earth, technically related to the twelve-year cycle of Jupiter, the largest object in the solar system besides the sun, representing the deepest part of our experience. The impression made at birth, when we first breathe in the Qi, or "wind," of the universe outside the womb, imprints a deep, deep pattern on us that we become and express our entire life. That moment is an incredible shock, which is probably why we cry, and it leaves a lasting impression.

The Qi of the year is the deepest, and the Qi of the hour is the most up-front. The hour imprints a surface expression, which then dances with the deeper expression of the year. These two together are primary. The month and day also imprint on us, but these patterns have more of an effect on our constitution, health, and life cycles in relation to the seasons.

We must remember that we are complex. The image of the year is basic, simple, and yet profound. As you read these chapters and consider your Qi Character, remember that these images are fundamental and only a doorway into the complexity of your astrological makeup. I encourage people to identify with the year and hour, but you also have Four Pillars, solar and lunar indicators, a Fate Chart, and so on. The wisdom of the year encourages us to find out what we have in common with others, rather than what makes us a unique snowflake.

So, now we move into the pattern of Horse Qi, which is part of my Qi Character. It is appropriate that the Horse is an ancient symbol of the wind, or *prana vayu*, Qi, and Lung (*rlung* in Tibetan). In Tantra and East and Central Asian shamanism, the image of the "Wind Horse," the Lungta, is an allegory for the human spirit of awakening.

The symbol of the Horse is an ancient and powerful shamanic symbol central to the cultures of Mongolia, China, and Tibet. To understand the symbol of the Horse, we must understand the role of the Horse in these ancient cultures as a symbol of freedom and expansion. The Horse, in many ways, shaped their history, primarily due to warfare.

The Horse spoken of in Chinese mythology is the Mongolian rather than the Arabian horse, which any equestrian person will tell you are very different kinds of horses. The Chinese attempted to train the Mongolian horse to work for a long time, but no amount of breeding and whipping coerced them to plow straight furrows, for they had no attention span and were wild. Eventually, the Chinese discovered the ox, or water buffalo, from the south, revolutionizing agriculture. But what about the horse?

Mongolians and the famous Genghis Khan would bring down the horse as an instrument of war. The Mongolian horse and the bow and arrow allowed Genghis and his grandson, Kublai, to dominate Asia and much of the Middle East and Eastern Europe. When the Chinese first saw Mongolians riding horses into battle, arrows and swords flying, they discovered the true power of the horse, which had been abandoned in China as a plow animal. The first depictions of the horse were a lot like the dragon, and many of these elements would make their way into the depiction of the dragon, for the horse could run so fast that it appeared to be flying.

People let the reins down, put on a war saddle, and the Horse came to life. With just a little direction rather than strict control, the Mongolian horse became the most productive tool in the Chinese military, aiding in the great expansion of the Tang dynasty. Emperors and generals bred them successfully for war throughout Chinese history, and they were always associated with martial arts and warriorship.

The image of the warhorse represents the Horse's Native Element, Yang Fire. The Fire Horse is an explosion of force, a wild stallion, uncontrollable yet capable of immense power and control if directed with skill. Like fire, the Horse represents a powerful tool that can be creative or destructive, depending on its use.

The genuine impulse of the Horse is to run free, be wild, and explode outward, which is why Horses and Tigers get along, for the Tiger represents a similar explosion of force. The Tiger, Yang Wood, is an immature, childlike impulse, while the Horse, Yang Fire, is the teenager—angsty, rebellious, leaping over boundaries and running wild. Each elemental version of the Horse represents a relationship to this impulse.

The impulse of Yang Fire is to energize, catalyze, activate, stimulate, transform, overpower and overcome, surprise, rebel, destroy, and excite. All Horse Characters have this lying in their nature. I was born on a Metal Horse Day, so this is part of my Character, albeit not as potent as my year and hour, the Fire Tiger and Metal Dragon. Hopefully, then, I can share some personal insight into the nature of the Horse, which is part of me.

The Metal Horse, or the "Horse in the Stall," of whom I know many (1990 is a Metal Horse Year), has a fundamental difficulty with its explosive nature: Horse's Fire "melts" Metal, leading to a kind of self-conflict and doubt. The Metal Horse wrestles between freedom and control, but their Metal exteriors make them capable of power and self-discipline in a way the Fire Horse is not.

The Fire Horse is a pure wild stallion. Traditionally in China, those born in these years would have been sent to the military as cannon fodder, along with Fire Tigers. On the opposite end of the spectrum, the Water Horse, the least "horsey" Horse, is more like a Clydesdale or the Budweiser horse: With the explosion extinguished, they are happy to be trained and trotted around.

The symbol of the Horse has a lot to do with the animal itself. Horses are big and physical; they are all muscles and tendons. The Mongolian horse has a huge hind quarter and legs, which makes them powerful runners and jumpers. This physicality represents a kind of embodiment, so Horse Qi is by nature very embodied: The Horse's impulse is to feel, be, and do rather than think.

In Chinese Medicine, the Horse symbolizes the Heart, exemplified by its powerful capacity to pump blood and run like the famous horse Secretariat. The Yang Fire of the Horse also symbolizes what Classical Chinese Medicine calls the Jun Huo, 君 火, the Sovereign Fire of the Heart, the spark of life that animates us, associated with the Horse's independence, power, and self-possession.

The Horse's opposite, the Rat, has the opposite impulse: Rat Qi tends to think and scheme, while the Horse represents what Chan Buddhism calls "no-mind." No-mind represents embodied action without thinking and planning. Horse Qi is "doing" without great premeditation, like a Chan monk sweeping the courtyard or raking stones in the garden. Horse Qi lends itself to the nonconceptual state.

Horse Qi is the wisdom of manifestation. Suppose the Rat represents everything splintered into pieces, needing to be organized and put back together. In that case, the Horse represents the final manifestation of this in the cycle of Time, everything manifesting and functioning efficiently. Horse is DIY and manufacturing—the strength to work and put things together. The Horse is all about working and doing, like the Ox, but they are the Yang version—muscle, speed, and power—and they can burn out, while Oxen can slowly plow forever.

Horse Qi is also the outcome of the Snake. Suppose Snake represents a cynical, piercing emptiness capable of disembodied depression. In that case, the flip side of Big Yin turning to Yang is a kind of straightforward, logical, no-nonsense practicality. The Snake questions whether the world even exists, and the Horse just gets to work. Emptiness roaring back to form. Why think about emptiness when there is stuff to do?

The Horse represents an "edgy" balance—part wild, part trained—and this gives the Horse a certain regal dignity; they allow us to use their strength, but if they want, they can leap the fence and take off. The Horse's strong, independent nature is extraordinarily successful when set to orderly tasks. For the Horse, "stuff" is for doing things with, and they tend not to need anything unless it represents "work," even if that work is spiritual.

Horse Hour, from 11 a.m. to 1 p.m., or high noon, is the full height of the sun. It is the time of day when we are at our peak and most productive. It is the time of the day for work, labor, and getting stuff done. It is Yang Fire, the bright, burning heat of summer when the light is the most active, warming, moving, catalyzing. If you were born between 11 a.m. and 1 p.m., you should also consider yourself part Horse.

MANIFESTATION/CHARACTER (形)

Now that we have covered the symbolism and energetic dynamics, let's get into key words for the Horse and talk about how this symbol manifests in and as people.

So, the first key words for the Horse are social, gregarious, yet independent. Horses in the wild are social animals, running in packs. Having a social life and seeking social interaction and engagement are important to the Horse Character. Like the Goat, the herd instinct is part of the Horse, but the social nature of the Horse is much different. Horses seek to be independent despite their herd mentality, so their social impulse is often somewhat competitive. Horses are showmen, like Clydesdales. They want to socialize, but they also want to run free and impress everyone with their speed and strength. They tend to be gregarious, friendly, and fond of parties and having fun. They can, of course, be introverted, but the direction of Yang Fire is outward moving. Horses can enjoy solitude, but their inward expression moves out.

At their best, Horses tend to be blessed with a sunny disposition. They can be bright, open, cheerful, and optimistic. Yang Fire tends to look on the bright side of life. The Horse's disposition tends toward innocence, which often attracts people to them. Their optimism lends naturally to humor. Horses are often jokesters; humor is critical to the Horse mentality, as in the term "horsing around." All the Horses I know like to play and fool around. They're natural comedians.

On the flip side, the independence and social qualities of the Horse can turn antisocial, even criminal, and violent. At their best, Horses are not loners, but the nature of Yang Fire is hot-tempered, angry, and rebellious. Their anger can lead to outbursts, which are often thoughtless. The tendency to do/act without thinking can have consequences. The bucking bronco can stamp on people, situations, or relationships. If their attempts at sociability don't go their way, they can ride off into the sunset, never to be seen again.

In general, the independent, wild quality of the Horse can never be held in. Like the Dragon and Tiger, any attempt to box in or control a Horse will be met with disaster. If restrained, they become bitter and exhibit destructive behavior. Horses can be "tamed," but their inside nature is wild; self-discipline for Horses is like harnessing a wild animal. The Horse's nature is fast; they do and act quickly, without hesitation.

With training and proper direction, Horse Qi can be put to work and is associated with strength and industry. Horses have an immense capacity to get shit done, to be the "workhorse," as we say. Horse Qi represents the all-American virtue of productivity: *just get me back to work*. For many Horses, life is about work, and without something to do, they get restless and bored and feel useless. Horse restlessness can be profound; they must direct themselves to tasks and projects, whether learning, reading, building, exercising, or organizing.

Horse Qi represents craft and trade work, DIY, and practical and functional art. Tiger or Monkey may represent abstract art, but you can sit in or do something with Horse art, like furniture or pottery, representing the dying virtue of the craft guilds. Liu Ming used to jokingly refer to Horses as being kind of like lumberjacks, carpenters, and handymen. Home Depot could be called "Horse Depot." Horses express themselves through creating and manifesting. If they do not create, they stagnate. Of course, not all Horses are handy, but they all express some fundamental need to manifest and create.

On a deeper level, this work mentality comes from embodiment, vitality, and physicality. Horses need to move and use their bodies. They need to run, hike, work out, or do anything to get moving, or else they will get restless. Horses, by nature, are also very "outdoorsy," for this physicality cannot stay indoors too long. Horses yearn for the great outdoors and open plains and must connect with the eternal blue sky.

On an even deeper level, this embodiment represents the Horse's profound capacity to feel. Despite their strong exteriors, Horses are very emotional, but they tend to express emotion more through doing rather than saying. Ming once joked about "Horse love" being a dad letting his son use his tools. The Horse may be affectionate, but they often show rather than tell, and not always through touchy-feely means. Horse Qi may not be all hugs, but if a Horse Dad makes his son a swing set, this is an expression pure love because he made it.

The thoughtless, active, and embodied quality of the Horse can be accident-prone. Horses can have a carelessness that tends toward not noticing. Physically, this can lead to self-injury, knocking things over, spilling coffee on your lap, falling off your bike, and so on. Mentally and emotionally, horses may have difficulty noticing and acknowledging other people's feelings, and they may speak and act carelessly, accidentally stomping all over others.

The reverse of being accident-prone is cleverness. Horse Qi represents what is now called "MacGyver" ingenuity—the ability to problem solve practically, throwing a bunch of stuff together into makeshift solutions. Horses can take something broken and find ten ways to assemble it. Or not. Horses can also be very clumsy.

This ingenuity also expresses the virtue of thoughtlessness, which is the ability to work efficiently through embodied skill. All the *Zen and the Art of*. . . books represent Horse Qi. You practice and practice and practice archery, each time getting in your own way because you keep thinking. Then, the thousandth time, you relax and release the arrow without effort. Watching master craftspeople, chefs, dancers, and anyone who embodies a skill is witnessing a Horse Qi ballet.

This cleverness also lends itself to eloquence and talkativeness. Think *Mr. Ed.* Horses make great orators and speakers, and they love to chat. Horse Qi can put their cleverness and ingenuity to work anywhere, including speech, and they love to impress people with their clever eloquence. This eloquence comes from a kind of direct honesty. Horses are honest because they don't overthink. And so, their rhetoric can be very profound; they say what others feel. This often creates a kind of magnetism. Horses are attractive people. Their strength, cleverness, and ability are what most people seek yet never find, for Horse Qi is full manifestation without complication.

This capacity can lead to arrogance and stubbornness, but horses are arrogant without realizing it. Horse stubbornness is a know-it-all show-off bravado, but it does not show off because it thinks it is better than people; it just loves showing off. They need to do something with all their strength.

Horses are stubborn, and it's hard for them not to give advice or tell people how to do things—they know best. Horse stubbornness is demonstrated in the old cliche of men not wanting to stop and ask for directions or call a repairman.

The Horse's personality is consistent and straightforward. Like the Ox, they tend to remain constant in their thoughts, actions, and lifestyle; they're not prone to significant changes in terms of personality. You may not see a Horse for ten years, and no matter how much they have changed, they seem like the same old person. They may be wild, adventurous, world-traveling people, but nonetheless, they seem consistent.

Some Characters, like the Snake, are a mystery. The Horse, being the outcome of Snake, is no mystery. What you see is what you get. Horse Qi is not about plumbing the depths. Which is not to say they're not deep. It's just that Horses do not play games; they do not mislead, misdirect, or manipulate—all that would require too much thinking. They just are and do.

The Horse symbol is of power, majesty, and freedom. The Lungta, the Wind Horse, symbolizes the human spirit of adventure but also aggression. The Horse is raw, dynamic power and strength, pure vitality. It rides hard and can burn out in a blaze of glory, dying with honor on the battlefield. The Horse characterizes the wild shamanic nomads of Central Asia, Mongolia, Tibet, and northern and western China. It is the wide-open expanse of the great plains and eternal blue sky. Freedom is the Horse's impulse, dancing with the edge of restraint.

Horse Qi is a turning point in the zodiac. From here, the Horse turns to Goat, and the cycle begins to resolve itself. The rest of the zodiac represents a kind of completion, a return to source.

In terms of the Five Horses, each has its unique characteristics that contribute to the overall understanding of the Horse zodiac sign. The Wood or Cloud Horse is the most restless, withdrawn, and unfocused of Horses, and they are shy but also self-assured. The Fire or Traveling Horse is the most natural of the Horses, and they are the most outspoken, quick-tempered, and skillful, but their restlessness is profound. The Earth or Corralled Horse is daring, impulsive, and strong, and the Earth helps them to stabilize and manifest. The Metal Horse or Horse in the Stall is the most restrained and frustrated but also the most talkative and insightful of Horses. And the Water or War Horse is the most emotional and least restless of the Horses, as the Water quells the blazing Fire. Understanding these different characteristics provides a comprehensive view of the Horse zodiac sign.

THE TWELVE CHARACTERS OF DESTINY, PART 9: GOAT QI

NATIVE ELEMENT: Yin Earth

HOUR AND MONTH: 1 p.m. to 3 p.m., 6th Moon

ORGAN NETWORK: Small Intestine

COMPATIBILITY TRINE: Rabbit, Pig

MARRIAGE PAIR: Horse

OPPOSITE: Ox

SYMBOLISM (象) AND QI (氣) DYNAMICS

HUMANS AND GOATS have been living happily together for a long, long time: at least 30,000 years. The goat is very happily domesticated. The symbol of the Goat in Chinese astrology is tied intimately to the goat's long-standing relationship with nomads and agrarian humans.

The Goat is most notably a symbol of sacrifice, specifically to the Ancestors. Humans have been ritually sacrificing goats for a long time, probably since before they were domesticated. This may sound grim for the goats, and it probably is from their perspective, but as a symbol, this sacrifice is more about being honored than being killed. I have seen many goat-related rituals, and believe it or not, they are very well taken care of, up until their throat is slit.

There is a significant Star in Polestar Astrology called Yang Ren, the Goat Blade Star, which we will discuss in later chapters. In Tantric iconography, dakinis are often depicted holding a hooked blade, used for draining a goat of its blood very quickly: This is Yang Ren. It represents a place where we are Fated to make a big sacrifice or encounter loss, for the kind of experience you look back at and say, "That was tough, but I would not be who I am today if I had not gone through that." Such is the nature of the Goat.

The Goat spoken of in Chinese astrology is the wild mountain goat and the big wooly ram as well as the domesticated goat. Despite the masculine image of rams butting heads, the Goat is decidedly Yin and represents the opposite of aggression. The Native Element of the Goat is Yin Earth, which it shares with its opposite, the Ox. Four Animals share the Native Element of Earth, and each portrays it in different ways.

The Goat's relationship to Yin Earth demonstrates the amazing ability of goats to be sure-footed and adaptable in all terrains. If you google mountain goats, you will find some incredible images of goats scaling sheer vertical cliffs. This is not a Yang skill. It must take astonishing finesse and delicate balance to do this. This image portrays a central theme of Goat Qi: adaptability. Goats are masters of adapting to their environment and have happily adapted wherever humans have taken them.

Yin Earth is all about cooperation, balance, nourishment, support, solidity, grounding, alliances, abundance, mothering, and nurturing. The Ox represents these qualities in the continuity of Earth, for the Ox is the steadfast container and maintainer of tradition. The Goat represents these same qualities in the refinement and reform of tradition, for the Goat is the wisdom of beauty, justice, symmetry, order, and harmony. In Classical Chinese Medicine, the Goat is associated with the small intestine, the place in the body where our food is harmonized, refined, and put to order.

The Ox preserves, and the Goat renews; it recognizes what has gotten old and stuffy and seeks to reinvigorate tradition. Unlike the Tiger, which aims to break the boundaries of tradition and liberate people from order, the Goat seeks to refine order to higher degrees. The Goat wants tradition, but it wants tradition to serve the people, so it wants a bloodless and peaceful revolution. The Tiger, the Horse, the Dragon, the Monkey, and the Dog all may shed blood, but the Goat will not. Don't mistake butting heads for aggression. I have lived with Goats, and this is an innocent and playful act; it's more about being flustered and horny.

In short, the Goat represents the virtues and difficulties of the dreaded word *politics*. Goats are the idealists, the most astute and aware of social circumstances. The Goat defines the herd animal and instinct. Having lived with Goats and watched them daily, I can see they have a hive mind. They run, jump, eat, and play together, and as soon as one takes off in a new direction, they all bounce along behind without hesitation. When a Goat is lost from the herd, it gets seriously distressed, but when it's with the clan, it is as happy as can be.

At a deeper level, the herd mentality of the Goat and of Goat Qi derives from a sense of inclusion that expresses an even more profound truth about the interconnected nature of everything. Goat Qi represents interbeing, interdependence, the intimate web of life, and the symbiotic relationships that define nature.

Of all the Twelve Characters, the Goat is said to be closest to this interbeing; they feel it on a deep, embodied level. Goats see the way everything is connected. And so, the impulse of the Goat is always for the herd, for the greater good. They sacrifice themselves for the benefit of others. The outer symbol of ritual sacrifice also communicates an inner one: Goats are willing to give up their own needs so others can thrive. They are the most egalitarian of all the signs.

The Goat is considered the most artistic and aesthetic of all the Twelve Qi Characters. The Goat feels connected to everything and wants everyone else to feel this way. But this interconnected web is beyond words. It cannot be described, so the instinct of the Goat is to express and communicate what is beyond words with art. Or better yet, with Qi. The Goat wants to convey the direct experience of Qi—the dynamic, flowing way everything relates to everything else.

The Goat seeks to make the world beautiful, harmonious, and balanced. Because Goats feel the deeper way in which everything is connected, they get flustered when the surface does not match the depths. Therefore, they seek order, to refine the outer expression to remind others of what lies beneath the surface.

Goat art is aesthetic and classical. Tiger art defies convention, while the Goat defines it. They are, therefore, in constant dialogue. Goat art expresses order, symmetry, tasteful arrangement, and elegance. Fengshui, the art and auspice of placement, is a Goat-like endeavor.

The Goat is the natural outcome of the Horse. The Horse manifests, constructs, and brings the World into being, and the Goat is sort of like the interior decorator. (But Fengshui is not interior decorating, by the way.) They take the Horse's raw and sometimes messy situation and make it orderly, expressing the harmonious relationships of Qi in space.

As we review these key words, remember this basic impulse: to communicate and express our connection beyond words. This is the heart of Goat Qi. The Goat also represents sustainability, social welfare, and responsibility; it represents the fact that we're all responsible for each other—always have been, and always will be. In Buddhism, this principle is called *sangha*.

Goat Qi is generally soft, peaceful, gentle, introverted, and Yin. It is impossible not to smile when watching goats. They are adorable and fundamentally goofy creatures, like big puppies. Within three hours of birth, kid goats jump around, happily bouncing with amusing playfulness, looking for a cliff to climb, nibbling on everything.

Goat Hour is from 1 p.m. to 3 p.m., which is time to "herd up." Since Goat Qi is associated with the herd—with social order, cooperation, compromising, harmony, justice, fairness, and so on—Goat Hour is the time to work and be with others, cultivating friendship and teamwork. This is the time to get together and do things in groups, to refine and adjust Horse Hour's productivity. Once we create something, we must adjust our creation according to social context and welfare. Building a table is useless if we do not sit down to eat, and what good is eating alone when your friends are hungry? Goat Hour is also the time for art and aesthetics. It is a time to paint, write, sing, or stare into the landscape and contemplate your humanity. If you were born during this time of the day, you are also part Goat.

MANIFESTATION/CHARACTER (形)

Now that we have covered the symbolism and energetic dynamics, let's explore the key words for the Goat and discuss how this symbol manifests in and as people.

The first key terms are easygoing, sweet, gentle, and agreeable. Goats have a naturally relaxed and slightly silly or goofy disposition. Earth Characters by nature, especially Yin Earth, are what we refer to as "chill." Yin Earth is stable, slow, and grounded. Goat Characters don't get worked up quickly and are happy to go with the flow and follow the group. Goats tend to be friendly, lovely, and kind people. Everyone can be friendly, of course, and the Goat symbolizes this quality in all of us. By respecting and acknowledging other people and their needs, by recognizing we are part of a herd, we naturally become kind, generous, and friendly. Self-centeredness is not part of Goat Qi.

The depleted version of this, however, is intolerance and crankiness. When Goats find themselves alone or isolated, or if they're raised in a poor community environment where their instincts are stunted, Goats tend to be fussy, cranky, moody, and even intolerant of others. At their best, the political vision of the Goat is all-inclusive, and the flip side of this is well-known the world over: We tolerate our in-group and hate the rest. The possibility for political unrest is most powerfully demonstrated in the Monkey and Tiger dynamics, but this begins in the Goat with the desire to create order, which turns almost immediately into its opposite in the cycle of time.

The next important key words are aesthetic and artistic, both visual and musical. Not all Goats are necessarily great artists and musicians, but this instinct to make the world beautiful and to express the ineffable must come out in some form. For some Goats, it may come out in how they dress, which may always match and be trendy. In others, it may be expressed through poetry or playing guitar. For others, it may be in their career as a graphic designer. And, of course, Goats are natural painters and artists in the classical sense—Michelangelo and Mark Twain were both Goats.

The gentle demeanor of Goat Qi goes hand in hand with another essential quality: cooperation. Like the Rabbit, the Goat seeks collaboration and compromise on all levels and hates confrontation. Goats want everyone to get along; they are peacemakers who offer solutions and treaties. They will often compromise their needs to make others happy, which depletes them in the long run.

If they keep compromising and cooperating to make others happy, Goats will eventually turn cranky and become unbelievably stubborn, hence the butting heads. Goats will dig in to their position, and compromise can turn into entrenched argumentation. Goats must commit to self-care and speak up about their needs. Otherwise, they will be nice, nice, nice, and then explode.

The Goat, naturally seeking communication and understanding, can become flustered and uncommunicative. Usually, they are quite eloquent, but when depleted and butting heads, Goats can hardly get out coherent sentences. They fear confrontation, so they tend to let things build until things turn to stubborn conflict.

On the flip side, Goats are masters of persuasion and charm. Goat Qi can eloquently and poetically express grand principles like harmony and justice; rhetoric both political and personal is a Goat affair. Their natural insight into social dynamics and structure offers them a social capacity unknown to many signs. They can read a group and know how to inspire and work up a crowd by invoking universal human principles. Goats tend to be very quiet and introverted but are prone to make dramatic speeches when provoked.

The calm, quiet, easygoing nature of Goat Qi can also turn impatient. Goats tend to be fussy perfectionists. They want everything to go just right, so they may try to engineer their life, relationships, and situations. Roosters and Rats tend to fuss over what, to the rest of us, are unimportant details, but the Goat fusses over the whole situation. If a Goat throws a dinner party, they don't mind how the table is arranged, but they will be sure to sit you next to someone who will change your life. They may work very hard to create the right social environment for magic, and if it falls apart, they may obsess over what went wrong, while the Rooster is still thinking about whether the silverware was in the right place.

With Pigs and Rabbits, Goats are part of the "social trine" of the Chinese zodiac. The social aspect of the Goat is all about generosity, encouragement, and social support. Goats need a herd of friends and family; without support, they wither, get depressed, and feel hopeless, anxious, and fearful. Alone, they worry and fret. Around others, they thrive and are the most supportive, encouraging, and generous people. Goats don't need a big herd per se—a small family and a few close friends are fine—but they can also get along in a big group, as long as that group represents "clan" or "tribe" for them. Alone, they will naturally seek to create a tribe. They make natural family people, such as parents, grandparents, and siblings. Goats easily take on social support roles, even if it is only for a select few. This need for social support is a key aspect of their personality and significantly influences their behavior and well-being.

Goats have a deep spiritual capacity to recognize relationships and interconnectedness. All the great spiritual traditions teach that we're all connected, everything is everything, and so on—you've probably heard it all before. This realization that we're all One is a Goat realization, so it is easier for Goat Characters to see this. Compassion and generosity, therefore, come naturally to them. This is not the case for all signs: Tigers, Snakes, and Dragons all need education in this regard, for their independent nature can disregard and struggle with the need to connect with other humans.

In terms of the Five Goats, each has its unique characteristics that contribute to the overall understanding of the Goat zodiac sign. The Wood or Respected Goat is the most industrious and sincere, but also the most naive and idealistic of Goats, and their artistic and aesthetic sense is strong. The Fire or Solitary Goat is the most high-strung and moody but also ambitious and successful of the Goats, and they are both argumentative and self-assured. The Earth Mountain Goat is the most natural and quintessential Goat, and they are proud, obstinate, and yet interconnected and deeply egalitarian. The Metal or Wealthy Goat is the most humble, gentle, forgiving, and aesthetic of Goats, as the Metal adds refinement and insight. And the Water or Herded Goat is the most talkative, sensitive, and persevering of Goats, with the strongest emotional attachments and universal idealisms. Understanding these different characteristics provides a comprehensive view of the Goat zodiac sign.

THE TWELVE CHARACTERS OF DESTINY, PART 10: MONKEY QI

NATIVE ELEMENT: Yang Metal

HOUR AND MONTH: 3 p.m. to 5 p.m., 7th Moon

ORGAN NETWORK: Bladder

COMPATIBILITY TRINE: Dragon, Rat

MARRIAGE PAIR: Snake

OPPOSITE: Tiger

SYMBOLISM (象) AND QI (氣) DYNAMICS

AS A TIGER, my opposite or "diametric" is Monkey Qi. Many misunderstand the diametric relationship in Chinese astrology. In most books on the Twelve Animals, they say, "Tiger–Monkey, Pig–Snake, Dragon–Dog—oh, very bad, incompatible!" However, that level of astrology assumes that ordinary people have little to no capacity for self-reflection. Which may be true, I don't know. But the diametric is a mirror relationship. Spiritually, they are complementary opposites, which tend to polarize and attract, creating a fascination with each other's differences. The relationship of opposites can be explosive and prone to volatility, but this explosive quality has tremendous potential for transformation, if met with self-reflection.

I have had many close Monkey friends, and I love all of them, for they are a mirror. When presented with the Monkey perspective, I scratch my head and go, *Wow, I would not have thought of that!* There is a great YouTube video of a monkey messing with tigers, jumping off the tree, pulling the tiger's tail, and then jumping out of reach—such is the Monkey–Tiger dance.

Asia adores the monkey. It is a vibrant symbol in Chinese cosmology. Monkeys are common all over Asia, particularly the gibbon and macaque, and many cultural myths surround them. Both China and Tibet share stories of having ancient monkey Ancestors; perhaps they had a natural understanding of evolution. Chinese folk religion regards monkeys as supernatural beings, and many myths about monkey spirits, monkey Demons, and monkey–human hybrids abound throughout China's history. Monkeys are generally depicted much like humans, both foolish and wise. In the Chinese zodiac, the Monkey represents a human flaw that has been heavily debated throughout the history of religion: desire.

We find the monkey in the transmission of Buddhism to China, which began around the second century B.C.E., most famously depicted in the sixteenth-century Ming dynasty novel *Journey to the West*, which English author Arthur Waley later abridged into the widely read novel *Monkey*.

In this story, the Buddha seeks a Chinese pilgrim to journey west to India and retrieve the Buddhist scriptures so that Chinese people can be enlightened (typical Buddhist evangelism, as if the Chinese Tradition was not rich enough). Based on the legendary Tang dynasty monk Xuanzang, the main character, Tripitika, volunteers and goes, has many trials and tribulations, and then successfully returns.

Gautama Buddha and the Bodhisattva Guan Yin enlist three protectors to help him along the way, including the famous Sun Wukong, the Monkey King. The Buddha imprisoned Sun Wukong under a mountain for rebelling against Heaven. Sun Wukong is a trickster, able to shapeshift and transform his appearance. In the journey, the Monkey King becomes a disciple of Tripitika and transforms from a trickster rebel to an enlightened sage.

Early Buddhism used many monkey similes. We have all heard of the famous "monkey mind." The Samyutta Nikaya says, "Just as a monkey roaming through a forest grabs hold of one branch, lets that go and grabs another, then lets that go and grabs still another, so too that which is called 'mind' and 'mentality' and 'consciousness' arises as one thing and ceases as another by day and by night." Monkeys helped transmit the Buddhist scriptures, so they became allegories for the transformation of the monkey mind to the enlightened mind.

The Monkey King was initially a Daoist immortal before being worked into Buddhism. Daoism, too, tells many tales of the monkey. Zhuangzi's famous story goes, "Once upon a time, there was a monkey keeper who was feeding little chestnuts to his charges. 'I'll give you three in the morning and four in the evening,' he told them. All the monkeys were angry. 'All right, then,' said the keeper, 'I'll give you four in the morning and three in the evening.' All the monkeys were happy with this arrangement. Without adversely affecting either the name or the reality of the amount that he fed them, the keeper acted in accordance with the feelings of the monkeys. He too recognized the mutual dependence of 'this' and 'that.' Consequently, the sage harmonizes the right and wrong of things and rests at the center of the celestial potter's wheel."[1] Here, the monkey-sage dichotomy depicts the transformation from delusion to enlightenment, implying that nothing happens other than a shift in perspective.

Liu Ming played with this famous tale in his book *Dragon's Play*. Here, Ming used the image of Monkey and Sage to represent our dual nature of energy and awareness. The delicate balancing act between these two, between freedom and control, is the dance of duality that every human must integrate to follow the Way.

At its core, Monkey Qi represents this perilous balancing act, like the monkey swinging through the trees, balancing from branch to branch. Monkeys are poised between the sacred and the profane, fluctuating between materialism and austerity, selfish fantasy and visionary wisdom. Every human has this dance inside them. Though depicted as godlike, Monkey Qi symbolizes the weakness commonly associated with humans: desire, which keeps them dancing between the poles.

This all may sound dramatic, but actually Monkey Qi is fundamentally playful. The Chinese never thought to demonize desire like the West. Even Buddhism could not make judgmental moralists of the Chinese (to the Chinese, morality is astrological). Monkey's balancing act is not a battle between good and evil, in which order wins over chaos. Both are natural aspects of our being, Yin and Yang. We must make friends with both, and Monkey Qi forever plays with this dynamic.

Ultimately, to tell a Monkey (or anyone) to sit still and control their monkey mind is stupid. Monkeys must play. They are the wisdom of playfulness and survival. The playfulness of Monkey Qi is a sleight of hand poking fun at the seriousness of good-and-evil, revealing duality as a game, a playful situation rather than the cause of suffering. If you put your monkey mind in a cage called meditation, how will this lead to freedom?

The myth that the mind must be trained is stupid; concentration (when excessive) is madness, especially to the Monkey. Training the Monkey, Ox, or Horse—whatever metaphor you want—implies that your Nature and duality are problematic. They're not; your Inner Nature is perfectly free as it is. Meditation is an expression of your Inner Nature, not an exercise in making it behave.

I lived on an island with monkeys in Thailand for some time and learned a lot by watching them. I found them to be very social creatures. They roamed the island in packs and would march down the beach in big monkey processions. Momma monkeys carried babies on their backs and had groups with leaders and sidekicks.

They were unbelievably curious, and everything they did was playful. They would wrestle around, jump on everything, and investigate everything they encountered. A monkey once jumped on my table while I was eating breakfast, snatched a handful of sugar packets off the table, ran off into the trees, and then proceeded to throw the sugar packets at me. They would also lunge at me, baring their teeth; perhaps they knew I was a Tiger. In Classical Chinese Medicine, the Monkey is associated with the bladder, which is also kind of a joke, because monkeys pee on everything, including themselves, scent marking territory, communicating with other monkeys, and self-anointing to attract mates. This behavior is called "urine washing." We find the impulse of Monkey Qi in its Native Element: Yang Metal. Yang Metal examines, refines, distills, and transforms; it is precision, ingenuity, and imagination, the active, conceptual mind used for problem-solving; it is our capacity for vision that internalizes, draws in, and goes toward Water, which is full-blown mysticism. This active, conceptual quality of Yang Metal is the so-called monkey mind, but the virtue of this is imagination, self-reflection, wit, and intellect, which are essential qualities.

Monkey Qi's impulse, which is Yang Metal's impulse, is to test the limit and push boundaries, seeking the release of Water. Monkeys define life by taking risks. Life without risk—why bother? Where is the fun in that? Monkeys like to poke, play, push, and test possibilities. They seek adventure and excitement to keep on moving. Stagnation is death to the Monkey. They seek to go as far out as possible into extreme situations, places, experiences, and so on, just so they can bounce back and say, "Wow, that was cool!"

Yang Metal generates what I call "scanning Qi." Monkeys in their natural environment constantly scan for danger: Where are the Tigers? Monkey Qi provides a broad, pervasive awareness of the environment and all the details within. Monkey feels the precise movement and activity of the jungle and is at home in chaos. Silence, stillness, serenity—this spells doom for the Monkey: *What's coming to kill me?* The monkey keeps moving, staying forever on its toes (or tail).

Monkeys and human beings share many similarities, and these similarities highlight many of the key terms we will discuss. Humans, arguably, became dominant because of our ability to use tools and problem-solve, which is primarily due to having thumbs.

Monkey Hour is from 3 p.m. to 5 p.m. Monkey Qi is associated with planning, strategizing, projecting, adapting, and imagining, so Monkey Hour is the time to look forward to the next day or week and plan. It is the time to cease productivity and to shift to imagination. During Monkey Hour, our Qi naturally anticipates the end of the day and the transition into night. It is a time of adaptation; soon, we must head home, but before we do, we must digest the day's experience, adapt accordingly, and anticipate what may come. Since Monkey Qi is playful, this is the time to end the seriousness of work; it's "quitting time," when you should joke and have fun with co-workers before heading home. If you were born during this time of the day, you are also part Monkey.

If the Goat teaches us about social responsibility, justice, order, harmony, fairness, and interconnection, then the Monkey teaches us that none of this is serious. When Goat gets on a high horse and their rhetoric starts working people up . . . here come the Monkeys.

MANIFESTATION/CHARACTER (形)

Now that we have covered the symbolism and energetic dynamics, let's get into key words for the Monkey and talk about how this symbol manifests in and as people.

The first key term, then, is curiosity. Think Curious George. Like the monkey stealing my sugar packets, Monkey people have an intense desire to investigate, understand, peek behind the curtain, get to the bottom of things, and pull the rug out from under people. They often seek professions, lifestyles, and hobbies that express this curiosity, and they tend to be spiritual seekers who rebel against committing to a single path, for there is always another branch, another tree, with more fruit. Monkeys are in danger of what Chögyam Trungpa called "spiritual materialism"—getting into the spiritual path because it offers fun and exciting experiences, which Monkey is very curious about. This curiosity goes hand in hand with the Monkey's naturally playful disposition.

Conversely, curiosity can turn to erratic and frantic behavior and monkey mind. By nature, Monkeys have a profound capacity for distraction. When depleted, their minds scatter, race, and push them into a thousand places at once. This erratic behavior can cause them to quit jobs, abandon projects, change their minds, and waffle back and forth, unable to make decisions. Monkey Qi defines compulsive (rather than impulsive) behavior, and they can easily spin out into addiction and self-destructive tendencies.

Monkeys are playful and funny; they joke and like to mess with people. In their hearts, Monkeys do not take life seriously. They are not grave or morbid. They view life as a playful act. Alan Watts once said life is musical, and we are supposed to dance while the music is being played. When other people are morbid, Monkeys want to tickle them. Monkeys wish to pull the rug out from under people's plans. When confronted with hard decisions, the Monkey's response is play! This can confound people who want them to commit and be responsible. Tiger, the Monkey's opposite, hates to be messed with, and we can tend toward moodiness, hence the Monkey pulling the Tiger's tail.

This playfulness is also imitative. Monkey see, monkey do. Monkey, like Snake, learns by imitating. They can watch someone do something and then do it better than them. While Snakes do this by becoming the teacher, Monkeys do so by adaptation and cleverness, which is part of the shapeshifting, trickster image. If you show off in front of a Monkey, they may just make a fool of you, and they are not afraid to make fools of themselves.

Monkeys have potent imaginations and are knowledgeable and innovative people. The Monkey's imagination is beyond visionary. Monkeys can climb high in the trees and see far beyond the branches. This imagination, being Yang, is creative, and Monkey ranks as one of the "artistic" types. If Monkeys can sit still, they are capable of being great artists. Monkey Qi expresses profound intelligence, the ability to learn and change how things are done.

Monkey Qi scans, schemes, plans, and looks for solutions. When confronted with a problem or danger, the Monkey will look for options and ways around; they want to sneak past danger and, with a sleight of hand, fool the Tiger. I was once sitting in traffic with my godmother, a Wood Monkey, and we hit a traffic jam. Her immediate response was to google alternate routes and look up traffic reports. My response was to sit there; it never even occurred to me that there was another option, for the Tiger's reaction to danger is to pounce forward like a freight train, while the Monkey is the acrobat, nimbly escaping obstacles.

Monkey Qi is resourceful. Monkeys can find, utilize, and manipulate resources to their advantage unlike any other sign. They can be amazingly productive when assigned these kinds of tasks, and demonstrate the human capacity to create and make tools for survival. I envy this immense social and professional skill, for it is beyond me. Monkeys are competent beings who can learn and master many skills. They tend, however, to be jacks-of-all-trades and masters of none.

When depleted, this capacity for imagination and innovation turns to fantasy and delusion. Monkeys are masters of creating and living in fantasy worlds and story lands. Their scheming can generate many versions of reality, and at their worst, Monkeys spin out into alternate realities, which they find fascinating and entertaining. Monkey Qi tends to indulge in fantasy because it is fun. Again, this is a playful act, so Monkeys can test the limits of sanity and bounce back.

Monkeys demonstrate that nothing is real or solid in the way you think it is. There is no actual, objective reality; everything is empty of inherent meaning. Insanity comes from taking the relative world too seriously; when we see the transparent nature of everything, we are likely to go crazy, but Monkeys think it's funny. Push this too far, and you will get madness.

Monkey defines adaptation, resilience, and responsiveness. Physically, they are one of the most resilient signs and can bounce back quickly from the most severe illness. They are likely to flirt with death and danger and then make fun of everyone for getting morbid. They heal fast and respond quickly to their environment. Monkeys can perceive the energetics of an environment with incredible precision; however, they are not very intuitive. They tend to make many stories about what they perceive, which may be inaccurate.

Monkeys can be very nervous, anxious, and paranoid. They constantly perceive themselves in a situation of danger or threat, and their tendency toward fantasy can produce panic, worry, and fear. The active nature of Monkey Qi will create danger and threat where there is none, which is an unconscious result of the Monkey's playfulness. They may develop stories and dangers to have something to do, something to overcome, so that they can have cool stories to tell their friends.

The Monkey's resourcefulness can turn cunning, crafty, and manipulative. Depleted, they may use their intelligence to mess with social situations, turn friends against each other, gossip, tell stories, and make drama. Monkeys can be very deceptive and act mischievous for fun. They can use their abilities to dominate others intellectually, and their wit can turn ruthless. If Monkey perceives the game of the world as cruel, then Monkey Qi can even turn criminal, like the Joker.

Finally, Monkeys can be avoidant. Rather than deal with things head-on, like the Tiger, they will dance around issues for a long time and never confront tough decisions. Of course, I'm a Tiger, so that's my bias. Confronting things head-on can be disastrous, and the Tiger impulse can leap over their actual situation. When not avoidant, Monkey Qi responsiveness knows when to duck and when to avoid confrontation, for it senses when danger is coming.

Monkeys often lead incredibly interesting and exciting lives. Their impulse for fun and adventure takes them to wild places. They always have interesting stories to tell and love to regale you with the tale about that time they almost died, while in the place, doing the thing.

Because of this impulse, Monkeys often dance between this world and the next. They have potent desires that propel them toward materialism, and at the same time, their instinct tells them the world is a game. Monkeys fluctuate between materialism and austerity. If they can reconcile this dance, they are capable of profound wisdom. They reveal the cosmic joke, the play of consciousness.

Reconciling the Monkey dance, again, has nothing to do with putting the Monkey in a cage. Monkeys need not punish themselves with harsh discipline because they are erratic. Monkeys need only to climb high into the tallest tree and see beyond the enormous context of Space. Our Inner Nature is something like Space, which hosts all duality equally. Harsh order and discipline exalt one side over the other, which only creates more chaos, which is what Monkey comes to show us.

In terms of the Five Monkeys, each has its unique characteristics that contribute to the overall understanding of the Monkey zodiac sign. The Wood or Climbing Monkey is the most versatile, adventurous, ambitious, playful, and the least serious and most resilient of Monkeys. The Fire or Mountain Monkey is vigorous, industrious, and frank, with strong energy and skill. The Earth or Solitary Monkey is more grounded but at odds with being on the ground, since their Monkey impulse tells them to swing. The Metal or Silver Fruit Monkeys are the most natural and at-home element, and so they are respectable, powerful, and versatile, with excellent capacities. And the Water or Elegant Monkey is high-strung, sharp, and observant, the most dramatic and emotional. They push the mischievous boundaries of Monkey Qi into unknown, possibly dark, mystical territories; not even Heaven can perceive what they're up to. Understanding these different characteristics provides a comprehensive view of the Monkey zodiac sign.

THE TWELVE CHARACTERS OF DESTINY, PART 11: ROOSTER QI

NATIVE ELEMENT: Yin Metal

HOUR AND MONTH: 5 p.m. to 7 p.m., 8th Moon

ORGAN NETWORK: Kidneys

COMPATIBILITY TRINE: Ox, Snake

MARRIAGE PAIR: Dragon

OPPOSITE: Rabbit

SYMBOLISM (象) AND QI (氣) DYNAMICS

THE MONKEY AND THE ROOSTER are a pair, for they share the Native Element of Metal. The Rooster is the Yin version of Metal, and the Monkey is the Yang version. Yin Metal is refined, hidden, matured, withdrawn, distilled, fermented, hardened, crystallized, designated, subtilized, sublimated, and conceptualized. It is symbolically portrayed as ore refined from the Earth through the process of alchemy (Yang Metal), such as silver or gold, gemstones, and so on. Metal sinks downward, drawing in.

I experience Yin Metal as the moment in time when I form an opinion, when I recognize a thought or a pattern, and when I refine my experience into ordered language and logic. Yang Metal represents the active moment of things becoming "thinged," or labeled; Yin Metal represents the subtle process of refining and drawing together all the details, and the Rooster is generally associated with "details," corresponding to Virgo in Western astrology.

I am happy to say that I am in part Fire Rooster. I was born in a Fire Rooster Month, so everything I am about to discuss is part of my Qi Character. Again, the month is not as potent as the year or hour, but it is part of me. Hopefully, my personal experience as part Fire Rooster can shed light on the nature of this symbol.

The Rooster symbol in China is complex and sometimes confusing due to some conflicting images. In general, the Rooster (also called Phoenix) includes all birds, such as the crane, owl, raven—anything with a beak. The Rooster of

Chinese astrology, however, refers to the cock, the male rooster, associated with fertility and aggression. However, it is a decidedly Yin symbol, hence the confusion. Originally, this Character was more associated with the owl, but over time the Chinese decided on the male rooster because of some specific symbolic qualities, which we will discuss.

Despite being a male symbol, the Rooster is also a symbol of the Empress and feminine Yin energy. Perhaps it represents the subjugation of the Feminine, the Rooster lording over the Hens. The Dragon is a symbol of the Emperor, and together, they constitute a classical marriage pair in Chinese synastry. Rooster, Bird, and Crane all represent the grace, elegance, deportment, and dominance associated with the empress of Chinese royalty. The Rooster does not dominate with physical aggression; it dominates with emotion, appearance, ideology, intellect, belief—what we call "Yin Power."

The Rooster symbol is obviously domestic, one of the barnyard signs. Remember, we're not talking about hens; the Rooster performs very specific functions on the family farm. These functions form the primary set of symbols associated with the Rooster.

The sharp beak is the first and most important symbolic aspect of the Rooster. The beak represents precision, accuracy, and the ability to peck things apart, like seeds or ideas, to get to the essential quality within (Yin Metal). Crane-style gongfu strikes at pressure points, hitting the opponent's weak spots to bring them down with little effort. In the Rooster, this represents a certain capacity for analysis and the possibility of getting fixated. Because roosters don't have much of a memory, if you put their beak to a chalk line, they get stuck there and will peck all day at the chalk line, hypnotized, unable to break free.

The second symbolic aspect of the Rooster is its wings and ability to "puff up." When challenged, roosters flap and beat their wings, taking in air and making themselves appear larger and more threatening than they are. This wing flapping often precedes the cockfight, in which roosters fight to the death. The wings represent a competitive and aggressive nature that appears very threatening but is all hot air.

The Rooster puffs up and looks big, but it does not have much physical strength, which is another reason why it is Yin. It makes a big show of wanting to fight but is weak and will not fight unless it knows it can win. When pushed or backed into a corner, the beak and the claws are vicious, and roosters can do some serious damage, but this is only after being abused.

Cockfighting is a cruel and abusive sport; the roosters don't want to fight, but when challenged, they will rip each other to shreds because of competitive pride. Roosters can't fly, so the wings are deceptive, Yin. It is strange that the only bird in the Chinese zodiac can't fly, a capacity found only in the Dragon, who has no wings.

The third symbolic aspect of the Rooster is its crow, calling to the sun at dawn and dusk. Roosters are very vocal creatures. I lived with chickens and roosters in Thailand, and they would crow all day, not just at dawn and dusk. Crowing represents a capacity for eloquence and "Yin extroversion," meaning Roosters have such an intense inner experience that they need to get out, and there outer expression often reflects the immense detail and complexity of their inner vision, which can intimidate others.

For example, I don't talk much until asked a question, after which I tend to fire-hose people with information they weren't expecting. I really try to tone it down, but the volume of my inner experience is enormous; I can't help it. People's eyes usually get wide as if to say, "Whoa, dude, slow down," and their facial expressions often communicate regret or overwhelm about fifteen seconds in.

The final symbolic aspect of the Rooster is sacrifice. Like the goat and ox, roosters were often sacrificed in Daoist rituals but for different reasons. Roosters were sacrificed only in rituals that required blood oaths. This symbolizes trust, a quality very important to Rooster Qi.

In Daoism, roosters were used to ward off poison, for roosters in the wild often eat snakes, scorpions, spiders, centipedes, and toads—what are called the Five Poisonous Creatures, which represent our different negative emotions. The Rooster has the capacity to digest and transform negative emotions into wisdom, and amulets were often made bearing the Chinese Character for Rooster to ward off the Five Poisonous Creatures and their respective negative emotions.

In Classical Chinese Medicine, the Rooster represents the kidneys, which are associated with reproduction. You need one rooster for every ten hens, and some can handle up to twenty, which says something about their capacity to reproduce. As I mentioned earlier, the Rooster and its opposite, the Rabbit, are considered the most "sexual" of the signs because both animals can reproduce like crazy.

To understand the nature of each Qi Character, we must get to the root impulse represented by the Native Element. Control is the main impulse of the Rooster, symbolized by the rooster lording over the hens. Yin Metal can be an inward struggle—trying to hold on, control, and keep things in order. Fire melts this control, which allows Metal to release and turn to Water, but as an impulse, Yin Metal holds on before death.

So, the Rooster can be wound a bit tight. Inwardly, their impulse is to subtly control, manipulate, and put their experience into order so that it does not lead to death (Water). This impulse has a lot of fear behind it, which the Rooster covers up with a world of intense conceptuality, like the five on the Enneagram.

Rooster is the natural outcome of Monkey in the cycle of Time. The Goat attempts to put order to everything based on idealistic principles of interconnectedness; the Monkey says that'll never happen and throws a wrench in the spokes, so to speak, potentially leaving behind a mess. Rooster, then, comes along and goes a bit crazy, working like mad to tidy up, organize all the shelves, label all the boxes, sweep everything under the rug, and put things back in their proper place, which the Dog then guards with its life so that the Pig can party.

Rooster Hour, from 5 p.m. to 7 p.m., is the time of completion. In China, this time of day is associated with "coming home to roost," the time when all the chickens and animals make their way back to the barn. It is a crepuscular hour, the transition from day to night. Rooster's opposite, the Rabbit, represents the other crepuscular hour, the dawn. Since Rooster Qi is associated with completion, precision, competition, and confidence, this is the time to go home and take pride in what you have done, to reflect and analyze. If you were born during this time of the day, you are also part Rooster.

MANIFESTATION/CHARACTER (形)

Now that we have covered the symbolism and energetic dynamics, let's explore the key words for the Rooster and discuss how this symbol manifests in and as people.

The first key terms are critical and analytical. Like the Rat, the Rooster zooms in close and uses its beak (intellect) to break everything apart. The Rat takes things apart to make them small enough to carry, but the Rooster breaks open the seed to get to the important stuff inside. In other words, Rat detail does not necessarily include analysis; Rooster Qi does. This analytic, critical nature, an aspect of Yin Metal, extends to all aspects of the Rooster Display. Inwardly, this is often expressed as thinking, thinking, thinking, going over and over details, analyzing, reasoning, and judging. Outwardly, this analysis penetrates behavior and speech; Roosters choose their actions very carefully, second-guessing and double-checking. Outwardly, they are meticulous and tidy; they love to clean and organize and are generally concerned with the outer appearance of things.

Naturally, this analytic nature lends itself to a certain kind of intelligence that is highly valued in our culture: problem-solving. Roosters make natural engineers, mathematicians, and scientists, but they also make great writers and artists—anything where they get to investigate and express detail and meaning. They make wonderful decorators, designers, and architects. The art critic is perhaps the most Roostery profession I can think of.

Rooster Qi is a kind of competence that can translate into many arenas. They have a tremendous capacity to learn systems, methods, approaches, and so on. They can apply these systems very adeptly to anything they want. There is no limit to what Rooster Qi can accomplish with efficiency, precision, and exactness. I'm sure this sounds wonderful, because our culture highly values these qualities and wants everyone to have them. Roosters are productive, but they have a difficult time relaxing.

Rooster Qi is naturally a bit high-strung, tense, and uptight. This intelligent and intense thinking mind can get obsessed, becoming close-minded and even fanatical. Roosters can fixate on problems to solve and situations to manage; they can go over things in their mind so much that they disconnect from reality. Of all the signs, I would say that Rooster Qi, especially Metal and Water Rooster Qi, is the most susceptible to mental health problems. They live in their heads, and the fixation (the beak) behind their Qi means they can get obsessive-compulsive, anal retentive, and a little crazy at times. They're prone to hypochondria.

Roosters benefit greatly from cultivating stillness, openness, and relaxation. They need to get into their bodies and out of their heads, which is a monumental task for them. When they try to drop into their bodies, their awareness tends to snap back up like a yo-yo.

Rooster intelligence and capacity have profound confidence. Like the male peacock, Rooster Qi tends to be confident and a bit of a show-off—not physically per se, but mentally for sure. They like to strut their stuff, tout their abilities, and talk a big game. This may manifest as certainty; they know they're correct, that their argument is valid, and will therefore attempt to dominate in conversation, which can lead to argument.

Confidence is a positive virtue, but it can easily lead to arrogance, rudeness, and pride. Roosters can be very proud. They tend to generate strong and rigid self-images that can't stand being challenged. This also leads to vanity, which can concern physical appearance but also what traditional cultures call "saving face," maintaining a good public image.

Roosters are trustworthy, honest, challenging, and forthright. They tend to speak very directly and concisely. They tend to challenge other people in conversation, for they like to debate. The Tibetan tradition of analytical debate is very Rooster. Tibetan Buddhists have a well-developed system of logic from Mahayana Buddhism, which they use to develop wisdom.

You begin with a statement and rebuttal from a defender and questioner. You clearly define all the terms you are using. You and your opponent put forth arguments. You attempt to find the *gakcha*, the crux of the other person's view, and then you use logic to undermine it, pointing to the emptiness of all fixed views. If done correctly, this process undermines our conceptual mind and shows us the structures of logic we use to construct false views about reality. Ultimately, it points to the nonconceptual state beyond all logic. Again, very Rooster.

The flip side turns harshly competitive, snobby, blunt, vulgar, and tactless. Rooster Qi can be volatile and erupt without consideration for others. They can be so sure of their view that they will argue it to the death, pecking and ripping with beak and claw. This impulse to challenge can be competitive, so much so that they will argue even if they know they're wrong, just so they can win and be in control. They may put down and criticize others, making them feel stupid, and they can do this unintentionally. Roosters need to develop big, open minds and include as many points of view as possible in their experience.

Rooster Qi tends to be very social and spontaneous. The Rooster is concerned with social dynamics regarding hierarchy, or pecking order, and structure. By nature, Roosters love socializing and fun; they like the dynamics of social interaction and relationships. Although they are prone to spontaneous displays of showmanship, invoking reactions from and interactions between others, they are acutely aware of social structure. They like to know where they stand with people; they feel secure knowing who is doing what and with whom. They think everyone should have a job and a role that is clearly defined. They like to know the reasons why people act the way they do. In the end, Roosters feel uncertain if these things are not defined, and they love being the ones to put everyone in order. This social certainty reflects the sacrifice of the Rooster, the blood oath, making a pact.

Depleted, Roosters can be aloof and closed off. If they lose face or if their ideas about how others perceive them and about their role in life fall apart, they may question everything and distance themselves until they can figure it out.

They can be overwhelmed by the amount of detail they take in, and if it is more than they can handle, they crumble.

It can be difficult to approach them when they close off; they need to relax and come to conclusions naturally to feel in control. If you confront them, they will likely snap back and get more entrenched in their difficulties. Roosters are adept at justifying their feelings, and if those feelings turn to self-hate or blame or to blaming others, they can't be talked out of their point of view. They will, however, respond to logic, if that logic is well presented and offers them a structure to work with.

Rooster Qi is intense and, by nature, alert, inspired, and insightful. Roosters on the farm are guardians. They are vigilant, observant, watchful, alert, aware, and perceptive. Rooster Qi can be luminous, awake, and present. At its best, Rooster Qi is bright and inspired by life, and they are psyched to wake up and crow. Roosters have a fantastic capacity to pay attention and focus. The category of meditation called Vipassana, which means to investigate with clear or distinct observation, is very Rooster. Vipassana is often translated as "insight meditation," and insight is the ideal outcome of the Rooster analysis.

I would, however, not recommend Vipassana to most Roosters, especially if they are depleted. They can be too focused, too analytical, or too vigilant, and Vipassana can make them even crazier. If clarity is not met with its sister, calm, then clarity and insight can produce agitation. Roosters can become hyperaware of how messed up everything is, and they may spin off into irritation and reactivity. Nonconceptual meditation, called Zuo Wang—Sitting and Forgetting—is much healthier for Roosters.

In terms of the Five Roosters, each has unique characteristics that contribute to the overall understanding of the Rooster zodiac sign. The Wood or Crowing Rooster is the most spontaneous, idealistic, inspired, and likely to forgive and forget. The Fire or Solitary Rooster is the most sensual and restless of the Roosters; they are bright and luminous, able to focus like laser beams, yet can collapse under too many difficulties. The Earth or Dawn Rooster is the most stable and conventional of the Roosters, but the capacity of Earth makes them so strong that they get easily overwhelmed by the amount of complexity they imagine they can handle. The Metal or Caged Rooster is the most natural and quintessential Rooster; they are the most meticulous, articulate, and fussy of the bunch, prone to mental instability, and often their ability to analyze is a cover for their delicate mental and emotional state. The Water or Nested Rooster puts their capacity over the edge into mystical territories, so much so that they lack the focus of other Roosters and are the most susceptible to instability and emotionality. Understanding these different characteristics provides a comprehensive view of the Rooster zodiac sign.

THE TWELVE CHARACTERS OF DESTINY, PART 12: DOG QI

NATIVE ELEMENT: Yang Earth

HOUR AND MONTH: 7 p.m. to 9 p.m., 9th Moon

ORGAN NETWORK: Pericardium

COMPATIBILITY TRINE: Tiger, Horse

MARRIAGE PAIR: Rabbit

OPPOSITE: Dragon

SYMBOLISM (象) AND QI (氣) DYNAMICS

TRADITIONALLY, THE DOG IS ELEVENTH in the series, but as you will recall, I started at the "end" with the Pig, in honor of Liu Ming, who was a Fire Pig. Since the Stem and Branch Cycles circle, there is no beginning or end, so it doesn't matter where we begin or end. I think the Dog is an excellent place to end this discussion, in many ways.

Humans have had a long relationship with dogs, which, strangely enough, began in China. People everywhere have been with wolves for a very long time; human hunters lived near and followed wolves and learned from them how to hunt. But for most of this time, we were separate and respected the independent nature of the wolf pack. At some point, to help us with the hunt, we captured wolf puppies and kept them close, slowly turning them to our side over time (cats, on the other hand, domesticated themselves).

According to legend, the Chinese were the first people to domesticate the wolf into a dog, which would make the first breed of dog the Chinese chow. All dogs come from wolves, which is hard to believe when you look at a chihuahua next to a mastiff. This shape-shifting quality also gives us a fundamental insight into Dog Qi that we can call subordination or adaptability.

The first dogs were bred for hunting and war. Soldiers trained dog companions to follow them into the heat of battle. They taught them to attack on command and to defend them to the death. When a soldier died, their dog remained and guarded the body, which is another insight about the Dog we can call faithfulness.

Dogs were also bred in Daoist families to guard temples, and you will still see "fu dogs," guardian statues, at the gates of most East Asian temples. The Daoist legend of Tiangou—a deity in the form of a black dog the size of a meteor, said to eat the sun or moon during an eclipse—is revered as a great protector who guards children and chases away harmful spirits and Demons.

From the Daoist point of view, the Dog represents strong Yin and Yang qualities—Yin when faithful and devoted, and Yang when acting as the fierce guardian. As we get into the key terms of Dog Qi, this Yinyang quality will become apparent, although we must say the Dog is a pure Yang Character.

Because our culture is obsessed with dogs, Dog Qi may be the easiest to understand. Tigers, too, for Tigers are basically house cats. The modern domesticated dog tells us everything we need to know. We can say that people born in the Dog Year generally have doglike characteristics. Energetically, Dog Qi is as complex and layered as all the other signs, but just like the domesticated dog, their core impulse is simple and easy to understand, which is why dogs were chosen as symbols of this pattern of Time. Remember, each of the Twelve Animals symbolizes a pattern of Time in a sequence.

In the sequence, the Monkey turns to a Rooster and then turns to the Dog. In other words, the Monkey breaks up the stuffy Goat, offering fun, excitement, adventure, and a bit of chaos. The Monkey makes a bit of a mess, and the Rooster puts everything back in order, offering precision, logic, reasoning, and hierarchy. The Rooster, then, needs the Dog to help. Once the Rooster sets everything to order, the Dog comes to take orders, protect, serve, guard, and love whatever the sequence of Time has created. Dog Qi does not care what has been produced; it follows orders and guards with its life no matter what.

Dog Hour is from 7 p.m. to 9 p.m., and it is when everything is complete but still active. We are supposed to be home and secure. Imagine the family guard dog, vigilant at their post while the family relaxes after a long day. The dog does not rest until everyone is safe, secure, and at ease. Dog Hour should be spent with family, friends, and those close to you, enjoying the company of those who share the virtue of loyalty. My best friend's dad is a Wood Dog, and he always stays up late; he will only go to sleep after everyone and everything is secure. If you were born during this time of the day, you are also part Dog.

The Native Element of the Dog is Yang Earth, which it shares with the Dragon, its opposite. For the Dragon, Yang Earth represents flight: breaking away from the ground through explosive, upward movement. For the Dog, Yang Earth represents territory. The impulse of Dog Qi surveys and guards the Earth and can traverse territory quickly through explosive movement. The Dog's keen senses cover the land and go for miles. Yang Earth for the Dog also represents support, stability, groundedness, solidity, and alliances.

Although they share the same Native Element, Dragons and Dogs are opposites. Again, the Dragon is the ultimate leader and represents the Emperor in Chinese cosmology. The Dog, on the other hand, is the ultimate follower, supporter, assistant, and subordinate; they find their Qi through subordination. The samurai's Bushido philosophy exemplifies the virtues of the Dog: to die on the battlefield protecting one's master.

Dogs are generally out of place in leadership positions. Strangely enough, three modern presidents are Fire Dogs, potentially the most territorial and aggressive of Dogs. Donald Trump, Bill Clinton, and George W. Bush are all interesting examples of what happens when Dogs are put in charge. But let's stay away from politics.

Despite being followers, Dogs are often complex and unique individuals. I am amazed at how many Dogs are famous artists and musicians: Elvis, John Waters, David Bowie, Cher, Leonard Cohen, and Prince, to name a few. Prince is a fitting example of Dog Qi. He was an amazingly complex individual, very private, and a revolutionary artist, and yet he was also a staunch and devoted Jehovah's Witness who devoted his life to serving and subordinating to evangelism. In this culture, Dogs often devote themselves to principles or symbols if they cannot find family or friends to protect.

To understand the Dog, we must look at territoriality and loyalty. Like the Tiger, the Dog has an alternating quality related to "territory," which is why they are in a trine together. Dog Qi functions based on a profound and simple principle of trust. When we meet a dog (the animal), we encounter a defensive territorial stance, so we put out our hand, and they sniff; we pet them and offer treats. If their human shows acceptance of you and lets you into their home, dogs can quickly switch from defenders to slobbering love machines. The Dog's instinct is to protect no matter what, so it perceives everything as a potential threat to those in its territory. But at its core, Dog Qi is overwhelmingly loving. So, Dogs alternate from growling to rolling over and showing you their belly. They go from "I can kill you!" to "Pet me!"

Dogs can be incredibly threatening and dangerous, but if well trained, we can feel comfortable with a giant mastiff guarding a newborn. This tells us what we need to know about Dog Qi. Dogs thrive and gain power from protecting, taking orders, and following. They are the great exemplars of the virtue of loyalty.

Loyalty is greatly misunderstood in our culture. We think that people need to earn our loyalty and trust by being "worthy." But your dog does not give a shit if you're worthy. You can be a total jerk, and they will still love you. Of course, you must feed them, take them for walks, and throw the ball. But your worthiness as a person is meaningless to them. They love unconditionally and purely.

Your dog is having an awesome time being loyal, which is true loyalty. Once you dedicate yourself to something or someone, you protect and defend no matter what. This is the samurai code. It doesn't matter if your master is corrupt; you die for them. There is wisdom in this, believe it or not. Many people change sides, defect, or drop loyalty at the first sign of corruption. We hold others to standards of perfection and then freak out and run away when they falter, mainly to protect ourselves, and this can sometimes be helpful. Of course, in today's world, so many leaders, teachers, and people in positions of power have proved themselves "unworthy." But the loyalty of Dog Qi is not about whom you serve or even why; it is about the transformative qualities of love, surrender, devotion, and service, not for others but for yourself. This is called "guru yoga" in Tantra.

You can open your heart to anything, and it will transform you if you do it from a deep place of self-love and acceptance without the need for trust. Without self-possession, devotion and surrender invite abuse. When trust gets involved, we get hurt or betrayed. Dogs can be betrayed, but their instinct is to open their hearts without reservation, to give completely. We can all learn something from this.

Liu Ming used to say that trust is stupid. Everything will disappoint you because everything is impermanent, unstable, and complex. If we put too much faith in others not to hurt us, we will be let down. Laozi said to trust the untrustworthy, which means giving up the notion that trust is valuable. This does not mean that you should mistrust people. On the contrary, it means accepting all people as valuable and worthy of your loyalty because they're human. What would it be like to accept and unconditionally love those who betray you without creating resentment? This is the virtue of Dog Qi.

Those born in the Year of the Dog have all these virtues as instinct. The impulse of Dog Qi is to protect, guard, follow, serve, and love without giving up their individuality. Dogs are complete people but find their power through subordination.

MANIFESTATION/CHARACTER (形)

Now that we have covered the symbolism and energetic dynamics, let's explore the key words for the Dog and discuss how this symbol manifests in and as people.

The first key term for the Dog is loyalty. Dogs are fantastic friends, partners, and family members. They often have close, select circles, people they have let into their world. When it comes to family, Dogs are loyal to the end. When it comes to friends, Dogs often have a process of choosing, sniffing out if you will, but once they accept you, they are great companions and bond very deeply in a relationship.

If a relationship or friendship ends, Dogs tend to carry the bond with them forever and may feel hurt for a long time. They can instantly recognize new "old friends" and are sometimes too eager to jump into things. People can be overwhelmed by how quickly a Dog seems to know and accept them. Or, they can be put off by a Dog's standoffishness or guard dog stance.

This loyalty is, by nature, protective. Dogs protect. They serve. This may take the form of protecting a younger sibling, child, friend, parent, partner, boss, teacher, co-worker, and so on. Dogs can also protect ideas, teachings, or principles. Dogs very naturally express the bodhisattva ideal that is so cherished in Mahayana Buddhism. The great Tibetan teacher Dilgo Khyentse Rinpoche was a Metal Dog, and if you watch footage of him, you will see that he served the Dharma and thousands of students but never put on shows about being a great master. He bowed to and honored everyone who came to him, and his love was vast and open.

Dogs naturally want to follow something or someone. Without this, their lives have no direction, no meaning. They often jump into devotion without forethought. Because of this, Dogs can stay in tough and even abusive situations for a long time out of misplaced loyalty; Pigs do this too, and so do Oxen. Once they are devoted, that's it. And it is hard for a Dog to break their bonds. They fear the ending of relationships, jobs, and community situations, for they may not know who they are outside these contexts. Dogs must cultivate solid boundaries and a sense of self; otherwise, their loyalty can endanger them.

Another flip side of this loyalty and protectiveness is territoriality, a rigid quality. If Dogs have trauma or wounds they have not integrated, if their loyalty was not nurtured early on, they can tend to growl. Dogs can put up enormous walls and feel very rigid to other people. Of course, behind this rigidness, Dogs are gushing with love. But, like attack dogs, their loyalty can be selective; they guard their territory. Again, this territory can be people, ideas, beliefs, and so on. They can lash out and hurt others to defend someone or something if they think they're right or justified. Sometimes, this is necessary; sometimes people need protection, and someone must be able to fight. Violence is available in the Dog. Dogs must, then, cultivate how to use their Yang aggressive qualities in appropriate ways: When is strong action necessary, and when is it paranoid?

Dog Qi cares very deeply. Whatever they do, in whomever they invest, wherever they choose to direct their Qi, Dogs give everything. They give too much. This caring quality can be unconditional in its true form. Of course, few people can actualize unconditional love and care, but Dogs are apt to accept people wholly. I am amazed when I look into the eyes of dogs (the animals) and see nothing but pure love, and Dog Qi has this abundance available.

Despite this quality of caring devotion, Dogs are by nature very private individuals. Every Dog has a touch of the lone wolf, which may be accentuated or understated depending on the individual. Dogs tend to have powerful private lives and love to be alone, which then alternates with their fierce companionship. When expressing their wolf side, Dogs feel at home in solitude. The flip side of this private individuality can be excessive vanity and concern with cultivating a unique self or appearance to give themselves power.

They tend to be very congenial, quiet, and respectful of others. They keep to themselves. For this reason, they fit in very well into situations with a chain of command, like the military. It is natural for them to slide into a role, take orders, and guard their platoon. They thrive in service-oriented professions and make great waiters, social workers, police officers, assistants, and anything that applies their energy to a greater cause. Dogs are naturally very just and like righting wrongs.

Dogs tend to be direct, blunt, and honest. This comes from their natural responsiveness, which allows them to react very directly to the present situation. Often, these reactions can be sudden and taken without consideration, like a dog barking at the mail carrier.

When depleted, these qualities can become stubborn, stingy, and spiteful. Dogs can be excessively critical of others based on their quick feelings and judgments. This blunt, straightforward attitude can appear to others as egotistical and argumentative. Dogs can get into barking matches if they think they need to defend themselves or if they are invested in protecting a situation.

The ears and the snout are important parts of the Dog symbol. The keen senses of the dog represent a kind of intuition and expansiveness. Dog Qi is very sensitive and picks up on even the slightest changes in the atmosphere. We have all noticed a dog lying on the ground, then all of a sudden their ears twitch, and they are up and barking before the humans realize anything has happened. This intuition feels the nature of situations, people, and environments in a sensory, embodied way. However, Dogs don't often know what to do with their intuition and look to others for guidance and direction. Still, a Dog can smell danger coming a mile away.

Their observant quality produces great insight, and Dogs often have a lot to offer in terms of seeing things from multiple angles and dimensions. When everyone is stuck, they can offer a new way to "smell" rather than just "see." Often, their energetic sensory insights are right without overthinking. Someone may appear a certain way, but if they don't smell right, the Dog knows something is off.

The warrior nature of the Dog is always ready to jump into battle. They feel at home in danger and chaos and act as sturdy pillars of calm. They are cool under fire. When everything goes to shit, Dogs are usually relaxed and ready to jump in and do what is necessary to help. Their senses and intuition come alive in high-intensity situations, which is great for sports and high-stress jobs.

When depleted or without training, Dogs can become rigid and frozen with anxiety, especially when emotions are high. Dogs take in the environment's energy, and if it is too much, they tremble, quake, and shiver with fear, unable to move, like a deer in the headlights. For this reason, Dogs need training and benefit greatly from the disciplined cultivation of sports, martial arts, debate, and so on, so that when they get into the heat of battle, their instincts can take over and they don't get frozen with fear. This frozen nature may translate into an inability to make life decisions or have tough conversations. When balanced, however, Dogs make quick decisions from the gut and don't second-guess things.

In terms of the Five Dogs, each has its unique characteristics that contribute to the overall understanding of the Dog zodiac sign. The Wood or Gate Dog is Puppy Qi, youthful, responsive, but naughty; they may tear up the sofa—that is, drain or ruin their good Fate resources. The Fire or Guard Dog can be trouble: forceful, vigorous, and with no fear of confrontation, without discipline, they will hurt others; with it, they make fierce and loyal guardians. The Earth or Mountain Dog is stable, sturdy, and dependable but likely to get stuck in patterns of stagnation. The Metal or Temple Dog possesses the keenest senses, intellect, and intuition but is prone to being too sensitive and potentially fixed in their loyalties. The Water or Family Dog is the most emotional, generous, and kind but tends toward devotion driven by sentiment and will devote themselves to hopeless causes. Understanding these different characteristics provides a comprehensive view of the Dog zodiac sign.

SYNTHESIZING THE QI CHARACTER OF THE YEAR AND HOUR

NOW THAT WE HAVE GONE THROUGH each of the Twelve Qi Characters of Destiny individually and in detail, we must understand how to synthesize them. In this tradition, we synthesize the Stem and Branch of the year and the hour in which a person was born to create an image of their Qi Character. We use the year and hour because these are the most important factors when calculating the position of the Stars in the Polestar chart. Again, the year is the primary image and is like a noun. The hour is the secondary image and is like an adjective, modifying the root image of the year. The first step when studying your Natal Chart or when giving a reading, after you introduce the View Teachings, of course, is to synthesize the year and hour and summarize the Qi Character, which is your basic capacity to resolve Fate. In this tradition, we basically ignore the Qi Character of the month and day, although these can be considered as well, for we are essentially a blend of our year, month, day, and hour. In this tradition, however, the month and day are considered to influence our physical body and constitution, while the year and hour are related more to our "personality display."

Here are the basic five steps you should take when synthesizing the Qi Character of any chart. I suggest you standardize this and take these five steps each time you do a reading. Steps 1 and 2 are virtually identical to steps 3 and 4.

STEP 1

Consider the Earthly Branch, or Zodiac Animal, of the year

This is the single most crucial factor in a person's Qi Character and the main factor determining Fate's auspice. This is the primary image that all the following factors will modify.

STEP 2

Consider the Influence of the Heavenly Stem, or Element, on the Earthly Branch of the year in relation to its Native Element

Now, we modify the Earthly Branch with its Heavenly Stem, which means that we add Yin or Yang and one of the Five Elements, so the Monkey turns into a Yang Wood Monkey, Yang Fire Monkey, Yang Earth Monkey, Yang Metal Monkey, or Yang Water Monkey. We must then consider this Outer Element's relationship with the Native Element of the Branch. The Native Element of the Monkey is Metal, and so if the person is born in a Water Monkey year, then we must consider the dynamic of Metal generating Water and how this modifies the Monkey image. If they were born in a Fire Monkey year, then we must consider the dynamic of Fire controlling Metal, how this modifies the Monkey image, and so on. We do this for each of the Earthly Branches.

STEP 3

Consider the Earthly Branch, or Zodiac Animal, of the Hour

Next, we do the same two steps but for the Hour. The hour is again the secondary image of Character, and it is like an adjective modifying the year. So, a person can then be a "Snakey" Monkey, a "Rabbity" Horse, a "Piggy" Tiger, a "Roostery" Dog, and so on.

STEP 4

Consider the Influence of the Heavenly Stem, or Element, on the Earthly Branch of the Hour

This is the same as step 2, but here we examine the dynamics of the Heavenly Stem on the Earthly Branch of the hour and how that Element modifies the basic Animal image.

STEP 5

Synthesize and Summarize the Earthly Branch and Heavenly Stem of the Year and Hour

Considering the dynamics of Yin and Yang, the Five Elements, and the nature of each zodiac Character and their trines of compatibility, we must attempt to synthesize or blend all this information into a single image. But how do we do this?

First, we consider the dynamics of Yin and Yang. In other words, a Yin and a Yang Earthly Branch will balance and complement each other. Two Yin Animals may make a Character who is too Yin, meaning they may be too inactive, tentative, stagnant, and so on. Likewise, two Yang Animals may be too Yang, and hence they may be too active, compulsive, restless, and so on. None of this is inherently problematic, but knowing how to work with it is very important.

Then, we consider the Five Element dynamics between the year and hour, so a Fire year and a Metal hour will be at odds, and the Animals will have more difficulty blending and will likely alternate or create conflict within the Character. However, a Wood year and Fire hour will be generative, and the year will empower the hour. An Earth year and Earth hour, too, will match and blend much easier, as they are identical. Here it becomes very important to understand the Five Element dynamics in terms of the Generative Cycle, or mother–child relationships, and the Controlling or Destructive Cycle. This is really a matter of creative application, and to do this, you must first understand the nature of each of the Five Elements and how they interact.

Then you can imagine how they affect one another. Here, you must also consider the direction of the Elements going from the year to the hour and vice versa. Consider what it means for the hour to control the year or the year to generate the hour. For example, if the Element of the year generates the hour, then the core personality will empower and strengthen the more superficial and outer personality traits. There are many dynamics that can happen here, and I leave it to you to explore all the possibilities. But I will give a few examples in a moment.

Finally, we consider the Animals themselves and if or how they are compatible. The trines of compatibility and marriage pairs mentioned in each Character section get along and blend well, and the opposites do not blend at all. People with their year and hour in opposite relationships will likely alternate and have a kind of split personality. Here, you must use your imagination and think of what it would be like for a Pig and Horse to blend into a single image. What about a Tiger and a Snake? How about a Rat and a Dragon?

There are simply too many combinations to explore everything: 60 times 60, to be exact. This book cannot cover everything but rather aims to examine each individual vocabulary term and the principles of interpretation in detail so that you can apply them to any given example.

Here are a few brief examples of synthesizing Qi Characters that I chose at random to highlight some important dynamics. I will give more real-life examples when I examine the example charts of myself and my parents. I suggest you do this for your own Qi Character and for a few friends and family members. This will be part of any chart reading, so practice with as many combinations as possible. The following is not meant to be comprehensive but rather to explore some of the ideas and get you thinking about how to blend all these images.

QI CHARACTER SYNTHESIS

Example 1

YEAR: Yin Water Rabbit

HOUR: Yang Wood Dog

STEP 1

Consider the Earthly Branch, or Zodiac Animal, of the Year

The Rabbit image is lunar and a symbol of the subterranean; the Rabbit represents the capacity of intuition and sensitivity to what lies beneath the surface. They are characterized by being vulnerable, and they hate confrontation. They are part of the domestic trine; they are dependent and need support and relationships to survive and thrive. The Rabbit is discreet, gentle, loving, supportive, quiet, peace-loving, intuitive, domestic, social, diverse, dependent, intelligent, aesthetic, and authoritative when charged. When depleted, they are gossipy, snobby, superficial, greedy, deceptive, opportunistic, paranoid, scattered, vain, promiscuous, conservative, stubborn, and lazy.

STEP 2

Consider the Influence of the Heavenly Stem, or Element, on the Earthly Branch of the Year

The Native Element of the Rabbit is Yin Wood, and the Heavenly Stem here is Yin Water. Water is the "mother" of Wood in the Five Element cycle, meaning the energetic direction is generative, supportive, and nurturing, as watering the soil gives birth to new sprouts. This dynamic has no conflict or control, so the Water Rabbit display has naturalness and ease. The power of Water enhances and exaggerates the Wood Element, and it adds drama, emotionality, increased sensitivity, and generosity to the Rabbit image, making the Water Rabbit an expansive, universal, and oceanic version of the Wood Rabbit, with all its emotional qualities dramatized.

STEP 3

Consider the Earthly Branch, or Zodiac Animal, of the Hour

The Dog symbolizes loyalty: the house guard and battlefield companion. The dog is independent and has an element of the lone wolf, but it is also fiercely dedicated and service oriented, in need of a mission to help, support, and follow others. When charged, the Dog is faithful, loyal, caring, protective, helpful, direct, insightful, just, direct, intuitive, expansive, congenial, private, quiet, and calm under fire. When depleted, the Dog is stubborn, argumentative, stingy, spiteful, rigid, vain, frozen with anxiety, and excessively critical.

STEP 4

Consider the influence of the Heavenly Stem, or Element, on the Earthly Branch of the Hour

The Native Element of the Dog is Yang Earth, but the Heavenly Stem here is Yang Wood. Yang Earth represents manifestation, confidence, alliance, leadership, wealth, abundance, balance, caring, and power. For the Dog, Yang Earth represents territory and the ability to intuit, cover, and protect the terrain. But in the Five Element structure, Wood "eats" Earth, so the pliant, youthful quality of Wood, which is like the roots of a sprout, aerating and breaking up the solid heaviness of Earth, is enlivening, lightening, and enriching and offers an innocent, childlike perspective to the Dog that is eternally fresh. So, the Wood Dog is essentially a puppy, adding a youthful responsiveness, ambition, and appetite for growth and knowledge to the Dog image. Wood Dogs are everyone's friend and loyal companion and are willing to subordinate and follow.

STEP 5

Synthesize and Summarize the Earthly Branch and Heavenly Stem of the Year and Hour

First, we see that we have a Yin and Yang Character, so in this sense, they will complement each other well. The Heavenly Stem of the year is Water, and the hour is Wood. Water is the mother of Wood, so the year is generative and supportive of the hour, which means that the Water Rabbit supports and blends well with the Wood Dog, and there is no conflict in the elemental makeup here.

In terms of the Animals, they are not in a trine or opposite, but the Animals are considered a special marriage pair as similar in that they are relationship-oriented and seek trust, protection, and loyalty in close partnership. The Dog is a follower and a protector, so this is very auspicious for the Rabbit. This Character will be very personable, and the Water Rabbit's social charm and the Wood Dog's lovability will make them very well liked and able to make friends. They will be social and dependent to a fault, as both the Dog and Rabbit take betrayal very seriously.

The Water Rabbit is very deep, serious, and spiritual, while the Wood Dog is a lot more lighthearted and fresher in their outlook, so this Character will have depth and profundity matched with a childlike, loving quality, which gives them a broad capacity to resolve the vicissitudes of Fate. These characters will be capable of a lot but struggle alone to find meaning and direction, so the relationship Houses and the career Houses will be important in their Chart (we will explore Houses in Step IV). There is a chance that these Characters will bring out both the best and worst of each other, as they will have very strong intuition but also very strong anxiety. This Character will be a champion for others and will be very protective and just.

QI CHARACTER SYNTHESIS

Example 2

YEAR: Yin Metal Snake

HOUR: Yin Earth Pig

STEP 1

Consider the Earthly Branch, or Zodiac Animal, of the Year

The snake is the mystical Yin image of the underworld, representing transformation, mystery, and magic. They shed their skin and are symbols of alchemy and the unknown, and their unknowable quality gives them a distinct depth and charm. The Snake is uniquely self-reflective and detached from the world. Their instinct is to hide, remain still, and disappear or be unseen. They can be "in the world but not 'of' it." When charged, the Snake is deeply reflective, wise, meditative, mystical, intelligent, inventive, philosophical, visionary, solitary, discreet, calm, slow, and evasive. When depleted, the Snake is paranoid, deceptive, secretive, negative, bitter, self-loathing, helpless, lazy, and possibly suicidal.

STEP 2

Consider the Influence of the Heavenly Stem, or Element, on the Earthly Branch of the Year

The Native Element of the Snake is Yin Fire, and the Heavenly Stem here is Yin Metal. In the Five Element cycle, Fire controls or melts Metal, which adds a conflicting dynamic to the Metal Snake, but paradoxically, the Snake seems very Metal. Metal adds refinement, discretion, and fastidiousness to the Snake image, and the Metal Snake is even more withdrawn, discreet, and self-reflective, with an enhanced capacity for intellectual, political, and spiritual matters. The Fire melts and softens the hardness and rigidness of the Metal qualities and instead gives way to further transcendence and mysticism. Metal Snakes are extremely sensitive and insightful, but their mental health is also challenged by too much vision into the unseen.

STEP 3

Consider the Earthly Branch, or Zodiac Animal, of the Hour

The Pig is the most domestic and worldly sign and a symbol of home and family. Pigs symbolize wealth, food, and abundance. Sensual in nature, Pigs see everything as food and art, and they love to indulge and enjoy life through the senses. They are also seen as powerful transformers, able to transform garbage into sweet white meat. They are the symbol of the wild mother boar, who is nature's most fierce protector, and they can be the most generous of all the signs. When charged, the Pig is honest, plain speaking, caring, sensuous, gregarious, funny, eloquent, tolerant, humanitarian, compromising, unselfish, hardworking, reliable, and lucky. The Pig is indulgent, luxury loving, flamboyant, self-destructive, secretive, long suffering, gullible, and self-indulgent when depleted.

STEP 4

Consider the Influence of the Heavenly Stem, or Element, on the Earthly Branch of the Hour

The Native Element of the Pig is Yin Water, and the Heavenly Stem here is Yin Earth. In the Five Element cycle, Earth controls or contains Water, so this is a conflicting dynamic. Earth can "dam" Water, meaning it can be shaped to control the flow of Water, which has no shape, into the form of rivers, aqueducts, canals, and so on. As such, the Earth Pig is more controlled and contained than the Water Pig, and they can be very hardworking, productive, and reliable. Earth adds groundedness, stability, conventionality, and maturity to the Pig image, and Earth Pigs are the most caring and confident of the Pigs. They can also be the most worldly, manifest, and interested in sensuality and indulgence. The Earth Element can bog them down, make them lethargic and aimless, and plague them with chronic dampness.

STEP 5

Synthesize and Summarize the Earthly Branch and Heavenly Stem of the Year and Hour

First, we can see that there are two Yin Animals here, so this Character is very, very Yin, meaning they will bring out the more inactive, sluggish, and slow dynamics in both Characters. The Heavenly Stems are supportive, and the Earth Element of the Pig Hour supports or generates the Outer Element of Metal in the Snake Year, so while these Characters are opposites, they are not elementally at odds, and there is less likely to be conflict between them. But they are opposites, and so this Character will likely have two personalities, and they will alternate between them.

The Snake and the Pig are very different: One stays hidden and detached from the world, and the other fully manifests and celebrates the world. So, there will be some deep confusion in this Character, and they may have times when they are reclusive and other times when they go crazy and have fun. The Pig is the least naturally depressed, and this balances out the Snake, who is the most naturally depressed. This could, however, create a manic-depressive quality. Overall, this Character will have to learn to balance these two sides, and ultimately, the Snake is the main image here and will win out.

They may indulge and act like a Pig in private, and this could lead to some self-destructive tendencies. They will likely have a deeply sensual and indulgent private personal life that they do not share with the world. They will find it difficult to come out and engage with the world and will have to watch out for stagnation and inactivity. If they can manage this, then this Character can have a profound, otherworld spiritual vision that they can express with the world and communicate with people through the senses. They can be both in the world fully, participating in a celebration of the senses, and at the same time, they can transcend.

QI CHARACTER SYNTHESIS

Example 3

YEAR: Yin Metal Rooster

HOUR: Yang Fire Rat

STEP 1

Consider the Earthly Branch, or Zodiac Animal, of the Year

The Rooster is the most competitive, extroverted, and challenging image of the Yin Animals, as the Rooster represents the cockfight, the duel to the death, and the rooster lording over the hens. However, they are also the Owl and the Phoenix and represent all symbols associated with "birds." The beak represents their precision and intellectual capacity to break things open to get to what is most essential. The wings and puffing up represent flight and competitive power, and the call to the sun at dusk and dawn represents their eloquence and honesty. Roosters were sacrificed in rituals that required oaths. When charged, the Rooster is analytical, critical, intelligent, confident, alert, social, dignified, articulate, forthright, spontaneous, inspired, financially adept, challenging, and meticulous. When depleted, the Rooster is volatile, rude, proud, argumentative, blunt, vulgar, tactless, close-minded, hypochondriac, vain, snobby, aloof, harshly competitive, and fanatical.

STEP 2

Consider the Influence of the Heavenly Stem, or Element, on the Earthly Branch of the Year

The Native Element of the Rooster is Yin Metal, and the Heavenly Stem here is Yin Metal, so this is the natural and most quintessential Rooster. Metal here represents the Rooster's precise, analytical qualities, adding refinement, confidence, and precision to the Rooster image, enhancing political, intellectual, and spiritual matters. The Metal Rooster is the most withdrawn, meticulous, and articulate of Roosters, able to use their best qualities with control and order, pecking with precision. Their ability to analyze is so strong that it can lead to belligerence and a compulsion to win. The Metal Element can also lead to delicate mental states and mental health challenges.

STEP 3

Consider the Earthly Branch, or Zodiac Animal, of the Hour

The Rat is the image of the grain rat and is associated with prosperity and a good harvest. They are the smallest and most zoomed-in of the signs and represent the wisdom of what is a composite because it is the nature of the Rat to take things apart to make them small enough to carry. Rats appear in packs and are social; individually, they are not strong, but when they work together, they can take down a whole building. They represent diligence and the capacity of the small to overcome the big. When charged, the Rat is analytical, charming, diligent, perseverant, methodical, sociable, cooperative, discreet, frugal, observant, capable, and fun-loving. When depleted, the Rat is complaining, nervous, nitpicky, stingy, overly analytical, secretive, scheming, cowardly, monomaniacal, and selfish.

STEP 4

Consider the Influence of the Heavenly Stem, or Element, on the Earthly Branch of the Hour

The Native Element of the Rat is Yang Water, and the Heavenly Stem here is Yang Fire. Water controls or douses Fire in the Five Element cycle, so there is a conflict in this dynamic. But here, the Water Element reins in some of the more aggressive qualities of Fire, which adds force, vigor, and courage to the meeker Rat image. Fire Rats are more aggressive and energized than other Rats, and they are excitable and brave Characters who have a Robin Hood–like quality. Fire Rats are the most ambitious and reckless of the Rats, but they can burn out, as the Fire and Water can boil away their inner resources.

STEP 5

Synthesize and Summarize the Earthly Branch and Heavenly Stem of the Year and Hour

Here, we see a Yin and a Yang Character, so they balance out and complement each other well in that regard, but both are paradoxical, for the Rooster can be very extroverted, which seems Yang, and the Rat very tentative and fearful, which seems Yin. In terms of the Five Elements, we see a conflict between the Fire and Metal Elements, and the Fire Element of the hour controls or melts the Metal of the year. The Fire Rat will temper the more aggressive, competitive, and challenging aspects of the Metal Rooster and make them more social, cooperative, and discreet.

The Rooster and the Rat are very similar, as they both represent a more precise, analytical, methodical, and detail-oriented energy. The Rat is very zoomed-in and compartmentalizes details, thoughts, emotions, and so on, and the Rooster is like a scalpel with razor-sharp intellect and analysis. Together, they make a very powerful team and have a strong capacity to resolve Fate: With both tool sets, this Character can accomplish a lot.

The Rat again adds a social, cooperative dynamic that the Rooster does not have, and the Rooster adds bravery and competitiveness that enhances the braver Fire Rat. Together, this is a powerhouse for success in business, science, and really anything that they set their mind to. The challenge here is being maniacal, overfocused, and too attached to the details, so much so that this Character can go crazy. They will likely have mental health challenges and have difficulty reining in their mind.

Again, these are just three examples of many possible combinations. I hope this gives you a sense of how to work with all these different factors and blend the images together. The key is to examine these dynamics through real people. So, look at your own year and hour and discover how these images blend within your own experience. Then, look at your family and friends. This is where you will see these factors come alive.

This, then, becomes a very powerful tool for self-reflection. You should spend a lot of time examining your Character before you engage with the images of Fate, for we do not want to confuse the two, and we also want to understand how they interact. The goal here, if there is such a thing, is to "release" our Characters, to be free to be ourselves. The more we understand and accept our Character and remember that it cannot be changed, the more we find freedom. The more we understand our Character as our capacity and skill set, the more we can utilize it to work with and resolve our Fate. In a way, this can become a kind of therapy; we can use this powerful set of symbols to look at ourselves and understand our behavior.

Now that we have covered the basic aspects of Qi Character, we can move on and begin to explore the complex dynamics of Fate in the Twelve Houses.

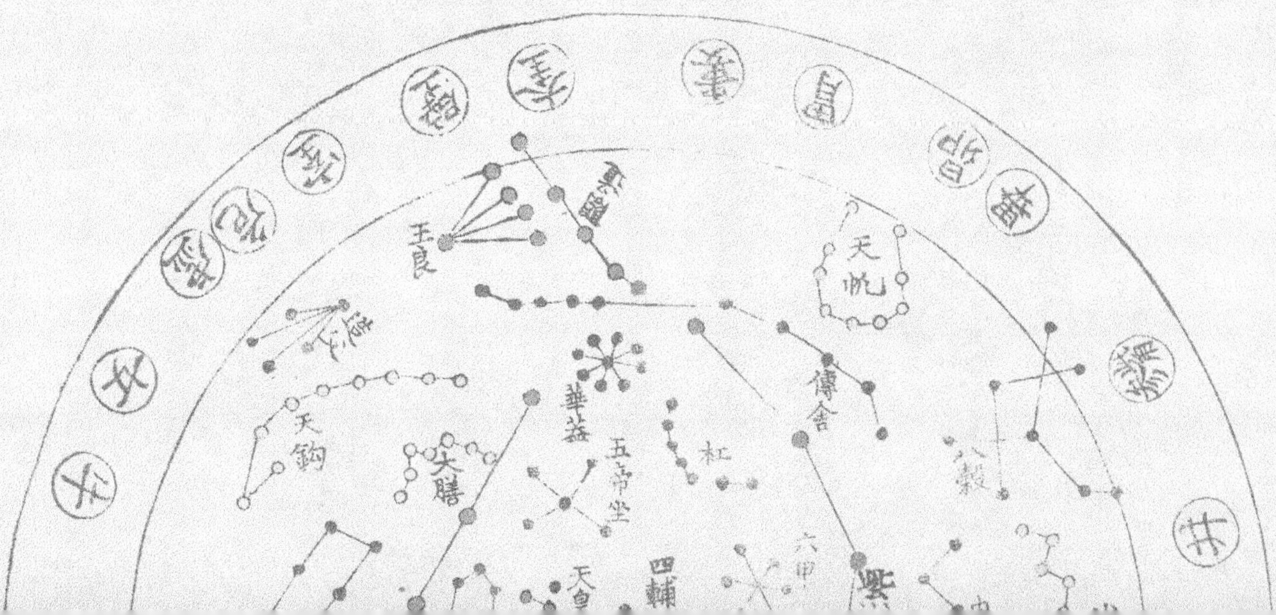

女
王良
天鈎
華蓋
五帝坐
杠
傳舍
八穀
六甲
四輔
井

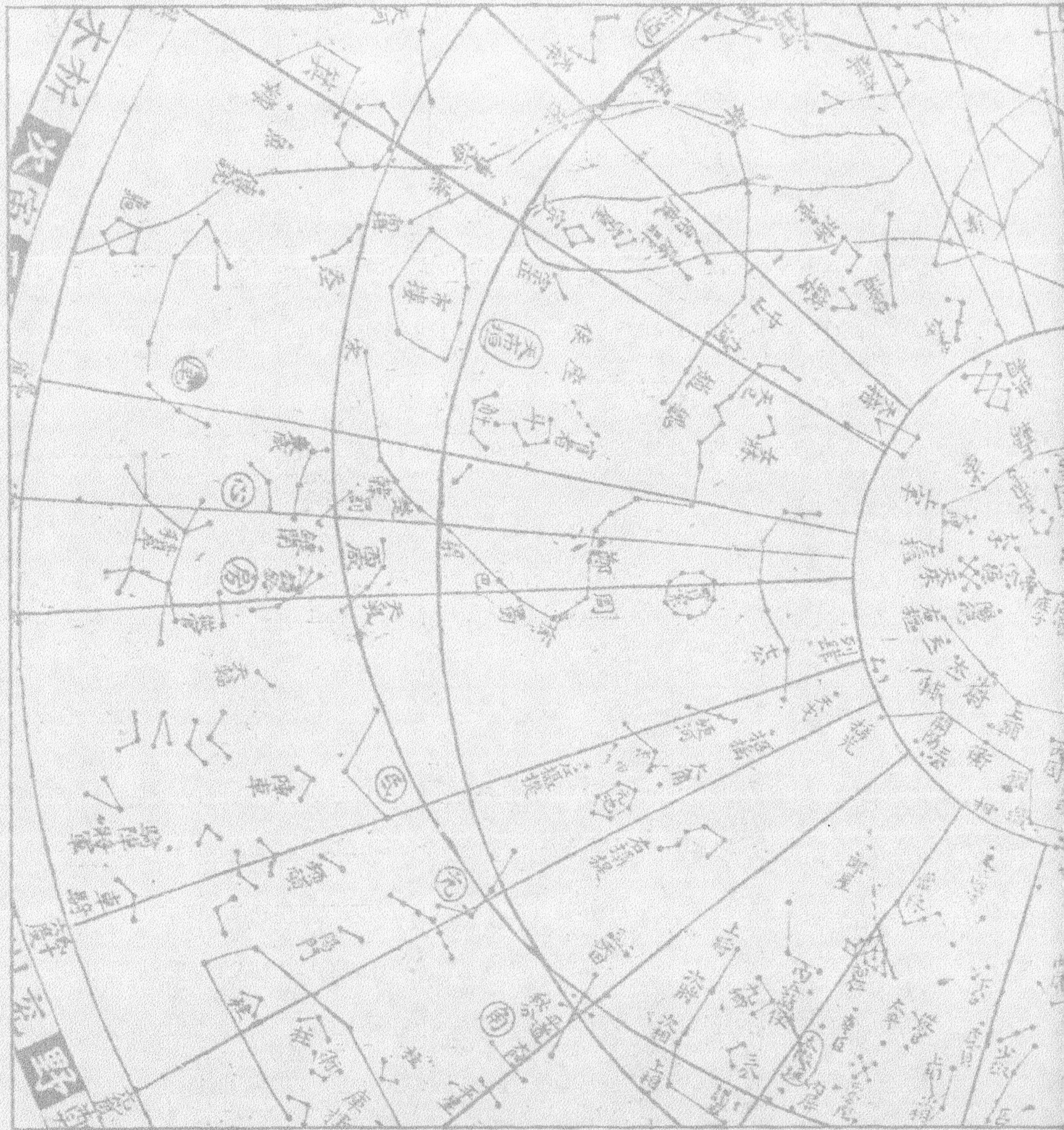

STEP IV

Method, or Shu
術

Part Two
Fate, or Ming (命)

MANTIC ARTISTRY, FATE CALCULATION, AND THE PRACTICE OF ZI WEI DOU SHU (紫微斗數)

MANTIC ARTISTRY AND THE CURRENTS OF FATE

WE NOW COME TO THE SUBJECT OF FATE, MING (命), and the art of interpreting it. And I say art rather than science, for this is a playful act, not fortune-telling. We have discussed the nature and origin of Fate at length, and we will now discuss the symbolic nature of each Star through the Twelve Houses of the Natal Chart. When read together in the context of your life, the Stars create Mingyun (命運), Currents of Fate. In other words, like currents in the ocean, Fate flows in cycles, and we are carried along by these cycles to different destinations. If we let go, we will ultimately be at the mercy of the ocean, and intersecting currents may pull our boat apart. If we understand the direction and timing of these currents, then we can navigate them and even correct our course.

Like Character, Fate is deeply symbolic. If we can understand the Qi of these symbols, we can play with their associations and "divine" them. The more we understand each symbol on its own, the more we can synthesize them and know how they interact with Character and the other symbols of Fate. We can become artists, and great plays and portraits can be envisioned. The past and future become soft; we can see them through a different lens. We can forgive ourselves and others. We can let go of mistakes, failures, or times that we fall short of perfection. We can go with the flow rather than against it. If you swim with the current, then the strength of the current is behind you.

Before we are introduced to the characters of the play in the form of the Stars of the Royal Court, we must familiarize ourselves with the stage and setting represented by the Twelve Houses.

THE TWELVE HOUSES OF POLESTAR ASTROLOGY

LIKE EVERY FORM OF NATAL ASTROLOGY, Polestar Astrology calculates and charts Fate in terms of twelve "Houses." In Western and Indian astrology, the Twelve Houses each comprise 30 degrees of the night's sky, adding up to a 360-degree picture of the heavens. While Polestar Astrology inherited this convention, I must again state that a Polestar chart does not depict the sky. However, the Twelve Houses of Polestar Astrology share many similarities with their Western and Indian counterparts. They also embody some stark differences.

Before we can delve into the Stars of Polestar Astrology, we must examine the Twelve Houses, for the meaning of any given Star is relative to its placement within a House. The Emperor Star in the Offspring Palace presents a very different image of Fate than this same Star in the Pleasure Palace, although both could result in children.

A Stem and Branch—an Element and a zodiac Animal—rule each House. There is a Dragon Palace, Snake Palace, Horse Palace, and so on. Depending on the individual calculation, your Youth Palace, for example, may be ruled by Yang Water Dragon. In addition to a ruling Star, a Heavenly Stem and an Earthly Branch—a Yinyang Element and a Zodiac Animal—rule each House, and these vary according to one's chart. Because of this, each of the Twelve Palaces—the Ming Palace, the Ancestors Palace, and so on—is sometimes referred to by the particular Earthly Branch that is ruling it: the Snake Palace or the Horse Palace, for example, according to one's chart. The influence of the Heavenly Stem and Earthly Branch on each House do not drastically affect the interpretation of the Stars but can sometimes diminish or exalt their influence. The Emperor Star, for example, is exalted in the Dragon and Horse Palaces. I will discuss this further when we discuss "luminous" Stars, "exalted" Houses, and Fate Thresholds.

Unlike Western and Indian astrology, the value system of the Twelve Houses is decidedly Confucian. Indian astrology is remarkably complex in its many layers of interpretation, and this kind of analysis is often necessary in a reading. Polestar Astrology, on the other hand, is not as concerned with that kind of detail. However, many details are available, such as influences from previous Houses, 120- and 180-degree influences (trines and opposites), borrowed Stars, auspicious Star Formations, and others. However, that kind of analysis often misses the forest for the trees.

Polestar Astrology is concerned with the "big picture" of our Fate regarding our relationships and participation in society. Each House has esoteric interpretations, but the mundane interpretation is the main one. The Houses, therefore, have a straightforward meaning. While any given House in Indian astrology may have hundreds of possible layers and meanings, in Polestar Astrology, the Offspring Palace is about your Fate as a parent, period. I appreciate the simplicity and power of the Twelve Houses, but if you're looking for psychology or insight into your deepest spiritual yearnings, maybe look to Jyotish.

Polestar Astrology is mainly concerned with our Fate in relationships and in the "world," which mostly means family and career in the modern context. It does not say much about the type of career you should have, but it does say whether your Fate will be resolved through your career and how and

<table>
<tr><td>MING
命宫
Snake Palace</td><td>ANCESTORS
父母宫
Horse Palace</td><td>PLEASURE
福德宫
Goat Palace</td><td>PROPERTY
田宅宫
Monkey Palace</td></tr>
<tr><td>YOUTH
兄弟宫
Dragon Palace</td><td colspan="2" rowspan="2"></td><td>SUPERIORS
官禄宫
Rooster Palace</td></tr>
<tr><td>PARTNERS
夫妻宫
Rabbit Palace</td><td>ASSISTANTS
交友宫
Dog Palace</td></tr>
<tr><td>OFFSPRING
子女宫
Tiger Palace</td><td>WEALTH
财帛宫
Ox Palace</td><td>HEALTH
疾厄宫
Rat Palace</td><td>CAREER/TRAVEL
遷移宫
Pig Palace</td></tr>
</table>

when that will likely happen. It offers a key to what we call "Fate Thresholds," which is not a matter of what but where, or which House. If your primary Fate is to be a parent, then your career is not as important, even if society tells you so.

The Twelve Houses provide a powerful yet straightforward map that shows where your Fate and opportunities in life will unfold. They cover just about every aspect of human life.

The first three Houses are read together, representing our overall Ancestral mandates.

MING PALACE

Summary of Fate and Hints of Character

The first House, or "Ascendant," is called the Ming Palace. Again, the Chinese character Ming (命) means life, Fate, Mandate of Heaven, destiny, purpose, and so on, but for our purposes, we leave it untranslated as the Ming Palace, for this idea is simply too broad to be captured in one English word. The character Gong (宫) means "palace" or "court" and is the same for each Palace, which we will also refer to as a House.

The Ming Palace gives us the big picture or a "principle" for unraveling Fate. The Star or Stars that appear here are your ruling Stars, which reveal the primary image or nature of your Fate in this lifetime. The attributes of your ruling Stars relate to your overall opportunities in life, and the Ming Palace is the only House that relates directly to your Character or capacity (the rest of the Houses are related indirectly).

The Stem and Branch of the year and hour you were born in give the primary image of your Character, but the ruling Star of the Ming Palace also give us an idea of what you're like as a person. My ruling Star is the Empress, but she's afflicted, so I'm like a moody Empress.

The Stars that appear here do not offer much insight into the specific events of Fate, but they indicate the "gravity" of our Fate. Since the Stars are organized in a hierarchy, the more potent Stars suggest a more potent or heavy Fate. A "heavy" or potent Fate is full of predestined affinities, responsibilities, and obligations, which requires our time and attention and usurps our freedom. A "light" Fate gives us more freedom and makes relationships and responsibilities less cumbersome.

The Ming Palace can be empty, which is called a Kong Gong (空宫), or Empty Palace, which means it is possible to be born without major Fate. An empty Ming Palace implies a life of Freedom to clear up minor details, help, and generally benefit others. It can manifest as confusion, lack of purpose, or lack of direction, for example, but it also implies an intentional birth, what Buddhists call a manifesting as a bodhisattva, in which you resolved your central Fate in a previous lifetime and came back intentionally to help and guide others. It can also imply that your Ancestors resolved your Fate for you and gave you a free pass this time around.

The nature of this House reveals the certainty or likelihood that you will resolve Fate in this lifetime. If one of the Four Rulers shows up here, then the resolution is almost guaranteed, provided you don't screw it up. If the primary image of Fate is afflicted, then life is characterized by a hue of struggle. Fate can, in this case, still be resolved, but we must use our freedom wisely and look to the other eleven Houses as to where that resolution can take place.

The Ming Palace is where we examine the essential astrological principle of Ganying (感應), or reciprocity. We look at how the overall nature of Fate will interact with a person's Character. If, like me, you have a very Yin Fate, characterized by the Empress Star, with a very Yang Character, like a Tiger born in Dragon hour, then this creates a certain dynamic that may result in struggle. This could be viewed as inauspicious. If you have a very exalted Yang Fate like the Emperor in this House and you're a Dragon, then this is a match of capacity meeting opportunity, which would be interpreted as very auspicious. The same situation would be inauspicious for a Rabbit or Snake, whose instinct is to hide and shy away from the spotlight.

The auspicious Ganying, or reciprocity, between Character (capacity) and Fate (opportunity) is what the Chinese call "Destiny." It is also simply called luck. The First House, when read with the Character, can tell us if a person potentially has Destiny, which would be something like an Exalted

Ming Palace with a good match between Character and Fate; this can create a threshold for Destiny, but the person must still use their Freedom wisely and step up to the opportunity, which not everyone does.

Traditionally, the Ming Palace is also said to offer an image of a person's appearance, but I have not found this to have much significance. It's too simplistic. However, I would say that I have an elegant and Empress-like demeanor, as she is my ruling Star.

This House is always read first and sometimes again last to reinforce the central image or "story" of Fate.

ANCESTORS PALACE

Ancestors and Parents: Elders, Filial Piety, Ancestral Mandates, Talents, Past Lives

Technically, the Fumu Gong (父母宮), or Ancestors Palace, is the twelfth and last House, but I always read it second with my clients and will do the same here and throughout the book. I do this because the Ancestor, Ming, and Youth Palaces are all intimately connected to the Fate with our family, parents, ancestors, and siblings, and these relationships deeply shape our lives. Together, they form the basis or background of a chart, so it useful to discuss it in the beginning rather than last. The characters Fumu (父母) literally mean "father/mother or parents," but in the Chinese Tradition, our parents are a lot more than our parents. Our father and mother represent the connection to our Ancestral lineage and symbolize our "precedent" or inheritance—everything that came before us and "caused" our birth.

Yang Stars represent our connection to our "Patriarchal" Ancestors, which can be every person on your father's side, including women, or it can be all the men in your family, including men from your mother's side. The Yin Stars represent our "Matriarchal" Ancestors, which can be all the women in the family or all the people on your mother's side, including men. It is up to you and your affinity, or your client's, to decide which is the case; it can also be both. The Stars in the Ancestors Palace represent the Yin and Yang of your heritage—your Ancestral or Source Qi, called Yuan Qi (元氣).

Superficially, this House can represent our Fated relationship with our parents, which can be the most meaningful relationship in our lives. It represents what the Chinese call Xiao (孝), or filial piety, which is our Fated responsibility to our parents and all that entails. You may be Fated to take care of your parents throughout life, and this House can reveal these mandated debts. It also tells us about their obligations to protect or take care of you.

It is easy to see family trauma and abuse here. In modern times, we "psychologize" our parental experience and spend a lot of energy examining the issues around our early nurturing with frameworks like attachment, family systems, and object relations theory. You can see that early nurturing in this House, as well as cues to the nature of the birth itself. This House represents more than the personal matter of sorting things out with your living Ancestors, but also the long line of dead people who reproduced successfully to give you a body. You can also, then, see inherited talents, abilities, and drives, as well as addictive and neurotic behaviors.

I read this House second because it represents our Fated affinity "behind the scenes"; it is a gate to the Spirit World, the unseen influences that shape our lives. In the Chinese Tradition, the dead profoundly affect the living. This House can represent up to and including seven generations of Ancestral patterning, depending on the arrangements that show up here. You may be connected to what the Chinese call an "Original Ancestor," or Yuan Zu (元祖): someone far, far back in the family line. You may have a deep-fated affinity with a great-great-grandmother whom you will never meet or even see a picture of. You may also have no connection whatsoever to the family you are born into.

Like the Ming Palace, the influence of this House reveals the nature of your Fate in all the Houses, for if your Ancestors bless your life, then no matter what difficulties you face, you will feel blessed. These Stars are like fairy godparents, protectors, or guardian angels. They conspire to provide you with opportunities, guidance, and connections.

However, you may also be born with an afflicted Ancestral Ghost pattern. Your life may be influenced by powerful self-destructive habits, Ancestral patterns of addiction, and illnesses that are not of your own making. You may receive a mountain of unfinished business that compels you into obsessive ambitions that have nothing to do with you. For example, you may inherit a family business and be raised to take it over, which you go along with, but secretly you want to be an artist and resent the burden of all the responsibility. You receive tremendous privilege and opportunity, though, so is this a blessing or a curse? That's up to you to decide, but this House tells us about our obligations to our Ancestors that must be fulfilled one way or another.

The Daoist interpretation of Polestar Astrology looks at this House in terms of what we call "Ghost profiling," and they take it to be the most significant House, spiritually speaking. Buddhists read this House as a picture of your previous lifetimes and past-life Fate. Both are acceptable interpretations.

When Ghost Stars show up here, or if they rule any House, I encourage people to study their genealogy and find as many stories as possible about who they come from. There is often a story somewhere in the family line that has been forgotten, a person who wants to be remembered for their struggle. You might continue to repeat their struggle until this story is told.

YOUTH PALACE

Time of Youth and Siblings: Childhood, Ancestral Mandates, School

The characters of the second House, Xiongdi (兄弟), are translated literally as "siblings," but we translate it as the Youth Palace, for it represents both our Fated relationship with siblings and the time of life that we call "youth," which is not clearly defined in our culture because we lack rites of passage. This House represents our possibility of resolving Fate in childhood through sibling relationships, early education, early life experience, and development.

All Chinese people receive three names, such as Mao Ze Dong (毛泽东): Dong is his personal name, Mao is his family name, and Ze is a name that he shares with his siblings. It represents the Chinese idea that we share a deep, Fated connection, a "shared body of Fate," with our siblings. So, this House can represent past-life connections with siblings.

Perhaps you were soldiers on the battlefield, and one of you died unable to protect the other, so now, as brothers, you shoot toy guns with each other and complete the circle. You may have been best friends in a past life and were so close that, this time around, you are brother and sister. It is also very possible that you have no Fated connection whatsoever to your siblings, and you grow up feeling like strangers. You may have half- or stepsiblings with whom you share a deep bond or no connection at all.

This House also represents the notion that one child in a family may receive more Ancestral Fate or mandates than another child. If the elder brother has a potent Star in the Youth Palace and the younger brother does not, then the elder brother may be responsible for completing the family's Fate. However, it was often the case that a younger sibling received this Fate and would be the one to take over a family business.

The Youth Palace may represent the distribution of resources, inheritance, and responsibilities in terms of family life. You may have to grow up early and become a second parent, raising your younger siblings, because Dad is out of the picture. Or, you may have an elder sister who protects and parents you more than your parents.

Sibling Fate may provide emotional support or be a source of affliction, argument, and discord that may never be resolved. Many clients have told me that they never speak to their siblings. Once, I had only begun to describe a Ghost Star in this House before the client replied, "Oh yeah, my brother is possessed!"

Potent Stars in this Palace can represent the strong influence of elders, mentors, aunts and uncles, and so on; it represents the presence of Ancestral Qi in our early life. Ghost Stars can represent unreliable, inappropriate adult protection or supervision in youth. An afflicted Youth Palace can represent early trauma, conflicts, and challenges that shape us for the rest of our lives, which can take place at home or school. In that sense, the influence of this House can extend far beyond youth, for so much of our lives now is spent processing our childhood.

The most important theme of this House is whether Fate is resolved in youth. I have an empty and afflicted Youth Palace, so although a lot happened to me during this time, these events did not resolve my Fate but rather created a tangle of traumatic Fate that I am resolving now as an adult. I often feel like a lot happened, but, in terms of completing my Fate, nothing happened. I did not exit childhood with any sense of resolution.

An exalted Youth Palace suggests that a person can complete their Fate in childhood, which I have seen many times, for these people are often at a loss about what to do with the rest of their lives, and therefore they consult an astrologer. Our culture does not accept the notion that a person can be complete in life before eighteen, but Fate-wise, this can be the case. It is possible to resolve your major Fate playing house with your sister—an idea that I try to communicate to clients, but I'm not sure people get it.

An exalted Youth Palace indicates what the Tibetans call a ***tulku***: that is, a person born with the Fated spiritual legacy, skills, and/or maturity of an adult. What in the West we might call an "old soul." People with exalted Youth Palaces basically pick up where they left off in their last life and tie up loose ends before they even exit grade school. These people are often precocious and show early signs of maturity, ambition, and so on. They often can't wait to be adults, and can spend their youth bucking authority, running away from home, and so on. They often feel like adults are idiots, or they may relate more to adults than to their peers, feeling above kid games. An exalted Youth Palace also implies that as an adult a person is then free to shape their life in whatever way they want, rather than continue to pursue Ancestral patterns of Fate.

The following two Houses are read together, for they relate to our Fate to partner and start our own family.

PARTNERS PALACE

Partners and Marriage: Long-Term Relationships

The characters for this House, Fu Qi (夫妻), literally mean "husband and wife," so we translate this as the Partners Palace. This House does not indicate other types of partnership, like business partnerships (that would be in the Assistants Palace) but refers specifically to our Fate with long-term relationship patterns.

This House expresses the Chinese concept of Yinyuan (姻緣), which refers to a predestined relationship. The image used to describe this is of two trees that appear separate, but beneath the surface, their roots are intertwined. Another term used here is "previously betrothed," which implies a past-life commitment that continues from life to life. This is somewhat similar but much less romantic than the Western idea of "soulmates," for this House also includes negative past-life connections. The variety of paired Stars that can appear in this House can play out in a dizzying array of possibilities that stretch the traditional Chinese intention and interpretation of this House, which refers to arranged marriage.

The Stars in this House reveal the depth and importance of relationships and partners in your life. Stars here can relate to your partner's appearance or character or to the nature of the relationship itself. They can also reveal a pattern of relating that has nothing to do with specific people but with your own desires and fantasies instead.

Major Stars often indicate specific Fated connections that may be resolved through marriage, or they can relate to many Fated partnerships. I once told someone born in the Year of the Pig struggling in marriage that they did not have Fate with one person but with many, which they knew but had been resisting due to the expectations of monogamy. This was a relief for them because Pigs have the tendency to fall in love with everyone, which goes to show the importance of Character when reading this House. Each Qi Character has a different relationship to relationships, and it is good to know these patterns well when interpreting this House.

Traditionally, the Chinese placed significant importance on the marriage ceremony itself as crucial in resolving Fate between two people, especially if the House is exalted or contains heavily "Ancestral" Stars, like the Oracle. Marriage, to the Chinese and to most traditional cultures, was not romantic but for joining two families. The ceremony was a ritual in which all the Ancestors of the two family lines, living and deceased, met and blessed the joining of two people.

So, traditionally, the main event in the liberation of Ancestral Fate is the marriage ceremony, not the marriage itself. Liu Ming often insisted that people with the Emperor or Empress in this House have a ceremony and invite as many family members as possible. Traditional Chinese and Indian marriage ceremonies include requesting permission from the family elders, somewhat like the European tradition of the father "giving away the bride"—a patriarchal custom, which in India is reversed: The man must ask permission from the matriarchy.

Significant Stars in this House imply that the unraveling of our Fate comes through our relationship with another person. Perhaps your life is stuck and stagnant, and then suddenly, you meet someone who whisks you into a world of adventure that introduces you to things you could never do without, and it changes you forever. Perhaps they create opportunities in your life that influence your career, spiritual path, and sense of purpose. Perhaps your relationship is boring by all appearances, but this person becomes your anchor in life, supporting you through all the ups and downs. This kind of Fate often unravels in terms of the next House, the Offspring Palace. For many people, family life becomes the center of their Fate.

Afflicted by Ghost Stars, this House can represent many patterns of struggle. Ghost Stars in this House suggest Ancestors who died feeling unloved, unwanted, betrayed, abandoned, or abused by their partners—a pattern you inherit to play out while "dating." Of course, our culture is profoundly disorganized and even sick when it comes to relationships, sex, and so on, so it may seem like everyone is playing out these kinds of patterns today, regardless of individual Fate. I am always refreshed to find normal monogamous couples who get along; it seems like a rarity these days.

Depending on Character, Ghost Stars may cause people to drift from one partner to another, disappointed, dissatisfied, and frustrated. They may prompt someone to repeatedly choose the wrong people, getting into or staying in abusive situations. Ghost Stars may cause quarrels, differences, and rifts between people that end in divorce. Their resolution often teaches people how to be in relationships. Perhaps you had a challenging relationship that taught you how to be a partner, and now you are free to have a healthy marriage.

Ghost Stars can also influence patterns of self-undermining—of always wanting what you can't have, holding impossible standards that no one can live up to, and so on—based on Ghostly needs and fantasies about the "perfect person" (who, of course, does not exist). Ghost Stars may cause some people to give up on their partnership altogether and choose to be alone, while deep down hoping to meet the right person. Or they may choose unconventional patterns of relationship that do not fit into social norms.

A classic story is about a young man who marries before going to war. Every day, he looks at the photo in his wallet, yearning to be home with his love. Back home, she waits patiently for him to return. He dies in battle, and his last thought is to return to her. In the Bardo, he searches for her and finds that she remarried and forgot about him. Or she never marries again and forever laments her long-lost love. Two generations later, you inherit the pattern of longing for your lost love from your great-uncle and spend your life searching for the perfect person, who is always out of reach.

It is also possible to have no significant Fate with a life partner, in which case you are free to choose or be chosen. Not everyone has a match made in heaven, and not everyone is Fated to struggle. People with empty Partners Palaces often feel disappointed, since there won't be a Prince Charming, but it may also mean that there will be fifty you must choose from. An empty Partners Palace means you build Fate with the person you choose so long as you remain together.

And yes, there is potential for love and happily-ever-after, but the Fate for this is rare. We hear stories of people marrying high-school sweethearts and growing old together. This kind of strong Fate often runs out; if people don't learn how to work with freedom in this regard, it can dissipate. Your Fate may be "done" with someone, in which case separating can be natural and not harmful; divorce is not always bad, and can often be a positive conclusion to a Fated relationship that is "done." Or, you can, of course, stay together as a celebration of choice and freedom, but you must continue to choose each other.

OFFSPRING PALACE

Offspring: Children, Adoption, Sexual Identity, Legacy

The characters for this House, Zinǚ (子女), means sons and daughters, so we translate it as the Offspring Palace. This House reveals our Ancestral mandate to create more Ancestors and our Fate with children and parenting. Traditionally, the fate of being a parent pays back a Fated debt, which is eighteen-plus years of taking care of someone who once took care of you in a previous life. You own them big, and give them human birth, which they then owe in return and must repay through gratitude and service. Parenting, in this sense, is about completing Fated obligations and letting go of personal freedom.

It is important to note that this House tells us more about your Fate as a parent and not so much about the Fate of your children, although it can give hints about their Character and Fate. If significant Stars show up here, completing the Fate indicated to have a fulfilling life is essential. People with significant Stars here who choose not to have children may miss out on a meaningful relationship that would otherwise have been crucial to their Fate.

Today, many people choose not to be parents for various reasons, and many have children much later in life. So, this House is getting harder and harder to interpret in today's culture. Essentially, this House represents our "Jing," our fundamental predilection toward embodiment, toward reproducing ourselves, so although it is primarily about children, there are other interpretations we can derive from this principle.

Clearly, some people are born to be parents. Strong Stars in this House mean that being a parent provides all the critical life lessons and becomes central to your understanding of what it means to be human. A Fated past-life connection with a child brings deep joy, meaning, and fulfillment in life. The unconditional love of parenthood transforms you beyond what you could have imagined, and you can't imagine life without your children.

From the Chinese perspective, that feeling of a past-life connection here can also indicate a "returning Ancestor," a person being reborn in the same family line. This may be a great-grandmother coming back as your child. In this case, the Chinese would often name children after Ancestors. If you research your genealogy, you may find that you are a dead ringer for one of your Ancestors, in which case you may be a returning Ancestor.

This House indicates how to be a parent. It may suggest conventional methods and/or go beyond the standard notions of parenting. Some children require a lot of attention, guidance, and advice. Others are "self-starters" who take charge of their parents' lives.

We assume that children are innocent and helpless, but this is almost never the case. Children are not *tabula rasa*, clean slates; they each come with their own Fate and need much less control than we often impose. Some kids need to be left alone to wander in the woods and skin their knees, while others are very sensitive and need a lot of protection to flourish.

Your Stars here can indicate the nature of your child or children. Yin Stars are often interpreted as girls, and Yang Stars are often interpreted as boys, and although this is somewhat accurate, it is not always the case. Yang Stars often represent independent, precocious children who do not need much parenting, and Yin Stars often represent more "sensitive" children who require a lot of support. The nature of the different Stars indicates what kind of support that may be. If you give birth to an Oracle who sees Ghosts, they may require a different kind of upbringing than a Vassal who should play team sports.

This House also brings up an essential idea that we have difficulty accepting in America: A child may resolve your

Fate for you. In China, they say, "A child brings honor to the family name," or Guangzong Yaozu (光宗耀祖). This means that your children may grow to be successful and fulfill your Fate in career and wealth for you. You may work hard in your career so your child can become the artist you always wanted to be. Or you may work hard to send them to college to become a doctor or lawyer and then support you in old age.

We also believe that children are expensive. Many say they will have kids when they get their lives in order, make enough money, or get the right job. But this House suggests that children might bring this Fate. Having a child may create the Fate opportunities you are seeking. You may be poor, but if you have the Fate to give birth to an Empress, and she demands a castle, then her Fate may cause you to get a promotion and raise. People with strong Fate here should have children even if their lives are imperfect, for the children bring order and resources. When I see strong Stars here without the affliction of Ghost Stars, I often emphatically say, "MAKE THE BABIES!!!"

When a person is childless or chooses not to have children and has major Stars in this House, we may interpret it differently. As I said earlier, this House is about Jing, so Fate here may reveal a Fated pattern around sexuality, sexual identity, or the reproductive system. I have seen many instances of this being the case, although it can be a sensitive subject that clients are shy about discussing.

Ghost Stars here can indicate miscarriages, abortions, difficulty conceiving, and so on. These incomplete pregnancies can "haunt" the mother or siblings for many years. Traditional cultures often have rituals for resolving children who don't make it to birth. These kinds of Ghosts can linger and produce the odd feeling that someone who is supposed to be here is absent. As an only child, you may have felt like you had a sister; you may have felt her presence, poured tea for her, talked to her, and so on. These feelings usually fade in adulthood, but many people remember having imaginary friends.

Ghosts can also indicate conflicted relationships between parents and their children. Ghost patterns can cause discord, arguments, and disagreements. Or they can create distance, separation, or the feeling that you have nothing in common. These children may leave home early, or rifts may cause you not to speak for many years. You may even lose a child to illness or accident.

If someone chooses not to have children or is childless for other reasons, then this House can become about legacy. Someone may create a product, a business, a brand, a book, a trust fund, and so on to leave behind for future generations. They may spend their lives working on a project that is like their "child." They may gestate, birth, nurture, and release something into the world that fulfills this Fate.

This House also indicates Fate to be a stepparent, to adopt, or to raise someone else's children. A friend of mine, for example, was adopted and has a very clear Fate to be a stepfather, which he has fulfilled. It can also indicate working with children as a nanny, a kindergarten teacher, and so on, in which case you parent many children. I had one client who worked with inner-city youth and felt like a parent to hundreds of kids. She never had kids of her own, yet she felt this aspect of her life was fulfilled.

It is also possible for men to have Fate with children and even with miscarriage and abortion that comes through women, which is perhaps difficult to grok. A woman may have no Fate to be a mother, but the father comes along, and his Ancestors take over the process.

It is very possible to have Fate with a child but not with a partner. Some women just need a sperm donor. Dad may be needed only for a few minutes, while the mother's Fate with the child lasts a lifetime. Or Dad may have the Fate and become a single father; it is rare for this to play out, but it does happen. He may also resolve Fate through being a "weekend" Dad. The time may be sparse, but it could be precious and resolve his Fate, being the only meaningful time in his life.

Traditionally, the influence of this House is said to fade for women during menopause. So, suppose a woman has significant Stars here and misses the opportunity. In that case, the relationship will be postponed until the next lifetime, and she may be reborn to complete the parenthood that never happened. That could even be the case for someone in this lifetime.

The Property and Wealth can be read together to determine a person's overall Fate with prosperity. The Property Palace, however, comes later as the tenth House.

WEALTH PALACE

Wealth: Finances, Resources, Inheritance, General Fortune

The Characters for this House, Cai Bo (財帛), are straightforward and literally mean "wealth": Cai means "money, resources, valuables," and so on, and Bo refers to silk, or "finery." So, we call this the Wealth Palace. This House reveals a person's Fate with cash, hard currency, investments, inheritance, windfall, and prosperity. It indicates their human capital and their ability to generate income and use and save money through industry and effort. It can also represent Fated connections with wealthy people.

In principle, it represents our Fate with managing our resources, which meant something much different in ancient China than today. In this sense, it should always be read with the Property Palace to understand a person's overall Fate with prosperity.

In an agricultural society, wealth was considered cyclical. In cyclical time, wealth varies according to the cycles and seasons. Spring brings the wealth of "new," summer the wealth of "abundance," fall the wealth of "harvest," and winter the wealth of "storage." In other words, when you live with the cycles of nature, especially if you are a hunter or farmer, you accept times of abundance and scarcity as demonstrations of Nature itself, nothing to get excited or panic about.

Our culture operates on the myth of linear time, which may be human history's greatest disaster. We view wealth as an endless, aggressive pursuit of acquisition; we attempt to live in eternal summer, which cannot be done. A select few have abundance, and the rest live in scarcity.

Obviously, the cyclical values of this tradition do not align with consumerist, American values. Then, we must interpret this House with the larger Fate of our culture in mind, which has most people in debt, living paycheck to paycheck, trying to make ends meet.

In the Chinese view, you are not poor if you have air to breathe, water to drink, food to eat, and good people in your life. Wealth is something that comes and goes in cycles in an atmosphere of nature's generosity. This House demonstrates the principle of wealth, although we often read it concerning money because that is what our society dictates.

Because our society has such a crude relationship to wealth, this House is straightforward in interpretation. The Stars in this House, especially Yang Stars, indicate how our Ancestral or past-life Fate comes to pay us back in the form of income. Most Stars are modest in interpretation. On the surface, they can indicate if you will be paid well, or fairly, for your efforts or whether your finances will increase steadily throughout your life. Yang Stars often indicate that your income is from direct sources; you may work a nine-to-five job and earn a paycheck. Yang Stars convey the American dream of hard work and getting paid for your effort, "pulling yourself up by your bootstraps."

Yin Stars, then, tend to indicate that your money comes from more indirect sources. This may be in the form of family money, inheritance, unexpected windfall, legal settlements, benefactors, financial loans, alimony checks, investments, savings, stocks, bonds, subscriptions, or side jobs. They could also indicate that you are a consultant, advisor, or philanthropist, and the money you earn, distribute, or manage is only tangentially related to the money you help produce.

Yin Stars also represent a flux in income that comes and goes. People with Yin Fate here may, at times, be interested in earning and doing well; at other times, they have no interest and are content with very little. Unafflicted by Ghost Stars, Yin Stars are considered a gift from your own past-life generosity or simply a privilege inherited from your Ancestors.

Ghost Stars usually indicate a struggle with finances that we interpret as Ancestral patterns around scarcity. Perhaps your great-grandfather worked his ass off to get the family started in America, but he died poor, worried about his family's future. You, then, inherit both his work ethic and insecurity, working sixty hours a week only to feel lack and want. This Fate may be resolved if your perseverance finally pays off: You get promoted, work less, or retire and feel satisfied, freeing the Ancestral pattern. Or it could be resolved by changing your relationship to money altogether, renouncing everything and living on a self-sustaining farm.

These Ghostly patterns can come in the form of debt: medical, legal, and so on. You may be Fated to work hard, only to lose everything in extensive legal battles. Or you may get sick and be overwhelmed by medical bills. You may inherit a family fortune that is fraught with challenges you did not expect. As we say, more money, more problems. Ghosts can certainly manifest as irresponsible, selfish, or careless behavior with money.

In some cases, Ghosts Stars are associated with "windfall," meaning sudden, unexpected income. This may come in the form of gambling: striking it big in Vegas or winning the lottery. Liu Ming would often tell people with certain patterns to test their luck in this regard. Traditionally, the windfall is viewed as a Ghost resolving through one last throw of the dice. However, the danger of this Ghost pattern is to win big and then lose big. If this happens, take the money and run!

An exalted Wealth Palace indicates that your major Fate is resolved through engaging with resources. The real crux of Fate's resolution in this House is the feeling of satisfaction, contentment, completion, and so on—the feeling that you are and have enough.

An exalted Wealth Palace can indicate doing very well financially. It can indicate prosperity, but if you get rich and feel no satisfaction, then you are not resolving Fate. If you are not generous and do not give back, then you are not resolving Fate. You may have a good Fate to earn a fortune, but if you are greedy, then this turns Ghostly very fast.

Your Fate may be a rags-to-riches story. You may be born into poverty, but if your Wealth Palace is exalted, doing well is not a matter of if but when. Again, it does not indicate the amount of money earned but the corresponding feeling of contentment and satisfaction that comes from having what you need, which inspires the feeling of generosity. Generosity is the natural outcome of abundance.

This House can also give us hints about career choices. Polestar Astrology does not indicate specific careers all that clearly, even in the career Houses, but the Wealth Palace can indicate being paid as a consultant, artist, doctor, healer, astrologer, spirit medium, teacher, and so on. Of course, you can do all these things without any astrological indication whatsoever.

HEALTH PALACE

Health: Physical Constitution, Illness, Death, Doctoring

The Characters for this House, Ji E (疾厄), literally mean "disease or sickness" and "distress or disaster," and traditionally this House was called the Death Palace. We, however, translate it as Health Palace, because death has become a little too morbid in our culture for us to relate to and because this House covers a lot of health-related factors. In fact, this is one of the more difficult Houses to interpret, due to the variety of experiences it can refer to.

The Stars appearing in this House can refer to a person's physical constitution, their Fate with illness and injury, their capacity to heal and recover, their relationships or Fate with doctors and healers, and their Fate with medical treatments. It also has implications concerning a person's longevity and the potential for early death or long life. The Stars here may reveal patterns around diet, exercise, and lifestyle. They may reveal Ancestral patterns of illness, congenital conditions and predispositions, and Fate for addiction, abuse, and so on. This House can also reveal a talent and affinity for practicing medicine and the Fate of becoming a healer, which often happens after a process of personal illness and recovery. We can say that the House refers to all aspects of health and well-being: mental, emotional, and physical.

The Polestar interpretations of the various Stars have many implications in Classical Chinese Medicine. Each Star has its own associations with illnesses, syndromes, and parts of the body, as well as organ networks and the Five Elements. The Stars also correlate to certain seasons and can tell us if a person heals best in the spring, summer, fall, winter, or in the seasonal transitions.

To understand this House, we must understand the basics of Chinese medicine. Chinese medicine seeks a certain balance and has no concept of an "ideal state" that exists separate from the individual. Our sense of normal is always in flux, changing relative to our age, the season, and the environment in which we live. In other words, there is no normal or healthy standard, for one person's medicine is another's poison. Chinese medicine is also not morbid; death may be the perfect resolution of illness or Fate, given certain situations. The hysterical preservation of life at all costs does not fit in with this tradition. It may be someone's Fate to go through a debilitating illness and not recover, for they may, in that process, understand the very meaning of life, and who are we to judge?

As symbolic representations of Ancestors, the Stars offer an image of inherited Ancestral patterns of illness, and the House can be read in correlation with the Ancestors Palace as an image of a person's inherited constitution and genetic memory, or what we now call "epigenetics." Illnesses that do not respond to standard treatments and that do not have clear medical diagnoses are thought of as being inherited from the unsettled dead.

It is important to note that the Stars in this House *cannot* be used to predict illness or disease, but they can maybe be used for prognosis. We cannot determine if someone will fall ill, but if they do, we can determine the nature of the condition in relation to Ancestral patterns, and we can determine the likelihood of recovery. Astrology is not an alternative to medical diagnosis but can be used as an effective tool to aid treatment. Many factors of Character also determine a person's elemental makeup, such as excessive Fire in a chart, which can tell us much about their health issues.

As astrologers, we must not jump to conclusions and predict illness, disease, or death. We are not fortune tellers. For example, I have looked at the chart of Stephen Hawking and many charts of people with debilitating illnesses. I have seen many people with the same Star arrangement as Hawking, who have very different expressions of the same Stars, and I have seen people with the same condition who have different Star arrangements. There is a vast range of potential possibilities in each Star, and we cannot predict how they will manifest. I have jumped to conclusions before and been very surprised by how different the client's situation is expressed. So, I always give as many interpretations as possible and do my best not to jump to conclusions and scare people who have a potentially challenging Health Palace. We also don't want to avoid complicated possibilities and sugarcoat a situation.

Ghost Stars here can create various experiences, ranging from chronic, subclinical, and minor conditions to allergies and food sensitivities, mental and emotional problems, and so on. An afflicted Health Palace may manifest for one person as an unhealthy obsession with illness, such as hypochondria. Or it may compel a person to seek medical attention constantly: They may go to an acupuncturist one day, a chiropractor the next, and a shamanic healer on the weekend, followed by a fast, a cleanse, and then an obsessive fixation on the next fad diet.

Ghosts can cause mistreatment, overtreatment, and improper or incorrect diagnosis due to constantly changing symptoms. Or, an afflicted Health Palace can manifest as accidents, injuries, accident-prone behavior, and even suicidal tendencies, risk-taking, and addictions that push the body's limits.

Again, Yang Stars traditionally relate to our Patriarchal Ancestors, and Yin Stars to our Matriarchal Ancestors. We can, therefore, determine where an Ancestral pattern may originate from. Again, Yang Stars can indicate anyone from your father's side or all men from both sides of your family, and Yin Stars can be your mother's side or all women in your family, regardless of side. We literally receive our bodies from our parents, and our strengths and weaknesses express the continuity of our heritage.

Yang Stars typically represent strength, endurance, and a straightforward experience of illness and recovery. People with Yang constitutions are more likely to be injured rather than ill. When they get sick, it usually goes away on its own, and if they see a doctor, they get treated and recover. The danger with strong or exalted Yang Stars here is being too strong for your own good. These people tend to overwork, overextend, and then burn out due to exhaustion. Think of the marathon runner who drops dead after running 26 miles. These people tend to ignore signs and symptoms and push through pain; they have difficulty resting, saying no, and shutting down productivity. They are restless, compulsive, active, and do well with routine and habit change. Yang constitutions usually have a high metabolism and pay less attention to diet. They tend to be less sensitive to environmental factors and mental issues.

Yin Stars typically represent sensitivity, receptivity, openness, susceptibility, and vulnerability. People with Yin Stars in their Health Palace do not have a straightforward experience of health. Their health comes from weakness rather than strength. They are sensitive to many influencing factors: environmental, mental-emotional, and so on.

Some Yin Stars make a person susceptible to what the Chinese call "possession," which implies that they are invaded by some kind of "outside" force due to poor boundaries, weak immunity, and insufficient defenses. People with Yin Stars here tend to be more lethargic and less active; they need to rest more and pay close attention to their health, which is changing all the time due to many complex factors. They may get stressed out and then catch a cold. They may hear about a friend's illness and then get the symptoms. Yin Stars, in general, are much more difficult to interpret.

An exalted Health Palace can indicate that a person's Fate revolves around a personal path of illness, healing, and recovery. Illness may be a spiritual experience, a call to wake up. These people are shamans. They are brought to death's door so they can return to heal others. Or an exalted Health Palace may indicate a long life of health with little to no illness or injury; they may be blessed with no Ancestral patterns of illness and the strength to overcome all minor conditions. They may inherit "good genes" and never experience health challenges, dying peacefully in old age. Some people become healers because they were healed and want to repay. Others become healers because they understand that their own health is a privilege and they want to use it to be of benefit.

Certain Stars indicate the potential for the study and practice of medicine. Others indicate the potential to excel at athletics and physical culture. A person's Character has a huge influence on how this turns out. A Horse or a Tiger will tend toward athletic expressions of physicality, while a Rabbit or a Goat may seek the intuitive art of medicine. Other Stars turn this House into a spiritual path and inspire people to practice yoga, meditation, and so on, using the body as the means to liberation.

The next three Houses, referred to as the career Houses, are read together to understand a person's Fate in the world through work or career and travel.

CAREER/TRAVEL PALACE

Career and Travel: Jobs, Skills, Talents, Immigration, Journeys

The Characters for this House, Qian Yi (遷移), literally mean "to immigrate, migrate, or move," but we translate this as the Career or Travel Palace. This House lies directly across from the Ming Palace and provides an image of your Fate "in the world"; it represents your life's journey outside your family and place of birth. It is read in conjunction with the Assistants and Superiors Palaces to give the overall shape of our work and life in the world.

For those born in modern industrial countries, this House may describe a professional career or the journey of discovering a suitable career through education, job hunting, experimentation, climbing the corporate ladder, or travel. It tells us how important or significant "working" will be in your life. The nature of that work is then refined in the following two Houses and may be indicated elsewhere in the chart, such as in the Wealth Palace (e.g., investor, banker), Health Palace (e.g., doctor, athlete), or Property Palace (e.g., real estate, architect).

First and foremost, this House tells us if you were born in the right place. Certain Stars can indicate if you "missed the mark" regarding birthplace and if you must travel to resolve your Fate. You may have died, been in the Bardo, and were circling the globe looking for Mongolia, but you crash-landed into Minnesota. You grow up feeling like home is somewhere else, and you go on a journey to find it. This House describes the potential success of that journey.

If you possess an exalted Career/Travel Palace, you may travel extensively, resolving past-life connections in different countries, states, and cities, searching for a home, meaning, or career. You may successfully immigrate. A new life or Fate may be waiting for you in a foreign land. The first time you arrive in Spain, you start speaking Spanish and never leave. Liu Ming referred to this as a "Fate Threshold" in the chart, a doorway to a new life.

Significant Stars here offer a journey of discovery through travel. I have the Emperor Star here and have traveled to over twenty countries and lived abroad. I personally feel that traveling is the best education you can receive. Stepping outside your comfort zone and experiencing other cultures, languages, and environments is extremely transformative. You may unravel your Fate here and discover yourself as a wayfarer, expat, or pilgrim. You may return to the place of your blood Ancestors by visiting the village in Norway your great-grandmother was born in, taking a pilgrimage to India, or traveling to Bhutan and discover a strong Fated affinity with Buddhism.

An afflicted House may suggest you have Fate for an unsuccessful immigration, like me, as if you just needed to complete some obligations, perhaps live a spell abroad followed by a pilgrimage home. It may also suggest a kind of wandering, moving from place to place, never feeling at home. Or you may journey abroad only to be met with disaster, illness, accidents, theft, and so on, which may be a perfect resolution of Fate.

If interpreted as the Career House, then significant Stars here can mean that your Fate unravels in the workplace. You may have no or minimal Fate for marriage or children and an exalted Career Palace. This does not mean that you won't or can't have kids, but it does suggest that your job will be an exciting, fulfilling place of interest and that your home life may be uneventful. You may love your kids, but at work you come alive, expressing your purpose and calling.

If the Superiors Palace is exalted, then, if read in conjunction, this House can indicate a "rise to success." You start as the janitor and work your way up to CEO. Or you start a business in your garage and sell it to Microsoft for millions of dollars. This House can indicate whether hard work, perseverance, and persistence will ultimately pay off.

It can also be modest and suggest a life of mediocrity or "quiet desperation," which is the case for many people. Remember, Fate is not about big or important things but about the feeling of completion. You may never have an exciting career, but if you die feeling satisfied with having tried your best, then this can be a resolution. If you die feeling incomplete and regretful for never having "made it," this may kick-start your Fate in the next lifetime.

Afflicted, you may wander from job to job, unfulfilled and bored. You may collect many skills and become a jack-of-all-trades, master of none. Ghost Stars may manifest as obstructions: You get fired, laid off, or passed over for promotions. Your startup fails, and you must start again with nothing. For many people, work is drudgery; they tough it out and work their fingers to the bone for little reward. But perhaps you have an exalted Offspring Palace, so work sucks, but you come home to your kids, who fill your life with joy. Everyone's chart balances out in some way.

A Yang Star indicates that work tends toward skill building and that success comes through getting good at something through discipline. Yang Fate in this House can manifest more "superficially," meaning your career may not be glamorous, spiritual, or flashy; you may rise to be the manager of a Home Depot. But that may be a perfect fit for a Horse with the Emperor Star here.

A Yang Star also implies that your work life is active, dynamic, eventful, and stressful. Yang can also mean physical; perhaps you become a carpenter, electrician, or hair stylist; you become skillful in using your body. Modest Yang Stars can be manual labor, retail, and so on. The Assistants Palace tends to indicate service work, but that can also show up here.

Yin Stars indicate that success comes through intuition rather than skill. Getting ahead, being promoted, and landing the job have more to do with feeling and being—and more to do with your deportment, even your appearance—rather than your resume or skill set. You may have an extensive skill set, but if your Fate here is Yin, it is the appropriate application of that skill at the right time through intuition that opens doors.

Yang Stars tend to be more about showing up and doing repetitive work. Yin Stars may be much more relaxed. Yin Stars can manifest as indirect, discrete, abstract, or intellectual work. You may sit at a desk all day moving numbers around on a screen and have no idea what you are doing, but you get a big paycheck. Or you may work behind the scenes, like all the people listed in movie credits. You never see them, but they make everything possible. Yin Stars may indicate that you get paid for your appearance (e.g., model, actor), intelligence (e.g., teacher, scientist, researcher), or presence (e.g., counselor, therapist, chaplain). You never "produce" anything tangible, but you help, inspire, and support others to do so.

Yang Stars indicate that you are "fresh," compelled by Fate to create and manifest your interests, sparked by Ancestral or past-life prompting. Yin Stars indicate that you may have done something for many lifetimes and that you need to "remember," which may manifest as a natural talent for something you have never trained for.

People with Yin Stars are "naturals" and pick things up immediately, while people with Yang Stars must work hard and may struggle to attain mastery. (Yin Fate is hard work, too, just a different kind.) You may be a natural at playing the piano but can't understand math enough to save your life. Or you may be a science wiz and practice guitar for ten years only to be mediocre. Everyone has past-life affinity somcwhcrc.

ASSISTANTS PALACE

Service: Friendship, Subordinates, Servants, Clients, Staff

The Characters for this House, Jiao You (交友), literally mean "to make friends," so we can translate this as the Friendship Palace, but practically, we call it the Assistants Palace. This House refers to a wide range of Fate possibilities and relationships, so it can be difficult to interpret. Overall, the House profiles our predestined help or harm that comes from nonfamily people and/or our Fate to help or harm others. It is important to note that this House (and the Superiors Palace) is bidirectional; it can refer to your role in life as an assistant or the influence of others assisting you.

This House represents the deeply held Chinese belief that we do nothing alone. Everything we do that is important is done through joint effort. Our primary support is family, but for many people, family is rough and they find their deepest connections in life through friendship. In the Confucian tradition, love is the primary characteristic of friendship rather than marriage. In work and career, our success often comes through our connections, teamwork, associations, and opportunities that come through others.

We read this House in two ways. First, as a relationship House, it indicates your Fate with friends, co-workers and colleagues, clients, schoolmates, and people you consider peers. It also indicates your Fate by receiving help from people who "assist" you in resolving your Fate.

Some people have little Fate with their birth family; they may have siblings, but they feel distant or difficult to connect with. Often, these people develop sibling-type bonds with friends. Perhaps you work in the same office for twenty years, and your co-workers become your family. Ming used the term a "circle of returners." In other words, you share deep past-life connections with friends, who become instrumental in resolving your Fate. Perhaps you were all in a platoon in a past life.

An exalted Assistants Palace can imply many important social connections, an avid social life, or several significant social events. You may have many people who are there for you, who show up when needed—a strong and well-knit social support network. You may be the life of the party and feel at home in social gatherings. Character makes a significant difference in this regard; a Dragon may have a hundred important friends, and a Rabbit may only have three. You may also constantly find yourself helping your friends; yours is the shoulder to cry on. Many American sitcoms portray exalted Assistants Palaces: Think Cheers, the bar where everyone knows your name.

Or, if afflicted, you may experience discord, betrayal, or a life-changing "falling out" with someone. You may try to connect with people, but they reject you. With every attempt going wrong, you may find connecting with others difficult or bewildering. You go to parties (if you even get invited) and stand in the corner feeling awkward. You may drift from one circle of friends to another, meeting many people but failing to form deep bonds or support. You may feel alone, like people aren't there for you, despite being in a crowd. Or you may give up and do everything alone, never asking for help or relying on others. Again, Character makes all the difference here. A Snake may be fine with self-reliance, but this could be a nightmare for a Pig.

If we interpret this as a career House, Stars here can indicate an assistant at work. Perhaps you are the boss or charismatic leader, but you cannot manage your appointments to save your life, so you have a stellar assistant who makes your career possible. Maybe you are that assistant. You may also be constantly promoted and helped due to the support, admiration, and recommendation of others. You may meet someone who changes your life at a conference, offering you a new and exciting career. You may also be credited with success without having done any real work.

If afflicted, you may experience scandal, confrontation, slander or gossip, and undermining in the workplace. You may experience competition with others that always gets the better of you. Others may make mistakes for which you get blamed. You may also follow others or be part of a team that loses or fails, leaving you without a job. You may hire an assistant who embezzles money from you and ruins your company. There are many ways this House can go wrong and many ways it can go right. A prized assistant may also make you a millionaire.

If this House has a significant Fate, it can indicate a life or a service career. This can be completely menial. You may be Fated to be a career waitperson or receptionist. My favorite restaurant back home has been staffed by the same people for over twenty years. I have been going there since I was a kid, and every time I return, I see the same waitstaff and chefs behind the counter. I imagine they all have exalted Assistants Palaces.

We can interpret many service-oriented careers from this House, from social work to teaching, consulting, and housekeeping. Many people dream big, but most end up "doing small"; not everyone becomes an astronaut. This House exemplifies those content to do simple, humble, or unrecognized work. Think Jeeves, the butler.

You may feel at home subordinating, following orders, or working with the chain of command, or you may be Fated to always rebel against it. You may excel in teamwork, networking, schmoozing, or hobnobbing with the rich. You may be a bodyguard, samurai, bouncer, or the like. Perhaps you are a professional athlete who makes a living because of a team.

I often use the phrase "behind the scenes" to describe this House, and I sometimes give the example of a politician who has the Emperor in their Superiors Palace and so has Fate to be a leader. His assistant, whom you've never heard of—who does all the work behind the scenes and without whom the politician could not function—may have the Emperor in their Assistants Palace. From this House, you may wield power from second place, from "behind the throne."

It is often the case that people have Fate in both the Superiors and Assistants Palaces, in which case, you may indeed become very well known, but you remain humble and use your position or voice to exalt and help others. You may have times in the spotlight but also do a lot of work behind the scenes that goes unnoticed.

An exalted Assistants Palace can propel you on a spiritual path of service and devotion. You may become a monk, join an ashram, and serve a community or a teacher. You may give up a distinguished career to feed the homeless. You may also dedicate yourself to starting intentional communities, bringing people together, and performing rituals. You may find your tribe in a sangha, kula, or witch coven. If afflicted, you may be at risk by following others; you may join a cult and end up "drinking the Kool-Aid."

If this House has a significant Fate, it suggests that your Ancestors manifest and work to bless you in your career by creating opportunities and connections. They may work as your protectors or guardian angels in the world, preventing you from meeting disaster. It may also be the case that a family business or family wealth is the key to all your success socially and politically, offering you connections to your career, for example, through the same fraternity your father and grandfather belonged to.

If this House is empty, then you have no Fated requirement for service. Rather, you may be a leader. This may also mean that you have little help, few friends, and must work hard to connect with people. It may also mean you must go at it alone. Often, this House is a "mixed bag," and I find it to be one of the most difficult to describe to clients.

SUPERIORS PALACE

Officials: Leadership, Teachers, Mentors, Bosses

The Characters for this House, Guan Lu (官祿), literally refer to the position of a Chinese government official, and we translate it as the Superiors Palace. Sometimes it is translated as the Official's Palace, for it gives the image of a person's "advancement and development" Fate. It shows how our Fate and achievement relate to authority. Like the Assistants Palace, it is bidirectional. It can refer to figures of authority in our life and/or our role in that regard. It also can be read as a relationship and/or career House. It is not always either/or and can offer a wide range of interpretations. It is important to note that this House refers to Fated relationships outside the family.

As the final or "highest" career House, it relates to success, achievement, ambition, and innovation and to being well-known, recognized, rewarded, or influential. An exalted Assistants Palace may mean that you become a doctor, but an exalted Superiors Palace could mean that your methods change the practice of medicine. This House can be the difference between being a mere salesperson or pioneering an innovative marketing tactic that changes our culture. It can also be the difference between simply moving abroad (Career/Travel Palace) or going down in history for introducing smallpox to the Aztecs.

If we interpret this as a relationship House, then Stars that show up here indicate the help or harm that comes to us from elders, teachers, mentors, bosses, employers, gurus, leaders, and so on. Fate connects us with people more experienced, advanced, or influential than us. These can simply be authority figures in the workplace whom you may or may not respect. Or they can be great teachers whom you respect, admire, or even revere.

Because of the potential trust we place in our superiors, the relationships here have the potential for great cause and effect. We can be greatly influenced, for better or worse, by those with power, and as we all know, power is easily corrupted and often abused. So, an afflicted Superiors Palace can manifest as abuse that comes from the throne, as strange relationships with teachers, or as harming others from one's own position of authority.

Stars in this House often imply a journey of apprenticeship. You meet a mentor, study with them, and follow in their footsteps, which has been the ideal model in most craft guilds. Perhaps you meet someone already practicing your dream job, so you work for them and learn the tricks of the trade. They may retire, leaving you the position, or you may do your own thing, having had them as a model.

This House can indicate becoming a boss, manager, and/or decision-maker. It denotes responsibility and leadership. You may be Fated to rise in the ranks to become the boss and make important decisions that influence people's lives. Traditionally, it refers to the role of government officials in China, which were the most prestigious jobs in the nation. Government officials were highly educated and respected members of the community who commanded others as "parents to the nation." This House indicates whether someone will become an official or simply meet officials, which is further inferred from other Houses.

Spiritually, this House can indicate a Fated relationship with a teacher or "guru," and traditionally, this House indicates connections to "lineage," a much-misunderstood term in modern times. The Ancestors Palace can indicate this as well, but this House tells us about what we can call your "Wisdom Ancestors"—inexplicable, Fated connections to people in traditions that are not from your culture, heritage, or country.

You may become a disciple, study with a master, and inherit a lineage, taking on students yourself. An exalted Superiors Palace can indicate that the major Fate of your life unravels by following a teacher, like Mr. Miyagi from

The Karate Kid. Completing this Fate is considered a complicated business in many traditions, especially in Tantra, where people vow to follow a teacher's lineage for as many lifetimes as it takes to become enlightened.

Again, Ghosts here can indicate abuse or betrayal from a teacher. It can indicate joining a cult and/or becoming a cult leader yourself. There are so many examples of fallen gurus in the modern spiritual scene that I don't even know where to start; it may, in fact, be all of them.

An afflicted Superiors Palace may simply indicate a strong distrust of authority—a rebel without a cause. You may rebel against your parents, teachers, cops, priests, and so on throughout your life, with or without cause. You may become an activist and work to dismantle oppression and patriarchy, which may have positive results but could leave you bitter, frustrated, and disillusioned. You may spend a lifetime fighting "the man" only to burn out. But, of course, you may change people's lives all along the way; such is the nature of Ghost resolution.

Gone wrong, this House can make you a crime boss, drug lord, or dictator—think Michael Corleone from *The Godfather*. It can lead to corruption, despotism, and jingoism of the worst order. All the worst acts in human history can be related to this House (and possibly the Assistants Palace), for it represents the power to influence people on a larger scale. We see here the importance of Character and Fate. You may have the character or capacity to be a great leader, like an Earth Dragon, but if this House is afflicted, you may become a gang leader in prison. In a different context, you may have become a general and been rewarded for your acts of aggression.

If we further interpret this as a career House, then it relates to the notion of success and achievement, contributing to your field. You may have an exalted Career/Travel Palace, in which case your career is important, but if your Superiors Palace is empty, afflicted, or debilitated, then you may work hard and not achieve success. You may never be recognized for your accomplishments. If they are both positive, then you will most likely do very well. You may even innovate. You may invent the next giz-widget, doohickey, or smartphone thingy.

This House is exemplified by inventors, contributors, and creative people who change the game. I like to think of Steve Jobs. It is also exemplified by great political leaders or by people who change the world with an act of defiance, like Rosa Parks.

It can also relate to fame and have nothing to do with talent. As we all know, many of the most talented people you will ever meet will never be famous, and many famous people are hacks. From an astrological point of view, this is all Fated. Hard work and talent do not always pay off. When they do, when Character and Fate match and someone rises to excellence, this again is called "Destiny."

Yang Stars here tend to relate more toward career and success. A strong Yang star here can create ambition, the drive to succeed, as well as the Fated connections to make it happen, especially if combined with an ambitious character. A Dragon with an exalted Superiors Palace is certainly auspicious, because they will try to rule the world anyway. A Rabbit, who may shy away from the spotlight, may feel tremendous anxiety if their Superiors Palace pushes them toward leadership.

Yang Stars indicate a "rise" to power based on perseverance and indicate that a great deal of Fate is resolved through career. They also suggest that a person will lead from an obvious or primary position, like an Emperor.

Yin Stars, like the Empress, suggest that power is wielded from a hidden, unusual, or secondary position, from behind the scenes. Ming introduced many people to the idea of "Yin Power," which is fundamentally difficult for Americans to understand. Yin Power is essentially passive, and for many, it appears manipulative. Yin Power is wielded through seduction, suggestion, and body language—through "psychological" tactics. Our culture looks down on this kind of power, although we use it extensively on each other and throughout the world, because Yin Power works. Marketing is based on Yin Power. A "damsel in distress" may achieve everything in life without ever lifting a finger.

Yin Stars suggest that your rise to success happens because of unseen factors that can appear lucky: being in the right place at the right time, meeting the right people, and/or being given opportunities that you did not appear to earn. To people with Yang Fate here who work their asses off to get ahead, Yin Fate appears unfair, for it looks effortless. Yin Fate can often manifest as privilege, family power, and influence; you may be promoted because your boss knows your father, or you may use family money to swing an election.

When read together with the previous two Houses, the Superiors Palace offers us a complete image of someone's participation in society through "work," which can be refined through other Houses. For example, an exalted Superiors Palace in conjunction with an exalted Property Palace means that one can exert their influence through real estate and material wealth.

The Property and Wealth Palaces are read together to determine a person's overall Fate with prosperity.

PROPERTY PALACE

Ownership: Home, Inheritance, Real Estate, Collections, Immigration, Fengshui

The Characters for this House, Tian Zhai (田宅), literally mean "farmland or field" and "residence or home," and we translate this as the Property Palace. This House has two distinct meanings. Primarily, the Stars here describe a person's relationship to material goods, real estate, and Fate with "ownership" of real property, whether through purchase or inheritance. Combined with the Wealth Palace, it creates a person's "stuff and home" Fate.

Secondarily, or perhaps on a deeper level, this House represents our Fate with the Chinese principle of Fengshui, or the auspice of placement. Like the Career/Travel Palace, it may tell us if we have a strong Fate with "place." Energetically, it represents home, so it can manifest as the Fate to create a home through owning land or a house, or through creating security via the possession of goods. Or it can imply that creating or looking for a home is a big deal for you. Is there a natural geographic or geomantic home for you? Perhaps you must find it, so this House can also indicate immigration.

As the Fengshui House, certain Stars can indicate if Fengshui is a major influence on you. You may be significantly affected by or connected to the land, nature, or objects in space. Perhaps you become ill, and nothing is working. You change the direction of your bed or the color of your sheets, and suddenly, you get better. You may be struggling in a new town. You move, and suddenly, everything clicks into place. You may be disoriented by disorganized arrangements and patterns and therefore have an instinct for design, in which case this House can indicate career architects, interior designers, and Fengshui consultants.

In the Chinese value system, ownership is not about accumulating stuff or "toys"—trying to "get yours" and die with the biggest pile. Fate with ownership of material goods or real estate is an opportunity to be generous. Real wealth is something that can be measured. Land can produce food; a home can provide shelter—sharing this with others is the greatest opportunity to be generous. Money is abstract, especially today; it is a play of numbers on screens. You may have a debilitated Wealth Palace and have no money but still have an exalted Property Palace and live on a farm with the benefit of everything nature provides.

Often, this House is straightforward and has to do with our Fate to buy, own, and sell property. It can represent the Fate of inheritance and family money. Or it can represent a career as a real estate broker, buying and selling properties at a profit. You may own several properties and rent out the rooms as an "Airbnb." You may manage an apartment building or become a landlord and collect passive income.

Major Fate in this House can indicate that many things in life revolve around your home. You may work from home. You may spend a fortune fixing up a piece of property, only to have it lead to all sorts of adventures, like in the movie *The Money Pit*. You may buy or move into a house only to have a series of complex situations happen with neighbors, roommates, city planning committees, and so on.

Fate here can impel you on a mission to find a home, wandering from place to place in search of belonging. You may never feel at home anywhere or even feel like your home is haunted. Ancestral Ghosts here can come from histories of war, exile, and migration.

Liu Ming told a remarkable story of a woman who bought and sold properties but never felt at home, especially in the kitchen. She never cooked, and as soon as she fixed up a house, she would sell it. Later, she uncovered a family story: During World War II, the whole family was sitting for dinner when the sirens went off. Her grandfather told them they were staying put, and the whole family died at the dinner table in an air raid. So, of course, she inherits an inexplicable fear of being in the kitchen.

This House can manifest as a wandering or nomad spirit. You may spend your entire adult life wandering; you may even feel claustrophobic, trapped after staying in one place for too long. You may be uprooted due to causes and conditions beyond your control, or you may move for work after being promoted to run the head office in Chicago. Or, you may have deep-fated connections to your hometown and never leave.

Many people throughout history were born and died in the same bed. And countless people have been exiled due to war. The Stars here indicate something of your Ancestral patterns around exile and migration, as does the Career/Travel Palace. Again, there is a Chinese saying that goes, "We only dig in our Ancestors," meaning we have lived on the same land for so long that the soil is made of the dead. You may inherit a family farm that has been there for generations; it could be a curse or a blessing.

This House may also indicate other kinds of possessions. You may buy, fix, and sell cars. You may own and operate a clothing company. You may produce artisan soaps and sell them at the farmer's market. Your life may be intimately connected to the material, the sensual, the manifest. You may cultivate the Earth and feel connected to the cycles and seasons. You may weave baskets, make goat cheese, or derive great power from a spiritual connection to objects. You may be a collector, and your Fate is tied to art, teapots, ritual bells, and so on. In Confucian culture, you are not considered a gentleperson until you have a collection. An art dealer is a perfect manifestation of this House.

Yang Stars in this House tend to manifest as more worldly Fate patterns. Yang Fate is to own, operate, and invest. Yang Stars can indicate careers in real estate, architecture, design, and so on. They may be connected to production: You may build your own House. As per usual, Yang Fate implies dynamism; working actively with challenges unravels Fate. In terms of inheritance, Yang Stars imply a Patriarchal Fate for inheritance.

Yin Stars often turn this House into a much more passive situation. You may inherit property or wealth and have everything taken care of for you, never having to work. Or, you may work with real estate and real goods, but the situations all manifest mysteriously, beyond your control. You may be constantly gifted things and return that fortune through generosity.

Yin Stars more easily manifest as generosity: spreading wealth through charity, philanthropy, and leaving behind a legacy or creating a foundation. Yin Stars are often associated with luxury, finery, comfort, and refinement. They also heighten the effect of Fengshui on a person as well as their regional, geographic, ethnic, or familial ties. Yin Stars indicate inheritance from the Matriarchal line.

PLEASURE PALACE

Pleasures: Luck, Hobbies, Interests, Enjoyment/Satisfaction

The Characters for this House, Fu De (福德), literally mean "happiness" and "virtue"—sometimes "blessed virtue"—and we translate this as the Pleasure Palace. I always read this House last, for it is the most important in many ways, for it tells us about our Fate to enjoy our life. It reveals Fated patterns of "inner experience" manifesting in our pursuit of satisfaction. We may have grand, exalted Fate, but if we don't have fun and are not satisfied when our Fate is complete, then what's the point?

Without satisfaction, we may very well create more Fate, which, from a Buddhist perspective, keeps us spinning in the wheel of samsara, for the relative world is by nature unsatisfactory and temporary. When we try to find permanent satisfaction, we experience discomfort. This tradition accepts the Buddhist principle of samsara but also shares a more Daoist belief that life alternates: Sometimes it is an awful place; sometimes it is a beautiful place. Happiness is possible but never permanent. This House reveals our capacity for temporary satisfaction as it comes and goes.

Some of us, after the sea of obligations has been fulfilled, after all the work has been done, are left with fond memories of joy and love. Others only remember the struggle, the battles fought, but here is the key: Some are Fated to be grumpy! We must let grumpy people be grumpy. If we tell pessimists to stop being negative, we turn them into hypocrites, and they spend their lives being a "nice person" until the day they snap. This goes hand in hand with understanding the Character: A Tiger with a grumpy Fate in the Pleasure Palace needs a lot of acceptance (this is me).

This House suggests that we may not be free to enjoy ourselves, which was a huge revelation to me. I've always wondered why some people are blessed with a sunny disposition and have such an easy time having fun while others find it so difficult. From this tradition's point of view, we may inherit patterns of either Ghostly inhibition or unbridled gregariousness from our Ancestors.

At its core, this House reveals our Fate around "satisfaction," but it manifests in patterns of enjoyment, pleasure, fun, hobbies, interests, entertainment, socializing, and so on. It tells us a crucial thing: Does fun provide you with Qi, or does it drain you of it?

Some people are at risk when they pursue pleasure. The first time they take a drink, they're an addict, and two years later, their life has gone down the toilet. Others may be Fated to "follow their fun." Liu Ming was a Fire Pig and had the Emperor Star in his Pleasure Palace, so according to him, his Fate unraveled when he followed his sense of enjoyment. So, for him, doing drugs was a much different Fate scenario than for others. This may be auspicious for some Characters, like Pigs, who will follow their fun anyway, and bewildering for others, like Snakes, who distrust the display of the senses.

Is fun like a battery for storing Qi? Are you a flirt who goes home glowing from flattery, or are you exhausted by trying to flirt? When you listen to an amazing musician, do you feel joy, or does it cause you to reflect on being a failed musician and feel bitter? When you work hard for something and achieve it, do you feel satisfied and accomplished, or are you already on to the next task, the next goal to accomplish? We often discuss these patterns as extrovert versus introvert, and type A versus B people, but they may also be viewed as Fated patterns.

When exalted, this House becomes difficult to interpret and often moves into a "spiritual" dimension. It means that a person's life revolves around a deeply personal sense of pleasure; they literally can't avoid it. It is easy to assume that these people are party animals, but when this House is exalted, we cannot say how it should manifest. A person may be utterly boring by our standards, but inside, this may be the perfect manifestation of their enjoyment. They may receive infinite pleasure from the fitting of a good pair of shoes or eating the same meal every day may be an enlightenment experience. They may even appear miserable from our perspective, but they may deeply love their struggle and turn it into amazing art, poetry, or music. Who are we to judge?

If this House is unafflicted, then a person can "trust" their sense of pleasure; it may even become a mandate. They can go to the party and festivals, do drugs, buy toys, and follow this to their heart's content. Doing so will catalyze their Fate and propel them in life. If strongly Fated, they may not be able to stop themselves. These people should know that this is okay, even if society calls them irresponsible. Often, these people turn their passion, interests, or hobby into their career. Their interests are so strong that they can't live life any other way. So, these people often become artists, musicians, humanitarians, and Dharma bums.

If the House is afflicted, then a person cannot trust their pleasure principle. Ghosts here imply that they inherited patterns of dissatisfaction, even addiction, and these can manifest as a wide range of harmful behaviors. This House can go very dark, but we must never jump to conclusions. My mother had a very afflicted Pleasure Palace and died of alcohol addiction.

Yet, I have seen others with similar arrangements and very different stories. However, the potential is always there, so we must read carefully. The darkest stories of addiction and abuse can undoubtedly manifest here.

Ghosts in this House represent Ancestors who could have died having fun (like an overdose), died from substance abuse, or never had a day of fun in their life. You may inherit a pattern of all work and no play and become very critical of pleasure. You may be Ebenezer Scrooge and think happy people are stupid. You may criticize people who go to clubs but secretly yearn to be a maniac on the dance floor.

Some Characters, like Horses or Oxen, tend to turn everything into an assignment or job, so affliction here may turn out well, or it may compound the already gloomy part of their Character. You may work at work, work at play, work in the gym, work on your spiritual path, and so on. You may be addicted to being busy, which is an epidemic in our culture. You may be unable to rest and do nothing, repeating the life pattern of your great-grandfather, who worked in a factory and never got a day off. You may only have fun at school or the gym, addicted to self-improvement.

Conversely, your grandparents may have worked every day of their lives, and now you are free to have a life of leisure. You inherit money, privilege, and opportunities and do not give a fig about bettering yourself. You may feel guilty because of the advantages you've received, but if it is Fated, then you should not. You have an Ancestral mandate to enjoy your life. The difficulty comes when this turns to entitlement. Inherent in this Fate is gratitude and generosity. Let your heart overflow with gratitude, and give back. Positive can also flow into positive: Your grandmother may be jolly, and so you are too.

Patterns here can create either creativity and spontaneity or routines and ruts. You may find yourself on wild adventures, meeting and connecting with amazing people, or you may do the same thing day in, day out, and hang out at the same bar with the same friends. You may be bursting with possibilities or have no idea what to do with yourself. But this can be made positive. If you tend to get stuck in a rut, then it means that you can enjoy discipline, which for some Characters is a nightmare. It can help you excel in activities that require rigorous practice.

Fate here may create deep affinities for art, music, sex, literature, history, performance, movies, and so on. You may have Fate to become a master calligrapher or ballerina. You may become the world's leading expert on ants. You may spend your life pursuing an unfulfilling career, while in your private life, you're obsessed with playing chess; you may retire or quit your day job and become a grand master, traveling the world playing chess tournaments.

Yang Stars here tend to manifest as more ordinary, socially acceptable pleasures. Yang Stars make people active pleasure-seekers. They may love socializing, parties, sports, travel, competition, and so on. Yang Stars may find it easy to accept trendy or popular enjoyments. Yang Fate makes for "divas," those who demand entertainment; if it isn't fun, it isn't worth doing. Yang Stars are more hedonic and likely to revel in food, sex, and song.

Yin Stars tend to manifest as a wide rainbow of "other possibilities." Yin Stars may create a deep affinity for the occult, astrology, tarot, ancient wisdom, and the like. Yin Stars are much more fluid in their expression; they compel people toward deep, hidden dimensions, which express an intuitive sense of enjoyment.

These people may be shy and wary of enjoyment because it may seem weird, strange, or taboo. They may appear normal but have a pleasure dungeon in their basement, or on weekends, they dress up as Klingons and attend sci-fi conventions. Yang Fate can express this way too, but would do so more for socializing and dressing up, while Yin Fate may feel a deep connection to the principles of *Star Trek*, which they can recite in Klingon.

Yin Fate here means that pleasure tends to find people naturally, while Yang Fate means that people pursue pleasure actively. If you have a major Fate here, then the rest of your life may manifest through this House. You may meet your partner at a sci-fi convention and start a business teaching Klingon to fellow Trekkies.

EMPTY COURT

The characters Kong Gong (空宫), literally mean "empty court," and this refers to a House that contains no ruling Stars. The message of an Empty Court is simple: no Fate. This means that freedom and choice are the main factors that have become very important. You must choose and create your Fate here, if you want it. And there may be few options. An Empty Court implies that you completed this Fate in a past life or that your Ancestors have freed you of it.

Some people have a few Empty Courts. I have four, which is the most you can have, and some people may have none. There is a tradition of "borrowing stars" from the opposite House, which act like a "Fate echo" and can tell the story of an Empty Palace. Borrowed Stars are read at half strength. However, I find freedom to be a much more important message, so except for the Offspring Palace of a parent, I do not read borrowed Stars and will not discuss them in this book. In a way, choice can activate the borrowed Stars, making them come alive. So, they represent potential but are otherwise not necessary.

BODY PALACE

The Character Shen (身) means body, so we translate this as the Body Palace. Due to certain Polestar calculations, one of the Twelve Houses becomes a secret 13th House, and this is the Body Palace. It can be any one of the Twelve Houses. My Body Palace is in the Wealth Palace. Whichever House it is, that House becomes connected to and expressed in some way through your body or embodiment. This is open to interpretation. It may indicate a career path, health and wellness, or situations surrounding your embodiment, such as being a doctor or athlete, or it may relate to an illness or recovery. I have seen many healthcare practitioners with a Body Palace in either the Wealth Palace (such as in my case) or one of the career Palaces. However, not a lot is taught or written about the Body Palace, and so as far as I am concerned, it is not all that important and will not be discussed in this book.

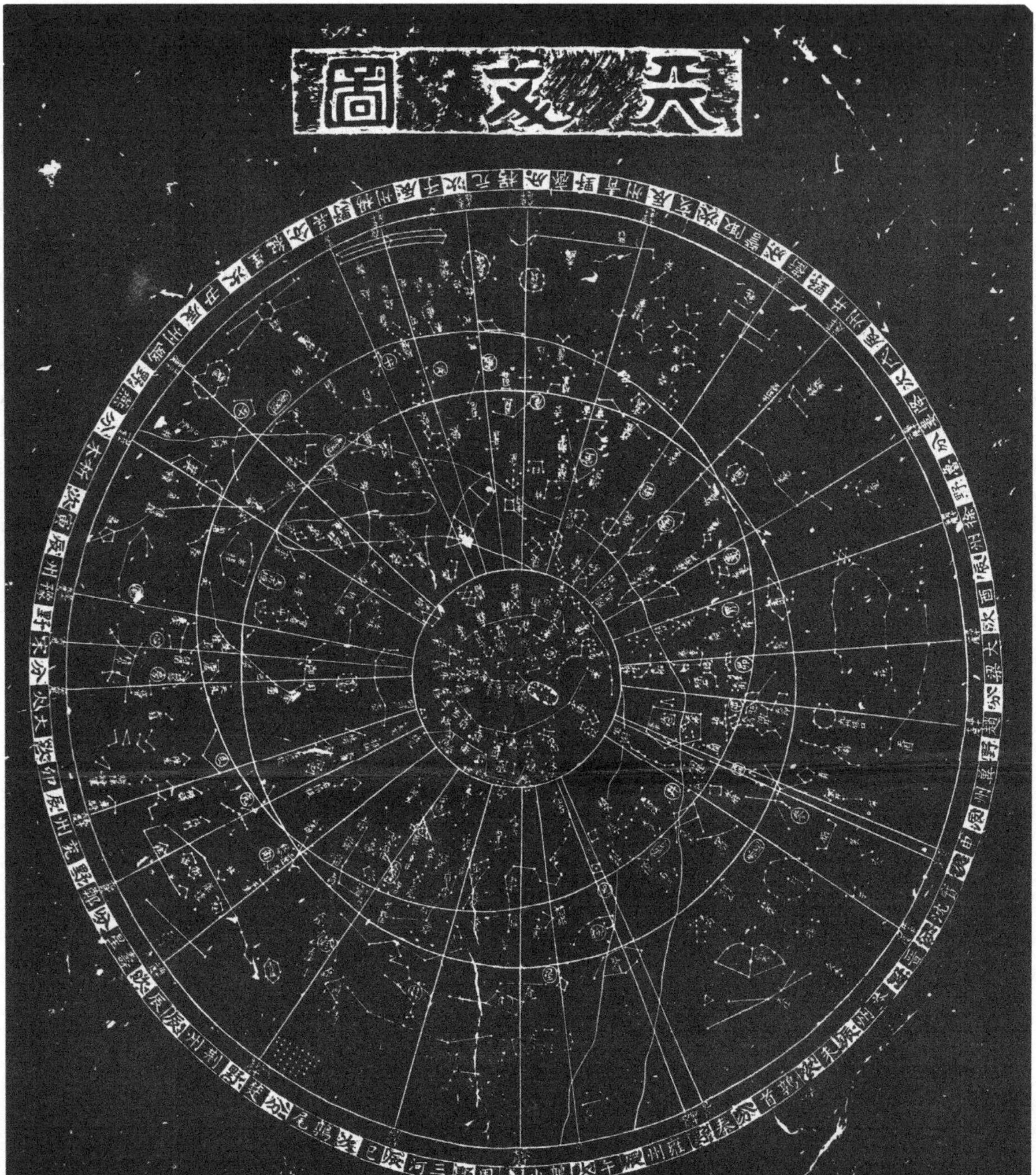

Reproduction of the Suzhou star chart[1]

XING MING (星命)—STAR POWER

WE WILL NOW SYSTEMATICALLY EXPLORE the Major and Minor Stars of the Polestar system. Unlike Western and Indian astrology, Polestar Astrology does not reference the planets of our solar system, but rather it refers to the nature of Stars in significant constellations like the Big Dipper. Some systems use up to 108 Stars and include more constellations, but we will focus on what are considered the most important 36, with an emphasis on the "Royal Court," or the Twelve Ruling Stars of Fate.

The Stars symbolically describe the nature of Fate inherited from our Ancestors. Since the system was developed for, by, and in the Chinese imperial court, each Major Star is a character in the Chinese imperial court, ruled by the Emperor and Empress. We use these character images to understand the Qi of the Star, as they ultimately represent patterns of cyclical time that manifest through and as human lives. Think of them as gateways or portals with shape, kind of like Play-Doh being pushed through a mold.

The Qi of each Star is a pattern, but we access these patterns through the cast of characters in the Royal Court. Think of it like a play: The Emperor, Empress, General, Tutor, Oracle, Prince, Princess, Vassal, Concubine, Executioner, Magistrate, Priest, and so on represent the complexities of human relationships, power dynamics, social and class struggles, and politics, and your chart is like the script, in which this cast are placed in certain areas of your life to enact a kind of drama or comedy. But this is not to be taken too literally, for we are interested in getting beneath these symbols to the Qi dynamics in the real events and relationships in our lives. It is quite profound to think that the underlying mathematical forces in the universe determine these plays.

It is very important to understand that Chinese astrology is ***not*** "astronomical" but mathematical. Polestar Astrology has astronomy in its distant past and uses the language of stars, but a Polestar chart does not depict the night sky. There is no illusion that it accurately depicts where these constellations were at the time of your birth. The system is said to have been "revealed" by patterns observed in the sky, but these patterns are mathematical and said to be an "independent influence" that forms or shapes the causes and conditions of Fate. Polestar charts are calculated by numerical equations and numerology, depicting sequences of time beyond the physical reality of stars in the sky. As such, it is better referred to as "chronology" rather than astrology.

Many of the actual constellations and stars with these names have disappeared by now, which, to the Chinese mind, makes them more potent, for they have gone to the realm of the Ancestors. So, although some of the Stars have the names of currently known astronomical bodies, what we call "Stars" in this system are better understood as poetical representations of Fate, mathematical patterns found in Nature, an endless spin of celestial Qi.

The Stars of the celestial Royal Court and their various arrangements, when interpreted, become a form of divination, or a mantic art. But who and what are being divined? The standard Chinese answer is the dead: our Ancestors, our life before birth. The Stars form an image of the precedent or cause of our birth and can be interpreted as both a symbolic and a literal picture of our Ancestors, which I will explain in more detail as we go through each Star. In short, the dead run the living.

On a practical level, they represent literal Ancestors in your family tree who died either resolved or unfinished. The Royal Court is your resolved Beneficial Ancestors who completed their human Fate but stayed in Heavenly Realms on their way toward Great Completion. They remain at their post, working toward the resolution of Fate for the entire line of Ancestors. The Emperor and Empress are often called your "Original Ancestors." And your Ancestors step into these roles to enact certain influence in this Royal Court.

The Stars, and therefore Fate, fall into two categories, Yang and Yin, or the Northern and Southern Array, led by the Emperor and Empress, respectively. The Yang Stars represent Patriarchal Fate, associated with action and doing, and the Yin Stars represent Matriarchal Fate, associated with receptivity and being. In this tradition, we are intimately connected with the dead, and we must play out the patterns of unfinished business we inherit at birth before we can experience the freedom of our Original Nature.

Ming used to say that we are the warm, wiggling end of thousands of dead people, responsible for at least seven generations of beings. When we get a human body, we inherit unfinished business, gifts, talents, and so on from all the bodies that preceded our body—it's the tax we pay for birth. Fate is said to be a "mandate" from our Ancestors to complete what they could not. The Twelve Ruling Stars, again, represent our accomplished Ancestors; the rest are what the Chinese refer to as Gui (鬼), or Ghosts, our "unfinished business."

The Buddhist interpretation suggests that the Stars represent our past-life Fate, which is the cause of our rebirth, and that we are here to finish our own unfinished Fate from past lives. Both are possible interpretations, and you can entertain and explore both. Ancestors are, however, much more tangible, because you can research your family tree and even ask your living Ancestors about their lives, which I highly recommend you do. The idea of past lives is a bit flimsy, and we are easily susceptible to fantasizing about them.

THE NORTHERN AND SOUTHERN ARRAY

THE STUDY OF FATE CALCULATION in Zi Wei Dou Shu focuses first on the Greater Twelve Ruling Stars, called the Royal Court, and secondarily on the Lesser Stars, all of which are found in two constellations: Ursa Major and the constellation of Sagittarius contain all the Greater and Lesser Stars. These two constellations are called the Northern and Southern Array, which follow the North Star, or Polestar, and an imaginary Southern Star. Some of these Stars are "imaginary" or "spirit" Stars, called Shen Sha (神煞), meaning they are not observable or no longer observable. Some of these imaginary Stars are Yin counterparts to Yang Stars. In other words, if there is a Yang, there must also be a Yin.

The Northern Array contains both Yin and Yang Stars but represents the Yang Fate associated with the Emperor Star, or Polestar, and your "Patriarchal" Ancestors, which can be interpreted as all the men in your family tree on both your father and mother's side *or* all the people on your father's side, including women. It is up to you to decide which is the case, and it can be both.

The Northern Array—otherwise known as Ursa Major, the Big Dipper, or the Zi Wei Cluster—is seen as the throne of Zi Wei (紫微), the Emperor, or of Shangdi (上帝), the Supreme Emperor, which is yet another name for the Polestar. This constellation contains seven stars that we can observe today plus two "hidden" stars. The Stars of the Northern Array include Tian Ji (天機), the Oracle; Tian Tong (天同), the Vassal; Lian Zhen (廉貞), the Concubine; Wu Qu (武曲), the General; You Bi (右弼), the Right Assistant; and Zuo Fu (左輔), the Left Assistant. We will also include Tai Yang (太陽), the Sun or Prince, which is a representation of the sun and follows the unraveling of Yang Fate.

The Southern Array also contains both Yin and Yang Stars but represents the Yin Fate associated with the Empress and your "Matriarchal" Ancestors, which, again, can be interpreted as all the women in your family tree on both your father and mother's side *or* all the people on your mother's side, including men. The Empress is not an observable star, but again, it is the Yin counterpart of the Polestar.

The Southern Array—otherwise known as Sagittarius or the Tian Fu Cluster—is ruled by Tian Fu (天府), the Empress. It includes Tian Xiang (天相), the Tutor; Tian Liang (天梁), the Roof Beam, Ju Men (巨門), the Great Gate; Qi Sha (七殺), the Seven Killings or Executioner; and Po Jun (破軍), the Rebel or Breaking Rank. We will also include Tai Yin (太陰), the Moon Lady or Princess, which is a representation of the moon and follows the resolution of Yin Fate.

Together, these two factions of the Northern and Southern Array, of Yin and Yang Fate, work synergistically to create the push and pull of our lives within the greater context of Nature, or Freedom. The relationships between all these characters are a complex web, and the art of Polestar Astrology is understanding how the complex dynamics of the Royal Court unfold in our lives. This is quite a challenge, so we start with our Natal Chart and examine each Star grouping through our own experience. We start with the Greater Stars and work our way down to the Lesser Stars.

The rest of the Lesser Stars are not so clear astronomically, and that's okay. Huo Xing (火星), the Fire Star, is the name of Mars but does not correlate with Mars the planet.

Ling Xing (鈴星), the Water or Ringing Star, is imaginary like the Empress; it is the Yin counterpart to the Fire Star but is not observable. Again, a Polestar chart is not "astronomical" and does not represent the sky, and it is important not to get hung up on whether these are "real" stars.

The categorization of the Lesser Stars is not as important, but they are organized into the Four Major Ghosts, the Four Minor Ghosts, the Four Incidentals, the Orphan Spirits, and the Four Transformers. While all these Stars are interesting, they are not nearly as influential as the Royal Court, and it is important to take them lightly. That being said, the Four Major and Four Minor Ghosts are the most potent of the Lesser Stars, and these deserve thorough contemplation, as their Ghostly influence can be powerful in the subtle way that they affect our lives. They represent the most significant "afflictions," and resolving the Fate associated with them can be considered "exorcistic."

Wen Qu (文曲), the Priest, and Wen Chang (文昌), the Magistrate—known as the Wen Stars—are a special pair associated with the year and hour and are sometimes grouped separately and also included among the Royal Court. Together, they represent a key to the resolution of Fate through self-cultivation and spiritual practice, and they will receive in-depth consideration here, for the resolution of Fate is our goal.

Again, the literal astronomical details are not so important, but if you make a chart by hand, you will see the relationships of each Star to one another and get a sense of their placement. What is essential to understand is that the Stars are in a fixed relationship, or position relative to each other in the chart, because they are constellations. They always appear in the same order and are always in specific patterns. The Oracle is always to the right hand of the Emperor Star, and the Moon is always to the left of the Empress. The Tutor is always across from the Rebel. The Seven Killings Star is always across from the Empress. These patterns are significant to understanding the patterns of Fate, but we will get into that later.

Also, because they are in fixed positions, there are a limited number of patterns and, therefore, charts that they can create. There is a fixed number of Polestar charts. It is possible for two people to have the same chart or to share the placement of the Northern or Southern Array. Two people can have the same (or similar) charts but lead very different lives; however, they may share similar themes, which is fascinating to study. Identical chart patterns in friends and family can sometimes indicate past-life connections that go beyond ancestry.

STAR POTENCY

UNDERSTANDING THAT THE STARS are not equal in strength or potency is crucial. Americans always want to exalt the Lesser Stars to make them all equal. So, let's clarify: The Emperor Star is the most essential and potent Star in a chart. The Empress is second. The Tutor and Oracle are equally third and fourth. These are the Four Rulers, the most powerful Stars in the chart. Every other Star is much less important and influential by comparison, so don't get caught up in worrying as much about all the other Stars. Focus on the Four Rulers, and you will not be led astray.

The Royal Court all represent Beneficial Ancestors and are a generally positive influence. They can be afflicted by the lesser Ghost Stars, but they are always to be read in a positive light. The Lesser Stars can be read as inauspicious or unfavorable, but they are minor in their influence on our lives. They represent weak self-undermining patterns of behavior and negative emotions, not significant Fate opportunities or disruptions.

The Ghost Stars are weak because Ghosts are weak. They can, however, be influential in their subtlety. But it is a mistake to focus on the Lesser Stars. The Royal Court is not a democracy; it is most certainly a monarchy with the Emperor Star at the top. All the Stars work in service of the Emperor Star, which is to say, toward the resolution of Fate.

LUMINOUS AND DIMINISHED STARS, LUMINOUS PAIRS, EXALTED HOUSES, AND FATE THRESHOLDS

THE PLACEMENT OF STARS is essential when understanding their potency. As in Indian and Western astrology, Stars are "exalted" or "luminous" in specific placements, and they are "debilitated" or "diminished" in others. In Polestar Astrology, the Zodiac Animal that rules the House determines the luminous nature of the Star. For example, the Emperor Star is luminous in the Dragon and Horse Palaces, which makes sense, as these are Yang Characters, and the Emperor Star rules Yang Fate. It is diminished in the Rooster and Rabbit Palaces, for these are Yin Characters, and their nature somewhat contradicts the Emperor's prerogative.

Furthermore, certain Stars belong in or are more compatible with certain Houses. For example, the Roof Beam Star is often called the Fengshui Star, and the Property Palace is the Fengshui House, so it makes sense that this Star is stronger or more luminous in this House. Also, particular Stars work well together in pairs and exalt each other and the House in which they appear. The Emperor and Empress together, for example, make the most auspicious pair in Polestar Astrology, called the Royal Procession, and they exalt the House and chart into the stratosphere. When the Wen Stars, the Priest and the Magistrate, appear together, they are highly auspicious but in a much different and more subtle way.

Certain Stars are also misplaced in certain Houses. The Concubine Star, for example, does not belong in the Superiors Palace, for she represents a place where we are Fated to be vulnerable and need help and guidance. She represents where we are clueless and don't know what to do, so to put her in charge of the House of Leadership is inauspicious. But, if she is paired with a strong leadership Star, like the Empress or Tutor, this exalts the House and becomes the image of mentorship or apprenticeship.

Exaltation or luminous placement means that the Star is stronger, for better or worse, which is not always good. A super-exalted Emperor in the Superiors Palace may be wonderful for a Dragon but a nightmare for a Rabbit. Having an exalted Star is like being on stage performing; it may be exhilarating, but it is a lot of pressure and can be exhausting. Strong may mean a lot of opportunities, or it may mean that certain opportunities are much more potent and meaningful. But we must always remember that we are free to resist Fate and ignore or miss opportunities, and as such, Fate Thresholds can be unintentionally missed, which is why it is helpful to study our chart.

Exalted Houses create what Liu Ming called "Fate Thresholds." In other words, the Fated opportunity in that House becomes the key to unraveling Fate in this lifetime, a potential threshold to a new life. A job opportunity, a compatible partner, a trip to study abroad, and so on can become a portal to a new life that forever changes your trajectory and shapes you into a new person. These are the most important things to identify and focus on in a chart. It is all too easy to focus on the debilitated Stars, but the wisdom of Polestar Astrology is to focus on the good stuff. If your Career Palaces are exalted but your Partners Palace is afflicted, and you obsess about this, it is a recipe for disaster. Put your energy into your career, and the Partners Fate will work itself out naturally. If you are called to step up and be a leader but are distracted by Ghosts in another House, you might miss a Fate Threshold and fail to resolve your Fate in this lifetime. It is, therefore, important to study our biggest opportunities in the chart so we can step up and actualize them.

Stars and Houses can also be afflicted or diminished in their potency by their placement or by the presence of Ghost Stars. When certain Zodiac Animals rule a House, they diminish particular Stars due to their opposing nature or simply because this is a convention of Polestar Astrology. For example, the Tutor Star is diminished in the Rooster Palace. And just like certain Stars can be exalted in pairs with other stars, they can also be afflicted by other Stars. The Ghost Stars are generally considered inauspicious and can afflict other Stars, especially when they gang up.

So what does affliction mean? The simple definition is that Ghost Stars are a negative influence that afflict. If they are alone in a House or rule a House, as is the case with the Four Ruling Ghosts, we say the House is afflicted. If they appear with Stars from the Royal Court, we say those Stars are afflicted in that House. The Stars of the Royal Court are always a more positive influence, so a House with Stars from the Royal Court afflicted by Ghost Stars is not necessarily an afflicted House, for the positive outweighs the negative.

What does affliction mean practically speaking? There is no easy answer, for what is auspicious and inauspicious is different for every Character. It can simply mean that a Star is weakened; therefore, you may struggle or have little to no opportunity in that House. You may work forever to be a musician but never get anywhere and spend your life playing cover songs. This may be your Career Fate, but perhaps you also have an exalted Offspring Palace, so even though you're disappointed that no one wants to listen to your original music and that you're stuck in a cover band, you thrive as a dad and sing your daughter bedtime songs, and this fills your life with meaning.

Affliction generally means negative emotions. The Ghost Stars represent patterns of negative emotions and self-destructive patterns inherited from negative Ancestral influence. An Ancestor may have died with tremendous fear, and as a result, we spend our lives afraid to take chances. Each Ghost Star represents a different set of negative emotions, and in studying them, we see the influence of our Ghost Ancestors and how they show up in our lives looking for resolution. We will explore the influence of the Ghost Stars and affliction in detail later. First, we must remember that Fate resolution is the "goal" of Polestar Astrology, which we will discuss again in brief.

THE RESOLUTION OF FATE

SO, NOW WE BEGIN OUR JOURNEY THROUGH THE STARS. I encourage you to have your own Natal Chart and the charts of a few friends and family members ready as we go through each Star in each House. This is a choose-your-own-adventure. You can read and study all the possibilities, or you can go through your chart, look at the placement of these Stars, read their image and interpretation, and reflect. Remember, you're the one in the chart, not me. The job of an astrologer is to provide as many interpretations as possible based on the nature of the symbol, but it is up to you to figure out what it means and choose how it manifests in your life. In that sense, we reverse engineer the meaning of these symbols. We find this through Yuanfen (缘分), which is a deep feeling of Fated affinity. No one can tell you what this is like, but you know it when you feel it.

For example, if you have the Polestar in the Career/Travel Palace, look at your own life and ask: *How have traveling, moving, and my desire to find a place, meaning, work, or life experience shaped my journey?* Ask yourself: *Am I really stepping up and working with this pattern?* If it is afflicted, look at how it is, find the patterns of self-undermining or obstruction, and ask: *Have I resolved this? Do I keep repeating the same pattern over and over?*

Remember, we are interested in unraveling and resolving Fate. But what does this mean? It means we inherit a certain pattern or momentum of experience from our Ancestors. We are compelled in life to do certain things and are given certain opportunities, which we call Yang Fate, and we are also Fated to go through specific experiences beyond our control, which we call Yin Fate. If we are thorough and present in our lives, then we learn what we need to learn, do what we need to do, and have a sense of satisfaction and completion. We want to feel finished and, therefore, free to pursue spiritual practice without being entangled in Fate.

How will you feel on your deathbed? If someone put a gun to your head right now, how would you feel about your life? Are you finished? Ready to go without regret or fear? If not, you are still bound to Fate. In other words, we can create more and more Fate and keep ourselves spinning in the endless cycles of rebirth. This is called samsara, the endless wheel of death and rebirth. We can create a positive Fate and ensure better rebirth and circumstances, or as Buddhists would say, we can use golden chains or red-hot iron chains to bind ourselves to the wheel, but either way, we are bound. Or we can seek to be free from the wheel altogether. While you are free to seek better and better circumstances, by the laws of Yinyang, these are still Fated to turn to misfortune eventually.

So, Polestar Astrology offers an insight into the patterns by which we are bound to Fate. We study our chart to see where we need to act, where we need to wait and receive, what we need to avoid, and so on, so that we can skillfully manage our Fate and ultimately be free of it. Again, freedom means being finished—no regrets on your deathbed. It also means resolving our worldly obligations so that we are not always tied to responsibilities, demands, retributions, results, and the like. Most important, it means being free of negative emotions and the negative Ancestral patterns we inherited at birth. We must become cycle breakers and free ourselves from cycles of addiction, abuse, anger, fear, and so on.

Remember the Threefold Training, the San Hui (三慧): learning, contemplation, and meditation. This practice bears the greatest fruition when we continue to study the symbols deeply until we have a thorough intellectual understanding.

We then contemplate them in our daily experience while maintaining a daily sitting practice. This allows insight and integration, and if you apply yourself to the study of your own chart, then endless revelations will flow. After more than a decade of studying my own chart, I continue to have revelations about it, and it never ceases to amaze me.

And finally, remember Part 1 of Step III, "Character." The key to understanding the dynamics at play in Fate is our Character. Each Animal will experience and manage the different patterns of Fate differently. If you are a Tiger born in Dragon Hour like me, you will resolve Fate much differently than a Rabbit born in Ox Hour. So, look at each pattern and ask how a Tiger (or insert your Character) would deal with this. Is this pattern due to your Fate or Character? Nature or nurture? In other words, am I being impatient because I am a Tiger, or is this the influence of the Fire Star, or both? If I am predisposed as a Rabbit to shy away from risk, how is the Concubine Star shaping this? Am I jumping into risk because I am a Monkey, or is the Emperor demanding that I move across the country? Remember, it is the Character that determines the auspice of Fate. This is the real practice of Polestar Astrology. Never forget that Character shapes Fate in the context of Freedom.

HOUSE RULERSHIP

WHEN INTERPRETING ANY GROUPING OF STARS in the Twelve Houses, you must first determine the "ruling Star." The strongest Star in the House is the ruling Star. Simple. The upcoming list of stars is hierarchical in groups from strongest to weakest, so this is easy enough. If two Stars are of equal strength—that is, from the same group—they share the ruling image. The ruling Star forms Fate's central image and story in that House, and all the weaker Stars modify that image.

So, it is essential to understand each Star in each House alone, and we will now walk through each Star in each House. We will get into the practice of synthesis later, but the art of Polestar interpretation is first to determine the ruling Star and deeply understand how that Star operates alone in the House and what kind of Fate patterns can be expressed there. Then, you look at all the other Stars in that House and all the Stars that influence it, whether from 180- or 120-degree influence (opposite or in a trine) or the proximal Houses, and then see how those influences modify the basic story in each House.

We will get to these influences, but let's look at an example. The Oracle, Moon, Priest, Left Assistant, Halberd, Travel, Destruction, and Red Bird Star all appear in the Career/Travel Palace with the Emperor and Empress in the adjacent or proximal Houses. That's quite an image, but it becomes much easier when you first determine that the Oracle rules the House. So first, you understand what the Oracle means in the Career/Travel Palace. Then you ask how the Moon, the next strongest Star, modifies that image. Then you add the influence of the Priest as another modifier—it doesn't change the basic story but modifies it and adds another flavor or dimension. And so on. You hold to the primary image of the ruling Star and then add the layers, remembering that they are not all equal. The weaker Stars are weaker in the way they modify that story. Once we get to the Ghost Stars, we are not changing the story but merely adding elements of negative emotion that can modify our behavior in self-undermining or obstructing ways but not alter our path.

In the following chapters, I will attempt to explore each Star alone in each House and meditate on each based on my study of Liu Ming's notes, through my own personal experience and understanding and my experience with clients. I hope to transmit something of the Qi of these symbols so that you can do your own exploration, self-reflect, and discover them in your own life. Therefore, some of these interpretations may apply to you and some may not, but hopefully you can get the gist. For this purpose, I will not yet give any "real-life" examples, but rather, I will be playing with the symbols so that you can see how to think about them as Xiang (象), as symbols.

In the example charts later, I will give real-life examples and interpretations from my chart and the charts of my parents so that you can get a sense of how these patterns of Ancestral Qi manifest in real life. Remember, everything that follows is playful; these are not definitive interpretations.

GREATER STARS—
THE CELESTIAL/ROYAL COURT
OF BENEFICIAL ANCESTORS

HERE IS A LIST OF THE 36 STARS representing every conceivable Fate pattern that we will explore. They are often grouped in a few different ways according to "potency," as the "Greater" Stars, called the Celestial or Royal Court, and the "Lesser," or "Minor," Stars. Again, they are grouped according to the Northern and Southern Array, as the Stars that follow the Emperor and Empress, respectively, representing the resolution of Yang and Yin Fate.

Traditionally, you would receive a Qi transmission of each of the following Stars in a ceremony. You would hear a description and then be shown an image and receive a mantra for each Star, and each was often thought of as a deity.

They are listed here in order of their potency, or strength.

THE FOUR RULERS

ZI WEI (紫微)—The Emperor or Polestar

TIAN FU (天府)—The Empress Star

TIAN XIANG (天相)—The Tutor Star

TIAN JI (天機)—The Oracle Star

THE FOUR HONORABLES

TAI YANG (太陽)—The Sun or Prince Star

WU QU (武曲)—The General Star

TAI YIN (太陰)—The Moon Lady or Princess Star

JU MEN (巨門)—The Great Gate Star

THE FOUR HIGH RANKING

TIAN TONG (天同)—The Vassal Star

TIAN LIANG (天梁)—The Roof Beam Star

WEN CHANG (文昌)—The Magistrate Star

WEN QU (文曲)—The Priest Star

LESSER STARS—GHOSTLY ANCESTORS, OR GUI (鬼)

THE FOUR MAJOR GHOSTS

LIAN ZHEN (廉貞)—The Concubine Star

QI SHA (七殺)—The Seven Killings or Executioner Star

TAN LANG (貪狼)—The Greedy Wolf Star

PO JUN (破軍)—The Rebel or Breaking Rank Star

THE FOUR MINOR GHOSTS

HUO XING (火星)—The Fire Star

LING XING (鈴星)—The Water or Ringing Star

QING YANG (擎羊) or **YANG REN** (羊刃)—the Goat Blade or Sacrificial Star

TUO LUO (駝羅)—The Humpback or Rejection Star

THE FOUR INCIDENTALS

YOU BI (右弼)—The Right Assistant Star

ZUO FU (左輔)—The Left Assistant Star

LU CUN (祿存)—The Storehouse Star

TIAN YAO (天姚)—The Beauty Star

THE ORPHAN SPIRITS

TIAN KUI (天魁)—The Leader Star

TIAN XI (天喜)—The Happiness Star

TIAN YUE (天鉞)—The Halberd Star

DE JIE (地劫)—The Loss Star

DI KONG (地空)—The Void or Empty Earth Star

TIAN XING (天刑)—The Punishment Star

TIAN MA (天馬)—The Travel or Heavenly Horse Star

HONG LUAN (紅鸞)—The Red Bird Star

THE FOUR TRANSFORMERS

HUA LU (化祿)—The Salary or Prosperity Star

HUA QUAN (化權)—The Authority Star

HUA KE (化科)—The Examination Star

HUA JI (化忌)—The Jealousy or Scandal Star

THE FOUR RULERS

WE BEGIN OUR JOURNEY WITH THE FOUR RULERS. Zi Wei (紫微) and Tian Fu (天府) are the Emperor and Empress of the Royal Court and the rulers of celestial Fate. Again, these are the two most important and potent Stars in any Natal Chart. When they appear together, they are called the Royal Procession—an image of a grand royal ceremony and ritual demonstrating the highest image of humanity and Icon of Essence.

We must remember that this does not reflect a modern democracy. The ancient Chinese had the highest reverence for the emperor and considered him the Son of Heaven, or Tianzi (天子). The Four Rulers are to be revered and understood as benevolent. Today, we do not trust or respect our political leaders, and we think of monarchies as being outdated, but the dynastic system of China, later adopted by Japan, is not to be interpreted through the lens of modern politics or culture. If you do this, you will not understand Polestar Astrology. We must entertain the idea of the benevolent Heavenly Ruler and bow in respect to the Emperor and Empress.

The first step in interpreting your chart is to examine the placement of these two Stars. This alone may be enough to ensure the resolution of Fate. Their potency is strong enough that their influence will happen regardless of your choice, but we must remember that our Character will determine how we relate to them and how our capacity meets the opportunities they represent.

Tian Xiang (天相), is the Tutor of the Emperor and is the Emperor's principal adviser on worldly matters. He is the power behind the throne and represents the highest Confucian ideal of self-cultivation. Tian Ji (天機), the Oracle, always sits to the right side of the Emperor Star and represents the voice of the Ancestors coming through the divination of a female shaman, Wu (巫), in a trance. The Oracle displays our most profound spiritual capacities and advises the Emperor about the unseen forces that govern our lives.

Together, these Four conspire to rule and direct our Fate. The patterns they represent are the most significant in our Chart, and everything else is minor by comparison. We will, therefore, spend the most time on these Stars when we study a chart. After placing them, study each in their own House and then look at how they relate to each other in their respective Houses. If any show up together in pairs, this is very powerful and represents a Fate Threshold. If any of these Four show up in the Ming Palace, you have a very high potential to resolve Fate in this lifetime and experience your Inner Nature.

The Four Rulers each represent our most beneficial and accomplished Ancestors, who shine from the Heavens looking out for our best interest. They can be afflicted but never fully eclipsed in their beneficial radiance. These are your guardian angels, your fairy godmothers, your original Ancestors. Learn to listen to their guidance and direction, for they shape the strongest Currents of Fate that guide our lives.

ZI WEI (紫微)—THE EMPEROR

Photo by Patrick McManaman on Unsplash.[1]

NAME AND TRANSLATIONS: Zi Wei (紫微), the Emperor Star, the Polestar

Zi, 紫—refers to the color purple, associated with the crepe myrtle flower, from lavender to violet, often a dark reddish-blue dye, traditionally produced from the root of Gromwell or the heartwood juice of sappanwood—the color is scarce in nature and is associated emblematically with royalty and the emperor; in the Tang dynasty, it was the color of robes worn by the highest bureaucratic grade. The color purple is associated with the depths of heaven, astral divinities, celestial phenomena, spectral visitations, cosmic totality, and wholeness; e.g., 紫虛 zixu, purple void, 紫冥 ziming, purple gulf, 紫宙 zizhou, purple firmament, all referring to heaven; 紫煙 ziyan, purple haze, 紫霞 zixia, purple auroras, which both refer to mystical mists; 紫曜明 ziyaoming, light of purple scintillance, an esoteric name for sun; 紫清 ziqing, Purple Clarity, alt. name for the heaven of Jade Clarity (玉清), highest of Dao. [Daoist] heavens; 紫雲 ziyun, purple clouds, an auspicious signal of heaven's support or protection; 紫河 zihe, Purple River, i.e., river in the deep sky, Milky Way.[2]

> *Wei*, 微—means faint, imperceptible, indiscernible, intangible, tenuous, subtle. a) what lies between wu 無 (of Dao) and you 有 (of phenomena)—this is a reference to the delicate nature of Fate and the difficulty of understanding and resolving it.[3]

Together, these characters can have many poetic meanings, but here, we translate them as the Emperor Star.

ELEMENT: Yin Earth due to its unmoving centrality, but it is the ruler of Yang Fate

TRADITIONAL IMAGE: Royalty, regality, authority, father or grandfather, leadership, maturity, natural accomplishment, majesty, unmoving, dignity, the Son of Heaven, the emperor, the Pivot of Fate, Ruling Power or Mandate of Heaven, depicted dressed in robes and armor[4]

ANCESTOR PROFILE: Original or highly accomplished Patriarchal Ancestor close to Great Completion: a father, grandfather, great-grandfather (etc.), a Great Elder, Ruler of Patriarchal Fate

LUMINOUS PLACEMENT: Dragon and Horse Palaces

DIMINISHED PLACEMENT: Rooster and Rabbit Palaces

AFFILIATIONS: Leader of the Northern Array but rules the Royal Court

We must, of course, begin with Zi Wei, the Polestar, the North Star, the Emperor Star, the pivot of all astrological calculations, and the central Star of Fate. Looking at a time-lapse photograph of the Polestar, you will see a fixed point in the night sky with the heavens spinning around it. For millennia, sailors and travelers have used the North Star to find their way home and navigate the world, for it is a fixed reference and always points north.

This is the most important image to contemplate, for obviously, it says something quite potent about our placement in the universe. How and why should our planet be fixed in relation to this Star? Due to the procession of the axial tilt of the Earth, the Polestar changes about every 40,000 years, which is also why Tropical Astrology is now 23.44 degrees off from its original calculations and from Sidereal Astrology. The current Polestar is Polaris, but a new Emperor will eventually ascend the throne.

Like the Polestar in the night sky, Zi Wei is the center of your Natal Chart, and all the Stars and Houses spin around it. It is, therefore, the central pivot of Fate and the key to unraveling it. It is considered the Emperor and likened to the emperor of China, the most dignified and respected of all symbols. It is associated with all things royal and regal and with leadership and the ruling power of Heaven. All the other Stars relate to the Polestar, and all patterns of Fate are in service of this central "mission" or "mandate" of Heaven.

In other words, if you focus on resolving this Fate, everything else will happen naturally. So, focus here first. Deeply contemplate the Polestar and its placement. The two most important takeaways from any chart are the Character of the Year and the placement of the Polestar. If you understand these, you can indeed understand and communicate the wisdom of Chinese Polestar Astrology.

Zi Wei rules Yang Fate. Again, Yang Fate is what you are born to "do." It is a catalyst. Yang Fate implies doing, acting, making connections, forming relationships, and making decisions and carrying them out. It is where we have the most significant opportunity and resources available to accomplish Fate. So, wherever it appears, you are called to action, but it is also where you have the most significant resources in the form of relationships, connections, abilities, and preordained successes.

The emperor didn't get his hands dirty but directed others, so although Zi Wei rules Yang Fate, the other Yang Stars often do the actual work. Make no mistake, though: Wherever it shows up is your most important mandate. It is, therefore, somewhat straightforward to interpret. For example, if it appears in the Offspring Palace, then you were born to be a parent, and all your most important Fate unravels after having kids.

The Emperor Star cannot fail. It represents all the blessings and inheritance of your greatest Ancestral patterns of accomplishment. It represents your Original Ancestor and can be a great-great-great-grandfather up to seven generations back, but it can also certainly manifest as the influence of a father or grandfather in this lifetime, as they act through the lineage of your Original Ancestors. It is the prompting of your patriarchy to do, grow, act, and accomplish. While Mom cradles and nurtures, Dad says, "Stand up, walk, play catch, get that college degree, go for that job!"

Wherever it appears, you are compelled and prompted by Fate. Its message is likely undeniable or unavoidable, but sometimes it can be confusing, for our culture has a very narrow image of Yang success. We pretty much limit Yang Fate to a career, but this is only represented in three or four Houses in the chart. So, what if it does not appear in a career House? Although you may be pressured or compelled by culture to pursue success in your career, you may not be Fated for it!

Perhaps you have the Polestar in the Pleasure or Partners Palace. Does this mean you cannot have a successful career? Of course not. It simply means that your career is not the central pivot of your Fate. A career isn't everything, so relax. Maybe it shows up in the Partners Palace, and you have a Lesser Star in Career; then, meeting your husband may change your life, and through him, you make connections that lead to a great job. The relationship becomes the context for all your greatest personal transformation.

As the most important Star, the Emperor cannot be ultimately afflicted or eclipsed, but it can still be afflicted. Alone, the Emperor and the Yang Fate he represents are clear; there is no confusion, and it is generally positive, although it is rare for it to show up completely alone in a House. Ultimately, no matter the affliction, the Yang Fate here will be accomplished to some degree, but it may not be pleasant. If the Emperor shows up with Ghost Stars, then the central resolution of Yang Fate can be a grind. Sometimes Fate is a series of bitter lessons, and we must go through a hero's trial.

Sometimes, an exalted Emperor can lead to greatness, like a shooting star—these are the rock stars, the CEOs, the great leaders and role models. A modest Emperor may mean owning a business, being a manager, being a great dad, or having a potent childhood. An afflicted Emperor could go through struggle, conflict, doubt, full of trial and error, but because it is the Polestar, this struggle is rewarding and can forge greatness through adversity.

The influence of Character here makes all the difference. Yang Characters are more suited to Yang Fate in Yang Houses. In other words, the Emperor in the Superiors Palace is auspicious for a Dragon, but a Dragon with the Emperor in the Offspring Palace may resent putting so much energy into the home, wishing they were off conquering the universe or having grand adventures. But for a Rabbit, the Emperor in the Offspring Palace is a blessing, and to have it in the Superiors Palace may feel like a curse: They resent having to go to work and wish they could stay home and play with their kids. In this scenario, the Dragon may pressure their kid to be the best baseball player ever to fulfill their own unrealized dreams, and the Rabbit may end up parenting their employees. As you go through the Houses, keep the Character dynamics in mind.

It cannot be repeated enough: Character determines how Fate unravels. And it may not be a match. The scenario just described could be you. You may have a strong Fate for something that is a mismatch for your Character. This is where the rubber meets the road. If this is the case, it is important to stick with the Emperor Star—it cannot be ignored. If you are a Rabbit and are Fated to be in the spotlight, this is inauspicious, but that's life. Knowing this may be half the battle. If you don't step up, you create negative Fate patterns that you pass on to your descendants. If this is so, look to other places in the chart, for there may well be an auspicious arrangement through other Stars more suited to your Character.

On a spiritual level, Zi Wei represents our most crucial path to Great Completion, enlightenment, the resolution of Fate, and the experience of our Original Nature. It is the light shining back from the Highest Heaven that represents our highest aspirations, matched only by the Empress, who is the mirror that reflects this Original Light. Once we get beyond the vagaries of worldly Fate, it turns us toward Great Completion, and its placement becomes an integral part of our spiritual path. As such, the placement of the Emperor and Empress always includes a contribution to society, generosity, compassion, altruism, and something greater than us. It doesn't need to be big, but it does need to be regal, royal, a place where we cultivate what Liu Ming called the Awesome Deportment. Please think of the Emperor as the best and most mature version of yourself, for the Emperor accomplishes through example; he is the ultimate benevolent leader.

All the Stars serve the Emperor, but the Northern Array supports and follows the Emperor most closely, so look to these Stars as the Emperor's closest allies.

Let's walk Zi Wei through the Twelve Houses.

Ming Palace

Zi Wei in the Ming Palace is the most significant and potent of placements in Polestar Astrology, and if you have this, you should feel blessed. For Yang Characters like the Dragon, Horse, or Tiger, it belongs here, and if it shows up in the Dragon or Horse Palace, then it is potent and exalted. If it is unafflicted, you are guaranteed to resolve Fate in this lifetime and at least have glimpses of your Original Nature. Here, you can go beyond personal happiness and contribute to society as a resource for others. You can go down as a significant person, a wisdom holder, or as a contributor to the world as an expert, innovator, or entrepreneur; you can influence history or at least be very influential to the people around you, especially if the Emperor is exalted or supported by other potent Stars.

If it appears here, then this life is a "big one." It means that your Ancestors conspired and gave you a lot to do, accomplish, and resolve and that all your past lives were a "buildup" that led to this one. Everything that preceded this life was a preparation, and you are here to do something important, which of course looks different for everyone. It means you will have a lot on your plate, but it also means that you will have an exciting, fulfilling, and rewarding life that you will look back on with a sense of satisfaction.

If you have spiritual aspirations, then the Emperor Star, or any of the Four Rulers, offers a high capacity for spiritual Fruition. You can live life so thoroughly that you see beyond it. It is important here to cultivate yourself, and you will naturally have a sense of dignity and elegance associated with wisdom. The Emperor Star is an Icon of Essence, a deity, and an image of enlightenment and compassion.

If Zi Wei is placed here, you will feel inspired, motivated, driven, and focused. Your Fate is strong. You will feel like you were born for a reason and a purpose; you will be on a mission. A sense of destiny, preordainment, and confidence will be clear to you from the beginning, and you will feel like you have unfinished business. Unafflicted, that mission could be clear, and you may take off like a rocket. If it is afflicted, then finding this mission may be a struggle, but it is in that search that you will unravel Fate.

Unfortunately, Zi Wei in the Ming Palace does not say much about what you are here to do specifically, but only that it is important. The Ming Palace is nonspecific and does not provide clear direction; it is more of an overarching sense of the big picture of life. In this sense, it doesn't really matter what you do; you only have to do it thoroughly, contributing and giving back to others. You must look to the other Houses to see the specifics of where this mission, or Mandate of Heaven, might unfold.

The Emperor in this House often means success in whatever you do: business, finances, passions, hobbies, relationships, and so on. It implies leadership, ambition, and industriousness, but these will change depending on your Character. Whatever you do, when it is done, you will feel a sense of true freedom and release. But for some, this feeling is never finished, and they work for themselves until the end, in service of a great vision or mission.

Zi Wei here has all the opportunity laid out before him—the Emperor Star cannot really fail. This means that you will have strong Fated opportunities, relationships, connections, and experiences. You will meet the right people at the right time in the right place. But you must step up and activate this Fate because Fate only brings you so far.

This placement means that your life is shaped, ruled, guided, and preordained by a very strong Patriarchal Ancestor and your Patriarchal Ancestors in general. Everything in your life goes according to their plan, which was arranged before your birth. You may very well be an accomplished Patriarchal Ancestor reborn.

You may possess the talent and disposition of this Ancestor, like inheriting a great musical ability or business acumen. We hear of these stories: Someone is born to a family of doctors, and graduates at the top of their class at twenty-two. Then, they see the true meaning of being a doctor, quit their hospital job at the age of twenty-seven, and go volunteer in clinics in South America, where they win a Nobel Prize for synthesizing a miracle drug from tree bark that saves millions of lives. This was the fruition of their Fate, and they are now free.

Ancestors Palace

If Zi Wei appears in the Ancestors Palace, then the influence of the Patriarchal Ancestors is even stronger than if it appears in the Ming Palace. This means that your life is not yours; it is theirs. The influence felt here is much more personal, and it manifests much stronger in family life. Your parents and grandparents have a very strong impact on your life, and if Zi Wei is unafflicted by Ghost Stars, then you likely have a very strong and positive relationship with them. You are strongly shaped, motivated, and guided by your parents, grandparents, and Ancestors, and you inherit their drives and ambitions. Here, you owe them a debt and are tied to family; you don't have much choice in the matter. If Zi Wei appears in one of the career Palaces, then this debt is much more open, but here it is tied to family, for better or worse. You are here to continue and resolve the family story—this is your main mission in life.

This can mean strong family inheritance, successorship, tradition, and wealth. You may strongly identify with your Ancestors, like you love being Scottish, and you go to the Highland Games, where you have a blast wearing a kilt and throwing cabers; you may have a lifelong tie to being a MacDonald and hear about the "old world" from Grandpa, who gives you his tartan. This story is where all your friends and connections are made in life. Or you live in the town that your Ancestors have been in for the past ten generations, and there are streets there named after your great-grandfather. You have strong ties there that give your life meaning and context.

It may mean entering the family business. Perhaps your dad is an electrician and owns his own company. At sixteen, you start helping, and by twenty-eight, you take over the business. Generally, it means receiving support and blessings from your Ancestors, but it takes the shape of having a mandate to continue, grow, or pass down a family tradition.

If you have the Emperor here, you can pray and call upon your Ancestors, who have your back. Often, this means that parental influence is strong, even overbearing and demanding. This can be the proverbial overbearing father who pushes you to succeed. As a kid, you hate it, but as an adult, you have gratitude, for he pushed you into mastery.

Zi Wei here can also be a strong spiritual connection to a teacher's lineage. You may meet your "true" Ancestors through a spiritual tradition. A teacher or mentor then becomes like a father, and your spiritual community becomes your family. This is much more common today in America, for we have very little connection to our Ancestral traditions, and we often seek meaning in other cultures.

If it is afflicted by Ghost Stars, reconnecting with your Ancestors could also be a mandate. Maybe you grew up in Australia, but your Ancestors are from Jakarta. So, you travel to meet them and discover a huge story of struggle, exile, and migration, then you start to dream of your grandfather after being handed your family kris knife. If afflicted, this placement can also mean inheriting strong Ancestral patterns of negativity, abuse, addiction, and so on, and you are tasked to liberate them—once you do, you are free, and your Ancestors are free.

It is essential to do genealogy and connect as deeply as possible with your Ancestors' story, land, tradition, religion, and language. It is equally important to pass this on to your kids and to help preserve your Ancestral heritage.

Youth Palace

If Zi Wei appears in the Youth Palace, it can be read in two ways. We must remember that this House represents Fate with siblings, but also Fate during the time of life that we call youth. So, first, it means a very powerful and important Fated connection with a sibling or with specific family members in your youth. The Emperor Star is a Yang star, so it implies a brother, often an older brother, but it can be a sister or younger brother as well, or even the presence of an uncle, grandfather, or role model in childhood.

Here, it means that you have strong Fated connections in youth from a past life or as an Ancestral debt and that this relationship will be central to your life from childhood and key to giving you guidance, education, and/or direction. It may be a strong ongoing, lifelong relationship. You and your brother or sibling may be best friends and rely on each other for the rest of your lives, and this anchor in life helps you unravel Fate. The relationship can go either way: It may represent an older mentor, or you may be the older mentor, and looking after your sibling may be central to your experience of growing up.

Zi Wei may also take the role of a teacher or mentor who appears in school or at church or as a coach on a sports team. Perhaps you have a football coach who believes in you, and you end up in the NFL. Without him, you never would have pursued football. Or it could be a music teacher who inspires you to take up violin, and later, you are playing for the London Symphony Orchestra. Or it could be a science teacher who inspires a passion for physics. Whoever it is, without them, your life would never have been the same.

The Youth Palace is one of the Ancestral mandate Houses, so it represents the strong presence of Patriarchal Ancestors in a very direct way in childhood. The difference between this and the Ancestors Palace is the debt. Here, the influence is strong in childhood, but you are liberated from this as an adult, whereas in the Ancestors Palace, it is with you lifelong. This could be a strong relationship with your father's side of the family—a sense of family tradition and heritage, like maybe you really love being Colombian. It means you have strong Ancestral guardians from your father's side watching over your childhood and shaping it.

If Zi Wei does not manifest specifically through siblings or the family, then it simply means that the time of life called youth is very significant and influential and that all the major Fate of your life happens in childhood. Your life starts big right from the beginning, and you have the life experience of an adult by age twenty. This could be having a big family drama or being born into war or political strife, or it could mean moving a lot and traveling as a child. It could mean being a child star or actor who is born with a clear sense of purpose and opportunities that manifest early. Often, this burns out in adulthood and is followed by a sense of loss or confusion.

Zi Wei here means you are born with the disposition of an adult. You may be a very precocious, talented, mature child—an "old soul." You may end up acting as a parent in your household, taking on great responsibility as a child, so you grow up fast. You reach the age of six and know right away that you want to be a doctor, and nothing stops you; you go on to graduate at the top of your class with a PhD at the age of twenty-two. Dragons, Tigers, Horses, and so on are the most likely to take this on in a big way.

Either way, having the Emperor in the Youth Palace means that your major Fate is over by the time you reach adulthood. This means you are free to do what you want for the rest of your life, but it can also mean feeling lost. You may go through a powerful and dramatic childhood and then not know what to do with yourself once you grow up. Or you are so driven to get that PhD that, once you get it, you lose your passion, for it was all just an inherited Ancestral drive from your great-grandfather who never got to go to school.

Here, it is important to look back at the Ancestral patterns from the patriarchal line and reflect on what you inherited because it was dumped on you as a child. If the Emperor is afflicted by Ghost Stars here, then childhood can be traumatic and abusive. But it also means that this shapes you in a very important way. For example, you may grow up as a child of a drug addict and then become a social worker helping children get out of the same kind of environment.

Partners Palace

If Zi Wei shows up in the Partners Palace, then you have a strong past-life or Ancestrally arranged Fate with a life partner. Meeting them becomes the pivot around which all your Fate unravels. Marriage becomes the center stage for the resolution of Fate: being in it changes you, shapes you, and makes you a better person. This is the kind of life that many people dream of having, but very few are Fated for. This can be the romanticized feeling of a twin flame or soulmate or simply a good match that happens easily and naturally and produces a myriad of great outcomes like family and livelihood. You may marry your high school sweetheart or meet your soulmate in college. Or you must go on a mission to find this person; you have a deep feeling that they are out there somewhere, and your life is a journey to find them. Once you do, you are released from Fate.

Zi Wei, however, is a bit serious, and it often means there is a bigger picture to the partnership. This is a match made by the Ancestors. The Chinese term is Yinyuan (姻緣), which is likened to two trees that appear separate, but beneath the ground, their roots are intertwined. This is not a light decision to partner; this means being tied together, for better or worse, until the Fate is complete.

If it is unafflicted by Ghost Stars, then it can be wonderful, and the relationship may be rewarding, fulfilling, and fruitful. Your partnership is the center of all your personal growth and transformation, and it also extends into the rest of your life. Your friends, family, work, business life, and so on all connect to your marriage in some way. Marriage here is key.

Traditionally, the marriage ceremony is very important if you have Zi Wei here. This is the meeting and joining of two Ancestral lines, and the ceremony is an important ritual for them to meet and give approval. Marriage and reproduction unite and cross Ancestors, and here, the partnership is preordained by Fate for this purpose. The marriage ceremony of Zi Wei is a celestial event, and the ritual is considered as important as the marriage itself. So, if you have it in this House, spend the money and make the event grand and meaningful—you are marrying an Emperor.

If it is afflicted by Ghost Stars, then the partnership can become explosive. Your meeting may be dramatic and powerful, and you fall deeply in love with passion and intensity. But eventually, you realize that you are very different and even incompatible when it comes to the mundanities of relating. Or you inherit a Ghost of Ancestral domestic abuse. So, you fight, argue, throw dishes, and the like, but you love them deeply, stick it out, work it out, and grow together. Because it is Zi Wei, you grow together, and Fate is slowly whittled away, melted in the furnace of relating.

Here, it gets tricky, for in some cases, it is worth sticking it out, but in others, divorce or separation is also important. Not all Fated relationships are Fated to last. Zi Wei with a powerful Ghost Star can be resolved through divorce, ending an abusive pattern and liberating the Ghosts of abused Ancestors.

Character matters a lot here. Rabbits, Pigs, and Goats are likely to seek out and stay in relationships, while independent Characters like Tigers, Dragons, or Monkeys are likely to avoid commitment if it means holding them down or forcing them to take accountability.

Traditionally, the Emperor here also implies meeting an older, more mature partner. Often, this is an older man with a younger woman, but it can go either way. They may offer resources, open new doors, and bring you into a world you otherwise would not have access to. They introduce you to new ideas and change the way you look at the world. They may bring you into a new and higher social circle as you marry "above your station." This is an image of hypergamy, or marrying "up."

Offspring Palace

Zi Wei in the Offspring Palace is easy to understand. It means you were born to be a parent. Having children is the central and most important aspect of your Fate, and being a parent is the crucible for all your greatest personal growth and transformation. So, make the babies! Zi Wei here makes the situation somewhat unavoidable. You will likely know early in life that you want to be a parent, but this is not always the case. Fate and a feeling of purpose in life may start as soon as you have kids; you may have been listless before, but now you know that the purpose of your life is to raise these kids, protect them, teach them, and so on.

Generally, this means you have a Fated past-life or Ancestral debt with your child. Traditionally, we are said to owe someone big, so now we must take care of them, change their diapers, feed them, and so on. If you have Zi Wei here, then you will feel a deep affinity to and profound love for your children. All parents feel this to some degree, but here there is a sense of debt and purpose. This is a lifelong relationship, and your children remain important throughout life. They then owe you and take care of you in old age.

This means you are giving birth to an Emperor, and this could mean giving birth to a returning or Original Ancestor. Generally, the Emperor implies a male child, but of course, it can go either way. More important, it means the child is bright, precocious, intelligent, talented, and easy to raise. You give birth to an "old soul," a self-starter. And, even more important, something about them changes your life for the better. Their arrival brings new resources, opportunities, and connections. Today, we think we must save money to have kids, but traditionally, it is believed that your kids bring you money, especially if you give birth to an Emperor.

But what if someone doesn't want to have kids or can't? Zi Wei here can then mean legacy. You create or give birth to something that is like your child. You create a legacy, invention, or idea that you pass down to the next generation. Or you act as a parent to many people. You may be a role model, teacher, mentor, or guide or work at an adoption agency and help many people be parents.

If afflicted by Ghost Stars, then parenthood may simply be postponed. Or, it could mean having to adopt, or that the journey of becoming a parent through medical intervention becomes significant. Affliction can also mean that the relationship becomes deeply troubled, but you are here to work it out, and this is central to your Fate.

Finally, this can mean a deep Fate with sexuality, for this Palace ultimately is about reproduction. You may not have kids, but you may practice a lot, and that could be central to your Fate. Beneath that urge are the Ancestors calling for children. It could mean Fate for sex work or being a sexual icon, or sexual identity, gender identity, or sexual orientation could be your most significant crux of Fate.

Wealth Palace

Zi Wei in the Wealth Palace goes beyond mere money and means your central Fate is about generating, receiving, or managing resources. Of course, money could play a significant part in this, but the principle of resources here is what matters most: redistribution, acquisition, generosity, abundance, philanthropy, and so on. Zi Wei here implies the Fate to make money, to earn, to grow, and to build wealth, but it doesn't mean a lot necessarily. Unafflicted or exalted, one may earn a lot, and it could very well mean getting rich. Or it could simply mean doing very well through a high salary or income.

Here it is the process that matters, and you receive the Ancestral Fate for seeking wealth that comes from previous generations. This could mean a significant inheritance or family money. Or it could mean growing up poor and inheriting the drive to get out of poverty. This drive could be the central theme of your Fate, and a poverty mentality may drive you your whole life. Even if you become successful, you may feel driven toward wealth.

Here, there are hints of a career. Zi Wei could mean working in banking, finance, or the stock market, and traditionally it meant working with fineries like gold or in the jewel trade. You may not make a lot of money, but you may work with rich people to make them richer. No matter the case, your Fate revolves around money, wealth, and resources. Wealth is resources—power, tangible and real products, and services—not just numbers on a screen. You may deal in lumber or steel, energy, food, or the wealth of information. These are true wealth because they're what we pay for.

If Zi Wei is afflicted by Ghost Stars here, you may build and lose a fortune. Or, you may be a "rags to riches" story like Andrew Carnegie. In the end, even if your fortunes are calamitous, you realize the true value of wealth and are satisfied with what you have. This brings to mind the story of Puyi, the last Emperor of China, who was forced to abdicate, imprisoned, and then ended his life as a humble gardener in the Beijing Botanical Gardens.

True fruition here and the royal nature of Zi Wei becomes generosity. You give back. You donate. You support others who are less fortunate, even if you have nothing, and this gives your life and your drive to get rich meaning and purpose. You may be Robin Hood: Rob the rich and give to the poor. Or you are Ebenezer Scrooge and must learn the real meaning of Christmas. Again, what is most important is that the true meaning of wealth is the central lesson of Fate, and that life unfolds around and due to this lesson.

Health Palace

Zi Wei in the Health Palace often takes on two different but often intertwined interpretations. First, it means that your body and constitution are directly linked to your Ancestors—if it is unafflicted by Ghost Stars, then you inherit a strong constitution and pattern of health and longevity from your Patriarchal Ancestors. This means a strong body, immunity, recovery, and resilience. It means having a strong Yang constitution that responds very well to "doing" things to cultivate health: exercise, diet, and treatments are all proactive and work well when you do them and comply with doctors. Sometimes, Zi Wei here is somewhat passive and means being strong and healthy, and this becomes a great basis for unraveling Fate. You rarely get sick, and when you do, you take medicine and get better.

Second, Zi Wei here means that your Fate revolves around and through your embodiment. In other words, your journey with health, healing, recovery, and so on becomes the central story. This is more often the case when the Emperor Star is afflicted by Ghost Stars; illness, disease, or lifelong sickness is the driving factor of all your personal transformation, and it affects your job, finances, relationships, and so on. Perhaps you get testicular cancer and go to China, where doctors heal you, and then you stay with them and study medicine to become a doctor yourself. If unafflicted, this placement can simply mean that being healthy is your Path; you live well, exercise, eat right, and help others to do the same. We often see yoga teachers, personal trainers, massage therapists, and so on with Zi Wei here.

In either case, we see a very strong Fate here for working in healthcare. Maybe you become sick and go on a healing journey, and then come back to help others with what you have learned. Or perhaps, you are called to help and heal others due to being health conscious all your life. Zi Wei here can mean a strong aptitude and passion for medicine. It can also mean having very strong routines and self-discipline that come from a powerful Ancestral guardian. You have a guardian angel who smacks your hand whenever you reach for a cookie.

If you get ill, there is a very strong likelihood that you will recover and that, in doing so, you will liberate a lot of Ancestral Ghosts. Here, your body becomes a vehicle for your Ancestors. Your strength and health are living it up for a long line of people who died with poor health, and your discipline and overcoming of bad habits are exorcising all kinds of negative patterns. Ghosts line up to get free of their chocolate addictions, which you conquer after a month of eating ice cream, after which you quit for good.

The danger here is being too strong for your own good. A Yang constitution means that you may have a high pain threshold and feel so strong that you push yourself all the time, burning the candle at both ends. You can work all day and not feel tired. You put yourself at risk by working forty hours a week and then climbing a mountain on the weekend. So, it is important here to cultivate balance and not overdo it.

Having a the Emperor here means that you heal best in the spring and summer, at morning and midday, and from being active and out and about. Generally, you respond to more conventional, standard medicine and to what we call "tonifying" treatment in Chinese medicine. It means that you have a very strong sense of survival, recovery, and resilience from all your Ancestors who made it.

Career/Travel Palace

If Zi Wei appears in the Career/Travel Palace, it is very similar to being in the Ming Palace, as it is the opposite House. Both represent very strong Fate in this lifetime, but the difference is that here, it means that your Fate manifests in your work in the world and your contribution to society outside the family. And, as the Travel Palace, it often means that you must go on a journey to find your Fate and express it. It could mean that you were born in the wrong place and that you must travel, immigrate, or move to another city. It is, therefore, often a Fate Threshold when it appears here, for it represents a new life other than the one you were born to. As such, this was considered an affliction in ancient China, for it was seen as a curse to be born in the wrong place and feel out of place. I have the Emperor Star here, and I have been to thirty countries, lived in two foreign countries, and moved many times to start my life over. My Emperor is afflicted by Qi Sha, so it has been a mess, but it has undoubtedly been the central unraveling of my Fate.

It can mean travel, but often it means moving. You missed the mark at birth, and your past-life and Ancestral Fate are scattered with relationships, connections, and opportunities all over the place. You must find the right place or series of places, following the breadcrumbs. Furthermore, it means that this traveling and/or moving is motivated by your sense of purpose or life's mission and goals. In other words, you don't move just for the sake of moving; you move for a job or career, for school, or in search of destiny.

You may feel like your life is out there waiting for you to discover. You may feel stifled, trapped, or simply out of place in your hometown. Life is boring until you move across the country for school; suddenly, you meet amazing people and go on great adventures. Or, you have an ordinary life and travel to Spain after three years of high school Spanish classes and find that you immediately feel at home and start speaking Spanish like a native. You marry a local and move there. If Zi Wei appears here, then you must do this. Your Fate will not unravel until you take the leap and make the journey.

This is also the first Career Palace, so it implies that your central Fate is in your work in the world. It doesn't say what that work is, but only that it is important and that moving and traveling must serve this. It generally means being successful in a career. Your career, job, and life purpose are where all the important stuff happens, and everything else unfolds as you follow this path. It often means doing something influential or important, and this could mean management, leadership, or business. Because it is the Emperor, it means doing something big, and contribution, altruism, service, and generosity are part of it.

It often means ambition: You inherit the patriarchal ambition for success and prosperity. Here, it means that Ancestral talents, past-life practice, and the opportunities cultivated from many lifetimes are involved. The job, purpose, and career that you find are not ordinary; they are the fruition of a long timeline of cultivation. You may become an architect and find that you dream in blueprints and see visions of great spaces in your mind; your hands and heart flow together, and you conduct a building like an orchestra.

If the Emperor is unafflicted by Ghost Stars, then this path may be clear, but if afflicted, then it could be a hero's trial. You must travel a lot and try out a lot of things before finding your calling. And it may never feel certain. But what is certain is that your Fate will unravel around your search for meaning, purpose, and place. Some Characters will jump to meet the adventure, and some will shy away. Character matters big time here. A Monkey or a Tiger (like me) may jump around, starting over compulsively, and a Snake may never move and just resent their station in life.

Assistants Palace

If Zi Wei appears in the Assistants or Friendship Palace, then you have strong and central Fate in two possible arenas. First, you are Fated to a life of helping others—to service and humility, working behind the scenes or in secondary or supportive roles. Second, it means that your Fate unravels through friends, co-workers, subordinates, and/or due to help from others. Zi Wei can appear here as a teacher, mentor, or helper who shows you the way and gives you a path to follow.

The Emperor is the supreme leader, so it is considered out of place here in the Assistants Palace. The Emperor is meant to be in the spotlight; here, it is behind the scenes. This can again be interpreted in two ways. In the first arena, you are Fated to a life of helping and supporting others. This often means service work: a career waiting tables, in a healthcare profession like nursing, or as an assistant to a more influential person. This is somewhat of a debt: You are paying back through helping. Some Characters are born for this, and others will resent it. A Rooster will not like being subordinate, but a Rabbit will feel safe behind the scenes. But because it is the Emperor, it means that you are a standout assistant, and you bring success to others. It is your organizational abilities, time management, and scheduling that keep them together, and without you, they would crash and burn. You may also be a counselor, therapist, or coach and help others shine, like the popular television character Ted Lasso. This is the strongest House for seeing Fate to be an astrologer as well.

The second interpretation is that someone owes you big. Your Fate is brought to you by a helper. You have a standout assistant or secretary who brings you success. You may be a visionary, but you are terrible at managing your schedule or finances. You are a mess until you hire someone, and then you take off and make it big, bringing them along with you.

However, here it could also mean you become the power behind the throne. Power is often wielded from a secondary position. You operate in the shadows or through a figurehead. Or, as an assistant, you do all the "real" work, and the manager is a joke but charismatic and, therefore, shines in the spotlight. Administrative work is often quite redundant in many organizations, and most of the real work is done by a small group of people who don't get credit.

The second arena here is Fate through friendship. This House represents all the relationships outside the family that fall under the category of friendship: co-workers, assistants, schoolmates, and so on. So, if the Emperor shows up here, it means that you have a significant Fate with these kinds of relationships. You may be part of a "circle of returners," a close-knit group of friends with past-life connections who find each other again. You may develop deep, meaningful connections with friends who feel like family. All the major unraveling of your Fate happens through and with these people. You may have great adventures, stories, parties, and so on with your clique.

Or, you have deep connections with co-workers, people you go to school with, and so on. Television shows like *The Office* demonstrate this kind of deep Fate with co-workers. Your office becomes your family, and you support each other through all kinds of ups and downs. In today's world, we spend most of our time at work with co-workers, so this makes sense. If it is afflicted by Ghost Stars, this can be a source of major drama and controversy.

Finally, this House can represent your students, clients, and customers. If you are a teacher, this House will represent your Fate with students, who may be vast in number. With the Emperor here, you may put out a course, and suddenly, thousands sign up, and you're touring the country as a motivational speaker. Or this is a strong Fate to have customers and clients: You set up a shingle and have a line out the door. If you build it, they will come.

Superiors Palace

Zi Wei is the Emperor and supreme icon of leadership, so it belongs in the Superiors Palace. If it appears here, it exalts the Star and House, especially if it appears with strong supporting Stars. Of all the Houses, this is the clearest match with the Emperor's mandate and the easiest to interpret. You have big things to do. It means you have a strong Fate for success and leadership, and you have the clearest potential to make a difference in the world through work, social contribution, innovation, politics, religion or spirituality, and so on.

This is the image of being "on top of the game." It means not only being successful at what you do but also being able to change the game. While a Lesser Star like the Sun could mean being a successful surgeon, the Emperor Star could mean inventing a new procedure that revolutionizes the way surgery is done, or you get promoted to Chief of Surgery and oversee an entire hospital. Here, the Emperor is in the spotlight, so it means being in a position of responsibility, with all eyes on you. The influence here spreads out, and with this placement, you have the capacity to influence the most people, and you can help many others in the resolution of their Fate.

There is strong potential here to start a business or be a manager, boss, CEO, executive director, or president. You will likely be promoted and find it easy and natural to work your way up the ranks. Some characters will thrive in this role, and others will struggle with the responsibility. Here, you will have to make big decisions that will affect the lives of others. You should lead by example, and there is a mandate here to self-cultivate for the sake of being a good leader.

You are a role model, and you set the standard. Here you are the Emperor and should cultivate a sense of regal deportment, without letting it get to your head. The Emperor is humble and compassionate, but some could easily turn this into being a despot, dictator, or just a jerk. A strong ego will likely abuse this power, and many people with strong Fate in leadership do become abusers, which is why self-cultivation becomes so important here.

You will likely have strong ambition and a hunger for success. People with this kind of Fate may work sixty-plus hours a week; they may sleep in the office; they may step over people and do anything to get ahead. Often, this placement generates a strong personal mission and vision: You want to create, inspire, and manifest something big in the world. So, you might create a brand, an invention, a new company, or the like. Of course, not all CEOs will have this here, for there are many ways that ambition and drive can show up in a chart, but this is the most direct, and the least likely to have ulterior motives.

This is also the House of teaching, successorship, and lineage. The Tutor and Wen Stars are more about academic teaching, but the Emperor indicates a larger influence or tradition and the likelihood of succession. You may have Fate to meet and study under a great teacher, boss, or mentor. You follow in the footsteps of a great artist, craftsperson, or master and then inherit their tradition or take over their business. They teach you everything they know, and the student then becomes the master. You may even surpass them in skill and ability.

Spiritually, this often means meeting a guru, lama, rabbi, saint, priest, and so on. You may be born on a quest for enlightenment and go off into the wilderness in search of a master who will show you the way. If the Emperor is here, then you will not only meet that person, but you may become them. Your Fate unravels after you meet your teacher. If it is afflicted by Ghost Stars, then it can often mean abuse at the hands of a teacher and/or becoming an abuser and misusing your power and authority.

If you resolve Fate in this House, then the influence of the Emperor means that you will be honored, remembered, and respected, for better or worse. You will make an impression of some kind, so make it a good one.

Property Palace

If Zi Wei appears in the Property Palace, then you have a strong Fate to own material goods, land, or property or with the practice of Fengshui. You may also have significant Fate around the concept of "home" or personal identity related to place, ethnicity, or cultural heritage.

The most straightforward interpretation here is the ownership of property. You will inherit or purchase land, buildings, cars, and other resources, and you will be successful due to that. Your Fate will unravel around owning and operating things. This House is connected to the Wealth Palace. The Wealth Palace indicates money, while the Property Palace indicates the things that money pays for, and the two feed off each other. So, you may be a landlord or work in real estate, material goods, or shipping. Either way, there is something tangible about the Fate in this House.

You may inherit property or a legacy of some kind, and that becomes the center of your Fate. There is often a strong connection to legacy, family money, family businesses, generational wealth, inheritance, and trust funds here. There is a link to the legacy of the Ancestors—they have built and provided everything for you. This may look like your family paying for college or setting you up to inherit the family fortune in a will. Or, you are stuck with a legacy of debt and junk, and your Fate is to sift through it and clean up the family mess. In either case, the Ancestors Palace will also provide clues to the nature of the inheritance.

This connection to Ancestors also implies a strong connection to land and place. So, often there is a strong Fate around your place of origin. You may have deep Fated connections to your hometown, the house you grew up in, or the "old world" where your relatives all came from. Maybe your family has lived in the same house for ten generations, and you sleep in the same room as your great-great-grandfather, and he visits you in dreams. Or, you have a spiritual connection to the landscape or nature of your childhood. Perhaps you grew up on a farm, and your Fate is tied intimately to wide-open pastures and raising cattle.

Often, the Emperor Star here means that your life is a "walkabout." In other words, you are displaced and must find a home, return home, create a home, or return to the place of your Ancestors. You move around from place to place, renting and looking for a home, and it isn't until you finally settle and "put down roots" that your Fate unravels. Buying or building a House is often a symbol of this. The Emperor here means that this will go smoothly, and it will become your palace. Creating a home gives you the power to become the Emperor. Building a legacy or home for your family is the center of your Fate, and through this process, you "grow up."

The Emperor here can also mean going on pilgrimage, either to a sacred place or to your Ancestral place of origin. You may have central Fate to go to Mecca or Bodhgaya or the Vatican. Or you must return to Auschwitz and pay respect to your Ancestors who died there, completing the circle. Along with the Travel Palace, we see the Fate of exile and migration here, but here the connection is to place, land, or property. There is Fate to make a physical connection, to touch something, to eat the food of your people, wear their clothes, hear their music, sing their songs and prayers. Here, you may feel called to do genealogy, learn an Ancestral language, kiss the Blarney Stone, and so on.

More simply, you may just start an Airbnb or own an apartment building, and that generates the money to buy another property, then another, and so on. This is a great Fate to work in real estate, sell cars, own and rent out retail space, and the like. It is also a strong indicator of working as an architect, contractor, carpenter, or designer.

The Emperor in this House means you have a strong sense of Fengshui, the art of placement. You deeply understand and intuit spaces and how people, energy, sound, weather, and so on flow through space. You have a strong internal compass; you are a divining rod. You can feel and sense the spirit of things, buildings, and landscapes. You naturally know how to rearrange the furniture. This is very similar to the Roof Beam Star here, but in this case it becomes the central pivot of unraveling Fate. You are looking to be in the right place or create the proper placement in life, and you can help others to do the same.

Pleasure Palace

If Zi Wei appears in the Pleasure Palace, then you were born to have fun! You were born to follow your sense of enjoyment, pleasure, fun, interest, adventure, and so on. Sounds pretty good, right? Liu Ming was born in the Year of the Pig and had the Polestar here, which he joked about a lot: This is an exalted placement for a Pig, for they are going to follow their fun anyway. For a Snake, a Rat, or an Ox, however, this could be inauspicious, for they are not likely to follow their fun. However, it just means that they will do what is fun *to them*, which for an Ox could be working all the time.

In our culture, living a life in pursuit of pleasure is both applauded and condemned. We all want to do this, but we also criticize others for achieving it. So, having the Emperor here can be confusing. Having an "ordinary" life, with a nine-to-five job and a heavy sense of duty and responsibility, will be tough to accept. You will be deeply drawn to a sense of enjoyment, so you must make your job something you love, or you will have to "work to play."

The key here is to dive deeply into your passions, hobbies, and interests and make them work for you. If you master what you love, then others will appreciate it, and you can make a life out of it. Or you can accept that work is not that important; just get a job to pay the bills and spend your free time pursuing what makes you happy.

Maybe you have a desk job, but at night you play pool for hours and make a ton of connections and community playing in tournaments. Or you spend all your hard-earned cash on collectibles, trading cards, antiques, and the like, and this gives you great pleasure. Eventually, you will sell your trading cards and get rich. Or you are a boring dentist, but every summer, you go wild doing drugs and partying at Burning Man, and this is where all your real Fate happens.

Perhaps you love video games and grow up to be a game designer or YouTube streamer. Here, we often see professional athletes, gamers, gamblers, musicians, performers, and so on. Some kind of hobby or sport, some way of playing, turned into a path. Things start as fun but then become your life. The Emperor turns the play into power.

The Emperor here pushes the boundaries of the senses; it drives you to find meaning and unravel Fate through experience. You will likely pursue sensual pleasure through travel, food, art, and music and become a connoisseur. You may indulge in drugs or drinking, but the purpose is to find meaning and to have deep experience. You will likely enjoy friendship and relationships, and sex could be a spiritual experience. You may love parties, concerts, performances, and so on.

It may be that your greatest joy is giving happiness and pleasure to others. If you have the Emperor here, then that becomes a mandate: You must go beyond personal enjoyment and find a way to give it back to the world. This is why we love professional athletes and actors and pay them so much; we love people who entertain us. This is a great placement for actors and entertainers, for they can truly lose themselves in their roles.

The Emperor means that, by following this mandate, all your Fate unravels, so life connections, relationships, jobs, and even personal transformation all happen by following your fun!

TIAN FU (天府)—THE EMPRESS

NAME AND TRANSLATIONS:

Tian Fu (天府), the Empress Star, the Southern Star, the Storehouse of Heaven

Tian, 天—refers to the sky or heavens; the highest cosmic principle or force. The Chinese concept of heaven includes not only the physical sky or space covering the earth but also weather and the seasons and the notion of nature and the forces and laws that govern it.[5]

Fu, 府—repository (of valuables), archive (of documents). a) Storehouse, treasury; depot. 2 princely headquarters, the administrative center of the government's establishment; palatine. 3 residences of a noble or high dignitary. 4 (med.)[medieval] prefectural administration in a capital city or strategic location; precincts. 5 (med.) SGL, or 府兵 fubing, in Tang [dynasty] times a military garrison, esp. in the militia system operating to rotate soldiers throughout the state. 6 開府 kaifu, the important title from Han through Tang, varying in application but indicating that the holder was permitted to open a headquarters with its own staff, in med. times often a military title. 7 receptacles, a set of inner organs of the human body, complementary to the 5 "viscera" (zang 臟), e.g., 六府 liufu.[6]

Together, the name of this Star can be translated as the Storehouse of Heaven, as it refers to a storehouse that holds all our accumulated good or positive Fate from our Beneficial Ancestors and past lives, to be distributed as gifts in this lifetime. As it is the Yin counterpart to the Emperor, we translate it as the Empress.

ELEMENT: Yang Earth, but it is the ruler of Yin Fate

TRADITIONAL IMAGE: A queen or empress, youthful or ageless, enthroned woman at court, elegantly dressed, surrounded by entourage of court ladies, eunuchs, and armed guards, Yin Power, effortless success, impeccability, persuasion, motherhood, nourishment[7]

ANCESTOR PROFILE: Original or highly accomplished Matriarchal Ancestor close to Great Completion: a mother, grandmother, or great-grandmother (etc.), a Great Elder, Ruler of Matriarchal Fate

LUMINOUS PLACEMENT: Ox and Goat Palaces

DIMINISHED PLACEMENT: Horse and Rooster Palaces

AFFILIATIONS: Leader of the Southern Array

Tian Fu is the Empress of the Royal Court and the Ruler of Yin Fate. Historically, there is great debate about whether this was a "real" Star. Some believe that it used to be visible in the southern sky but has since passed out of view due to the axial tilt of the Earth, and others believe that it is simply an imaginary Star. Logically, if there is a Yang in the form of the Emperor or North Polestar, there must be a Yin, so we have the Empress, or Southern Polestar. Together with the Emperor, she is the second most potent Star in the Royal Court, and in many ways, she is more powerful, for she represents what is certain and already accomplished.

The Empress is difficult for Westerners to understand. The Emperor is easy: This is what you are here to "do"; this is where you have Yang Fate. There is a mission, a goal, things to accomplish. But the Empress represents "being." There is nothing to "do" here regarding productivity, but there is something to demonstrate through "being." This is the classic dynamic between Yin and Yang.

The emperor had a job; he had to make decisions and carry much responsibility for the empire. The empress did not have a job; she was an icon. Her job was to demonstrate royalty. She set the standard for beauty, and she was an object of worship for the empire. She, therefore, had to be impeccable in the way that she is dressed, the way that she moved, and the way that she spoke. Her deportment was elegant, graceful, and highly mannered. But she did this seemingly without effort, for she was trained to be in this role since birth. By the time she became empress, it is natural and effortless. In your chart, Tian Fu represents where you are the most accomplished, gifted, and graceful, and where you receive the most fruition from past efforts.

The name of the Star, Tian Fu (天府), means the Storehouse of Heaven. The Empress was brought and given gifts as part of the ritual of court, which she placed in the Lu Cun (祿存), the

Storehouse, the name of a Lesser Star, which is a place in the chart where you receive financial and worldly boons. The Empress is the storehouse of all your Ancestral gifts; it is the record where all that your Ancestors accomplished is written. It can also be interpreted as the positive momentum of all your past lives—everything here has already been done, and in this lifetime, you are Fated to receive and experience the results. You just need to sit back and receive them.

This is the definition of Yin Fate. We are Fated to go through certain experiences, be given opportunities, and have things happen to us that are beyond our control. This is because the causes happened before we were born. Our Ancestors already did things, or we did things in past lives. And now we get to experience the results and rewards. We all know what it is like to feel like things happen to us, and we ask, *Why me? What did I do to deserve this?* We search our past and can't find a good explanation or reason for things. This is Yin Fate. But the Empress is wholly positive. She represents all the beneficial results. She can be afflicted, but this only makes her moody. Some Characters can make the most positive situations negative, but no matter the affliction, everyone has a wealth of good fortune with the Empress, no matter how dark things seem. It is up to us to make good on that fortune and not squander it, ignore it, or reject it.

The Empress, then, represents birth talent and skill. We may naturally take to playing the piano, or mathematics, or art, or dance. Perhaps we are born intelligent, resourceful, and highly organized, despite no positive reinforcement at school or home. We may be born into a wealthy family or beautiful surroundings. We may be gifted with college tuition, a great job, or a trip, or we might inherit a role, a title, or a plot of land. We may meet people who change our lives; we follow them, and then one day realize that our lives would have never been the same without them.

Tian Fu represents opportunities, gifts, connections, and so on that seem to happen naturally or at least easily. You meet the right person at the right time. You get a job offer that you are not qualified for because a friend or relative put in a good word. You happen to be naturally gifted at something, opening a world of possibilities. But remember, the job of the Empress is to receive and follow the opportunity and breadcrumbs left behind.

Yin Fate is about waiting, listening, receiving, following the signs, and letting others work for you. You do not have to do anything when the Empress shows up. Relax and let it happen, for all the groundwork has been laid. This is called Wuwei, which we can translate as effortless effort, non-striving, non-doing, going with the flow. There are, of course, places in our chart where we must work hard and strive, but not here. Here, we are gifted.

The Empress represents Yin Power. This is the power the Empress wields in the Royal Court. This is the power of women, which has been devalued in our modern understanding of history, because we only understand Yang Power and force. We think that women need to be like men to be equal. Yin Power represents seduction, perception, subtlety, manipulation, and empathy—the capacity to influence and control through body language, a subtle glance, and a well-timed remark. It is social skill and perception. It is calculating and reading patterns to know when a tiny push can have a tremendous effect. It is the power of alliance, so often there is the potential for great networking and social connection wherever she shows up.

While some of this may sound mysterious, the Empress also represents our greatest capacity for love, compassion, and generosity, and she is the center of our greatest spiritual fruition. Wherever she shows up is a great place to practice meditation, yoga, self-cultivation, and self-reflection to bring out our best inherent qualities. Most important, it is crucial to understand that, like the Emperor, the Empress cannot fail. Wherever she shows up, Fate is guaranteed to unravel without effort, without us having to strive.

But as such, she is mysterious. We don't get to understand our Yin Fate, and we don't have to. The Empress represents a great mystery. We are so hard-pressed to know what to do and how to work things out, but there is no figuring her out. So, take to heart that the Empress represents a place where we can trust in the unknown and let things happen. We only need to get out of the way.

All the Stars revere the Empress, but the Southern Array supports and follows her most closely, so look to these Stars as the Empress's closest allies.

Let's walk Tian Fu through the Twelve Houses.

Ming Palace

Tian Fu in the Ming Palace is one of the most exalted but mysterious placements in Polestar Astrology. In general, having one of the Four Rulers in the Ming Palace means you have "Big Fate" and guarantees a strong resolution of Fate in this lifetime: The Emperor is the most significant in terms of having a Yang Fate agenda with lots of stuff to do and accomplish, but the Empress means everything is already done, which is hard to understand, as life will still of course require effort. If the Empress in particular arrives in the Ming Palace, you are truly blessed, for you can trust that the unraveling of your Fate will unfold exactly as it is meant to. You are along for the ride.

If you have the Emperor in the Ming Palace, it means this life is a "Big One," but if Tian Fu arrives here, it means that your last lifetime was a "Big One." And now you get to experience the rewards and results of that work. It means that all the work of your Ancestors has culminated in your birth, and everything was a setup. Life has a script, an itinerary, but unfortunately, you never get to see it. This is the definition of Yin Fate, and the only perhaps more mysterious Yin Fate is that of the Moon and Concubine, for their Fate is out of their control. The Empress is in control, but she has no specific mandate other than to be an Icon of Essence.

This can be very frustrating for some proactive Characters, like Tigers, Dragons, Roosters, or Horses. They are always looking to be active and busy and often want to control their agenda. They can be compulsive in their "doing," so a Yin Fate of waiting, listening, and simply being is tough. With the Empress in the Ming Palace, we take leaps of faith, but we must be cautious not to leap *over* our Fate.

Tian Fu here means that you have a noble, elegant, dignified, seductive, mysterious, and even regal countenance or that you will eventually cultivate one. Often it means having talent, intelligence, and skills that are inherited at birth. You have tremendous "memory" from your Ancestors or past lives, which may result in a deep feeling of having been here and done that before. Because you did. It's kind of like you finished everything but decided to come back for one more lifetime to help out and benefit others, similar to the bodhisattva ideal of Buddhism.

Because of this, the Empress in the Ming Palace is considered one of the highest (if not the highest) capacities for spiritual practice. If you have this Star in this House, nothing else will make sense. Worldly goals and striving have already been done, and you are here to be or demonstrate something. You will likely feel a deep calling toward meditation, yoga, prayer, and inner cultivation, and you can excel at them. Furthermore, the Empress is the icon of compassion and altruism, for the empress's work was often charitable. So, the Four Immeasurables of compassion, loving-kindness, joy, and equanimity come naturally to her, and you should cultivate and express them to the best of your ability.

If unafflicted by Ghost Stars, you will feel blessed and protected and will likely experience a great deal of luck. Often, this will be due to the actions and influences of others. An exalted Empress gets cared for, which can be like being born with a silver spoon, but not necessarily. It can simply mean that you "want for not," as others provide for you. No effort is required for prosperity, and learning to receive is an important part of your Fate. You are gifted Fate—this means opportunity often falls in your lap if you pay attention. The Empress is gifted Fate because of who she is; your deportment and character will attract others and opportunities to you.

This means that the agenda of your Fate is subtle, complex, and mysterious. It is written in fine print, and often, there are breadcrumbs that you must follow. If you have the Empress here, you can trust your instinct and gut feelings (to a point). And you can follow the signs, the connections, the serendipitous, and the synchronicitous. And you should. This is your Fate. Your Fate will unravel as you follow your heart rather than your head. The more your head gets in the way, the more you will complicate things. This means that life may be a strange and circuitous story, but it will all work out for the best.

And just as you must learn to receive, you must also learn to give. The empress is a leader and does have that responsibility, for all eyes are on her. She must cultivate benevolence and generosity, but what she gives is love, beauty, and wisdom. She is a patron of the arts and humanities. Whatever good fortune you receive, you have a responsibility to pay it forward and to give back.

Ultimately, you are Fated to succeed in all aspects of Fate with ease, grace, and style. Everything you do, you can do well. Like the Emperor, the Empress cannot be truly afflicted, but she can be made moody and frustrated by the likes of the Ghostly Stars, so pay extra care if she is afflicted, for it can be easy to make a mess of such subtle and complex Fate.

Ancestors Palace

If Tian Fu arrives in the Ancestors Palace, it means that your life is strongly influenced and shaped by your Matriarchal Ancestors, which again, can mean either all the women in your family or everyone on your mother's side. You have a very strong female Ancestral guardian, or many of them. It kind of means that you come from a long line of badass women, and all of them have ganged up to make sure that your life is a demonstration of everything they have worked for and probably could not have.

Women have historically been disadvantaged in agricultural and industrial societies, and it is only in the past few decades that this has turned. This means that we all have a lot of frustrated and oppressed women in our Ancestral line who were likely not given the chance to fulfill their true potential. If you have the Empress here, then they are all behind you, raining down blessings and working behind the scenes to give you the life they desire. So, there is a mandate to live this life for them and to accomplish and experience the freedom and opportunities they were denied. There may be a lot of pain and sadness in this, but ultimately, you are liberating all your female Ancestors through your life.

Like the Empress in the Ming Palace, there is a strong agenda of Yin Fate, which is mysterious and subtle. But here, it is much more closely aligned with the Ancestors, and therefore, you may identify very strongly with clan, ethnicity, and geography, as well as receive gifts and messages from lineage. There is a responsibility here to connect with them, while in the Ming Palace, life is much more open and free. Your Matriarchal Ancestors give you promptings, messages, dreams, and signs in life. Perhaps your great-grandmother would have excelled if she were put in charge of the family business, but she wasn't, and your grandfather ran it into the ground. Now, you get the job as a manager or become a CEO as an expression of her unused talents.

You may feel very close to your mother, grandmother, or your mother's side of the family. They may strongly influence your life and provide protection, education, and guidance. Often, this is the image of closeness to a matriarch that extends into all aspects of life, and you may feel closer to your mother than your father.

You will receive talents, strengths, and behavioral patterns from your Matriarchal Ancestors, and you may be an Original Ancestor reborn. This often means having big genetic gifts in the arts and a sense of style, elegance, and grace that comes from a long line of family tradition. Family tradition here is important and must be carried on. So, learn the songs and stories of your grandparents, for their wisdom shapes your life. And look for inheritance and heirlooms, especially those with stories.

Youth Palace

If Tian Fu appears in the Youth Palace, then your Matriarchal Ancestors have a very strong and influential presence in your early life. This often means a strong connection to one or many siblings and that your mother and/or grandmother are very present when raising you. Your mother or grandmother may give you education and guidance, and you may be very close to them emotionally, or at the very least, they are very influential and possibly even overbearing.

Also, like the Emperor in this House, it means that you have a lot of Fate resolution that happens in childhood, but again, it is Yin in this case, so much of it is beyond your control. You are Fated to go through a lot: Your youth may be a whirlwind of experience that carries you along, and you may not realize how profound it was until much later in life. You may grow up jet-setting with your CEO mother or expat parents, going to private schools and learning foreign languages, or you may grow up cooking with your grandmother, who tells you stories about the war and teaches you Yiddish. This may seem normal, but then, as an adult, you realize it was a great privilege.

Often, this means a very strong connection with a sibling or an older family member. Because it is the Empress, it may be a sister or aunt, but this is not always the case. You may have an influential older sister, or you may be one. It could mean a big family, like you are one of ten kids, and your youth is an absolute circus. But in general, this is very positive, and a lot of deep Fated connections are made and unraveled here. The Ancestral or past-life Fate here is very strong but natural. It is like you have known each other for lifetimes, because you have. These kinds of sibling connections are deep and last a lifetime; you may be connected at the hip and continue to rely on each other as adults.

Like the Emperor, it can mean being a very talented and precocious child. You are born an old soul, with the character of an adult by the time you're ten. Often, it means a lot of inborn talents and gifts that come alive in childhood and may even come to fruition, like winning the state championship spelling bee or going to nationals at anything. The Emperor is more active here, needing to accomplish a great task, but the Empress is more about maturity, talent, and character that gets rewarded—think Shirley Temple.

Finally, it may mean a lot of complex social dynamics at home and school. The Empress represents Yin Power and all the power dynamics of the Royal Court. She makes and breaks alliances, manipulates power behind the scenes, and influences the nation through gossip and glances. This suggests the many Hollywood movies of high school drama—you may be part of a cheerleader cabal that runs the school.

Either way, you enter adulthood very prepared, and there may even be a sense of uncertainty as an adult, for your childhood was so rich. It is important to look to the Emperor in this case to see where the work is still to be done.

Partners Palace

Tian Fu in the Partners Palace is very similar to the Emperor here, but the difference is that the Empress has an effortless quality that makes this placement much more relaxed and less dramatic. The Empress here means you have very strong Yinyuan (姻缘), past-life or Ancestrally arranged Fate with a life partner. You are "previously betrothed."

This kind of Fate has a naturalness and easy flow. You immediately feel that you have known each other for lifetimes, and there is an "of course" factor. It just seems to happen without effort, and you will likely be very compatible. Short-term passion can easily come and then fizzle out, but long-term compatibility is very difficult to find. Here, there is a very strong basis for a stable, long-term partnership that resolves the Fate of both partners. This is pretty much the ideal Fate for marriage, and most people dream of this, but few find it. There are stronger Stars for romance and love, but this Star is supreme for marriage.

If it is unafflicted, then you will have a bright, supportive, and attractive partner with whom you may share a significant social life. As with the Emperor in this House, the wedding is very important; because it is also about the union of clans and Ancestors, it is a celestial event. So, if you have this placement, make the wedding glorious, and invite the whole family. This can release you from a lot of heavy Fate.

In contrast to the Emperor, the Empress is much more likely to be chosen. The Emperor may denote a mission to find a soulmate, while for the Empress, your soulmate may show up and choose you. Often, this person is older or at least more mature, more worldly, more sophisticated. They sweep you off your feet, or you become enamored with them. You are more likely to follow and serve them; you are their queen—and yes, this applies to men too. You may have a partner who serves and worships you, or you may adore your partner and serve them like a queen. Either way, service is an important component.

Here, your Fate is to give, nurture, and support. The job of the empress was to be an icon of royalty sitting beside the emperor, so the term *trophy wife/husband* could be applicable. There could be Fate to be fully supported by your partner as a stay-at-home parent. They could offer financial support: They may buy you your dream home or pay all the bills. Or, vice versa: You may work to support your partner, but they provide endless love and emotional support and look after the home.

The Empress is hard to afflict here. If afflicted by Ghost Stars, you may have a supportive, easy marriage, but there's no love or passion. It may lack content but be very functional and natural. There could be arguing or incompatibility, but you stick it out and work together in the long run. This is very traditional. Marriage, for most of history, was just a social arrangement to raise children, and the idea of romance was not common until modern times. Love, however, is deep here, even if there are problems, for love is and always has been important for human pair bonding.

Offspring Palace

If you have Tian Fu in the Offspring Palace, then you have a very strong Fate as a parent with at least one, if not multiple, children. Being a parent is also easy and second nature, naturally unraveling your Fate. You so easily take to being a parent that you cannot picture your life without kids. Your children will follow and respect you and play a big part in your life, especially as they age. This is like giving birth to old friends. You will have a very strong Fate with your children from past lives, and/or you are giving birth to returning Ancestors. This may be a significant or Original Ancestor coming back. Either way, you may feel as though you know each other or are reuniting.

Like the Emperor here, with the Empress there is a sense of debt: You were born to serve, protect, and educate your children. You are their provider and advocate throughout life. Everything you do for them is a given, natural, and you don't have to think about it. Your Fate unfolds around them without a choice in the matter. You owe them, so you must provide, and in turn, they take care of you in old age. If unafflicted, this is a very supportive and close relationship throughout life. Your kids become your best friends, and they will love you and seek your help and guidance, even to a fault. You may even have to shove them out of the nest.

Naturally, the Empress implies daughters, but this is not always true. You may have sons, but you may also have a significant Fated connection to a daughter. In other words, you may have two sons, but as soon as the daughter comes along, you find your best friend. There is something special and magical about a particular child, and you become intertwined for life. Or, you are the Empress, and it is your mandate to give birth to a son, as was the demand of empresses historically. Remember that Fate can always go both ways.

The Empress implies giving birth to an old soul, a self-starter, a bright, precocious child with the Fate legacy of an adult. They are naturally gifted, talented, beautiful, and mature right from the start. There is something "easy" about raising them. Parenthood is never easy, but the Empress implies that they are born having already learned the important lessons; they just need a little reminder.

Finally, like the Emperor Star here, if a person does not want to or cannot have kids, then legacy or sexuality can become important. Parenting also happens whether you have children or not. You are so naturally a parent that you take care of everyone around you, and your employees or students may be like your children, and you may be the mother of your company or social circle.

Here, sexuality, especially regarding your appearance, is often more prominent than with the Emperor. Sexuality may become a big bargaining chip in your life. You radiate youth and fertility, and everyone is attracted to you; everyone wants you and is magnetized to you, looking to reproduce. This may lead to modeling, acting, dancing, or simply that you use your sexuality to unravel your Fate. Every man may become sweaty and compliant in your presence, willing to buy you things and give you what you want. Or you are tall, dark, and handsome, and everyone just submits to your charm.

Wealth Palace

Tian Fu in the Wealth Palace is what everyone thinks they want, but it often comes with challenges. It implies a lot of positive Fate and resources coming back to you from past lives and/or from Ancestral inheritance. It means that your Fate with money and resources is very Yin, which means it is out of your control and often indirect. It means being dependent and being cared for by others, and potentially that money is never a concern. If it is unafflicted by Ghost Stars, then you are like Queen Elizabeth or Oprah: You inherit or make a fortune without apparent effort and are capable of greatly expanding wealth with investment and through "speculative investment" like the stock market, branding, fine art, collectibles, or manipulating foreign currency. Your wealth becomes a way of influencing and helping others.

The empress did not work or handle money. Empresses often had a bursar, a person who would handle their money. The empress would just point at things she wanted, and the bursar would take care of everything; she came home, and everything was already at the palace. While the Emperor often denotes a drive or mission to earn, the Empress does not; she may even disdain money, but she has it and wields it.

The Empress denotes finery and having elegant and expensive taste. You may cultivate a regal appearance through jewelry and clothing, and you only shop at the most expensive stores. This is a classic Yin display of power and status: an expensive handbag that says, "I am high-value." Following and displaying the latest fashion or trends is very Empress. This is Madison Avenue, glamor, high fashion, and the like. But it does not need to be popular; it can be a very personal and unique expression of appearance.

Tian Fu can mean family money, inheritance, or windfall. You may acquire wealth unexpectedly or get a very high-paying job in which you suddenly have more money than you know what to do with. The Yin nature of the Fate here often means that finances tend to fluctuate a lot throughout your life and that this is beyond your control. You are dependent on others, on luck, on the kindness of strangers. This is very Blanche DuBois. If it is afflicted by Ghosts, then this can be the case.

This is the very nature of the stock market: One day, it is up, and the other, it plummets. The Empress is all about knowing when to wait, buy, or sell. It is about adaptability and intuition; it is about using what you've got to get ahead, what used to be called "feminine wiles," regardless of your gender.

As with the Emperor in this House, generosity is very important. The job of the empress was, again, often philanthropic and charitable. This is about giving back. So, if Fate smiles on you in this way, then it is important not to be selfish and to spread the wealth. This Star does not always mean you are rich or have inherited a fortune, but it means that money is not a concern or interest for you. But it is for most people. Generosity does not have to be big, and you do not have to be rich to give. You may have this Star and be broke, but you will probably have everything you need, wanting for naught. If you have this placement, giving a buck to a person on the street goes a long way. You have the capacity to change people's lives with even the humblest generosity, and you can liberate Ghosts by giving. You become a conduit for wealth; it comes to you to get redistributed.

Health Palace

If you have Tian Fu in the Health Palace, then you have the definition of a Yin constitution, and the Empress's placement here is much more about health and well-being than about active Fate like the Emperor. The Emperor implies two interpretations, one about inheriting a Yang constitution from the Patriarchal Ancestors, and the other about the crux of your Fate manifesting through the body, through health cultivation, or even through the practice of medicine. But again, the Empress is simply about "being." There is no agenda of doing anything here, although a lot may manifest around your embodiment. Here, the Yin nature of this Star in this House is all about demonstrating your nature.

As the strongest Yin Star, the Empress means that you inherit your constitution, immunity, and physicality from your Matriarchal Ancestors, and in a way, your body is a direct expression of their wisdom and experience. You have a very direct connection to your Ancestors through the body. You may have your grandmother's intuition and love of baking, and by drinking afternoon tea as she did for fifty years, you can heal any illness. Or you may find a photo of your great-aunt, and you were a dead ringer for her in high school; perhaps, you have an instinct to crochet like she did, and it comes naturally. They may speak to you through signs, dreams, and omens; you have a direct line of communication with other realms. You likely inherit their strongest talents and predispositions, and with that, a strong capacity to heal yourself and others.

In general, this means inheriting very strong immunity and sturdy health; you rarely get sick and can recover very well through rest and treatment. Health comes naturally, and self-care and care for others happen without effort. This is a very strong "mama bear" type of energy—nurturing, protective, and caring—for it comes from all the mothers and grandmothers you come from. You radiate a kind of restful, rejuvenating energy, so you will naturally be a nurturing presence to others. You may become a healer, but this is second nature, not an active pursuit.

You can excel at yoga, meditation, traditional medicine, and all medicine, but it is not likely a job or mission in life. If you have strong Stars in the career Palaces, this can indicate a career in healthcare, but it stems from being a person who naturally has a remedy for everything and who naturally tends to and cares for yourself and others.

A strong Yin constitution means having a very strong sense of empathy and understanding that illness and healing are a matter of emotions. You can feel and experience what others feel, which can be strongly emphasized in certain Characters like Rabbits, Goats, or Pigs. You get ill due to negative emotions and get better when you work them out. You may perceive when others are not well and be able to help them with a few kind words or a hug.

A Yin constitution means that you heal best in autumn and winter, in the afternoon and nighttime, and that you heal best through sleep. Depending on Character, you may have a strong disposition to sleep and rest, and stillness and inactivity are natural. Active Characters will, of course, fight this but then benefit from it.

Having a Yin constitution also means responding well to medical treatment and doctors with good medical compliance, especially to unconventional, alternative, or traditional medicine. This is the energy of shamans, midwives, and doulas; of herbalism, massage, diet, and acupuncture; and of healing through nature. You can heal from being in the forest, mountains, or ocean or respond easily to a home remedy, a home-cooked meal, or a healing touch. You have the natural capacity to resolve Fate and the Fate of others through healing, but again this happens without effort or contrivance; it is simply an expression of your embodiment.

Finally, like the Ming Palace, this is a place where the Empress shines with a sense of elegance, grace, and naturalness. You will radiate love, compassion, and caring to others, and your deportment and countenance represent the skills and cultivation of a geisha, which means "art person." You may be adept at things like dance, flower arranging, performing the tea ceremony, or calligraphy.

Career/Travel Palace

Tian Fu in the Career/Travel Palace is one of the more mysterious placements and not so easy to understand to those living it. It is like having the Emperor here, as it denotes a strong Fate to travel or immigrate or that Career will be very significant, but like having the Empress in the Ming Palace, the nature of that Fate and how it will unravel is a mystery beyond your control. You will naturally fall into it; it will "just happen." You will look back a million miles from where you started and have no idea how you got to where you are, but it will all make sense in hindsight and have worked out for the best.

The Emperor means that you are on a mission to travel and find your path in life, while the Empress is gifted with these things. If unafflicted, then you will likely travel a great deal. The opportunity to travel will happen through association. You may travel with family, friends, or a partner or get a job that pays to fly you worldwide. You will go places, meet people, and make connections that all come from previous patterns of Fate or past-life connections. It will be like returning home or reuniting with old friends. You may find yourself on the streets of London, and intuitively, you walk down old streets and know how to find your way back to a special pub. Or, you arrive in Chile and immediately start picking up Spanish, conversing with locals and being invited to parties. Before you know it, you move there.

You may have a very strong Fate to move or immigrate, but again, it will happen naturally. This can be a Fate Threshold to reconnect with past-life or Ancestral Fate in a foreign place. I have met many of these kinds of people traveling—expats who seem like they were just born in the wrong place and are at home as soon as they get to Thailand, or Spain, or Australia. They fall into a new life and easily adapt.

In terms of career, it is likely that you have strong talent or ability that naturally unfolds into a suitable career. Empress Fate here denotes a smooth and natural progression into something by just going with the flow. Whatever you do, it was like you were born to do it. It comes as second nature. Or opportunity comes to you without your having to work your way up a long and arduous ladder. Your boss spots your managerial potential and promotes you to supervisor. Maybe you will publish, or win an award in college, which will land you a big interview. Or maybe you run into an old friend, and they put in a good word with their boss, and you rocket to the top.

The Empress here also denotes more Yin, or passive, work rather than industrious productivity or manual labor. The Empress was often a diplomat, and her role was more social than productive. This can mean managerial work, overseeing others, networking and community outreach, charity and social work, and so on. Often, it means a helping or listening profession, but more so in the next House. It can represent work as a therapist, counselor, or local religious leader. Healing, doctoring, and nursing are also very Empress. Compassion and altruism are important themes, for the Empress is not interested in industry but people.

The Empress does not have a clearly defined job or path here. Things may be cobbled together, or it may seem random and strange. Or you may not work at all but be provided for and allowed to follow your other passions. Maybe you sell your company and retire at thirty. Or perhaps you love being a stay-at-home mom.

The arts and humanities are emphasized here, so you may work at things that others don't consider work; this is all about Yin Power and changing the world by being rather than doing. Or you may invent a job that did not previously exist, which is more and more possible now in the information age. Being an "influencer" is very Empress. Either way, the Fate here is Yin and mysterious, but ultimately it will work out for the best.

Assistants Palace

If Tian Fu arrives in the Assistants or Friendship House, it exalts the House. Just like the Emperor belongs in the Superiors Palace, the Empress belongs here, for her role is supportive, and she wields power from behind the scenes. She is also strong in the Superiors Palace, but she thrives here, for this is all about Yin Power.

This House can always be interpreted in two ways: as a career House or as a relationship House. As a career House, this exalts all helping and service professions. You were born to serve and help others with compassion and care. You have an immense capacity to influence others by supporting them and lifting them up. You are a cheerleader, advocate, and benefactor. So, of course, careers in the service industry, like waiting tables, being a cashier, and so on, can be influential. When you say, "Have a nice day," and hand someone their change, you can change their life; maybe they were in a bad mood, and you cheered them up, and then they treat their kids better when they get home.

You also have a strong Fate to wield and manipulate social dynamics, hopefully for the benefit of others. This capacity can obviously be abused, so Character matters a lot here. In the royal court, the empress was always watching, waiting, observing, and gossiping. She had spies and informants everywhere, listening in to the emperor, the generals, the concubines, and so on. She had dirt on everyone and knew how to alter the course of history through a well-timed and precise comment. Again, this is Yin Power. Here, you may wield a strong social influence through a huge network of friends, associates, and connections. This could be at work or in your personal life. If afflicted, this can lead to a lot of interpersonal drama, gossip, and so on.

The Empress in the Assistants Palace can mean a huge circle of friends. You may have many Fated past-life connections with friends, co-workers, fellow students, and so on. These kinds of connections find you, and they naturally feel like family. As with the Emperor here, you find your people, your tribe, and have deeply rewarding connections with a "circle of returners."

Or you may simply be an exemplary friend, as you are Fated so deeply to support others. You always stay in touch, send birthday cards, and call people to reconnect. You are a great listener, and people come to you for advice, guidance, and support. You may naturally fall into this role with everyone; you are the mother of your friend group, or you are like a parent to your students or clients. This is again mama-bear protective energy, so you go to bat for people, and you fight for the underdog, the marginalized, and the oppressed. As a teacher or healer, it may mean having a lot of Fated connections with students and patients.

In your career, this can mean that you are an excellent assistant or are Fated to have an excellent assistant who brings you success. You may be second to a powerful person and work as their organizer, time manager, and bookkeeper. You enjoy working behind the scenes, in the shadows, and out of the spotlight. You love greeting people, talking to customers, and booking clients so that your boss can be successful. Or, you are Fated to have such an assistant who works tirelessly for you, and because of them, you succeed without effort.

Superiors Palace

Tian Fu is strong here because she is royalty, but she is slightly out of place. The Empress shines when she is in a supportive role rather than being in charge. She so naturally supports others that even when she is in the Superiors Palace, she wields power from a secondary or apparently subordinate position. That being said, this is a strong Fate for success in your career, but this success comes due to your character, not skill. You model what to do rather than tell people what to do.

This is a natural success that comes without apparent effort. Like royalty, it may mean inheriting a position or title, which is a strong indicator of family business. It may denote some natural charm, charisma, beauty, or advantage that brings you power or influence. This can mean being so naturally gifted and talented that you are rocketed to fame or at least get acknowledged and rewarded for your talent. This doesn't have to be big, but it does mean that others recognize and maybe even follow you.

This is like Oprah Winfrey or Tony Robbins—people who become successful by giving advice or by coaching and motivating others. This is also like overseeing a philanthropic organization, and it comes with the responsibility to give back and redistribute wealth and power. You may be in the spotlight and have a lot of responsibility, but you downplay this and are humble and gracious as a leader, despite being way overqualified for everything.

You may become a role model, an example, an influencer, or a trendsetter. Social media now lends itself to these roles; many try to achieve them, but few do. Anyone can get on social media and have a worldwide platform, but if you have the Empress in the Superiors Palace, then you may find yourself going viral. You may then make millions posting a few photos a week and can now travel and "live your best life."

As the main House of lineage, you may also have a strong Fate with a teacher, and possibly as a teacher, in a line of succession. You may have a very strong Fate with many mentors, guides, and gurus who show you the way. You may also have the Fate to pursue a spiritual path and be interested in tradition. And you will likely have a lot of very deep connections here and connect with a lineage.

This looks very different from the Emperor placed here. The Emperor is comfortable in the spotlight and with creating hierarchy, and often this kind of teacher is on a "throne" and others bow and grovel. However, the Empress is more interested in creating community and uplifting others, which creates a very different type of school. Liu Ming had this, and he said many times that he was not the leader, and he undermined those who tried to make him a guru.

Despite being out of place here, this is a very strong indicator of success and being overqualified for life. You will likely find success easily and be given opportunities and promoted often. Like every placement of the Empress, generosity is important. Here, she potentially wields the most power and influence, so it is even more important to have self-cultivation and to practice what you preach. Here, you must really be a great role model, and the more power and influence you have, the more responsibility there is to use that power and voice for good.

Property Palace

Tian Fu in the Property Palace is a very auspicious and fortunate placement, as it is one of the strongest indicators of inheritance and having a good Fate to own, receive, manage, and distribute property. Here, it also exalts the Fates of legacy and charity. The Empress was given everything: a palace, a title, land, and so on. You will likely inherit, be given, or acquire property in your lifetime and benefit greatly from it, possibly from your Matriarchal Ancestors.

This may be a family inheritance such as a farm, house, apartment building, empty lot, or car. It may also be family heirlooms or something connected to your Ancestors, like old photos, journals, love letters, trinkets, and so on. It may also be in the form of stories, such as sitting around a fire with Grandpa.

It may be modest, but something is coming your way, and you can do very well with what you receive through real estate and/or investing. Here you are also likely to be housed and supported by others throughout life. Perhaps your parents will pay your rent. You could also live in a monastery or convent. It also denotes general good luck with landlords and realtors, finding good places to live, and living in beautiful or even luxurious surroundings. There is a deep appreciation here for luxury, as you have the taste of an Empress. This may also be a keen eye for architecture, landscaping, interior design, and Fengshui. Like the Emperor, Fengshui plays a significant role in your Fate, but rather than having an internal compass or divining rod pointing you to a new home, you are already there, and it is a matter of fully realizing that home is an Ancestral altar.

You may have a strong connection to Ancestors and tradition, like living under the same roof with three generations of relatives or on the same plot of land that your Ancestors migrated to and cultivated. Identity with place, ethnicity, name, title, and religion is strong. You may feel a deep connection to this, especially to the Matriarchal Ancestors or specifically to a great-grandmother. It is powerful to do genealogy here, but it requires special attention to place, land, towns, homes, and so on.

If unafflicted by Ghost Stars, you may have a strong connection to your birthplace. You are deeply connected to your home, hometown, and community and spend your whole life there. Legacy is very important here: connecting to it, creating it, maintaining it, and passing it down. The Emperor in this House can denote a "walkabout"—having to leave home to find it—but the Empress is more likely to have strong roots and water them. You are weakened if you leave home.

This is one of the strongest placements for receiving and/or building generational wealth, not just in the form of money but in the form of real, tangible property and institutions. Like always, it is important to spread the wealth, for charity is the job of the Empress; of course, humans are selfish, and wealth often stays in the family, but this keeps us bound to Fate. The more you can give away selflessly, the more you are freed of Fate in this House.

Pleasure Palace

Tian Fu in the Pleasure Palace is like the Emperor here, but less specific in that you have a strong Fate to pursue pleasure and follow your fun, but it is not imperative. It is more of an auspicious bonus in life that you are deeply Fated to enjoy, but without pressure. As such, this is a very auspicious placement, especially for Characters like Pigs, Dragons, Monkeys, or any of the Characters who are bound to live playfully and pursue pleasure.

The Empress, of course, has fine taste. So, this means enjoying high class, culture, music, art, food, and drink. You may have a wine collection or be a sommelier. You may be an art critic, a museum curator, or a reviewer of fine food for a magazine. The French term for you is *gourmet* rather than *gourmand*. You appreciate the details, craftsmanship, and the soul of things. Whether it be art, music, or food, you can feel the heart of those who created it, and you can create it yourself.

This is a strong indicator of being a visual artist, musician, chef, or the like. It denotes talent inherited from the Ancestors that you express for the love of it. This is the true meaning of being an amateur. Being an amateur does not mean you lack talent or skill; it simply means that you do something for the love of it rather than for the money. We also see rich hobbies and personal interests here. All this comes naturally, and you follow your passion like breathing.

Often, this means being a flirt, enjoying a social life, and letting your hair down. Parties, dances, banquets, dinners, box socials, and so on draw you to connect with others. This means that your biggest pleasure in life is sharing what you love with others. So, you deeply enjoy friendship, sex, and experience. Life for you is measured in experience and having stories to tell.

There is also usually a great draw to nature, the countryside, and rustic settings where you can feel a greater sense of connection to joy. If the Empress is unafflicted, she brings a deep sense of natural, poetic, and even spiritual joy. This is also a strong drive toward a spiritual path, often through loving-kindness, compassion, and so on, rather than a personal drive to be free of suffering. Therefore, this placement greatly supports working in charity, volunteering, and supporting others, especially in education, entertainment, and the arts. If you have this Star in this House, you should feel blessed and enjoy life to the fullest, because few do.

TIAN XIANG (天相)—THE TUTOR

NAME AND TRANSLATIONS:

Tian Xiang (天相), the Tutor Star, the Imperial Tutor, Celestial Magistrate

Tian, 天—refers to the sky or heavens; the highest cosmic principle or force.[8]

Xiang, 相—to assist; adjuvant, minister, esp. of government; often short for 丞相 chengxiang, prime minister, chancellor, or 宰相 zaixiang, grand councilor, chief minister. a) a ministry; governmental organ or physical location associated with ministerial functions. 2 support, enhance, add a supplemental element to, e.g., 相質 xiangzhi, enhance the substance. 3 appraise, assess, inspect, ken, esp. appraise the inner qualities of a person or animal by means of its physical aspects a) gauge or estimate character or destiny. 4 In Buddhism, it is a translation of the Sanskrit nimita or lakṣaṇa, external mark, manifested aspect, characteristic mark, physical sign, esp. of a cakravartin or buddha; the phenomenal, as opp. to the noumenal 理 li. a) an attribute or characteristic. b) physical appearance, e.g., 相好 xianghao, physical features.[9]

Together, we can translate this Star as the Celestial Magistrate, Heavenly Minister, or Sky Chancellor, for example. However, it refers to a specific role in the royal court, that of tutor and primary adviser to the emperor, so we call this the Imperial Tutor or Tutor.

ELEMENT: Yang Water

TRADITIONAL IMAGE: The highest order of Confucian magistrate and of high court; an icon of dignity and nobility, depicted as impeccably dressed in robes with a long beard, scholar's hat, books, ink brush, and official insignia[10]

ANCESTOR PROFILE: Patriarchal Ancestor, highly accomplished and a responsible leader in their lifetime; represents the force of knowledge, education, intelligence, and social responsibility

LUMINOUS PLACEMENT: Ox Palace

DIMINISHED PLACEMENT: Rat and Rooster Palaces

AFFILIATIONS: Southern Array—derives power from the Empress but serves the Emperor

Tian Xiang, or the imperial tutor, was the personal tutor and primary adviser to the emperor as well as the highest-ranking magistrate in the Chinese government and of the royal court. Although the emperor and empress ruled the royal court, the tutor, in many ways, ran the show. The emperor and empress could not be bothered by the mundane details of rulership. The emperor had the final say and made the big decisions, so the placement of the Emperor Star is the central crux of Fate, showing us where we must act and initiate the unraveling of our Fate through action. But the Emperor is informed and educated by Tian Xiang, or the Imperial Tutor.

The tutor worked day and night, meeting with all the magistrates, the generals, the vassals, and so on, reading all the reports, evaluating all the information coming to the imperial palace. He gathered, organized, and summarized all the information needed to rule and delivered it in pith form to the emperor, who made the final decisions. But those decisions were based on whatever the tutor presented, so he became the man behind the throne and wielded a kind of true power. He, therefore, had to be of the highest character, for a corrupt tutor could bring down the government or even seize power.

His job was to educate and train the emperor from birth on how to be an emperor. His guidance and wisdom shaped the emperor. He was, therefore, an older man who was wise, experienced, and above all, selfless. The tutor gave everything to the emperor in service of the dynasty, which in our case means in service of the Fate of the Ancestral line that we come from. The tutor ensured the lineage would survive and thrive.

This was, however, an appointed position and not an inherited one. He was not related to the emperor, which is why the Star belongs to the Southern Array. The tutor was elected to serve in this role, so he had to be the most outstanding and immaculate character. He was the most accomplished, most educated, and highly revered of the magistrates, and his Star is, therefore, associated with success and achievement through perseverance, hard work, education, self-reflection, and good judgment. The tutor represents the highest of Confucian ideals and is like a Confucian superhero. The images of Confucius and Mencius are good icons for this Star, as it is very conventional, traditional, and even a bit stuffy.

Tian Xiang represents the fruition and demonstration of the term ***self-cultivation***, or Xiuyang (修養). But he also represents self-cultivation applied to the unraveling and resolution of Fate. This is not a naval-gazing Star that self-reflects; it is tirelessly in action and, therefore, represents the place in our chart where hard work, professionalism, and long-term success are most likely to occur. This is not a "fun" Star and has little association with "being." This is all about "doing."

Wherever this Star appears, we are Fated to be at the top of our game and demonstrate our highest achievements. The resolution of Fate in whatever House it shows up in is very strong, although not central in the same way as the Emperor; it is secondary but just as hardworking, if not more so. The difference is that the Emperor catalyzes our Fate, and then the Tutor gets put to work. For example, you may have the Emperor in the Travel Palace and Tutor in the Superiors Palace—you must first immigrate or move, and when you do, you get a job where you then demonstrate your highest capacity.

> Wherever the Tutor appears, the Fate is likely associated with education, teaching, expertise, and the like. It represents our professional life and responsibilities in the world, contributing to society through work, leadership, and service. It is, therefore, exalted in the career Houses—that is, the Career/Travel, Assistants, and Superiors Palaces—and functions well in the Wealth, Property, and Ming Palaces, but it is somewhat out of place in the rest of the Houses. This is a Yang accomplishing Star, so wherever it shows up, you have work to do, and it may be tireless, thankless, and you may not see the rewards for many years. Nonetheless, it is not easily afflicted and will ultimately resolve Fate in time through perseverance.
>
> Look to the Southern Array for the Tutor's allies but remember that he serves the Emperor and unites the Northern and Southern Array in their mission to resolve Fate.
>
> Let's walk the Tutor through the twelve Houses.

Ming Palace

As one of the Four Rulers, if Tian Xiang, the Tutor, arrives in the Ming Palace, then you have a very strong capacity and likelihood of resolving Fate in this lifetime. This is "Big Fate" like the Emperor here, but much more modest and self-sacrificing, and you should look at the placement of the Emperor to understand the direction of this Fate. Overall, you will have a clear path in life and a feeling of needing to get to work—this is Yang Fate, and there will be a significant agenda full of tasks and projects. You will be driven to gain the knowledge and skills that you need and undergo significant education and training, working your way up the ranks or through a series of progressions, working slowly and methodically.

Your life is greatly influenced by a very accomplished, hardworking, and dignified Patriarchal Ancestor, possibly on the mother's side, as this is part of the Southern Array. You inherit their drive, talent, and sense of moral responsibility and conventionality. You are continuing or following in their footsteps as a leader or authority who will be responsible for managing others or contributing as a professional, expert, or innovator.

Education, training, teachers, mentors, and guides will be important on your path, and you will likely end up in this role after your training is complete and you gain real-world experience. Confucian education and self-cultivation are crucial: this means self-reflection applied to community, family, and society; this also means stellar conduct and practicing what you preach. Above all, this means Ren (仁), cultivating kindness as a reflection of human-heartedness and basic goodness.

This education will be connected to a sense of tradition and values that may be connected to family or religion, and you will feel part of a stream or lineage. You will be born into a stream of helpful people, family members, friends, acquaintances, and so on, who help you to understand your role and direct you toward your path as a valued member of that lineage.

This path will undoubtedly be directed at something greater, bigger, and beyond the "greater good." This Star comes with a sense of duty and moral responsibility, so it matches very well with Characters like the Ox, Goat, and Dog, and more rebellious and unconventional Characters will fight against this. This Star seeks to uphold that mission toward the greater good through service and self-sacrifice, so you will probably work very hard for others and put yourself last. This may be a pattern that happens everywhere—work, relationships, family. You give everything and don't ask for anything in return.

This Star is not as grand or dramatic as the Emperor, so fame, renown, and the spotlight are less likely. Rather, you may receive recognition and respect for continuous hard work and consistency. This Star is all about consistency. Like the tortoise, slow and steady wins the race. You will feel accomplished at the end of life but maintain humility. You may leave behind a legacy of academic, literary, or intellectual achievement.

Ancestors Palace

If Tian Xiang appears in the Ancestors Palace, you have a very strong connection to your parents and Ancestors that is somewhat strict and stuffy but all-around positive. This is not a warm and cuddly relationship; it is more likely that your parents, grandparents, and family provide a strong and stern sense of duty and responsibility. This may be a very strong father figure or influence from a great Ancestor that runs your life but also gives you direction, confidence, and inspiration. A strong mentor may appear somewhere in the family.

You are continuing a strong family tradition: This may be through business, community, education, or religion. Cultural identity, ethnicity, and tribe are strong. This often means a big family with many aunts, uncles, cousins, and so on who all feel pride in being an O'Malley, Nguyen, or Chen. You may go to church on Sundays or Chinese School on the weekends; maybe you always have Thanksgiving together, or the boys go hunting every month, or your Grandpa shows you how to fix cars and takes you to car shows. Tradition and rituals are important; you will likely continue them with your kids.

Your parents or father will teach you, guide you, and give you a lot of support. This may feel overbearing and confining. This is like having a dad who disciplines you to practice piano for two hours every day after school. As a kid, you hate it, but you grow up to play recitals in front of audiences who weep at your performances, and you realize that you would never have gotten there without your dad pushing you.

This often means being a dutiful, respectful, and obedient child who wants to honor your parents. In turn, they want to mold you into a responsible person, so you grow up with a strong compass: Always say please and thank-you, look both ways before crossing the street, and so on. You honor your elders and eventually become an honored elder. Through this process, you resolve a lot of Ancestral Ghosts, who see your conduct as a threshold. The purpose of such conduct is to open gateways for the unsettled dead to be released, for it is the simple acts of custom, like saying please and thank-you, that generate selflessness and allow Ghosts to ride through that to the other side. This is the recipe for a good Confucian life of service and contribution.

Youth Palace

Tian Xiang in the Youth Palace is very similar to being in the Ancestors Palace, but often, the mentor relationship appears as an older sibling, or you act as a mentor to a younger sibling. The sibling connection is strong, and you resolve a lot of Fate through this relationship. It is very traditional for the eldest child to become like a third parent and take care of the younger siblings, which becomes a lifelong duty. If this is you, then you will likely mature very quickly and take on the role of protector with your siblings and peers. You may be the "leader" in your friend group, as they look to you for guidance.

The sense of family duty, responsibility, and tradition is also strong here, but it takes on the extra dimension of resolving Fate during youth. This is often done at school through education, and you may be a precocious and hardworking youth. You may be the valedictorian, honor student, or teacher's pet. You will win the admiration of your teachers, and you may converse with them like peers. You will have more in common with adults and teachers than kids your own age. You may stay after school and do extracurricular activities or work for extra credit. The Tutor may also represent a significant teacher or role model at school, like a math teacher who encourages you to join the "mathletes," which takes you to the state championship and gets you into a good college.

Sometimes, this represents few or no siblings, and often, it represents being an only child who relates more to adults and must raise themself. Or it is the dutiful sibling who supports the whole family. Either way, this is not a fun and silly childhood but one full of rules, discipline, and responsibilities. This is a great setup for adulthood, but often, there is regret for having missed out on just being a kid.

Partners Palace

Tian Xiang in the Partners Palace is a bit misplaced, as this is not a romantic Star. This placement often turns relationships into a job with a sense of duty. You serve your partner, support them financially, care for them, do all the chores, take care of the kids, and so on. You "work" on the relationship and try to use it as a means for self-cultivation, which can go well if your partner is on board, but often it leads to imbalances. If both are on board, then relationships can be a source of cultivation and transformation, but sometimes they lack fun, spontaneity, and romance. They can be loving and content but not passionate, with more of a sense of duty to create a stable family to benefit society, which is a very old-world value.

Or you may be married to your job and never home. You may meet your partner at work and share a professional life together. Maybe your wife runs the front end, does the books, and handles the money while you deal with clients. Or you perform or compete, and your husband cooks for you and does the chores so you can focus on being your best. It can also mean meeting your partner at school or college, someone who shares with you a very particular interest or set of values.

There is often some kind of discrepancy in the relationship—something odd, such as disparities in age, status, education, ethnicity, background, or worldview. This often means that one partner becomes the teacher or mentor of the other. You bring respectability and maturity to them, or they do to you. It is very common for one partner to be much older, which is common all over the world. With this Star in this House, it is very common for an older, accomplished man to marry a younger woman.

This can be like an arranged marriage—a sensible, practical affair: The daughter of the lumber mill owner marries the son of a forester, and the families go into business. Here, the Ancestors may choose a suitable partner for your betterment or for the betterment of the family. Generally, the partnership is peaceful and resolves Fate in a very predictable way.

Offspring Palace

If you have Tian Xiang in the Offspring Palace, then you have a strong Fate to be a parent. However, it is possible that this will occur late in life or that you will be a "late bloomer" sexually. Generally, the Tutor is considered very auspicious here, for it represents a precocious, intelligent, and successful child who will be a great pride for the family.

Often, it means having a small family, and it often means that you have a very strong, special connection as a mentor and educator to your child. You place a great emphasis and care on their upbringing, raising them with strong values. You may be a strict parent, but you do so because you want the best for your child. You instill in them a strong moral compass and do so by being a great role model. This goes beyond telling your kids what to do; it means showing them how to do it. You are their idol.

This means that you will work very hard for your children throughout life. You will work hard to support them financially, put a roof over their head, and so on; this is the classic self-sacrifice of a parent. Your mission and purpose in life are to give them a good life. You mature and learn all the important life lessons through being a parent, and this leads to advancement in your own professional life. You realize that success is not for you; it is for them, so you work harder than ever to succeed.

Here, your kids carry on the Ancestral lineage and family traditions, and the Tutor may be a significant Ancestor reborn. Your children will grow up to be better and more successful than you, and they will outclass you, but this makes you happy. They will become dutiful and respectful children who grow up to take care of you in old age. Their success benefits you; this is the classic story of the mom who gives everything so that then the child grows up, wins the championship, thanks his mom, and buys her a house. Here, children become your legacy; the greatest gift to the world may be the child you produce.

As it relates to sexuality, this may mean being a bit asexual or uninterested in sex. Again, it may mean being a late bloomer sexually, coming into yourself in midlife.

Wealth Palace

Tian Xiang in the Wealth Palace is an auspicious but modest placement. The tutor was not interested in getting rich. He was interested in integrity, sacrifice, and service, and he worked tirelessly without thought of reward. He was successful and paid well, but the pay was secondary: purpose and meaning were primary. Therefore, if you have this placement, you are likely to work very hard and be successful and compensated well, but wealth will never be the primary motivation in your life.

It is possible that you will work in the service of rich and powerful people, and that your wealth is linked to others, possibly coming through social contacts, networking, and as a reward for helping others succeed. Success here comes from diligent hard work, perseverance, and climbing your way up the ladder to a position of management, leadership, or even ownership, likely in an academic, political, or corporate position. However, the source of this work must have integrity and include service and contributing to society, or you will not be interested, and your Fate here will not be resolved.

This is a wise and frugal Star who saves and invests and does not spend money irresponsibly. You will likely be responsible with money and handle it very well, and therefore long-term success, retirement, and being wealthy in old age are very possible. This is a slow and steady approach—compound interest over a long period of time—adding just enough to the savings that one day you become wealthy.

There is also an element of luck with this Star, which is the result of a positive Fate generated from Ancestral and past-life honesty, integrity, and generosity. You may receive the beneficial results of this through bonuses, raises, positive investments, and windfall. But you will not be greedy, and you will use this money wisely. You can resolve Fate here through generosity and using wealth for the greater good and social service. You may be a champion for the poor and seek social justice through the redistribution of wealth.

Health Palace

This is considered one of the best placements of Tian Xiang, as it represents a very strong, even "bulletproof," constitution that is upheld by very strong personal discipline and health rituals. This is the Fate of diligent hard work and self-honesty applied to health cultivation that comes from deep Ancestral patterns of wellness.

Human beings know how to be healthy; before modern industrial food, we didn't have another option, for we could only eat what could be grown, hunted, or gathered, and we had to work to produce food and shelter. These kinds of patterns of health are deeply ingrained in us—they are modest but powerful. Previously, illness came from hardship and scarcity; today, it comes from comfort and abundance (and a predatory business model of sick-care). If we could apply the disciplined patterns of our Ancestors to modern life, we would thrive, for we have mostly eliminated the previous hardships that killed our Ancestors.

The Tutor represents longevity that comes from good conduct. As a Yang Star, it represents being active, and the only danger here is working too hard. The Tutor is likely to exhaust himself by overdoing it, but he also has a tremendous capacity for work. If you have this unafflicted, then you can work all day and night and be okay, but you should probably learn to hold back and take it easy. The Tutor here will burn the candle at both ends in pursuit of their life goals, and a sense of work and purpose sustains them and gives them health. Without work, the Tutor will fall ill. The Tutor has no limit in their ability to care for others over themselves, and caring for others heals them.

The Tutor easily develops good spiritual hygiene and what Ayurveda calls *dinacharya*, or daily routines. Sleep, exercise, diet, meditation, cleanliness, attention to personal appearance, and so on come naturally. So does the practice of medicine. This is an excellent placement for both receiving and practicing medicine. You will likely be the perfect, compliant patient and do everything the doctor orders. You respond well to the "standard of care" and conventional medicine.

The Tutor in this House makes an excellent doctor who can master the more intellectual sides of medicine, like diagnosis and prescription. The Tutor is not an empathic, touchy-feely Star, so the bedside manner may not be great, but you can give excellent care through a deep understanding of principles and training, and you are likely to get better at this with age and experience.

If you do get ill or injured, you can recover through the skill of expert physicians and specialists, and this placement is a good Fate to meet them. Generally, it means a preference for self-discipline, and the Tutor can heal themself through personal health practices. But you will likely seek the guidance of experts before doing so. You may research your illness or injury, read all the studies, and do what it takes to get better. "Stress" is the most likely root cause of all the Tutor's troubles, as you often don't pay attention to yourself until you are worked to the bone.

This Star here means you heal best in autumn and get stronger in old age. The Tutor represents a good Fate for longevity, and traditionally, they say many people will attend your funeral. The Tutor is deeply connected to their role in society and community, so you get ill and well in connection with others. You heal to help others, not yourself.

Career/Travel Palace

If Tian Xiang appears in this or any of the career Houses, it exalts the House, for this is the "professional" Star. The next three Houses are very similar in their interpretation. If the Tutor shows up here, you were born to work, and you will likely travel and/or move to make this happen. A significant portion of your Fate will happen at work or through traveling, which will likely be done with a purpose or mission in life. The Tutor is the head magistrate, and the symbol represents the story of him working from being a small-town magistrate to the tutor at the imperial palace.

There is a long story here of self-sacrifice, hard work, and determination. The Tutor will likely travel extensively either for work or in search of it, but once you find your place, then success in your career is Fated to unfold and go well. A job or career is central to your life and gives you purpose and direction. You may even become famous or renowned for the work that you do, and you can be paid well as an expert. You may end up a workaholic and give everything to your professional development and pursuit of success.

As we have already mentioned, the Tutor is all about contribution, integrity, and working for the greater good. So, your career must inspire you as such, although this can be deeply personal and different for everyone. There are many ways to contribute, but here, it is personal and connected to your vision of a greater society.

As this Star is connected to education and training, you may work in education, academia, or STEM (science, technology, engineering, and math). But it also shows an affinity for corporate structure, business, finance, law, and consultation. Really, this Star can be successful at anything if it is purposeful. Education will be important, and you may pursue higher education; the more prestigious, the better. This can provide a solid Fate for research and publishing as well as for receiving honors and rewards.

Regarding travel, you will probably have to move away from where you were born; if you stay there, you are not as likely to find success. You may move for school and then return home, but a journey must be made. Travel here is not frivolous or for fun but with a higher purpose in mind.

The likelihood that you will earn a good living, retire well, and teach others at some point is very high, as this Star is a role model. Succession and apprenticeship are also important and may be a significant part of the journey. Like the other strong Yang Stars, this is the continuation of a long line of Patriarchal ambition and success; your drive for success is motivated by your Ancestors, and you want to succeed because of their hard work. This may be the fruition of a lot of Ancestral preparation, and you have a great backup in the form of Ancestral guardians in your life's work.

Assistants Palace

Tian Xiang in the Friendship or Assistants Palace is also an exalted position, and its interpretation is very similar to the previous and next House but with a few distinct differences. Here, you are strongly Fated for career and work, but the role of public service, as teacher, mentor, or assistant, is exalted and pushed to the forefront. The work of the Tutor here takes on the role of subordinate and servant to others, which in many ways, is his most suitable role.

As always, this House can go both ways—this is you as an assistant or your Fate to have such an assistant. So, in the first case, you may be an outstanding assistant and support a great leader, boss, teacher, and so on. Your Fate is truly to be the tutor of the emperor, so you advise and help someone, and your professional Fate revolves around this. You work tirelessly behind the scenes and take on organization, management, and service, and this role suits you well, depending on your Character. Or, in the second case, depending on your Superiors Palace, you may have Fate to have such an assistant who helps you and brings you success. Your subordinates support and expand your work, or you may have an important Tutor who guides you.

At the core, you really want to help and serve. You are a dedicated servant for a higher purpose, and your own success is not important. You want to lift and exalt others so that they can shine. Sometimes, this has the reverse effect: You are so humble and want to help so badly that you end up in charge, because the leader that people truly need is the one who is reluctant and just wants to serve. Social justice and charity drive the Tutor in this House; he hears the cries of those who are suffering, and he wants to help. This is the image of a bodhisattva.

This placement also exalts teaching. So, if you have this, you will make an excellent teacher, professor, tutor, or the like. Academic pursuits will be highly fruitful, and you can research, write, publish, work at a university, and contribute to human knowledge. You will be a great student, which is the prerequisite to being a great teacher. And you may have a lot of students who come to you for guidance.

There is also a strong connection to traditional or classical knowledge, especially of the humanities, as well as to Confucian self-reflection and self-cultivation. Self-cultivation is critical here, and there is strong potential for a connection to lineage and to a spiritual path based on tradition. Succession and apprenticeship are also important here and may play a central role in the transmission of knowledge and skill.

Superiors Palace

Tian Xiang in the Superiors Palace is very similar to being in the past two Houses, but here he gets placed in the spotlight as a leader, manager, teacher, or government official. The role of the Tutor is naturally one of leadership and service. To the emperor, he was the humble servant, but to the rest of the imperial court, he was a leader; he was the second-in-command and the one who did all the practical work of the government. The emperor made the big decisions, but the tutor made thousands of small ones that ran the government.

So, this is a strong Fate for career success and leadership, and success in community, industry, and commerce are also much stronger. This is being at the top of the game and contributing to your field as an expert, innovator, or teacher. This is the most successful version of the tutor's story of working his way up the ladder to the top. If you have this, then you can be successful no matter what you do, but as always, it must include service, integrity, the greater good, and so on. You will be a public servant dedicated to justice and equality, a champion and advocate for others.

In this House, you will likely have a much larger scope of influence and advice for many people than in the previous two Houses. You will also be much more in the spotlight and in a leadership role. This may be big, like government work, or it may mean being the manager of twenty people in a landscaping business. Either way, you have a scope of influence that can change the world for the better, so you must use it responsibly.

Education is again exalted, but here you are likely to have a strong connection to an outstanding leader, lineage holder, or spiritual teacher, and you may succeed them and become a teacher yourself. You may train and educate others, who will become successful and bring you prestige, recognition, and admiration. Here, it again becomes very important that you practice what you preach and be a good role model, for this is where you gain power and influence and can do the most harm or the most good.

Traditionally, they say this means success comes late, and that life "begins" in your fifties. This is a late-blooming success—the image of a wise and accomplished older magistrate who is chosen to lead because of their years of experience. So, your greatest achievements may not come until later in life, but when they do, they will be more meaningful because they will be based on real wisdom rather than mere intellect or idealism.

Again, behind this is a great Ancestral precedent and drive for success that comes from the Patriarchal Ancestors. Here they achieve their highest goals through you.

Property Palace

Tian Xiang in the Property Palace, like the Wealth Palace, is modest but successful with a strong affinity for the ownership of property but with little interest in it, for the priority of the Tutor is not getting rich but doing something with purpose and meaning for the betterment of society. So, if you have this placement, you will likely use this Fate for a purpose as a landlord, local leader, politician, environmentalist, land developer, architect, engineer, or the like.

The Tutor is driven away from the accumulation of wealth and property for its own sake, but as the highest government official, he is given everything he needs. Fate for inheritance or acquiring property is solid, and the likelihood of getting your living arrangements taken care of through work is high. You will have good luck with homes and real estate and will benefit from rules, regulations, contracts, and the like. This also implies that property and ownership increase and get better with age; you may retire well and live in the countryside in a nice home.

The Tutor represents standards and law, so this is good support for studying architecture, engineering, and Fengshui, and we can see hints of careers here in related fields. As the tutor was a government official, government work in land, community, housing, transit, agriculture, and development, especially with a concern for the greater good, is also very likely. You may dedicate yourself to large-scale environmental concerns and campaigns to protect the environment through policy and activism. This placement can also push you into politics to achieve these kinds of goals.

This Star can also inspire a strong interest in place, history, genealogy, and so on. This may be personal, so you research your own family history and enjoy discovering their stories and tracking down their artifacts. But it also expands to include the history and stories of your local area and out to the world at large. However, the Tutor has a real interest in people and places, so you may get involved in local government or leadership after researching your local history in the hopes of improving your own community. Either way, your work involves getting involved in the community at the level of policy.

There may be a connection to family land, inherited homes, and heirlooms, or a long history in a place, so that the town you live in has streets named after your Ancestors. Traditionally, they say the Tutor in this House means you may have monuments named after you when you die and leave behind a legacy on property, with a plaque about you on benches or buildings.

Pleasure Palace

The Pleasure Palace is an odd placement for Tian Xiang, for the Tutor is not really a "fun" Star; it is sort of "all work and no play." So, it is likely that you enjoy work; you enjoy being busy and productive. You only have fun when you are learning, doing, creating, contributing, and so on. Self-improvement and discipline are fun to you. You probably cannot conceive of personal or frivolous enjoyment for its own sake, and you may be critical of this kind of pleasure. This may even border on masochistic, and you may feel guilty if you're not working.

This often means being studious, well-read, and educated in the classical humanities. You get a deep sense of enjoyment, meaning, and purpose from learning because it shapes you into a better human. The Tutor here is connected to the "classics," and his tastes are very conventional:

history, philosophy, literature, art, religion, and so on. The Tutor can be practically artistic, but more often this manifests as a deep appreciation for the "arts"—music, museums, opera, theater, art galleries—with attention to history, cultural context, and aesthetics. This Star is more of an appreciative art critic than an artist.

The Tutor does not enjoy things unless they include others, so this placement involves community events. This may be concerts, fairs, farmer's markets, and so on, not for their content but because they uplift and better the community. The Tutor wants to donate to worthy causes and perform community service, so you will likely enjoy helping and teaching others. You may love organizing parties, weddings, galas, or public events, especially if it is for charity. Charity and philanthropy are also highly supported by this placement.

The Tutor also derives a sense of identity and, therefore, enjoyment from staying up to date on politics and current affairs. You will probably follow the news and may get really involved in politics, identifying strongly as a Democrat, Republican, Libertarian, or whatever. You are deeply moved by the rhetoric of justice, equality, fairness, harmony, and world peace—the Tutor here may want to save the world or liberate all sentient beings from suffering. It is a deeply idealistic Star, for better or worse.

As such, this Star makes a great base for a spiritual path. You will be able to enjoy discipline, hard work, and practice. Meditation, routine conduct, ritual, prayer, and self-reflection all come naturally to this Star, and because the Tutor is dedicated to the welfare of others and seeks purpose and meaning, you will be compelled toward religion, spirituality, and the idea of a "path." The bodhisattva ideal of Buddhism works very well here.

TIAN JI (天機)—THE ORACLE

NAME AND TRANSLATION: Tian Ji (天機), the Oracle Star

Tian, 天—refers to the sky or heavens; the highest cosmic principle or force.[11]

Ji, 機—Heaven's workings; natural spontaneity. 2 key, a turning point; crux, crucial; exigency; e.g., 時機, shiji, critical moment, timely circumstances. a) opportunity, opportune moment; conducive; advantageous. 3 motive (power), stimulus, impulse, impetus; synapse; leading action > foretoken(ing); e.g., 見機 jianji, "see the springs of action," i.e., clairvoyant. a) energy; faculty; function(al), action. b) operative; effective, efficient. 4 dexterity, skill; ingenuity, ingenious; cleverness. a) perspicacity; judgment. b) calculating, contriving; e.g., 無(亡)機 wuji, guileless. 5 loom (weaving); e.g., 機杼 jizhu, loom and shuttle; also, conception and arrangement of lit-

> erary composition. 6 天機 tianji, "Heaven's Armil," 3rd star of Big Dipper (γ Ursae Majoris, = Phecdra); 機衡 jiheng, abb. of 璇機玉衡 xuanji yuheng, "Jadestone Armil and Jade Transverse," the bowl and handle of the Dipper; also, reputedly the ancient armillary sphere and sighting tube; also > the dome of heaven. mechanism (n.) {as in 病機 bing ji, pathomechanism} dynamic (n.) {as in 氣機 qi ji, qi dynamic}. The spring, or motive principle, machine, contrivance, artifice, occasion, opportunity, basis, root or germ, natural bent, fundamental quality. Adjective—secret or clandestine.[12]

The character Ji (機), is complex and has many meanings, but here refers to the inner workings or Qi dynamics of Heaven and to the clairvoyance and ingenuity that comes from seeing into the secrets of the universe. It refers to the dynamics that are secret, hidden, and beneath the surface of everything. Together, this Star can be translated in many ways, such as Heaven's Secret, Heaven's Pillar, and Sky Loom, but as it is an image of the Wu (巫) or Xi (覡), the "spirit medium" in a trance, we translate it as the Oracle of the Royal Court.

ELEMENT: Yin Wood

TRADITIONAL IMAGE: The state oracle, an image of the Wu (巫) or Xi (覡), the female or male "spirit medium" in a trance; a witch or wizard dressed in Daoist or gossamer robes, dancing to ritual court music, eyes rolled back, possessed of the Ancestors, speaking in tongues[13]

ANCESTOR PROFILE: Highly accomplished Matriarchal Ancestor(s), having their intuition or prophecy

LUMINOUS PLACEMENT: Rat and Horse Palaces

DIMINISHED PLACEMENT: Tiger and Ox Palaces

AFFILIATIONS: Northern Array—always to the right side of the Emperor; primary voice of the Ancestors; close to the General

Tian Ji, the Oracle, is the State Oracle of the Royal Court and always appears to the right of the Emperor Star. Although it is a Yin Star and represents the Matriarchal Ancestors, it is an androgynous, nonbinary, or gender-fluid image, as both men and women historically filled this role, but they were traditionally dressed as female. As one of the Four Rulers, the Oracle serves as the second primary adviser to the Emperor. The Tutor is the Emperor's Yang adviser, who offers counsel on worldly and political affairs. But the Oracle is his Yin adviser, who provides counsel on spiritual matters and serves as a trance medium and voice of the Emperor's Ancestors. The oracle was the emperor's direct connection to Heaven, to the unseen world of the dead, and to the various gods, goddesses, nature spirits, and so on, that influence Earth. The Oracle represents divination in all its forms, like the famous oracle bones of ancient China.

It has been customary in China and many Asian countries (and worldwide) to have a state oracle, such as the Nechung Oracle of Tibet or the Pythia at Delphi. China had an extensive system of discovering and training young children to be oracles through networks of Daoist temples centered at the sacred mountain Maoshan. The highest and most accomplished oracle would be sent to the royal palace to serve the emperor.

If children displayed sensitivity and prophetic vision—seeing spirits, talking to the dead, and so on—they would be sent to local temples for training. It tended to be girls—the Wu (巫)—but there were also boys—called Xi (覡)—who were dressed as female, hence the nonbinary image. If they could not be trained out of their sensitivity (to be able to participate in farming instead), they would continue their training and work their way up the ranks as oracles in higher and higher stations, serving local governors, vassals, magistrates, and so on. The most gifted would go to Maoshan, and the most gifted of those would be chosen to serve the royal palace as a voice of divination for the whole empire or even dynasty.

The image of the Oracle is one of trance: The oracle held a mirror and whirled in ritual dance. The character Wu (巫), developed from the early Seal script, depicts Oracles dancing. As they dance, they lose themselves, and their body is taken; they are possessed; they look through the mirror and see visions. They are a vessel of divination.

But what was being divined through the oracle? Primarily the voice of the Ancestors—the Ancestors of the emperor but also of any powerful spirits, gods, or protectors communicating the Mandate of Heaven. In your chart, the Oracle represents your Ancestors' most potent communication, guidance, and intuition. It represents their stories, resolved and unresolved. Wherever it shows up is where they are speaking the loudest—it is a divining rod pointing you where to go, and there is some wisdom connected to their stories. This manifests as intuition, inspiration, creativity, intelligence, psychic ability, and sensitivity, and as signs, omens, gut feelings, special connections, and so on. It manifests through dreams and daydreams. Wherever it shows up, weird stuff tends to happen.

It represents all your Ancestors, but as a Yin Star it is associated with the Matriarchal Ancestors and is often described as a kind of fairy godmother or guardian angel, a strong and beneficent female Ancestor who is guiding you. It represents all the collective wisdom and intuition of your Ancestors in relation to spiritual matters—to our deeper callings for meaning, belonging, transcendence, enlightenment, realization, and liberation. It represents your spiritual path and the resolution of "otherworldly," rather than worldly, Fate, although sometimes these two things blur.

The Oracle is deeply connected to the feelings, wishes, hopes, fears, and longings of the Ancestors, as well as their love, compassion, and empathy. It is a "feeling" Star, operating through "other" ways of knowing besides the rational mind, but it is also deeply intelligent and intuitive. It represents the influence of the unseen: the deeper principles, dynamics—called Ji (機)—and laws of nature that govern Earth from the Heavens (and the Underworlds).

As a feeling Star, it easily becomes confused, muddled, obsessive, and conflicted when afflicted. It is also open to mediumship and possession from Ghosts, spirits, and Beneficial Ancestors; this is where you get possessed by your Ancestors, working their Fate out through you.

This Star is deeply connected to the Emperor and the General, to whom it helps to communicate strategy and foresee negative omens.

Let's walk the Oracle through the Twelve Houses.

Ming Palace

If Tian Ji, the Oracle Star, shows up in the Ming Palace, then you are an oracle. Life will be quite strange by ordinary standards; to you, it will seem normal, but your life will be bizarre, extraordinary, and even mystical to others. Your Ancestral Fate is powerful, and your life is driven by the Ancestors through an irrational process based on dreams, intuition, gut feelings, omens, strange or serendipitous connections, and so on, and not by a rational, linear timeline. You are a vessel, a medium, and you can see through to "other" worlds and experience altered states, and this may start early in life. You will likely have a strong sense of otherworldliness, spiritual transcendence, or at the very least, a deep sense of meaning and purpose that makes you feel different.

As one of the Four Rulers, the Oracle means that the capacity to resolve Fate in this lifetime is very strong, but the resolution of Fate in this case will come through spiritual means, and it will unravel in a direct link to your Ancestors, possibly as the expression of a specific Ancestral guardian or "fairy godmother," who is blessing you, waving her magic wand, and setting out a path before you. Your job is simply to surrender and "follow your weird" in your own way.

Often, this means being very intelligent, high-strung, gifted, talented, sensitive, and so on, and this sensitivity is unavoidable and will likely take training to manage. It can manifest as musical or artistic ability, profound creativity, and/or wisdom beyond your years that comes through a deeply spiritual drive to connect to a higher power or means.

You will receive visions, dreams, signs, omens, and so on; if you ignore them, you will fail to resolve Fate. The Ancestors will be speaking to you somewhere, and you must listen, so pay attention. Record your dreams. It may be a call to religion or travel. It may be artistic, and you may need to put a brush or instrument in front of the stream of passionate voices and feelings speaking through you. It may be a call to study foreign languages, culture, and religion. It may require you to travel, immigrate, or go on a journey to fulfill your purpose.

And often, this purpose is divination or medicine. This can manifest as being an adviser, consultant, therapist, psychiatrist, counselor, or doctor—or, even stranger, as an astrologer, psychic, trance medium, shaman, priest, or doctor of traditional medicines like herbalism. Fate here is usually resolved by using your gift to help or guide others. You will also be called to meet, study, and receive help from such people. You may have a significant Fate with a teacher of these arts who will show you the way.

The call to be an oracle, shaman, or healer of some kind may involve a healing or awakening journey that brings you close to death, puts you through a hero's trial or vision quest, or subjects you to deep and transformational training, retreat, and testing. Mediation, yoga, visualization, prayer, chanting, dance, martial arts, plant medicine/drugs, rituals, and so on could be an important part of your journey, and necessary to resolve your Fate.

Ancestors Palace

Tian Ji in the Ancestors Palace is like the Ming Palace, but there is less Fate to be an oracle yourself and even more of an overarching influence of the Ancestors on your life from "behind the scenes." Your Ancestors are the main influence on your life, but this may not be as obvious as a direct connection to your immediate family. It may mean a very strong, even psychic, connection to both parents, but usually to your mother, grandmother, or especially to a great-(or great-great-)grandmother, who acts as the fairy godmother. Here, they are a very strong influence and may show up in dreams and intuition or as talent, creativity, and so on.

Your life and Fate directly result from their unresolved energies, and your Fate will unravel as they resolve. This means that you inherit a lot of unfinished business to work out, which is not to say Ghosts, but Ghost Stars very easily influence the Oracle here. Your life may not feel like your own. It may feel out of control, or like you don't know who you are, as you go through a lot of phases, chapters, ups, and downs, trying on different personalities, professions, addictions, passions, journeys, and so on. You are possessed of a long line of Ancestors finishing out their stories, so you might have to move to Thailand for two years to run a hostel on a beach but then return to South Africa to become a lawyer, only to then quit and be an activist, to then go through drug addiction, clean up your act, and become a counselor who understands the law and helps at-risk youth. These kinds of life-changing reversals of Fate free you of Ancestral burdens and break cycles of negativity for the better.

Like Tian Ji in the Ming Palace, you may hear voices, receive visions, dreams, omens, and so on. It is important to listen, but you may not have to follow them. Here, they are not as central to your Fate story but still seek to be resolved. It is more important to hear their story, get the message, and feel the feelings so they can be released. Many Ancestors need their stories to be heard, so do genealogy if you can. This may be a call to connect back to Ancestral origins that were lost in histories of exile, migration, slavery, and so on. Because their histories are lost, they can only communicate them in dreams.

This could also mean that you have a very high capacity for spiritual practice and a Fate connection to lineage, or past-life connections to teachers and traditions outside your direct Ancestral line. You may be called to wisdom traditions of the past, compelled by deep drives for transcendence, awakening, release, resolution, and so on. Here, you inherit the Ancestral drive to completion, and so this is a very strong basis for meditation, yoga, and spiritual practice of all kinds. You may have a strong Fate with a teacher who downloads their tradition to you, and you become a "lineage holder." There is some kind of strong spiritual inheritance to find here.

Youth Palace

Tian Ji in the Youth Palace is, again, like in the Ming and Ancestors Palace in that the Ancestors are a very strong influence on your life, and you have Fate to be an oracle. The difference is that this Fate manifests and resolves earlier in life and can be complete by adulthood. The influence of your Ancestors, especially Matriarchal Ancestors, will lead to a strong resolution of Fate in childhood through dreams, imagination, and play.

In short, you will be a weird kid and/or have a very weird childhood. Or you will have a very strange and fragile connection to, or relationship with, your siblings. With the Oracle in this House, you may be a very sensitive, artistic, creative, otherworldly child who sees Ghosts, has imaginary friends (who are probably real), and plays in a rich world of imagination that is full of life, stories, and experiences that are difficult for others, both peers and adults, to understand. You will not be like other kids; your dad may say, "That boy ain't right."

When you play with imaginary friends, toys, video games, and so on, you are working out a vast sea of Ancestors who easily connect to your childlike innocence and sensitivity. When you play war with toy guns, all the soldiers in your family who died in war line up and work out their stuff. When you play house, you may pour tea to a dead aunt or miscarried sibling. Your play is their play. Ancestral spirits and guardians fill your childhood and often become like a third parent.

It is important to let children like this play and never tell them that their imaginary friends are not real. If they come to you and say there is a Ghost in the closet or a monster under the bed, do not tell them it isn't real or that there is no such thing as a Ghost. It is much better to believe them, calmly ask them what the Ghost wants, and then find out. Ghosts are just looking for help, so let's help them. These children are oracles, and they can help lost spirits with their kindness. It is also helpful to train children with these experiences, so art, prayer, playful meditations, yoga practices, and so on are very powerful. These are the kids who end up at the Daoist temple. They need protection and not to be judged for their strangeness. These kids are empathetic and feel the pain of others. They may cry and not know why, but someone else is in pain just down the road, or two thousand miles away, Grandma died or a war may have started.

This placement may also mean having a strong psychic and spiritual connection to your siblings; now you are brother and sister, but heaven only knows what you were in a past life. You may be enemies reuniting to work out their previous Fate by roughhousing and making forts out of couch cushions. Often, this relationship is fragile because you're just kids but have the Fate of generations working through you. Often, these relationships are deep but need to be worked out and maintained as adults. Otherwise, you grow distant. You may feel it from two states away when your sister is ill or sad.

Often, this means that childhood is unstable. Sometimes, it means that home is a turbulent place where Ancestral Fate is being worked out through family relations, and there may be a lot of fighting, arguing, bickering, and so on. Your sensitivity may also hinder you if you are born into a family or culture that does not honor it. You may have to learn to manage and even overcome that sensitivity to function in the world. It may be repressed or traumatized by the harshness of modernity or by a rough family life. It may mean that you are a late bloomer and that you don't stabilize your gifts until later in adulthood. Often, these kids become very kind, mature, and sensitive adults.

This may also manifest as a strange childhood, like growing up in a cult or religious household that is very different from the mainstream. It can be growing up in a foreign country as a child of expats, or maybe your parents run a strange business, and you grow up in a lot of unusual circumstances. It can also mean being an outsider, outcast, or "black sheep." Your family may be outcasts or black sheep, or you may be the odd one in the family and so get treated differently.

Finally, you may develop a spiritual path very early. You may be what the Tibetans call a tulku, a spiritual practitioner reborn intentionally to get right back on the path. You may be drawn to church, temples, rituals, and spiritual practices early. You may be an "old soul" who is wise beyond your years. You might go to a temple and see the monks or nuns and want to be one. You may be exposed to spirituality early and have a sense of enlightenment, God, or the sacred before you have a sense of "what you want to be when you grow up." You will also likely have a deep and spiritual connection to nature and the place or environment of your childhood.

Partners Palace

Tian Ji in the Partners Palace is a mixed bag. There is a strong Fate resolution through partnership and a deep spiritual, psychic connection with a partner. However, this connection is easily afflicted and emotionally shaky, and there is also a strong influence of the Ancestors here. They may be choosing for you, and you may be Fated to work out Ancestral patterns through marriage. So, family patterns of making bad choices or of abuse are possible and need to be worked out to make the best of this.

The connections here are deeply Fated and not easy to understand. You and your partner will likely be drawn to each other powerfully and mysteriously and feel like there is a past-life or soulmate connection. Often, the partner is attractive and mesmerizing. You may read each other's minds and be intuitively wired. When they are having a bad day, you can feel it. You think about them, and they call you.

This deep connection can also be a hindrance, for you may not be compatible or mature but stay together because of this feeling of being connected. Sometimes, this means staying in a bad relationship.

You may also have this Fate with multiple people, and it is part of your path of growth and maturation to work out your issues and Ancestral or past-life patterns through being in relationships. This means that relationships are dramatic, powerful, deeply meaningful, and equally devastating. Relationships can become like a religion, and some people turn them into everything, seeking God or enlightenment through union. But often, this is tumultuous, as it is unleashing our deep sexual, instinctual energies.

However, with maturation, this can become wonderful. A partner and marriage may become a powerful container for growth, and with the Oracle in this House, it is possible that the partner opens you to a spiritual path. In that case, the partnership can weather the difficulties of life and become a source of great meaning and support. The term "Dharma partnership" applies, as does "mindful marriage."

There is often a discrepancy in the relationship. Sometimes, it is age, but often, it is maturity, as partners find it difficult to express their emotions. The Ancestors are speaking here, and a lot of stuff is being worked out, so it is touchy. Traditionally, they say that one partner may outlive the other and that one may live alone for a long time.

Finally, you may be drawn to being a monk or nun, especially if this is afflicted by Ghost Stars. You may be married to Jesus. Or you can work out your difficulties with relationships by renouncing them altogether. You may also practice Tantric or Daoist sex rituals and practices and/or practice Karma Mudra, visualizing yourself in sexual union with a deity.

Offspring Palace

If you have Tian Ji in the Offspring Palace, then you will likely give birth to an oracle. You may be Fated to have a very sensitive, spiritual, artistic, or unusual child. As a Yin Star, this Star means it may be a daughter, but not necessarily. This child will be empathic and intuitive and display "oracular" qualities, like seeing spirits or Ghosts, having foresight into the future, and so on. They will need protection, guidance, education, and training to help with their abilities, which may range from being talented to full-blown psychic. They may be odd, but they tell you about strange dreams, feelings, and so on. They may also possess deep insights into people that are well beyond their age. It is important to nurture these gifts and not squash them; their imaginary friends are real, and there really is a Ghost in the closet. As previously stated, it is better to have them engage with curiosity rather than tell them these things aren't real.

They are Fated to use their abilities and talents to help you resolve your Fate. You will have a deep spiritual connection to them and to being a parent. Being a parent may very well awaken your own oracular abilities. You become psychically linked to your children and can sense their moods and needs, and this awakens your empathy for others. After having kids, you develop a sense of compassion that you never had, and this deepens your life and creates a sense of the spiritual or sacred. It may even start you on a spiritual path.

You never knew what unconditional love was until you had kids, and this breaks you open and heals your past wounds. You can forgive and forget, because nothing else matters. You will care deeply, even too deeply, for your children, which could lead you to become overbearing. So, protect them, but learn to let them go. You grow very close to them, and this closeness deepens over time. Children may end your search for a home, connect you to your Ancestors, and give you sense of family continuity.

If you have this Star in this House, your Fate with reproduction is a direct conduit for the Ancestors; your child or children are returning Ancestors with a strong link to your Ancestral origins; they may seek to connect or reconnect back to where you come from—the traditions, religions, language, land, and so on. Whenever you have sex, the Ancestors start to gather and queue up. They are calling for children. A child may resemble a great-great-grandmother and have the same interests and talents. Having kids inspires you to research genealogy and family history, and this brings with it a wealth of insights and resolution.

Finally, sex may be a mystical experience that opens realms of previously closed-off experiences. You lose yourself and achieve states of unity or transcendence through sex. Like in the previous House, Tian Ji here may make you apt to adopt Tantric or Daoist sex rituals and practices and to benefit from seeing the world through the lens of Yin-yang—everything coming into being through sex-paired opposites—or even to transcend this through gender-fluid, nonbinary, polyamorous explorations, seeing sex and gender as empty.

Wealth Palace

If you have Tian Ji in the Wealth Palace, then you have a possible Fate to work or make money as an oracle. Overall, this Fate with Wealth is very uneven; it is very much like the stock market, with lots of ups and downs—very volatile, and with a very abstract relationship to money.

The most straightforward interpretation is work as an oracle—as an astrologer, psychic, spirit medium, spiritual guide, or the like, or in the culturally accepted forms of this kind of work: counselor, therapist, psychiatrist, doctor, musician, artist, and so on. You may predict the weather or stock market or work in investing, trading, and speculation—anything that involves statistics and prediction. This could also manifest in gambling: casinos, sports betting, and so on. Las Vegas is very Oracle. If you have this unafflicted, then you should go to Vegas and let the Oracle speak. Maybe play the lottery regularly, letting the numbers come to you.

Either way, intuition, intelligence, and foresight—not skill, ability, or competence—bring you success. Money and wealth may be very indirect; this is not an ordinary salary or paycheck, and money may be acquired indirectly or through association. But the Ancestors are speaking here, offering you wisdom and guidance from all their mistakes, failures, and successes. This could also manifest as family money or inheritance from the Ancestors: Your grandfather, whom you never met, dies and leaves you a fortune.

Because of this, wealth tends to fluctuate a lot: You can go from rags to riches and back again. Character matters a lot here, as well as the placement of other Stars, because some characters, like the Ox, may be naturally responsible and conservative with money and, therefore, not likely to gamble it away or risk it all on a big investment. But some, like the Monkey, for example, may take big risks and therefore lose or win big.

Health Palace

Tian Ji in the Health Palace is a powerful placement. Like other placements, it means that you are an oracle, but this oracular capacity manifests very strongly through your embodiment and health. Your body is a very direct expression of your Ancestors and their patterns, resolved and unresolved. You have a lot coming through you that is working itself out. Therefore, health and wellness may be a bit of a roller coaster. Health is not straightforward and is even quite strange.

Generally, this means having a very sensitive constitution, but you are not weak. You have a very strong capacity to resolve Ancestral Fate through illness and healing, and your healing process is resolving Ghosts, which may appear exorcistic. The Ancestors are lining up to finish their stuff through you, so you may have strange illnesses, accidents, and a host of miraculous occurrences around getting sick or injured and recovering.

Diagnosing you, then, is not so simple. You may have all kinds of strange, unexplainable symptoms with no obvious cause. The term *wind* in Chinese medicine is very applicable—changing, moving, and coming from unknown directions. This often manifests as nervous disorders, skin conditions, mental health problems, autoimmune conditions, allergies, sensitivities, and often as genetic or inherited patterns of illness.

You may be a sickly child, and after a rough childhood, you learn how to maintain your health in a very personal and strange way, but this gives you longevity. You may become a hypochondriac and worry about your health all the time because you can feel yourself getting sick from all kinds of things that don't make sense to others. Cultivating very strong health routines and practices is, therefore, very important. You must build very strong "gates," or boundaries, for you are very open to influence.

Here, you are very susceptible to "possession" from Ancestral Ghosts and various types of spirits. This is a kind of openness and sensitivity that draws all kinds of things to you; you may see Ghosts, spirits, auras, channels, chakras, and so on. You may have very strong empathy and therefore take on the feelings and even illnesses of others. You may also have a very strong connection to the seasons, to seasonal and weather changes, and to the host of spirits that ride what Chinese medicine calls damp, cold, wind, and so on. This is like knowing a storm is coming because you can feel it in your joints.

Emotions compromise you; if you are stressed or upset, you may get ill. If you are tired, you may easily get ill from all kinds of sources, from the basic compromised immunity to absorbing other people's problems to getting possessed by a lost wood spirit while hiking. The person next to you has a headache, and you start to get one. A family member, partner, or friend may be stressed, and so you start to feel upset even though you are fifty miles away. You watch an upsetting story on the news and get sick. There's a war on the other side of the world, and you start crying. Again, you are an oracle, so learning to manage this will be important, because your health depends on it. Here, you can get ill or well through miraculous means; a shaman may pull a chicken gizzard out of you, but it works. Or you may suddenly walk after being in a wheelchair during a faith revival.

This is again the image of the Wu, or shaman, which in the Health Palace means that sickness, illness, injury, and so on may be your spiritual path. You may be Fated to be brought close to death as a kind of vision quest, and your healing journey may be central to your Fate resolution. Here, there may be a mandate to heal others as repayment of a debt. This is generally a strong Fate with doctors and healers of all kinds, both to meet them and potentially to become one. A shaman or medicine person may heal you. In being healed and/or healing yourself, you may learn to heal others. As a sick child, you may learn all kinds of things along the way that will benefit others. And the Oracle's capacity for feeling, empathy, and understanding is very strong here. Becoming a doctor, healer, shaman, or the like may be second nature.

Tian Ji in this House is connected to traditional medicine, Indigenous medicine, faith healing, and so on, with more of a connection to herbs, energy work, diet and lifestyle, yoga, meditation, talismans, prayers, and so on. So, if you have the calling, then you can study and practice medicine. It can manifest in traditional medicine, but when it does, it appears a lot more intuitive, relational, and mystical, and it makes you good at diagnosis. It will probably give you a more holistic outlook rather than a reductionist one, but reading a lab report also may be a kind of divination.

Longevity is possible here, but it comes through a lot of very personal health routines that are based on trial, error, and intuition. Worry and stress can wear you out prematurely, but your weird routines will give you longevity if you can learn to manage things. Maybe you take huge handfuls of supplements, follow a very odd diet, or do cold plunges every morning. It doesn't matter what the studies say; it matters how you feel. Traditionally, they say you heal best in the transitions between seasons, the "Eight Gates"—the two equinoxes, the two solstices, and the points between.

Career/Travel Palace

If Tian Ji appears in the Career/Travel Palace or any of the career Houses, then your Ancestors are pushing you to use your oracular abilities to contribute to society through your work in the world, and your Ancestral Fate is resolved through travel and work. But if it appears in the Career/Travel Palace, then there is a strong likelihood that you will have to go on a journey to discover, train, and manifest your unique abilities. This journey may be strange, mystical, and feel beyond your control, as if dictated by otherworldly forces or callings. Life may include a very powerful journey of personal and spiritual transformation to become an oracle and express those abilities. There will be a strong significance to where you were born, but there will also be something calling you that you must find.

This is often a strong Fate Threshold for a new life in a new place. It may be immigrating to a new country, but it can also be a strong Fate in a new town, city, state, or geographic location. When you get there, a new life starts, and it is not until then that your Fate unravels. The story of the Ancestors will likely play a role in this—either as a connection to places of Ancestral origin or in the details of the Ancestors' story, which is often of exile, migration, immigration, slavery, war, occupation, and so on. The Ancestral patterns of movement, travel, and relocating are strong, and you will play this out in your experience, seeking to resolve these stories. This may result in starting over again or discovering a place that causes your Fate to unravel. It may also be a call to continue a family line of work that is oracular, like coming from a long line of musicians.

Your life may be a walkabout, and you may be a wanderer, traveling from place to place, seeking a home, until the Fate here is resolved and manifests fully when you put down roots and serve as an oracle. Here, all the deep, spiritual experiences of your Ancestors are guiding you, speaking through you in the hope of finding "the promised land" or returning to a homeland. Or they were forced to relocate because of war, exile, or the like, and your experience working in the world becomes a vessel for them; you experience freedom as you tell these stories and shed generations of struggle. This often manifests as art, music, storytelling, and writing, but also in the seeking of truth, which could be journalism, activism, environmentalism, and so on.

This placement also denotes a strong calling to spiritual and religious matters. You may be called to practice a foreign religion or to reconnect to the religion of your Ancestors. It may be a calling to rediscover myths, legends, and stories and to find other ways of knowing and being in the world, beyond modern consumer-corporate myths, scientific atheism, or Judeo-Christian beliefs.

The call to prayer, divination, meditation, ritual, exegesis, study, learning, and so on will be strong and seek transformation, both personally and globally. You will want to share and use these practices to better the world, your community, the environment, and so on. This may mean working as a support to others as a counselor, social worker, community leader, or therapist, but also in the stranger guise of psychic, astrologer, medium, healer, or spiritual guide. You want to connect with people and the community, especially through stories and myths.

Intuition and sensitivity are key here: Your Ancestors are a divining rod; they are calling you to where the work is to be done. You must listen to your intuition and your gut feelings and follow the signs. It may be in one place or several, but you are on a journey of discovery, working to help others with your unique abilities, talents, vision, and so on. You may travel widely in search of this. You may live in many places and seek grand adventures, but there is a call to meaning and transformation out there beyond the horizon.

Assistants Palace

Tian Ji in the Assistants Palace is considered a somewhat disadvantaged position, but it does exalt the Oracle's role as a support for others. This is considered a classical placement for practicing astrology and medicine (I have this here) and for all kinds of divination or simply service professions done with a spiritual motivation. This also exalts spiritual practice in the form of service, compassion, and loving-kindness, as this House places others first and puts you in a secondary and selfless position.

Tian Ji in this House is disadvantaged because the Oracle needs support, strong boundaries, and freedom. It must be able to do its thing without constraint, judgment, or conspiracy, because it is weird. Here, the Oracle is shaky and not good for friendship; if you have good support, then it goes well, but if not, then things can go badly. The Oracle's intuition can become paranoid and self-conscious around others, and this can cause you to misunderstand others or for others to misunderstand you. The strange nature of this Star can cause confusion and misinterpretation, and people can take advantage of you. When we are dealing with empaths and negative emotions, things get touchy. You are at risk of scandal and your intuition going haywire. Without good training, your judgment can be poor and put yourself and others at risk. Certain characters, like Rabbits, Goats, and Pigs, need to be very mindful of relationship boundaries.

It is, therefore, important to have strong training in spiritual hygiene, boundaries, and honest self-reflection. Buddhist training in Emptiness and no-self can be powerful aids to mitigate magical thinking and delusion here. It is also important to ensure you have good people around you; they need to earn your trust and prove themselves to be the best support. If you are too trusting and don't see warning signs, then your intuition may fail to protect you. It may be best to go it alone, and you may feel more confident alone until you feel strong enough and have good enough boundaries to let people into your inner circle. Entrepreneurial work is a good way to manage this; be your own boss, and come up with your own unique job.

There are potentially strong and deep spiritual past-life connections with friends and people outside the family. As with the Emperor in this House, you may be part of a "circle of returners," but here, the connection is spiritual, mystical, and connected to spiritual goals, community, or experience. This may manifest as a very strong community at a church or temple, or it may manifest as doing psychedelics in the desert at Burning Man. Also, because the Oracle is an Ancestral Star, you may find your true Ancestors or family through friendship, work, community, parish, lineage, and so on. You may practice a foreign tradition, medicine, or religion and find past-life continuity through lineage and a teacher, guru, or mentor.

The best manifestation of this Star is service: There is a calling to use your talents and oracular abilities to help others, and it connects you to the momentum of wisdom traditions. This exalts all service professions as a spiritual path. It doesn't really matter what you do. You can be a waiter, a janitor, a bus driver, a schoolteacher, a yoga teacher; it doesn't matter. What matters is your connection to others and the path of service and contribution. Here, you serve to serve; this is about giving selflessly without thought of return or getting an advantage. Be the best damn bus driver you can be, and you can touch many lives in a positive way. This is about cultivating the Four Immeasurables: compassion, loving-kindness, sympathetic joy, and equanimity. Equanimity—relaxed, nonjudgmental awareness with love—is key to resolving Fate here. See everyone as the Buddha. With this Star in this House, you have the capacity to connect to the deepest insights of spiritual work through selflessness.

Superiors Palace

Tian Ji is exalted in the Superiors Palace. This is where it is meant to be; here, the Oracle is given the best position and support to express its gifts. This is the image of the fully realized state oracle at the right hand of the emperor. This is one of the best placements to excel in work that changes the world and that expresses your Ancestors' highest aspirations and values. In this professional House, the Oracle enables you to succeed as an oracle in your work; it may be through art, music, religion, academia, or culture, but you can benefit and change the world or at least your community at large. This gives you a platform for influence, and the Oracle here can set trends, change opinions, and inspire people.

Divination can take many forms and encompass many professions, but whatever you do, you must use your intuition, your foresight, and your sensitivities. This is what brings you success. In this placement, there is the opportunity to find and express a unique voice. Your weirdness, your personality, and your charisma can bring you success. Unique talents and gifts can also have a strong influence; you may invent a new giz-widget, method, or technique that may change your profession, industry, or even just office logistics. This has a high potential for success and excellence. This usually comes with a vision, so starting a company and running your own business can be powerful here. You want to change the world for the better, and you can. It can be with new technology or just by selling top-of-the-line lawnmowers.

Tian Ji in this House has a strong connection to high honors in academia and the humanities: writing, literature, poetry, philosophy, art, music, theater, history, and so on.

The purpose of studying these things is to make you a better human and to exalt the themes that run through the humanities: myth, meaning, purpose, and human virtue. To become the oracle, you must actualize these; you must live them.

This placement is strongly associated with the teacher–student relationship and with mentorship and succession. This may be in the workplace as the path to becoming a journeyman. It may mean inheriting a job through succession. Or it may be through a spiritual teacher or lineage. It may also be through a family business that you take over and take to the next level. Here you are, a prodigy, a rising star on the path to mastery.

This is considered one of the best placements for spiritual practice in the traditional sense, as it exalts religion and lineage. This is the image of the disciple connecting with a guru, lama, priest, or the like, who shows them the way. This is a deep spiritual yearning and calling. You may be compelled on a spiritual path to discover the meaning of life, enlightenment, salvation, and so on. You may be compelled to find a teacher—as the adage goes, "When the student is ready, the master will appear." This may be formal and involve initiation into a tradition and taking vows. Or it may manifest in a more worldly way, like finding a coach or therapist who helps you succeed. This is a strong precedent for following and completing a spiritual path of meditation, retreat, yoga, or any disciplined practice and experiencing great Fruition. The resolution of Fate and the experience of enlightenment is strong in this House.

Like this Star in the other career Houses, in this placement your work in the world and contribution to society are your spiritual path and your way of resolving Ancestral Fate. But here, you are in the spotlight and may have a strong influence through oracular means. You can influence people through ideas, myths, stories, and politics. You could even go so far as being a cult leader or following a cult leader. There can be a kind of religious fervor or belief here that can be very powerful.

Property Palace

Tian Ji in the Property Palace is considered a poor placement for the more worldly and solid meanings of this House. There is little affinity for the Oracle here to own property, material wealth, or goods. The oracle often had to leave home and move from temple to temple for training, and eventually lived in the Palace Temple. So, the Fate here is very transient, and you may drift from place to place and never feel at home in the world. You may be unattached to worldly possessions and feel comfortable having only the clothes on your back—"Wherever I lay my hat is home."

However, this may not be a bad thing; like this Star in the Travel Palace, your life may be a "walkabout." There is a calling here for a spiritual journey, and the image is one of renunciation and retreat.

The oracle was always given housing, so there is no sense of being poor or homeless, but rather that home and property are indirect and provided by others. This can be as mundane as always renting and never putting down roots because your Fate is never to be attached to a place—always mobile and ready for the next adventure. Or it can be living as a monk or nun or wandering yogi of sorts in a monastery, hermitage, faculty housing, or the like.

Often, this life of being a nomad or a wandering yogi is resolved with a spiritual maturation that happens later in life when you decide to put down roots. You spend your life looking for a home, and this is resolved when you choose to stay put. You may purchase a property or some land and build a cabin in the woods, where you finally escape life's chaos and find peace. You may love traveling and will likely travel extensively, and this Star in this House can be a strong indicator of migrating or retiring to a foreign country after a life of being rootless or feeling disconnected from the culture you were born in. It could also mean finding a true family or past-life connection in a foreign place, like Liu Ming, who was adopted by a family in Taiwan.

In this placement, factors of Fate drive the Oracle to relocate; this is often part of your Ancestral Fate and connected to Ancestral patterns of exile and migration; we have seen this in other Houses, but here it is deeply connected to home. The history of the world is often one of exile, migration, war, genocide, and so on. There are no Indigenous people, really—no one is originally from anywhere, strictly speaking—but sometimes we manage to build a tradition for enough generations to create culture, religion, language, and so on. Very often, we go to war over land and resources, seeking the wealth of others, displacing people from these long histories.

The Oracle here is the voice of these stories, which will manifest according to your Ancestors' unique stories—this may be stories of immigration due to hardship, slavery, apartheid, or war, which causes the unsettled wandering, looking to return to or find a home. Here, doing genealogy and traveling to the places of your Ancestors and discovering their stories are very powerful and liberate you from their Fate. Many people have been displaced by slavery and war, so genealogy is not so easy. These could be the voices of those Ancestral guardians calling you back to Africa or to find the tribe you come from. This could be a call from the deep to reconnect to your Ancestral roots, like going beyond being Scottish to being Gaelic, or it may mean going on a pilgrimage to Mecca, Jerusalem, Bodhgaya, Mount Kailash, the Vatican, and so on. Once you go on the pilgrimage, you are free.

This placement is a strong basis for doing long spiritual retreats and being a hermit or yogi in a cave. You may be called to be in solitude in the wilderness, the mountains, a lighthouse by the ocean, and so on. You may feel a deep spiritual connection to the wild or to a specific environment like the desert or beach. Your spiritual path is found in renouncing everything and going into the wild. There is a strong connection to Fengshui here, and the Ancestors again act like a divining rod, a compass pointing you where you will be liberated or happy.

There can also be strange Fate here with property, like inheriting a haunted house or being connected to local spirits, nature spirits, or Ghosts. Maybe you move into a house and start having dreams of a previous owner's death. Or you get possessed by the spirit of a place: You move to Texas and find yourself wearing boots and big belt buckles and wanting to be a cowboy. Or you travel to Indonesia and feel more like yourself when you wear a sarong.

Pleasure Palace

Tian Ji in the Pleasure Palace denotes a strong interest in spiritual matters and in enjoying all things oracular. This is one of the most direct placements for spiritual practice, because this House is not connected to worldly matters but more to our inner personal experience. The Oracle here is free from obligation, responsibility, and pressure to fit into the world. So, the deepest aspirations and enjoyments come forth as mystical experiences. Your greatest sense of joy and meaning will come from religion, spirituality, philosophy, mythology, and so on. You will be called to understand the big picture, the true meaning of life, and the reason why we are all here. You can't imagine something more important. You will enjoy everything that expresses these deep human callings for meaning, purpose, transcendence, connection, liberation, and salvation and seek them for their own sake.

This can be traditional or deeply personal. You may love culture, religion, art, music, and history, but this love may be very specific to your own personal sense of meaning that you create through your experience. You may eventually turn this love into a path or occupation later in life. Like, you may be an avid punk rocker, and your deepest experiences are in a mosh pit. Now you're in your forties and work a dead-end job, but you still want to rock out on the weekends. So, you go all in and buy a dying music venue, and now you are deeply fulfilled by providing a space for young, up-and-coming bands. Or it may be a very specific Ancestral call to enjoyment, like learning traditional West African dance and then teaching this to inner-city youth.

Spiritual community and human connection are very important here. This is the Ancestors calling for communion. You get great joy from friendship, family, lovers, and partners, but it is the spirit of what brings you together that is important, like communion in the Holy Spirit or gathering for a shared love of muscle cars. These things become

Icons of Essence and spirit and connect you to the "other side." Rituals and going to places of worship are very important here; you may lose yourself singing hymns or chanting sutras. Here the love of these things is pure, for its own sake and purpose, not for any ulterior motives. You love it because generations have loved it, and that is what brings your family together. This may also create a great love for genealogy and lineage and an enjoyment of your Ancestors' traditions.

Spiritual practice and discipline here can actually be fun. Sitting in meditation, saying Hail Marys, visualizing Green Tara, or doing *paschimottanasana* is a blast. You love learning about the history and meaning of these practices and can't wait to do them. Things like astrology and tarot may fascinate you. Perhaps the suffering of Catholic saints or ascetic yogis in loincloths excites you, and you imagine being them. The dangers here are imagination and spiritual materialism, which can get out of hand. Some people fantasize about spiritual Fruition because it becomes a new identity to grasp onto that fits a higher purpose. But it also gives you the advantage of enjoying practice, which means you are more likely to do it. Here, you also connect to your Ancestors and past-life spiritual Fruition and may have a strong momentum in these kinds of practices. They may come forth in dreams, visions, and natural talents in wisdom traditions like astrology, medicine, and yoga.

You may have a long list of strange or unusual interests and hobbies. You may be a Trekkie and lose yourself when you cosplay as a Klingon fighting for the glory of the Empire. Or you may feel most at purpose when leading your Dungeons and Dragons group. Whatever your interests, they go beyond mere enjoyment to become mystical experiences where you lose yourself or connect to a higher power.

THE FOUR HONORABLES

NOW THAT WE HAVE FINISHED OUR EXPLORATION of the Four Rulers—the four most important Stars in the Polestar Pantheon—we must now continue our journey with the next most potent grouping: the Four Honorables. These are Tai Yang (太陽), the Sun or Prince; Tai Yin (太陰), the Moon Lady or Princess; Wu Qu (武曲), the General; and Ju Men (巨門), the Great Gate. These Stars are strongly connected to the inner sanctum of the Four Rulers and the image of government and royalty.

These Stars are secondary in the big picture of Fate, and they are not as essential or integral to our most important patterns of Fate as the Four Rulers. However, they do represent significant Fate patterns that are often more practical, and could even feel more important, because they usually involve a path of "becoming" or accomplishment—especially in the case of the Sun and Moon—or of struggle, as it is with the General. These patterns often involve a lot of raw work and challenges to overcome, but these patterns are in service of the Four Rulers. We must never forget that the Emperor and Empress represent the key patterns of Fate in the chart, and everything else supports those two Stars. So, while there is work here, the bigger mission or purpose is often elsewhere.

The two most potent of the Four Honorables are Tai Yang, the Sun, who is the Prince of the Royal Court and son of the Emperor, and Tai Yin, the Moon Lady, who is the Princess of the Royal Court. These compose the second-most potent Yin and Yang pair in our chart. They are obviously astronomical bodies—the Sun and Moon—but they do not represent the literal Sun and Moon; rather, they are poetic representations of them.

The Sun Star is called Tai Yang, meaning Great Yang, and is obviously connected to our Yang Fate of doing, acting, becoming, and accomplishing. The Sun is the prince, whose job is to ascend the throne and prove his right to become the emperor. He is youthful, brash, and unformed, but he has great strength and potential. The Moon, called Tai Yin, or Great Yin, is, of course, connected to our Yin Fate of being, waiting, and responding. The Moon is the princess, whose job it is to prove her right to become an empress, often married off to another kingdom as an emissary. She does not have to work to ascend the throne so much as she must adapt to strange circumstances and respond to the whims of others in a role, like the Empress's, of deportment and cultivation.

Wu Qu, the General, is the most accomplished general of the dynasty and is the highest military adviser to the emperor. He is a retired general who has survived a life of war and is now advising the emperor on matters of war and strategy. He is like the famous Sunzi and his famous book, *The Art of War* (孫子兵法). The General represents accomplishment, strategy, and the wisdom that comes through hardship and experience. It is the oldest Star in the Pantheon and deeply connected to the military.

Finally, Ju Men, the Great Gate, is an odd Star, as it is not actually a character in the royal court, per se, but rather is the image of a wide-open gate. It represents a "Fate turnstile," a place where there is a lot of open, unfixed potential. It is represented in the court as an elder statesman who brings great opportunity to the court but is not connected to politics or the royal family. This Star is mixed in auspice, and its meaning is often formed by the Stars that show up with it.

TAI YANG (太陽)—THE SUN OR PRINCE

NAME AND TRANSLATIONS: Tai Yang (太陽), the Sun Star, the Prince Star

Tai, 太—great(est), grand(est) a) indicating extreme, maximum, or superlative status of the following word; e.g., 太煞 taishai, most extreme, ultimate. b) (med.) excessive, undue. 2 honorific markers of seniority, age, or importance; e.g., 太子 taizi, the Grand Heir, Grand Scion, heir-designate; 太祖 taizu, Grand Forefather, usu. indicating a dynasty's founding emperor.[1]

Yang, 陽—sunlight; sun-lit, hot-lit; solar(city); e.g., 夕陽 xiyang, evening sunlight, eventide; 陽臺 yangtai, sun-lit terrace; 陽燧 yangsui, "solar kindler," concave bronze mirror also used as burning-glass. a) brilliance, light. 2 south side of a mountain, north side of a river, esp. in place-names. 3 warm(th); lively, full of life; seasons of spring and summer; e.g., 陽春 yangchun, springtime as the season when light, warmth, and life are renewed. a) revive, renew. 4 masculine principles (opp. 陰 yin), associated with the sun, heaven, light, warmth, strength, hardness, height, mastery, potency, action, etc. a) unbroken lines in Yijing hexagrams. b) symbolic of the number 9 as the most fully Yang of the nine fundamental numerals, e.g., 重陽 chongyang, "double ninth," the ninth day of the ninth month; 陽九 yangjiu, end of a cosmic cycle, owing to the exhaustion of Yang energy. 5 on the surface (as opposed to recessed), e.g., 陽文 yangwen, characters carved in relief. a) superficial; feign, simulate.[2]

Together, we simply translate "Great Yang" as the Sun, but in the Royal Court, he is the image of the Crown Prince.

ELEMENT: Yang Fire

TRADITIONAL IMAGE: The crown prince of the royal court, depicted as young and without a beard, wearing a helmet and carrying a sword[3]

ANCESTOR PROFILE: An unfinished but beneficial Patriarchal Ancestor, represents the ambition of Patriarchal Ancestors for worldly success and wealth

LUMINOUS PLACEMENt: Rabbit, Dragon, and Horse Palaces

DIMINISHED PLACEMENT: Rat Palace

AFFILIATIONS: Northern Array; closely affiliated with the Emperor and Vassal

Tai Yang, the Sun, again represents the Crown Prince of the Royal Court and is the son of the Emperor. As the name suggests, this Star is very Yang and is perhaps the most forceful and obvious Yang influence in our chart. Although the Emperor represents our most important and significant Yang Fate, he represents mature Yang, which is much more subtle, as the name Wei (微), meaning "subtle," suggests. The Emperor is the pivot and crux of Fate, but the emperor himself did not do the menial tasks or hard labor; he oversaw and directed through decrees and mandates. In the Royal Court, he often directs the government of Fate through his Tutor first and the hard work through his son, the Sun or Prince, and then, to a lesser degree, through the Vassal—this hierarchy is important to understand.

The Sun is the Emperor in training and is a kind of working Emperor, and the Fate of this placement is like the Emperor here but with less pressure or huge life-changing occurrences. The key to the Sun is that the prince must prove his right to ascend the throne through accomplishment. He was given jobs, tasks, and missions that he must do as part of his training. However, as the prince, he was given all the support that he needed to succeed, and many chances, for he must succeed, but he must also fail, fail, and fail better. Therefore, the Sun represents some of our most positive Fate to succeed, but it is unformed and must be forged through fire into the image of the Emperor.

The Prince is represented as a young man, brash, headstrong, ambitious, and eager to prove himself. He is inexperienced but strong and capable. The Sun is obviously Yang: It's a huge burning ball of fire in the sky; there is nothing subtle or uncertain about it. It represents male potency and a very worldly, brute force. It rises and sets in a predictable manner, and so it represents constancy. The Fate here is reliable and predictable but hardworking. Wherever the Sun shows up, there is work to do in service of our greater Fate. But, again, we must always refer to the placement of the Emperor, for the Sun does not have his own mission yet. He works for his Father, so wherever he shows up, there is a lot of opportunity and action, but it does not turn the Great Wheel, meaning its rewards show up and are directed elsewhere.

Wherever the Sun shows up, expect opportunity and challenges: Wear a helmet, and prepare to eat humble pie. The Fate here is somewhat ordinary, modest, and "blue collar," and generally auspicious wherever it is placed. The Prince was sent to work with the ordinary folk to learn humility. The Sun has a great capacity but lacks subtlety, refinement, and manners. The Sun cannot be afflicted but can be distracted, as he is young and spoiled. Here you must learn the true lessons of Fate and prove yourself worthy to your Ancestors.

Let's walk the Sun through the Twelve Houses.

Ming Palace

Tai Yang in the Ming Palace is considered very auspicious for modern people because it is probably the Fate that we all want; it is very "American." In some ways, it is better than having the Emperor here because we are given a lot of opportunity and capacity but without the heavy responsibilities that weigh on the head that wears the crown. This placement is natural for strong Yang characters like Dragons, Tigers, Horses, and Dogs and an auspicious boost for the more hardworking Yin Animals like Ox, Pigs, and Roosters.

Generally, this means that you have a very strong and full agenda of Fate that is somewhat obvious, clear, and predictable, like the Sun. The challenges and opportunities in life arise and set in a reliable fashion. You know what needs to be done, and a path opens before you; you must simply step up and do the work. You are strong and capable and have a lot of raw talent and ability that must be forged and molded. You also have everything you need to succeed and are given all the support. The crux of this Fate is that you are given the perfect amount of work that you are capable of because the Prince must succeed, but he also must be tested. So, you will be tested in life, but in such a way that makes you shine.

You will be born into a stream of very supportive and reliable people, and you are given a lot of opportunities in life—these will manifest along the way as clear roles, tasks, jobs, and so on. This could mean having a supportive family, getting into a good school, getting a decent job out of college, getting promotions, and so on—again, very American. The prototype of this Fate is what most Americans expect and want, but very few get. It can, of course, manifest in many ways, but if this Star shows up in the Ming Palace, life is somewhat straightforward, which is the opposite of having the Prince's sister here—the Moon—who is anything but clear. Your capacity and opportunity are well matched, and you can be successful and productive, which is the great American dream, and pastime.

Here you are Fated to be a Prince, which can mean that you are somewhat cocky, confident, obsessive, and even aggressive. You may "have a chip on your shoulder." The Sun has great ambition, for he is eager to sit on the throne. So, you may want and expect big things in life; you may have a grand vision, but this vision often starts out immature and unformed. On the more negative side, this can make you complacent and entitled, expecting everything to be given to you; you want the rewards without the work. The Sun expects reliability and constancy in life and can't handle Yin uncertainty and confusion. Therefore, the central theme of the Sun is very strong in your life if it shows up here—you must go on a path of maturing and becoming.

You will be put to work and put to the test, and you must humble yourself as a student. You must temper your aggression and learn to submit to the will of the Emperor. If you are to ascend the throne, you must prove yourself, and in doing so, there is a very high capacity for success and accomplishment in life. Expect challenges and trials, but if this is not afflicted, then you can succeed with flying colors. The overall resolution of Fate in this lifetime will be ordinary and worldly but fulfilling and rewarding. Great Completion is not likely, though, as this life is a kind of preparation: You are working hard for the Ancestors to accomplish their worldly goals. This Star represents the accumulation of positive Fate for the success of the family.

Here, the Patriarchal Ancestors and influence of the Emperor are very strong, and the agenda of Fate may be very clearly linked to your Patriarchal ancestry and the influence of your father, grandfathers, and/or the men in the family.

Ancestors Palace

If Tai Yang arrives in the Ancestors Palace, then there is a very strong influence from the Patriarchal Ancestors, but unlike the Emperor here, you inherit all their blessings and all their unresolved Fate, with an emphasis on the latter. The Emperor represents all the resolved, positive Fate that has already been accomplished, but the Sun represents all the things the Emperor has yet to achieve.

The Sun is the Prince, so he inherits the vision of the future that he must accomplish for the good of the family and the empire. This is generally a positive inheritance and comes with all the previous momentum of accomplishment and success. So, you will inherit opportunity and talent from the Ancestors, but it comes with a lot of obligation. This Star represents all the ambitions, desires, hopes, and dreams of the Ancestors to succeed in life. They want wealth, power, land, and so on, so they can provide for their children and future generations. This represents the Ancestors' desire for their descendants to have a better life than they did.

You may inherit a strong unconscious drive for success and to prove yourself. This is like this Star in the Ming Palace, but more unconscious, and it carries a stronger "story" of becoming and earning that is inherited from the Ancestors. There may be a very strong, even overbearing, influence to succeed from your parents and grandparents, especially from your father. It may be literal and come as constant lessons on responsibility, obligation, and "being a man." You are the family's prince and must succeed for them to be happy.

Maybe your father or grandfather worked hard laying bricks so that you could go to a good school and live in a good neighborhood. Now, you are pressured to succeed because of his sacrifices. Perhaps your dad is a doctor, and you are strongly pushed to follow in his footsteps, even though you want to be an artist. You are chastised, "No son of mine will be an artist," so you repress your artistic talents and resent your father but become a great doctor. Or, on the more positive side, you may love being a doctor and become the fourth generation to succeed at this, but it comes with a strong pressure and expectation. You may even be named after a Patriarchal Ancestor; traditionally if a boy has this, they are considered an incarnation and given the father's name.

Essentially, with this placement, you become your father, which means that you inherit and carry on the same Ancestral patterns of Yang Fate, for better or worse. You will receive all his unfinished business along with his positive momentum. If afflicted by Ghost Stars, this can mean inheriting patterns of addiction, abuse, failure, and so on. But in general, the Fate here is "worldly," ordinary, and based on continuing Fate in the world as a householder.

The simplest interpretation is having a very positive and beneficial relationship with your parents and family, especially with your father or with a grandfather or male role model. You have a soulmate in your family who cares for and looks after you. You model yourself after their guidance and continue in their footsteps. Here, you continue a strong sense of tradition, but in something ordinary, like you grow up watching football with your dad and then love to watch football with your children.

Youth Palace

Tai Yang in the Youth Palace is somewhat straightforward and should be first interpreted as a strong Fated connection to siblings, especially to a brother or as a brother. This is a close, loyal, and mutually supportive relationship that resolves a lot of important Fate in childhood. You may have a brother or many siblings, and the Fated connection here is strong. You are close, and your childhood is shared with them; either they are an older role model, or you are. Either way, this relationship strongly influences you, and you remain close throughout life.

The Sun here is a very typical, ordinary childhood, the one that we all wish we had. It is exalted here, being one of the best Stars to have in the Youth Palace. It is the image of rough-and-tumble play and adventures full of imagination and fun. It is just being a kid and having a nice maturation process through conduct and education. You play games with your siblings and help each other grow at school and at home. If the Sun is unafflicted by Ghost Stars, then youth is a very rich and rewarding time in life, and you will look back on it fondly.

The Sun is the Prince and represents youthful becoming. Here he is allowed to be immature and grow up in the ordinary fashion. This means being a typical rambunctious youth and having a playful, active childhood. Again, this is auspicious because it matches the image of the House; there is constancy and harmony in development, and you grow up to fulfill and meet the obligations of becoming an adult, showing early but expected maturation. You may have a strong experience of maturing as the older sibling or through the influence of one. You may be an ambitious and precocious child who is outgoing and social. This may be captain of the football team, head cheerleader, or captain of the debate team.

The Patriarchal Ancestors are a strong influence here, and family, relatives, cousins, and so on may be very important. There may be a strong sense of clan or tribe with strong but ordinary family traditions—like you all go Christmas caroling or something. In the best sense, this looks like a sitcom family. So, consider yourself lucky if you have this Star here.

Partners Palace

Tai Yang in the Partners Palace is also considered one of the best possible placements, because it represents what most people want. If unafflicted by Ghost Stars, this is a strong and positive Fate resolution with a partner. This is an "arranged" marriage, Yinyuan (姻緣), for the Prince and Princess were "betrothed." This may feel like a strong past-life connection or predestined affinity, and if it is unafflicted, it should go smoothly. The personal connection is obvious, and you don't have to think about it. You marry someone just like you, and stay together for a long time.

Because this Star is Yang, yours is an active and lively relationship. Your partner is attractive and brings you social connections and benefits. There may be a sense that your partner brings you into a new life and opens a world of possibilities. As an obvious Yang Star, it is likely that the circumstances of life, work, school, friendship, and so on will bring you together. This is like marrying your high school sweetheart, college girlfriend, or best friend. You may have a nice story of how you met that you can tell at your wedding. It may even manifest as Prince Charming.

As a Yang Star and as the Prince, this Star means you will have a clear path to maturing, growing up, becoming a better person, and so on through relationships and especially marriage. This will be a place where you learn a lot of lessons that lead to greater prosperity in life. You will also grow together, and while this could be rocky and involve a lot of friction, it will be rewarding. You may get married as "kids" out of high school or college and go through all the ups and downs together, having kids and becoming mature adults in the process.

Or you must go through this process of maturing and becoming a complete adult before you can meet the right partner and be a good partner. Often, this means a lot of trial and error. The Prince here can mean a lot of opportunity, so there can be quite a bit of promiscuity, sowing wild oats, and casual relationships. You may date a lot. There may be a lot of sport-sex or conquest. You may also have a period of delayed adolescence, experimenting and exploring through sex and relationships before settling down. After all this, you mature and start a family, ready to put the wild days behind you. Once you choose to settle down, you meet the right person, for the prince cannot just marry anyone; he must marry a princess.

Offspring Palace

Tai Yang in the Offspring Palace is again considered an auspicious placement, especially in the traditional Chinese sense. As a Yang Star, this Star implies the birth of a son, but it can, of course, go either way. It represents having a supportive, active, and bright child who will be independent but responsible and carry on the family tradition. This is the best scenario for the Chinese and most traditional cultures who see the firstborn son as the family's future. Even if it is a daughter, the Sun here means she takes on the family mantle and cares for the family, especially the parents, as they age.

It means giving birth to a prince (or princely child) who will ascend the throne. Generally, the child's Fate is connected to the Patriarchal Ancestors, and traditionally, they would be named after a grandparent. In some way, they will continue the same patterns of the Ancestors and inherit their momentum.

This placement represents a strong affinity for being a parent and a smooth but challenging resolution of Fate through parenthood. It is not as central or life-changing as the Emperor or Empress here but represents a very typical, ordinary experience of parenthood in the smoothest sense. You grow, mature, and come into your own as a parent. Important life lessons are learned, but there is not as much pressure as with the Emperor; they can smoothly happen in the background of life.

As a Yang Star, the Prince here can also manifest as an early sexual awakening or maturing, or it can become a strong sexual appetite, for it represents the Patriarchal Ancestral drive to reproduce. As the Prince, this Star is immature and like a teenage boy, so if you have this here, you may have the ongoing sex drive of a teenage boy. This also, then, may imply having a lot of children.

Wealth Palace

Tai Yang in the Wealth Palace is an excellent placement, for it represents all the good things we associate with the Sun: consistency, timeliness, and steady ascendance. You will likely do well in financial matters, be paid well for your work, and experience steady and reliable improvement throughout your life—this is what all Americans want. Income will likely be steady and dependable, and Fate around wealth will turn out well, even with setbacks and obstacles.

This is the Prince; he is rewarded for his hard work and supported in all his endeavors. The prince of the empire was given opportunities and was also set to inherit the throne, so although he was not yet in command of great wealth, he would be. So, this means profitable and successful investment and retirement. You should invest in the stock market, open CDs, start a business, and so on. Traditionally, this Star is associated with the gem trade and gold, which is the color of the Sun.

As usual, there is a maturation process here, so you may start out immature with money, spending too much and living beyond your means, but it turns out well in the long run; you will have to learn a lot through lessons with money, but you will ultimately be responsible and smart with it. After this maturation, you can do well in all financial matters and even work well in the finance industry.

The Sun is abundant and gives its light to everyone; this is generosity, for the Prince wants to show off and share wealth. So, initially, you may be ostentatious and have fancy, expensive tastes. You may be a diva and demand the finest things or at least want the finest things. But you will be generous to those close to you, and this Fate is resolved well through giving, especially to those less fortunate. As you mature, your tastes will mature and become regal.

As a Yang Star, the Sun here represents the Patriarchal Ancestors' patterns around money, which you may inherit for better or worse. If afflicted by Ghost Stars, these may include patterns around gambling, debt, and mismanaging finances. You may also inherit money and wealth, gems and jewelry, or a family business, and your wealth may come from family.

Health Palace

Tai Yang is the most obvious definition of inheriting or having a Yang constitution from the Patriarchal Ancestors. This means being strong and very physical. This is like the Emperor here, but more raw and immature, less capable of rest and being inactive, so more prone to injury, overwork, and burnout. The Emperor represents a very strong Yang constitution but is more mature and capable of being skillful with health cultivation. The Sun is Yang Fire—all work, burning the candle at both ends.

So, you will likely feel very strong and capable and almost bulletproof. This can continue steadily for a while, but without maintaining and developing Yin, you may burn out and collapse sometime in midlife. This is a common story. People are hardcore active all their lives, and then a big injury or illness takes them out; they then lament not being able to run marathons or climb mountains anymore, wondering what went wrong. People with the Sun here are more likely to squander their energy because they feel invincible and then collapse.

As a Yang Star, you will naturally love being active, and this is good. Exercise, a strong routine (rising and setting like the Sun), and competition are important and can lead to longevity, if you can learn to balance them with proper rest, nutrition, and inactivity. Learning to incorporate these into your routines becomes a great basis for health, as Yang is the principle of life, movement, and circulation. The Sun bolsters and builds, and this is your strength.

Again, the danger is injury from overwork, collapse from fatigue, sudden death from accidents, or from being stupid and going to extremes. Yes, you may be in great health, but you also might fall off a cliff mountain biking, freeze to death climbing Mount Everest, or have a heart attack after a triathlon. So, take it easy; learn to hold back; be careful. Yes, do everything—you must feel normal and happy—but be aware that you can burn out and get injured.

Generally, the Sun learns from mistakes and matures. There will again be a process of maturation where you learn to take care of yourself and not overdo it. The Prince is easily influenced, which can lead to many bad habits, following health trends, yo-yo dieting, and so on. You may learn a lot from this process, and maturity comes from trial and error here.

Sometimes, this manifests itself as being athletic and competitive in youth and then becoming rundown and shabby in old age. Maybe you were captain of the football team, and now you are overweight with bad knees in your forties, watching football on the couch and reminiscing about the good old days. Maybe you were a smoke show at twenty-two, but you lose your looks and resort to plastic surgery. This is the image of bright and shiny youth, so be careful about aging; it happens to all of us. No one is excused from old age, illness, or death, and it hits those with Yang constitutions hardest because they are so used to being strong that weakness becomes difficult to handle.

Yang Fire is especially associated with the heart and heart conditions, as well as small intestine and digestive disorders. Traditionally, they say you will heal and feel best in the summer and during the day, and that you will respond the best to "tonifying" treatment. Again, inactivity is not supported, so you must cultivate some Yin to balance things out: Rest, relax, and incorporate some aimless wandering.

As usual, Yang Stars are associated with the Patriarchal Ancestors, and here you inherit all their strengths and weaknesses. So, look for Ancestral patterns of behavior and illness. You may inherit their athleticism but also their predisposition for something like heart disease. This is like your dad playing soccer with you as a kid, which ingrains a lifelong love of exercising. But Dad also has a weak heart, and as you get older, you realize you have the same weakness.

Career/Travel Palace

If Tai Yang appears in the Career/Travel Palace or one of the other career Houses, then you have a strong but modest Fate resolution through career and travel. A career is not as central or important as with the Emperor here, but you will nonetheless have a lot of work to do. The Sun in this House is generally more modest and ordinary, like you get up and go to work every day and earn a paycheck. Simple. You like your job, work hard, and get decent pay. It is likely that the Emperor and your more important Fate reside elsewhere. Maybe your central Fate is to be a parent or partner, and the job is just a job.

However, you have a very strong likelihood of having rewarding success in a suitable career. Like the sun that rises and sets every day, you are persevering and diligent, and this is the real strength here. You can roll up your sleeves and get to work. The Sun in this House often manifests as Yang careers: active, busy, physical labor, maybe outdoors, creating, producing, building, making stuff—not too complex, not "information" work. Often it is repetitive but consistent, humble, and "working class." Most jobs are ordinary, though, and society is supported by the ordinary working-class folks who do their jobs.

This placement is associated with craft, skill, and working with your hands. It is associated with strength and male-dominated jobs: construction, firefighting, military jobs, plumbing, truck driving, and so on. These are dominated by men because they are the most dangerous, and men are generally considered expendable in most cultures; ours is no exception.

Work will be very rewarding and offer a path to maturity. Again, the story here is of the prince who must prove his right to ascend the throne. Wherever the Prince shows up, there is a process of learning the ropes, being tested, challenged, and having to step up and grow. Progressing in your career will be tough, but you will steadily grow to maturity through it. Eventually, this can lead to becoming very successful. This often includes a path of apprenticeship and succession. You may inherit your position from a mentor or follow a journeyman's path of becoming a professional.

Often, there is great ambition here. You may be forceful, aggressive, and determined. You are inheriting the Patriarchal drive for success and to support the family. There may be a strong drive here to succeed where your father failed or to continue a family business or skill. But with this placement, it looks more like taking up your father's plumbing business or becoming a carpenter or electrician. You may become your father, and this can be a source of pride and tradition.

The Sun is also considered very strong for travel, but it is not as pivotal as the Emperor. You may have and cultivate the opportunity to travel widely. You are the prince, born free to go wherever you would like. You will mature from traveling and seeing the world, especially going to places where life is much rougher. You can work and live in many places; you are adaptable, make connections, and find opportunities everywhere you go. Sometimes, this can be a strong Fate Threshold for immigrating and starting a new life elsewhere. If this is the case, then staying near your home will hold you back. You must travel and find your "true home" far from your birthplace. However, as the Prince, this may be a story of the Prodigal Son, and you may return home to reconnect and claim the throne after being abroad for a spell.

Assistants Palace

Tai Yang in the House of Friends and Assistants is considered a mixed bag but mostly auspicious. In some ways, it belongs here; the Sun is the crown prince and naturally falls into a secondary position. This is the image of the prince learning to lead through making connections, making alliances, and supporting others to do their work so that the empire could succeed as a unit. The true role of leadership is one of service, and the Prince must learn to help; he must learn humility and overcome his nature, which is brash, impulsive, immature, and eager to be in command.

This means that the maturation process may involve some humility and humbling yourself. The Prince must mingle with ordinary folks and learn the way of the people. The Sun here can shine as an assistant, and so service work may be very powerful. You may develop and mature through supporting an important leader. But the Sun is bright and illuminates; it manifests best through networking, teamwork, team building, and integration. This placement means you magnetize others to you for support, and you have a natural quality to lead a team. You are a natural team captain, manager, community organizer, and so on. This is how you advance in your career.

Friendship is important, but this is where the mixed bag comes into play. The Prince naturally attracts help, but people may have ulterior motives. People are jealous. They want to help you, but it could be for their own good. They want to take your power and resources or gain status through association. So, some people will be helpful, and some will not. There is a tendency here for professional challenges with people undermining you or being two-faced. There may also be a lot of older people who seek to help and support you, and this may lead to mentorship, but it may also be awkward and open to controversy and being taken advantage of.

Generally, the Prince is given everything to succeed, which means getting much help in life. You may receive many opportunities, gifts, and so on that advance your career. You will get a lot of chances and always find support in your endeavors. When paired with other strong Stars in your career, this is a great foundation for success, so seek help through scholarships, grants, loans and funding, benefactors, and so on. If you build it, they will come.

The Sun naturally makes a lot of friends, and the image is generous, outgoing, and fun. This is usually a good Fate for having a fun and active social life with many parties and a big social circle. But sometimes, it is superficial and has trouble with depth and closeness. You may have a big circle of friends but few you can rely on. The auspice of this depends a lot on Character.

Superiors Palace

If you have Tai Yang in the Superiors Palace, then you will resolve a lot of important Fate through your career and work in the world. This is an exalted placement for the Prince because it forces him to step up into the role he was born for. He is clear-headed, ambitious, and in a direct line to inherit the throne. But here, there is often a very important affinity with a teacher, mentor, boss, guru, or the like who is needed for your success. The prince was not yet the emperor, but he was surrounded by teachers who would help him. If you have this, model yourself after the success you want, and seek out people who have done it and follow in their footsteps.

As a Yang Star, like in the Career/Travel Palace, Tai Yang is associated with active, dynamic, and skillful work, but here it is a step up and more connected with leadership and ownership. So, while it is still associated with more "blue-collar" work, it can mean owning a construction business rather than just working for one. But this process often includes meeting a mentor who shows you the way. You become an apprentice and then become a successor, taking over a role or business and stepping into leadership. This person will be like a father to you. You will owe everything to them.

Like the consistency of the sun, rising and setting, there is steady progress, and there can be many opportunities for advancement and success. It means being very hardworking and ambitious, even monomaniacal, in your goals. You want to be emperor and will do whatever it takes. This could mean climbing the corporate ladder, and you may step over people on your way to your goals. Once you achieve your goals, you will work even harder; you may work late, on weekends, and even past retirement age.

But we must remember that the Sun is not the pivot of Fate. The Emperor is the Polestar, not the Sun, so while you may work very hard here and be driven to succeed, it may not be deeply or ultimately fulfilling. You may work hard your whole life to achieve a dream but then realize that you wasted your life chasing after something without knowing the reason why. This drive may be the inheritance of a Patriarchal Ancestor who was driven to succeed but did not finish; you may inherit this and finish, but it was never yours to begin with.

Like the Emperor or any strong Star here, there is a capacity to affect the world and change things, but this is more modest, for the Sun is not the Emperor. So, maybe you invent a longer-lasting lightbulb or manufacture the world's best lawn mower; no one really cares, but it still changes the world. Modest goals can be very important and can still lead to great success. The world needs innovation in the ordinary.

Property Palace

Like in the Wealth Palace, Tai Yang in the Property Palace is modest but auspicious and generally positive. The Sun here is usually linked to inheritance, as the prince is in line to inherit everything that comes with the throne. So, family property and associated wealth may be coming your way, but work will be involved in the acquisition and transition. As always, the Sun must mature and be tested. You will have to grow up in the process of establishing a home, property, legacy, and wealth.

As the Prince, if it is unafflicted by Ghost Stars, this Star may look like having a "silver spoon," but it only looks that way. You get support but must strike out on your own and find independence. You may have a strong identity around where you are from through culture, religion, or language, but you are not attached, and attachment would even cause conflict. The Sun's brightness pushes you out of the nest here, so you will likely travel, move a lot, and seek to find and establish your own sense of home, place, and identity, apart from the Ancestors.

The Sun is consistent and rhythmic and represents abundance. You will be given many chances and rewards here. Housing, homes, apartments, and so on will be reliable, and you will always have a roof over your head. You will generally have good luck finding places, but they will be modest. You will probably not live in luxury, but you will appreciate and want a nice home and even feel entitled to higher quality. The Sun is a bit of a diva here, but you must work hard for what you have. There may be property ownership later in life, but this looks like renting a lot until you either inherit something or finally get your life together to buy, and this may have to be in partnership with others.

With this placement, the Patriarchal Ancestors have a legacy to build and establish. There is sort of an immigrant, explorer, pioneer, settler, homesteader, and/or pilgrim vibe. As the Prince Star is not the Emperor, it is not yet established, but there is ambition. You may have a strong drive and ambition to create a home, acquire property, build wealth, and establish yourself. Look to genealogy here for patterns of colonialism and/or immigration.

This is a good basis for working in real estate: buying and selling and turning property into profit. It's nothing fancy; it may just be a job, but it can do well as a side hustle or secondary source of income to support other endeavors in life.

Pleasure Palace

If you have Tai Yang in the Pleasure Palace, then you may be a diva. Character makes a big difference in how this will manifest, but often, the Sun here makes you a pleasure-seeker. You love to have fun, and you love and want things that are expensive, luxurious, glamorous, posh, and so on. But often, the sense of pleasure is more superficial and not concerned with the finer nuances of art, culture, music, cuisine, and so on. This comes with a sense of status, so you may want a sports car, not because it is a great car but because you want to show it off and look wealthy. The Prince wants to hang out with wealthy, powerful people and fit in.

The Sun or Prince thrives on a sense of competition, action, and productivity. The Prince wants to acquire and demonstrate. He wants to win and competes with everyone, even close friends. So, you may love competitive sports and identify with local sports teams with a sense of pride, shouting and celebrating when they win and taking it personally when they lose. You may love playing sports and are driven by a competitive spirit to win and a hatred of losing. It may also manifest as a sexual conquest and status seeking through sex and relationships, like seeking a trophy spouse.

This placement is connected to popular culture, fashion, and trends, and it is very active and social. You may follow pop culture and learn about all the celebrity gossip. You may pride yourself in being cool, hip, or whatever the kids are calling it these days. As you age, you may stay stuck in your generation and then have a crisis when you no longer fit in. You will mature as you grow out of your youthful identity, but this may require a midlife crisis, when you buy a sports car, get a tattoo, or the like. You may also be a follower, taking your enjoyment from others and not knowing what you actually enjoy; this crisis may force you to rediscover yourself and find what you truly love to do.

The Sun here wants to push the limits and seeks new and novel experiences. You may love parties and drugs and seek extreme experiences like skydiving, bungee jumping, race car driving, and so on for the high of adrenaline or the thrill of danger. This can lead to addictive patterns, so watch out for drinking and drugs. You may love being high, but not so much as to explore altered states but because it makes you feel alive and part of the crowd.

The Prince is a bit immature here and can go a little crazy; it is a bit like having an expense account or credit card without limits. You may be a party animal, but you also love to share wealth. The Sun loves friendship and company and experiences fun in relationships with other people. You want others to have fun, and you cannot conceive of fun by yourself. Usually, you mature out of this as you age and come to love solitude later in life, in contrast to your wild youth.

Sometimes, depending on Character, this can manifest in the opposite way, as all work and no play. You may find all the above frivolous and instead be driven to work, accomplish, produce, and so on, with no sense of fun. Work is fun, but it's likely that beneath that "fun" is that same sense of status or power seeking, perhaps to prove yourself or as an Ancestral drive to be successful no matter what. The Patriarchal Ancestors may push you to abandon personal pleasure to work yourself to the bone.

WU QU (武曲)—THE GENERAL

NAME AND TRANSLATIONS:

Wu Qu (武曲), the General Star, Generalissimo, Military Music, Military Minister

> Wu, 武—pertaining to the military or martial, as opposed to (ant.) [antonym] 文 wen, cultured, civil. a) warrior, soldier, fighter. 2 warlike prowess; courageous; militant, aggressive, bellicose; violent.[4]

> Qu, 曲—musical tune, an air. a) (med.) 法曲 faqu, pseudo-classical ritual music popular in Tang times, using handbells, cymbals, large bells, lithophones, steamered syrinxes, and lutes.[5]

The term Wu (武) refers to anything associated with the military. The term Qu (曲) refers specifically to a kind of ritual music played in court during the Tang dynasty, and the character is an actual picture of the instrument. Together, they refer to the music associated with the military that inspired people to go to battle, so we can translate this as Military Music. However, in the image of the royal court, it refers specifically to the emperor's primary military adviser, and so we translate it as the General Star, or the "Generalissimo," the general of all the generals.

ELEMENT: Yin Metal

TRADITIONAL IMAGE: An elderly, retired general, dressed in armor and helmet but without a sword to depict that he is no longer fighting; accompanied by war dead, his face in a grimace[6]

ANCESTOR PROFILE: A very ancient, Original Ancestor, far back in the family line, very accomplished, closely associated with Ancestors in the military or who died at war, exorcist of Ancestral Ghosts

LUMINOUS PLACEMENT: Ox Palace

DIMINISHED PLACEMENT: Snake Palace

AFFILIATIONS: The Northern Array—always in a trine with the Emperor; in close connection to everyone as adviser and protector

Wu Qu, the General, is the image of an old, retired general who has spent his whole life in the military. This is an image of an accomplished warrior. He survived everything through discipline, grit, determination, intelligent use of strategy, and luck. He was highly respected and revered in the royal court and chosen from among all the generals by the emperor to be his primary adviser on military and political strategy and to lead the military as the "generalissimo," or general to all the generals.

The key aspect of the General is that he is retired from battle. Although this is a military image and is associated with war, fighting, death, and so on, it is important that the general himself is no longer fighting. He is the result of war. He spent his life on the battlefield and has seen death, defeat, and victory. He has sent young kids off to die and knows the dark side of war and military expansion. He represents all the hard-earned lessons of war and death and has dedicated himself to stratagem, tactics, planning, and so on to avoid unnecessary death while still accomplishing what needs to be done to secure the dynasty.

The General is best understood and represented through the Chinese martial arts: wushu (武術), gongfu (功夫), and the Sunzi Bingfa (孫子兵法), or *The Art of War*, an ancient Chinese military treatise dating from the Late Spring and Autumn Period (roughly the fifth century B.C.E.). This treatise is arguably the most influential strategy text in East Asian warfare and has influenced many nonmilitary endeavors in the modern world, including espionage, culture, politics, business, and sports, as it is about how to outsmart your opponent without engaging in physical battle. Like Sunzi, the General understands that war is grave and must be avoided at all costs.

The nature of the General is reluctant. He is grizzled, old, grumpy, beat-up, but dignified. His life has not been pleasant, and yet now, in retirement, he is given a palatial estate, money, a young wife, servants, and so on. But he doesn't know what to do with these things, because he spent his life sleeping in tents, fighting in battle, and sleeping with prostitutes on Flower Boats. He hates the politicians who sent him to war and ordered him to fight and send kids to their deaths. And now he must work with them and advise them on things they know nothing about. He slightly resents the spoiled royals but is also very loyal and dedicated to the service of the Emperor, Empress, Prince, Princess, and Tutor. He is withdrawn and tired. His body is in pain from old injuries. But he is still sharp and critical, with years of hard-earned wisdom. The General is old-fashioned, traditional, conventional, and out of touch with the youth and with the fancy rituals of court life.

In our chart, Wu Qu represents the deep givens of our Fate, the well-worn groves. It represents all the wisdom of accomplishment and experience that comes from our Ancestors, especially from fighting, hardship, struggle, hard work, failure turned to achievement, and of course, from war. The General represents warriorship, discipline, sacrifice, skill, strategy, wisdom, experience, and maturity applied to our life in service of our greater Fate. But often, it represents where we already have these abilities in some way; it is where we are already a grumpy old man. It shows us our innate wisdom.

The General is often directly connected to our Ancestral Fate around war and the military, which almost everyone has. Human history, especially the past few hundred years, has been full of war, and most people alive today are connected in some way to the two World Wars or another major conflict of the last century. We are lucky now to be living in the safest, most prosperous time in history, but war still rages today and is not going anywhere anytime soon.

Wherever the General shows up, it postpones and slows things down. It represents retirement and late-blooming success. As such, Wu Qu is generally out of place in the Youth Palace and the relationship and family Houses and postpones or diminishes the Fate there. The General represents the grace of decline and the dignity of old age, elders, and death and is connected to our oldest Ancestors and deepest Ancestral patterns. It represents a hard-fought path that turns out well in the end because we survive. So, it is auspicious, but that auspice is often delayed and/or not easy to see.

The General represents a tremendous capacity to resolve Fate, but this Fate is not so clear, as it often involves the need to strategize, make plans, follow a discipline, and wait. Wherever it shows up may be a long road full of challenges, but in the end, it will be fruitful.

The General also represents the most powerful "exorcistic" force in our chart. The general could smell a spy in the emperor's court from a mile away. He can be afflicted, but he is the least open to affliction from the Ghost Stars. He generally eclipses the Ghost Stars from their most grievous qualities, but when afflicted, he can turn to dullness, struggle, depression, resentment, and violence in his darkest aspects. He sometimes feels like an affliction due to the grumpy nature of the Star, but we must remember that he is the wisdom of old age and experience. There is a difference between realism and negativity. He is not negative but has seen the full spectrum of humanity. Human nature includes violence, and we are all capable of it in the right context. He is about accepting our darker nature and using wisdom to turn that darkness into light.

Let's walk the General through the Twelve Houses.

Ming Palace

If Wu Qu arrives in the Ming Palace, then life may, unfortunately, be a long, hard-fought but nonetheless successful road. The big picture of your Fate is intractable, hard to understand and deal with, but you are a warrior who will fight until the end. Life may feel like a battle, but thankfully, you also inherit a tremendous capacity to resolve all your Fate and settle all your Ancestors in this lifetime. We must remember that the General is retired; he has survived everything and come out the other side. In some cases, this can mean starting out this way, and that life is basically a retirement from your previous life, and/or you are inheriting all the rewards of your Ancestors' hard work. But more often, it means life is the path of becoming the General, which means your Fate is "late-blooming."

If it is unafflicted by Ghost Stars and Fate is clear elsewhere, then this can mean that life is smooth sailing. You are born mature and wise beyond your years; you are capable, disciplined, and skilled and can easily handle everything that comes your way. It may not even feel like a challenge. You may feel way overqualified for life, as you are inheriting all the results of your previous life, and/or you channel the intelligence, wisdom, and experience of all your Ancestors.

No matter how complicated life gets, you are more than capable of working it out. You are born retired, so practically speaking, you may retire early, as you feel all the work is already done.

If afflicted by Ghost Stars or with a more complex picture of Fate, the General here may be at war. You may inherit a long list of battles to fight and finish. Life may be a constant struggle that feels out of your control; you are ordered by the demands of Fate to go from place to place, where you will be put to the test. You may face a lot of puzzles, challenges, and obstacles that require very precise strategy. Life may also be very stern and minimalistic, even bleak. But, again, you are more than capable of dealing with everything, though the work may feel endless and the rewards distant.

You may resist retiring and stay at war for a long time—life, fun, freedom, and so on may not begin until your late fifties, sixties, or beyond—but in the end, you retire and experience peace. It will come. Many people work until the end and then feel out of place sitting on a beach drinking a mai tai, as if they missed their youth and are unsure how to make up for it. And you may be too tired to enjoy it. Or success may be delayed until later in life. You may work hard with little to no reward and then finally have a breakthrough in your fifties and become successful. The General here postpones everything until later, so patience is a virtue.

Here, you are deeply connected to a very old or ancient Ancestral guardian. The General reaches way back into the family line, possibly to an Original Ancestor, especially if the family story is connected to war, exile, or migration or immigration due to struggle, famine, and so on. Your Fate may be very intimately linked to the military or war. You may repeat these patterns and work in the military or in a related or similar job—anything that requires strategy and discipline.

You may have family in the military or a significant family war story that you are here to resolve, like a great-grandfather who died in WWI. This is especially true in the Ancestors Palace, where you inherit Ancestors' emotions and memories, but in this House, your life plays out a very important theme from their unfinished Fate, and you may not know what it is. Perhaps your great-grandfather left behind a business and a small child to go to war and died, so now you must do the same but survive and finish that story. With this placement, it is important to do genealogy to connect with the stories and find the parallels.

Because of the exorcist quality of the General, having it here or in the Ancestors Palace often means inheriting a lot of minor family Ghosts to resolve, or maybe even a big one. Your Ancestors give you a lot of work to do; this life is a cleanup job, working out a lot of minor negativities in the family through disciplined habits and overcoming challenges. Eventually, this dark fog lifts, and you experience peace. Or you may be given a Demon to resolve; you may have to go through a big trauma or healing event, like overcoming suicidal depression or an addiction. The General would then go to AA for the next forty-plus years and keep telling the story of how they tried to kill themselves when they were eighteen.

The General here can create a serious, stern, even grumpy demeanor. You may be all work and no play and see life as a mission to accomplish. You may have a very hard-boiled look at life and see everything as war, struggle, violence, and so on. It is important to accept this and not "try to be positive." It's okay to be grumpy and to accept grumpy people. If you force grumpy people to be positive, they will pretend to be positive and resent it, which never ends well.

No matter what, the General in the Ming Palace is long-lived and becomes a source of wisdom for others.

Ancestors Palace

Wu Qu in the Ancestors Palace is like in the Ming Palace, but it less central to the story of your personal Fate; here, you inherit a graveyard of Ghosts. This often means inheriting a lot of weak Ghostly patterns and obligations that muddle and weaken your connection to your parents and family. You may have a weak affinity with your birth parents and Ancestors but are born with a lot of subtle negativities in the family to overcome. Sometimes you must leave or escape your family to be free of this. Or, it means slowly working through many old family Ghosts, which means a lot of complex and subtle Fate: struggle, challenges, obstructions, and so on. You eventually work through all this and are liberated later in life.

With the General in the Ancestors Palace, you are again connected to a very old or Original Ancestor, but he is less of a guardian/exorcist here and more of a long and distant story to connect to. Someone far back is reaching out, but it is unclear, muddled, and maybe dark. You do not inherit as much of the direct skill and wisdom of the Ancestors, but you do inherit a lot of their old, unfinished emotions, making this somewhat intractable and hard to work through. Genealogy can be helpful here, but it may open a can of worms.

Again, this placement may be connected to early Ancestors who migrated, went to war, or were displaced by war, famine, or the like. You may have a direct connection to the military, like coming from a military family or growing up an army brat. Sometimes, there is a sense of punishment that comes with this Star; you may feel like you are being punished for the wrongdoings of an Ancestor or the mistakes of your parents. Their negative Fate becomes yours.

The General here can also be the strong influence of a stern father figure, maybe a grandfather. Your dad or guardian may be strict, critical, and demanding. They enforce a lot of rules, and discipline you harshly. They are distant emotionally and hard to connect with, but they teach you many life lessons and skills, putting you through the wringer to learn them. This may lead to rejecting your father, parents, or Ancestors. You may rebel and "fight the power." Often, though, people become their parents and repeat the same patterns when they have kids.

The simplest manifestation is a grandfather who becomes a prominent influence or father figure who raises you. This could be due to the loss of, or punishment of, a parent.

Youth Palace

Wu Qu is out of place and diminished or weak in the Youth Palace (and in the next two Houses). The image of an old man simply doesn't match with the energy of youth. The simplest interpretation is the appearance of an older mentor, elderly parent, grandparent, protector, or half-sibling that appears in youth as a significant part of your Fate. Perhaps Grandma dies, and Grandpa must move into your room with you as a kid. You grow up with him as a third parent, and he tells you all his stories. This can be very positive or create discord, as he may feel out of place, or he may be ill. You may become like a caregiver and have a lot of responsibilities early in life.

This can manifest as an elder parent. Men can have kids until quite late in life, and with modern medicine, many people are having children much older. You may care for an elderly parent as part of your Fate and family obligation. Often, this means being an only child with little to no Fate with siblings, and sometimes, it means a weak fate with cousins and/or extended family. It can also mean half-siblings and that a parent has a second family.

The General here may also mean growing up alone and maturing early as an only child, or that you must grow up fast due to a lot of responsibilities or trauma. You may not have a childhood as such, as you are born with the Fate of an old man. You may be a grumpy old man before you are twenty, or you may also be a troubled youth. You may be a juvenile delinquent and rebel against authority. You want to grow up fast, so you hang out with older kids or adults and get into trouble. You may not fit in with kids your age, so you do what it takes to fit in with the older crowd.

The General here may simply postpone Fate. You resolve little to no Fate in childhood. You are a late bloomer, and everything is postponed until much later in life. The General is simply out of place here and can't resolve Fate.

We can also see the military influence here, like growing up a military brat, moving around from base to base, going to military school, or having a family military tradition. Your dad or parents may also be militant and strict, have a lot of rules, and discipline you harshly. You may reject or rebel against this, and/or it may take the fun out of childhood.

Partners Palace

Wu Qu is also misplaced in the Partners Palace, so the Fate here is weak or diminished. The General is a little too old for romance, and even in his younger years, it was not a priority. He spent his life in battle; if he was married, he was away for long periods of time. So, the most straightforward interpretation is that you will partner much later in life, possibly even after forty. Work, life circumstances, and so on take priority, and either you don't have the time, or those circumstances get in the way. Maybe you are always on the move, or you have a job that forces you to work odd hours or in strange conditions. Once you settle down, you meet someone suitable. Or, maybe you are in the military and on tour for long periods; once you retire, you marry.

The General is given a young bride in retirement, which is often associated with marrying someone much older or younger, someone from a different generation. Either you are very young and marry someone much older, or you live out the scenario of working a lot until late in life, then wanting a family and settling down. It is a common story for men to become successful in their late forties or fifties and then decide to have a family and marry a much younger woman. In that case, the image applies both ways.

Often, there is a big discrepancy in age between partners, but sometimes this leads to a match in maturity. The General is depicted as wise and skillful at war but with the emotional maturity of someone much younger, as he has simply never been in a relationship. In this case, the age mismatch can be a good fit, as women mature much earlier than men. Or, the marriage is for money or security, and the two have little in common.

This placement can also indicate never marrying and living alone. Some people just never meet the right person. It can also indicate becoming a widow or widower or having an early divorce, leading to being alone for the rest of your life. The classic image is the couple who marry young, the husband goes off to war and never comes back, and the girl never marries again. It can also indicate one partner being ill and the other becoming a caregiver.

However this manifests, there is little romance available. This is an Ancestral pattern of loneliness, solitude, and struggle: Most men in history did not reproduce (something like 80 percent), and many were sent to war or the military or into religion for this reason.

Offspring Palace

Wu Qu is out of place in the Offspring Palace as well; obviously, the image of an old man does not match the image of children. Again, the simplest interpretation is that the Fate here is postponed until much later in life. In traditional cultures, late in life would be late twenties or early thirties, but today this means more like late thirties or early forties and beyond for men.

The same scenario applies as with the Partners Palace: Life circumstances, or, in many cases, maturity, gets in the way. There is some reluctance or fear of growing up or having kids. Fate is not necessarily obstructed, but the Ancestral pattern is that of war, struggle, and survival; it doesn't leave much room for kids. So that must be worked out. Sometimes life takes priority. Once you settle down and figure out finances or security, then you may have kids.

Or this placement can create the desire never to have kids. Maybe it seems too hard or too expensive, or maybe you feel that the world is a cruel place and that the future is too uncertain. Or maybe you just don't like kids and cannot see yourself as a parent. Work and career, personal goals, individual freedom, and so on may be more important to you. You want your freedom and money. It's possible you just never met a partner, so looking at the Partners Palace is important here. Or you may also be asexual and have no desire to reproduce.

This Star's Ancestral pattern of struggle and survival can obstruct children in many ways. A child may die or be taken from you due to war, divorce, illness, or legal issues. There are many scenarios in which children are taken from parents, especially from men, as they have fewer legal rights to children. This could be a Fate as a single Dad who never gets to see his kids.

The kids may also struggle: They reject your guidance, argue with you, or run away from home. Maybe your children haven't called you in twenty years. The General can lead to being a strict, militant parent or to unstable environments for raising children—again, the war image—and this can create distance and trauma between parent and child.

Sometimes this placement manifests as adoption or being a stepparent; you marry or remarry much later in life to someone who has kids. You never wanted kids, but now you are a stepdad to someone in their twenties. It can also represent parenting orphans or working with orphans, children in foster care, inner-city at-risk youth, and so on.

Finally, you may have disciples, students, or subordinates at work who are like children to you or whom you mentor. Your life is work, and you may command a platoon of people who look to you, like a parent, for guidance.

Wealth Palace

Wu Qu in the Wealth Palace is solid but not what most people want. As usual, the General represents late-blooming prosperity and retirement. This is slow prosperity that is preceded by struggle and survival. The General has little interest in money and wealth in early life because he is on a mission. He is given a stipend and supported by the military, which often means a period of indirect finances, like living off family support, student loans, a military stipend, the help of a patron, investments, savings, or the like.

The general worked very hard in the service of the emperor but didn't expect much in return. This Star means a sense of duty and obligation with a deeper vision of purpose and meaning; the General has a mission in life, and getting rich is not a priority. Often, this means working tough jobs for little pay that are in service of your path; you are always working toward something greater but have difficulty experiencing the rewards. The General doesn't want to get rich, so money is unimportant, but he is also smart and strategic. It's not that he is bad with money; it just doesn't matter.

The General is a minimalist. So, you may be happy with very little but have great wealth through experience. You can sell everything you own and live out of a suitcase, which makes you happy. You are free from attachment to material possessions and from the status seeking of wealth. You can be a monk or nun with only a robe and bowl. Your happy place may be living in a tent in the wilderness, hunting and gathering. You may become a renunciate and reject worldly concerns. You may also volunteer, give away your time, and seek to end poverty and inequality.

Wealth here accumulates slowly and steadily, but this may take a while. You may not begin to save or build wealth until much later in life, but it does happen, and you retire well. The General is the image of retirement; at the end of his journey, he is rewarded and given everything. The key is "slow and steady": compound interest over time—a little in the savings account that eventually goes a long way. The General does well here with investing and modest risk through speculation. You may leave behind a strong legacy through building a home or business, and traditionally, they say this placement means you may have a tomb or monument somewhere.

The General in this House often comes with a sense of scarcity and survival. This is the Ancestral pattern of those scattered to the wind due to war or of those who immigrated to escape poverty or persecution. Poverty mentality is hard to get out of here, and the General has a tough time asking for money. He is more likely to give everything away in the desire to help others. The General has strong moral values around money and may even despise the rich.

Sometimes, depending on the Ancestral patterns, the deep desire to escape poverty takes over here. But the General in the Wealth Palace is more like working hard so that your children and grandchildren can thrive. You work three jobs to put your kids through college, and they reward you by buying you a house so that you can retire. This Fate is exemplified in the patterns of immigrants to America.

Health Palace

As an image of old age, Wu Qu in the Health Palace means longevity, but as an image associated with war, it also means injury and danger. So, this is a somewhat paradoxical image. The paradox is that injuries, illness, and the potential for danger create caution, carefulness, and, of course, strategy with discipline.

The general was a soldier; this means boot camp. He spent a lifetime training for war. This means martial arts, push-ups, pull-ups, running in the mud, doing drills, and so on. The General is often very physical and disciplined and pushes you into vigilance to survive. There is a sense of danger and incoming threats that lead you to be on edge, ready for battle and prepared for anything. You may expect the worst, but this again makes you take charge of your health and creates discipline. All physical disciplines, especially martial arts, yoga, and strength and athletic skill training, are essential here.

This is the Ancestral pattern of survival in dire circumstances. This is the pattern of war, exile, immigration, and so on: How can we survive and live to fight another day? Often, this leads to longevity because you do what you must to survive. The General in this House creates disciplined routines with sleep, exercise, and diet, which often can be rugged, tough, and minimalist. This also comes with a sense of worry, anxiety, and fear of the future because war may be coming. You inherit your Ancestors' fear for survival, which can translate to many areas of life as a sense of scarcity, danger, or caution. Even if you live in the suburbs, you may have survival gear and provisions ready for an emergency. This creates worry, which weakens the heart and lungs.

The General in the Health Palace is associated with bodily injury, physical trauma, wounds, scars, and so on. You may have a lot of minor scars, cuts and scrapes, and perhaps a few broken bones. This can lead to physical trauma from accidents and wounds from war, fights, or being attacked. It can also be a chronic illness like asthma or childhood allergies that makes you aware very early of your mortality. Often, this creates illness or injury early in life, which gives you a lot of caution and, therefore, creates longevity. The General here is too tough and ornery to die; he is stubborn and lives long, even with scars and a limp. This General has a lot of war stories here.

In this placement you age gracefully and get stronger with age, and traditionally they say that you will be well prepared for death and die well. The General knows war and understands mortality. He expects it, so that he can go into it with awareness and without fear. Death is natural, and those who have seen it a lot understand the wisdom of aging, death, and dying. No one is excused from it; it is an opportunity to let go and be liberated from our attachments. If you have the General here, you can die well before you die well.

The General here means you respond well to doctors and conventional treatment. The General understands the chain of command and takes orders well. He is very compliant and will follow protocols. You easily maintain personal discipline and routines that become the basis for your longevity. As a Yin Metal Star, the General here means you heal best in autumn but have a constitutional lung weakness.

As generals have seen some things, there are often issues with grief, worry, PTSD, and mental health challenges. Psychotherapy and the like can be very powerful. Genealogical research is also important, because you inherit the patterns of war, survival, and struggle, and exploring them can liberate many Ancestral Ghosts. The exorcist power of the General is at work here, and you can liberate family Ghosts through self-discipline and healing.

Career/Travel Palace

If you have Wu Qu in the Career/Travel Palace or one of the other career Houses, then you are a warrior in this life. You will be very hardworking and self-sacrificing. You will resolve a lot of Fate through travel and your work in the world, and a sense of warriorship will define your path. Success will be slow, gradual, and hard-earned but inevitable. Self-discipline, perseverance, and strategy will be crucial to your journey. The circumstances of Fate will be full of challenges that will force you to adapt constantly. Your life may feel like a battle, and you may be called to something: to war, on a mission or journey, to fight for a worthy cause. And you may be a bit grumpy about it all.

Here, travel will likely be an important part of your life, and it may even feel like wandering or moving from place to place in search of the next mission. Being on the road, going where life demands, will become home. You may even live like a minimalist, living out of a suitcase in airports and in hotels, ready to drop everything and get to work. Your purpose takes precedence, and you are willing to give everything up in service of service. You will likely die far from where you were born, and staying close to home will hinder you. Your life may be an odyssey.

You will take your accomplishments lightly and not be attached to success or wealth, as you will have high personal standards and morals. Success is certainly possible, but it is gradual and late blooming. It may take a long time to figure out what you are doing or where you are going, but if you keep a moral compass and vision connected to a higher ideal, then you will eventually get there. Eventually, you will contribute and be recognized for your work, especially in retirement. This is the life of the quiet soldier, fighting the good fight for the underdogs. Service work, social work, politics, and, of course, the military are suitable.

You may be a jack-of-all-trades. You go from job to job building skills, and eventually you synthesize them into a career later in life. This is good for business but not great for ownership or entrepreneurship, as the General is a reluctant leader and more suited to following orders. This is more of a consultant image; people hire you for your advice, expertise, and strategy. This is the wisdom of *The Art of War*—one of the greatest texts ever written about military strategy and tactics—put to the test. This is a life lived according to these kinds of philosophies. The General and Vassal Stars align with Bushido, or the Way of the Warrior, the moral and ethical code of conduct for samurai. Confucian morals are also very suitable, as they put the service to family and country first.

Here, the Ancestors are pushing you to complete their unresolved Fate of struggle, survival, and escape from war, immigration, persecution, exile, migration, and so on. Family history is important here, especially if you have these patterns in your recent history. Stories from the World Wars, from political and social upheaval over the past hundred years, from immigration and global imperialism and expansion all over the world, from the conquerors and the conquered, are all very applicable. It may be recent, like you are the child of immigrants or refugees, or it may be very distant, like you are fulfilling a dream of people stepping off the *Mayflower*.

Here, peace in life begins in retirement, and you may experience a "second childhood." Life is a battle until you retire, and then you finally get to relax and have fun. You become childlike in old age. You may struggle and not feel successful in life, but the gradual, progressive, and cumulative nature of your growth ends up making life very stable and fruitful in the end. You may not be rich, but the General doesn't need much; he feels rich, though he could also struggle with some PTSD later. Life's battles may weigh heavily on you in the end, but it will make for an excellent memoir.

Assistants Palace

Wu Qu is somewhat exalted in the Assistants Palace because of the clear chain of command. The general was a masterful team leader, but he always took orders from the emperor; in retirement, he was a counselor and an adviser, and he consulted the emperor on war and politics in the style of *The Art of War*. Here, that chain of command works very well for you, and you either are an excellent adviser or you have one who brings you great success. In this House, the General gets to serve selflessly and give himself to the Emperor like a samurai.

Through hard work and integrity, you will earn respect and become a highly sought-after consultant, adviser, or team leader. This is excellent for a career, and like usual, social work and the service professions are exalted, especially jobs that require intelligence, strategy, tactics, and so on. The late-blooming nature of the General often means, like in the previous House, that success is slow and gradual and not fully realized until much later in life. You may also be a jack-of-all-trades, but eventually, you put everything together very successfully late in life and are able to apply your skills and experience to a specific industry or job.

As usual, integrity and living and working according to a code of conduct are important. This is Bushido, the Way of the Warrior, in practice. This image borders on stuffy and uptight regarding personal integrity applied to life and work, but this is a strength. So, follow a code of honor and stay true to that sense of integrity, but watch out for others who lack integrity, as they can be your undoing.

The General is somewhat vulnerable here if the chain of command is obstructed or afflicted. The possibility of scandal or being undermined by a subordinate, employee, lawyer, consultant, and so on is very high. The General is stronger in the Superiors Palace for these kinds of mishaps. Here, he can be disgraced, and this can lead to losing face, losing a business, losing friends, losing money, or the like. This can degrade into espionage, blackmail, revolution, and revolt. This can also lead to being stuck in the chain—unable to progress, always in middle management, or forever a cog in the machine.

Here, the General applies his discipline and practices to help others. This is like a drill sergeant leading a platoon. There is a chain of command and a clear hierarchy. You thrive in this situation and work your way up the ranks. Sometimes it is helpful to have someone bark orders at you; you are relieved of having to think and get to just do what you're told. If it comes from a place of integrity, then having an experienced leader guide you can be a powerful path of transformation, especially in youth. Let's face it: No one knows what they want to do early in life. This leader can be a powerful role model, teacher, or coach who guides you early with "tough love." Going into the military can work well with this placement.

Wu Qu in this House can be mixed in terms of friendship but is great for co-workers, as the energy of teamwork is strong. This looks like a squad, a platoon—a well-organized unit. So, this placement can work well if you have a mission that you band together with co-workers, teammates, school chums, and so on to accomplish. But the image of the General is not fun and freewheeling, and casual friendship may be challenging. You may find your best friends on a local amateur sports team or league, where you get to enact a chain of command.

You may also be Fated to have a very hardworking assistant who follows you into battle. This person may give you everything, do all the hard work, and bring you success. This works well when you are a skilled and charismatic leader who is horrible at managing small stuff. Having a General to assist you can make a huge difference.

Superiors Palace

Wu Qu is very comfortable and auspicious in the Superiors Palace, as he is given full command to lead here. We must remember that the General is not the Emperor, not the ruler, so the story of Fate here is not central to your life, but there is a lot of work to do. You work and lead reluctantly but with a sense of duty and honor.

The general was fundamentally an adviser to the emperor, but he also oversaw the military. Here, he is given the most power and freedom to lead and offer his wisdom. With this placement, chain of command will be important in your life, as in the previous House, but here, the General is very clearly the squad leader or team captain. Your career will be very important, and you will resolve a lot of Fate in this House by applying strategy, discipline, and, most important, the wisdom of leadership. Because he has seen the horrors of war, the General is a reluctant leader, making him the best leader. This is the image of a boss who cares, who listens and learns from mistakes, and who wants the best for everyone involved. The General has humility and little to no ego. He leads because he must.

This is an all-around auspicious placement for career success. Here, the hard work, perseverance, and discipline of the General go smoothly, and you progress steadily to a very productive career. You may never reach the top or be CEO, owner, and so on, but you will do well in upper management, where you can make big decisions and handle a lot of responsibility. Wu Qu in this House does well in corporate, business, government, and, of course, military environments. Here, you are given responsibility after proving yourself to be wise, capable, and effective. Success for the General may still be late blooming and take a while, but it is the most immediate in this House.

You may serve as an adviser to a powerful person, and this person will honor and respect you. You will be a generous and effective manager, leader, or boss, and your employees or followers will respect and listen to you. You can apply the wisdom of *The Art of War* very effectively, and you become a source of guidance and wisdom for others. Here, you can make the biggest difference and have the most influence on the world. This may be modest, like you become the local sheriff, and the mayor comes to you for advice on managing crime; you make suggestions, leading to policy change that affects local government, and violent crime goes down.

Traditionally, they say this placement means you will be honored in old age, especially at your funeral. As usual, retirement is very significant, and here, it will be well earned and very rewarding. Old age will be when you make your greatest contributions. This is like the book called the *Hagakure: The Way of the Samurai*, written by an old samurai who survived until old age and could pass on his wisdom. You may write memoirs or a book of strategy that others will follow.

Property Palace

If Wu Qu appears in the Property Palace, then you will have a strong affinity for the ownership of property and goods later in life, but you will be unattached to local identity, wealth, or ownership. This makes this a somewhat paradoxical image: The general is rewarded in retirement with a grand palatial estate, but he has spent his life living on the battlefield in a tent. Therefore, this is a very auspicious placement to be rewarded for hard work and not fall victim to the trappings of wealth, for you are not greedy and do not require safety and harmony.

The General here may cause you to be on the move a lot in response to the demands of Fate. You may move, uproot, and feel happy with very little. However, this is still a good Fate to be given good living circumstances as a reward for your work. For example, you get a job that pays for your moving and living expenses, or you are set up in community housing, a dorm, or a nice hotel. You may live a life of austerity, living out of a suitcase, but again, you are unattached. The road is home.

The General is accustomed to danger, war, and constant upheaval. This is the Ancestral pattern of migration and movement in response to changing tides. Unafflicted by Ghost Stars, it represents resolving these patterns and settling the Ancestors. After a life of war, they return home. So, you may move a lot but find great peace when you settle down and put down roots. You may reestablish an Ancestral connection and build a spiritual, religious, or cultural community far from where you were born. This is like settling a colony of refugees and rebuilding a broken culture with great success. Afflicted, this can be connected to the dark stories of exile, war, migration, and so on, but often it represents a resolution of these negativities.

This placement is a very strong guarantee of success late in life, with the end of your life full of rewards. This is the ultimate Chinese success story: a life of hard work and service that is rewarded at the end. You can retire well and spend your twilight years on a palatial estate in the countryside. Your investments, stocks, savings, and so on will mature and be very fruitful. There is also an association here with having a great collection or that your collection of goods is very valuable. However, the General doesn't know what to do in the lap of luxury and will probably end up giving it all away and living in a cabin in the woods.

This is the image of the Tomb of the Unknown Soldier. You may have a monument built for you or a park bench with your name on it somewhere. You may have a legacy, but it will be others who establish it in remembrance of you. Everyone you helped or took care of will take care of you and honor you in your old age.

In the most ordinary sense, this is also greatly applicable to working in real estate or property management, but there is a greater sense of social work. You may work to provide shelter for unhoused people, refugees, war veterans, and so on.

Pleasure Palace

If you have Wu Qu in the Pleasure Palace, then you are likely to struggle with enjoyment. Again, this is the image of a grumpy old man who has spent his life in battle. This placement creates a rather serious, stern demeanor that may or may not reflect your inner or true self. You are born "old" and may be a very serious, mature child who was wise beyond your years. You will probably not relate to kids your age and will spend more time talking to and relating with adults. However, this seriousness lightens with age, and you will enjoy yourself more and more as you get older. You have a kind of second childhood, for the General is retired and is now free to enjoy himself, though he still finds it difficult because of his past.

You inherit this sense of hardship and seriousness from your Ancestors' struggles. Many of your Ancestors had to work hard all their lives; maybe they never got to relax and have a good time. Or maybe they went through war, persecution, or the like. It weighs on you right from the start, and you must learn to lighten up and release the sense of struggle, seriousness, and hardship. You may be critical of fun, silliness, and relaxation and find it frivolous. You may be "uptight," and you may find participating in parties, dancing, and games to be a challenge: You either can't relax and let loose, or you would rather be working. You may be all work and no play.

It's not that the General does not experience pleasure; it's that he takes pleasure in work, discipline, and challenge. He enjoys suffering. The General wants to be on a mission and have a purpose. He enjoys tasks, timetables, drills, and routines. He takes pleasure in working hard for others and being productive. This is both an advantage and a disadvantage. It is better to lean into it as an advantage, for if you can enjoy discipline, then you can accomplish a lot. You can apply yourself diligently to learning skills and accomplishing goals. So, sports, martial arts, and personal discipline come easy for the General. He can do well in sports, not because they are fun, but because he likes doing push-ups. Martial arts are an excellent expression of this, so a kid with Wu Qu in this House should definitely go to karate class.

The disadvantage is, of course, not having traditional fun. But, again, this lightens with age. It is better to let serious and grumpy people be themselves, and if you are a serious, grumpy person, then it is good to lighten up and learn to relax without feeling guilty. But embrace the love of discipline and training, and apply yourself diligently. It is a good idea to get out of your comfort zone and go to parties or dance, but it is also okay to hate dancing. Not everyone has to love dancing.

The General would rather pour himself into solitary acts of enjoyment, and this Star tends to create interest in unusual or niche hobbies that require a lot of skill, strength, and discipline. Sports like golf, pool, chess, weight lifting, bodybuilding, martial arts, boxing, and track and field interest the General. If the General likes team sports, it is usually because of the chain of command and running plays; American football is very warlike. The General makes a good coach or drill sergeant.

Again, with this placement, true relaxation and fun come at the end of life and as you get older. Retirement becomes a second childhood, and you become carefree and soft in old age. You may have even missed out on your first childhood due to seriousness, and so now you want to make up for it by buying toys, playing games, and throwing parties. The term "seenager"—"senior teenager," or "senile teenager"—is applicable. You retire, and now you have money. You don't have to go to work or school. You have no curfew or responsibilities. Maybe the kids are all grown up, so now you are finally free to go wild. But you may be too tired and worn out to appreciate it.

TAI YIN (太陰)—THE MOON LADY OR PRINCESS

NAME AND TRANSLATIONS:

Tai Yin (太陰), the Moon Star, Moon Lady, the Princess Star

Tai, 太—great(est), grand(est) a) indicating extreme, maximum, or superlative status of the following word; e.g., 太煞 taishai, most extreme, ultimate.[7]

Yin, 陰—shade(d), shadow(ed); cold-lit. a) dark(ness), dim(ly). 2 north side of a mountain, south side of a river, esp. in place-names. 3 cold(ness); inactivity, declining strength, seasons of autumn and winter; e.g., 陰氣 yinqi, cool vapors and aura of autumn and winter; 陰風 yinfeng, cold wind, esp. north wind. a) decline, weaken. 4 feminine principles (opp. 陽 yang), associated with the moon, earth, darkness, cold, weakness, softness, hiddenness, latency, stillness, etc. a) broken lines in Yijing hexagrams. b) symbolic of the number 6 as the most fully Yin of the nine fundamental numerals. 5 below the surface, secretive, out of sight; retract(ed); e.g., 陰德 yinde, actions helpful for others done without their knowledge; 陰室 yinshi, private room(s); 陰通 yintong, secret communications. a) suggest(ion), intimation; innuendo.[8]

Together we translate "Great Yin" as the Moon, but in the Royal Court she is the image of the Princess.

ELEMENT: Yin Water

TRADITIONAL IMAGE: Young, beautiful princess at court, fashionably dressed, seductive, face obscured, bathing in the moonlight, ascending to the moon with Yuetu, the Moon Rabbit, and living in the Moon Palace[9]

ANCESTOR PROFILE: Matriarchal Ancestors, matrons who use intuition and Yin/feminine power to survive; fear and pressing need of Matriarchal retribution

LUMINOUS PLACEMENT: Rat, Rooster, Dog, and Pig Palaces

DIMINISHED PLACEMENT: Tiger, Dragon, and Horse Palaces

AFFILIATIONS: Southern Array—always at the left hand of the Empress

Tai Yin is the astronomical name of the Moon, but in the Royal Court, the Moon represents the Princess and daughter of the Emperor and Empress. She is also called the Moon Lady and represents Yin Power and femininity as the beautiful and mysterious Chang'e (嫦娥), the Goddess of the Moon, living in the Moon Palace. She is depicted as lunar, soft, and mysterious, representing the indefinable power of beauty and seduction but also of innocence and mutability.

She is like the Empress in many ways, as she also represents the legacy of the Matriarchal Ancestors and what we have already called Yin Fate, associated with being, waiting, listening, following, restraint, intuition, and so on. While the Empress represents our major Yin Fate and is the storehouse of our most positive gifts in this lifetime, the Moon represents our more subtle, indefinable, changeable, and uneven Yin Fate, associated with our somewhat lesser Matriarchal Ancestors, the women whose lives were very much out of their control and who had to adapt to new and foreign circumstances.

It has long been the custom in patriarchal and gerontocratic societies to marry off daughters through an arranged marriage, and so women would often have to leave their families at a young age and leave behind their social support networks to find themselves in what was often an unwelcome environment. Historically, women have adapted to make alliances, friends, and alloparents, and they are very affected by gossip, status, hierarchy, and so on, while men were sent off to work and war. She, therefore, represents the subtle and powerful role of socializing.

The Moon represents the Fate of the princess of the royal court, whose Fate was very much out of her own control, for she was married off to a foreign prince to make political alliances. There, she would have to learn a new language and new customs and act as a bridge between factions. As the Fate of the Sun is to work and prove his right to become the Emperor, the Moon must train to be an Empress. There were often many princesses of the court, and they were often foreign dignitaries or emissaries sent to use their powers of seduction to bargain and broker deals for strategic purposes.

The job of the Princess, then, is all about social skills via self-cultivation and deportment, how she learns to manipulate using beauty, emotion, seduction, empathy, and language. She is like the Empress and the Star called the Concubine, but she is somewhat in the middle. All three stars represent the Yin Fate that is out of our hands, but the Empress has the most power, and the Concubine has the least. The Fate of the Princess is middling, as much of it is out of her own hands; however, through Yin Power, she can alter and change her own Fate and the Fate of others. If a Princess is successful in her alliances, she can be very powerful and become an Empress. But she must leave home to do so, so her Fate is often a journey to a strange land.

The Fate of the Moon is very much the opposite of the Sun. The sun itself is obvious, bright, and shiny and makes steady progress. Wherever the Moon shows up, Fate is strange, mysterious, uneven, but also renewable and strangely confident. This is the image of the moon. The moon is Great Yin, and it is always changing. The moon waxes and wanes; it is always altering its appearance, slowly progressing toward fullness and then disappearing back into darkness. Sometimes it is bright; sometimes it is hidden. It does not have light of its own, but rather it reflects back light from the sun as cool, soft, and delicate moonlight. The moon is fickle and mysterious and has always inspired images of sensual romance and artistic inspiration. The Fate here is associated with all things lunar: emotion, spirituality, intuition, potentiality, art, love, music, poetry, sensual pleasure, and so on. Wherever the Moon Star shows up is imbued with a sense of spirituality and the sacred.

The Fate of the Moon or Princess is often episodic and unfolds in chapters. Our opportunities and circumstances there wax and wane, and the sense of progression in that House is uneven and uncertain. If it is unafflicted, it offers a smooth resolution of Fate that happens naturally but mysteriously. Wherever it shows up, expect magical weirdness. If it is afflicted, it is easily swayed by the negativity of other Stars and can become even more unreliable, so expect that weirdness to turn wonky. The lunar nature of the Moon can easily slip into darkness and self-destruction.

Let's walk the Moon Lady through the Twelve Houses.

Ming Palace

If Tai Yin arrives in the Ming Palace, then the overall nature of your Fate is obscure and mysterious but fortunate and associated with all things lunar. Like the moon itself, your Fate will wax and wane; it will be episodic, with many seemingly related and unrelated chapters, constantly changing; it will include many ups and downs, periods of brightness and darkness. It will unravel slowly, and while your life may involve a great deal of effort, the promptings of Fate that change your life and lead toward resolution will happen all by themselves, and you will not understand them at first, or maybe ever. Fate is revealed slowly, like the Moon in the night sky.

Fate is decidedly and effectively Yin, meaning it is more about being than doing; it requires waiting, listening, following, and holding back, and it depends on others. Others will show you the way, and you must make alliances and friends and follow signs and gut instincts. The details of Fate are subtle, obscure, and often hidden. Your capacity to unravel Fate is found in your ability to maneuver relationships, circumstances, and obstacles subtly via feelings, emotion, empathy, gentleness, and social skill.

Traditionally, this placement is associated with being elegant, attractive, charming, and seductive, and your Fate requires you to take advantage of what used to be called "feminine wiles"—and yes, this applies to men as well. Your success and prosperity will depend on your self-cultivation, social skills, deportment, and countenance rather than on your intellectual and physical skill or labor. But modesty is also key, for the Fate here cannot be overcome with force, aggression, or effort. The Moon is Yin Water and uses what is soft, gentle, and relaxed to overcome what is hard.

You must learn to use Yin Power, and if you have Tai Yin here or in the Ancestors Palace, then you inherit the Yin Power of your Matriarchal Ancestors. This is the skill, grace, and intuition of all the women in your family. You inherit the legacy of their experience, their skills and demeanor, and their stories, and you are Fated to resolve their unfinished business. Your Fate will be an extension of them, so your mother, grandmother, aunts, and so on may be an important presence in your life, and understanding your genealogy and connecting to them will be important. You have an army of female guardian spirits behind you, and they send gifts, signs, omens, and subtle hints and promptings to guide you in life. You must learn to listen and follow your heart.

You are the princess of the royal court sent off to a foreign land as a dignitary or to be married off to a prince. This means that life may involve making a significant journey or a series of journeys with the purpose of making alliances. You may travel widely, immigrate, or move to a new home or city.

You may have to adapt to strange circumstances and learn new languages, customs, and so on. The Princess is given everything she needs to succeed, and others support her. You must learn to rely on other people—family, friends, partners, and so on—and your Fates will be mutually beneficial.

The Moon is easily afflicted and often swayed by others, so if Ghost Stars show up with her, then she can be unseated, which often leads to her being lazy, entitled, moody, distracted, depressed, and unthorough. She can also be a "succubus" and steal energy from others in a desire to avoid hard work. Afflicted, the Moon can be very strange, weird, confusing, and slippery. In general, emotionality undermines the success of the Moon, but it is also her greatest strength.

Your Fate is very connected to your emotions, feelings, intuitions, and inspirations. The Moon can very easily go haywire if emotions get out of check, but she can also express great artistic vision and beauty in life. You are here to feel and love deeply and express beauty. You will have a deep feeling of spirituality and the sacred. If the Moon is unafflicted, or if affliction is overcome, then Fate unravels with a sense of freedom, beauty, and awe at the mystery of life. The key is to let go and go with the flow; be like water, and everything will happen as it should. You will demonstrate your Freedom through your deportment, and you can be an example or icon for others to emulate and follow.

Ancestors Palace

If Tai Yin arrives in the Ancestors Palace, then you have a strong but potentially uneven connection with your parents and Ancestors, and as a Yin Star, it especially strengthens the connection with your mother and Matriarchal Ancestors. Like the Empress, the Moon connects you deeply to the stories, feelings, and influence of all the women in your family and/or to your mother's side of the family. You are their living dream; their influence greatly shapes your life. You may even be a returning Ancestor or greatly resemble one.

In the Ming Palace, this influence drives the greater patterns of your Fate in the world, and there is more freedom to express those influences in a deeply personal way, but here it flows much more directly through your parents and through familial relations. Your story is closely aligned with them. Your relationship with your mother, grandmother, or mother's family is crucial; you are close, or at least you are very impacted by their Fate. This relationship may be tenuous and troubled, and it may wax and wane throughout life. You will inherit their unfinished business, their stories, their fears, their inhibitions, and their dreams, and you are Fated to fulfill these stories. So, it is important to hear the stories and connect with the wisdom of your mother, grandmothers, aunts, and so on.

Find out who you are and where you come from, especially the untold, unacknowledged stories of your family. If accompanied by Ghost Stars, this inheritance could include stories of pain and hardship that you are here to liberate. Your Matriarchal Ancestors are with you on a spiritual path to liberate the Ghosts of the family. You have a spiritual connection to the "feminine," and you may have something to square with women (even if you are a woman), which may mean resolving patterns of Ancestral abuse. Women may also be the main source of help and friendship in your life, as this puts you in touch with your "feminine side."

The lunar nature of the Moon here connects you strongly with the dead, and you will receive guidance, protection, and inspiration from them. Your life may involve a lot of cathartic releases as you work through the patterns of the unsettled dead. This link is psychic and may appear in dreams, visions, premonitions, signs, omens, and so on. Your dream life will be very active, as will your imagination and creativity. You may inherit talents and abilities, but they are more artistic and emotional rather than physical and productive (like those imparted by the Sun).

Like when this Star is in the Ming Palace and Career/Travel Palace, life may be episodic and full of chapters that appear incongruent. You are living out Ancestral patterns, so you may have a period of traveling, a period as an artist, a period of loneliness and isolation, a period of family, and so on, and they may be in different places with different people. Eventually, this will make sense, but until then life may seem like a mess. It will have a lot of ups and downs and bright and dark periods, like the Moon. This waxing and waning quality may also apply to family: Sometimes, the connection may be strong, and sometimes, it may be nonexistent.

Youth Palace

If you have Tai Yin in the Youth Palace, then the Fate of your childhood and with siblings is delicate, uneven, and very Yin. Here, the stories and unfinished business of your Matriarchal Ancestors and the presence of your mother shape your childhood in strong, even overbearing, ways.

You are also likely Fated to be a very sensitive, shy, and imaginative child. You may be a "late bloomer" and not come into your own until much later in life. You will need to learn to overcome shyness as you mature so you can blossom and share your gifts, which are likely great. But you may be distracted, aloof, and uninterested as a child, making it hard to engage at school and with the process of "growing up." This Star is vulnerable to trauma in this House, and the wounds of childhood may affect you strongly. Getting over these wounds means growing into adulthood may be stunted, and you may have delayed adolescence or arrested development, leading to liberation and a wild period when you finally begin to bloom.

This placement often means having few siblings or no siblings. If that is the case, then the sense of being a loner and late bloomer is amplified. Your sensitivity will make it difficult to integrate at school and to play with siblings. You may want to be alone and live in a world of imagination. You may naturally feel a connection to nature and have a sense of the sacred and numinous. Playing with toys or playing games will have a depth of meaning unknown to others, and this may fade as you get older, or it may be lost as you are forced to adapt to the unimaginative, boring harshness of adult life. Childhood may also involve deep fascination and obsessions—like, you love the ocean and want to learn everything there is to know about sharks, or you read fantasy novels and want to be a dark elf. Because you are late to develop, socially and possibly physically, middle school and high school may be rough.

If you have siblings, those relationships are potentially very deep, even psychic, but likely uneven and complex. As a Yin Star, this Star here could mean a sister, or you may have a stronger or deeper relationship with a sister over your brother. You and your sister may be an inseparable pair when you are young, but a wedge may divide you—like, the older sister goes to high school and gets a boyfriend and no longer wants to stay home with you watching Disney movies while drinking chocolate milk. The lunar, waxing and waning quality of the Moon in this House implies that sibling relationships are uneven; you may grow apart but reconnect later in life as adults.

This waxing and waning may also make youth itself sporadic and uneven. The Yin nature of this Star means a lot of your Fate is out of your control and may be hard to understand. It may be full of life-changing events and chapters. You may move a lot due to a parent's job or to their financial instability. You may have a chapter in California, then Colorado, and then Massachusetts. Or you may go from living in a house to living in an apartment to living out of a car and then back again. You may yourself go through a lot of phases, like a punk phase, a goth phase, a cheerleader phase, and so on. You may play out and try on a lot of identities, seeking to discover yourself.

Partners Palace

Tai Yin in the Partners Palace is definitely the basis for a rom-com. There is a strong Fate to meet a partner or many partners, but the Fate is based on attraction and appearance, at least in the beginning. And the Yin nature of the Fate and waxing and waning quality of the moon makes for a lot of ups and downs, coming together and apart. So it's very Hollywood; there's definitely a movie here.

The image of the Moon is of the beautiful princess betrothed to a foreign prince, so there is Yinyuan (姻緣) here, meaning past-life or Ancestrally arranged Fate with a life partner. You are "previously betrothed," but for the purpose of survival and making alliances. Therefore, it can be strongly swayed and could be interested in status and safety seeking through partnership, especially with certain characters, like Rabbits. Often, this is associated with being chosen rather than choosing.

Superficially, this Star is associated with attraction and attractiveness and is somewhat shallow until it matures. So, you may be focused on looks, money, or status, or simply be immature and naive when it comes to partner choices—like, you're really into tall guys or tattoos. The Fate to meet an attractive and alluring partner is strong, but you may be too preoccupied with meeting Prince Charming or with wanting a beautiful partner.

You may be chosen or pursued for the same reason. Someone may want you as a trophy or arm candy. Sometimes, there is a discrepancy in age here, and you marry "up." You may also have the Fate to drift about and change partners a lot in constant pursuit of perfection, unable to settle down and unsure about what you want, or because you confuse romance with compatibility. This process matures and can eventually lead to stability and finding Mr. or Mrs. Right, but first you must overcome uncertainty and immaturity.

This placement may be the Fate to marry young and immature as well. You marry a high school sweetheart but are ill-equipped for long-term relationships and separate; if it is unafflicted by Ghost Stars, then you may come together and apart and eventually have a solid partnership. Afflicted, it can lead to heartbreak. In general, this marriage may have a lot of ups and downs, a lot of challenges and uncertainty. Again, the lunar waxing and waning make stability difficult, but there is also the strong potential for a deep emotional and spiritual connection, which is not the same as compatibility. You may feel deeply sexually or spiritually attracted to someone with whom you are incompatible, and the boring monotony of marriage is a very different challenge—you may love staring into each other's eyes but argue about who takes out the garbage.

Offspring Palace

Tai Yin in the Offspring Palace is very auspicious for children and Fate resolution through parenting. As a Yin Star, it is associated with having a daughter or daughters or having a special connection with a particular daughter over a son. She may also be a delicate, sensitive, and/or precious child that needs a lot of protection, nurturing, and care. The connection and closeness here are strong, and children help you manage your Fate and will take care of you later in life. Traditionally, they say this placement means the child will marry well and support you in old age.

The Moon in this House often makes the circumstances and Fate around parenting somewhat delicate and precarious. It may take many tries to get pregnant, or you may wait until later in life, which makes it harder. So, the child becomes more precious. Or, you wait too long and can't have kids, so you may adopt a child. Your Fated child may be waiting for you in another country. Or your life may be too unstable; you can't find a stable partner or job, or your job or career may be too demanding to take time off and have kids, so you wait. This is a common story today, as we are seeing record-low birth rates all over the world, and the main reasons given are money, time, and circumstances.

If you are a father, then this is Daddy's little girl; it means giving birth to a princess on whom you lavish attention. You may be overprotective and intimidate the boys she brings home. Or you have special daddy-daughter days that you continue into her adulthood. The Moon is not always a daughter, though, and may also indicate a sensitive, special child. They may possess unusual qualities or be very beautiful. They may be artistic, talented, or shy and require a lot of protection and guidance to blossom.

The circumstances and experience of parenthood also wax and wane a lot. Your interest in being a parent may come and go, which could be why you wait to have them. Or, you really love the baby phase but hate the toddler phase. You may love it when they win at baseball or impress everyone at their piano recital, but you are annoyed when they waste their twenties refusing to get a real job. You love them deeply, but they may come and go out of your life a lot. Sometimes, they are needy and want money, and other times, they don't call or need you at all.

The Moon here is also associated with your own sexual attractiveness and can be related to being very sexually active very early or experiencing early sexual trauma. If you are attractive and mature early, then you may receive a lot of sexual attention, which forces you to grow up. If afflicted by Ghost Stars, this can mean abuse and trauma, and this placement is also traditionally associated with sexually transmitted diseases, miscarriage, and abortion.

Wealth Palace

If you have Tai Yin in the Wealth Palace, then your Fate with finances is indirect and uneven, both practically speaking and in terms of interest. Here, the waxing and waning quality of the moon is strong, and the image of the Princess is one of patronage and support. The Princess does not have a standard nine-to-five job; her family supports her, and she "wants for not."

Therefore, this Star often represents an indirect source of income: You may live off family money, inheritance, or a trust fund; you may have a parent, patron, or partner who supports you; or you may make money through a side job or hustle or through investments. Student loans and grant money for research also fit this image. This Star works well with investing—stocks, bonds, CDs, and so on. You may sit at the computer in your underwear at 3 A.M. doing online trading, and somewhere, someone sends you a check—very lunar. It also works well today with income from the internet, apps, and subscriptions, and from information work, paid sponsors, endorsements, and so on through social media and from "content creators." Ten-plus years ago, this would not have been a thing, but today, there are many more lunar sources of income. In general, this placement means money doesn't come through a paycheck or standard salaried job. You will have a varied financial life.

Tai Yin in this House can manifest as all kinds of "strange" work, including illegal activities, black or gray markets, sex work, pimping, and so on. Modeling is very lunar and Princess: You get paid to be pretty. You may be a circus performer, acrobat, artist, comedian, podcaster, or the like. If it is odd, indirect, unusual, and fluctuating, it fits. You may also manage other people's money and/or work as a consultant, or work through intuition, prediction, speculation, and feeling. A career as a counselor, therapist, or doctor also makes sense here, as does being a foreign diplomat or politician, as this often was the job of the princess. It is not your skill or competence but your feeling and intuition that get you paid.

The waxing and waning qualities of the moon imply that income and wealth fluctuate a lot here. If it is unafflicted by Ghost Stars, then wealth can steadily increase through things like investments, but it is likely to go up and down a lot. You have periods of wealth and poverty, feast and famine. This may be a struggle, and you may worry a great deal about finances. But it often means that your interest in money waxes and wanes; you generally don't care, and may even find money abhorrent. You may resent the rich or responsibility and find yourself comfortable with very little or ideologically opposed to luxury, so you embrace minimalism. But then, as you get older, you become a diva and only want the finest things. You may have a princess mentality: You are complacent and expect things to be handed to you. You may manipulate others to support you, or you may seek a sugar daddy or mama and move from one person to the next.

Health Palace

Tai Yin in the Health Palace is very similar to the Empress here but much more vulnerable, as the Princess is not as mature, and the image of the Moon is very unstable. You inherit a very delicate and sensitive Yin constitution from your Matriarchal Ancestors, and you inherit their emotionality and vulnerability. You have a very strong sense of feeling and a kind of psychic embodiment. This is not "weak" in a bad sense, but it is soft, delicate, and easily compromised. The strength of the Moon is the capacity to feel and sense, and this translates to very strong empathy, love, and compassion. The Moon here makes for a great healer and listener and exalts the practice of alternative, traditional, or energy-based medicine.

The Moon is compromised by emotionality, and while this is true for everyone to some degree, here, it is the basis of all illness and recovery. Illness and recovery, then, become mysterious and may seem uncontrollable. The Moon naturally goes through a process of waxing and waning, and your health may have these kinds of cycles. You will be very connected to nature, astrology, the seasons, and to the Moon, of course. You need to learn to go with these cycles, to rest and act appropriately, and to gather and expend strength in rhythms. If you try to push all the time like the Sun, you will burn out. For women, this makes the menstrual cycle very important, so learn to embrace and find wisdom in the cycle, as it connects you to nature in a very profound way. For men, it adds a dimension of sensitivity that is uncharacteristic for most men, so you will likely be more emotional and less "macho."

Again, negative emotions are the basis for illness. So, it is very important to practice self-cultivation and reflection. Therapy is very helpful, and in turn, this makes for being a good therapist yourself. You need to learn to be "in touch" with your emotions: Be aware of them while they are happening so they do not spin out of control. Here, you will feel them deeply in the body, and they can manifest with psychical symptoms as "nervous disorders," like you easily catch a cold or upper respiratory infection when you are stressed, tired, and sad, or you get digestive disturbances when nervous or angry, or you get headaches as you get frustrated, or your back and knees hurt when you're worried about the future. You may worry a great deal and become a hypochondriac. Your mind may be out of control, and this causes hysteria, neurosis, stress, and all kinds of strange, otherwise inexplicable symptoms, like panic attacks, a racing heartbeat, dizziness or vertigo, and shortness of breath, even when all the lab reports are negative.

You may deal with illnesses that are not fully recognized or acknowledged by Western medicine, like Lyme disease. You will also be easily misdiagnosed and mistreated by Western medicine and given inappropriate medications or surgical treatments, so be cautious. The Moon is also traditionally associated with reproductive disorders, STDs, infertility, and so on.

The Moon is very susceptible to possession from both Ancestral Ghosts and local Ghosts. If this shows up with Ghost Stars, then you are likely to inherit a lot of unresolved Ancestral Fate from the Matriarchy, and this may manifest as strange and cyclical illnesses. You are liberating Ghosts through illness. Your sickness is you finishing and concluding Ancestral Ghosts, and this may be physical or mental, manifesting as unexplained or ungrounded fears, worries, and unspecified anxiety from all the women in your Ancestral line. But you also inherit their positive qualities and talents, love, compassion, nurturing, and so on. You inherit their resilience and power to recover, which is part of their Yin Power.

You may also be susceptible to local Ghosts and Fengshui portals—like, you get nervous and pick up on other people's negative emotions just being around them. You walk through a park and inhale a bunch of displaced wood spirits from a local forest that was cut down or earth spirits set loose by a construction project. It is important to emphasize that this gives you the capacity to feel, release, and resolve these kinds of Ghosts rather than being taken over by them. If Ghosts rule the Health Palace, then you can be taken over. Here, you feel them deeply, but you can release them with love.

You are much more likely to respond to feeling-based medicine, energy medicine, traditional medicine, and so on. Healing with herbs, diet, and lifestyle are key, especially in connection to nature, the seasons, the moon, and so on. It is important to develop an emotional connection with doctors and healers, and this rapport is more important than their skill. The placebo effect is very powerful here. If you feel safe and heard, you can heal no matter what they do. The Moon is reliably unreliable, so healers need to understand that you do not respond directly to treatment but rather indirectly—you will not heal in an obvious way. Onset and recovery are not obvious like with the Sun, and it may involve a deep emotional process.

It is also important to develop a very strong practice of self-cultivation, meditation, and prayer. Prayer especially can go a long way; you can pray and heal others, and connecting to a higher power or healing force is also powerful. Whatever you do, it must be personal, but it is important to comply and develop consistency, as the waxing and waning quality is all over the place. Compliance will be difficult, and you may be addicted to changing your habits, practices, and routines every time you change your mind. It is important not to get stuck in an eternal healing process or addicted to treatment. The Moon heals best in winter, at night, through sleep, rest, and inactivity.

Career/Travel Palace

If you have Tai Yin in the Career/Travel Palace, then you will have a bizarre, unconventional, and possibly disjointed resume or life path that will eventually make sense and blossom into a fulfilling and inspired sense of purpose. You will naturally and effortlessly resolve Fate here by following your intuition and innate abilities. This Star is the opposite of the Sun, who is driven on a path of productivity to prove himself. Here, for purpose and meaning, the Moon is driven to express and unfurl natural, innate abilities, talents, and gifts based on deep personal feelings.

Your path in life will be slow, circuitous, indirect, and, as usual, it will wax and wane. There will be periods of bright and dark, rise and fall, but you will be supported in this process. For the moon reflects, or is "given," the light of the sun; it is not its own. This is the image of the Princess, who is gifted with a path of self-expression.

You may be born with a silver spoon, or you may find a way to use privilege to your advantage. If not, then you will find a way to compromise so that you may live minimally, and you do so because you are an artist at heart. The Moon wants to contribute to the world through feeling, and it is associated with the arts, learning, music, spirituality, and so on. As usual, the Moon is connected to empathy, love, and compassion for others, so the desire to help, heal, and support people will be behind everything you do, not out of high ideals but because you really care and feel their pain and suffering.

As the princess was often sent as a diplomat or dignitary or married off to a foreign prince, it is likely that you will travel widely for work and pleasure. This placement is possibly a strong Fate Threshold for relocating and starting a new life in a new place. Travel and moving will be based on feelings and intuition. For example, you have always wanted to go to Kyoto, and when you arrive, you will take a job teaching English. Or you may drift from place to place, working as a waiter to support yourself as a guitar player, doing open mic nights and hoping to get discovered. You may take odd jobs, but really, you just want to paint or dance or do magic tricks. However, you will feel at risk away from home and away from family, so you should be cautious and seek alliance and friendship wherever you go, as you are vulnerable if isolated.

You will likely be gifted in some way, and you inherit these gifts from the Matriarchal Ancestors; they are behind you, seeking to fulfill their dreams through your work in the world. The Sun dreams of success and productivity, while the Moon dreams of helping, charity, and self-expression. You want to help, so this often manifests in helping and service professions, and it often has an activist bent. You may be a heroic empath, a bleeding-heart liberal, and a social justice warrior. You want equity, inclusion, and justice, especially for the marginalized, oppressed, and minorities. You may work with immigrants and victims of abuse, poverty, war, and so on. This sometimes comes from a place of privilege, which allows you to see these things from the outside. If you experience them from the inside, then they manifest more directly as a voice for the oppressed through art, protest, and service. You seek to do this kind of work through alliance and through associates—power in numbers. Eventually, you will mature into a very generous and sincere person who cares deeply and wants to make the world a better place. You may be drawn to politics, but you are not likely to follow the traditional political path.

Your path in life and career development will be slow and steady; you will discreetly rise to prominence and success, but you may try on several careers and make many changes along the way. Your resume may be all over the place, but you can piece it together into a unique job or service.

Your life will also be episodic and have many chapters, moving from place to place, job to job, and so on. These chapters will not seem related at first, but in the bigger picture of your life, they will make sense. You will look back and feel like you would not be where you are without having followed such a strange and circuitous path; each step leads to the next and makes sense in hindsight. All along, you will be driven by and feel a deep sense of spiritual purpose, seeking the sacred or transcendent. However, negative emotions, fear, and doubt will hold you back, and confidence will never be certain.

Assistants Palace

Tai Yin is strong and somewhat exalted in the Assistants Palace, as the role of the princess was naturally secondary or behind the scenes. Her job was to support others and to make alliances, which is the theme of this House. The only thing that makes this placement potentially inauspicious is the unreliable and unstable nature of the Moon, for the waxing and waning quality here does not help friendship or career.

Generally, however, this Star in this House means that you have a strong, predestined affinity with help and friendship, especially female help, and with subordinates, coworkers, community members, schoolmates, and so on. You will receive a lot of help and support in life in terms of opportunities, jobs, finances, and the like. Depending on your Character, you naturally attract others who want to help and support you. Often, this means that others are attracted to you because of your appearance or demeanor, and you can use beauty, charm, or seduction to your advantage or your detriment. You are naturally predisposed to making friends, connecting with people, and serving them. You want to help others and make the world a better place, and this magnetizes like-minded people with similar values to yours. You effortlessly build and create community and are egalitarian and welcoming.

This is the Ancestral inheritance from the women in your family, who welcome everyone to the hearth and dinner table. If this is unafflicted, then you will find love and support from friends and the community, who will become like family. This may manifest at work, through religious community, or through a meaningful and varied social life. If it is afflicted, this can unfortunately devolve into gossip, slander, or scandal in these spheres. People may want to take advantage of you, and you may even be betrayed. If you depend on people too much, you are more vulnerable to betrayal and rescue, and your life circumstances may be too much in the control of others. You may find yourself entangled with people socially, and this can get complicated.

However, you also have the capacity to liberate a lot of Ghosts here through generosity, acceptance, and service, and selflessness goes a long way toward resolving Fate in this House. This is the strong foundation for a spiritual path and a lifelong interest in lunar activities, with the added motivation of contribution. You are drawn to work in the arts, humanities, medicine, divination, healing, and so on; again, you want to serve, help out, and make the world a better place. This makes you a lifelong student and an excellent assistant. Being a monk, nun, priest, or yogi would make sense here.

This exalts you in a secondary position, and as a career House, this House offers Fate resolution through service work. You may serve a powerful person as second-in-command, such as an assistant, organizer, networker, accountant, or the like. The kinds of professions here are often humble, and this can represent a lot of work that has now been undervalued and demonized as "lesser" or even demeaning. You may work as an administrative assistant, receptionist, cashier, or janitor, or as a model, sex worker, camgirl, dancer, or escort. The Princess may also manifest in a diplomat-like position, but here, you will not be recognized or known for your work; rather, you will work silently behind the scenes like a secret agent. This may be the key to your success, as the spotlight could make things difficult for you, and there is an aspect of espionage here.

The challenge is that the waxing and waning quality of the Moon makes long-term stability at work and with friends difficult; relationships are uneven. You may have a lot of ups and downs in your career, moving and changing jobs, making it hard to develop long-term prospects. You may have many chapters in life, and this results in a lot of different friend groups all over the place. You may have pockets of alliances in different towns after different stints in different places. You may not feel like you really belong anywhere, so you are drifting from job to job, community to community, seeking a home, family, tribe, or parish. You make a lot of friends and alliances and have connections everywhere but no true home. The princess was sent to live in a foreign land and marry into a different family, so you may feel like an outsider trying to gain trust and acceptance.

Superiors Palace

Tai Yin in the Superiors Palace exalts your Fate to contribute to the world through "lunar" work as an artist, healer, teacher, politician, performer, or diviner. Here, the Moon as the Princess is given the spotlight, but she is not the Empress and not yet a leader. She is celebrated for something else, which exalts more artistic or iconic positions. You will achieve success and be celebrated for something "special," which could be your appearance, artistic ability, or singing voice, for example. Of course, this does not mean that you will be famous; you may just wow your church group by singing hymns in front of the congregation, but this kind of thing can lead to alliances that will bring success in life.

You succeed through social grace and intuition, sensitivity, and generosity. Although the Princess is not the Empress, this placement can be a great help for success in a different kind of leadership: You exalt the community and give a voice to the people. This creates a lot of help and backup; you may receive support, donations, and the like, which can lead to success in politics and government work, and the image of the foreign diplomat or dignitary fits very well here. You may run for local office, create a charitable organization, or work in community outreach. Here, you are still suited to be second-in-command and work through service, but on a larger, more public, more influential scale. You can use your privilege and influence to help the little guy. You may also serve a powerful person who works in the public eye and be able to influence things by influencing them.

You will never feel confident or certain, but you will succeed slowly and steadily and have a happy and prosperous life. This placement is not as strong and effortless as the Empress, and the Moon here must work and go through more of a process of waxing and waning to become the icon she is meant to be. Often, this is associated with meeting and learning from a mentor, spiritual teacher, or guide who will train you and help you on your path. There is a process of maturing and growing up through stepping up into a bigger, more responsible position. This may be scary and strenuous and feel uncertain, but this Star here is also associated with good luck. You will be in the right place at the right time and receive all the support that you need in life. The Prince and Princess, Sun and Moon, are always given what they need to succeed, but they must be tested. Here, the Princess has more of a responsibility to lead by example and set the standard, but she must earn it first.

This placement can create a very strong, lifelong interest in spirituality, art, music, literature, and so on. You may be an inspired artist, and here you have the backup to be recognized and celebrated for your gifts. You will be unique, weird, strange, unusual, and talented in some way, and this can be the key to your success in life, so bring it out and show off. Strut your stuff; as the saying goes, if you got it, flaunt it. You may be a witch or wizard, alchemist, healer, diviner, or the like, so experiment and play. This may also manifest through tech work or science, and you may do something like work in a lab, but you do so from a deeper interest in playing with the forces of nature.

However, if the spiritual aspiration is strong, this can also lead to renunciation, and being a monk, nun, hermit, or yogi works well with this image. You may go off into a cabin and chant or pray for the welfare of all beings. Through your practices, you may become like Guanyin and be a force for peace and well-being in the world.

Property Palace

Tai Yin in the Property Palace is very similar to being in the Wealth Palace, in that your association with property and ownership will often be indirect and gradual. If it is unafflicted, then this placement can lead to steady growth and acquisition, but this may not occur until later in life. This is a mix of certain and uncertain factors.

As the image of the Princess implies, you will be provided for, and where you live will be taken care of or shared with others. You may have a parent or partner or family money or inheritance that takes care of housing. Maybe your dad pays your rent while you go to school, or you lived in your uncle's house at one point and then moved in with a friend and stayed on their couch before heading to live on a commune. You may have roommates and/or live in a communal space, college dorm, parish, monastery or convent, or in assisted living. You may seek an intentional community with like-minded people.

The Princess is unaware of the responsibilities of ownership and property; it is taken care of for her. So, you may be privileged or just good at avoiding responsibility through social manipulation. You may even be a "deadbeat"—a couch-surfing hippie who doesn't believe in ownership. Or, where you live may be out of your hands; you go where you are told and may move to and live in certain places for work or family obligations.

The waxing and waning quality of the Moon here can mean a lot of ups and downs, both in terms of interest and actual place of residence. You may move a lot and live in a variety of circumstances. You may live in luxury and poverty as a princess and a pauper. You can live in the countryside or in the big city. You may live with people or alone in the woods. Often, this placement means being drawn more to nature and to living in rural or remote places. You may feel a deep spiritual attraction to a particular landscape and seek the ocean, mountains, or desert. You may seek to do meditation retreats in a cave. Your life may be a walkabout, and you may wander, drift, and move from place to place on a kind of pilgrimage. You may even be drawn to a religious pilgrimage or an Ancestral return. You may leave home and travel throughout your life and then return to your place of birth as you get old.

More practically speaking, you may be set up for inheritance or be given property. This can be in the form of housing or material goods like family heirlooms. If this is unafflicted, then you may be able to gradually acquire land and property and hold on to property that you inherit. There is a strong basis for living as a landlord or landlady, for this supports you indirectly and is a way of working without working. You may be able to use this indirect income to buy more property and so on, owning a lot of property in old age. This is a gradual process and will involve many gifts and graces.

Pleasure Palace

If you have Tai Yin in the Pleasure Palace, then you will probably be pretty weird. In short, you're an artist and love beauty. The lunar nature of the Moon here is very flexible and changeable, and it seeks to feel intuition and to express a spiritual, artistic, and aesthetic sense of things. You will be attracted to and take great pleasure in all things lunar, such as art, music, and personal expression, but it is the feelings beneath and behind the art that you love. You will feel deeply, and revel in expressions of love, devotion, mood, sensation, and so on. This leads to a natural disposition toward drama, theater, performance, and ritual and is often more associated with the blues, melodrama, and morbidity, as the Moon is moody.

The Moon here is clairvoyant and psychic and seeks to divine the ways of Heaven and Earth. You may love things like astrology, Fengshui, personality typing, meditation, yoga, alchemy, and so on. You may be attracted to drugs and altered states and seek to learn and follow a spiritual path through embodiment, feeling, pleasure, sacred sex, and so on. Or this placement may take a more secular route and express through a love of science, physics, or chemistry, but the Moon will draw you to things like black holes, quantum physics, theories of relativity, and so on. You are a mystic, and it must come out somewhere in what you enjoy.

The Moon loves stories of both history and fiction. The Moon wants to lose itself in the drama, so you may read about the past and then dress up and do historical reenactments. Or you may love science fiction and dress as a Vulcan or learn Klingon. You may love Italian opera and watching people pretend to betray and murder each other while singing at the top of their lungs. You are an enthusiastic audience and cry at movies and plays, especially when it comes to love, romance, devotion, loss, and so on. The Moon here is considered a flirt and loves sex and the attention of the opposite sex. You may be a "lady's man" or seductress and enjoy giving and getting attention.

The Moon is fluid and changeable, and the waxing and waning quality means that you may explore and alter what you love in search of certain moods, feelings, or experiences. You can take pleasure in a wide variety of things, and your interests will change throughout your life and go through a lot of phases. You may have a punk phase and lose yourself in mosh pits; two years later, you may be listening to country or bluegrass and wearing big belt buckles. You will develop a broad sense of enjoyment as you follow your intuitions, feelings, and emotions. The Moon may even lead to confusion in this sense—you don't know what you like, because it isn't about the thing itself but about feelings. The Moon is also a bit nonbinary here, and you may be fluid regarding gender expression and sexuality.

The Moon is often associated with a love of nature, and you may travel a lot in search of beauty. You will be attracted to dramatic scenes of beauty like the Grand Canyon or Rocky Mountains. You will seek wilderness and landscapes to be inspired. As you age, you may be drawn more and more toward solitude in the wild. You may be drawn to travel widely but will seek culture, art, and beauty. You will go to cathedrals and temples but also want to go hiking in search of the perfect vista.

As the Princess, this Star also loves giving and charity. You may be drawn toward community service, volunteering, and humanitarian work. You have great empathy and feel the suffering of others, and so you enjoy the feeling of connection that you get from helping them. You may enjoy nursing and taking care of the sick or elderly. Working in a soup kitchen, homeless shelter, or church or community outreach program may be your idea of a good time.

If the Moon is afflicted here, then you may be weary, shy, and confused in matters of enjoyment. All that fluid changeability may go into stranger, darker dimensions, and you may not feel comfortable or safe expressing yourself. You may then seek to enjoy yourself in secret or in underground or private places with other oddballs. This may lead toward fetishes and obsessions as well.

JU MEN (巨門)—THE GREAT GATE

NAME AND TRANSLATION:

Ju Men (巨門), the Great Gate, Great Door, Huge Portal, Gate of Indecision, Gate of Possibilities

Ju, 巨—gigantic, gargantuan; beyond measure; immense.[10]

Men, 門—1 gateway, usu. with two leaves; portal, outer door; entrance (cf. 戶 hu, single-leaved or inner door); e.g., 門人 menren, 門子 menzi, 門徒 mentu, gatekeeper; (Dao.) 天門 tianmen, celestial gate, esoteric term for mouth. a) access, approach to; key, solution to a situation or problem; means, way to do something. b) orifice, sense-organ. 2 family, group, faction, sect, community associated with a particular individual or teaching; e.g., 門人 menren, 門子 menzi, 門徒 mentu, retainer, disciple; 門附 menfu, a dependent; (med.) 道門 daomen, the Daoist community. 3 class, category; section.[11]

Together, we simply translate this as the Great Gate.

ELEMENT: Yin Earth, Yin Water, Yin Metal

TRADITIONAL IMAGE: Elder statesman, disheveled, wearing ill-fitting and unfashionable robes, depicted asleep holding a long beard[12]

ANCESTOR PROFILE: Beneficial Ancestor(s) without specific mandates—represents accumulated possibilities, opportunities, and potentials but unfixed and unassociated with either the Patriarchy or Matriarchy

LUMINOUS PLACEMENT: Rat, Rabbit, and Horse Palaces

DIMINISHED PLACEMENT: Ox, Snake, and Dog Palaces

AFFILIATIONS: Southern Array

Ju Men, the Great Gate, is a bit of a wild card in the Polestar Pantheon, as it is, again, not really a character in the Royal Court. The Great Gate is hard to describe and interpret because it is neither auspicious nor inauspicious; it is not associated with any specific Ancestor, although it is a Yin Star and part of the Southern Array, and so could be attributed to the Matriarchy. Ironically, it is traditionally associated with Earth, Metal, and Water, probably because no one could decide what it is. It is the image of a huge, wide-open gate; that's all.

In the image of the royal court, Ju Men is depicted as a very old elder statesman with a long beard wearing disheveled clothing, who has fallen asleep in the back of the court, holding his long beard aside like a wizard. The idea is that he is very wealthy and connected to a vast fortune and is politically unaffiliated but shows support for whomever is in power. He is supplicated for support and supplies a vast budget to the government for whatever projects they want, as long as he gets to maintain his seat on the court. However, there is little to no oversight into how to spend the funds; they are there and represent great potential. Without direction, the funds go unused and nothing gets done, but with direction, it expands the possibilities.

Liu Ming called this the Mr. Magoo Star. Mr. Magoo is an elderly cartoon character who constantly gets into comedic situations because of his extreme nearsightedness, compounded by his stubborn refusal to admit to the problem. However, through uncanny streaks of luck, his situation always works itself out, leaving him no worse off than before. That pretty much sums up the Great Gate. It is where we stumble about, unsure about who and where we are and what we are doing, but everything still seems to work itself out.

Interpreting the Great Gate is difficult when it is alone and rules a House, because it does not indicate anything other than a lot of potential possibilities and unobstructed opportunities. The Character then makes a big difference in how that possibility will be focused, and it often magnifies the values of the Character, for better or worse. If it is alone, it starts to sound like an affliction because it does not provide focus, values, or direction and can often lead to confusion, indecision, and distractedness. It magnifies the Character, so if the Character is compulsive, like a Tiger, they might be very compulsive. Or, if they are promiscuous and opportunistic, like a depleted Rabbit, then this may get amplified if it shows up in the Partners Palace.

Alone, it can offer too many opportunities and lead to indecision. Like, how do you choose from fifty different brands of toothpaste? This is called analysis paralysis: When everything is equal, and you have a lot of choices, how do you choose? This Star can make us feel lost, uncertain, and spaced out. It, therefore, is mixed but tends to be more auspicious or inauspicious in certain Houses; it is great in the Wealth Palace due to ample opportunity but tough in the Partners Palace, as it can make commitment difficult.

The auspice of the Star is, then, given by the Stars that show up with it, and it is easily boosted or afflicted. If it shows up with other beneficial Stars, then it magnifies the possibilities and makes the influence vast. With the Emperor, it can push us into the stratosphere of life. If it shows up with Ghost Stars, then it can magnify the disorder and affliction and make our addictions and negative emotions even more difficult to overcome.

As an Ancestral Star, this is not associated with any specific Ancestor or with the Matriarchy or Patriarchy, but rather it is kind of a savings account from all the Ancestors. This is where their accumulated opportunity, choice, and possibilities are stored for many potential futures. It is a wide-open door that makes anything possible, so wherever it shows up requires focus, clarity, and discipline to make good of the abundance.

Let's walk Ju Men through the Twelve Houses, assuming that it is alone and rules the House.

Ming Palace

If Ju Men arrives in the Ming Palace as the central image of Fate, then the predestined choreography of your Fate is open, loose, and unfixed but full of possibilities. It is as if all your Ancestors showed up and gave you a blank slate with a trust fund or expense account and said, "Do whatever you want." This is not literal in the sense—it doesn't mean you are wealthy or have a trust fund—but it implies that your life is very open and unobstructed, and in a way, it means that you have no fixed Fate. You are free to choose, free to make of life what you will, which is not something many people can say. Despite the many myths of freedom in the modern world, most of us are quite driven by the patterns of our Ancestral inheritance and past-life predilections. The Great Gate doesn't free us from Ancestral Fate, but if it shows up here, it breaks the centrality of that narrative and lets you form it however you want.

It is difficult to say if this is good or bad, and as is the case with every House, any other Stars that show up with the Great Gate will alter its image. Alone, it tells us almost nothing specific, so it is important to look at your Character and other Houses to form a story. Look to the Emperor, and focus there if you feel lost. However, the message of freedom and choice is important. And you must choose.

If you are waiting for a feeling of purpose, direction, and meaning to come into your life, it may not come. Or you may find it all over the place. You may be presented with an abundance of possibilities; many possible paths, passions, and directions may open before you. All your Ancestors shape your Fate, but nothing is demanded of you here. Your parents and family may not pressure you, and you may even be privileged to have abundant choices and opportunities. You may have many talents, interests, and abilities, but none feel like "the one." Clarity and discipline then become very important, as do Character and conduct.

Your Character gets amplified in the lack of clear direction, so your good and bad qualities may get blown out of proportion, and life may be a demonstration of your Character rather than an unraveling of Fate. Dragons with a ton of ambition and energy may become self-destructive in their endless adventuring; Monkeys may take a lot of huge risks and swing from branch to branch endlessly, playing with all the possibilities. The more dependable and reliable Characters like Oxen, Horses, Roosters, Goats, and Pigs may be able to put this toward greater possibilities like work and service, and the Character image can then hold the key to manifestation. More erratic and emotional Characters like Dragons, Tigers, Monkeys, and Rabbits will struggle without direction or support. It's too big for Rats and means almost nothing for Snakes. Without direction and something to follow, Dogs will become lost.

If it is afflicted, then life may feel like a struggle; you may feel lost, uncertain, unfocused, and without direction or purpose. You may muddle about and feel clueless. Your ineptitude may attract others, and you may then turn to them, following or copying them and trying on all kinds of things looking for answers, but nothing feels right. Without a clear focus, this can spiral out of control, and if Ghosts influence it, the affliction can get magnified in life very strongly. Spiritual practice and direction then become important to give you purpose, meaning, and a way to exorcise the Ghosts.

If it is unafflicted by Ghost Stars, then it is possible to experience great freedom, as this is the Great Gate. Freedom may be wonderful, and you can be benevolent and generous. You may relax and enjoy having a life that is unencumbered by strong pressure and demands. You may be clueless, but this doesn't matter, and life slowly and completely unfolds as you go with the flow. You may just live in the present and react to what the moment presents. Just deal with what is in front of you, and things will work out. If you choose a specific path, then you can have a vast scale of influence and do big things. There is no limit. But you must keep choosing, as whatever you choose will not choose you back. Nothing is what it seems, and you are not what you seem to others. Unafflicted, literally anything is possible here; this is a blank canvas with all the tools.

Ancestors Palace

If you have Ju Men in the Ancestors Palace, then you have an unclear and confusing relationship with your parents and Ancestors. This is almost like having an empty Ancestors Palace. It is not that you are not connected to them, but that connection is open, unfixed, and, unfortunately, vulnerable to all kinds of Ghostly influence. Your Ancestral image is that of a huge portal in which everything comes and goes freely. It is possible to tap into a great wellspring, but it is also possible to feel like there is a black hole that attracts an endless purgatory of unresolved Ancestors.

Practically speaking, you may have an uneven and unsupportive relationship with your parents, grandparents, and family growing up. They are there, but their love feels insufficient, inappropriate, or empty. You don't feel connected or identified; you don't feel Chinese, Irish, Australian, or whatever. You may not have strong connections to grandparents or any warmth around family tradition or values. This may lead to resentment or separation. You may drift apart and struggle to relate. You or your parents may be aloof and distant. The relationship may become imbalanced, even abusive or vampiric.

You may also be adopted and live in a family that you have no blood connection to. You may grow up in an orphanage, foster home, or even homeless. If this is the case, it may be difficult to find or connect with your birth parents. If it shows up in this House with another strong Star, then this connection can be made and turn out well.

The openness of this placement is kind of a vacuum that can attract a lot of unresolved Ancestors and Ghosts; if Ju Men shows up with Ghosts, then the haunting and affliction can be very strong and possibly very dark. Ghosts with the Great Gate in this House are very tough to resolve and may require renunciation. You do not inherit specific Ancestral debts, but rather you suck up a lot of minor Ghosts like a vacuum. Life then may have a lot of muddled, negative emotions, confusion, and a lack of direction. You may feel undermined and like you are constantly messing up, choosing the wrong things, or getting obstructed by minor hindrances and messes for "no reason." When you pray to the Ancestors, you come up empty; they only offer confusion, so it is important here to choose wisely when seeking advice or help spiritually.

If it is unafflicted, then this can be simply an Ancestral pass. You can choose to leave the family or marry into another family, or you may take up a spiritual name and connect with a tradition or religious lineage as your new family. You can become a Chu Jiaren (出家人), "one who leaves the family," which is the Chinese term for monk or nun. This also may be the way to resolve Ghosts and afflictions: You simply need to sever ties and disappear.

It is also possible to tap into a wellspring here, as the Great Gate is generally auspicious and represents a lot of possibilities. You may be able to tap the great resources of your Ancestors and express great generosity. You may be able to attain great freedom and become unattached and unburdened by Ancestral responsibilities and obligations. You are without a name, without origin, and this can become a source of spiritual liberation.

Youth Palace

If Ju Men appears in the Youth Palace, then as in the previous House, you have an uneven, unsupportive, and confusing relationship with your siblings, and youth itself may be a wash. The Great Gate alone doesn't fare well in the relationship Houses and Ancestral Palace either, for it breaks connection where connection is key. Also, the Ancestors and Youth Palaces are a place where Ancestral Ghosts can cause "hauntings," and the openness of this placement makes you susceptible to possession.

If this is unafflicted, it simply means that you have or feel little connection with siblings or family. It is like you are a stranger: *Who are these people? What am I doing here?* You may have no siblings, but if you do, you are probably not close, and you may have little to nothing in common. This is not likely to change, and you may continue to grow apart as you get older.

You may also feel little to no connection to your family and place of origin. You do not feel connected to your hometown, to your school, to your family's religion or traditions, and so on. You may go along with everything, but deep down, you feel out of place and may question everything. You may even be spoiled, but you don't care. You may do well at school, but you get little out of your education.

You may feel listless, uninterested, unengaged, and spaced out. You may have a vivid imagination and live in other worlds, hide in your room, or escape into TV, comics, music, and so on, just to get away from the boring place you live. You may snap out of this as you get older, but you will likely mature slowly. You may be a late bloomer and not find direction until later in adulthood. This may feel like coming out of a fog or depression. The Great Gate simply makes things open, uncertain, unclear, and without direction.

If it is afflicted, then you may experience hauntings in youth and with sibling relationships. The Ghost Stars can become strong here if paired with the Great Gate, as you are opening a portal into the unsettled dead. This may manifest as a vivid imagination or, at worst, trauma, arguments, abuse, addictions, and uncertain and negative family circumstances, like homelessness, eviction, or poverty. These may infect sibling relations and create disconnect, abuse, or arguments between you.

Partners Palace

The auspices of Ju Men in the Partners Palace change a lot depending on Character, for it means that you have no specific Fate with a life partner, and the openness of the Great Gate creates a lot of potential possibilities that make it difficult to choose or settle down. It creates ambivalence, indecisiveness, and possibly promiscuity. So, Character matters. Social and dependent Characters like Pigs, Dogs, Goats, and Rabbits may want and flirt with everyone, making monogamy difficult. Independent Characters like Tigers, Monkeys, Dragons, and Horses may find it very difficult to form attachments, and this can make partners dispensable. More cerebral Characters like Roosters, Snakes, and Rats may have little to no interest at all. Oxen can commit but may be unromantic and have a marriage based on tolerance and routine.

Often, this creates the pattern of going from partner to partner, of going through the motions until one day you are chosen. Someone locks you down, and you go along with it. There is a lot of freedom here. Although it isn't necessarily afflicted or obstructed, the Fate is unfixed and potentially spread all over the place. So, attaining the deep feeling of finding "the one" or forming a lasting connection is difficult. Often, the other person does it for you or at you, and you either accept it and settle down or keep wandering, looking for something elusive you can't find and may not even want. You may be forever single—always the bridesmaid, never a bride. You may also be asexual and not understand what everyone is so worked up about. Or you may be hypersexual, with an insatiable appetite that one person can never satisfy.

Even if you settle down, you may find it easy to be unfaithful, or you may end the relationship when you find something better. You may choose based on resources, security, or social status, and you may marry more than once. You may also marry due to social convenience or religious expectations, and you may want a partner in order to have children, because they are who your Fate is with. In that case, it is better to just get a sperm donor.

The Great Gate is easily influenced by the Stars that show up with it, so another, stronger Star here can add more depth and Fate with a partner, but even then, you will never feel 100 percent sure. But you may be able to commit and put in the work. If Ghost Stars show up, then this placement can easily lead to arguments, abuse, or simply being afraid of or uninterested in relationships. You may very easily "Ghost" others or be "Ghosted." Divorce is very likely when the Great Gate is afflicted, and it may be for trivial reasons.

Offspring Palace

If you have Ju Men in the Offspring Palace, then you have an open and potentially uneven Fate as a parent. This can mean that you have little to no interest in being a parent or that you have no strong Fate connection with your children. Either way, it leads to ambivalence.

You may have no interest, but you have children because your partner wants them. You, of course, love them as a parent but may not be very close, connected, or careful in your relationship with them. You may be aloof, distant, or busy with your other Fate obligations, so you are never home and always working, or you stay out with friends at night while your kids are at home. It may be difficult to maintain your interest as a parent, so this could mean you're a deadbeat parent, or you may make a lot of excuses not to have kids or not take care of them—like, you don't have money or time, or you are irresponsible. Either way, having children or the idea of having children brings discomfort.

You may have Fate with difficult, unconventional, or antisocial children. They are troublesome, reject your authority, reject the family or family values, argue with you, leave home early, run away, marry early, or the like. They may also simply be very different, and so you don't connect well. You have nothing in common; they don't want to be around you and are distant and aloof themselves. You will likely not be very close, and maintaining a relationship throughout life will be difficult. If it is unafflicted, then there is simply openness and freedom. They may not be troublesome, but it is easy for them to leave home, drift apart, and be unattached.

If it is afflicted, then you will likely be haunted by unborn children, incomplete pregnancies, abortions, miscarriage, infertility, and possible circumstantial obstructions like money, timing, and difficulties in a partnership. This can be just as true for men and women; men can have Fate for abortion and miscarriage. You may have a lot of hardship and stress when it comes to your relationship with your kids. They may need medical care or have special needs. Or circumstances may force you to work two jobs, and so you never get to see them.

This may also mean that you have an enormous sexual appetite, rebellious sexuality, asexuality, gender dysphoria, or antisocial sexual conduct. You may, therefore, never have kids or have a lot of illegitimate children, or this could mean that you adopt, become a stepparent, or work with kids who are not your own.

Wealth Palace

If Ju Men shows up in the Wealth Palace, then your Fate with money, wealth, and income will be varied, uncertain, and unfixed but not necessarily obstructed. You simply have no clear Fate with money, but you also have great potential and a lot of opportunities to earn money and will likely do well financially despite yourself. The image of openness here can manifest in many ways, and as usual, Character matters, for the interest in money will vary a lot among those with this placement. More ambitious Characters will pursue and make use of the opportunities, and more conservative Characters will likely have anxiety due to the uncertainty here.

The Great Gate alone and unafflicted means that you may not be all that interested in money and that you don't take it seriously; it just isn't a concern, which is not to say that you are well off. You can be happy either way; rich or poor, it doesn't matter. You can be happy as a stay-at-home mom or dad or with a humble job.

You may be frugal and save your spare change in jars or collect coupon codes. You may work a bunch of side jobs; you might wait tables and save your tips. Maybe you live in a studio, make arts and crafts, sell them at a farmer's market, and use the money to buy more supplies. You don't spend money on anything other than what you need. In the long run, this pays off, and you may do very well in the end, despite never earning anything significant. You may work a very ordinary job with very average pay, but you consistently add to the pension fund and retire well-off.

Traditionally, this placement is associated with "windfall": inheritance or money from secondary and unusual sources. The money earned from a salary, wages, and more ordinary sources may not be significant, but you may have significant wealth from family money and investments, and you should probably play the lottery from time to time, because this placement is also associated with sudden big money from out of nowhere. Stocks, bonds, and so on are advised.

If this is afflicted, it can create many struggles with money. You may not do well with the uncertainty, and the image of windfall can turn to loss; you may bet and lose big. Or you may experience bankruptcy, debt, or poverty, struggling to make ends meet. You may juggle a lot of part-time jobs, live paycheck to paycheck, and not know where the next meal will come from. You may also be foolish, naive, or stupid with money. You may be duped, robbed, or conned out of it. You may also have expensive tastes but no money, so you live beyond your means and get yourself into trouble.

Health Palace

Ju Men in the Health Palace is very difficult to interpret, as it makes you a bit of a medical mystery. Your constitutional immunity is a wide-open gate, a revolving door, and both illness and recovery are open, uncertain, and potentially vulnerable to outside influences and internal possession. Your health is characterized by inconsistency and unevenness, and there is no easy story to tell. You do not conform to standard diagnosis and treatment, for something about you defies explanation.

As an Ancestral inheritance, this placement is a strange gate between illness and recovery: You have inherited the pivot place where Ancestral energy comes and goes freely, inviting both Ghosts and Beneficial Ancestors, but none stick around. You are a conduit. So, what does this mean?

Your state is always changing; you may be sick often and can go from well to sick and back again seemingly without cause. You may suffer from many strange and inexplicable symptoms that come and go and change all the time. This is called "wind" in Chinese medicine. The openness of the Great Gate means that, without strong boundaries, you are easily "possessed" by outside influences physically, mentally, emotionally, spiritually, and so on. Physically, you are easily invaded by cold, wind, and damp weather. Mentally, you can be influenced by others and take on their symptoms. Emotionally, you are very empathic and can take on others' negative emotions. Spiritually, you are easily possessed by the unsettled dead, Ancestral or otherwise. The hordes of unsettled dead in your family get easy access to you as a path to resolution, but you are also open to being possessed by local Ghosts and nature spirits, so you may get sick on a hike, riding the bus, or walking through a dark alley.

You are, in general, very vulnerable to getting sick, and during your life, you may contract several things that turn into subclinical, low-grade illnesses, like Lyme disease, Epstein-Barr, mold toxicity, fungal infections, malaria, fibromyalgia, and so on. You may collect a host of symptoms that doctors cannot explain or treat, and so your complaints get disregarded and you are told that it's all in your head. You may manifest a one-in-a-million medical mystery illness that will appear in textbooks. You may be accident-prone and illness-prone, and this can also lead to sudden onset of illness, strange infections, and accidents that come out of nowhere.

You may experience misdiagnosis, mistreatment, overtreatment, and potentially harmful medical advice. The doctors think you have something, so they give you medicine, but this causes more problems. So, they treat that with new drugs and cause more problems, all without ever understanding or treating the original problem. You may spiral into a series of health problems caused by medicine and not know how to get out of it. Your medical condition may end up so complex that no one can understand it. It is important, then, not to get overtreated and not to get caught up in hypochondria and addicted to treatment, which is very possible here. For you, overindulgence and poor choices can lead to chronic digestive disorders and poor health.

You also may get better suddenly without cause. You are prone to miraculous cures as well as strange diseases. You may go into miraculous remission, walk after being in a wheelchair, regain your sight, or the like. You are capable of faith healing, the placebo effect, and healing through prayer, ritual, meditation, and psychedelics. With all that being said, it is impossible to rely on any of that, because there is no system to how the Great Gate works. Caution is best, but you will also be drawn to trying anything and everything.

Unafflicted by Ghost Stars or sharing this House with stronger Stars, this can all be very benign and go well. You may not be suffering from anything dramatic—just lots of little things. Another, strong Star here can help create structure, as you may struggle with constant distractedness when it comes to health routines: You forget to take your pills, miss appointments, and have many ups and downs with diet, lifestyle, exercise, treatment, and so on.

This lack of focus makes compliance difficult, so it is very important to cultivate strong self-discipline and routines. And it is equally important to stick to one system and not jump all over the place looking for new practices—dig one well a hundred feet deep rather than a hundred wells one foot deep. Don't try Ayurveda, then Traditional Chinese Medicine, then go to the hospital for antibiotics, then fly to Peru to do ayahuasca, then go for a colonic, followed by a vegan crash diet chased down with handfuls of supplements. This is a recipe for disaster, so pick one of these and stick to it. Seek out qualified, highly skilled, and experienced doctors, for you will be very easily misunderstood.

This placement is traditionally associated with purgative treatments like traditional Panchakarma in Ayurveda. From time to time, purgative treatment can be beneficial because you tend to accumulate a lot of gunk, both physically and mentally. Just don't overdo it and get addicted to purging, for purging can easily be overdone.

Strong Stars can become a large gateway for healing, and with careful study and practice, you can turn your own patterns of illness into a way to heal others. When it shows up with the Great Gate, the Oracle can be miraculous and you can heal many as a conduit of something greater. When it shows up with the Magistrate or Priest, you can become a great learned doctor or spiritual healer.

If this is afflicted by Ghost Stars, things can go very dark, making it even more important to cultivate strong boundaries and routines. This may very well manifest as an intractable and incurable disease that starts during a sickly youth or from an accident. You may also be quite affected by strong negative emotions that not only undermine your health but cause you to make decisions that get worse and worse until they undo you. This can spiral out of control easily. Like always, Character makes a huge difference here. More hypochondriac or erratic Characters can spin out of control because of the Great Gate, and the more disciplined and routine ones can contain it.

Career/Travel Palace

If you have Ju Men in the Career/Travel Palace, then your Fate with your work in the world and your contribution to society, as well as with traveling and your relationship to your birthplace, is unfixed and likely to create a life of wandering, confusion, and uncertainty. You are not strongly connected to your place of birth, and your Ancestral mandate for work in the world is not set: Your Ancestors set you free to choose, which may show up as a supportive family who does not pressure you and provides a lot of opportunity. Or it may mean that you are not connected to your family at all. If the Great Gate shows with strong supporting Stars, then this may give you a direction in life, but alone here, it is a bit confusing and also potentially liberating. This is the case for Ju Men in any of the career Houses.

You will not likely feel a strong calling or purpose or have a clear direction in life. You may feel like the world is your oyster and that there are many possibilities, but you don't know what to do. This openness often leads to a strong interest in travel, and you will probably travel widely. You may work in a traveling profession and even live abroad, which can sometimes offer a Fate Threshold to a new life in a new place. However, if the Great Gate is alone, you will not feel truly at home anywhere, so you become more of a nomad. You may wander through life with a strong sense of freedom or frustration. On the one hand, you can become a wandering yogi and live a life free of attachment to purpose or place. You may be born in Idaho and end up a monk in Thailand. But, without a spiritual path, this Star here can lead to despondency.

You may change jobs and careers often, looking for something meaningful, but never find it. Your resume may be all over the place, and you may be a jack-of-all-trades, master of none. You may settle into something eventually, but it is best to look elsewhere in your chart for meaning. Perhaps you have a strong Fate with family, children, or pleasure. A career isn't everything. With strong Stars in the other career Houses, this can turn out well and open into something powerful, for the Great Gate can magnify influence. But it will take some searching. If not, then it is best to embrace being free. You can change jobs every few years, travel a lot, and enjoy the journey of being unfixed and open to change.

Like a secret agent, you can powerfully reinvent yourself and become a new person. You can change your name, appearance, and profession and start over multiple times. This placement lends itself to jobs that are open, like consulting, traveling sales, acting, performing music, and now, digital nomadship. The trouble here is getting traction. You may work very hard and not feel like you are getting anywhere; progress or "success" may be at a standstill, as is your commitment and dedication. So, it is good to be strategic and find a way to link all of your experience, skills, and interests together into something unique.

If this Star is afflicted by Ghost Stars, then it can go dark; you may be forced to change jobs, immigrate, or be exiled due to war, or you may experience many negative emotions that make the open, unfixed nature of this Star even more difficult to deal with, leading to compulsive or impulsive decisions that could upend and even ruin your life.

Assistants Palace

Ju Men in the Assistants Palace doesn't mean much, especially if it is alone and rules the House. If it shows up with other Stars, then it can lead to moderate success in more open-ended, service-oriented professions like consultant work, but otherwise, this is not a strong indication of a career. Your Fate regarding service, helping others, and being an assistant is unclear and not a mandate.

This placement can even mean that your attempts to help others fail, especially if it is afflicted by Ghost Stars. Affliction here means that you do not have a strong foundation for helping others and little traction for service work. So, you may be well intentioned and work hard, but things can go very wrong. Perhaps you can't get funding or clients, or no one hires you. You may be indecisive and full of doubt regarding work, which could undermine you and even turn others against you. You may have big, innovative ideas, but affliction here can lead to disaster for yourself or your subordinates due to poor planning, communication, or execution. People may lie, cheat, steal, or embezzle money from you or your company, or you may be possessed to do the same. They may also make accusations, false or otherwise, against you: of criminal activity, abuse or harassment, or various "isms"—racism, sexism, ageism, ableism, and so on. So, caution when starting a business is a good idea. Also, Ancestral Ghosts can manifest in some dark ways here, so self-reflect before making big decisions.

Often, this placement relates more to relationships with friends, co-workers, schoolmates, and so on. You may struggle to make friends and build lasting relationships or community with people outside of your family. You may meet many people and have a huge social circle, but have few to no close friends. Or friendship just doesn't last, because you move, change jobs, and so on, and constantly must start over again with people. Your Fate with support from others is uneven, and people easily lose interest in or forget about you. You may be abandoned.

Exalted and/or with strong positive Stars, the Great Gate here can lead to luck and success from others, such as helpers, employees, or friends. It can also expand your scope of influence through service work. If you start a nonprofit, charity, or altruistic organization, it can help and reach many people. You may have a big audience, lots of clients, patients, donors, and so on.

Superiors Palace

The more open and unfixed nature of Ju Men tends to go well in the Superiors Palace. As usual, alone this Star doesn't say much, but it can be strongly shaped by positive Stars that show up with it. You will likely have big dreams and ambitions but may be unfocused. Therefore, other Stars that show up in this House can help provide direction, especially through teachers, mentors, guides, gurus, and so on. Strong Stars can be very influential teachers, and the Great Gate may mean that you have many teachers and/or many opportunities. This can also lead to apprenticeship or succession into a role, eventually becoming a strong leader.

Often, this role matures later in life, after you change jobs and directions a few times. There are big dreams here, and sometimes it takes a few tries to find something suitable or realistic. You will feel unbounded and struggle with boundaries, borders, definitions, or limitations. So, you may have to hone your dream through many explorations, then, later in life, you settle into something lucrative and succeed. You have the potential to make big changes, and eventually you will be honored and appreciated. The Great Gate means you can reach and influence many people and make whatever you do big and grand.

Unafflicted by Ghost Stars, the world is your oyster; you may have a lot of opportunities to succeed, and you can manifest great generosity and influence. You can be imaginative and innovative, with great resources. However, affliction here can cause you to wander from job to job. Because of the unfixed nature of this Star, you can be unstable, unfocused, and easily lose interest. Nothing sticks, and you can't choose what to do. Or, like in the previous Houses, you may work very hard but cannot get traction. You take one step forward and two steps back—incomplete work, training, and so on—which can make it hard to finish things or make progress. Generally, it is your own lack of focus or enthusiasm that undermines you here, as this is one of the more auspicious placements for this Star.

Property Palace

If you have Ju Men in the Property Palace, then you have little fixed Fate with place or ownership of property. This is a mixed bag. Like many placements, this can create a wandering life; you may not feel at home anywhere. You may feel little connection to your birthplace, culture of origin, family religion or traditions, native language, and so on. This is common among second- and third-generation immigrants—even more so today, when it is so easy to pick up and move to a new place. Some Stars create a "walkabout," meaning a life of pilgrimage, but not this one, for here there is no ideal or set destination you are trying to reach; you are just not connected to where you are. But this is not inherently a bad thing unless it is afflicted, which can lead to a dark and haunted sense of eternal wandering.

If it is unafflicted by Ghost Stars, you will likely move a lot, always renting, never owning much. You can pick up and move to a new town or a new country with relative ease. You are never stuck anywhere, but this may come with the challenges of not feeling rooted or developing long-term friendships and community. But life can be an adventure with many opportunities. You may travel a lot, move abroad, and live out of a suitcase occasionally. For the most part, you can be fine with this, depending on your Character, but in the long run it may be unfulfilling. This can be sorted out, and you can settle later in life and eventually own property, but more domestic and Yin Characters will struggle with transiency, making it an affliction.

If Ju Men has the support of strong Stars, then property ownership can happen sooner, but it will likely come through connections with other people. Even if you settle down and put down roots, though, you will not feel like you have a forever home. You will still be drawn to travel, and you may still move around. The best outcome is to own property but either sell or rent it, so you can move and travel freely. Owning anything will always be tentative. Positive Stars also support investment, speculation, and growing wealth through property, for the Great Gate can always enhance and magnify possibilities.

If this is afflicted, then Ancestral Ghosts will haunt your sense of home and stability and cause you to wander sporadically. You may be homeless, never owning anything, or you may always rent a place and live in poor conditions. This is difficult to confront, but looking into family histories of exile, migration, war, immigration, and so on, can help you understand why home feels haunted. Ghost Stars often mean that Ancestors died at home, and the Great Gate can magnify these feelings and create astro-geomantic patterns that push you around in life, making home and ownership very unstable.

Pleasure Palace

If you have Ju Men in the Pleasure Palace, then pleasure is not fixed; it is wide open, and so you may struggle with finding a deep or meaningful sense of personal satisfaction or pleasure, which can lead to a sense of searching, boredom, and even longing. Character and supporting Stars then make a big difference, as the openness of the Great Gate magnifies character traits and pursuits. If it is alone and unafflicted, then it simply means you are adaptable and open-minded; your sense of pleasure is not fixed, and you can enjoy almost anything. Often, this means taking on the interests of others and/or being easily distracted.

While this is not a bad thing, it may be hard to achieve depth or mastery in any one thing, for you are attracted to and interested in just about everything. You are broad and unbiased and find everything fascinating. You may jump around and study a little bit of it all, taking up new hobbies all the time, reading books on various subjects, and changing your interests on a whim. You are flexible and can find something to love about everything. This can be shallow, and you may love pop culture and easily take up new trends. You love every movie you see and every song you hear and find it hard to be critical. Or you may be easily swayed and follow people with strong personalities, charisma, and conviction, for you lack these things and find them attractive.

The Great Gate can lead to boredom—nothing to do, no sense of fun, confusion, indecisiveness, and so on—and you may then struggle with enjoyment and relaxation. So, you might always work because you can't handle the spaciousness of having nothing to do. You are always busy—working out, cleaning, organizing, planning—to keep boredom at bay; this is especially true with the more active Yang Characters. Yin Characters will be more apt to embrace boredom and be at home doing nothing.

Without fixed worldly interests, this placement can lead to spiritual interests; the bigness of the Great Gate can lead you to be interested in big, universal, spiritual ideas. So, you find pleasure in absolutes like God, the universe, and enlightenment.

This can also lead to a big appetite for fun and pleasure, especially with strong Yang Stars. You may be a glutton and easily overindulge in food, drink, and sensual pleasure. This can also lead to promiscuity, and you may be attracted to anyone who wants to have a good time. Compulsive and adventurous characters like Pigs, Dragons, Monkeys, and Tigers may struggle more in this case. You may also love being in the limelight, as you want to be big, grand, or famous.

Afflicted, this placement can lead to dark places: overindulgence, drugs, addiction, and so on. Ghosts in this House can be magnified and lead to risky behavior, bad judgment, and dangerous miscalculations. You may also have trouble understanding the value of things or people, which can be very destructive. You may never have a sense of enjoyment, and life can be devoid of meaning and purpose.

THE FOUR HIGH RANKING STARS

NOW THAT WE HAVE COMPLETED OUR DISCUSSION OF THE FOUR HONORABLES, the more secondary influences in the unraveling of Fate, we can now move on to discuss the Four High Ranking Stars. These Stars are naturally "tertiary" in the big picture of Ancestral Fate, but they can nonetheless be very influential. These are Tian Tong (天同), the Vassal; Tian Liang (天梁), the Roof Beam; and the two Wen Stars, Wen Chang (文昌), the Magistrate, and Wen Qu (文曲), the Priest. Together, these Stars represent the underpinning influences of our support systems, alliances, education, and Fengshui that are often integral to the big picture of our lives.

In the image of the Royal Court, the previous four Stars—the Sun, Moon, and General, with the Great Gate being a wild card—were strongly connected to the royalty and the inner sanctum of the Emperor and Empress. The Sun and Moon represent the strong Fate of becoming, and the General represents our Fate of survival and strategy. Their patterns are often deep and meaningful in our lives, but they serve the Currents of Fate represented in the Emperor and Empress. The Four High Ranking Stars are not in the inner sanctum but represent an important bridge between the royal court and the outer kingdom. These Stars, again, represent allegiance, position or Fengshui, and education. They represent the structure and operation of the royal court through protocol, law, rules, regulations, and tradition.

The first Star, Tian Tong, the Vassal, is not related to the Emperor but is very close to the Prince or Sun. A vassal is a military image, sort of like a duke, and represents the emperor's loyal local leaders, who served the emperor and ran the various states in the kingdom. They were how law and royal decrees were distributed to the kingdom. They were sort of like samurai, for their power came through their loyalty, and they received protection and land in return for loyalty and military service. Without loyalty, they had nothing and could be replaced. Therefore, they had to be very hardworking, and they had to maintain and forge political alliances. The Vassal Star represents a strong, hardworking Yang Fate resolution through unity, loyalty, and service.

The second Star, Tian Liang, the Roof Beam, is not so much a person, although it is depicted as a senior statesman in the royal court. The Roof Beam is the image of real estate and national and local identity in the kingdom, and it represents the roof beam in a traditional Chinese house, which was central in any home and put in place before construction. As such, it represents architecture, Fengshui, and the importance of placement and space in our lives.

The third and fourth High Ranking Stars are a pair associated with the Chinese term Wen (文), which is connected to language, culture, writing, and civility. Wen Chang, the Magistrate, and Wen Qu, the Priest, are a special Confucian pair that represents how two different aspects of education and training help us unravel our Fate. The Magistrate is associated with formal education, school, college, and so on. It is the deity associated with taking exams and becoming a magistrate. The Priest is associated with religious and spiritual education and represents Daoist court ritual, music, and study. The Priest represents how inner work, meditation, and religion and spirituality help us to unravel Fate.

If the Wen Stars show up together, they are very powerful and can be a threshold to unraveling Fate in the entire Chart through spiritual revelation. It is important to understand that these Stars are supportive, and their patterns manifest more through conduct than through larger patterns of Fated occurrences.

TIAN TONG (天同)—THE VASSAL

NAME AND TRANSLATIONS:

Tian Tong (天同), the Vassal, Celestial Unity, the Heavenly Allegiance, the Sky Fellowship

> Tian, 天—refers to the sky or heavens; the highest cosmic principle or force.[1]
>
> Tong, 同—share with or in; join. a) coincide with, conform with. b) similar(ity), like(ness); 同心 tongxin, of like mind. c) same(ness), identity; coequal; e.g., 同時 tongshi, at the same time, simultaneously; 同人 tongren, the same person. d) identical to, no more than. 2 together, in concert; e.g., 同坐 tongzuo, sit together. 3 同人 tongren, "fellowship," name of the 13th hexagram of the Yijing.[2]

The term Tong (同) means to come together or unite in allegiance, so these two characters together can be translated in many ways, such as "celestial unity," "heavenly allegiance," or even "sky fellowship," but we know this as the Vassal of the Royal Court, whose power comes through allegiance to the Emperor.

ELEMENT: Yang Water—active connection and alliance

TRADITIONAL IMAGE: Depicted as a bright young military officer wearing a helmet and armor, holding a sword, in a ready, fighting stance[3]

ANCESTOR PROFILE: Beneficial Patriarchal Ancestor(s), direct or aunts and uncles, cousins, step-relations, and so on; strongly connected to uniting tribes and clans; seeking loyalty, benefit, and accomplishment through family allegiances

LUMINOUS PLACEMENT: Rat Palace

DIMINISHED PLACEMENT: Monkey Palace

AFFILIATIONS: Northern Array—strong allegiance to the Emperor and close to or competitive with the Prince

Tian Tong, the Vassal, is a lesser but nonetheless very powerful, accomplishing Yang Star. Despite being among the tertiary influences, it can play a very significant role in the unraveling of our more worldly and familial Fate, so much so that it often sounds like a greater Star. When it is unafflicted by Ghost Stars, it offers dedication, hard work, creative adaptation, sociability, cooperation, self-sacrifice, motivation, and Yang Fate resolution that can be very significant in career and relationships and in the acquisition of wealth, property, and resources. However, as a Lesser Star, it is easily afflicted, and therefore its benefits are often lost to pettiness, competitiveness, excessive idealism or ambition, ineptitude, argument, and so on. This Star is tribal, feudal, and associated with the dark side of human clan, tribe, and cult behavior, including the manipulation and abuse of power and resources.

What is a vassal? A vassal was a person who received protection and land from a lord, king, emperor, or the like in return for military loyalty and service. So, the vassal was not related to the emperor but was given a title, land, and money to govern an area of the kingdom. Vassals collected taxes, enforced the law, and conscripted people into a local army, which they would then run. A vassal is like a duke or earl, as they owed homage and loyalty to the emperor in exchange for the right to hold land. This is an image of feudalism, which was central to ancient China, just as it was in most of the medieval world as the basis of clans and tribes. Tian Tong reports back to the Emperor Star and serves the bigger picture of our Yang Fate in a tertiary way, working out issues of Ancestral Fate and loyalty that can sometimes help us but sometimes lead us astray.

Astrologically, this Star translates to very specific aspects of our Ancestral Fate. Specifically, it relates to how our Yang or Patriarchal Ancestors made, brokered, forged, and maintained alliances to survive. It represents the loyalty of the family and the politics that ensue through marriage, business, and war. It is hardworking and dedicated but easily falls into the darkness of politics, negotiating and seeking benefit through self-interest or family interest, very much like Vito Corleone in *The Godfather*. This can represent direct Ancestors, but often, the Fate of the Vassal is associated with aunts and uncles, cousins, step-relations, and so on.

So, wherever this Star shows up, you inherit the legacy of these kinds of Ancestral patterns. The Fate in that House, then, is often relational and involves working to forge and maintain alliances. It is often tribal and comes with complex familial patterns. At its best, it generates strength, love, and loyalty from these patterns and is very active and thorough in resolving Fate.

The Vassal is also a military image, and as such, this Star is associated with bravery, courage, and strategy, which is very similar to the General. It is disciplined and follows a code of conduct, like a samurai. But, unlike the General's, its loyalty can change. Afflicted, this Star can represent feuds, betrayals, arguments, personal grudges, and so on. This can be how an alliance goes bad. The Fate here can get complex and sticky, but this darkness is resolved through working it out with others.

The tertiary aspect of this Fate here also implies that it can keep you entwined in worldly Fate, rather than leading you to become free of Fate altogether.

Let's walk the Vassal through the Twelve Houses.

Ming Palace

If Tian Tong, the Vassal, shows up in the Ming Palace, then your Fate is very Yang, and there is a lot to do, but you are also quite capable and have good leadership and social skills that will translate easily into business, medicine, politics, and so on. You are also Fated to be disciplined, strategic, and naturally dignified, strong, modest, and charming.

The nature of this Fate, and the central theme of unraveling it, is alliance. You are not alone and cannot be. You are here to work it out with others; you need them, and they need you. This can come in the form of a strong and central relationship—one that will require loyalty and dedication, like a teacher, colleague, or close friend—but often there is a tribe or clan here. This can be your blood family or a community that you create or join, and/or a business or career that you create that becomes central to your life and relies on you working with others.

You inherit the family legacy of clan, tribe, and community. As a Yang Star, Tian Tong represents Patriarchy and connects you either to your father's side or to all the men in your family. You will likely be surrounded and supported by family and friends, and you will have a strong connection to both the living and dead in your family. You may have a lot of siblings, aunts, uncles, cousins, and so on, and you are born embedded into a complex family tree with a lot of ongoing deep relationships and stories, and possibly age-old feuds, legacies, debts, and so on. This is also the case in the Ancestors and Youth Palaces.

Loyalty and the family are important here; this placement is very *Godfather*—you never go against the family—and your Fate could unravel around and through them in a very central way. Strongly social, loyal, and domestic Characters like Goats, Ox, Dogs, Pigs, and Rabbits will take to this, but more independent and rebellious Characters like Tigers, Dragons, Monkeys, and Snakes will struggle. If it is afflicted, this can lead to some complex relationship dynamics and consequences.

Because of the more worldly nature of this Star, life and Fate may feel like they keep you entwined or embroiled in drama, arguments, feuds, disagreements, and so on, especially if it is afflicted. There may be a mandate to work a lot of this stuff out, and an afflicted Vassal can be hard to resolve. The more you reject the drama here, the more it will come back to haunt you. The more you work it out, however, the more you will be free to focus on the more personal, central aspects of your Fate, like the Emperor in your chart.

Again, it is all about alliance, about getting help and giving it. This Star follows and serves the Emperor, and it does so as a Vassal. The more you focus on creating community and making alliances, the more your Fate will unravel. It is through relationships that things happen. You may be called to lead and create, but you may also be a mediator and work in service of something greater. This is the "samurai Star," so you may be called to serve selflessly, with unquestioning loyalty. This may be to a person or to the family, but it could also include a higher ideal, cause, or goal, like your purpose is to serve your church, synagogue, or sangha as something like a rabbi, priest, monk, or the like. Or you may own a shop, restaurant, or cafe or lead a team, committee, or volunteer organization that serves and connects people.

If this is unafflicted by Ghost Stars, then you will have a life of accomplishment with just rewards. You can succeed, be financially well off, and become a leader or honorable person in society and/or in your local community. You can resolve Fate in this lifetime but will likely stay connected and obligated to your tribe, clan, or community. You will have many supporters who stick with you and honor you, and you will be respected for a life of service and commitment.

Ancestors Palace

If you have Tian Tong in the Ancestors Palace, then you have a strong Fated connection with your Ancestors, with the family tribe or clan, and potentially with a hardworking, vassal-like Patriarchal Ancestor, who may be a parent, grandparent, or a significant aunt or uncle, cousin, or the like; as this is a Yang Star, it can be anyone from your father's side or from among all the men in the family. You will feel great family loyalty and may want to serve the family like a vassal. With this placement there may be a very strong, very big family clan; this is also the case for Tian Tong in the Youth Palace.

If this is not afflicted by any Ghost Star, then Ancestral Qi is a blessing in life and a source of great inspiration. You will likely feel an affinity with a particular stream within the family and associate them with a feeling of lineage and inheritance, which could be material, religious, intellectual, or based on talent. It is worth doing genealogy here and connecting to your lineage; you may have a soulmate in your family line whom you identify with and learn from. You may inherit their skills and disposition.

Your parents will be very proud of you and adore you, and if this is not afflicted, then you will be very close to them. With affliction, however, there can be tribal or clan disputes, family feuds, and so on. This Star tends toward passion and can lead to warlike factional mindsets, so pride, adoration, and love can easily turn to criticism, rejection, neglect, or abuse. You may also struggle with specific aspects of your Ancestral inheritance and find darkness in their stories; this may cause inner conflict and problems with self-esteem, but it may also harden you and cause you to identify with an Ancestral cause like persecution, oppression, and so on. Loyalty and identity are crucial here; you may feel the plight of your people deeply, and you may be subject to the same struggle and Fate to liberate those family cycles.

The Vassal is hardworking and practical and serves the Emperor, and this may manifest as a very hardworking parent who does everything they can for their child and family. This is the classic story of a parent who works hard to give their kid a better life than they had, which is a common theme in history. So, look to your parents and grandparents and find out what they gave up and sacrificed for you; gratitude and debt then turn into mutual support, and you may support them in old age as they supported you.

The Vassal is also a military image, so there could be military history here, like a grandfather who served in war or a parent in the military. Or there is simply something disciplined, structured, and routine about the way your parents raised you—enforcing rules, lessons, chores, and so on. They may have forced you to play sports or learn a musical instrument as a kid, which you might have hated. However, you then grew up with a tremendous skill or sense of personal responsibility that you are very grateful for, as it becomes the key to your success. Your life and career may be a continuation and expression of the hard work and struggle of your parents or Ancestors and the lessons they taught you.

Youth Palace

If you have Tian Tong in the Youth Palace, then the same sense of tribe, clan, and family unity applies, and it manifests more directly as a strong influence in your childhood and sibling relationships. This placement often manifests as a large family with many siblings, cousins, aunts, uncles, nieces, nephews, and so on, spanning generations, with big family gatherings, reunions, and a sense of tradition, religion, and so on that color and shape your childhood.

As a Yang Star, the Vassal here means there is a strong basis for the resolution of Fate in childhood, and you may do and accomplish a lot as a youth. You may be a precocious, talented child who is the pride of your family and community. You may win spelling bees, be football team captain, or help with the family business. The military image here is very "team sports." The Vassal is depicted as youthful, so the Star fits well in this House, but it wants to grow up quickly and act like an adult. You may spend your childhood trying to be a grown-up, and your youth may be so busy that you miss out on the wild or silly fun.

You may have a strong sense of tribe, clan, and connection with your brothers and/or sisters. You may be part of a team, a squadron, or a unit, and the military image here binds you with a sense of duty, mission, or service to the family. These relationships resolve a lot of Fate and can be strong throughout life. If this is not afflicted, then you may give and receive support from your siblings throughout life, and holidays, family reunions, and so on will be full of ritual, meaning, and nostalgia.

If this is afflicted, then sibling and family relations can get dark—full of betrayal, arguments, and abuse. Again, the tribal nature of this Star can tend toward feuds, and in this House, blood feuds can lead to bitterness and resentment later in life. These entanglements can shake family loyalty and drive people apart. But working that stuff out can be profound and lead to healing family wounds, trauma, and so on. Negative emotions and Ghosts easily unseat the Vassal, and in this House, there is something generational about these conflicts that plays out with your siblings.

Partners Palace

Tian Tong in the Partners Palace is a very strong basis for Fate resolution through partnership, but it is easily unseated here by negative emotions and Ghosts. Affliction here is very important to work with and through. In general, in this placement there is a strong Fated connection with someone via deep emotional ties based on loyalty and mutual benefit and alliance.

If this is unafflicted, then that strong Fate can turn into a successful and devoted partnership. You are likely to be very compatible, mutually attracted, and able to work extremely well together. You will make an excellent team, and the military image here manifests itself as a very practical, efficient, and devoted partnership that has good communication and is able to have both romance and a shared sense of duty and responsibility. Marriage can become a wellspring of happiness, and strong loyalty can lead to a lifelong friendship. You can and will accomplish a lot together and create a strong sense of family and clan through partnership.

However, if this is afflicted by Ghost Stars, then it tends to lead to arguments, insults, and betrayal, and that strong loyalty and connection can cause you to be deeply hurt. Unfortunately, your sense of loyalty can also lead to staying in bad relationships that get plagued with arguments and feuds. Eventually, this often does lead to divorce, which can be depleting and devastating. If you work it out, then you can remain friends and/or be great separated parents. Experiencing this sense of hurt and betrayal can also lead you to give up on relationships altogether and become celibate or monastic. This placement can also manifest as being widowed.

Offspring Palace

Tian Tong in the Offspring Palace provides a strong basis for the resolution of Fate through being a parent, and its military image associated with loyalty calls to mind the sense of duty and responsibility of both parenting and of children to their parents. As a Yang Star, the Vassal here implies the birth of a son, but traditionally, this placement is associated with daughters, so really it can be either. Either way, your children are Fated to be talented, precocious, and active but also respectful, well behaved, disciplined, and easy to care for. They will be a source of great pride, and if this is unafflicted, then you will have a strong relationship throughout life, and your children will return the sacrifice and take care of you in old age.

The military image of this Star means that you will sacrifice a lot and work very hard for your children. You will feel a strong sense of duty, responsibility, and loyalty and, therefore, work to be a competent parent with well-defined family values, rules, and standards. You may be a strict and firm parent who enforces bedtimes, chores, and so on. You will have timetables and take your kids to scheduled soccer practices and playdates. Everyone brushes their teeth and goes to bed on time. The family you create may be like a platoon that works well together, but you will also create a sense of tribe and tradition. The blood ties and sense of closeness here are powerful. Likewise, your kids may be very hardworking, responsible, and disciplined, doing well at school and in extracurricular activities and ultimately doing well in life.

As a tertiary Star, the Vassal will cause a lot of Fate resolutions here that will be rewarding, but they will not be central to life. The process of parenting will be a support and duty that you must work at, but it may feel like it is in service of the greater good, as the Vassal serves the Emperor.

As usual, Ghost Stars can unseat the Vassal, and this can create conflict. Your children may rebel against you, disobey orders, and find it difficult to relate to you and your values. You try to enforce rules or share or create a tradition, and they reject it. Loyalty means that this is workable, but you may need to work through a lot of issues later in life. Ghost

Stars here can also manifest as miscarriage, difficult pregnancy, and difficulty with the circumstances of parenting, such as being a hardworking single parent who sacrifices everything with little help or reward.

Wealth Palace

Tian Tong in the Wealth Palace is generally auspicious and signifies what most people expect from work. It indicates prosperity through effort that improves over time and through frugal discipline and saving. It represents being paid fairly for hard work, and it is often associated with the service industry, as the Vassal is a loyal servant to the Emperor. This can manifest as a wide variety of professions, but the key is loyal service and achieving success through someone or something else. This placement does not lend itself to solo or entrepreneurial ventures, but you can flourish in managerial positions and administration; this is very middle management. Owning and operating a franchise would also be very Vassal-like.

If this is unafflicted, then it is a solid basis to do well in life and eventually establish wealth and prosperity. Discipline, frugality, and a bit of austerity are key. Stability and security come from enforcing a value system and sticking to it. You must and will develop good habits around work, saving money, paying bills, managing credit, and investing intelligently. This is the slow and steady improvement of compound interest over time that eventually pays off. This strategy can also work well in the Property Palace to build wealth through property and real estate. Sometimes this placement is associated with modest family inheritance, as there are always themes of clan, tribe, and alliance here, but again, it is modest and will come with a lot of work.

If the Vassal is afflicted by Ghost Stars, then this can lead to a lot of Fated troubles with money. You may be very hardworking but mismanage your finances, lose money, and accrue debt. You may worry a great deal about money and struggle with things like medical or legal bills, maxed-out credit cards, or poor, miscalculated investments, and sometimes the discipline of this Star can be applied in a very compulsive way, like becoming a professional gambler or obsessive collector who blows all your money on some addiction. You may be haunted by Ancestral Ghosts that push you toward a lifestyle you cannot afford, and so you go into debt and leave behind no other legacy.

Health Palace

Tian Tong is generally very auspicious in the Health Palace, as it is moderately strong and inspires great personal discipline. As a Yang Star, the Vassal here represents a constitutional inheritance from the Patriarchy: the active, dynamic cultivation of health through "work." This is the health of the Ancestors who thrived working together cooperatively in the community. Your sense of self and health will depend on your sense of community and of working with and toward a purpose.

Health, longevity, and strength are made from disciplined, consistent routines and regularity, as this Star is a military image that thrives with structure, order, and clear direction. As a tertiary Star, the Vassal here implies a strong resolution of Fate through health cultivation, but the pursuit of health is not central to life. You will actively resolve Fate by engaging with health cultivation, but as an underpinning of life that feeds into everything else and helps to establish a basis for things like work and relationships.

You will thrive through exercise and physical practices, and you will likely be coordinated and athletic and skilled at sports. You may have a lot of routines, like waking early, taking supplements, and being intentional about diet, lifestyle, and hygiene. These will create structure, and if they break down, so does your health. As a Yang Star, Tian Tong means you will rarely be sick, and you will likely tough it out and try to cure yourself when you are. If you are injured or ill, you would rather work on it with home remedies than seek help.

However, if you do seek doctors or healers, you will make the ultimate patient, following orders and complying with directions, especially if you respect the doctor. You will be very thorough and respond well to conventional treatments.

Unlike other placements, the Vassal here is a strong contender against Ghost Stars and easily exorcises Ghosts through personal discipline. In this House, the Vassal does not get easily tangled in negative emotions, which is not the case in other Houses.

If the Vassal is afflicted by Ghost Stars, then you may struggle with psychosomatic issues and a lot of minor, subclinical complaints, but again, you will manage them well with a healthy routine, exercise, and self-discipline. The Vassal tends to suffer from physical issues like pain and problems with mobility and circulation, and as such, it is associated with heart and blood conditions. As a Yang Star, it tends more toward excess and injury, and the resulting stasis and stagnation, than infection or deficiency problems. However, Tian Tong is traditionally said to be susceptible to poison and toxins.

The Vassal heals best in spring, and rest and sleep can be a very powerful form of recovery; burnout and overdoing it are likely, as this is a very active Star. Sometimes, you can undermine yourself with too many routines and practices, and you can make this worse by trying too hard. Your body and mind may be at odds, and you may be too controlling when it comes to health. However, this discipline ultimately leads to longevity and survival.

Career/Travel Palace

Tian Tong is very much at home and somewhat exalted in the Career/Travel Palace and the other career Houses, as they exemplify the nature of the symbol. The Vassal is a very Yang, hardworking Star, eager to follow and willing to fight to prove itself and its loyalty. It seeks power, advancement, and promotion and is generally ambitious and willing to work with others to achieve goals. The Vassal is persevering and driven by a mission, so you will likely find a career and stick to it, eventually finding success and happiness. This is the Ancestral inheritance of those who worked hard to succeed through alliance, and your Ancestors have given you everything you need, from stick-to-itiveness to the necessary connections. As such, you will resolve a great deal of Ancestral Fate through your work in the world, and this may require travel or relocating.

The key to success here often comes through others; you will have an affinity with mentors, teachers, and bosses, and you may be an apprentice, successor, or subordinate. You will succeed with the help of others through networking and connections, and opportunities will come from loyalty and from the chain of command. With this placement, it works well to stay with a job, work your way up the ranks, and eventually become an owner, manager, or team leader. The sense of teamwork and tribe is strong, and this can translate to a family business or a business that feels like a family. You will also do well to work for powerful people, as the Vassal is like a samurai. If you faithfully serve someone or something, you will succeed. Indecision, laziness, and doubt will undermine your career and progression in life.

The Vassal here is considered a strong Fate Threshold for immigration or living and working abroad. You may travel a great deal in search of your place, tribe, or family, and this Star may require you to relocate and start a new life in a new place. This may be crucial for the manifestation of your Fate. Vassals were often appointed to manage a faraway territory and often had to move at the behest of the emperor. Your career or life's mission or purpose may demand that you move; this may be to a whole new country where you must learn a new language and culture, but you will thrive there and find your true home.

As usual, Ghost Stars easily afflict the Vassal, which can lead to anger, frustration, and wasted energy in this House. You may be betrayed, duped, or undermined by others on your path in life. You may work very hard but struggle to get ahead, missing opportunities and promotions. You may even be overqualified; resolving affliction here often means working beneath yourself with humility and accepting help from others. However, the disciplined, hardworking, and consistent nature of the Vassal will eventually figure things out, and you will always land on your feet. You will likely have a fascinating resume, and you may have a late-blooming career or faulty start in life that does not really manifest results until you move or travel.

Assistants Palace

Tian Tong is most at home and exalted in the Assistants Palace, as it is the Star of loyalty, self-sacrifice, and service. As such, the interpretation of this Star is straightforward here: The vassal is not the emperor but the emperor's loyal servant. You will resolve a lot of Ancestral Fate through helping others, and you will thrive in service professions or as a subordinate or second-in-command. This represents unquestioning support and loyalty, and again, like a samurai, you will naturally become an outstanding assistant and friend. You are likely to be generous to a fault, depending on your Character.

The act of being such a loyal and generous helper will also inspire many to help and support you. You will have lots of friends, helpers, cheerleaders, and so on, and this may involve a very active social life. This is the Ancestral Fate of connection and clan, and you will have a lot of Fated support and opportunities that come from working together with others as a team with a shared mission or goal. Following the chain of command and working your way up the ranks works well for you, and the learning process of apprenticeship and successorship may be an integral part of your path.

Any teamwork is exalted here, as are all professions of service and assistance to others. You were born to serve; this is where your power lies. You naturally connect with others and connect people with each other. You lead through teamwork and lifting others up. You work behind the scenes and wield power and influence through others. The Fate of your career depends on other people, networking, and giving and receiving help. You will be honored and respected by those you help and benefit from those relationships. Respect and loyalty here come from integrity and kindness.

As usual, the Vassal is vulnerable to affliction from Ghost Stars, which in this House can lead to being taken advantage of and to misplaced or abused loyalty. You may be too nice, naive, or trusting, which may be a disaster. You may also follow or work for someone who lacks integrity, and you may suffer from their mistakes or abuse. Scandal may be part of your Fate. Here, it is essential to remember that the power of loyalty does not come from being perfect or worthy; sometimes, our path involves having to atone and save face with others, even when we are not at fault. We should not abandon people, and occasionally true friendship means sticking with someone, within reason. You may have to help and serve someone who falls from grace, or you yourself may fall from grace and must apologize and make good publicly. Many Ghosts can be resolved in this process, for this is the Ancestral Fate of work in the community, which is where so many of our Ghosts lie.

Superiors Palace

Tian Tong is also very much at home in the Superiors Palace, but here it gets pushed more into roles of leadership and enhances your opportunities for success, contribution, and Fate resolution through career and work. The Vassal is by nature more at home in service through the Assistants Palace in service of the Emperor, but the role of the Vassal is also one of leadership. The key is that leadership here is more reluctant and done with political motives to help and benefit others. The affinity for service and helping professions is therefore still strong, such as working in healthcare, education, public service, politics, and so on. But here, the Vassal may thrust you into leadership in these fields, or at least increase your spheres of influence and your ability to reach and help more people. This may be modest, or it may be significant. It may also increase your ability to innovate and contribute to your field as an expert.

Either way, you inherit the Ancestral pattern of communal hard work and determination, and you will become very capable and eventually respected. You will slowly work your way to the top of your chosen path, and you may lead a team, manage a company, or get involved in politics and government. Positions like mayor, governor, judge, congressperson, and so on are very Vassal-like. Personal habits, discipline, and Character matter a great deal here, and if this is unafflicted, then you will likely have a powerful work ethic and persevere with a strong sense of mission, purpose, and determination, like a soldier or samurai. Loyalty to a worthy cause is important.

This is the Ancestral Fate associated with clans and tribes, so your path will include the welfare and interests of the community, and you will want to make life better for others. Work should include these notions of contribution, and the more you get involved in local leadership, whether through work or religious community, the more you will be fulfilling these Ancestral mandates.

Here, the possibility of success from the chain of command, from apprenticeship, or from inheriting a role, job, or position through a boss, mentor, or teacher is greatly enhanced. You may have a significant Fate with a teacher or mentor, and you will learn from them, follow in their footsteps, and eventually take over in their place. This may manifest through career, but it could also be through a spiritual or religious lineage, and you may form a relationship with a guru, priest, rabbi, or the like.

If this is afflicted, then your life and career may have a rough start and many ups and downs. Your path may be a battle, but you have the capacity to fight through it. You may be too focused and intense in your determination, and this can lead down some dark roads and generate a lot of negativities or create blind spots in your integrity. You may also be challenged or caught up in scandal with others who lack integrity, especially people in authority. Be cautious of leaders, teachers, and authority figures in whom you place trust and loyalty, and likewise, be cautious in these roles yourself, as you may abuse the loyalty of others.

Property Palace

Tian Tong is of mixed auspice in the Property Palace. Despite its connection to clan and tribe, it is not considered a strong basis for the ownership of property or for having or establishing a strong local identity. The emperor put the vassal in charge of managing land or territory, but their sense of ownership was very conditional and tentative. They moved at the behest of the emperor and had to leave everything behind if ordered. In the Career/Travel Palace, this can mean moving to a new country, town, or state for a job, but in this House, you move all the time, often rent, and live and die far from where you were born. Where you live is determined by all the other aspects of Fate, such as work, relationships, and family matters. You may return to your Ancestral home many times, but you will not stay there or remain connected in any practical way.

Although this placement is generally weak for ownership, you can acquire property later in life and will eventually settle down. You can become a landlord and rent to others, but you yourself will not feel identified with any specific place. You will likely not be interested in material possessions or local/cultural identity, but you will not be poor, homeless, or bereft of community either. The Vassal here can get involved in local government or community and eventually develop a sense of home, but often, this is much later in life, once all the other matters of Fate are settled.

If this is afflicted, then this can lead to loss of house or home or difficulties with renting, landlords, and so on. But the Fate here is steady, and despite ups and downs, you will always be able to work things out and land on your feet. The military image of this Star means that you will be responsible and disciplined with possessions but also minimalist and happy with very little. Anywhere you lay your hat can become home, and you will likely travel a great deal, live in many places, and be able to start over again and again.

Pleasure Palace

If you have Tian Tong in the Pleasure Palace, then your sense of enjoyment is deeply connected to others and a sense of shared loyalty and tradition. Here, the feeling of tribe, clan, and community is central, and the Vassal is associated with being a traditionalist. Character can alter this a great deal, but enjoyment is generally social. It is also very physical and connected to your sense of work, purpose, and discipline.

So, you will enjoy friendship, companionship, and the admiration and company of others. You will want to enjoy yourself with others and share in a sense of camaraderie, teamwork, unity, and social harmony. Individual or private enjoyment will seem odd to you. Therefore, you will love things like watching and playing team sports and participating in political, cultural, or religious events that bring people together. Concerts, festivals, parades, and so on will naturally draw you in, especially if they are connected to a sense of loyalty, tradition, cultural identity, ethnicity, or tribe. So, you may love to go to the local Greek festival, pride parade, Chinese lantern festival, Dia de Los Muertos, European and South American Carnival, Oktoberfest, and so on. The Vassal loves these kinds of traditions, so things like opera, classical and traditional music, museums, and the like will inspire you.

You will also be attracted to others and draw others to you. You will be naturally flirtatious and gregarious, and you will magnetize and gather people to you; you will, therefore, be good at initiating parties, gatherings, and so on. This is the Ancestral pattern of gathering people in the clan together for a shared purpose, so you may be the life of the party or a great social influencer. This can translate to many different spheres or arenas—social, religious, political, and so on—but for many Characters, your greatest pleasure in life will be in connecting people and socializing. Afflicted, this can lead to scandal and conflict.

This placement can manifest, if not socially, then as the military image of physical discipline. You may love and be obsessed with work, working out, training, cleaning, and so on. You may be all work and no play, but your work *is* your play, especially if it is connected to a sense of purpose, a worthy cause, or a mission that benefits others. If this is afflicted, then it can lead to obsession, addiction, and overdoing it, creating discord in all of the above.

TIAN LIANG (天梁)—THE ROOF BEAM

NAME AND TRANSLATIONS:

Tian Liang (天梁), the Roof Beam Star, the Milky Way, Heaven's Ridgepole

Tian, 天—refers to the sky or heavens; the highest cosmic principle or force.[4]

Liang, 梁—1 bridge; plank bridge; sometimes pontoon bridge. 2 roofbeam, ridgepole. a) rafter, crossbeam. b) lintel, a door or window. 3 fishing-sluice, fish-weir. a) dam.[5]

Here we have the usual term Tian (天), and the term Liang (梁), which is specifically associated with the placement and Fengshui of the central roof beam, or ridgepole, of the traditional Chinese home, later adopted by Japanese architecture. So, we translate it as the Roof Beam Star or Heaven's Ridgepole, but it is also associated with the Milky Way.

ELEMENT: Yang Earth—associated with the dynamics of placement

TRADITIONAL IMAGE: Elderly senior statesman with white hair in an official cap and gown carrying a tally, account book, and abacus; not associated with politics but with land, home, architecture, geomancy, and Fengshui; a conduit of imperial favor[6]

ANCESTOR PROFILE: Beneficial Ancestors and Ancestral legacy of placement, acquisition, inheritance, and legacy associated with home, land, property and real estate, and resources

LUMINOUS PLACEMENT: Rat, Rabbit, and Horse Palaces

DIMINISHED PLACEMENT: Snake, Goat, and Rooster Palaces

AFFILIATIONS: Southern Array

Tian Liang, or the Roof Beam Star, is associated with the Milky Way, which appears like a spine, bridge, or ridgepole in the Heavens, and it is unique among the Twelve Ruling Stars as an architectural image, representing astrology's connection to geomancy or Fengshui, the auspice of placement. Again, the term Liang refers to the central roof beam of a traditional Chinese home, but it also represents bridges, planks, dams, and anything that supports a structure and dictates the flow of Qi through a space. As such, it represents the principles of geomancy and Fengshui as they unfold in our chart in specific relation to our Ancestors' connection to place, land, home, identity, ethnicity, nationality, and so on.

Traditionally, when building a home, it was customary first to choose an auspicious location that accorded with the principles of Fengshui. Then, an auspicious day would be chosen for construction, and the roof beam would be ceremoniously placed first, before any other construction began. The names of the Ancestors would be carved into the beam, representing the family's lineage and connection to the land, and the rest of the home would then be constructed around the roof beam. It would henceforth act as the hearth and center of family life. The family would cook, eat, gather, and tell stories around the roof beam.

In the image of the royal court, Tian Liang is not so much a person, although it is depicted as an elderly senior statesman who oversees the allocation of property, real estate, construction, and engineering projects and of building and maintaining national and local identity within the kingdom. The effect of the Roof Beam, then, is multifold but often very physical, practical, and grounded in place and position. In the Royal Court, the Roof Beam is not directly connected to the Emperor but to all the Stars; it relates to the security and protection derived from position, reputation, and identity gained from living in certain places over long periods of time. Politics and national, cultural, or ethnic identity are very much a factor of location over time, for the history of the world is one of ever-shifting, dynamic borders, territories, and languages; it is from these that we build traditions, and it is due to these that we go to war.

Interpreting the Roof Beam Star begins, then, with the principles of Fengshui, and wherever it shows up, we must first ask the question of placement, especially in the Houses associated with travel, career, and property. Are we in the right place? This is the most fundamental question. Fengshui, simply put, is the idea that things flow properly if they are in the right place, and the laws of nature and space function in such a way that, if you place things correctly, you produce harmony. If things, people, buildings, furniture, and so on are not placed properly, they generate discord. Similarly, the theory of aesthetics states that nothing is inherently ugly; it is only misplaced.

The Roof Beam can indicate either a strong connection to the place you already are, which is rich with Fated opportunities and connections, or it can indicate that you are in the wrong place and that these Fated connections are elsewhere. Life may be a walkabout or a pilgrimage to your proper place. As your Fate may not unravel until you are placed properly, this Star can be very significant when making interpretations.

In relationship Houses, Tian Liang can indicate that your Fate with particular people is connected to a specific place, and you may meet an important person somewhere specific or in a certain Fated environment. This may be after a long search or in a serendipitous meeting, and this Star is associated with romance as such. It represents continuity over time, and seeking feelings of familiarity and destiny from the well-worn grooves of the past. Sometimes these are obvious and sometimes not, for we as modern people are quite displaced, and sometimes these grooves come to us from distant Ancestors.

Regarding career, wealth, and property, the Roof Beam represents real stuff and real estate and practical skills associated with the tangible world, architecture being the most obvious example. It can manifest as a felt connection to buildings, cathedrals, temples, pagodas, tombs, and so on, and also as a love and appreciation for the beauty of materials like stone and wood, for the texture of cloth and clay, and for trinkets, objects, and collectibles.

In our body and health, the Roof Beam represents our spine, bones, and physical structure; it is our physical and Ancestral inheritance from a place, like being able to digest dairy because you come from a long line of farmers or nomads. It represents the connection of our spirit to the body, which may be solid or otherwise. It also represents a spiritual connection to land, nature, geography, and the spirits of mountains, rivers, plains, and so on and a connection to directions, seasons, and astrological transits.

The Roof Beam is generally auspicious and considered positive, but it can be challenging, for it may call us to travel, move, or go on a pilgrimage. It may be a call to connect with your Ancestors and their ancient land, or it may simply represent the boons of already living in intimate interconnection with the land and your tradition. When afflicted, it calls to mind the Ghosts of land, borders, territories, migration, immigration, exile, and even war, for all these things determine where and how we live.

Let's walk the Roof Beam through the Twelve Houses.

Ming Palace

If Tian Liang appears in the Ming Palace, then the most central and important theme of your life is Fengshui, and the auspice of placement is crucial to the unfolding of your Fate. There are many ways to interpret this, but it begins by looking at where you are and asking, *am I in the right place?* This is not an easy question to answer, but it is a deeply personal one that only you can determine. If you have the Roof Beam here, then you were born with a divining rod, an inner compass pointing you where to go and even digging at you with this question of place. You are inherently sensitive to the principles of Fengshui and to the auspice of placement. You can feel if things, people, buildings, and so on are misplaced, and you are sensitive to nature, seasons, astrological transits, and so on. You will naturally seek to harmonize yourself and the environment.

If the Roof Beam is unafflicted, then the answer here tends to be *yes, I am in the right place.* However, it can also inspire a meaningful and positive path of searching for, finding, and relocating to a new and true home. Life will inevitably feel like a journey home, both physically and spiritually. Affliction by Ghost Stars, however, tends to make the answer *no, I am not in the right place*, but this is not a rule. It can go either way, and many of the themes are the same either way. Regardless, your Fate is intimately connected to the stories of your Ancestors—their connection to land, place, tradition, identity, ethnicity, religion, language, and so on—and how these stories play out in your search for home. Character, naturally, plays a big role in this, for domestic Characters like Rabbits, Pigs, and Goats will make home very easily, and more independent Characters like Tigers, Dragons, and Horses will seek adventure and strike out on their own much more readily.

If the answer is a yes, then your Fate is deeply connected to the home, town or city, and so on, that you were born in, and you will strongly identify with that place, your people, and/or the geography of your home. You are intertwined with your Ancestors. You may have strong ties to family and/or land. This may come with some continuity of inheritance, which may be in the form of tradition, language, or religion—like perhaps you are born the son of a rabbi in Brooklyn, and you make aliyah to Israel—but it may also be physical in the form of inherited land, property, finances, or business, like being born into a family of cattle ranchers.

If the answer is no, and if the Roof Beam is afflicted by Ghost Stars, then you will not feel like you are in the right place. You may feel or even be displaced, and you must find your true home. You may not identify at all with the people or place where you were born, and so you search, and the path of finding your place and people is where your Fate unravels. This may mean immigration, learning a new language, practicing a new religion, or following a foreign teacher. Your Fate in your birthplace may even be chaotic, violent, or war-torn, and you may be a refugee or immigrant. Ghost Stars here can reveal stories of death, tragedy, exile, and injustice in relation to land, community, and home. Your Fate of relocation may be out of your hands, and you may be along for the ride through patterns of escape, rejection, or revolution.

Sometimes, the Roof Beam in the Ming Palace manifests as a deep calling to work with Fengshui, architecture, design, art, craft, and so on. You may be inherently talented or skilled in these arts and crafts, and you are born to express them. Sometimes, it can simply indicate that your physical home or environment is crucial and central to your flourishing, like once you get your own home, it becomes your fortress, and everything falls into place.

Ancestors Palace

If Tian Liang appears in the Ancestors Palace, then you have a mandate to connect or reconnect to your Ancestors and their homeland. You have a deep physical and spiritual connection with your Ancestors and their traditions, language, and geography. Here, the ties to your direct family—parents, grandparents, and so on—are stronger, and the theme of home and finding a home are not as important. The sense of inheritance and connection is key. This is all about the clan, tribe, or lineage. Your inheritance can be substantial here, and it may be physical or financial, in the form of money, property, or heirlooms.

If this is unafflicted, then you will likely be very close with your parents and grandparents; you are connected to family elders, and Ancestral energy permeates your life with richness. This, again, may take the form of tradition, religion, language, rituals, customs, and stories. Genealogy can be very powerful here, and the more you know and inherit from your Ancestors, the more they become a wellspring of positive energy. Learn their language, and call to them in dreams. You may find a soulmate among your Ancestors, and you may either be a returning Ancestor or have a call or mandate to return.

This placement traditionally indicates a strong call to return to place in the form of a pilgrimage. So, if you have this, book a ticket back to where your Ancestors are from. I can't stress enough how important it is to go there and make contact physically. Find out the towns and villages they came from; touch their graves, clean the gravestones, and make offerings. Go to the temples or churches they visited. Meet your cousins and distant relatives. Eat their food, wear their clothes, sing their songs, and listen to their stories. This will be a profound source of transformation, and it will liberate many of the family Ghosts. Again, if you have Tian Liang in this House, go and stand on Poland, Indonesia, India, or wherever. Going there is the most important, for wherever connections are calling you back will find you and unfold when you do.

If Ghost Stars are afflicting the Roof Beam, then this process of pilgrimage and return may be full of pain and suffering, but this only makes the liberation and exorcism more profound and cathartic. You may discover dark stories of tragedy, betrayal, and loss. You may inherit deep feelings and emotions from these experiences as well as stories that may or may not make sense. The more you learn, the more revelatory the experience.

If you already live in the place of your Ancestors and have a deep continuity there, then you have the charge to maintain and preserve it through custom and tradition. You are the steward of your family. This may mean becoming a priest or lineage holder yourself. You will receive lineage teachings and stories and carry them on for another generation. This may be a family tradition, or you may be called to practice and inherit a foreign tradition. You may have spiritual Ancestors outside your family line that you must reconnect with. The call to pilgrimage here may be traditionally religious, and it can be powerful to go to Bodhgaya, Mecca, Jerusalem, the Vatican, or the Kumbh Mela, for example.

The Roof Beam here generally means that your parents are long-lived and remain a positive influence in your life. It can also represent a strong and influential relationship with a grandparent who is a mentor and guide. It may indicate taking over and inheriting a family business. And, as always with this Star, Fengshui is key, so the auspice of placement—opening the pathways for the connection, flow, and return of Ancestral Qi—is important.

Youth Palace

If Tian Liang appears in the Youth Palace, then the Fengshui of your childhood is very significant, and the environment you grow up in plays a significant role in the unraveling of your Fate. Your sense of home and the geography of your youth shape who you are and your sense of self. Home, family, and your connection to your siblings are rich and filled with a sense of place, tradition, and even literal texture, like having deep memories of the shag carpet or wallpaper of your childhood home. Fengshui here may manifest as moving a lot, like as an army brat, or as a significant move to a new home that shapes you. This placement may also manifest as the strong presence of a family business or tradition that you work in or contribute to as a kid.

Your childhood home, neighborhood, and other places of your upbringing are deeply imprinted on your memory and fill you with nostalgia. You are likely a shy, imaginative child who loses yourself in imagination, wonder, and play. You may have imaginary friends and go on adventures with your toys and stuffed animals. This placement often means having few or no siblings, but if you do, then you will play vivid, imaginative games together and go on adventures outside and inside. Your connection to your siblings and childhood friends will be deep and based on these shared adventures, games, and places. You may play war with toy guns and relive the memories of Ancestors who died on the battlefield.

You will feel a deep connection to the landscape, hills, rivers, creeks, forests, and city streets of your childhood and explore them after school and during summer vacation. Hollywood movies like *The Sandlot* come to mind, where something like playing baseball as a kid is an important memory for your whole life. The place and culture of your childhood become central to your identity, like growing up as a hippie, greaser, or rebel without a cause. A significant place, like the location of a summer camp or band camp, a vacation or travel location, or where you had adventures with the Boy Scouts, can also shape you.

You will be drawn to nature—playing outside with your hands in the dirt, going swimming in the lake, climbing trees. This is the childhood most people idealize and hope to give their kids but seem to fear more and more these days. If this is unafflicted by Ghost Stars, then you will develop a strong body and a sturdy sense of physicality and adventure as a kid.

If this is afflicted, then all these things can be haunted by Ancestral Ghosts, which may cause a disruption in your sense of home that also leaves a deep impression on you for life. You may be stuck, forever dreaming about trauma in your childhood home or reliving your childhood patterns. Your home may be filled with arguments and abuse, and this may cause you to leave home early and strike out on your own to look for a new home or family or a sense of freedom and independence.

Partners Palace

Tian Liang in the Partners Palace is considered an auspicious placement for romance and love, and the influence of Fengshui implies an influential factor of place or property in the relationship. Traditionally, this placement is associated with a discrepancy in age, so you may partner with someone much older or younger. This also may manifest as a discrepancy in class, language, culture, ethnicity, and so on—a difference that comes from partnering with someone from a different place. This partnership may give you social status or prestige, or it may involve moving together to a new life.

Here, the Roof Beam implies that something about Fengshui plays an important role in meeting and partnering with someone. So, you may meet them in a specific place, like school, work, or church, but there is something serendipitous and special about the environment that brings you together. The relationship may bloom and blossom in that place or in relation to that place. Or, your courtship may involve special places, memories, trips, adventures, and so on that make the relationship special and give you a sense of nostalgia about meeting. The relationship may also develop and become stable through living or working together, and it is in that environment that you bond. In general, the relationship will have a process of stabilizing and becoming solid, maturing, and forming solid boundaries and a sense of home. If you have this, you should focus on creating a home and family together. Finally, this placement may mean that you must move, travel, or live abroad to meet your partner. They may move to your country, or you to theirs.

Often, Tian Liang in this House means meeting a like-minded and attractive partner. You will share mutual interests, views, and values. This may bring you together across a cultural or religious divide, or it may be the thing that attracts you to each other in a disparate environment. If this is unafflicted by Ghost Stars, then you can fall in love and be very close and mutually supportive. Hence, the association with love and romance can go beyond infatuation into long-term stability. You will share resources, property, land, and wealth. This is a partnership ordained of Heaven and Earth, and you should feel fortunate to have this. The marriage ceremony, too, should be special and involve Fengshui, cultural and religious elements, and strong family ties.

If this is afflicted, then there can be division over property, wealth, resources, and place, and these elements may play a significant role in discord. You may marry for money or lose money and property in a divorce. You may argue or fight a lot in the home; living together may make you fight, as you may find the relationship plagued by differences in lifestyle or means. The strong potential for love here makes the potential for heartbreak all the stronger, but this can be a path of maturation, and the positive nature of this Star means it can be worked out for the better because of the deep ties that you share. Love here can grow stronger over time.

Offspring Palace

As a Yin Star, Tian Liang in the Offspring Palace implies a strong Fated connection with a daughter or a shy or sensitive son. Traditionally, this Star has a feminine aspect, and sons are said to rebel or reject authority at home. As per usual, this Star is associated with Fengshui and the home. So, creating a home and a sense of family is an important part of this Fate. The environment may also play a significant role in raising children. Growing up on the mean streets of New Orleans or in the rural backwaters of Appalachia may be crucial to their development and Fate. Their physical house, too, may be very influential in their development, and you may even homeschool.

Having children may be the beginning of an important process of maturation that forces you to become stable and create a home. The Star brings the sense of home and the auspice of property and placement through being born. So, you may actually find a home, buy a house, or settle down with their arrival, when before you were nomadic or irresponsible. They may bring you a better job, more money and resources, or better luck with property simply through being born. You may give birth to a "princess" who demands a "castle." The Roof Beam here forces you to put down roots and grow up.

The home you create will be very important and meaningful. You should and will create a strong sense of family, tradition, and values, whatever that means to you. Creating special or unique family traditions, perhaps around holidays, sports, or meals, will be part of your family legacy. Creating legacy and inheritance is important. This may be financial or in the form of property, but again, it may also be a legacy of ideas, values, or life lessons. Your kids will remember and honor what you teach them, and their gratitude will cause them to love and support you in old age. This is all about giving and receiving support, and the more support you show them in childhood, the more they will, in turn, show you as adults.

Unafflicted by Ghost Stars, children are very obedient and resourceful and do well at school. But affliction here can amplify differences and disharmony at home, especially if your children are boys, although this tends to resolve as they mature. You may create too much structure, and they may find it overbearing or suffocating. There is a tendency to overparent here, and too much control can spark a rebellion. Affliction may involve a child running away, relocating with a relative, living with the other parent, or being sent to a military school or juvenile hall.

Wealth Palace

Tian Liang in the Wealth Palace is considered auspicious for prosperity associated with property, real estate, products, material goods, or manufacturing. It is also traditionally associated with being paid to utilize Fengshui through interior design, architecture, construction, landscaping, graphic design, art, sculpture, or the like. It also has an association with teaching and practicing medicine or astrology. Again, Fengshui is the key principle, and here it can manifest in a variety of ways.

Your income and wealth may be connected to property and equity, and you may be a successful landlord or property manager. You can do well investing or receive money from an inheritance, a legacy, or a settlement. You are capable and responsible with money and will be and/or have a very competent financial adviser or advisers. This is about the legacy of the Ancestors, so you may inherit family money, title, or property; however, if this is afflicted by Ghost Stars, you may inherit their debt or legacy of problems.

Generally, this placement means that wealth grows steadily throughout your life, you are very well off in your later years, and you will leave behind an inheritance to your kids or a legacy in the form of a business, organization, or charity. The

Fengshui aspect implies that you retire with a very nice home and many possessions, or you may be a collector of fine art, muscle cars, Persian rugs, antiques, and so on. It also implies that location may be crucial to your success. You may be in the wrong place, and moving to the right place, getting the right job, or getting connected with the right people may be the determining factor in building wealth.

Your wealth may be tied to others, and a community, parish, or donations may support you. It may be tied to land or collateral. If not, wealth may manifest through creative means, so if you have a talent for Fengshui as an artist, designer, decorator, builder, craftsperson, or doctor, you can be paid well for it. On a deeper level, the Roof Beam here is about real wealth, which is skill, material, intelligence, resources, and so on rather than just paper money.

If this is afflicted, then your investments can go poorly. You may lose property or a business or have things stolen from you, or you may be spread thin over many complex investments. This can create debt and loss, but you may also receive a resulting windfall, like through insurance settlements. You may become motivated to build and create wealth and a legacy by an experience of failure or from a drive to transcend the poverty of your family or upbringing. Yours may be a rags-to-riches story, or it may involve renouncing wealth altogether to be a monk or hermit.

Health Palace

If you have Tian Liang in the Health Palace, then your health is intimately connected to Fengshui, to nature, to seasons, and to all your Ancestors. If this is unafflicted, then you inherit a very strong constitution and immunity provided by all your Ancestors; you are the embodiment of your Ancestors and connected to their land, food, and traditions. As such, it is important to connect with their traditions, foods, and practices, and going on a pilgrimage to the places of your Ancestral roots could be integral to your health, especially if this House is afflicted by Ghost Stars. Going on a pilgrimage can liberate Ancestral Ghosts and potentially heal you of illness.

Essentially, you are the product of your environment and connected to it physically and spiritually. Of course, everyone is, to a degree, but if you have this placement, this connection to place is part of your Fate. Your health is affected directly by both your immediate environment and that of your Ancestors, so if they are different, then you have two dynamics at play.

The first dynamic is that your health responds to your immediate architecture and Fengshui, which means to the buildings and structures you live and work in and to the shifting dynamics of nature: the hills, rivers, mountains, local nature spirits, and seasons and seasonal changes. You may heal and recover in response to the dynamics of these places and to the Qi of the calendar; as such, your health may feel like a mystery, especially if you are in a city and work in a cubicle. Simple things like cleaning and rearranging your furniture, too, can have a profound impact on your health, as can living in dirty, disorganized environments. You may be ill or unable to heal because you are in the wrong place! So, hire a Fengshui consultant.

The second dynamic is that the particulars of your Ancestors also shape your health, so whether they were farmers, fishermen, nomads, or city dwellers, this patterns you, and going against it will cause disharmony. This is why it is crucial to connect with their history and live according to their patterns to a degree. This may mean eating like they ate or taking up some form of farming, fishing, praying, and so on.

The Roof Beam here symbolizes the spine and structure, so bones, joints, sinews, ligaments, and so on are affected. This can manifest as both health and illness in these structures. It can be chronic neck, knee, or back pain and general musculoskeletal injury, but it is also physicality, athleticism, and strength. Being very physical often means being more prone to injury from activity.

You are a perfect candidate for massage, chiropractic medicine, spa treatments, and so on. Exercise, sports, dancing, yoga, Qigong, going for walks in nature, and resting can all be powerful medicine; healthy habits and routines go a long way. You are also cured by food, especially from your grandmother, and by seasonal shifts, and traditionally this placement is connected to herbal medicine, more so if your Ancestors practiced it. You generally respond well to medical treatment and traditional medicine, and the Ancestral continuity of this Star is a strong basis for recovery. Tian Liang here can also inspire a sensitivity to Fengshui and design as well as to the practice of medicine, so you should apply this to yourself first; then, once you heal yourself, this can be the basis for helping others with these skills, too.

The Ancestral connection here can translate to epigenetics, or genetic predisposition to certain illnesses. So, you may inherit a specific disease pattern from a parent or Ancestor and die in the same way. If heart disease, cancer, or autoimmunity runs in your family, find out, as it may have deep Ancestral roots. You may also have "phantom" pains or illnesses from the death of an Ancestor. They may have been killed in battle or an accident, and so you relieve this pain in some way, like getting into an accident yourself. Learning the stories of how your Ancestors died can help liberate these patterns. Going to Ancestral sites, too, can liberate Ghosts and bring about recovery. Clean your Ancestors' graves.

Career/Travel Palace

If you have Tian Liang in the Career/Travel Palace or one of the other career Houses, then Fengshui is crucial to your work in the world and contribution to society. This is very similar to having it in the Ming Palace, as it makes this question central: *Am I in the right place?* It is important to ask this question, but the difference between the Roof Beam here and in the Ming Palace is that here it is more specifically about your "career" or work in the world and about applying the skills of Fengshui to that work. In the Ming Palace, there are more questions about home, finding a home, making a home, and so on.

Again, with both placements, if the Roof Beam is unafflicted, then the answer tends to be *yes, I am in the right place.* If it is afflicted, then these Ghosts tend to undermine this feeling and set you on a quest to find the proper placement. However, this may not be the case, and this Star here can be a threshold for immigrating to a new place, finding a new Fated family, and starting a new life in a new country, state, town, and so on. You may need to find the correct place to express your gifts, and when you do, everything falls into place. Until you find this place, your life purpose, work or career, talents, and so on may be in a state of arrested development. Find the right place, and suddenly, you make connections, get offers, find support, and take off. You may love or hate to travel, and it is either key to your Fate or completely unnecessary, as you are deeply connected to your home.

If unafflicted, this tends to mean that your work or career, life purpose, and contribution are connected to home and/or expressed through the principles of Fengshui. This can be as simple as working from home, which is easy in today's information economy, or starting a home-based business; or this can be a family business that you inherit or have worked in since childhood and simply continue. Maybe your parents own a bakery, coffee shop, or laundromat, for example; you work there as a teen and take it over as an adult. Or maybe your parents are horse trainers, carpenters, plumbers, doctors, or teachers, and so you become one too.

Parents, family, and relatives may be key to your success. You may learn a skill or trade from them, or you may be an apprentice and inherit your role from a mentor, role model, or teacher. This placement is excellent for the apprenticeship route, especially when it comes to "old world" skills and trades that involve working with your hands, with materials, and with building, creating, designing, and so on.

This placement is also excellent for all Fengshui-related careers, which is the case for this Star in any of the career Houses. This includes Fengshui, interior design, architecture, engineering, contracting, real estate, carpentry, and so on. Tian Liang here is also traditionally associated with government service but also with healing, medicine, and really any service profession. It relates to the continuity of traditions, so your work can be anything that involves lineage or at least a line of teachers and professionals that you follow in the footsteps of.

This Star's connection with home, identity, culture, tradition, and place implies that your work and contribution to society are connected to these things. You may be deeply involved in the local community, government, religious institutions, and businesses or in social work, and you have, inherit, or develop strong ties with—and work for the improvement of—your community and its people. This may also be the inverse case and manifest as working in international business, travel, or government.

Generally, this Star is hardworking, industrious, and practical. If it is unafflicted, then you will be successful, but this tends to be late blooming and requires a process of "building." If it is afflicted, then your location, connections, skills, and so on can be haunted, and you may have to search for the proper Fengshui arrangement, which could be elusive. This Star tends to be solid here and not strongly affected by Ghost Stars, however, except as temporary obstacles and setbacks that make you more focused.

Assistants Palace

Tian Liang in the Assistants Palace is considered one of the most auspicious of placements. It is at home here, using the skills of Fengshui as a service to others. The Roof Beam is the image of support and structure; it is the central pillar of the home that upholds it. So, having Tian Liang here exalts supporting and helping others. If you have this placement, then you are a great friend and reliable helper. You have an instinct from your Beneficial Ancestors to help and serve. Service to others has great results, and the benefits go both ways.

You inherit a naturally modest and supportive character that invites others to help and support you. You inherit Ancestral connections that come to your aid and help you in life through others. This may manifest at school, work, or in the community. People help you and are loyal to you. An assistant, friend, or subordinate may bring you success and uphold that success with loyalty, and you may do this for someone else. This is all about creating supportive and connected networks of help and service. It is about being modest and wanting to help, and this energy attracts support and goodwill. Your Fate will resolve with the help of others, and in turn you will help them to resolve their Fate.

The Roof Beam here is traditionally associated with the mantic arts and with astrology, Fengshui, traditional medicine, and spiritual tradition or lineage, as these are service oriented and often based on lineage and the continuity of tradition. So, learning these kinds of traditional arts can not only be rewarding, but they may also make an excellent career and path in life. You are naturally adept at wisdom and wellness traditions.

You may meet a great teacher, guru, genius, saint, leader, or boss and uphold them as their apprentice, following in their footsteps. But if you do, you will be humble and lead from a secondary position or from behind the scenes. You are suited to being in a secondary position, depending on what Star you have in the Superiors Palace. This placement is also excellent for government, social, and political work. Everything practical, like architecture, construction, engineering, design, or real estate, applies, but here the service aspect is emphasized.

The Fengshui aspect of this Star implies that your people, tribe, community, or teacher may be in a special or specific location or placement that you must find. If this is unafflicted, then you may be born into this community or find it easily, making friends into family as the Roof Beam guides you; your vibe attracts your tribe. If it is afflicted, then you may not be born into the right community, and you may have to find them, which could be contentious. Affliction by Ghost Stars here can cause conflict with others through negative emotions, misunderstandings, arguments, and scandals, and your relationship with the community in certain places may have a lot of ups and downs. Affliction here can also limit your scope of influence and limit your ability to help people. Afflicted, you may be stuck in a more meager or humble service position, like bus driver, delivery person, cop, or security guard—something that makes you relate to a place.

Superiors Palace

Tian Liang here is like the last two placements, but it exalts the role of leadership, teaching, and helping others on a larger scale or with a bigger scope of influence. This placement is traditionally associated with a strong Fated relationship with a teacher, guru, mentor, genius, or guide who shows you the way. They may be much older or in a much more advanced or successful position. You serve them, and this gives you a great advantage, as they have done all the work and laid out a path for you to follow. You may inherit their position when they retire, succeed them as an apprentice, and follow in their footsteps. The difference between this and the last House is that, here, you are more propelled through this path into a position of leadership. You may be thrust into the spotlight, and you will serve others as a team or community leader, guide, teacher, guru, or mentor. Traditionally, this exalts spiritual lineage and practice, and you may have a strong Fated connection with a guru that you must travel to meet.

Again, the Fengshui influence suggests that a teacher or mentor may be in a particular place that you must find or that your success or career may require finding the correct placement. You may work very hard to no avail, and as soon as you move to a certain city or start at a certain job, suddenly you meet an influential teacher or a big promotion, and everything is set in motion from there.

If you do not meet a teacher, this House may represent the "ladder" of success that you climb. You will be industrious, hardworking, and practical. You will receive constant promotions and advance in your career into a place of importance, power, influence, and leadership. This is great for starting your own business and entrepreneurship if it is service oriented and involves creating something tangible, such as owning your own shop, making goods and products, and/or applying your Fengshui skills. This Star here excels at government, politics, academia, and all Fengshui-related professions: architecture, landscape, agriculture, transit, engineering, design, real estate, construction, contracting, carpentry, traditional medicine, astrology, mantic arts, and so on. You will work and find great success in anything that involves the auspice of placement and space.

In this House, the ability to apply the principles of Fengshui at a great scale becomes much more potent. You can influence large communities, cities, swaths of land, and so on. Your work may influence many people. You may influence politics, policies, laws, and so on, or you can at least work in and engage with these things on a larger scale. If you work in real estate, construction, or design, you may build bridges or skyscrapers, design city parks, or buy or sell strategic and important properties. If you work in government or law, you may create or change policies that affect waterways, agriculture, public transportation, and so on.

This placement represents the inherited Ancestral pattern of successful community survival in relation to working with the land, with tradition, and with nature. You inherit the desire to see people and communities thrive and become successful, and you inherit the Fate of leadership to guide people or organizations to make this happen. You want to serve and help, but you want to help on a big scale. You want to make a difference in the world and affect the flow of things, connect people and places, and make things more beautiful, practical, accessible, and so on.

If this is unafflicted by Ghost Stars, then you will be successful and honored in your success. Traditionally, they say you will have a monument erected in your honor. This is the kind of success available; you will leave a lasting impression and may change things enough to be memorialized. This may mean a plaque on a park bench or a brick, or a statue may be made of your likeness. This may also be some physical legacy in the form of books, art, or construction projects; you will leave behind tangible works. Your contribution and success will also lead to others honoring and supporting you in old age.

If this is afflicted, you may have many ups and downs and setbacks, but the Roof Beam can work through these challenges. You may encounter obstacles to your work and even get embroiled in controversy, legal disputes, scandals, or opposition, but in the long run these will only serve you on your path.

Property Palace

Tian Liang is exalted and at home in the Property Palace, for this is the Fengshui Star in the Fengshui House. If you have this placement, then you inherit the deep wisdom of Ancestors' relationship to Fengshui and divination and are attuned to divination in a special way that can have a multitude of different manifestations, from the spiritual to the most practical and physical.

From the spiritual perspective, this is a deep sensitivity to the principles of Fengshui and divination and the ability to use them practically. You can feel the nature of how things flow in and relate to space, from the mountains, rivers, and wind to the way people and objects flow in and through structures, houses, cities, and so on. This sensitivity affects you deeply, and if things are off, your Fate will not unravel. You will be called to arrange yourself, your life, your home, your family, your friends, and your job in accordance with what feels right and is most auspicious. You have a deep connection to nature, to the turning of the seasons, and to how these all relate to human well-being. You also have a deep connection to home—making a home, finding a home—and much of your Fate will resolve from and through home. These may all just be instincts, but they can be brought out and made explicit with training.

You may, therefore, pursue training through art, design, engineering, mathematics, aesthetics, astrology, spirituality or religion, or through traditional Fengshui itself. This may be a hobby or become a career. Either way, it is fundamental to life and the unfolding of Fate. This placement can translate to a career in any of these fields, most obviously in real estate: buying and selling property, designing buildings or landscapes, and so on. It could also be used to play the stock market, bet on horse races, or invest speculatively. You may also build your own home or work with your hands and build things for others.

You may have a strong Fate for ownership, inheritance, and acquiring property, goods, and objects, and you can increase your wealth and property steadily and retire very well, or even own a great deal of land and achieve status. This may come from family inheritance in the form of a home, land, an apartment building, a family business, or the like, which you may then manage, increase, and generate income from. But it may also come with a strong inheritance of name, title, identity, religion, tradition, language, and story. You are, again, deeply connected to the story of your Ancestors and their connection to the land. You may identify strongly with nationality, ethnicity, religion, language, and so on, and be called to carry them on as a lineage holder.

If this is afflicted, then these stories may be haunted by war, exile, migration, persecution, and so on. You may be caught up in these ongoing conflicts based on where you were born, or there may be a story in your deep family history that you inherit and must unravel. You may inherit dreams, feelings, and fears associated with land and home. This Star here may be a call to pilgrimage to an Ancestral or spiritual home to resolve Ghosts. Wandering, searching for a home, and going on pilgrimage exorcise Ghost Stars in this House, so you should do genealogy and learn any patterns of pain that may be buried here. Negativity and obstruction to home or property are Ancestral Ghost patterns seeking resolution.

This can be a call to immigrate or move to a new home. This can be a Fate Threshold for a new life in a new country, state, or city. Your life may also be a walkabout in which you must search for meaning through wandering. You may be called to embark on a vision quest, spiritual retreat, or rite of passage. In this House, the Roof Beam is a divining rod, and you must feel into it and let it guide you. The practical manifestations are specific to your Ancestors, and Fengshui will dictate how they unfold.

Pleasure Palace

Tian Liang is very auspicious in the Pleasure Palace and similar to the previous placement, with the difference being that here, placement is much more of a hobby and less central to the unraveling of Fate. As in the previous House, here you are deeply connected to Fengshui, and these principles govern your sense of enjoyment and pleasure in life. You enjoy things based on the auspice of their placement and as an extension of the spiritual principles of nature. This placement makes for a classic artist, poet, or diviner.

You enjoy nature, traveling, and exploring, and you love seeing the different and unique vistas, landscapes, and natural formations of distinct places. You love the diversity of culture, art, and history and to see the manifestations of this through architecture, cities, and parks. When you travel, you have an itinerary to see these kinds of places. You connect with places on a deeply felt spiritual level that is beyond words; you connect with the Qi of things. You, therefore, connect with the soul of poets, artists, and great thinkers and may become one yourself. You will have a deep, broad, and unprejudiced appreciation of culture, art, and music.

Here, the Roof Beam can manifest through art, design, poetry, music, and so on—anything that expresses Fengshui, aesthetics, beauty, and so on. You will make an excellent designer, architect, or astrologer, but here there is no pressure to use this as a career to unravel Fate. It may simply manifest as a hobby or collection, and you may express the true meaning of amateur: someone who does something purely to enjoy it.

On the deepest level, having the Roof Beam here means that you understand the nature of pleasure as a principle of nature and how it connects to all beings and things. The universe is enjoying itself, demonstrated through people, places, and things. You will, therefore, enjoy life deeply and be able to appreciate and take pleasure in everything, from the fit of a good pair of shoes to the smell of fresh-cut grass. You will see the bright side of things and be able to offer fresh insight and appreciation, no matter the circumstances. If this is afflicted by Ghost Stars, it may inhibit your ability to express joy, but it does not inhibit inner joy. Even in prison, you can enjoy the song of birds outside your cell or the taste of prison meatloaf. This gives you unique insight that can and will be expressed through art of some kind, no matter how modest. You may be artful in the way you dress and talk, and even your affect expresses Fengshui.

THE WEN (文) STARS

The Wen Stars are a special pair associated with the Chinese term Wen (文), which is associated with language, culture, writing, and civility, and both are traditional deities, or Di (帝), associated with imperial examinations and literary affairs and with the governing of scholarship and examinations. They are prayed to all over China to this day.

There is some debate about whether these Stars belong to the Royal Court or are strong enough to "rule a House." If they are alone in a House, I say that they do indeed rule it, but the Fate there is not central: The influence of these Stars supports the greater currents of Fate within the chart. However, if they arrive together, they are very powerful, and special attention should be paid to that House, as it represents a kind of Fate Threshold through which all a person's spiritual and worldly Fate can be transcended through the application of spiritual means and technologies.

WEN CHANG (文昌)—THE MAGISTRATE

NAME AND TRANSLATIONS:

Wen Chang (文昌), the Magistrate Star, the Scholar Star, Literary Brilliance

Wen, 文—natural pattern of lines, incl. distinctive markings on animals and natural phenomena. 2 designed or incised pattern, surface ornament, elaboration, as added to (ant.) 質 zhi, basic stuff, plainness; cf. 理 li, inherent pattern; cog. [cognate with] 紋 wen, reticulated, embroidered. 3

ornament(ed); ornate. 4 the refined, civil, or cultured qualities, as opp. to (ant.) 武 wu, martial attainments or prowess. a) culture and the arts associated with it. b) written text; consciously devised pattern of words; literature. 5 well-patterned; artful. 6 a graph consisting of a single component only; cf. zi 字, graph consisting of 2 or more components. 7 (med.) rhymed or refined writings, as distinguished from 筆 bi, unrhymed or utilitarian writings. 8 prose or prosomeric writings, as distinguished from 詩 shi, "verse."[7]

Chang, 昌—splendid, shining, brilliance; glory, glorious. 2 flourishing; prosperous. 3 positive; exact; e.g., 昌言 changyan, straightforward or veracious words.[8]

Traditionally, Wen Changdi (文昌帝), is the Chinese god of literature or at least one of many governing scholarships and examinations. Here, we translate the Star as the Magistrate of the Royal Court. We can also translate it as the Scholar Star, Literary Prosperity, or Literary Brilliance.

ELEMENT: Yang Metal

TRADITIONAL IMAGE: Traditional Confucian magistrate, scholarly, wearing an official cap and gown, carrying scrolls of protocol, standing with impeccable posture, carrying out exams and rituals[9]

ANCESTOR PROFILE: Our ambitious, learned, accomplished Ancestors that resolved their Fate through education, learning, schooling, exams, work, study, self-reflection, and promotion

LUMINOUS PLACEMENt: Rat, Ox, Rabbit, Goat, Rooster, and Pig Palaces

DIMINISHED PLACEMENT: None

AFFILIATIONS: Northern Array—affiliated with the Tutor

Wen Chang, the Magistrate, and Wen Qu, the Priest, are a unique pair associated with the word Wen, which again encapsulates everything the Chinese associate with culture, art, history, education, and self-cultivation—as opposed to the term Wu (武), which is associated with the martial arts. The Magistrate and Priest represent different aspects of self-cultivation as a Yinyang pair, with the Magistrate being Yang, representing the more "outer," or exoteric, forms of cultivation, and the Priest being Yin, representing the more "inner," or esoteric, forms. The Magistrate is Yang Metal, representing rules, regulation, etiquette, and timing.

As already stated, Wen Chang is also Wen Changdi (文昌帝)—Di (帝) indicating a deity—meaning this is one of many gods of literature that governs scholarship and examination, and as such, there are temples all over China dedicated to this god. To this day, many people pray to him for good luck on tests, job interviews, promotions, and so on.

Traditionally, this god governed and symbolized the process of becoming a Confucian county or local magistrate in ancient China, known as Xianling (縣令). County magistrates had face-to-face relations with the people and administered all aspects of government on behalf of the emperor. The emperor would appoint magistrates from among those who passed the imperial examinations, and they were educated in the Confucian Classics, which molded the officials with a shared ideology that helped to unify the empire. After assuming office, magistrates would acquire specialized skills related to their posts, so their education would continue long after graduation.

Wen Chang, the magistrate of the royal court, was the official and highest ranked magistrate in the empire, serving the emperor, Zi Wei, and the royal court as the master of protocol. It was the magistrate's job to enforce manners, roles, obligations, rules, and regulations in the court and to keep everyone in their place. This position was training to eventually be considered for the role of imperial tutor, Tian Xiang (天相), one of the Four Rulers in Polestar Astrology, which we have already discussed. The Magistrate is very similar in that sense to the Tutor Star, but it is much more subtle and specifically focused on the role of education, learning, and schooling. It is an icon of education and the development of character. It is the Tutor Star in training.

As such, Wen Chang in our chart often represents a path of "becoming" through education. Again, it represents an aspect of our Fate that is related to the successful use of education, and it manifests as achievement in Wen, or culture, art, literature, and so on—what we would now call the "humanities." The Star represents that which nourishes our humanity and creates sensitive and functional leaders and teachers. That being said, it represents any successful education used to resolve Fate, so it can include "STEM" subjects (science, technology, engineering, and mathematics).

This Star is a kind of energetic momentum inherited from our learned Ancestors, the ones who successfully improved their station in life and helped others through learning, schooling, apprenticing, teaching, and so on as well as those who achieved social, political, or professional prominence through bettering themselves, learning a skill, or self-cultivation. This Star may represent an educated or learned parent or grandparent, but it can also be a thought connection or affinity with a specific Ancestor and their self-cultivation far back in the family line. For example, you may be born with a deep interest in learning to play music, only to find out you had a great-grandfather who was a composer. While the Fate here can be associated with spiritual or religious education, often it is more "worldly" and related to community and practical affairs. Wen Qu (文曲), the Priest, represents spiritual and religious training.

The Fate represented by this Star can be minor and more subtle when alone, but it can rise to significance, especially when paired with stronger Stars. It can add a deeper flavor or dimension of education and teaching to a significant Star like the Emperor. Often, it implies a path of learning, community engagement and service, and sometimes teaching or passing on knowledge.

Let's walk the Magistrate through the Twelve Houses.

Ming Palace

If you have Wen Chang in the Ming Palace, then you are Fated to be a magistrate. Your life and the unraveling of your Fate will include a strong dimension of education, self-cultivation, and possibly teaching. You are connected to the lineage of education and self-cultivation in your family, and your life and character are an expression of that cultivation. All their learning and knowledge, skills, and accomplishments flow through you and benefit your life. You may inherit a noble, refined, courteous, and well-mannered (even stuffy) character that develops as you grow and learn. This well-mannered and considerate nature will bring you good fortune and be central to the unraveling of your Fate.

School, education, training, learning, and eventually teaching or leadership will be an essential and central part of your life. Much of your Fate may happen at school, and you may pursue a life of learning. This may be formal and include higher education and institutionalized learning, but it also may be independent and self-initiated. Either way, you have a deep desire to learn, grow, and better yourself. This may come with a mandate to help others and contribute to society through the benefits of your learning. So, careers in education, research, and academia are a natural outcome, but this could become work in government or social services and involve leadership and community engagement.

Although this placement often means you are born with an inherent intelligence and sense of cultivation, a lifelong process of learning and growth will be revelatory and central to your Fate. Self-cultivation is central and is the key to actualizing your dreams. It will remain central throughout life and be a defining aspect of your person. Contribution and community, helping and seeing others succeed, will also be great sources of meaning and happiness for you.

This path of cultivation will be very different for different Characters, and often it can be remedial for more independent Characters who struggle with selfishness and impulsivity. So, Tigers, Monkeys, Dragons, Dogs, and Horses will struggle but ultimately benefit greatly from this placement, as it will temper them and help them to participate and contribute to society more easily. Social and domestic characters with a sense of responsibility, like Goats, Rabbits, Oxen, and Pigs, will exalt the nature of this Star and more naturally express it. The more intellectual or mental Characters like Roosters, Rats, and Snakes will focus much more on the rules, regulations, and revelations of this Star.

Alone, this Star is not strong, so look elsewhere in the chart for where this education and self-cultivation will manifest most strongly. If the Magistrate shows up with a stronger Star, then this path of cultivation can become much stronger. If it is afflicted by Ghost Stars, then this path can be fraught with deep struggle and challenges but ultimately be resolved and released through education and self-cultivation.

Ancestors Palace

If Wen Chang arrives in the Ancestors Palace, then you have a deep, Fated connection with a specific learned Ancestor and/or with the lineage of education and learning in your family. In general, this is a strong affinity with all your Ancestors and represents the fruition of their betterment, contribution, and accomplishments. Ancestral Qi is, therefore, a blessing and a guiding force that manifests through your education, learning, and personal and professional development. Here, the momentum of your Ancestors flows through you and guides you to happiness and fulfillment. Like in the Ming Palace, you inherit a noble, refined, courteous, considerate, and well-mannered character, but here these are likely imposed on you by your parents or through family pressure.

Your parents and grandparents will be proud and supportive, and they may even raise you with a strong sense of lineage, tradition, or identity. Your upbringing may involve rules, lessons, guidelines, and so on. This may be religious or worldly and come from a deep sense of character. A parent or grandparent may be an important teacher or mentor who guides and shapes your life so that you develop "character."

Sometimes this placement manifests a specific connection to a learned Ancestor that you have a Fated bond and connection with through time. You may have a soulmate among your Ancestors whom you connect with through education.

You inherit their desire to learn something, or you inherit the momentum of their education as a talent or predestined affinity for something. You may be drawn to art, literature, music, or poetry and come from a long line of intellectuals or literati. Maybe your great-grandmother was a musician or poet, and so you are too. You should connect with these legacies: Read their poetry, journals, or letters; find their arts or crafts; and learn about their lives and drives.

Often, this placement manifests as a deep desire to learn that you are born with. But it also manifests as an inherited affinity for learning or ability to learn, so you do it easily and are naturally disciplined, studious, and organized. This predisposition will benefit you throughout life and flow into everything you do. It can be overtly intellectual, or it can be as simple as learning to knit quilts from your grandmother.

The Magistrate here may also mean a family lineage and tradition of education or training of some kind. Perhaps everyone in your family is a lawyer, doctor, or professor, so you become one, too. Or maybe everyone in your family goes to Stanford, West Point, or Cambridge; or maybe they belong to a fraternity, sorority, or group like the Freemasons. You grow up with a sense of values shaped by these institutions and carry on in a tradition. You may grow up in a house full of books, where learning, reading, and self-improvement are normal and encouraged.

If this is afflicted, then this connection to learning may be challenged with negative emotions, arguments, or disagreements. Your parents may be overbearing and force an education on you that you find suffocating, and therefore, you rebel against them. Education may even be abusive and strict to the point of becoming traumatic. Family expectations may be stuffy, old, or outdated, or they may be judgmental of you, should you fail to live up to expectations or defy the rules.

Youth Palace

If Wen Chang appears in the Youth Palace, then the themes of education and the setting of school will be a very significant part of your childhood. You will likely have a strong affinity with supportive siblings, but sibling Fate here is often mild. If you do have siblings, then the relationship will be supportive, and you may have an older sibling who teaches and mentors you. Or you will teach and mentor a younger sibling. The Magistrate implies a sense of social responsibility in your family that you must rise to and develop the character to enact. You may have the mantle of the older sibling and must grow up quickly, becoming a second parent and/or helping out with the family responsibilities. This can manifest as involvement in a family business; you may work in that business after school, or the business may be influential in your youth.

The Magistrate here can mean some kind of significant mentor, teacher, coach, or the like who guides you and influences the rest of your life. This may involve learning a skill, but more important, it involves life lessons and becomes a source of personal growth and character development in which you learn and grow as a human in the Confucian sense. This mentor may be a family member—a parent, older sibling, or uncle maybe—or it may be someone outside the family you meet through school, sports, music lessons, the gym, and so on. This can also manifest as friends, and you may be the leader or responsible one in your friend group, guiding and organizing adventures and activities. You may act as a mediator, arbiter, or liaison between friends, family, schoolmates, and so on.

Often, this placement means you are a naturally mature, responsible, and studious youth. You may be precocious, eager to learn, and ambitious academically. You may be a geek, nerd, or bookworm. School, learning, and smarts are where it is at. You will do well at school and be liked by your teachers and by adults in general. You may have more in common with adults than kids your age. This may distance you, and you may be alone without friends, finding solace in books and imagination. You may be on the honor roll, top of the class, teacher's pet, AP student, and so on. This may manifest as success in extracurricular activities like chess club, debate team, mathletes, and the like.

Youth will involve a lot of growth, learning, development, and maturity, and you will become a responsible and professional adult. This will translate to early success. You may graduate early and get into a great college. If it is afflicted, then significant challenges or conflicts can occur at school, with teachers, or in the politics of the family or family business.

Partners Palace

Wen Chang is generally auspicious but not particularly strong in the Partners Palace. If it is unafflicted by Ghost Stars, then it can mean Fate with a supportive and compatible partner. The partnership will likely be characterized more by duty or social responsibility than romance. This looks more like a classic "arranged marriage," bringing together two families, or it may be a "smart match" or sensible arrangement. You may come together for more practical means and work very well together, creating a well-functioning family unit. This is the Ancestral pattern of successful and practical marriage for social reasons, which is most marriages throughout history. Before modern times, romance was unimportant; people married to create and maintain society.

You may meet this partner at work or school or through some kind of shared hobby or activity that you meet doing or do together. This shared activity or interest may be crucial for your bonding, or it may even be central to your partnership. You might meet at a conference, event, or convention. You may marry your high school or college sweetheart, administrative assistant, or person in the cubicle next to you, or you may even fall for a teacher. The partnership may involve community, social responsibilities, business, or work in some way. You may both be intellectuals, and it is important that you share similar values and worldviews.

You will communicate well, learn from each other, and grow from the partnership. Marriage, and relationships in general, will be a source of self-cultivation, reflection, and personal growth. You will become a better person and grow in your humanity through relating with others and the self-sacrifice and service that it requires.

If this is afflicted, then this growth and cultivation may involve arguments, conflict, and patterns of negative emotion that prevent you from finding the right person, but eventually, these can be overcome because you learn and grow from your mistakes. You may also be married to your job. This may get in the way of a partnership or meeting someone, or it may come between you and a partner. You simply may not have the time to date; you are always at work or busy, so you are alone. Your "nerdiness" may also isolate you and make you hard to understand or connect with.

Offspring Palace

Wen Chang is very auspicious in the Offspring Palace, as it denotes Fate to be a parent that is successful but not central, as this is a tertiary Star. It is successful because the Magistrate manifests itself as bright, well-behaved, and intelligent children with potentially delicate constitutions who do well in school and become a source of great pride. You give birth to a little magistrate who listens, learns, follows the rules, and has a sense of others. As a Yang Star, this Star can mean the birth of a son, but it can, of course, go either way. They may be studious, nerdy, and get good grades. They may be on the honor roll, in AP classes, and so on. They will grow up to be responsible and take care of you in old age.

School, education, and learning will be an important aspect of parenting for you personally, and the school environment will play an important role in the Fate here. You are deeply invested in their education and may seek out the best schools or private schools, or you may homeschool them. You will be their mentor and teacher and pass on life lessons and values. These may be family or religious values coming from a sense of tradition, or they may be much more secular and come from your own education and personal beliefs. You may raise your kids with a strong sense of secular values—a belief in reason, logic, science, and so on. You may instill political, social, or economic beliefs in them as well, and these may characterize conversation around the dinner table. Rules, regulations, structure, and discipline will be part of your parenting.

As usual, this Star implies that being a parent is a path of self-cultivation and a source of personal growth for you.

Your child is your greatest teacher. Being a parent forces you to grow up, mature, and become socially responsible. It may also force you to get a better job, seek promotion, and earn more money. The birth of a child may be the Fate that catalyzes your success. You may also raise them in a community; a village may be involved in their upbringing.

If this is afflicted by Ghost Stars, then they may rebel against school and authority. They may reject your values and beliefs. You may be too strict, overbearing, and suffocating, and they may resent you for being too harsh or judgmental or never being able to live up to your expectations. Arguments with your kids may revolve around political or financial disagreements. These can be overcome through self-reflection and learning to let go of harsh rules, discipline, and structure.

Wealth Palace

If you have Wen Chang the Wealth Palace, then you are Fated to prosper through work as a magistrate, which is not guided or motivated by the pursuit of money but rather by ideals and a sense of duty, social justice, and service. The Fate is quite like the Tutor Star here but much more modest. This is ideal for most people, as it represents being well paid and holding down a steady job in the most basic sense. Furthermore, it represents what most people imagine to be the acceptable path in our culture: Go to school and get a good job in your chosen field. Many people pursue this route, but few are initially successful. Here, you inherit the Ancestral pattern of successfully using education to resolve Fate, and you can follow this precedent to make money.

As usual, we see hints of career in this House, and magistrate work is, again, motivated by ideals. You are probably not interested in getting rich and may even be very critical of money and consumerism. You want to serve people and society; you want to make the world a better place. The Magistrate here is drawn to work that demonstrates these ideals and involves a process of learning and applying education—so, any field that requires licensing and certainly any field that has an ethos: law, medicine and healthcare, social work, psychology, service work, and so on. You can also earn through Wen: culture, art, history, education, and self-cultivation. Money and wealth will become a pivot of your self-cultivation, and you will learn and grow through relating to money and wealth as resources that expand to include higher principles and ideas.

You will likely go to school, earn a degree, possibly apprentice, get licensed, and serve people, society, and/or a chosen community. This placement may even manifest as political aspirations, and you may go from being a lawyer to being a politician. The most direct manifestation would be a government job and salary, as magistrates were an extension of the government. Or you may swing toward activism and social justice, wanting to change society with a sense of heroism. All that being said, you may also be a stockbroker and adept at making money and/or managing money for other people as a social service, and the Magistrate may apply toward learning how to manipulate money.

Teaching is also a very direct manifestation of this placement. You may follow the traditional academic path, pursuing higher education and going into teaching or research. Depending on your Character, you may be a professor, but teaching high school, middle school, and even preschool makes sense here. Wen Chang's sense of duty and responsibility may also drive you into management, so you may become the school principal or head of the PTA. You may also become an independent teacher, writer, or lecturer. Writing books, giving talks, teaching courses, and so on also make sense here.

Generally, this Star is frugal, resourceful, responsible, and modest. You may earn a decent living, but this is unlikely to generate great wealth, and you are not likely to be interested in getting rich for the sake of it. Depending on your Character, you may save and invest, and even have rules around money and spending. You will probably not be ostentatious or showy, and even if you become wealthy, you will be happy with a modest apartment and an average car. You will likely apply your money toward goals and slowly achieve them. You will have a sense of purpose, generosity, and charity. You feel it is not your money but "ours." This may mean sharing it with family, helping relatives, giving to charity, or donating to church or religious tithings.

If this is afflicted, then you can struggle with modesty, and wealth can become a grind. Ghost Stars here may push you into mediocrity and keep you stuck earning little, struggling to get by in a middling profession that you resent. Maybe you get fired as an assistant professor at a community college and lose your meager pension due to a market crash. You may pursue a career with high-minded aspirations but get burnt out, disillusioned, bitter, and resentful, and having to earn a living, pay the bills, and so on may become a source of frustration and hate. This may push you to hate money and "the system" and swing toward activism. You may start pushing for things like socialism or communism with the same misguided idealism, hating the system and post-capitalist consumerism.

Health Palace

Wen Chang is considered somewhat weak in the Health Palace; alone, it doesn't offer a strong Fate here. The Wen Stars represent somewhat frail, aged, scholarly figures with gray hair, so the image is that of inheriting a weak constitution that may experience premature aging. But, as the Magistrate, it also represents a thoughtful, caring, and systematic approach to health. Here it represents the Wen—the culture, art, history, education, and self-cultivation—of health, and medicine. It means excellent care and willingness to work to help others, and the Ancestral pattern of teaching and learning are applied to your health cultivation, which will flow through you to others.

This placement makes for an astute and compliant patient. It is also considered a good Fate for finding good doctors and receiving suitable treatments, as it represents the return of past service to others that benefits you. It also means being thorough and intelligent in your choice of doctors. The Magistrate is willing to research health and wellness, follow instructions, and comply with doctor's orders. You may study medicine and research treatment protocols. If you are diagnosed with something, you will learn everything about the condition and be able to converse with doctors and advocate for yourself. You may also be an excellent advocate for others, and this could lead to an interest in public health.

As such, this placement is an excellent base for the study and practice of medicine as a clinician or for working in healthcare or public health. The Magistrate represents a more intellectual approach to self-cultivation: studying medical classics, memorizing formulas and prescriptions, and so on. This applies to both traditional and conventional medicine. However, the nature of the Magistrate is Confucian. He is dedicated to public service, so you will likely work very hard to help others; however, this can weaken the spleen and eventually the kidneys. The Magistrate is more likely to burn out from working too much and never resting or retiring, and may suffer from nervous disorders from excessive rumination, worry, and anxiety, which then affect other organs and lead to more complex conditions.

If Ghosts afflict this Star, then it can lead to a lot of complex mental and emotional disorders and subclinical chronic conditions made worse by negative emotions. However, with care and an intellectual application of medicine and healthcare practices, you can create longevity, likely involving a complex and organized routine. This may manifest as becoming a doctor who works tirelessly to help others despite their health problems. Others will be very grateful for your service, and traditionally, they say many friends will attend your funeral and give touching eulogies. In short, if you have this Star here, you will likely want to learn and practice medicine.

Career/Travel Palace

If Wen Chang appears in the Career/Travel Palace, you will likely have to travel widely, move to a new city or state, and possibly even immigrate to catalyze your Fate in the world and your career successfully. Magistrates often had to leave home and travel to the big city to undergo education and take the imperial exams. They were then assigned to work in cities other than the ones they were born in. Magistrates acted as judges and arbiters; they enforced and upheld all aspects of government on behalf of the emperor. It was therefore considered problematic to return to work in your hometown, many of which were small, for there may be conflicts of interest with family members and relatives there. So, this is a Fate Threshold for relocating and returning home on pilgrimage, which magistrates would often do as town heroes. So, travel, live and study abroad, and be willing to move to manifest your Fate.

This placement is auspicious for all kinds of magisterial work or simply for the successful application of Wen: again, culture, art, history, education, and self-cultivation. So, if you have this Star here or in one of the other career Houses, you should follow the traditional route of going to college and grad school and even pursuing doctoral work. This is the pattern of successfully using education to resolve Fate, so get educated, and follow your interests into a career. Symbolically, this looks like traditional academia, but it can be any kind of education, including trade work or apprenticeship.

Magisterial work involves learning and education, such as teaching, tutoring, professorship, and research—anything from preschool or kindergarten to tenured professor. This placement also works very well for legal work, public health, politics, and anything involving community service, especially anything with a theory, code of conduct, philosophy, and so on. The Magistrate is about applying ideals from Confucianism, Daoism, and Buddhism in China, but they can come from anywhere. It can be personal, like your Christian faith supports you as a social worker, or it can be embedded in the job, like working as a doctor and taking the Hippocratic oath. This placement may also involve learning multiple languages, traditions, or cultures and being a translator or mediator between cultures. In general, it implies mediation, service, and community work.

Often, this represents a slow but steady path of progression. You must go to school and go through a process of learning and transformation to then apply that to work. Many try to do this, but few follow this model successfully. Most go to school but end up far away from what they studied and often bounce around before settling into something eventually. This Star here is at least the foundation to follow a clearly chosen path: You (or your parents) always wanted to be a lawyer, so you go to school, become an intern, take and pass the boards, and then work for a law firm.

If this is afflicted by Ghost Stars, this process can be fraught with negative emotions, challenges, and doubt, which often seems to be the case. But here, challenges are overcome by applying what you learn and practicing what you preach. Also, Ghost Stars here are often liberated by moving to a new city, state, or country. Staying close to home can perpetuate Ghost patterns and inhibit you from releasing them.

Assistants Palace

Wen Chang is exalted in the Assistants Palace and belongs here, as it is symbolic of this House, perhaps even more so than the Tutor, for the Tutor is the "head" magistrate and leader, thriving in the Superiors Palace, while the Magistrate Star is purely in the role of service. Here, the Magistrate manifests strongly through service-oriented professions, community engagement, and friendship. Everything we have mentioned so far as Magistrate work applies, and again, it follows the path of successfully applying education toward the resolution of Fate. For you, service work becomes your path of self-cultivation, and you grow by working to help others.

So, work in education, academia, healthcare, social work, government, politics, and so on all apply—again, anything with an ethos, philosophy, or higher purpose, anything that involves Wen. The Magistrate pursues their path with profound ideals and aspirations to help others and improve the world. This represents successfully going to school, apprenticing, getting higher education, getting licensed, and getting an excellent job in your chosen field. But here, the Star is given the added boost of inheriting the good Fate associated with your Ancestors' previous generosity, community engagement, and work behind the scenes to serve others. This will galvanize help, love, and support from friends, co-workers, students, and so on. Others will come together, show up, and help you so that you can help others. Group effort and joint business of any kind go well. Depending on your Character, you may have a lot of reliable and helpful friends who surround you, and you help each other in life. You may be part of a network or friends, and you become the magistrate and arbiter of disputes.

You will be generous and serve others selflessly. This generosity will be reciprocated, and you will receive much help from others. However, you serve because you are an extension of your generous Ancestors, and it comes naturally. So, you pay it back and forth, spreading wealth and love. This manifests very well through any personal and professional teamwork, team building, joint business, and so on. You may start social clubs, sports teams, community engagement activities, and so on. Or it may manifest through professional or political networking. But here, you are not seeking leadership or being in the spotlight; that's the next House. Here, you want to work behind the scenes, in the shadows, in subordinate or secondary positions.

Wen Chang here can manifest in a more blue-collar or bureaucratic service position, but you will likely be driven into middle management and behind-the-scenes community or team organizing. Government work, social work, and so on are given the added dimension of community and teamwork. This placement also works very well for being a teacher or researcher and can be applied toward STEM, but again, it is all about working in teams with some higher ideal or purpose, like working together to find a cure for cancer. You may work your way up the ranks and slowly achieve success, but you will likely stay subordinate unless you have strong Stars in the next House. The Magistrate is happy, and thrives, in a team helping others or in a position to exalt others.

If this is afflicted, then Ghosts can undermine teamwork and create discord with others or with leadership. Affliction can also create drama with friends, co-workers, and the community, leading to career challenges and delays in progress. You may get stuck in a middle position, like assistant manager at a restaurant, and stall there; you write the schedule, do payroll, and lead the team, but this doesn't amount to much. Affliction here can also cause disillusionment and frustration. You want to help and try to, but it doesn't go well, so you must abandon your ideals and soul-search for meaning and purpose. This may be exorcistic, and you may have to dig deep to find your true purpose and connect with a higher calling that sustains you in service to others.

Superiors Palace

If Wen Chang appears in the Superiors Palace, he gets pushed toward leadership and higher success as the Magistrate. This looks more like a magistrate becoming the tutor and finding a higher position in education, government, or service. If you are a lawyer, you may become a judge. You might go from district attorney to governor. Or you may go from being a teacher to being the principal. Everything here gets pushed to the next level, and success means your ideals can reach many more people. You want to change the world, and you can do so through ideas, laws, rules, and regulations, as well as teaching and creating community. This can also lead to exalted and triumphant expression of Wen.

Again, the Magistrate represents pursuing education and service with high-minded ideals, but in this House, it gets more ambitious and has a wider sphere of influence. Whatever you do, you can take it to the next level and affect more people. You may teach what you do and lead the next generation of people in your profession, art, or cultural practice. You can be an excellent teacher or mentor, and you will be able to take pride in your students' accomplishments as an extension of yourself. You may end up changing the way your profession is done by changing laws, practices, and norms. You can leave behind a legacy of ideas in the form of a memoir, autobiography, or book.

Here, teaching, academics, writing, and research are powerful, but rather than being behind the scenes, you get pushed into the public and become a leading researcher, renowned lecturer, artist, musician, or respected public intellectual. You may start humble, but success can lead to recognition. You can become a thought leader, influencer, and public commentator. You may be interviewed for your expertise; this may be small and local, or you may end up being asked your opinion about politics on the news.

Generally, this placement is an excellent basis for career success, and you will be hardworking, responsible, diligent, and persevering. Success and teaching will become your path of self-cultivation and personal growth. You can successfully use education, and this House exalts higher education and intellectual accomplishment. As always, it represents service, and the Magistrate is the epitome of following the rules, working your way up the ranks, passing exams, and getting promotions.

This placement can equally be applied toward success at owning a business or entrepreneurship, for you create your own ladder for others to climb. You will make a great manager, boss, or owner, as you will be socially responsible and governed by higher ideals, which your business will radiate into the world. If you create a brand, it will stand for something.

This can also represent a connection to traditional lineage and spiritual teachings. You may strongly connect to a religious or spiritual teacher in a "teaching lineage." This means that the tradition will have a solid academic and literary component; you may study scripture and classical or ancient texts. You may succeed your teacher and receive a lineage. But here, Wen Chang is more about the teachings and less about practice. You must grasp and preserve the correct intellectual understanding of teachings and pass them on, doing your best to practice what you preach, but this may not manifest as being a yogi (this is more the Priest Star). You may be something like a rabbi, preacher, geshe, or pundit. So, self-cultivation becomes central.

If this is afflicted, then Ghost Stars can produce drama and discord through your work in the world. You may share and disseminate bad or harmful ideas that create trouble. Or you may be fired or forced to resign as a chairperson, president, or spokesperson due to misspeaking, lying, or falsifying records or research. You may have to apologize publicly to save face, or you may be relegated to a lesser position, change professions, or go on trial. You may break or bend the rules, and this could lead to disaster.

Property Palace

Wen Chang is auspicious but modest in the Property Palace. The Magistrate represents doing government work, getting paid a decent salary, and receiving good benefits so you can save, buy a house, and retire well. So, this is a sound basis for owning property and doing well in life, but it is not extravagant, plush, or showy. Generally, it means that in youth your interest in owning property is weak and subordinate to the demands of your career path, but that you will live in comfort and can do much better in your later years.

The Magistrate often means moving to the big city to live and work, retiring in the countryside, and returning to your birth home in old age. Magistrates had to leave home and move to the capital to take imperial exams; they were then sent to different prefectures, where they were appointed local magistrate to enforce government law. They would often work in an area for a few years and then move or get promoted to a higher position. Therefore, this usually means repeatedly moving for work and relocating for different positions. You may also live on a stipend or in government-provided housing. You will likely leave home for school and again when you find a job. You may live in apartments, rentals, and so on, but you are okay with this and are a happy minimalist.

Applied to real estate and ownership, this placement makes for a good application of rule and law, so you may be a landlord, work in real estate, or invest and make good on a family inheritance. More appropriately, this represents government or legal work that deals with land, property, zoning, city or community planning rules and regulations, and so on. Applied to Fengshui, this is an excellent basis for learning and applying the principles of Fengshui so that you make a great designer, architect, or planner. You can intuitively understand how space, architecture, and interior design affect people and communities through more considerable influences like laws, such as access to water or public transportation. You may have high ideals about these kinds of laws and work to change them and affect communities for the better. You may also collect, create, or sell items or creations of Wen—artifacts of culture, art, history, and so on.

The Magistrate is frugal and responsible, so you can invest and do well, but alone, this placement is unlikely to manifest as significant property ownership. If it is afflicted, then Ancestral Ghosts can obstruct property ownership and management through rules and regulations. You fail to build "to code" and must pay fines and rebuild, and you get bogged down in legalistic bureaucratic complications. Affliction can mean living in very meager, humble conditions and struggling to break out of renting into ownership. You may end up disillusioned and lose your high ideals, intentionally living in community housing or unhoused on principle.

Pleasure Palace

If Wen Chang arrives in the Pleasure Palace, then your sense of enjoyment and pleasure is connected to Wen, which again encapsulates everything the Chinese associate with culture, art, history, literature, education, and self-cultivation. This is an auspicious placement because you actually enjoy self-cultivation; inversely, you can self-cultivate through enjoyment. Enjoyment is connected to others and a sense of community, culture, and tradition; you enjoy seeing others succeed and supporting others through service. You receive true satisfaction and joy from seeing others benefit and receive recognition and rewards.

You will likely be a lifelong learner deeply nourished by everything associated with Wen. You will love museums, libraries, festivals, rituals, and concerts; you are more likely to connect with traditional expressions, but this is not always the case. If it represents a connection to more profound principles and ideals, then any form of Wen will be moving and meaningful. You can enjoy studying, reading, painting, learning to play an instrument, and so on because you love these as a form of meditation, reflection, and growth. You can enjoy discipline and routine practice and grow as a human being by pursuing these practices. Of course, everyone can benefit from these things, but here, you inherit these interests from your Ancestors and carry the momentum of their cultivation forward as joy.

You will enjoy service and can even enjoy work if it is in the service of others and higher ideals. Essentially, you are a Magistrate in the purest sense, which means that you cultivate for enjoyment rather than as a duty or job. An amateur pursues something for the pure love of the act rather than to earn money as a professional; when passions become jobs, you lose the magic. Here, you love the magic of Wen and are happy to practice, and you want to share the essence of these things with others. You can connect with the essence more quickly because it is not bogged down by duty or responsibility. You can turn your hobbies and passions into a career, but this will be more of a certainty than a goal. You will love to do things, and it is only natural that eventually you will get paid for it.

Your hobbies, passions, and interests may or may not be connected to Wen in the traditional sense. You are not necessarily a nerd or scholar. Connection to tradition can take many forms and will be deeply personal. You will have a deep desire to share your interests with others for their benefit. You will also not be able to conceive of enjoying things alone and may cultivate a community based on your interests. This small, connected community will be based on a shared, mutual sense of Wen—of creating or continuing culture or art.

You may also have no connection whatsoever to Wen, but you create a sense of cultivation with whatever you love. In other words, whatever your path of enjoyment, you turn it into a practice for self-cultivation, and this may manifest simply as relating to others through kindness and generosity. Or, what you enjoy may be mundane and uncultured, but you do it so well that you make an art of it. You grow as a human simply by following your path of enjoyment and learning from the process.

WEN QU (文曲)—THE PRIEST

NAME AND TRANSLATIONS:

Wen Qu (文曲), the Priest Star, Protocol Master,
Master of Rights, Master of Music, Ritual Music Star

Wen, 文—a natural pattern of lines, incl. distinctive markings on animals and natural phenomena. 2 designed or incised pattern, surface ornament, elaboration, as added to (ant.) 質 zhi, basic stuff, plainness; cf. 理 li, inherent pattern; cog. 紋 wen, reticulated, embroidered. 3 ornaments(ed); ornate. 4 the refined, civil, or cultured qualities, as opposed to (ant.) 武 wu, penciled martial attainments or prowess. a) culture and the arts associated with it. b) written text; consciously devised pattern of words; literature. 5 well-patterned; artful. 6 a graph consisting of a single component only; cf. zi 字, graph consisting of 2 or more components. 7 (med.) rhymed or refined writings, as distinguished from 筆 bi, unrhymed or utilitarian writings. 8 prose or prosomeric writings, as distinguished from 詩 shi, "verse."[10]

Qu, 曲—musical tune, an air. a) (med.) 法曲 faqu, pseudo-classical ritual music popular in Tang times, using handbells, cymbals, large bells, lithophones, steamered syrinxes, and lutes.[11]

Wen Qudi (文曲帝) is another Chinese deity of imperial examinations and literary affairs and a constellation governing scholarship and examinations. Here, we translate this Star as the Priest or Protocol Master of the Royal Court. It may also be translated as the Ritual Master of the Music of the Tang Dynasty Court.

ELEMENT: Yin Water

TRADITIONAL IMAGE: Depicted as a Daoist priest, wearing the colorful robes, cap, and gown of the coronation ritual, head and hands bowing in prayer position or holding talismans[12]

ANCESTOR PROFILE: Our spiritual and religious Ancestors who practiced and resolved their Fate through prayer, meditation, scripture, ritual, magic, and wisdom

LUMINOUS PLACEMENT: Rat, Ox, Rabbit, Goat, Rooster, and Pig Palaces

DIMINISHED PLACEMENT: None

AFFILIATIONS: Southern Array—affiliated with the Oracle

As we have already discussed, Wen Chang, the Magistrate, and Wen Qu, the Priest, are a unique pair associated with the word Wen (文), which again encapsulates everything the Chinese associate with culture, art, history, education, and self-cultivation, in opposition to the term Wu (武), which is associated with the martial arts. As a Yinyang pair, the Magistrate and Priest represent different aspects of self-cultivation. We have now discussed the Magistrate as the Yang figure, representing the more "outer," exoteric, or worldly forms of cultivation and education, and we can now look at the Priest as the Yin counterpart, representing the more "inner" or esoteric forms.

The Magistrate is Yang Metal, representing rules, regulation, propriety, and timing, and the Priest is Yin Water, representing dissolution, meditation, spiritual connectivity, prayer, trance, mystical experience, and transcendence. Like Wen Changdi, Wen Qudi (文曲帝) is a Chinese deity of imperial examinations and literary affairs governing scholarship and examinations, but he is more associated with religious ritual rather than academia.

This character is complex and multifaceted, as it is the image of a Daoist priest but also what was called the "protocol master" of the royal court. This figure was well versed in the spiritual meaning and obligations of the royal court and was responsible for maintaining the court's connection to Heaven through ritual. As the protocol master, the priest was allowed to critique everyone in the court, including the emperor, so that they would follow proper ritual observance. Daoist court ritual was a precise and intentional act whose goal was dissolution and trance for those participating, especially for the oracle, to which it is similar, which we have already discussed. The priest or protocol master governed the dress, actions, and speech of the court members and maintained the ritual so that it could function as a bridge between the living and the dead, between Heaven and Earth, but with decorum.

The Priest is the image of a Daoist priest who has undergone extensive religious study and training in ritual. As such, it represents our Ancestral connection to spiritual study and culture and the successful application of religion and spirituality to resolve fate. It is like the Magistrate, but the self-cultivation of the Priest is associated with the education and study that leads to spiritual wisdom rather than worldly wisdom, and the difference here is crucial. Spiritual wisdom reveals our Original Nature and connects us to the Dao and Heaven, Tian (天), while worldly wisdom may follow the Dao, but it connects us to humanity, Ren (人), rather than Heaven.

As an astrological influence, the Priest is generally auspicious. Like the Magistrate, it is not central but supportive, as it adds a dimension or flavor of spiritual or religious wisdom that can be a literal connection to religion or can be a place of more profound spiritual cultivation. It represents a connection to the religious study, mystical experience, and spiritual cultivation of our Ancestors, systematic or not, that we inherit to unravel our Fate.

The term Qu (曲), is the picture of an instrument called Bianzhong (編鐘), which was a set of bronze bells on a rack, and it refers to the ritual music played on this instrument at the royal court. The priest would conduct this music while orchestrating the ritual observances. This took much training and cultivation, which was connected to Daoist practices, principles, and transmission. It, therefore, represents spiritual training and a connection to music, art, poetry, and creativity in general, which is a more accessible dimension of spiritual cultivation and, more often, how these principles manifest in people's lives. Not everyone has an obvious spiritual or religious dimension, but everyone has a place where creativity and deeper artistic impulses manifest. Wherever Wen Qu appears, you are called to something more profound and connected to the spiritual wisdom of your Ancestors.

Let's walk the Priest through the Twelve Houses.

Ming Palace

If Wen Qu arrives in the Ming Palace, you are Fated to have a deep connection to religion, spirituality, esoteric "secret" teachings, and self-cultivation in the pursuit of wisdom. You inherit a connection to your Ancestors' religious or spiritual heritage as a central aspect of your Fate, and your Ancestors guide your life toward spiritual revelation. This may be overtly religious or simply an auspicious blessing that manifests as a stream of creativity, meaning, or inspiration that guides you. This inspiration may manifest through spiritual pursuits and artistic, musical, or literary talents. It may also be scientific or empirical, but either way, you want to understand the nature of reality and how things work.

You inherit the basis for a quiet, deeply considerate character and spiritual deportment from your Ancestors' wisdom. You are born with a natural wisdom and spiritual sense of things. You are an "old soul," displaying maturity and self-cultivation from an early age. You may also manifest many natural talents and be predisposed to be a gifted musician, composer, artist, or poet. This artistic expression may be central to unraveling your Fate as a "calling." You may also be deeply ritualistic and even ceremonial in your conduct.

You are a born mystic and may have spiritual experiences from an early age. This could make you a "weird" child; you may be "different" and not connect with kids your age, adults, or the conventional culture around you. You may be born with a yearning for wisdom, God, transcendence, and so on, and be deeply drawn to prayer, meditation, religion, churches, temples, and the like. You may begin asking deep questions about life and the universe at an early age, or you may be drawn to understanding things deeply, which may lead you down a path of study early on. You may manifest this through science or religion, but either way, you want to understand the nature of reality, no matter the means. Science and experimentation can become like a religion, as it brings you closer to truth.

This placement may manifest as a specific religious or spiritual presence in your life or, again, as a tradition of study or inquiry, like being the child of a quantum physicist. You may be born into a religious family connected to a tradition like Catholicism, Judaism, Buddhism, or Hinduism, for example. Religious tradition may be central to your experience, and you may meet a spiritual teacher early in life. This may shape you and influence the unraveling of your Fate.

Your Fate may include a religious or spiritual "calling," which may manifest as a vocation. This can be the Fate to become a monk, nun, priest, yogi, rabbi, pastor, or the like. You may be called to seminary, divinity school, or rabbinical school, and end up ordained as a religious figure wearing vestments. This placement can be a connection to lineage, and you may inherit a tradition as a lineage holder. This connection can also be worldly and come in the form of inheriting a deeper pursuit of truth, like you become an artist or physicist following in the footsteps of a wise mentor.

The core theme here is that the unraveling of your Fate will have a deeper spiritual component and calling, which may resolve through spiritual or mystical experience, revelation, awakening, or enlightenment. It may also involve significant rituals or rites of passage. Your life is a spiritual path, and you must pursue it. While this may sound highfalutin and mystical, it may add a deep dimension of ritual and protocol to your character. You may be very attuned to ritual, propriety, and decorum, and this can even manifest through you legalistically or through high ideals of justice.

If this is afflicted by Ghost Stars, your path of spiritual cultivation and practice may involve exorcising Demons and Ghosts, and spiritual revelation may be cathartic. You may be called to resolve Ancestral Ghosts and break dark patterns through spiritual means, and this may be central to your Fate. Afflictions may come in the form of dark visions or emotions you do not understand, but you can release them and grow wise.

Ancestors Palace

If you have Wen Qu in the Ancestors Palace, you are directly connected to your Ancestors' religious or spiritual inheritance. In general, this represents a connection with all your Ancestors, but it may also be a direct connection to a specific Wisdom Ancestor whose religious or spiritual cultivation flows into your life. Your Ancestors are a blessing, and their wisdom guides you to spiritual fulfillment and Fruition. You will be a source of pride for your Ancestors and represent their spiritual aspirations.

Religion or spiritual cultivation may play a significant role in your Ancestors' lives, coming to you through your parents or grandparents or a specific Ancestor. Your family may be devoutly Catholic, Hasidic, Shaivite, Theravada Buddhist, or something else, and your parents may enforce these beliefs through ritual, family prayer, attending church or temple, or simply by transmitting a worldview and set of religious values to you. You may have a particular parent or grandparent who is spiritual or wise and who shapes your worldview.

The Priest in this House can also manifest as a deep and central focus on spirituality and religion that does not come from your Ancestral blood family but rather from a "spiritual family." You may have Fated connections with a spiritual lineage, wisdom holders, or religious traditions outside your family or from a different culture. This lineage may be your "true" family, and a spiritual teacher, guru, or guide may become like a parent. You are Fated to practice a foreign spiritual tradition and even inherit that tradition as a practitioner or priest. This placement also may be a call to revitalize a spiritual tradition in your family and help them remember their spiritual roots. You may be an "adept" and readily take up meditation, prayer, yoga, chanting, and so on. These esoteric practices will be like memories rather than things you must learn. You have the potential to follow these practices to Fruition and experience enlightenment, awakening, or salvation, as you are following the momentum of your Wisdom Ancestors who have already done the work. This may also manifest as an artistic, musical, or poetic gift inherited from the Ancestors that expresses deeper and more spiritual insights and aspirations.

This Star here can manifest as a deep fascination with and talent for the mantic arts: divination, astrology, Fengshui, tarot, palm reading, and so on. You will be drawn to secret teachings, mystery, and magic. You may also experience visions or prophetic dreams. You will be a vivid dreamer and oneironaut, able to have lucid dreams and connect with teachers, guides, spirits, and Ancestors while sleeping and potentially even when awake. You may naturally become adept at trance, dance, and losing yourself in rituals, fasting, and prayer. You can learn all these things with ease—again, as if you are remembering them.

If this is afflicted by Ghost Stars, then you may be caught up in a lot of the negativity that comes with religion. You may join a cult and experience abuse, or you may have negative experiences at a church or from a religious or spiritual teacher who mistreats, abuses, or confuses you. You may have a lot of dark, negative emotions around religion, like guilt, shame, fear, or punishment and retribution. Your path may involve releasing these negative emotions. You may also be haunted in your meditation practice, trance, or prayer, and you may become possessed by negative spirits or Ghosts. Spirituality and religion may then become a confusing and dark path that you must either release or let go of and become secular.

Youth Palace

If Wen Qu arrives in the Youth Palace, religion and spirituality will deeply influence your Fate with siblings or your Fate in youth. This Star may manifest as a sensitive or spiritual sibling, or your relationship with your siblings may be deeply meaningful and bordering on spiritual. You may have a past-life or Ancestral connections with them to help and guide each other toward spiritual goals. An older sibling may be a strong spiritual role model and influence you toward a more meaningful life, or you may be this role model for your younger siblings.

This placement often means your connection to siblings is weak, so you may be an only child or the "weird" child who feels little or no connection to your siblings or family. You may be a sensitive and spiritual child who lives in your own world. You distance yourself from everyone and become a shy loner, drawn to renunciation and solitude. You may connect more with adults, as you may be an "old soul" who exhibits wisdom, maturity, and a spiritual sense of things early in life. You start a spiritual path and practice meditation, yoga, or prayer early, and you may manifest spiritual experiences, visions, or trance at an early age.

You may be drawn to wisdom, religion, and spirituality early in life, or religion may be an important factor in your youth. You and your family may spend a lot of time at church or temple, and a religious community could be a significant influence; that religious community may support and influence your childhood and be full of Fated friendships and deep connections. This Star here may also represent an essential spiritual figure or mentor in youth. A priest, pastor, monk, rabbi, or the like might be a role model and influence your upbringing. It may also manifest as a parochial, private, or religious school, like Sunday school, Yeshiva, or Chinese school for immigrant families, where you learn traditional values outside of your public education.

Youth may be full of significant rituals, rites of passage, or protocol. Your family may be strict and observe religious protocol, or you may be drawn to performing rituals. You may be highly organized, disciplined, and ritualistic in your conduct. You may organize people, places, and things according to intuition or a natural feeling of Fengshui.

This may also be expressed as musical, artistic, or poetic talents early in life. You may take up an instrument or paintbrush or start writing early with precocious, even competitive, talent and long-term goals. This may draw you to find a community or to seek others who share your gifts.

If this is afflicted by Ghost Stars, you may experience darkness at church or through religion early on. You may endure abuse at the hands of religion or a religious figure, and this may put you off religion for the rest of your life. You may be burdened with the guilt, shame, or fear put into you by religion as a child. You may also be open to possession and experiences with Ghosts or spirits during trance or visions, as your haunted Ancestors may be drawn to your spiritual sensitivity and receptivity. You may have exorcistic experiences as a youth, and you may have to repress these memories.

Partners Palace

Wen Qu is generally auspicious in the Partners Palace and can manifest in two directions. First, you may be Fated to meet a kind, gentle, and spiritual partner, and relationships may be a source of spiritual cultivation. Second, it can manifest as renunciation, celibacy, or living the life of a monk or nun who abstains from marriage. If this is afflicted, then it tends toward the latter.

The Priest may manifest as a Fated spiritual connection with a partner. Your partner may be spiritual, or you may meet them through connections with a religious or spiritual community. Sometimes but not always, this person is older, and they may choose you. Or it may be a partnership that happens later in life or is arranged via astrology. Partnership, in general, is quiet, spiritual, and more characterized by modesty and respect than wild romance here. Partnership will be a powerful source of spiritual growth and self-cultivation, and you can grow wise and even develop a Dharma partnership. This may manifest as intentional spiritual cultivation in the form of Daoism or Tantra, or it may be informed by traditional religious values on marriage, adhering to something like Jewish or Islamic law. You may also practice Karma Mudra, Maithuna, sexual yoga, and so on, and actualize yourselves as deities in sexual union. Or your partnership may simply involve a lot of protocols, rituals, or routines that become a source of insight and growth.

You may also be Fated to live as a monk or nun and renounce married life. You may cry when you see monks and nuns and feel you are supposed to be one. You may know early on that you are asexual or have no interest in partnership or having children. Your spiritual path may involve taking vows of celibacy, and you may not be able to marry due to religious restrictions. This may be intentional and welcomed or simply something you must deal with. You may also be a hermit and live alone in the mountains; you may be interested in partners but never meet them because you are alone. Or this placement may force you into being alone. You can also be like Saint Catherine of Alexandria or Teresa of Avila and be mystically married to Christ.

If this is afflicted by Ghost Stars, you may turn toward renunciation or celibacy out of negative experiences. You may be abused or hurt by a partner, and so you give up on relationships altogether and live alone out of fear of being hurt again. You may experience trauma early in life that makes you asexual as an adult. You may also constantly play out or relive negative, abusive patterns in relationships, and this may drive you to be alone due to many failed partnerships. Working through these patterns may be a source of spiritual revelation and growth.

Offspring Palace

If Wen Qu arrives in the Offspring Palace, you are Fated to have well-behaved, sensitive, and spiritual children who will care for you in old age. As a Yin Star, this implies having daughters, but traditionally, the Priest represents a son. Either way, at least one child will have a natural spiritual disposition or be emotionally sensitive. They may be sickly and have a delicate constitution, but they will be intelligent, wise, and long-lived due to their self-discipline and cultivation.

This placement potentially indicates a spiritual past-life or Ancestral connection with someone you have a debt to. Your children or one of your children may be a returning spiritual friend or teacher who has come to teach you everything you need to know. Taking care of them fulfills a debt; as the old Tibetan adage goes, every sentient being has at one point been your mother, so now you must be their mother, and so on. So, you change their diapers, which develops compassion, equanimity, and loving-kindness.

Having a child may initiate you on a spiritual path, and the challenges and joys of being a parent may be a primary source of spiritual growth. Taking care of them may be your spiritual path, as it again cultivates the Four Immeasurables of equanimity, compassion, joy, and loving-kindness. You may grow up and mature immensely after having kids, as you must now care for others and be a role model. You may also have great insight into the nature of birth, life, death, and immortality from having kids.

You may also be inspired to raise your kids in a religious household or make spirituality and religion an essential part of raising them. Maybe having kids makes you find religion, as you want them to have community and values. You may baptize them or perform Jatakarma or Brit Milah. You may give them a religious name; traditionally, it was the custom sometimes to send off the third-born to be a monk, nun, or priest.

Affliction by Ghost Stars here can lead to the child being sickly or delicate, to the point that they need much more attention or help. You may also have a child who is too sensitive for their own good; they may see Ghosts and spirits and be open to possession. Affliction can also lead to difficulty conceiving, which could become a spiritual dilemma and a source of deep reflection and soul searching. Also, religious restrictions on sexuality—such as prudence, purity, and modesty, and avoiding having sex, and children, out of wedlock—could be a hindrance and source of negativity in your life that you rebel against, or they might be directives you enforce on others.

Wealth Palace

Wen Qu, a symbol of frugality, resourcefulness, and "protocol," is auspicious in the Wealth Palace. It does not represent the pursuit of vast wealth but rather the image of the priest or protocol master, who was a figure of high organization, ceremony, and selflessness in the royal court. This symbol is also associated with earning from religious or spiritual work.

In the more secular view, as the Protocol Master, this Star means you will again be responsible, organized, frugal, and resourceful with money so that you can do well with just about anything and even excel at consulting, advising, and managing businesses. This can translate to direct work in finance, accounting, banking, investing, and so on. It can also easily translate to any coaching or work helping people create or enforce protocols, rituals, regulations, and the like.

However, by nature, the Priest is not interested in money for worldly gains; instead, he has high spiritual aspirations. So, you will not likely be driven by money or the desire for worldly satisfaction, but earning money will be directed toward a higher sense of purpose, aspiration, or religious and spiritual values. This may include giving money to charity, donating to a temple, or giving tithings to a church. You will direct funds toward your spiritual goals, and generating wealth will be done to create good "merit" and to pay it forward. You will be inspired to spread wealth, give to the poor, and generate charity, generosity, and goodwill by honestly acquiring wealth and resources.

You may even follow religious or spiritual protocols for earning money—what Buddhism calls "right livelihood"—which means no trading in weapons or living beings, meat, liquor, or poisons. Generating wealth will be a ritual in which you guide and channel the forces of the universe; you will see money, goods, services, and information as forces of nature that you direct with ritual protocol. Deep down, your actual wealth will be spiritual and internal; you will find wealth in well-being, peace of mind, and wisdom, and you will be satisfied with anything if you are helping others and generating good merit and wisdom.

In the more religious manifestations, you may work as an ordained priest, rabbi, sheikh, or the like and earn your livelihood as a spiritual leader. This may also manifest as a renunciation of money as a monk or nun who takes a vow of poverty, and you can subsist only on what is given to you through donations or gifts. You may have only a robe and bowl and eat only what strangers put in the bowl. In the less religious manifestations, you may work and be paid well as an astrologer, psychic, yoga teacher, chaplain, spiritual counselor, or coach. You may be a hospice worker or hospital chaplain and counsel people on deathbeds or perform marriage ceremonies.

If this is afflicted by Ghost Stars, you may struggle with poverty and resent your renunciation, which you do out of spite for the world. Unable to make a career work, you may give up and renounce wealth but never truly, as you may have spite and bitterness. You may try to be a wandering yogi or carefree Daoist but end up a wandering bum who mooches off others. You may be a "hippie" who doesn't want to work due to misplaced spiritual ideals, and so you become a burden on others. You may also lose money or end up in poverty as a kind of spiritual hero's trial, in which you must be poor as penance or punishment for the lawlessness of an Ancestor. Affliction may also look like stealing money from the collection plate or embezzling money through untaxed religious organizations.

Health Palace

Wen Qu is considered to have mixed auspices in the Health Palace, which depend significantly on self-cultivation and aligning with a spiritual path. This placement means that you inherit a deep and embodied spiritual sensitivity from your Ancestors. You inherit their hopes, dreams, and prayers for salvation, their hopes for the eternal, for God, for enlightenment for the benefit of all beings.

This sensitivity gives you a delicate constitution; you may have a weaker physical disposition, weak kidneys, and a weak heart. This sensitivity may translate to your environment, physically, mentally, and emotionally: You may have a host of environmental and food allergies and be prone to many autoimmune disorders, skin rashes, digestive disorders, and affliction of the lungs due to dampness, phlegm, wind, cold, and heat. These conditions will be diagnosable, but you can overcome them by self-cultivation and working to strengthen your "gates," or your defensive Qi.

You may also be very sensitive to mental and emotional disorders. You may be naturally empathic and quickly pick up on the stress and negative emotions of others. You may take on their negativity, and this can stress you out and manifest as unexplainable symptoms like heart racing, dizziness, migraines, IBS, and so on. When you are in stressful environments, you manifest these symptoms, and when you leave, they go away. You may be prone to what looks like miraculous recovery, but this is because your conditions are psychic, mental, emotional, and so on, which is not to downplay them, for this ability can be very powerful. Managing stress and developing strong personal health disciplines that evoke protection from harmful influences become very important. Living in nature, seeking solitude, and exiting complex, stressful, or confusing environments are also essential.

As the indicator of spiritual Fate, this also means that your health is aligned with your spiritual and religious aspirations. When you are internally, spiritually aligned, then you are healthy. When you are not following your path or misaligned, you start to get ill. It will be essential to align your life with these deep aspirations and values; otherwise, you may get very sick. You will also generate health from spiritual practices like meditation, yoga, alchemy, and prayer. Prayer and positive visualization, the "placebo effect," will be powerful forms of healing, as will ritual and spiritual community. A spiritual or religious community will be essential to keep you on your path, support you, and create a positive environment crucial to your well-being. You may need to go see Jesus on the cross or bow and make offerings to the Buddha to be healthy.

This also indicates a high aptitude for healthcare and medicine in the traditional sense, as a wisdom path, but also more simply as a means of expressing compassion and cultivating good merit. You can excel at traditional cultivation practices associated with medicine, like Qigong, and you can quickly learn and understand the energy dynamics of herbs and poisons as medicine. You can also be disciplined and organized enough in your study to excel at modern medicine, but unless it is guided by a spiritual goal of service or compassion, this endeavor will not succeed. If you are aligned with these goals, you can make an excellent doctor, counselor, therapist, or health coach.

Traditionally, this placement means that you will be adept at yoga, meditation, and alchemy, and you can be a high-level practitioner and experience great Fruition. This Star here can indicate doing long retreats or extensive practice. Because of this, you can die very well; your Ancestors will appear to greet you in death, and you may manifest miraculous signs at the time of death. You may even perform miracles and heal others.

If this is afflicted, it aggravates the above tendencies for sensitivity, and Ghost Stars here can make nervous, autoimmune, and mental-emotional disorders much worse. They may become an expression of dark Ancestral energy that must be resolved through adverse health and illness and released with prayer, meditation, and even cathartic exorcism. These kinds of unexplained medical conditions can get more grievous, and internal conflict, struggle, suffering, and so on could tear you up inside and become a spiritual trial that degrades your spirit and manifests as severe illness. Affliction may generate illness from improper spiritual practices like yoga and Inner Alchemy or from the inappropriate use of medicine, psychedelics, or poisons.

Career/Travel Palace

If Wen Qu appears in the Career/Travel Palace, then the fundamental flavor of your work in the world, your contribution to society, and any travel you do will take on a spiritual or religious nature. This is a call to connect with and express your Ancestors' religious or spiritual values through your work in the world, which is true of this Star in all the career Houses.

Like magistrates, priests were also called away from their home, and often, kids with spiritual aptitude were taken from home at an early age and placed in various temples for training. If they had a high aptitude, they might have been taken to the holiest temples and sacred mountains, and eventually, they would become official priests at designated temples. The Protocol Master was the highest-ranking Daoist priest who served the royal court. So, their Fate was to leave home, and it manifested far from home. As such, this is often a Fate Threshold to move far from home to a new town, city, or country, and your Fate may not flower until you move or travel to find it. It may involve a spiritual calling or vocation that you must seek. Your Fate in the world is a spiritual path, which may be outwardly religious or internally based on spiritual principles.

As such, this placement is a strong indicator of a religious or spiritual profession, or at least a profession as a Protocol Master. Again, you may be a priest, pastor, rabbi, sheikh, or the like, but your profession may also simply involve working for a religious institution as a layperson. Your work life may be intimately tied to your religious community.

You can also excel at any work that involves spiritual or religious technology: astrologer, healer, medium, psychic, and so on. It may also include being a translator or interpreter, and you may study classical or sacred texts. Your work may involve the transmission of lineage or traditional knowledge that you must study and master. This may manifest as a Fated meeting with a spiritual teacher, guru, or guide with whom you apprentice. You may, in turn, become a spiritual teacher, guide, or coach, and guide others.

This Star here can manifest as being the most extreme version of a monk, yogi, or hermit. You may renounce the world and go off to a monastery, convent, or hermitage. You may dedicate your life to meditation, yoga, alchemy, and so on. You may be solely focused on enlightenment and liberation for the benefit of all beings, and you must travel and leave home on pilgrimage to complete your path. This may happen early in life, or you may retire to the mountains in old age.

In the more secular sense of being the Protocol Master, you will again be responsible, organized, frugal, and resourceful and can do well with just about anything that involves consulting, advising, and managing business; you can work in finance, accounting, banking, or investing, or do any coaching or work to help people create or enforce protocols, rituals, or regulations. Managing and directing the actions of others are crucial, especially at any institution with solid values and organizing principles. You may also make an excellent diplomat, public relations person, or officer who enforces rules or laws.

You will do these things with a sense of purpose and potentially as an expression of your higher spiritual aspirations and ideals, which may be an expression of your Ancestors or past lives. Your work in the world must be aligned with your deeper values. These may be religious and come directly from a religious source, or they may be personal, whether Ancestral or derived from your own spiritual life. If your work is not aligned with your values, it will be stunted and not progress until you become aligned.

If this is afflicted by Ghost Stars, you may be burdened with spiritual aspirations you cannot fulfill. You may struggle to integrate into the world because of your spiritual nature. You may be unable to "play the game" of society. You may curse the rat race, the struggle of samsara. This may become resentful, and ordinary life may become a grind. You may not be in a place to renounce the world, however, and your lack of motivation leads you to become poor; as in the Wealth Palace, you may intend to be a wandering yogi but become a wandering bum. You may seek a spiritual path, teacher, or profession but cannot find it; this may turn to longing and sadness. You may be haunted by the Ghosts of religion in your life and be unable to live up to them. You may also incur scandal or drama at or through a religious institution that affects your career or makes you leave town and start over somewhere new.

Assistants Palace

Wen Qu is exalted and belongs in the Assistants Palace, as does the Magistrate Star, as these Stars are both images of selfless service. This placement exemplifies the more profound role of "selfless" service and values like compassion, generosity, charity, and loving-kindness, as exemplified in various religious and spiritual traditions. If you have this here, no matter what you do, you will serve others with a deeper spiritual purpose and cultivate a sense of selflessness by helping others. You will develop these virtues through your work in the world. At heart, this is a call to connect with and express your Ancestors' religious or spiritual values through your work in the world in service of others.

This can be formally religious, and this Star can bring out a connection to spiritual or religious lineage; you may have a Fated connection with a spiritual teacher, guru, mentor, or the like whom you serve and succeed. You may have many older or wiser mentors who love and guide you.

The Priest here may also mean a deep connection to a spiritual or religious community, parish, convent, or school filled with people you rely on and work with toward a greater purpose or spiritual mission. These people support you, and you may depend heavily on each other but serve each other well so that you can serve the world or the greater community. Again, this may be a temple, church group, synagogue, mosque, and so on, even more so if you have an Ancestral connection to that tradition. It may also be an academic, educational, healthcare, or social service organization with some connection to tradition or a clear mandate or goal to serve. As the Protocol Master, you will make an excellent teammate and team leader or organizer. You may be adept at managing others, but you will not be a leader; instead, you will uphold others from behind.

As the House of Friendship, this may also mean a deep spiritual connection to a group of friends. You may be Fated to meet many people with whom you share a spiritual connection. You will be part of a "circle of returners" who reconnect through spiritual values. This can also manifest through a group of co-workers with whom you share a spiritual connection. You meet and serve many other people who all have the same mission in life. Perhaps you become a social worker, doctor, or therapist, and you have a deep kinship with the people you work with, because you were all brought up on the same path for the same reason.

This placement can manifest as a calling to practice religion or spiritual technologies. You may be drawn to meditation, yoga, prayer, and so on. You may study these formally, or they may become essential to your life and support your work. Your job may have nothing to do with religion or spirituality, but you bring a deep sense of prayer or meditation to it. You may just "cut wood and carry water," as they say in Zen: You may be a farmer, janitor, barista, or whatever, but you serve and work selflessly as a form of meditation or worship and spirituality. Indian traditions call this karma yoga; you work and do your duty with no thought of fame, privilege, or financial reward; work is simply a dedication to a higher spiritual purpose. Generally, you are an excellent servant, assistant, helper, and friend, as you are more naturally selfless. This is an Ancestral inheritance.

At the most basic level, Wen Qu here can also be a force of creativity in music, art, poetry, and so on. You may work in a creative, innovative, or cutting-edge field, in something that borders on the mystical but could be very practical. You may be talented and imaginative; in this House, these passions and hobbies can become a job, but you will likely remain behind the scenes. Something mystical, creative, and deep inspires and guides you, and it could come out as secular and scientific or more "woo woo" and esoteric. You may be drawn to work in cutting-edge technology that looks like magic or in actual magic. You may create art, music, or tech that guides people toward a more spiritual experience or connection or that simply creates a sense of inspiration and aspiration toward something better.

If this is afflicted by Ghost Stars, you may incur scandal or conflict through a religious or spiritual community or a spiritual teacher. Your spiritual aspirations may bog you down and hinder you through excessive idealism, unrealistic or distorted understandings of the "real world," or cloistered, cultlike brainwashing. You may be in an actual cult or be delusional enough to try and start one. You may be a failed guru or spiritual teacher. Your spiritual path and practices may also be haunted by Ancestral Ghosts and require exorcist catharsis. Or, more simply, your creative work may be haunted and stuck in mediocrity, despair, failure, and conflict patterns.

Superiors Palace

Wen Qu is also very strong in the Superiors Palace and exemplifies work as a Priest or Protocol Master. This is also one of the most vital indicators of experiencing spiritual lineage or meeting a spiritual teacher, guru, mentor, or the like and for successfully following a spiritual path to Fruition in this lifetime. So, you may have a spiritual calling or vocation and be drawn to seek a teacher and follow a path. This may be overtly religious, or it may be more secular and manifest through your work, but here in the Superiors Palace, you can reach and influence more people and express and disseminate spiritual ideas to a broader audience. You can be a successful Priest, whatever that means.

As usual, there is a call here to connect with your Ancestors' spiritual or religious traditions, which may be blood Ancestors or past-life Wisdom Ancestors. You may have a strong connection with a tradition outside your family, which may be initiated through meeting a teacher or encountering esoteric teachings. You may be a "professional" yogi. You may feel called or be groomed to be a monk, nun, rabbi, imam, or guru. This may be a personal spiritual path in which you go off to the mountains, or you may undergo deep training at a temple or school, but in general, this comes with the mandate to teach and help others as a leader. It comes with a strong precedent for having spiritual realization and Fruition, as it has the momentum of previous practice from Ancestors.

Often, this placement indicates a serious teacher–student relationship or apprenticeship. You may undergo intense training with a spiritual teacher, guru, or mentor who mirrors your limitations and shortcomings and helps you grow. This may be formally spiritual, like in Zen or Tantra, or it may take the form of a professional or personal mentor who helps you grow. You may receive "transmission" from this teacher and carry on their lineage or follow in your mentor's footsteps. You can also contribute to and expand the teachings; you can write a spiritual text, innovating and creating your own system of knowledge.

In the more secular sense, Wen Qu may manifest as creativity through music, art, or writing, but here, you may be successful, which so few artists are. It is challenging to "make it" as an artist, musician, or creative person in this culture, but if you have this placement, then a career as an artist may be viable, and you can find an audience and support; people will appreciate your work and pay you for it. Your work may be public: You may perform or share your work with the world. The secret to success will be heartfelt and genuine expression and authenticity that people can connect with. Of course, you must also be a good artist. This Star here also means the ability to innovate and generate evocative, exciting, and new art.

In the even more secular sense of the Protocol Master, you may be an excellent organizer and leader of people. You may be drawn to leadership, management, and educational work. You will be naturally gifted at protocol and "ritual" and can use this professionally. You will be a kind and gentle leader, but you can also be strict and enforce rules and protocols, and you will excel at work that has a ritual aspect. Whatever you do will be guided by more profound religious or spiritual principles and values, by a "greater good."

If this is afflicted by Ghost Stars, then you may experience abuse or trauma at the hands of a spiritual or religious teacher, institution, or cult. Your spiritual path may involve exorcising a lot of Ancestral Ghosts, which may lead to many ups and downs and turmoil on the path that are ultimately cathartic and enlightening. Your creative work may also be challenged by many negative emotions, self-doubt, and anger, but this may color your work and make it unique.

Property Palace

If Wen Qu shows up in the Property Palace, then you will have a religious or spiritual connection to land and property or be sensitive to Fengshui. You will also likely have a deep spiritual connection to nature, wilderness, countryside, sacred spaces, and architecture. This directly connects to property like churches, temples, synagogues, mosques, pagodas, and shrines, which you may own, manage, build, make offerings to, or visit on pilgrimage. A significant piece of your Fate may be catalyzed by or in "sacred spaces." This placement also means a connection to any piece of property, inheritance, or heirloom considered sacred or personal or that carries on or continues an Ancestral story of meaning or purpose.

So, you may inherit or receive property, inheritance, or heirlooms that carry deep religious, Ancestral, or personal meaning. This may be physical property, like a house or plot of land, but it may also come in the form of personal items like letters, photos, artifacts, and so on. Fate may connect you to religiously significant land or property, like inheriting the deed to a church or a place where your Ancestors worshipped (and perhaps still do). But you may also be called to doing genealogy, manifesting as receiving an inheritance of old letters and photos you sort through and organize. You feel a spiritual connection to their stories, which come alive through old black-and-white photos and letters in another language.

In general, property ownership and management can go well, and property will increase in value, but your interest in owning property for financial reasons may be weak. You may be more called to practice minimalism, non-attachment, and renunciation. This is the image of a priest, but it may be more like a monk who only possesses a robe and bowl. You may sell all your possessions and keep only what you can store in a backpack or suitcase. You may live in religious housing like a monastery, hermitage, or commune, and you may undergo significant training there. You may also spend a lot of time on meditation retreats, both group and solo. Or you may simply live in partnership or cooperation with others. Your living situation may be provided for by a benefactor, community, or charity. You may also live in housing provided by the government or social services. Either way, at some point, you may not have to pay for your living situation.

This Star here also manifests as a connection and sensitivity to Fengshui and the mantic arts of geomancy and placement. You feel a spiritual connection to nature and space and how energy flows through space and influences people and spirits. This can manifest as a connection to spirits, Ghosts, Demons, and so on, which you may see, feel, or perceive through the medium of space. For example, spirits tend to gather in nature at ascension points, like at the base of mountains, and you may intuit these things. Because you may be sensitive to Fengshui, your health and well-being may be affected by your location and the organization or arrangement of the people, buildings, and objects in the spaces of your life.

You may also be talented at Fengshui and can work as a consultant. This talent is a skill and a spiritual gift that is embodied and felt. It is expressed in a visionary and creative way. Your designs, arrangements, and projects are not just based on practical principles but on spiritual ones. They express realizations, insights, and intuitions rather than rational or intellectual understandings. This understanding can make you feel more connected and validated in your abilities.

If this is afflicted, you may be open to Ancestral Ghosts and possessions in and through sacred places. You may be attuned to the Ghosts of religion and the moral, physical, and psychological violence perpetrated by religion. Your sense of Fengshui and spirits may open you to possession, and you may experience irrational or strange, negative emotions in certain places or places of religious or Ancestral significance. You may also lose property or experience a disaster or the destruction of a sacred place.

Pleasure Palace

If you have Wen Qu in the Pleasure Palace, you will enjoy and be able to take pleasure in all things religious, spiritual, esoteric, or occult. You will be fascinated by meaning-making, soteriology, ontology, cosmology, and so on. You may also enjoy the physical manifestations of religion through people and places. You may be very interested in and connected to the specific religion that you inherit; you may be born into a religion, and your sense of enjoyment in life comes through its influence—maybe you let Jesus take the wheel, or you may see everything as a manifestation of Lila, the divine play of Shiva. Or you may be fascinated by religion in general and study much of it, as you are drawn to esoteric wisdom and occult knowledge. Here, you inherit the pure love of wisdom without ulterior worldly motives, and you have the desire to manifest and actualize that wisdom from your Ancestors.

You may study and be naturally talented at various esoteric or occult practices, like astrology, Fengshui, palmistry, and so on. You may also be a natural psychic or medium. Or you may take a more traditional route and study Buddhism, Daoism, Hinduism, Sufism, Kabbalah, Christian Mysticism, and so on. Still, you are drawn to the more mystical sides of religion rather than the purely moral or legalistic. You want to experience the wisdom these traditions point to. You may be interested in altered states, trance, and revelation and be drawn to practice meditation, yoga, and prayer because you want to experience these states, and this is because you enjoy them. You may also seek these states through drugs, dance, music, ritual, or sex. You may enjoy the otherness or contrast of these states from ordinary consciousness, or you may enjoy them intellectually or experientially as they are felt in the body. It doesn't matter how you enjoy them, but you do. This makes the Fruition of the spiritual path easier because you can also enjoy the discipline of these practices.

If this placement does not manifest as religious or spiritual, you may simply be "weird." You may be drawn to odd, different, niche, rare, nerdy, geeky, or quirky hobbies and things. Again, it doesn't matter what you enjoy; it is that your enjoyment of things borders on the mystical. Whatever you enjoy becomes a spiritual experience. Enjoyment is deeply personal and deeply felt, and here it expresses something "beyond," other, secret, mystical, and so on. This can come through fantasy, science fiction, history, technology, video games, role-play—you name it. This can also manifest as a deep musical, artistic, or poetic talent that, again, becomes a spiritual experience. You may turn these hobbies and interests into a job, but this will be challenging because they tend to alienate people due to their strangeness.

If this is afflicted by Ghost Stars, then these altered states of consciousness can become dark, and you may be open to possession. This may be Ancestral, and you may be haunted by Ancestors who suffered through religion, or you may open yourself to any variety of external phenomena that possesses you. This may be in the form of spirits, Ghosts, Demons, and so on, but you may also be open to weird, strange, delusional, or dangerous ideas that cause you great confusion and lead to negative emotions, obsession, and even self-harm.

If afflicted, this placement may also lead to substance abuse and addiction or to being addicted to experiences like video games, pornography, or sex. You may have strange, otherworldly experiences of aliens, angels, and so on that become an obsession or experience of persecution. The border between spiritual realization and being crazy is flimsy, and when this Star is afflicted, it can push that border into going crazy. You may also experience struggle due to being weird, different, or other. You may become obsessed with things in a way that undermines your life and makes it difficult to fit in or get a regular job.

GHOSTLY ANCESTORS (鬼)

NOW THAT WE HAVE COMPLETED OUR JOURNEY of the Twelve Ruling Stars through all the Twelve Houses, we can now begin to study the Lesser Stars of Polestar Astrology and the concept of "affliction," which we call Gui (鬼), or Ghosts. These Stars vary in strength but are generally much weaker than the Twelve Ruling Stars. Except for the Four Major Ghosts, their influence is considered minor or insignificant; hence, we call them "Lesser" Stars.

It is important to note that, except for the Four Major Ghosts, these Stars are not strong enough to rule a House; this cannot be overstated. They are weak in nature, but sometimes weakness can be persistent and lead to negativity. Think of these Stars like mosquito bites or, better yet, cigarettes: One cigarette will not kill you and can hardly be proved be harmful. But they are addictive, and many cigarettes over a long period can become very destructive. So it is with Ghosts.

Many of these Stars represent very small, subtle, and weak influences that can become harmful or frustrating over time. They do not represent significant patterns of Fate but rather subtle aspects of behavior, and again, except for the Four Major Ghosts, they cannot "rule" a House. So, if these Stars show up alone in a House without a Major Star, then that House is considered "empty" and has no significant Fate. These influences can lead to subtle flavors, patterns, and textures of experience, but they are not strong enough to drastically shape or direct Fate.

We call these Stars "Gui," or Ghosts. Ghosts are the uncomfortable or painful "story" or conflicted mental-emotional states of an Ancestor who died physically but was unable to complete the process of death emotionally. These unresolved emotions and thought patterns are called Ghosts and do not "stop" in death. Instead, they lose the body/mind/Qi context that generated them, and without the reference of human embodiment, they cannot resolve. Therefore, they seek embodiment to "finish" and cross over. In Buddhism, these negative emotions are known as *kleshas*, or "poisons" (desire, hatred, ignorance, pride, envy), and are seen as the root cause of suffering. In Polestar Astrology, we are said to inherit predispositions for these poisons from our Ghostly Ancestors.

All the following Stars represent our inherited patterns of Ancestral negativity and incomplete experience that we must finish, complete, or resolve. This is where the Twelve Ruling Stars come in. They represent our Beneficial Ancestors, who often gang up in our chart to help resolve negative Ancestral Fate. This may sound heroic or dramatic, but these should not be taken too seriously. Americans get very excited about Ghosts and Demons, but this is itself "Ghost" behavior, so relax.

That being said, the Four Major Ghosts can represent "strong" patterns of unresolved or negative emotion and story, inexplicable experiences of anger, jealousy, delusion, and so on, that we inherit, especially Qi Sha (七殺), the Seven Killings or Executioner Star, and Po Jun (破軍), the Rebel or Breaking Rank Star. These can be very dark and influential, so it is essential to examine these thoroughly, as they can rule a House.

Qi Sha, the Seven Killings or Executioner Star, can become "Demonic," and as such, it is the darkest force in Polestar Astrology. Otherwise, these Stars represent inherited patterns of negative emotions and self-imposed limitations from our unresolved Ancestors. And we can be free of them. We can persist and be liberated if we follow a path with sincerity and consistency. Our job is to liberate these Ghosts so we can be free of them and free our Ancestors of these ongoing stories and burdens.

The Lesser Stars are divided into five categories: the Four Major Ghosts, the Four Minor Ghosts, the Four Incidentals, the Orphan Spirits, and the Four Transformers. We will walk the Four Major Ghosts through the Twelve Houses, because these Stars are strong enough to affect the shape and direction of our Fate. They should not be taken lightly, as they can significantly alter our life's path. We will discuss the others but not walk them through the Houses, for these Stars are not strong enough to alter Fate; they mostly just make us moody. It is essential not to overanalyze or exalt these Stars to the same level as the Royal Court. They are not equal; the Royal Court is not a democracy. Many of the Lesser Stars can even be ignored or thrown out.

THE FOUR MAJOR GHOSTS

THE FOUR MAJOR GHOSTS are Lian Zhen (廉貞), the Concubine Star; Qi Sha (七殺), the Seven Killings or Executioner Star; Tan Lang (貪狼), the Greedy Wolf Star; and Po Jun (破軍), the Rebel or Breaking Rank Star. These are, again, the "strongest" of the Ghost Stars and represent the most significant patterns of affliction in our charts, except for the Concubine, which is not really an affliction but can be an undermining or limiting force that can amplify affliction.

Again, these Stars represent our most significant Ancestral Ghosts that we inherit at birth. In a way, we are "charged" with resolving these negative or limiting factors. If we do not, these patterns tend to repeat and reinforce themselves in our own lives and down the generations of future Ancestors. They do not get resolved because people perpetuate them; we gnaw and tear at old wounds like a dog that tastes its own blood.

Again, these are the living stories of negativity inherited from our unresolved Ancestors. They represent generalized forces in our chart, but each chart must be understood on a case-by-case, individual basis concerning your actual Ancestors. In other words, they represent real stories that may or may not be dramatic and may or may not be significant. And they can be "eclipsed." If these Stars show up with other, stronger Stars, they can be eclipsed to some degree, sometimes wholly, especially if they show up with the General or Emperor Star.

Often, Major Ghosts add an extra dimension of "struggle": limitations, obstacles, and obstructions. They add patterns that are usually self-imposed but can also be experienced as "external." They can represent conflict with other people as well as accidents, losses, disaster, and hardship. However, it is important to self-reflect and see these as patterns that, at the very least, we contribute to, if they are not in fact caused by our behavior, attitudes, and negative emotions. Each represents different kinds of conflicting and negative emotion. For example, Qi Sha can represent anger, hatred, and rage when it rules a House, and when it gets eclipsed by a Star like the Emperor, that anger can turn inward and become more subtle patterns of frustration, self-hate, and bitterness that obstruct the Emperor's path to resolving Fate.

Behind each of the Four Major Ghosts is a story from an Ancestor who died with heavy negative emotions that were unresolved. They may have died in old age full of regret, grief, sadness, or anger, but they also may have died young suddenly or tragically. They may have died in an accident, from a debilitating illness or disease, drugged in a hospital, or perhaps they were betrayed, murdered, or killed in war or combat. For whatever reason, they were unable to resolve their negative emotions and have a complete experience of death, and they passed these emotions down to you to resolve. You experience them as patterns of negativity or neurotic behavior that you have no explanation for in this lifetime.

You may inherit these emotions from anyone up to seven generations back, and some of these dark patterns repeat for generations without being resolved. Sometimes they come to us from or through parents, siblings, or partners, and sometimes we experience them in our career and work. Sometimes we experience them only in certain places or during certain periods, and sometimes they are pervasive and experienced all the time. They can be dark and dramatic, or they can be subtle; either way, they can be powerful in the way they control our lives.

It is essential to do the Ancestral work of these Stars, especially Qi Sha, the Seven Killings or Executioner Star, and Po Jun, The Rebel or Breaking Rank Star. In other words, do genealogy, talk to your parents and grandparents, and find out the stories here. It would be best if you discovered the dark stories in your family: stories of hardship, heartache, betrayal, death, suicide, depression, fear, addiction, and so on. Discover what patterns you might be charged with liberating. It is crucial to connect with these stories because they may still be alive in you.

Your unresolved Ancestors call you to free them, and sometimes, their stories need to be heard or told. Sometimes, their patterns make us say, "I can't believe I did that again!" These bitter lessons of Fate are hard to learn, listen to, and let go of, because they represent the darkest patterns that we cannot often see about ourselves. But these patterns do not belong to us; we inherit them. For example, you may just be playing out the fears of your great-grandfather, who died on the battlefield.

Once these patterns are liberated, they no longer significantly influence your chart; you are free of them. They may linger as memories, but they don't remain relevant after they are resolved. However, they can be tricky: We may think we are done with something only to have it come back stronger in the future. It is up to us to be done with things but also be careful not to fool yourself. Once they are liberated, these resolved emotions turn into wisdom and become the source of our most significant personal transformation and catharsis. We should liberate them but remember them, so we do not repeat them.

Lian Zhen, the Concubine Star, represents our Ancestral patterns of inexperience, vulnerability, compliance, innocence, and youth that are easily lost, corrupted, or betrayed. It is the image of a young girl sent to the palace to be a concubine to the emperor. She is young and innocent, and her Fate is out of her control; what is coming is unknown and could be dark, and she is always in the process of waiting for an uncertain future. If she has a positive influence, this Fate can go very well. But her Fate can turn very dark if she shows up with other Ghosts.

Tan Lang, the Greedy Wolf Star, represents our Ancestral patterns of independence, isolation, struggle, loss, and hardship, but also of ingenuity, entrepreneurship, and creative adaptation; it describes patterns of exile, migration, immigration, and potentially persecution and escape. It is the image of an old lone wolf cast out of the pack to go off alone. It represents where we are Fated to struggle alone and in isolation and to adapt accordingly. It represents independence, selfishness, and at best, self-reliance—which can be a boon in modern culture, but traditionally, this was considered a nightmare.

Po Jun, the Rebel or Breaking Rank Star, represents Ancestral patterns of defiance, revolt, and revolution; it represents patterns of self-inflicted negativity born from delusions, misunderstandings, and confusions. It is the image of a military officer who realizes he is cannon fodder and "breaks rank," defying the general's orders to save himself and his platoon. As a result of his rebellion, he disrupts the general's larger plan and gets thousands killed. So, it represents patterns of behavior in which we think we are doing something good or heroic for ourselves or others but then accidentally incur negative or even disastrous consequences. We may do this over and over until we learn the lesson.

Qi Sha, the Seven Killings or Executioner Star, represents our darkest Ancestral patterns: death, murder, suicide, betrayal, loss, revenge, spite, and even hate. It represents a dark story that has potentially turned "Demonic." It is no longer a Ghost and is on its way to becoming a Demon, forgetting its humanity. As such, it is the most potent afflicting force in Polestar Astrology and the only Star that we can call genuinely hostile.

It is, again, essential to remember that these Four Stars are as dark as it gets and detail the worst of all human stories. Otherwise, everything else in Polestar Astrology is considered a positive influence. These four Stars cannot rule a House, technically, but they are strong enough to dictate and shape Fate if they arrive alone, so we will walk them through the Twelve Houses. It is common for a Chart to have at least one and possibly up to four Houses shaped by the Four Major Ghosts, and these Houses must be considered carefully. Otherwise, we must consider these Ghost Stars as augmenting or shaping the nature of one of the Twelve Ruling Stars. We must always ask how they affect the story of the stronger Stars.

LIAN ZHEN (廉貞)—THE CONCUBINE

NAME AND TRANSLATIONS:

Lian Zhen (廉貞), the Concubine Star, Pure Virtue, the Bride Star, the Celestial Favorite, the Chastity Star

Lian, 廉—incorruptible; irreproachable; blameless; probity, integrity; scrupulous; disinterested. 2 grave reserve, keep one's own counsel. a) (med.) withdraw(n), retreat; yield. 3 side-portions of a hall or large room. a) angle, corner > pointed in attention or intelligence. 4 inspect, scrutinize; examine, investigate.[1]

Zhen, 貞—real, true < true to its own nature; natural, authentic, genuine. a) what is supposed to be (cf. 實 shi, what actually is or happens to be). b) pure, perfect, of thoroughgoing genuineness; e.g., 真金 zhenjin, pure gold, finest gold. c) realize(d), perfect(ed), actualize or bring to completion one's inherent qualities; e.g., (Dao.) 真人 zhenren, Realized Persons, the Perfected, term found as early as the 6th chapter of Zhuangzi and used in various movements, but esp. influential in Shang Qing Dao. to designate the highest class of divine beings whose home is in the Shang Qing heaven and who are completely spiritualized. d) ideal, worthy to be imitated. 2 true < what is real and not illusory.[2]

These two characters can be translated in many ways, including "true or pure virtue" or as "Chastity Star," as it represents the energy of youth, childhood, and innocence in the form of a young girl who is sent to the palace to be a concubine, bride, or favorite to the emperor. So, here we translate them as the Concubine Star.

ELEMENT: Yang Wood, Yin Fire, Yang Earth

TRADITIONAL IMAGE: A naturally beautiful but frail young girl, bowed in compliant gesture, dressed as a concubine, geisha, or bride[3]

GHOST PROFILE: A young, inexperienced, subordinate, or oppressed Ancestor who died young, dispossessed, lost, or at the hands of others

RESOLUTION/EXORCISM: Resolved through confidence, self-possession, maturity, and courage; helped by mature guidance from stronger Stars

LUMINOUS PLACEMENT: Monkey and Dog Palaces

DIMINISHED PLACEMENT: Rabbit, Snake, Rooster, and Pig Palaces

AFFILIATIONS: Northern Array—in a trine with the Emperor and General

Lian Zhen, which we translate as the Concubine Star, is the first of the Four Major Ghosts, and alone, she may be the least negative or afflicting of the group. The auspice of this Star is often determined by the Stars that show up with it, for this is the Star of "compliance" and following. If she shows up with strong, positive Stars, it usually becomes a positive story and often represents a teacher–student relationship, mentorship, or apprenticeship; it represents where we are clueless and follow someone older, wiser, or more experienced with positive results. If she shows up with other Ghost Stars, then she becomes a negative influence and represents the worst kind of naive, abused, and misguided youth; the combination of this Star with Qi Sha, the Seven Killings or Executioner Star; with Po Jun, the Rebel or Breaking Rank Star; or with any of the Four Minor Ghosts is a recipe for disaster. It can become a story of trauma, abuse, excessive passion, addiction, and darkness.

Lian Zhen is the image of an innocent young girl—the Chinese characters mean "Pure Virtue"—who comes from a poor family. Eager to gain wealth, connection, and upward social mobility, the family forces their daughter to become a concubine, which was a common practice in China. The English term *concubine* here refers to the term Pinfei (嬪妃), or "Imperial Concubine," which was an official position that could potentially carry a very high rank. The emperor would often have many concubines through which he would seek male heirs or indulge his sexual desire. The practice of concubinage in China was outlawed when the Chinese Communist Party came to power in 1949, but in premodern China, it was common. It was illegal and considered socially disreputable for a man to have more than one wife, but it was acceptable to have concubines. From the earliest times, wealthy men purchased concubines and added them to their households in addition to their wives. Concubines were like servants or enslaved people but had a higher social status.

So, if a poor family could sell one of their daughters, they could earn money and gain social mobility, even more so if she were sold to a wealthy man or, in this case, to the emperor. If a family could send their daughter off to be an imperial concubine, a Pinfei, then this created a tremendously valuable connection that could lead to greater wealth, political power, and upward social mobility. This was a great boon for the family, but it was terrible for the girl, as she was essentially sold into sexual slavery.

In this image, the young girl's Fate is out of her hands, and in our chart, it represents Fate that is very much out of our hands. She is forced into a life she did not choose, and the life ahead of her may involve doing things she doesn't want to do but must do for her family's and her own survival. She is also dependent on others for everything and cannot provide for herself alone; she gets her power by manipulating others to do things for her, which is her only source of strength.

The image of the Concubine Star is, more specifically, of a young girl chosen to be a royal concubine who is on her way to the royal court but has not yet arrived. She is young, still innocent, and has not yet been "corrupted." Alone, she still maintains her "Pure Virtue." She does not know what is coming, but she knows that it could be dark but that it could also lead to significant benefits for her and her family. So, she must do it, and she can also manipulate this energy through Yin Power: seduction, beauty, pleasure, and dalliance. While this Star represents innocence, it also represents the potential for great power, such as that of Yehe Nara Xingzhen, who was selected as a concubine of the Xianfeng Emperor and eventually rose to power as the Empress Dowager Cixi and ruled China for fifty years.

It is also associated with the gossip and politics of the royal court. The emperor would often have many concubines, both male and female. The male concubines were called "favorites," or Ningxing (佞幸), and even Mao Ze Dong had favorites. The concubines usually lived in the back of the palace in a separate compound, and they would fight for the attention of the emperor; some would never even meet him. There is poetry written by gray-haired concubines still waiting for the emperor to arrive.

The concubine would also be in competition with the empress to have a male heir, and these two Stars have an interesting dynamic in Polestar Astrology, for the Empress represents mature Yin, and the Concubine represents immature Yin. The Concubine Star is often associated with the complexity of social interaction and the play of Yin Power associated with manipulation, seduction, and gossip used to gain advantage or survive. It is important to note that all these principles apply the same to men and women. Despite this Star's being an image of a young girl, its influence manifests differently depending on gender and Character.

This Star represents a place where we are clueless, innocent, naive, and unformed but also have great potential and are looking for help and guidance. If this Star shows up alone, we are clueless and lost; we feel inexperienced and unprepared and remain that way until we learn self-possession and self-reliance. If it shows up alone, we struggle to grow, mature, and find our way. It is important to emphasize that she is on her way to the palace; it represents the Qi of transition, limbo, becoming, and uncertainness. This Star is, therefore, an interesting "affliction," for it is unclear whether it is harmful; it can go either way. Again, if it shows up with strong Stars, then the Concubine gets a mentor, and she can rise to become the empress dowager. But, if she shows up with other Ghosts, she can head down a dark path leading to the worst tragedies.

As an Ancestral Ghost, the Concubine represents any Ancestors who died young, before their Fate was formed and finished. Although today it is much more rare, it has been common throughout history for people to die young, so this is not ultimately unusual. This Star represents the force of youth in our family line and how that gets shaped and formed for good or bad by the factors of Fate.

The Concubine also represents the Ghosts of our Ancestors who were, for lack of a better word, weak, meek, ineffectual, clueless, and compliant. Many people in history followed authority and did what they were told, for better or worse. This kind of compliance can lead to all sorts of darkness, which was very evident during the Second World War, for example, in the Holocaust, during which the whole of Europe was essentially complicit in funneling Jews into the gas chambers. How many people have gone along with the crowd? Would we stand up and fight for what's right? We would all like to think that we would, but it is hard to be sure, for it is often easier to comply than defy.

Finally, this Star represents your Ancestral connection to all the women in your family whose Fate was out of their control and who had to do what they needed to survive. Often, this is the case with affliction; it can represent the darkness of abuse and being taken advantage of.

The image of a Concubine is by nature sexual and associated with images of beauty, and although it is a female image, this applies equally to men. This Star can represent a place where we attract others who want to take advantage of us, and they may. At its best, it represents the natural power of innocence, youth, and wisdom "from the mouth of babes." It can represent delight, happiness, and the straightforward enjoyment of being a child. But it also represents the transformation of this innocence into trauma, seduction, sexuality, and passion and all the ways that these things can become perverted.

It is again important to understand and interpret this Star in relation to the Stars that show up with it, so we will discuss what happens if the Concubine shows up alone, with a mentor, or with affliction.

Let's walk the Concubine through the Twelve Houses.

Ming Palace

If Lian Zhen arrives in the Ming Palace alone, your Fate is delicate and out of your hands. If she is alone, it is imperative to look at the rest of the chart to determine whether this goes well or poorly. You must ask, *where is my mentor*? Life will be all about mentor relationships, so if you have a strong Star in the Partners or Offspring House or in one of the career Houses, this may be a clue.

If the Concubine is alone here as the central image of Fate, then you enter life without much predestined affinity apart from others; you may have an innocent, naive, and soft or weak demeanor, depending on your Character, and the outcome of your Fate is very dependent on others and how they do or do not help you. Your Fate is in a kind of limbo characterized by uncertainty; remember, the Concubine is on her way to the palace and unsure of what lies in wait. Your Fate could be very harsh or very prosperous, depending on how you use your Yin Power; you may have to seduce, manipulate, and learn to control others to prosper.

Your Fate may be strongly influenced and shaped by an Ancestor who died young and who never matured enough to understand and complete their Fate. Or, you may be influenced by all your female Ancestors, who had to use Yin Power to survive. So, you may feel clueless, lost, and unsure of what to do with your life. You may feel timid, afraid, and uncertain. You may feel compelled to use Yin Power and whatever advantage you have to get ahead, get safe, or prosper. Your appearance and sexuality may play an essential role in your Fate. Or, you may be innocent and open to many possibilities, looking to others for help and guidance, which may or may not come. You may also be influenced by all Ancestral forces, especially by women who could not control their own lives.

You are potentially very reliant on others. You may be dependent, which could be good or bad. You may have benefactors and people who help you, or you may be Blanche DuBois and always depend on the kindness of strangers, leading to a life of "loose morals." Your innocence could attract others who want to help or take advantage of you, and this may be a central theme of Fate. This innocence can become a source of power or detriment. We must, therefore, see who shows up with this Star. If she arrives with a strong Star, she finds a mentor and guide. As part of the Northern Array, she can only show up with Stars from the Southern Array, like the Empress or Tutor, and if she does, then your life may be a Cinderella, or "rags to riches," story. If she shows up with the Empress, you may be the empress dowager and rise from a lowly place to a position of high power. You will succeed through the help of powerful and influential people. If she shows up with the Tutor, you may be protected, educated, and guided by an excellent mentor. If she shows up with any strong Star, your life is a path to becoming the image of the stronger Star. You may have an influential teacher, student, or apprentice-like relationship in which you rise to become the teacher or master from humble or ignorant beginnings. Your life will be about graciously accepting the help of others or about learning to masterfully manipulate resources to your advantage.

It must be said that, if the Concubine arrives with other Ghost Stars here, this can lead to the worst possible circumstances that may harden Fate and be challenging to resolve. This can go very dark. You may be born into inhospitable, dangerous, and even violent circumstances that you must escape. Your family and friends may be a danger to you, and you may experience some of the darkest abuse. Your story may be harsh, tragic, and disastrous. If you survive to maturity, it means you will have escaped, and you must learn heroic survival skills and do whatever it takes to survive.

Again, if you have this afflicted in the Ming Palace, then you inherit a very dark Ancestral story or curse, and you must liberate this or become victim to it. This may come in the form of abuse from others or as a dark inner pattern that turns to addiction, violence, or illegal activities. Somewhere in your family is the story of someone young and innocent or of women who were abused, manipulated, and taken advantage of. This can include things like rape and sexual abuse; it can also include drugs and crime. This placement manifests as significant health challenges, illness, and accidents.

There is simply no way to describe how dark this can go if it is further afflicted, especially by Qi Sha, the Seven Killings or Executioner Star. If you have something like this, then you are charged with liberating a dark Ancestral curse, the resolution of which is not clear or easy and may be antisocial. You must do family research and genealogy to discover any dark Ancestral stories that may be behind your struggles. At best, affliction here can cause your cluelessness or naivety to become haunted by negative emotions, resentment, or pretenses that cause you to stay stuck in hopeless causes and unable to mature and grow up.

Ancestors Palace

If Lian Zhen arrives alone in the Ancestors Palace, you have a weak connection to your Ancestors and will not receive much help or guidance from them. They may be distant, uninvolved, and unloving, and at the worst, they may abandon, abuse, or disown you. They may "send you off the palace," or in other words, they may use you to their advantage. You may grow up apart from your immediate family and live with another relative or in an orphanage, halfway home, or foster home. Your Ancestors may fail to protect you, or they may not offer much support, and this can lead to a life struggle in which you fail to mature and grow up due to a lack of support, education, and protection. You may then feel inadequate, ineffectual, or lost and clueless.

Your Ancestors may have a lot of unfinished business due to being ineffectual, and you inherit this, or you may inherit the longing of Ancestors who died young, before their Fate was formed and finished. You, therefore, feel clueless, lost, sad, and lack direction or inspiration. You may feel distant and disconnected from your Ancestors and their story. You also may inherit the Fate of all the women in your family whose Fate was out of their control and who had to do what they needed to survive; you may be put in this situation, too.

If other Ghosts Stars appear with the Concubine here, this can represent the darkness of abuse, the betrayal of innocence, and the consequences of being taken advantage of. Afflicted this way, this placement can represent arguing and discord with parents, or it can be the worst kind of sexual, emotional, verbal, or physical abuse from a parent or grandparent. It can also manifest as your being orphaned, adopted, or separated from your parents, or as running away from home to escape abuse. It can also continue patterns of drug, alcohol, or gambling addiction and even falling into crime.

If further afflicted, escape is often the best option; you may have to cut ties and even hide to resolve your Fate. It can be powerful to do genealogy here, as you may inherit a very dark family curse that can be exorcised, though it may need to be exorcised through your own dark story and trauma. You can stay and fight for survival, or you may need to escape. The presence of other Ghosts here with Lian Zhen can lead to the darkest of Ancestral curses and the worst kind of familial trauma.

If the Concubine shows up with a powerful positive Star, you may find a strong role model, teacher, or guide among your Ancestors, but you may never feel truly connected to them. Your relationship may never be clear. You may be cared for or financially supported but not receive much love and affection. Circumstances beyond your control may also separate you from your family; you may be sent to military, boarding, or religious schools. This may not be negative, and it may even avert more severe negativity. Outside forces may shape your Ancestral Fate, and people you don't know may run your life.

Youth Palace

If Lian Zhen arrives in the Youth Palace, you have little basis for resolving Fate in childhood or with your siblings; your Fated connection to siblings may be difficult and cause struggle. It seems like the Concubine, as an image of youth, should belong in the Youth Palace, but it is misplaced here, as it is the image of lost youth, a young person sent away from home into a potentially complex and unknown situation. The nature of this Star's immaturity, dependence, vulnerability, and innocence can go very badly here, especially if it is afflicted by other Ghosts.

If the Concubine shows up alone here, you may be lost in youth. Your childhood may be uneven, traumatic, and rough, and you may have to grow up very quickly due to negative relationships with your parents, relatives, or siblings or due to challenging circumstances at home or school. Childhood may be full of painful memories that haunt you for the rest of your life. These may come as the result of abuse, neglect, abandonment, or betrayal from family members.

The Concubine is looking for help and guidance, but she does not find it alone. She is sent off to the palace to be a concubine to the emperor. Your parents may send you away, neglect you, give you up for adoption, lose you to child services, or get divorced and create one or more unstable homes. One parent may leave, so you may struggle being raised by a single parent. You may lose a parent due to an accident or illness. You may be raised by an older sibling who is not mature enough for the task. You may grow up and live in poverty or have parents who struggle with substance addiction. Parents or siblings may be physically or emotionally abusive. You may even be homeless for some time or live in a camper or out of a car. You may be put to work early and even forced to do inappropriate things for your age. You may be drawn to drugs, crime, or rebellion if you "fall in with the wrong crowd."

Or, you may be lost, distant, and lonely as a child. You may be an only child or separated from your siblings. You may struggle to make friends and fit in, and you may experience bullying. Your innocence and vulnerability may attract the wrong people, who exploit you. Looking for help, you get misled, misguided, or lied to. You may spend your childhood lost in a fantasy world and stay stuck for a long time in arrested development. All the above gets worse or darker if other Ghost Stars appear with the Concubine here, and intense affliction of the Concubine can lead to a very traumatic and dark Fate in childhood. You may only barely survive youth, and while this affliction can be resolved in your youth, the escape of this dark Fate could be with you for life.

If the Concubine shows up with a stronger Star, she gets a guide, mentor, or protector, which can go much better, and she can bloom. This may be an older sibling, aunt or uncle, grandparent, or the like who helps and protects you in difficult circumstances. Alternatively, you may take this role for a younger sibling. You may have to grow up and defend them or work to support them as a third parent. But, even if Lian Zhen shows up with stronger Stars, your siblings, family members, and elders will not be much help in resolving your Fate. You may be surrounded by incompetent adults and siblings who only make things worse for you, despite trying to help. They pose at protecting you but fail or try their best and are ineffectual. A stronger Star may also mean you find a mentor from school, church, or an afterschool program who helps you escape the negativity or neglect at home.

Partners Palace

If you have Lian Zhen in the Partners Palace, you have a strong Fate with a partner or many partners. Still, it may be harmful, as it represents a pattern of dependency and vulnerability that can be taken advantage of, especially if you marry or partner early. The image of the concubine as a young girl sold as a sexual slave to the emperor doesn't bode well for partnership. However, partnership is the concubine's only source of livelihood, so if you have this Star here, relationships often become a harmful obsession. This image of a young, inexperienced girl often means an Ancestral pattern of immaturity and fantasy in relationships, and Character matters a lot in determining how this plays out.

If the Concubine is alone in this House, you may have an ongoing pattern of making poor, immature relationship choices. You may be dependent and unable to do things independently, so you seek older or wealthy partners to care for you. You may use seduction or manipulation to get into relationships and then abuse people for your gain. Or they may abuse and misuse you for your looks or money. You may be shallow and opportunistic and partner with others for money or status or to get ahead in life. You may even be forced into these circumstances by family or because of poverty or being a single parent. Your partnerships may be codependent, and you may stay in bad relationships because you cannot survive alone.

You may also be emotionally immature and seek a fantasy relationship, a prince or princess, a knight in shining armor, a savior, a parent figure, a soulmate, and so on. You may go from person to person, unable to find your "perfect match." You may have a lot of immature, unrealistic, or unreasonable expectations and desires and never find a partner who is good enough. You may also obsess repeatedly about why you are not married or why you can't find a good man or woman, which may be the very thing that prevents you from "settling." You may also be promiscuous, polyamorous, afraid of commitment, or sexually experimental. Unable to make committed relationships, you may struggle to find substitutes that never really work or fulfill you, leaving you longing for that thing you could never find.

This is an image of youth, and often, these patterns are stronger earlier in life and made worse if you marry or partner early. You may be Fated to marry early, and this relationship may be immature and full of irreconcilable differences, ending in divorce. However, if this is the case, you can be free of Fate after that relationship ends, for you may mature and learn how to be a partner. Or you may go through a long pattern of immaturity and failed relationships and eventually grow up and liberate this pattern. The primary way to liberate the negative Fate here is to "settle" and to partner later in life, after you "grow up." Celibacy, being a monk or nun, or intentionally avoiding relationships is also a way to avoid this Fate, but you may never actually grow up if you do this.

If this is further afflicted by other Ghost Stars, then all the above gets worse and can turn into one or many nightmare relationships. You may physically or emotionally abuse or be abused by a partner; this may be an inherited Ancestral pattern of abuse in marriage, which was a lot more common in previous generations, as women were more financially dependent on men and religious influences were much stronger and forbade divorce. People often got married much earlier and had to do a lot of growing up in marriage. Domestic violence also was more accepted once, and unfortunately is still accepted in many parts of the world. And while most domestic abuse victims are, of course, women, it is important to note that one in three victims are male in the US,[4] and this Fate applies to men too. You may be Fated to go through a nightmare relationship, abuse, rejection, and separation. After this, you may be free of Fate in this House and able to partner with someone, provided you learn the lessons you need to learn to avoid this dynamic or not perpetuate it.

If the Concubine shows up with a stronger Star, this can go much better, but you may be subordinate or seek to subordinate a partner. Your partner may be your protector, provider, and teacher, or you may be in this role to someone else. Your relationship may be good, but it may be more about protection and providing than romance. You may marry someone much older or younger, creating the above dependency dynamics. You may also be a housewife, trophy spouse, or arranged partner chosen by the family or chosen for advantageous circumstances like getting a green card.

Offspring Palace

If Lian Zhen arrives in the Offspring Palace, you have a weak affinity with being a parent, and your life as a parent may be filled with uncertainty and potential loss. This is, again, the image of a young teenage girl who is sent to the palace to be a sexual slave, but also potentially to bear an heir to the throne. If she did bear an heir, she would likely never get to see her child, and if she did not, during certain early dynasties, like the Qin and the early Ming dynasty, some concubines who had not borne children were forced to commit suicide or were killed to be buried with the deceased emperor and serve him in the afterlife. Ultimately, this is not a happy situation. Here, Lian Zhen represents the Ancestral pattern of disadvantaged young mothers.

The best-case scenario with this placement is to be a young or immature parent. This may be fine, but it will be a challenge, as you will have to grow up and mature in the process of being a parent. This Star may be an image of you but also of your child, who may also struggle to grow up; they may be immature and stuck in arrested development, always looking to you for help. They may be dependent on you and unable to take care of themselves. This could be simply from immaturity, but it may also be from a disability or illness.

You may be Fated to have no children or struggle to have or conceive children, or you may be Fated to lose one or more of your children. This can be due to infertility, miscarriage, abortion, complicated pregnancies, or childhood illness, or you may have a child while very young and must give it up for adoption. You may be unable to provide for your children and have to give them to relatives or have them taken away by child services. You may be a young single parent and struggle with immaturity, having to grow up early to take this role. You may have to be a heroic parent and raise a child in unusual circumstances, alone and without support. You may struggle with an unwanted or unexpected pregnancy. You may also either be or use a surrogate mother or undergo artificial insemination or in-vitro fertilization. All this could stem from an Ancestor who died in childbirth or died before being able to reproduce.

If this Star is further afflicted, then it makes everything more uncertain and hostile, and more Ghost Stars here can lead to hauntings as well as to things like your own death in childbirth, child disabilities or illnesses, abortions, or the loss of a child in infancy. You may also hurt or be hurt by your child as they grow up. This placement can also mean child abuse and neglect or arguments and discord between parent and child. You may be separated from your children due to war or political strife, or they may be kidnapped, die in an accident, or be murdered. You may be haunted by unborn or lost children or long for a child you never had, and these Ghosts may follow you in life. It is then essential to have proper ceremonies to liberate these orphaned spirits. Intense affliction here can also lead to rape, sexual abuse or assault, sex work, and sexually transmitted diseases. Again, this can get very dark.

If the Concubine shows up with a stronger Star here, things can go well, especially if you partner with someone with a solid and positive Fate to be a parent. You may have to continually be a guide, role model, protector, or advocate for your children. You may have multiple kids, and one may serve as a parent or protector to the younger or more vulnerable child. You may also raise someone else's children as a stepparent or even run a successful daycare center, orphanage, or school.

Wealth Palace

If you have Lian Zhen in the Wealth Palace, you are Fated to be financially dependent on others. Again, this is the image of a young girl who cannot provide for herself; she falls into a "job," but everything is out of her hands. Everything is provided for her by the palace, as she lives in the palace and has no responsibilities other than to provide the services of a concubine.

The most positive manifestation of this is to have a patron or patrons. You may be born into a wealthy family and not have to work. You may also inherit family money; perhaps your parents pay your rent or give you a monthly allowance. You may also marry into wealth, and this can be the image of a housewife or at least having a sugar daddy/mama. If this Star is not further afflicted, this can be considered a good thing, as it may give you a lot of freedom to pursue other things. The downside is being immature and remaining that way due to not having financial responsibilities. You may never have to go through the grind of a nine-to-five job. You may pursue endless side jobs, hobbies, or vanity projects, because you do not have to worry about the bills.

This is all the more so if the Concubine shows up with a stronger Star like the Empress or Tutor, as you may be very well patronized and connected to people who are wealthy, and live comfortably your whole life. It also increases the likelihood of investing your inheritance profitably and turning it into acts of generosity and legacy. This is also like the image of Cinderella, and your appearance may bring wealth, fame, or status. You may be a model or actress and work in television, movies, or magazines.

Stronger Stars here with Lian Zhen may also indicate inheriting or creating a unique business, skill, or legacy that leads to prosperity. It often indicates wealth from unexpected, unusual, and even illegal sources, like gambling. They may also represent meeting a role model, mentor, boss, or teacher who guides you to financial success. You may start as a nobody and then get rich in the stock market after meeting a successful investor who shows you the way. Strong Stars with the Concubine can be very profitable, and their effects can increase steadily over time, leading to great wealth, generosity, and legacy—a "rags to riches" story. You may start poor but never forget where you came from. Stronger Stars add a dimension of work and a connection between work and prosperity that the Concubine alone does not have.

If this is further afflicted, then your relationship with money can turn dark and disastrous. As the Concubine represents immaturity, other Ghost Stars often become a bad influence and connect this Star to crime, gambling, addiction, drugs, and sex work. You may long for money but resent the wealthy. You may inherit money and squander it through gambling. You may spend other people's money until they cut you off, then realize you have no skills to earn your own. You may be born into poverty, grow up in a trailer park, and be unable to get out. Affliction here turns to desperation, and you may turn to theft, crime, sex work, compulsive gambling, and so on; again, this image of a Concubine represents what we might consider illicit, explicit, and socially unacceptable behavior. You may live way beyond your means and get into debt. You may attempt illegal moneymaking schemes that fail.

If further afflicted, this can represent an Ancestral curse around money, debt, gambling, addiction, and so on. You may have an Ancestor who was killed over money or who died poor and in the gutter. If this is heavily afflicted, things can go very badly. However, there is a chance to turn these circumstances into something empowering; even sex workers can go on to live dignified and prosperous lives.

Health Palace

If you have Lian Zhen alone in the Health Palace, you inherit a weak and vulnerable Yin constitution from your Matriarchal Ancestors. This Star is the image of youth, dependence, and immaturity that must work hard to protect itself, so with solid self-discipline, this can turn out well and become a source of longevity. However, this longevity will be hard-won, and you must make great effort to protect yourself and become strong. This placement represents a Yin openness, susceptibility, and vulnerability to outside forces—mentally, physically, and emotionally.

You may be naturally weak, frail, or slight. As the Concubine is an image of youth, it often represents childhood illness, so you may be a child stricken with a childhood disease or who gets sick all the time. You may have a variety of chronic illnesses, such as asthma, allergies, food sensitivities, a physical handicap, or other weaknesses. You may be very dependent and need a lot of help, support, and attention, constantly going to doctors and specialists. While this may be an affliction, it may cause you to develop many healthcare routines and healthy habits early on. You may have to work hard to overcome childhood illness and to mature, and these conditions may be with you for life. This may make you very cautious and give you a long life.

Essentially, this placement means you are vulnerable and may be susceptible to many things. Physically, you may have a lot of allergies and sensitivities. You may be unable to eat many foods or develop respiratory or skin problems due to environmental factors. From a traditional perspective, you are susceptible to "wind," which means you are hard to diagnose, your symptoms are constantly changing, and you can be "invaded." Therefore, you are difficult to treat and may respond poorly to conventional treatment. You may also distrust doctors, hospitals, and conventional treatments and even be the victim of iatrogenic illness, which is an illness caused by medical treatment. However, you generally respond well to primary care, food, herbs, home remedies, and the help of caregivers, family, and relatives.

Lian Zhen here means that you are mentally and emotionally vulnerable as well, so you may be highly empathic and respond strongly to the emotions of others. You may take on their emotions and have trouble distinguishing between what is yours and what is not. You may also get ill due to emotions and have many physical symptoms associated with emotionality, such as hives, dizziness, irregular bowels, and so on. These may flare up when you are stressed, nervous, or anxious. You will likely be very emotional, experiencing a flood of emotions all the time. You may be neurotic, and this will be something you must learn to manage, mainly because it will be influenced, and even made worse, by your surroundings, friends, and the media. The more negative emotions you have, the worse you get physically, and you can quickly spiral out of control.

Traditionally, this placement is associated with kidney weakness, which means slowness to mature and prosper, what could be called a "failure to thrive," and an overall constitutional weakness. It is also associated with urinary and sexual disorders and even STDs and other contagious diseases. Therefore, it is important to be cautious in many ways: You must protect yourself from all kinds of invasion and influence, from within and without.

If this Star shows up with stronger Stars, your constitution will be strengthened; you will still be delicate and vulnerable, but your response will be much stronger. You will respond better to doctors, treatments, and health cultivation practices. If the Concubine has support, you will not be as dependent and will be better able to care for yourself and others. Stronger Stars with the Concubine mean that vulnerability becomes a strength; you become more sensitive, caring, and compassionate to the vulnerability and suffering of others, and caring for others will give you strength. It also strengthens the relationship you have with healers and physicians. Your weakness may inspire a spiritual path or path of health cultivation that becomes a way to help yourself and others. Even with stronger Stars, your health will wax and wane; you will always need to tend to that vulnerability.

If the Concubine is further afflicted, again, this can become very negative here. Combined with the vulnerability and susceptibility of the Concubine, further affliction will cause all the above patterns of negative emotions, allergies, and psychosomatic sensitivities to get worse—more severe, less responsive to treatment, and so on. More Ghost Stars means that your health is afflicted by your unresolved Ancestors, who may have died of illness, accident, war, murder, suicide, and so on; you may have to suffer illness, accidents, improper diagnosis and treatment, disease, and even death to resolve these Ghosts. You will be harder to diagnose and treat, for in this case you are not ill in the conventional sense but "spiritually ill," possessed of the unresolved dead. You may have a cathartic recovery from something like cancer or a horrific car accident and become a survivor. Or, something like this may take your life early. It is essential to do genealogy and find any negative death stories that may be haunting you. Spiritual means may be necessary to resolve them.

Career/Travel Palace

If Lian Zhen arrives in the Career/Travel Palace, then you are Fated to leave home and potentially struggle with a lot of uncertainty in life, and your Fate here may be fixed and out of your hands. It may be chosen for you, and you must follow it, for better or worse. The concubine was sent off to the palace as a young girl; her life path was chosen. The image is of her on her way to the palace, but she never arrives. Her future is unknown, and possibly dark.

You may have an outside influence that governs your path in life. You may be at the mercy of others—family, government, and societal circumstances—when you are young and vulnerable, and this may set you on a life path that is out of your control. Due to your family situation, you may have to move somewhere and start a new life. You may be commanded to go somewhere, or you might choose a path based on immature decisions. You may run away or be forced to leave home at an early age. You will likely travel and move to a new city, town, state, or country. You can successfully immigrate or start a new life, but you will likely be young, immature, and inexperienced in the new place. You may live life as a foreigner, outsider, or expat. You may have benefactors and move with all the factors set up for you, like through the military, or you may be alone and vulnerable and seeking a mentor.

If the Concubine shows up with stronger Stars, you will likely meet and follow a mentor, teacher, guru, guide, friend, or older family member on your path. If you run away or leave home early, you may be adopted by a mentor, stranger, foreigner, new friend group, gang, or the like. They may help and protect you and give you asylum. You may also mentor younger, more vulnerable people as a teacher, social worker, or mentor. This placement may be a path to getting into social work because a social worker helps you when you are vulnerable and alone. You may also have a benefactor who takes care of things, so you are free to do what you want. Still, you may need guidance as to what to do with that freedom.

Stronger Stars also indicate the potential for success through working for wealthy or influential people or as a helper, companion, assistant, or subordinate to a strong leader or businessperson. The Concubine often signifies work that is based on your unique appearance or personal talents. This could translate to entrepreneurial work or a job that is unique to you or a career as a model, actor, singer, musician, television personality, housewife, and so on. Or, it could simply mean that you are hired for a job because of your physical attractiveness. This placement could also mean that you don't need to work; you may be able to rely on family money, welfare, disability, or charity. Stronger Stars can also indicate the use of certain means to get what you need, perhaps particular skills, cunning, cleverness, or manipulation. The Concubine must do whatever she can to survive, but the Star is weak alone, so stronger Stars can offer a path out.

In general, Lian Zhen in this House means being somewhat lost, clueless, immature, and uncertain about your path in life and needing to grow up and find your way. This may create a kind of arrested development regarding your career. You may be Peter Pan and not want to grow up, or you may be selfish and want to stay in your parents' basement playing video games. Stronger Stars make this placement about finding and locking onto a mentor whom you admire. They may shake you out of complacency and entitlement.

If this Star is further afflicted, you may head down a dark path in life and make bad choices. Ghost Stars become a bad influence here, and you may become lazy, antisocial, and fall into bad crowds. You may spend your life on the run: You may get involved in crime and illegal schemes and get arrested early in life, lose everything, turn to drugs or addiction, or even go to jail or prison. Further affliction can therefore be powerful here, as it can alter your life significantly in a very negative way. These kinds of stories are out there and can be very dramatic. However, not everyone who has this placement goes to prison.

If you do have additional Ghost Stars here, then these circumstances are an Ancestral affliction. You may be paying for the sins of your Ancestors, doomed to repeat their negativity unless you can break free. Strong affliction in this House can also come from Ancestors whose life path was derailed by war, violence, famine, oppression, and genocide, causing them to uproot and leave home in a vulnerable state. You may be Fated to continue these patterns and either liberate them or continue them through your own struggle. So, doing genealogy and finding familiar stories of struggle are essential to breaking the cycle.

Assistants Palace

The Assistants Palace is a tricky placement for Lian Zhen. If she is unafflicted or shows up with stronger Stars, this placement is auspicious and can go well. This House is about people showing up to help you, and the Concubine needs help. However, if she is afflicted, it can go very badly because in this House she may be the most vulnerable to being taken advantage of by Ghost Stars. This is like Little Red Riding Hood and the Big Bad Wolf. As a career House, however, it is also tricky: Alone, the Concubine means that you may lack skills, maturity, or direction, but with a stronger Star, it can mean an excellent path of apprenticeship and growth. It is essential, then, to check this placement for affliction and act accordingly.

If this Star shows up alone and unafflicted, you have a fragile relationship with friends, co-workers, subordinates, and so on. Your status as a helper is also dependent and fragile. The Concubine is always in limbo or transition; she is on her way to the palace and looking for help. You may be in a position to be duped or taken advantage of earlier in life, and depending on Character, you may be naive, gullible, and vulnerable to outside influences. You may be scared, untrusting, aloof, and hesitant about people, but you need them and must seek help. You may trust others too quickly, leading to you being abused or taken advantage of if you choose poorly. You may be Fated to attract others looking to help you, like the "damsel in distress," and they may or may not have your best interest at heart. If they do, then you are successfully aided and guided by older, wiser, more mature people. If not, then this can, again, go very badly. If the Concubine is alone in this House, you must always be careful about who you follow, trust, and let help you. You must also be cautious about whom you support, for it too may have conditions and consequences.

In general, this placement suits you to helping professions and to being subordinate, as the Concubine is in a position of following. However, this can be turned into a position of power. This is about learning to yield Yin Power from a place of weakness or disadvantage. You may have to learn to use your appearance, seduction, manipulation, lying, guile, wit, charm, and so on to get ahead. This is about understanding the psychology of people—what makes them tick and what makes them vulnerable. This may sound bad, but it may be necessary to survive. You can also turn these skills into a positive force to benefit others, if you have good intentions. It is essential, then, to check your intentions.

If Lian Zhen shows up with Stronger Stars, you may be Fated to find and follow a mentor or guide, and older people will aid you. You may have a guardian angel and receive help at very auspicious junctures in life. When you are vulnerable and need help, the right people, or the same person, will show up to the rescue. Remember, this House represents relationships outside the family, so your rescuer is likely a friend, co-worker, schoolmate, or the like. An older mentor or successful person may take you under their wing, and your career and success may be brought to you through the help of another. You may be Fated to be an apprentice and succeed someone in your career or on a spiritual path. And again, the role can always be reversed. If this shows up with stronger Stars, you may be Fated to be a rescuer. You may be constantly helping out others in need and may be suited to careers like social work, therapy, healthcare professions, and even something like being a firefighter, police officer, security guard, or soldier. You may rescue or protect people for a living. This placement can turn out very heroic.

If this is further afflicted, then the Concubine turns into Little Red Riding Hood. You may have Fate with attracting and associating with the wrong people. You may be tricked, duped, used, abused, and exploited by others. This can be a more subtle pattern of being taken advantage of that may not be dramatically negative but that constantly undermines you, holds you back, drains your energy and resources, and so on. You may be too kind, trusting, and generous, and others may use or treat you like a doormat or pawn. You may be unable to stand up for yourself, and they may abandon you, steal from you, or mess things up at work or in your personal life.

You may be hired or used for your appearance. This can lead to misunderstandings, slander, libel, gossip, and rumors. You may also imagine that you are competent and then fail miserably. All these things can lead to bitterness, disillusionment, mistrust, and fear of others. It can lead to jealousy, revenge, and hate. Stronger affliction here can even lead to assault, sexual abuse or harassment, robbery, and worse. You may be hurt or killed by someone, or vice versa.

Traditionally, Lian Zhen in this House is seen as a Fated debt from your Ancestors who either needed help and never got it or who themselves hurt, cheated, or took advantage of others, and now you must pay the consequences. This is most easily resolved through spiritual service: Your Ancestors hurt others, so now you must serve others and pay penance. Generosity, compassion, loving-kindness, and equanimity go a long way to liberate Ghosts in this House, but you may have to face some unavoidable negativity. Or your Ancestors may have been abused or hurt, and now you are following down the same path, unable to learn the lesson. You may have to learn to stand up for yourself and fight back, or to go it alone without help. Traditionally, people who come to you for help are people you have a debt with, so you must help them to liberate your adverse Fate.

Superiors Palace

Surprisingly, the Superiors Palace is the most auspicious placement for Lian Zhen, but as usual, further affliction by other Ghosts can lead to many negativities. Here, she is put in the most advantageous position to rise above her vulnerable and disadvantaged circumstances, especially if she shows up with stronger Stars. This placement is all about being able to work and wield power from unusual, underprivileged, or hidden positions and rise through the ranks with Yin Power. This is the image of the Dragon Empress, the Concubine who successfully took over China. Here, your unique disposition and talents can become a power and bring you success and status.

If this Lian Zhen is not afflicted, the Concubine is protected and can lead a prosperous and safe life. You can successfully use Yin Power to your advantage, and you may be successful at ownership, managerial work, or helping others, but you will not be in the spotlight. You will lead from behind the scenes and somehow wield power through others. Others will serve you and do your bidding. You will be repeatedly guided, helped, and protected by older, more powerful people. You may be provided for, and a suitable career may come to you through associations with others or superiors at work.

Your appearance, demeanor, and disposition will draw others to help you; by "working" these associations, you can make your way in life. This is all about networking, making connections, and using charm, wit, and social skills to your advantage, which may include seduction, flattery, and so on. The Concubine here can also lead to a successful career through your appearance, physical or sexual attractiveness, or allure. So, being a model, actor, musician, spokesperson, mascot, and so on all apply, or you may get the job or promotions due to "pretty privilege" or the "halo effect." People may inherently trust you, give you things, offer you help or advice, or even do things for you just to get in your favor. You may also be the "face" of a business or organization, chosen to represent the company because of your looks or demeanor.

If Lian Zhen shows up with stronger Stars, you will have excellent teachers, mentors, bosses, and so on who protect, educate, and guide you. Someone older, wiser, or more successful may take you under their wing. You can succeed through apprenticeship and succession, which will be a path of "growing up" and maturing through learning from a teacher, like Daniel-san in *The Karate Kid*. This may be a solid Fated relationship with a mentor or boss who becomes the key to your success. However, this can also be an important academic or spiritual teacher, guru, or the like. You will resolve a great deal of Fate through this relationship; you are here to complete this Fate and become the teacher. This can lead to great success and alliance in your career. Spiritually, this can be a deep connection to lineage and express the fruition of the teacher–student relationship. You may then be Fated to be a teacher yourself and guide younger seekers.

If this placement is further afflicted by Ghost Stars, you may be Fated to choose or work for poor teachers, bosses, and so on, and be led astray or hindered in your career or path because of their incompetence, misguidance, or failures. Your teachers or bosses may lack integrity, and you may have to pay for this because you work for them. You may even be abused, harassed, or attacked by a boss, teacher, or person in power. You may be taken in by a false guru, cult leader, or radical mentor and get caught up in their world. You may be drawn into a cult, illegal business, pyramid scheme, or scam and suffer disastrous consequences. You may even be brainwashed into protecting, defending, or identifying with your abuser, as with Stockholm syndrome. You may be caught up in illegal activity, "black arts," get-rich-quick schemes, fraud, money laundering, drug rings, shady underworlds, and so on.

Further affliction here can also mean that you are lost, clueless, immature, and naive in your career or life path, unable to grow up and work successfully. You may make repeated mistakes, and your negative emotions constantly undermine your ability to work and resolve Fate. You may end up with more Fate entanglements in life than you started with, due to constant mistakes and failures, immaturity, constantly changing your mind, or outright failure and disaster or because of negative associations with others who drag you into their mess. Your naivety may also lead to idealism and choosing a life path that cannot be fulfilled. You may stay stuck in a negative cycle of mediocrity, unable to grow or progress, or stuck in arrested development.

Property Palace

If Lian Zhen shows up in the Property Palace, then you have a weak Fate with owning property, but you will likely be dependent on others and provided for or helped by them somehow. Your relationship to property is uneven, but you can own or share property with others, or it may be gifted to you through inheritance or from benefactors. The concubine was sent off to the palace where she lived and was provided for with the other concubines; she never owned property herself, but she had her material needs met. Affliction here tends not to be all that negative, but it can strongly relate to negative Ancestral Fate associated with place, immigration, exile, migration, displacement from war, political strife, difficult homelife, and so on.

Alone in this House, the Concubine often means that others provide for your property, housing, and possessions, or you may struggle to provide them for yourself. You may live off your parents, family, inheritance, allowance, government welfare, alimony, child support, disability, unemployment, or the dole. You may be poor and unable to provide for yourself, but you will not likely be homeless, as others will want to help you somehow. You may be a bum, mooch, or squatter, living on other people's couches, or you may live in a partner's house. You may get into relationships to have a place to live and to have someone to provide for you as a sugar daddy/mama. Or you may always rent and never be able to own anything or to be entirely on your own. You may be able to hold on to and own the property you inherit or receive as a gift, but this is unlikely if you are alone.

If the Concubine shows up with stronger Stars, then you may own property, but you will need, and receive, a lot of help from others. If there is no further affliction, then inheritance here can be significant, and you may have a lot of family money, but you will be dependent. You may have to own property with others and end up sharing property or land with others and living in a more communal situation. You may buy property only once you get married and always must share a lease or deed with a partner. You may always need a cosigner for everything, but you will always have one.

Stronger Stars may also be helpers, mentors, or older, more experienced people who help you with everything practical related to property or home ownership. You may have a parent or older relative who fixes everything, repairs your plumbing, or enables you to fix up your home. You may need to be more knowledgeable about home or property maintenance, but you will always have someone to call to work things out for you.

Further affliction here from the Seven Killings Star, despite being the most negative Star, tends to go well and can be associated with windfall and receiving surprise inheritance, gifts, prizes, and so on. So, you may inherit a huge property or plot of land or win big in Vegas. However, often these things come with a price and can be more of a curse than a blessing. That being said, Ghost Stars here with the Concubine can represent Ancestors who died at home or far from home, or who died or struggled in their relationship to land, property, place, ethnicity, identity, and so on. They may have been displaced and made vulnerable or lost their resources due to war, political strife, exile, migration, and so on. Genealogy and family history are important here because you may have an Ancestral Ghost associated with your home, inheritance, or Ancestral homeland. This can cause fear at home, fear of being alone or vulnerable, or specific fears of drowning or being burned alive, attacked at home, bombings, violence, and so on.

Pleasure Palace

Lian Zhen is considered generally inauspicious in the Pleasure Palace, but as usual, the Stars that show up with it determine how this turns out. This Star doesn't say much alone, but the image is one of youth, inexperience, and even a kind of "purity." Innocence and immaturity are very open to influence here, and the Concubine often becomes about testing the limits, experimenting, and trying new things. This is like being a teenager just after puberty—hormones raging, eager to grow up, keen to discover new things. If the Concubine shows up with stronger Stars, things go much better, but affliction by other Ghosts in this House can create some of the darkest scenarios in Polestar Astrology.

If this Star is alone and unafflicted, then it is not so bad; you are Fated to be a bit immature and fun-seeking, like a teenager just opening into the adult world. You will enjoy trying new things and testing the limits of your body and mind. You may seek parties, novel experiences, thrills, excitement, strenuous exercise, extreme sports, and so on, and this can lead to eager experimentation with drugs, sex, alcohol, food, and travel. This can border on sadomasochism, and you may even be drawn to BDSM and the like. At best, you may be a perpetual noob with an eternal sense of innocence and wonder. You may have no idea what you enjoy and remain clueless.

Traditionally, they say this placement means you will love to dress up and try on new identities and will be a bit vain. You may enjoy dressing in such a way as to stand out, and you may go through phases: goth, steampunk, retro, whatever. You may be in your late thirties and still have blue hair or wear metal spikes on your jacket. As this is an image of sexuality and beauty, you may be very fashionable, stylish, and even a bit shallow when it comes to appearance. But you will enjoy altering your appearance and expressing a sense of sensuality or sexuality through your countenance.

If the Concubine shows up with stronger Stars, you will be fully dedicated to pursuing pleasure, but it may come in the form of the stronger Star. You may be a follower, and your sense of enjoyment in life may come from copying others. Here, cluelessness tends to make you follow others rather than have a strong sense of personal enjoyment. You may go through phases after meeting or dating new people. You may bounce from hobby to hobby, adventure to adventure, party to party, looking to others to show you what to like. You may get into something just because your partner is into it. You may even enjoy the protection of others and the sense of company you get from being included in a group. When young, you may seek out older people to have fun with to feel cool; when you get old, you may seek younger people so that you don't feel old.

If other Ghost Stars appear with the Concubine here, then she can turn very dark, and all the negative sides of sex, drugs, and rock and roll can become dangerous, especially if she shows up with Qi Sha, the Seven Killings Star. This combination usually leads to a short life, and affliction here can lead to addiction, sexual abuse, STDs, and even death or suicide. We can imagine many possible dark stories, but this is one of the places where affliction can come for your life. This is an Ancestor who died enjoying themselves, but not in a good way. This can represent the darkest cycles of drug addiction, violence, abuse, and especially sexual abuse. You may have to survive this, but it is possible, and you will come out the other side a true "survivor."

QI SHA (七殺)—THE SEVEN KILLINGS OR EXECUTIONER

NAME AND TRANSLATIONS:

Qi Sha (七殺), the Seven Killings Star, the Executioner Star, Robber's Curse

Qi, 七—seven, seventh, sevenfold.[5]

Sha, 殺—terminate. a) bring to a close, put an end to, conclude, complete, wrap up. b) put to death, kill; slaughter; assail, wound, strip of. 2 fail, be at the end of; decay(ed), wear away; spoil. 3 (med.) following VB or ADJ [verb or adjective], extremely, to the maximal extent; e.g., 愁殺 chousha, as sad as can be. a) (med.) 可殺 kesha, extremely, very, exceedingly; e.g., 可殺濕 keshashi, excessively wet.[6]

This translation is simple: Qi (七), just means seven, and Sha (殺), means to kill or put to death, so we translate this as Seven Killings or Executioner Star.

ELEMENT: Yin Metal, Yang Fire

TRADITIONAL IMAGE: An executioner or brute with a ruddy, blank, expressionless face, wielding a large and bloody sword or ax[7]

GHOST PROFILE: A ghost king or demon that represents a dark or Demonic force in our Ancestors, that leads and controls the unsettled dead in our family inheritance; Ghostly Ancestor with a dark story, untimely death, or suicide who has been forgotten, repressed, or abandoned and is on the verge of becoming a Demon

RESOLUTION/EXORCISM: Resolved with great difficulty—there is no confidence about antidotes or cures for this affliction, for it represents our most bitter and fatal inner flaws and blind spots; it can never completely eclipsed but can be mitigated and mostly eclipsed by the General or Emperor

LUMINOUS PLACEMENT: None

DIMINISHED PLACEMENT: None

AFFILIATIONS: Southern Array—always across from the Empress; leader of the Ghost Stars but has no affiliations with the Royal Court

Qi Sha, or the Seven Killings/Executioner Star, is the darkest and most afflicting Ghost Star in Polestar Astrology. It has a special place in this exploration of Stars, for it is the only Star powerful enough to truly afflict or haunt a House or other Stars, and it is the only Star that can become irreversible in its negativity. All the Ghost Stars discussed in this section can create hauntings in the form of negative emotions and perceived obstruction from outer circumstances, but these are more obvious and can be resolved with some confidence, dedication, and persistence. We tend to understand these afflictions relatively easily, and they can be more easily resolved with clear principles. But Qi Sha represents our most significant "blind eye"—our most Fated inner flaws—and it is characterized by a diabolical sneakiness due to our inability to learn from experience.

Qi Sha contains the darkest and most painful stories from the unsettled dead in our family up to seven generations back, hence the name. Qi (七), seven, is an unlucky number in Chinese cosmology and represents death. In its more subtle forms, the Seven Killings Star manifests as a pattern we don't see about ourselves and may even deny, which is why it is so difficult to resolve. We may also repeat its core pattern of negativity, perhaps up to seven times before it is resolved. Qi Sha is an inner flaw mistaken for outer circumstances, and therefore, it is misperceived and underestimated. In its more negative manifestations, it can create inexplicable negative emotions, anxiety, and self-destructive behavior. At worst, it can create violence, calamity, and death from suicide, accidents, addictions, and illnesses, which, at the root, come from within.

So, what is Qi Sha, and how does it get created? Qi Sha is an unsettled or unresolved Ghost in our Ancestral line that is enraged and full of fury and even vengeance. And it is coming for your life, especially in the Ming, Ancestor, or Health Palace. It is likely an Ancestor who had a tragic, painful, or traumatic death, but this is not always the case. It is someone in our Ancestral line from as far back as seven generations whose negativity at the time of death and the story surrounding their death have been forgotten, repressed, covered up, lied about, denied, or ignored by the family.

Ghosts seek help from their Ancestors to resolve them, and Qi Sha has been ignored or forgotten. This Ancestor's story may have been shameful, dark, bitter, or blasphemous, so the family ignored them and doesn't want to discuss it. They also may have just been lost and forgotten in war, or more tragically, they received an improper burial or inappropriate funeral or have a damaged burial site.

The key is that they have been forgotten, and the family has not dealt with their negativity, so it has compounded and continues to get passed down for up to seven generations. The Seven Killings Star has been spinning in negativity for so long that it has forgotten its humanity, become angry, hurtful, and vengeful, and wants retribution. It wants to be heard and will do anything to achieve this. It is a Ghost on the verge of becoming a Demon, and in some cases, it can be a full-blown Demon in your chart.

If it is alone and rules the House or shows up with other Ghost Stars, then the Seven Killings Star becomes very powerful, which may mean you inherited a Demon. Ghosts and Demons both feed on negativity, but Demons are coming for your life. Ghosts want to wallow forever in negativity and stay feeding on the human realm, but Demons wish to resolve and go to the Hell Realms, and they can resolve if they take your life as revenge or retribution. This may sound scary, but this force represents much of the darkness and negativity in the world, and it is the only thing in Chinese cosmology that can be called "evil."

So, if the Seven Killings Star rules a House in your chart, you'd better pay attention. But remember, this is always done on a case-by-case basis, and there is no guarantee that there is a Demon in your family. The test is to look at your life. If there is any ongoing pattern of negativity that you can't seem to resolve, especially in the House it rules, then you must look at Qi Sha. You must deeply self-reflect and do genealogy to find the source of this negativity. You have been charged with resolving a long unresolved pattern of Ancestral negativity, and you must resolve it, or it may kill you or harm others through you.

If it shows up with a stronger Star, Qi Sha's negativity can be mitigated but never fully eclipsed. The General Star is the most potent exorcistic or eclipsing force in the chart, and if Qi Sha shows up with the General, then you have a strong Ancestral guardian who has taken care of this Demon for you, and it is mostly eclipsed. Here, the best Qi Sha can do is delay, postpone, or create subtle fear and self-doubt about the Fate in that House. The Emperor is the second strongest eclipsing force, and although the Fate of the Emperor can never be stopped, Qi Sha can haunt you with intense self-doubt, limiting self-undermining behavior, and obstruction. The combination of the Emperor with Qi Sha can make the central resolution of Fate a slow, tedious, and ponderous grind, in which you slowly wear down your Fate, and resolving it becomes about overcoming this central haunting represented by Qi Sha.

If other, but more minor, Stars from the Royal Court show up with the Seven Killings Star, they represent the "way out," which may be through education or meditation like with the Magistrate and Priest, but the negativity tends to be stronger and more challenging. If more Ghosts gang up with it, then the chances of this turning into a Demon and going full-blown negative increase.

All the Ghost Stars represent negative emotions that come from Ancestors who died with "unfinished business" and whose negative emotions characterized their moment of death, making them unable to "resolve" in death. And we each inherit a smattering of this across the Twelve Houses. But most of these are "weak" and can be overcome with self-reflection and discipline, because these Ghosts remember their humanity, but Qi Sha doesn't and doesn't follow human behavior. Wherever Qi Sha appears, you cannot manage your thoughts, emotions, and fears. Qi Sha "possesses" you and makes you blind, unreasonable, and irrational. It can bring up many confusing, conflicting, and painful emotions that seem to come from nowhere, meaning you did nothing in this life to create them. They represent an inscrutable message coming from the anxious voices of your unsettled dead Ancestors, trying to be heard by making you reenact their negativity, but the message has been long buried and cannot be easily heard.

This influence can create patterns of undermining yourself with compulsive negative actions, hostility, and arguments. It may cause you to act out or lash out to prove, defend, or assert yourself, or it may cause you to self-destruct, harm or hurt yourself, fail repeatedly, and so on. It can cause miscalculations, misjudgments, and misunderstandings. It inspires addiction, abuse, and trauma and seeks to repeat these patterns until it kills you or others. It is an unlearnable lesson, causing us to ask ourselves, *Why does this keep happening to me? I can't believe I did that again!* So, how is this pattern resolved?

This may sound dramatic, but it all comes down to your unique circumstances, as this Ghost comes from your Ancestors and whatever dark stories they have not dealt with. So, there are innumerable ways this can manifest in actual people. We all have this Star somewhere, and if stronger Stars partially eclipse it, then it likely represents more banal forms of self-limiting behavior and negative emotions that will work themselves out and resolve by sticking with your path. For example, if you have the Emperor and Qi Sha in a career House, then you will slowly grind down Qi Sha through your work in the world, but it may be filled with self-doubt, obstacles, and negative emotions. Eventually, you will get there and feel free and resolved.

If it rules a House, then the resolution is more "exorcistic," cathartic, and dramatic, and you need to do genealogy and uncover the Ancestral story behind the affliction. Somewhere in your family is a dark story that no one talks about, and that story is likely related to whatever House the Seven Killings Star shows up in. So, ask your parents and grandparents. Perhaps someone died in an accident, killed themselves, or was murdered, lost at sea, lost in war, betrayed, bereft, homeless, or the like. Find their story, and tell it. It may involve family therapy. Look at the House and how this story manifests in your life. Qi Sha is tricky and will keep undermining you; you may think it is resolved, but then it comes back with a vengeance. How many times have you thought you were done with something, only to have it happen again but worse? This is Qi Sha.

Resolution may, and should, involve a more profound spiritual dimension. It may require prayer, priests, ritual, deep self-reflection, meditation, and a lot of help, compassion, and kindness from yourself and others, for it is coming from within you, but it is not yours. It may manifest as violence, addiction, illness, and accidents, and you may have to go through these to resolve Qi Sha. These things may be Fated. Not all accidents or illnesses are Fated and evident in a chart; some are just accidents. However, if they are in the chart, they are "Ancestral illnesses." If you do, say, get cancer or try to kill yourself and come out the other side stronger, then Qi Sha is likely resolved. You may feel it "leave you." Only you can determine if it is done, but remember, it will try to trick you. You must also look at the other Houses in a chart to see and follow the positive energy. Remember, this all sounds dramatic, but it is important not to obsess over this or any other Ghost Star, for in the end, this just makes them stronger.

Let's walk the Seven Killings Star through the Twelve Houses. We will discuss them as if this Ghost Star is alone and ruling each House. The interpretation for each of the Twelve Houses is similar and follows the same message: that House's area of life is governed by an Ancestral negativity that must be resolved.

Ming Palace

If Qi Sha rules the Ming Palace, your life is governed by an Ancestral Ghost or Demon that has come for your life; this placement represents a challenging and complicated life! The same goes for the Ancestors and Health Palaces. If there are no other afflicting Stars, then it can be resolved, and you can live a successful life. However, if it shows up with other afflicting Stars, then you may die young from an accident, suicide, murder, illness, or death on the battlefield. Of course, this is not guaranteed; you may be Fated to go through a cathartic or exorcistic event that comes close to claiming your life, but you may survive such an act and liberate this Ghost. If you survive, Qi Sha is likely cleared, and life can continue without further negativity. You must look to the Ancestors Palace and other strong Houses to see if you have Ancestral protection.

Sometimes, our Ancestors set us up or offer us as a sacrifice to resolve Qi Sha. If the Ancestors Palace is exalted or the Emperor and Empress appear together in the House across from the Seven Killings Star, you know it is a setup. You may be overcome with negative emotions and try to kill yourself or go through a horrendous car accident or assault but survive. During that experience, Qi Sha is exorcised, and you are free of it. When you remember trying to kill yourself, it may even feel like it was happening to someone else. Qi Sha needed to relieve an Ancestor's death or suicide through you to be finished. However, you may carry prominent scars or emotional wounds for the rest of your life.

If you do not go through a dramatic or cathartic exorcism in the form of an illness, accident, or attack, then you will likely have a more subtle haunting by Qi Sha. You may have inexplicable anxiety, fear, hatred, or addictive or compulsive actions that have no basis in this life. These may manifest in early childhood or adolescence or come on suddenly at some point in life. You inherit the dark story of Qi Sha as a central part of your Fate, and it can create powerful forms of self-undermining negativity. You must deal with and heal it, or it will ruin your life. Character becomes very important here, and "strong" Characters like Dragons, Oxen, Tigers, and so on can handle this much better than more emotional or anxious characters like Rabbits, Snakes, or Rats. You must take great care here if you are a Rabbit or Snake.

There are many ways this negativity can manifest. But remember, Qi Sha "possesses" you and makes you blind, unreasonable, and irrational. It can bring up many confusing, conflicting, and painful emotions that seem to come from nowhere, meaning you did nothing in this life to create them. The Seven Killings Star represents an inscrutable message coming from the anxious voices of your unsettled dead Ancestors, and you inherit this as the central image of your Fate. You are here to resolve the most negative story of your Ancestors; they are trying to be heard by driving you to reenact their negativity. The best way to resolve this Ghost, though, is not to reenact their story! But to do this, you must see the pattern and have enough self-possession to stop it.

Unfortunately, the Seven Killings Star's influence can create patterns of undermining yourself with compulsive negative actions, hostility, and arguments. It may cause you to act out or lash out to prove, defend, or assert yourself, or it may cause you to self-destruct, harm or hurt yourself, fail repeatedly, and so on. It can cause miscalculations, misjudgments, and misunderstandings. It inspires addiction, abuse, and trauma and seeks to repeat these patterns until it kills you or others. It is a seemingly unlearnable lesson: *Why does this keep happening to me? I can't believe I did that again!* If Qi Sha shows up with more Ghosts, it makes all these patterns of negativity stronger, more challenging to see, and harder to resolve, and it increases the likelihood of this all becoming more hostile. A stronger Star from the Royal Court can offer a path out, so follow the principle of that Star. Despite Qi Sha's negativity, every Star from the Royal Court is much stronger and can ultimately help to resolve this.

Again, if you have the Seven Killings Star here, you may have to go through some very dark and challenging experiences that come close to taking your life. As always, you must do genealogy and uncover the Ancestral story behind the affliction. Somewhere in your family is a dark story that no one talks about: Someone died in an accident, killed themselves, or was murdered, lost at sea, lost in war, betrayed, bereft, homeless, or the like. Their death haunts you. Find their story, and tell it; seek therapy and help.

Qi Sha is tricky and will keep undermining you; you may think it is gone, but then it comes back with a vengeance. This is a hard life. There's no way around it, but remember, it is not your fault! The struggle comes from your Ancestors. Still, you must also remember not to blame or curse them. If you inherit Qi Sha as a central image of your Fate, then you were chosen by your Ancestors because they believe you are strong enough to resolve this family Ghost or Demon. You can do it.

Ancestors Palace

If Qi Sha rules the Ancestors Palace, then your Ancestral Fate and relationship to the family is a Ghostly or Demonic curse. The centrality of negativity here is similar to in the Ming Palace, and potentially has a strong effect on the Health Palace as well. However, in this House the negative influence manifests much more powerfully through your parents, grandparents, and other direct family members. In other words, in the Ming Palace, the Seven Killings Star affects your life more generally, but here, it comes at you through your parents or grandparents, sometimes as irreconcilable anxiety and mental illness.

You have a direct connection with Qi Sha as an Ancestor who had an untimely, tragic, or traumatic death, the story of which was repressed, forgotten, and even disavowed by the family. If Qi Sha rules this House, it is angry and is coming for your life. If other Ghost Stars are present, the Seven Killings Star here can be one of the darkest placements in Polestar Astrology. As part of your Fate, your Ancestors have charged you with a difficult exorcism, which is likely an ongoing, dark pattern of suffering in the family. Qi Sha will try to possess you and replay this pattern.

There are many ways that Qi Sha can possess and come after you in this House, the most straightforward of which is child abuse, trauma, and specifically, intergenerational trauma that gets played out through the parent–child relationship. Your parents may be possessed by Qi Sha, and they may hurt, neglect, and physically, emotionally, or sexually abuse you, depending on the Ancestral pattern you inherited. They may also play out this possession through addiction, drugs, alcohol, gambling, crime, and so on, and abuse may be intertwined with that. Your parents are likely doing something that was done to them. Perhaps your dad's dad was an alcoholic who beat him, and unconsciously, he ends up doing the same thing to you. This can play out in many ways, so you must examine your family dynamics, do genealogy, and look backward to find out where and how this pattern started. Somewhere is a dark origin story of sadness, death, suicide, war, or other tragedy. If it has not been dealt with, you get it directly as a family pattern of negativity. You can either perpetuate or liberate it, but first, you must recognize it.

This pattern can haunt you past childhood and into adulthood, and your whole life may be an expression of the anxiety and pain you experienced in childhood. You may grow up with anger, shame, guilt, fear, and so on because of what happened to you, and this can lead to risky behavior, drugs, crime, and so on. You may rebel against the family, run away, and change your name. You may take your own survival lightly, as Qi Sha enjoys your life being at risk. So, you get into dangerous situations, make poor choices, and perpetuate the negativity of your childhood. You may be prone to accidents, injuries, addictions, and abuses. You may die early in an accident, fight, drug overdose, or suicide or on the battlefield. You may become the abuser and repeat the abuse you received, either directly or indirectly, through your anger, lashing out at those who try to help you. Or, you may keep all this inside and abuse yourself. This can be overt or subtle, but either way, you must face a dark pattern here, or it will keep hurting you and others. Obstacles, challenges, and setbacks may also beset your life, despite everything else seeming fine.

The Seven Killings Star here can lead to dark mental states, anxiety, depression, and mental illness that have no cause in this lifetime. This placement does not guarantee parental abuse—your parents may be fine—but you may be possessed by a Ghostly or Demonic Ancestor who creates dark mental states. You may be overcome by them and have nightmares, inexplicable fears, or hallucinations, and you may try to take your own life or lash out at others. Therapy can be helpful, but therapists will struggle to understand why you feel this way, because the causes are not from this life but from that of an Ancestor. You may try and fail at killing yourself, but in this process, Qi Sha is liberated, and you are then free. Or, you may struggle for years with mental illness and eventually be able to free this pattern through therapy.

Again, genealogy is important, and a ritual to connect with and exorcise this pattern may be necessary. Traditionally, you would be sent to a priest. Qi Sha here rejects the family and is angry at the family for what they did to it, and it is holding you accountable. You must open up the darkness around this Ancestor's story and bring it into the light. This may involve having to deal with guilt, shame, denial, or grief from family members who don't want to admit to or face the darkness in the family. You may run away, change your name, or become a monk to avoid this.

The Seven Killings Star in the Ancestors Palace also strongly affects the Health Palace, which is directly across from it, and can lead to Ancestral or genetic illness. You may have a genetic predisposition to die young, or you may suffer from a childhood illness that comes close to taking your life if it doesn't. Illness may come at you later in life as well. You may be struck with a severe or terminal illness that runs in the family, like cancer, heart disease, brain disease, and so on. If more Ghost Stars are present, the likelihood of illness, injury, or accident becomes more severe, as it tends to compound the negativity. Stronger Stars can significantly mitigate that negativity and make it less life-threatening. If you do not deal with Qi Sha during life, then it may consume you in the moment of dying, making death a fearful or horrific process.

Youth Palace

If Qi Sha appears in the Youth Palace, it generally has two possible manifestations. The first is that Qi Sha haunts the Fate you share with your sibling and becomes irresolvable. The second is that Qi Sha haunts your childhood, making it harsh, dark, and traumatic; this may involve negativity from your siblings, parents, and even teachers and friends. Either way, your youth will involve a Demonic element that comes from the Ghost of an Ancestor, who may have died young or at the hands of a sibling. This may be a blood feud between siblings from generations back.

It may be that one of your siblings is possessed by Qi Sha. They may be troubled, angry, irresponsible, or abusive to you or other family members. They may hurt and even torment you emotionally or physically. They may be older and abandon you or fail to protect you. Or the relationship itself may be haunted and full of betrayal, arguments, and negative emotions. Or you may lose a sibling to suicide, accidental or sudden death, or illness. Or you may be possessed yourself, and harm your siblings. The Seven Killings Star may also act through an uncle, cousin, or protector who harms, abuses, or betrays you during your youth. You may be adopted or go through foster care, where you are hurt or abused. Sibling or family relationships may need to be severed, and the relationships may always be troubled; you may never reconcile. Liberating Qi Sha may involve resolving things with these family members, which can include cutting ties and holding boundaries. You may also have no siblings, which may be an affliction during one's youth.

Qi Sha may have died young, and their experience haunts you, looking for resolution. This may make you an "at risk," reclusive, antisocial, or rebellious child. You may put yourself in danger, run away from home, or get involved with drugs, gangs, or crime early in life. Your sexuality may bloom early and cause you to mature too soon, or it may result in sexual abuse, assault, or rape from older people. You may be a delinquent and go to juvenile hall or deal with homelessness or neglect.

The reason for all of this is the negative promptings of the unsettled dead, who create inexplicable feelings of danger, fear, persecution, and the need to rebel or escape, and who want you to perpetuate their negativity and be at risk. You may try to commit suicide in youth. You may do something you barely survive, or escape something by the skin of your teeth. You may remember the difficulties of youth and be haunted by them for the rest of your life, which can become a detriment, or you may remember the struggles you rose above and use them as a source of strength.

The Seven Killings Star here may also manifest as an early childhood illness, injury, or death. You may get a severe or terminal illness in childhood; if you survive, you will be free of Qi Sha. You may also get into a severe accident and become injured. This may also manifest as a serious mental illness early in life, and you may experience anxiety, depression, or hallucinations. Again, all these come from Qi Sha, so therapists and parents will not be able to understand where it comes from. You may grow out of this as you mature, and your Ancestors may have set you up to liberate Qi Sha as a child. The more Ghost Stars present, however, the more likely all the above negativities may get worse or harsher. As always, doing genealogy is essential here, but this may be retrospective because you will already be an adult by the time you get to it. Although it may all be a memory by then, the trauma may still be with you, or your sibling relationships may still be haunted.

In this House, it is likely that an Ancestor died in youth in a harsh way that did not allow them to have a complete death, so the negative promptings of Qi Sha tend to be more immature and irrational here, as we are not emotionally mature as children. This placement may also mean a blood feud between siblings was never resolved and has been passed down. Siblings may have been at war with each other or even killed each other. You may have to tell their story and resolve the original grievance with your siblings. Again, you may also have to escape this Fate to be free, to cut ties with family and never return.

Partners Palace

If you have Qi Sha in the Partners Palace, then you inherit an Ancestral pattern of abuse in partnership or marriage or a pattern of loss and loneliness that comes from losing a partner early, possibly from war. As a result, you will likely struggle with relationships; you may abuse or be abused, get divorced, or be hurt by a partner. It is likely that Qi Sha here is an Ancestor who was abused by their partner and may even have been killed by them. There may be a history of spousal abuse in your family, or of bad marriages that are full of arguments, discord, and domestic violence. This abuse may be emotional, physical, or sexual. Your parents or grandparents may have had a bad marriage, and you may be Fated to play out their negative patterns.

There are many ways this placement can manifest. The first is difficulty getting into or maintaining relationships in the first place. You may have many fears, neuroticisms, apprehensions, fantasies, or projections about relationships that come from Qi Sha. Qi Sha possesses you when it comes to relationships. This may prevent you from meeting someone or make you abandon relationships due to irrational concerns. Jealousy, insecurity, suspicion, low self-worth, or fear of abandonment or rejection may plague you. You may also be very confused by the emotion of love, and it may be mixed with many other negative emotions, causing you to behave irrationally. You may have childhood fantasies of a Prince Charming, soulmate, or twin flame that cause unrealistic expectations and impossible standards that can never be fulfilled. You may become obsessive about, attached to, and fixated on finding "the one."

You may get into many relationships, lack self-reflection, and even get married and divorced due to the above confusion. You may use and abuse people or be used and abused. These patterns may be unconscious, a blind eye. You may be drawn again and again to the same kind of lousy partner and repeat the same patterns of abuse or rejection that you cannot admit to or even see. You may also be drawn back again and again to the very same partner who abuses you, thinking you can change them or hoping they will change. Your relationships may be full of arguments, discord, and incompatibility. You may partner with someone incompatible, or your partner may change personality after the wedding, going from sweet to Demonic.

You may be stuck in a lousy marriage and unable to get out. Again, you may be subject to physical, emotional, or sexual abuse at the hands of your partner, or you may be the abuser, playing out the same patterns of abuse that your parents did to each other. You may be Fated for one or many nightmare partnerships until you can either see the negative patterns you are playing out and choose differently or grow out of the core patterns. You may also be Fated to lose a partner and be widowed tragically; they may die in war, from an illness, or in an accident, and you may become bereft, never to love again. But it is better to have loved and lost than never to have loved at all.

You may also be asexual or afraid of partnership. You may be uninterested in or incapable of partnership due to your fears or insecurities. You may be a loner or "incel" (involuntarily celibate). You may be poor, unattractive, and have no prospects but are unwilling to do the work on yourself to become a worthy partner. Then you may become bitter and resentful that you cannot find a partner and become antagonistic toward the opposite sex.

As always, genealogy and evaluating your parents' marriage are essential here. The more Ghost Stars are present in this House, the darker this can get. Qi Sha may have been abused or killed by a partner in your family line. Or you may have a history of domestic violence and spousal abuse that is caused or made worse by drugs, alcohol, or trauma, or simply from lack of self-reflection and personal growth. This may be a dark pattern the family doesn't discuss or deal with.

Domestic abuse has been common throughout history and is worse or more accepted in certain cultures and religions; historically, I doubt many people "worked" on themselves much to be better partners. And remember, while the majority of domestic abuse victims are women, this can affect men too. However, if you have Qi Sha in this House, partnership can become a dark obsession or the source of a lot of negativities, so there may be a lot of self-work to do to liberate this. Or you may have to avoid it, stay single, or become a monk or nun. A lot of the negativity here can also be avoided by getting married later in life, after you have grown up, but you still may have to go through a lot of negativities to mature because sometimes our immaturity does not come out until we are in a relationship.

Offspring Palace

If Qi Sha rules the Offspring Palace, then the circumstances and the whole experience of being a parent are haunted by unsettled dead in your family. Qi Sha here may be an Ancestor who died giving birth or lost a child early. They may have been infertile or otherwise unable to conceive, and died full of longing. They may have been killed, betrayed, or hurt by their children. Or, you are haunted by a child who died as an orphan—alone, unprotected, and resentful—or who died because of their parents' negligence or disownment, or a child who died during birth, in the womb, or later from a childhood illness or injury. Either way, this haunting will either create an irrational fear of being a parent or an inability to fulfill parenthood, or it will complicate the process of pregnancy or parenting itself. It should be said that these influences can affect men and women the same.

The most common scenario is the fear of being a parent. This fear may be irrational, like the very idea scares you, or it may be perfectly rational and justified. You may have specific fears of dying in childbirth or of inadequacy or insufficiency at being a parent. Maybe you fear losing your freedom or money. Perhaps you are too immature and unable to grow up. But those fears are somewhat justified here, as you are at risk as a parent. Qi Sha is Demonic and provokes medical and psychological problems, especially if it shows up with more Ghost Stars.

You may want children, but you struggle with infertility, impotence, irregular menstrual cycles, or other health problems that produce infertility as a side effect. You may have multiple miscarriages, abortions, or incomplete pregnancies. You may have complications from surgeries or spend a fortune on invasive medical treatments like in vitro fertilization, only to have them fail. Childbirth itself may be painful and complicated, and you or your child may die or suffer from medical complications. Your child may also be born with a chronic medical condition; they may require constant medical care, maybe for life. This may be a burden, draining your time and money. Here, Qi Sha is coming for your life, and childbirth can be hazardous, even for fathers, whose health may somehow decline after childbirth.

If the pregnancy goes well, you may be Fated to have a difficult child. They may be rebellious and disagreeable or entirely reject you and your authority. This may create a lifelong struggle, and although you try your best, you still struggle being a parent. It may be awkward, uncomfortable, and unnatural; you may even hate being a parent. You may have never wanted to be a parent in the first place, and so you are a bad parent as a result. I'm sure everyone tries their best, but ask around: Many people are, simply put, bad parents.

This placement may be an Ancestral curse that causes child abuse, physical, sexual, and/or emotional violence, or abandonment and neglect. You may give children up for adoption or foster care or leave them to be raised by strangers or other family members. Your children may also hurt you, physically or emotionally. They may steal from you, manipulate you, or drain you of resources. They may constantly get in trouble and need your help, never listening to advice or growing up. They may never leave home and live in your basement, or they may run away early and join a gang. Military school or something similar can be a good option here.

There are two ways to resolve this Fate. One is simply to avoid having kids, which may be easy if you don't want them. Even if this is the case, the Seven Killings Star here can still create medical issues around sexuality and reproduction. The second is to wait and postpone having kids until later in life, which is easier for men, since they can have kids pretty much until they die. For women, most of the negativity should be cleared by thirty-eight, but then it may be much more complex to conceive, and you are likely to get into the scenario of medical difficulty and expense. A third option is to adopt, but this, too, can be fraught with peril. As always, do genealogy and find any negative stories around Ancestors who may have died in childbirth or lost children or were unable to have kids.

Wealth Palace

The Wealth Palace is considered the only beneficial placement for Qi Sha, and it may not be an affliction at all if it shows up alone or with stronger Stars. Strangely, the Seven Killings Star here is considered an auspicious placement for gaining and earning money by unexpected means, such as playing the lottery. It is associated with "windfall," gambling, wild speculation, inheritance, and investment. Qi Sha is considered a harmful Ancestral curse around money that actually comes back to benefit you. However, it can be very afflicting if it shows up with other Ghost Stars. An Ancestor may have died poor or with outstanding debts; they may have been robbed or been a robber. This may be an Ancestral curse of poverty and a struggle for success.

If it shows up alone or with stronger Stars, you should buy a weekly lottery ticket, and you should go to Vegas occasionally and try your luck. You may also be in line to receive a large, unexpected inheritance or settlement from an insurance claim or lawsuit. You may slip and fall in a grocery store, winning millions in the settlement. Or you may invest in a start-up and make millions on the IPO. Gambling and taking risks can go very well. You may also lose a fortune and gain it back, only to lose it again. The Seven Killings Star is wild here and can have a lot of ups and downs. There may be a one-off source of windfall, or it may be a pattern that you can capitalize on. I would say be careful, but also don't be too afraid to take risks.

This placement can also indicate making money illegally. You may be a criminal. This can manifest as blackmail, extortion, theft, or embezzlement. You may do this, or it may be done to you. The more Ghost Stars, the more likely this will go poorly and be a disaster. You may have an Ancestor who was a criminal and are Fated to pay for their sins. Jail time and legal troubles are possible here.

If the Seven Killings Star shows up with more Ghost Stars, you may struggle significantly with money all your life. You may be unable to pull yourself up by your bootstraps. You may be poor, homeless, and lose everything. You may be racked with medical bills, legal fees, alimony, or child support payments. You may be delinquent or in deep with a loan shark or the mafia. Or you may be a loan shark or in the mafia yourself. You may hate and resent money or the wealthy, but you are nonetheless obsessed with money—wanting it, unable to get it, or rejecting it altogether. You may be humiliated either by poverty or by status or become a deadbeat.

The easiest way to resolve this Ghost Star is to become a monk or nun and take vows of poverty and charity. Generosity also resolves Qi Sha here, so if you receive a considerable windfall, give it away, at least in part. Part of the curse is that those who receive windfall, like in Vegas, go right back to gambling and lose it all again. The more you do something positive and generous with your money, the more you are likely to liberate negative family curses around cash. As always, do genealogy: If you have a criminal relative, you may be connected to their Fate.

Health Palace

If Qi Sha rules the Health Palace, then a Ghostly and possibly Demonic Ancestral force will negatively affect your health. If Qi Sha appears in the Ming, Ancestors, Pleasure, or Health Palace (and possibly in the Offspring Palace), its negativity can become a threat to your life, especially here. As such, this is a very inauspicious placement, especially if it shows up with more Ghost Stars.

Here, your health and well-being are directly connected to Qi Sha; you are "possessed" in some way by this Ghost Star, and as a result, you will be tough to diagnose and treat. You will likely suffer from a weak constitution and possibly from many chronic and even severe illnesses or accidents. The exorcism of Qi Sha is part of your Fate, but this process is challenging to understand, for you can make things worse very easily by obsessing over health and healing and getting addicted to treatment and even to being ill. Character matters a lot here, as this has the potential to go much worse for more nervous and sensitive Characters.

The effects of this placement can run the gamut in terms of symptoms; they will be characterized by "wind," which means they are always moving and changing and, therefore, are hard to understand and diagnose. You may be a medical mystery. The key is understanding Qi Sha itself, which means doing genealogy and finding the Ancestor who is coming for you. Somewhere in your family is a very dark story, and here, an Ancestor most likely had a tragic, traumatic, or painful death, and they probably died full of fear, anger, hate, confusion, and so on. They were unable to process or complete their death, and so they will possess you and try to complete it through you, reliving their pain. The specific symptoms you have will be directly related to their story, but they can manifest in many unpredictable and strange ways.

First, it must be understood that the Seven Killings Star is possibly the most devious in this House; it can manifest as mental, emotional, and physical symptoms, but underlying these is probably an addictive pattern of self-inflicted pain. You may have inexplicable anxiety, depression, neuroses, irrational fears, addictions, vices, bad habits, poor self-control or self-discipline, risk-taking and accident-prone behavior, and so on, and you may be blind to these traits or trapped by them in such a way that they are very difficult to resolve or process. Your symptoms may then lead to addictive behavior patterns including poor eating patterns, substance abuse, or drug addiction or to physical abuse, sexual abuse, and so on, which may be inflicted on you or which you may inflict on others. Beneath all these is a pain pattern trying to be fulfilled. So, identifying that is critical to resolving it. These dark patterns can lead to suicidal ideation and attempted suicide, both fast by taking your own life or long and slow in the form of something like drug addiction, in which you gradually kill yourself over time.

This placement can manifest as a weak constitution that is susceptible to illness; you may be weak and sickly in childhood and develop disease patterns that continue into adulthood. You may have many subclinical chronic illnesses, digestive disorders, sleep disorders, and adrenal fatigue, and your life may be a constant health struggle. You may become addicted to medical treatment, cures, fasting, and purging, and you may be dependent on doctors, healers, therapists, and so on. You may be a professional patient and carry a binder of diagnoses and test results. You may alienate your caregivers because of your obsession. You may take handfuls of supplements and pharmaceutical medications. You may have a long list of surgeries and subsequent surgeries resulting from complications from past surgeries. Your medical bills may bankrupt you. You may be the victim of iatrogenic disease and die at a hospital from a botched surgery, post-op infection, improper drug administration, and so on. Qi Sha can even possess those trying to help you, making things worse.

You may, at some point, be given a dire diagnosis like cancer. Going through something like this may be part of your Fate; you may survive and resolve Qi Sha, and you may not. You may also be Fated to go through a severe accident and be severely injured, liberating Qi Sha in the process. You may die on the battlefield or be murdered. You may have perfect health for most of your life, to have it all suddenly deteriorate or be taken from you. Or none of this may ever happen. It is important not to obsess over negative details and possibilities here, but we must acknowledge the worst that can happen. Obsessing here makes the Seven Killings Star stronger and more likely to make you addicted to seeking help and healing and, in the process, make things worse.

We can go on and on about the possible negativity here, but none of it is certain, and this placement must be taken on a case-by-case basis. Stronger Stars can mitigate these patterns, but health challenges are still very likely. Resolving Qi Sha here is exorcistic and may be dramatic and cathartic. Again, do genealogy, talk to elders in your family, and find out what dark Ancestral pattern you have inherited. Tell the Ancestor's story, complete it, and resolve their hardship through forgiveness and love.

This placement may also be a spiritual call to prayer, meditation, pilgrimage, and ritual. You may need a "shaman" or priest to help resolve this Ghost. The more you can practice generosity, selfless service, loving-kindness, equanimity, and compassion, the more likely this will become a spiritual release and source of wisdom. Remember, this Star may be a Demon, but it's also your relative. If you treat Qi Sha like a grandmother would treat a disobedient grandchild, it will resolve in time. And if it takes your life, no worries: Birth is the cause of death, and no one really dies.

Career/Travel Palace

If Qi Sha rules the Career/Travel Palace, then you will likely struggle with work and travel, working hard and making sacrifices with little reward, but you are a good place to resolve Ancestral negativity through these things. As such, this and the other career Houses are a more auspicious placement for Qi Sha, especially for active and adventurous Yang Characters. Qi Sha here represents and Ancestor who died far from where they were born, maybe at work or on the battlefield. The Ghost seeks to find home and fulfillment but is lost and cannot find their way. Qi Sha can turn angry and frustrated here, and it is usually resolved through the grind of finding your way in the world and facing many obstacles and challenges.

You may feel a deep sense of not belonging and of needing to find yourself through travel. Or you may feel a deep longing but lack of purpose and direction. You may feel profoundly unsettled and called to wander in life in search of something unknown. You may, therefore, travel widely and even move far from where you were born. You may leave home to escape a hostile family. This may resolve Qi Sha, as you may be more at risk if you stay home. Or Qi Sha may be calling you to die far from home like they did. Many hundreds of millions of people have been killed in war, far from home, in the past 150 years. Many tens of millions of people became refugees and were forced to flee due to war, the forging of modern nation-states, and ethnic struggles. The Seven Killings Star here can be related to such struggles and may be seeking to resolve Ancestors' unsettled pain through your wandering. This pain can turn angry and cause you a deep sense of pain, anger, and frustration that inspires feelings of vengeance, retribution, or violence toward those who wronged you or your Ancestors.

This placement can manifest as a deep uncertainty about what to do with your life. You may travel a lot, change jobs many times, and pursue many paths in search of meaning or purpose, never to find it. You may change jobs often but develop neither skills nor a meaningful profession. You may work hard your whole life without success and never live up to your potential. You may be suited to be a wandering artist or writer, traveling salesperson or musician, career student, or spiritual nomad.

The Seven Killings Star here can also make you aggressive and risk-taking, seeking danger to relive your Ancestor's death. You may be drawn to danger, combat, or violence, so the military is an excellent way to resolve this. You may also be drawn to strange or dangerous professions, like being an undertaker, surgeon, spy, police officer, firefighter, boxer or martial artist, skydiver, extreme sports enthusiast, or hostage negotiator. And it must be said that this placement can manifest as a crime. Qi Sha may be the Ghost of an Ancestor who was a criminal or died committing a crime. So, you may gamble, commit a crime, join a gang, or go to prison. You may also become a refugee or be forced to leave home due to war, violence, or political strife. Your life may be in danger, and you may live in a constant state of peril. You may also lose everything and be homeless at some point.

The more Ghost Stars show up with the Seven Killings Star, the more likely career and travel will represent a negative and dark path. This may manifest as constant and repeated failure and obstacles. Qi Sha can possess you and make you undermine yourself through poor choices, abandoning things that get hard, acting on irrational fear, taking unnecessary risks, or alternatively, being afraid to take risks.

You will likely resolve a great deal of Fate through traveling and work, and it will likely be a unique and deeply personal journey that reshapes you. This path may involve deep character growth or become an apophatic spiritual path of letting go of delusions, fantasies, failed dreams, unrealistic hopes, and unfulfilled expectations. You become who and what you are by discovering what you are not. You also may be hardened by life and its unfairness and challenges. Qi Sha may make you bitter and resentful, or you may release Qi Sha and gain wisdom, for it is only after we have lost everything that we are free to do anything.

Assistants Palace

If Qi Sha rules the Assistants Palace, then you have an Ancestor who likely died at the hands of a friend, co-worker, or person who either was or seemed to be trying to help them. This is the pattern of righteous victimhood and the resulting consequences. Qi Sha here represents an Ancestor who may have been betrayed, abandoned, robbed, or hurt by someone outside the family who was trying to assist them. You inherit this dark pattern of betrayal or victimhood. As in all the career Houses, the auspice of placement here is both good and bad, for this is an excellent place to resolve Qi Sha, but you will likely struggle a lot and potentially experience a lot of negativities in relationships and your career. But through patience, kindness, generosity, and service, you can resolve and liberate Qi Sha and overcome selfishness and fear.

In this House, the Seven Killings Star possesses you when you try to make friends and help others, and potentially possesses those trying to help you too. You may have inexplicable fears of abandonment and betrayal that keep you from taking risks, working with others, making friends, and advancing in your career. You may be a lousy judge of character and choose bad friends, harmful helpers, or unreliable and even sneaky subordinates. You may be undermined, betrayed, robbed, or abandoned by people who are supposed to be helping you. This may be a pattern or a dramatic Fated episode of scandal or drama at work or school or in a community. You may also be possessed, betrayed, hurt, or taken advantage of by others. As always, you must look in the mirror and ask if you are the villain.

You may be generous and kind, but others may take advantage of this. Your generosity may be miscalculated and lead to loss. You may constantly blame, fear, or mistrust others, or they may do this to you. Here, all this is due to an Ancestral Ghost who died with a negative story of betrayal. They seek retribution or revenge through you and may cause you to relive this pattern repeatedly until you can resolve it. You will have to learn some vital lessons about people, and they may not be pretty. If you take revenge or act out of blame or suspicion, the Seven Killings Star becomes more assertive, creating more enemies, more people to blame, and more victim mentality.

There are three ways to resolve this Ghost. The first is to work alone and be self-reliant; if you work alone, you avoid drama, which may work for some Characters, like Dragons or Snakes, but this is not the best way to live. And it may still suck you in. There is a lot of potential for scandal, arguments, misunderstandings, and betrayal from friends, schoolmates, or co-workers here. You may try to avoid it, but it may be inevitable, as we are rarely isolated individuals. You can also self-efface and try to be as meek, modest, and unassuming as possible, trying to avoid negativity, but this may also invite it.

The second way is to stand there and take it. You accept all the stones thrown at you with a smile. You turn the other cheek and love thy enemy. You dedicate yourself to serving others as selflessly as possible. You give no matter what, without the thought of getting anything in return. You accept accusations even if they are false, for the truth will come out if they are. If any allegations are true, then you take responsibility; this is all about taking responsibility for your actions. Do not blame, just serve others.

The third way is to become a monk, nun, or yogi. Spiritual practice, prayer, mediation, confession, and ritual are powerful here for resolving Qi Sha.

Traditionally, they say to do service work if you have this placement, and everyone who comes to you for help will be someone you or your Ancestors wronged in a past life. So, if you are a doctor, all your patients are people you have a debt with. If you do social work, then all the people you help are people who once helped you or people you wronged, and now you are paying them back. And if you have the Seven Killings Star in this House, you have a long list of people you or your Ancestors wronged, so you must go through many negativities, scandals, or acts of selfless service to right those wrongs. So, do the work, and do not blame others or ask, ***why me***? The more Ghost Stars, the worse and more dramatic the scandal can get, and the harder it is to avoid victimhood and blaming.

Superiors Palace

The Superiors Palace is considered one of the best placements for resolving Qi Sha; if it appears here, it is somewhat unaffected by other Stars. It is similar here as in the other career Houses, but here, Qi Sha is an Ancestor who may have died at the hands of a teacher, guide, boss, or authority figure. They may have been hurt, betrayed, or abandoned by a person or people in power, and you inherit their struggle with authority. They may also have been a social or political leader or someone who was responsible for others but failed them, abused their power, or hurt those they were accountable to protect. They may have died at work or doing something dangerous for a great purpose or mission. Qi Sha here thrives on your life being at risk and will seek to avenge themself. It may also drive you to seek power or authority or to make those in power pay.

With Qi Sha here, you inherit a struggle with power, authority, or risk-taking. This will significantly affect your career and purpose in life, and the consequences can affect many people. You may inherit the negative impacts of an Ancestor's failure. You may hate authority, those in power, and "the man," and you may project this onto your work or society in general. You may struggle with deep feelings about race, class, status, money and wealth, power, social justice, and so on, willing to die for your cause. Your work in the world and even your career may be related to social justice and power and resolving these imbalances and inequalities. You may be a champion for the underdog, for underprivileged, marginalized, and oppressed people. You may become a revolutionary, criminal, or gang leader or at least aspire or pretend to be one.

The Seven Killings Star here may also mean an Ancestorhad great aspirations for power or success but failed to achieve anything, so they died feeling cheated, frustrated, or like a failure. You may work very hard and have great aspirations but be ignored, passed over, and receive no recognition or respect. You may struggle with anger and blame authority. You may achieve success but do many negative things to get there, such as hurting and taking advantage of others along the way. Your success may be "dirty." You may be justly or unjustly accused of breaking the law and be punished. This is the curse of an Ancestor, but you must take responsibility and suffer the consequences of your, and their, actions.

You may also be Fated to have a negative experience with a teacher, boss, guru, mentor, or authority figure. You may be abused, robbed, or taken advantage of by a person in power. You may be drawn into a cult where you are sexually or emotionally abused. You may seek a spiritual teacher and find they are corrupt, phony, or sleeping with students. You may be duped by a scam or pyramid scheme through a boss or someone pretending to be a mentor. And as always, you must look in the mirror and ask if you are the villain. You may be the abuser possessed by Qi Sha, seeking power, fame, wealth, sex, or status, and you may be willing to do anything to get it.

You may also be drawn to dangerous professions or excel at hazardous work or work that is distasteful or disgraceful to others. You may work in the prison system, social welfare, or better yet, the military. Traditionally, they say the military is the best way to resolve this placement, especially if you must go through a robust disciplinary system where you are yelled at by drill sergeants and forced to do push-ups. The more you can take orders, follow discipline, and learn patience, the more you will resolve this pattern. So, with things like martial arts, sports, and disciplined spiritual practices like yoga, you are in a powerful position to resolve the Seven Killings Star and help others through discipline and self-sacrifice.

Property Palace

If Qi Sha rules the Property Palace, then the notion of home, safety, national or cultural identity, and place will be haunted by a Ghostly and possibly Demonic force. An Ancestor likely died at home, which will create a feeling of never being safe and even an irrational fear of being home or being trapped, unable to escape. You may have claustrophobia or agoraphobia. Your Ancestor may have been safe at home only to be bombed in an air raid or to have their home collapse in an earthquake. As a result, your home is haunted, and you always feel uneasy. You never feel safe or secure, and you are constantly moving, changing or buying and selling homes, changing rooms, rearranging furniture, buying new security systems, and so on, trying to get safe. Maybe an Ancestor died while they were in their kitchen, so now you always feel uneasy in kitchens and hate cooking. You may disdain homebodies and always feel like you must be out and about. At home, you feel trapped, claustrophobic, and in danger. Your life will be unsettled until you resolve this Ghost. With further affliction, you may actually be in danger, and you may be attacked, robbed, sexually assaulted, or experience imminent danger or calamity in your home from war or natural disasters.

Or maybe an Ancestor died far from home, perhaps lost and trying to get home or longing for home. They may have been killed in war, at sea, or accidentally while on vacation or traveling. As a result, you are always searching for a home with a deep sense of unfinished business or of being lost, lonely, or out of place. Unable to find a home, your life may become a walkabout, and you may become a wandering nomad, vagabond, or constant expat, moving from place to place. You may be drawn to boats and then almost drown, reliving an Ancestor's death experience. Qi Sha is resolved when you put down roots and find that place to stay, but this may require letting go of the need for a proper home and realizing that home is where you make it.

This Ghost Star also thrives by your being at risk and unsafe, so here you may be forced into exile or refugee status due to war, political strife, or ethnic struggles. Qi Sha may be a curse associated with your Ancestral ethnic group, and you may be haunted by Ancestors who were forced to flee or subjected to genocide or ethnic cleansing, which was many hundreds of millions of people over the past century. Qi Sha may be Ancestors who are angry and vengeful and have a deep hatred for those who attacked their people, and you may continue this strife. You will likely die far from home; you may die on the run, fleeing home or trying to get back home. You may start over somewhere but never feel naturalized in your new home, longing to return to your Ancestral homeland. You may also hate the people you come from and be ashamed of what they did to others. Your Ancestors may have participated directly or indirectly in war, genocide, or ethnic cleansing, and you inherit the shame and guilt as well as the consequences.

Strangely enough, Qi Sha here is similar to this Star in the Wealth Palace, and this placement can sometimes turn out positive. As such, it is associated with windfall and inheritance from out of the blue. So, you may inherit property out of nowhere from a distant or unknown relative. You may also win a car or boat at the slot machines in Vegas. But this is sort of like in those TV shows where you have to stay the night in a haunted house to receive the prize. The Seven Killings Star here can be a haunted house. You may inherit an old house that has been in the family for ten generations, but it is falling apart, haunted by Ghosts, and may even be a death trap. You may sink a fortune into a "money pit" that seems appealing but bankrupts you. You may move in and then suddenly become plagued with anxiety, fear, and suicidal ideation. Qi Sha possesses you after you move in and comes after your life; you may experience visions and "bumps in the night." Qi Sha here may also make you irresponsible with money and property. You may get into severe debt, gamble your money away, and lose everything; the bank forecloses on your home and takes your car. This placement can also mean you are a squatter and live in an abandoned house.

If there is no other affliction, you can acquire real estate, buy and sell property, and make a profit. But the Seven Killings Star often means that it comes with a price: You may profit at the expense of others, or you may end up being a slumlord. Possessed by Qi Sha, you become greedy and hustle people out of their money, lying, cheating, and stealing to get rich and own land. You may also end up being a "snake oil salesman," used car dealer, con artist, hustler, pimp, and so on. You may inherit the dark Fate of Ancestors who bought, sold, and exploited people as slaves, which happened all over the world throughout history, not just in America. There are an estimated 50 million slaves still today, far more than even at the peak of the African slave trade; this is not a thing of the past but a present-day reality that affects many countries. The sex trade, child labor, and all sorts of human trafficking are also very real, and your Fate may be tied to these in some way. This placement may also represent involvement in the black or gray market, racketeering, and illegal counterfeiting. You may lie, cheat on your taxes, and inflate your wealth only to get in trouble with the IRS.

As always, it is essential to do genealogy and talk to the elders in your family. Find out if you have any dark stories of Ancestors who died at home, at war, at sea, and so on. Find out if any were the victim or perpetrator of ethnic violence. If you inherit a House, find out if anyone died or committed suicide there. Whatever pattern you are playing out is directly related to these stories, and the only way to resolve them is to find the story and finish it. This may involve an exorcism, and you may need a priest. You may have to cleanse or perform a ritual in a house or piece of land to appease evil spirits.

Qi Sha may be an "earthbound spirit" connected to a specific piece of property, such as a house, kris sword, family heirloom, or the like. You may have to clean an Ancestor's grave and give them a proper burial if they died at sea or war and never received one. You may have to return to your Ancestral homeland on a pilgrimage to confront the Ghost of the past, so be prepared. You may have to forgive those who wronged your people. You may receive reparations of some kind.

Pleasure Palace

If Qi Sha rules the Pleasure Palace, it makes one of the darkest placements in Polestar Astrology. This is one of the places where Qi Sha is truly coming for your life, and it can lead to dark, addictive, abusive, and self-destructive patterns. Here, you are haunted by Qi Sha, the Ghost of an Ancestor who died having too much fun, in the bad sense of the word, or who died from something that is usually associated with pleasure. They may have died from drug or alcohol addiction. They may have suffered sexual abuse, rape, or assault. They may have been a glutton or died of starvation. They may have gotten into a lot of trouble having fun with friends; maybe things got out of hand, and they had an accident and hurt or killed someone. They may have become addicted to the high or thrill of high-risk, bad behavior and gotten involved in crime, gang violence, or theft. Here, unfortunately, Qi Sha can become a pattern of sadomasochism, and you may end up enjoying pain or enjoying inflicting pain on others. This placement can be host to many dark, negative emotions, and it will drive you to put yourself at risk, seeking the furthest edges of pain and pleasure.

This can turn very dark. There are countless ways the Seven Killings Star can spin out into very dark behavior patterns here, especially if it shows up with more Ghost Stars. As always, it is essential to do genealogy, talk to the elders in your family, and come to understand this pattern. Hopefully, it is not too late, for this one can easily lead to a lot of suffering and an untimely death. You may be the victim of sexual abuse, drug or alcohol addiction, or many compulsive, self-destructive behaviors. You may be drawn to pleasure-seeking in such a way that it gets out of control. You may be drawn to others who are out of control. Qi Sha here wants to indulge; it wants you to go too far.

If it shows up with other Ghost Stars, then you will likely die young from the consequences of some form of bad behavior, or you may commit suicide or be killed. You may also enjoy hurting others and committing violence. You may die a slow and painful death that is tortured with negative emotions, or you may die in a drugged-up coma so that death is hardly experienced. If you are lucky enough to survive, you will be a "survivor." You will have a dark story of recovering from addiction and hitting rock bottom, which is what it may take to liberate this Ghost. You should most certainly seek help and therapy and do whatever you can to be free of it.

The Seven Killings Star here may also manifest as "all work and no play." You may be unable to have fun. The nature of your Ancestor's death may make you deeply fearful of having fun, to the point where it is impossible. You may be deathly serious, rude, stern, and critical of anything frivolous. You may be antisocial, a loner, or isolated and outcast. You may also experience deep, irrational anxiety or fear at the prospect of having fun. You may dissociate and leave your body out of fear. You may also fall into deep depression and never experience joy. You may be possessed of religious judgment and fear-based morality and condemn all pleasure as the devil.

The best result would be renunciation; you can resolve this Ghost by being a monk or nun. But be careful of repression, for there have been many priests who abused children. Qi Sha here must never be repressed, suppressed, or ignored, for its darkness will come out somewhere else, which can be the worst form of this affliction. You must engage and work directly with these dark patterns. As always, do genealogy, talk to the elders in your family, and find out where this Ancestral Ghost comes from. Qi Sha here wants a slow and painful death; he wants to enjoy you slowly killing yourself with addiction and depression. Again, this can get very dark, so if you have this Ghost Star here, remember it does not belong to you. You inherited it and can be free of it if you dare to go through the darkness and come out the other side.

TAN LANG (貪狼)—THE GREEDY WOLF

NAME AND TRANSLATION: Tan Lang (貪狼), the Greedy Wolf Star

> *Tan*, 貪—avid for, greedy, covetous, insatiate, esurient; crave, lust after, pursue obsessively. a) avaricious(ness), cupidity; cling to. b) (Budd.) trns. [translation] Skt. raga, sensual attachment, clinging to desires of this world. 2 (med.) wish to, prefer to (without pejorative implication). 3探 tan, search out; probe.[8]
>
> *Lang*, 狼—wolf. 2 狼尾草 langweicao, foxtail grass, fountain-grass (*Pennisetum alopecuroides*); syn. [synonym] 董蓈 donglang. 3 cmpd. [compound] 狼籍, 狼藉 langji, strewn in a clutter, littered and jumbled, in a total mess; (med.) cmpd. 狼狽 langbei, fall stupidly out of step, stumble and blunder unwittingly; disconnected(ly), disconcerted(ly) (< 2 animals, 1 with front legs too short, 1 with back legs too short, who must lean on each other to go forward).[9]

This translation is also simple: Tan (貪) means "greedy," and Lang (狼) means "wolf," so we translate this as Greedy Wolf Star. The name also implies being obsessive, attached, and desirous and also disordered, cluttered, and out of step.

ELEMENT: Yang Wood, Yin Water

TRADITIONAL IMAGE: A mercenary or hired official with a cloak and dagger, scruffy robes, dark, beady eyes, weak but fearsome[10]

GHOST PROFILE: Ancestral Ghost who was abandoned, rejected, cast out, or fiercely independent, who struck out on their own; image of Ancestral isolation, alienation, exile, migration, refugeedom, immigration, and struggle without help or resources

RESOLUTION/EXORCISM: Resolved through creativity, self-reliance, and individuality that forgoes selfishness and can ask for and receive help, reforming into community and renewed life

LUMINOUS PLACEMENT: Rat, Dragon, and Horse Palaces

DIMINISHED PLACEMENT: Snake and Pig Palaces

AFFILIATIONS: Southern Array—image of a lone wolf with no affiliations

Tan Lang, or the Greedy Wolf Star, is the third of the Four Major Ghosts and probably the most "positive" of the Ghost Stars for modern people, for the pattern it represents often aligns with our individualist, atomized, and "DIY" culture. So we can call this the "American Star." However, the pattern is very much the opposite of traditional culture, which was usually collectivist, inclusive, and tribal. As such, this is traditionally considered a big affliction, but there are now many ways we can use this to our advantage and make the best out of it, for we are a culture of lone wolves, and we love the "underdog."

This is the image of a lone wolf cast out of the wolf pack. Tan Lang has become too old to hunt and has become a burden, so it is cast out to wander alone and fend for itself. The term Tan Lang means "Greedy Wolf," so there is also the sense that it was cast out or exiled from the pack for being selfish and greedy and for not working well with the group.

This Star is, therefore, the symbol of isolation, alienation, and struggle. It is also the Star of greed, and it can represent our Ancestors' desire for money, power, fame, status, sex, prestige, and so on. It represents not "fitting in" but doing whatever you must do to survive on your own. As such, it can be the most hardworking, resourceful, and practical of the Ghost Stars and can manifest great success in a limited sense of the word. But it is still petty, greedy, selfish, and often narrow-minded and can devolve into lazy entitlement. Alone, it is certainly an affliction, but when it shows up with stronger Stars, it can simply become eccentricity, alternative and unconventional means or lifestyles, or a unique and quirky personality.

Tan Lang is also traditionally associated with the image of the shaman, mystic, prophet, or charismatic leader. It is associated with the "vision quest": To become a healer, the shaman must go out alone into the desert, jungle, or forest. They must be brought close to death, then they come out the other side with the power to heal. The experience of prophets is often unique, and their visions start religions or new sects. The shaman's power comes from almost dying themself; they come to the edge of death, cross over, and can communicate between worlds. Tan Lang can represent this kind of Ancestor and path, especially in the Health Palace. This can represent the charisma and charm that creates cults, followings, or movements.

As an Ancestral energy or Ghost, the Greedy Wolf represents an Ancestral pattern of abandonment and rejection. It represents a person or a group who was cast out or who was fiercely independent and struck out on their own. It is the image of Ancestral isolation, alienation, exile, migration, and immigration, as well as struggle without help or resources. There were hundreds of millions of people displaced as refugees over the past century who had to make it alone in a foreign environment. Many more struck out as immigrants to the "New Worlds" of the Americans or Australia, looking for opportunity and to escape poverty, religious persecution, war, political or ethnic strife, or famine. These people left behind generations of tradition, heritage, language, religion, and so on. They may have lived for a hundred generations on the same land only to get on a boat with a pocket full of silver and the hope of a new life. This takes great courage, and more important, it takes resourcefulness, self-reliance, and ingenuity. You must learn a new language and adapt to a new environment and culture as an "outsider." Eventually, you integrate and make a new life. This adaptation is the resolution of Tan Lang. To remain an outsider or refugee instead makes Tan Lang stronger and more entrenched in their struggle.

The worst aspect of Tan Lang is the struggle to do everything yourself. If this Ghost Star rules a House, you are haunted by an Ancestor(s) who struggled alone and never adapted or got help. They are stuck in the pattern of having to do everything alone or for themselves. The more afflicted that House, the more antisocial, aggressive, argumentative, narcissistic, petty, greedy, selfish, deceitful, dishonest, vengeful, and ruthless the Greedy Wolf becomes. It will do anything to survive; it struggles and strives and is addicted to the struggle and stress. It feeds on it, like a dog chewing on a bone, cutting its gums, and liking the taste of its own blood. It doesn't want help or need it—at least, that is what it thinks. It alienates people and isolates you. It can indicate loss, entrapment, and conflict with others. It can represent degenerative disease and deteriorating circumstances that lead to losing everything.

But Tan Lang also inspires resourcefulness, creativity, adaptation, unconventionality, rugged individualism, and personal success. It is about contradiction and paradox and finding a way through. At its best, it can become entrepreneurship and be a harbinger of success and wealth on a strictly personal level. However, this success often comes with a cost, as you may burn bridges, take advantage of others, and step over people as you climb the ladder. As such, this Star tends to do well in our modern culture because we embrace and celebrate the "underdog," entrepreneurship, hard work, rugged individualism, uniqueness, unconventionality, ingenuity, "elbow grease," and the do-it-yourself, "pull yourself up by your own bootstraps" mentality that characterized the founding of the U.S. It is very much the "American" Star, though much of the world is adopting this mindset. We are becoming a culture of atomized individuals, trying to make it as "digital nomads." But is this sustainable? Are we happier? I'm not so sure.

Tan Lang is resolved when you embrace others and rejoin the wolf pack, when you let go of selfishness and individualism and embrace the herd. Generosity, selflessness, kindness, and putting others first transform the Greedy Wolf, and their resourcefulness can then become a boon to others. Unlike Qi Sha and Po Jun, this Star can be resolved with some confidence and turned into a positive force.

Let's walk the Greedy Wolf through the Twelve Houses.

Ming Palace

If Tan Lang rules the Ming Palace, then you are ruled by an unsettled and possibly aggressive, ambitious, or courageous Ancestral Ghost who was forced into isolation, alienation, exile, migration, immigration, or struggle. They were forced to become self-reliant and do everything alone or apart from their place of heritage. Your Fate is shaped and motivated by their struggle, and your life is a continuation or expression of their story. This may be a direct connection to Ancestors who migrated, immigrated, and broke away from tradition. It may also be connected to Ancestors who were displaced by war, natural disaster, or ethnic or political strife.

Your Ancestors, or an Ancestor, had to struggle to survive, and you inherit this struggle in some way; it shapes you, directly or indirectly, and overcoming it forms the central image of your Fate. Many people in the Americas and Australia have these kinds of immigrant stories, and many people in Europe, Africa, and the Middle East have been displaced due to war and strife over the past few centuries, as have Indigenous people all over the world.

Your Fate is possibly mismatched with the circumstances, time, or place of your birth in such a way that causes you to strike out on your own on a path of self-discovery, independence, or survival. You may have to immigrate, move, or travel widely. The details of your Fate are hidden in the fine print and details, and you have a mix of good and bad Fate that you must work hard to integrate and overcome. You inherit grit, determination, and confidence from your independent Ancestors, and you may even be aggressive, wolflike, or obsessed with success, survival, struggle, or overcoming opposition or oppression. This struggle may be real or (at least in part) self-created.

You may be Fated to struggle alone or be alone a great deal. You may experience a lot of isolation, solitude, and even exile. You may be forced to be on your own and do everything yourself. If this House is not further afflicted, you may thrive this way and even like or prefer the situation. Again, your isolation may be partly due to your actions, but it may be hard to see this about yourself. You may alienate others but think that you are in the right and that everyone else is incompetent or out to get you. You may be paranoid or fear help from others due to being burned in the past or because your people are being or have been oppressed.

You may be an "underdog," outcast, loner, foreigner, or weirdo and identify as such. This may have been set off by a significant experience of ostracization. You also may be born with a very different, quirky, and unique personality that sets you apart. This image may be central to your Fate. It may isolate you or exalt you to a special position. You can work this image to your advantage and use it to get ahead, influence people, or even intimidate them. You may build a life on your uniqueness, and this can manifest as successful entrepreneurship or any solo path, like acting, modeling, or writing. You may be a stand-up comic, athlete, or podcaster. You may invent your own unique path or capitalize on a unique talent or skill. This is all about innovation and self-created ingenuity. You may become a champion or hero for the underdog, the marginalized, or the outcast.

You may also be a kind of shaman, healer, mystic, or charismatic leader. Tan Lang is associated with the shaman or healer who must go out on their own into the desert, forest, or jungle and be brought close to death. This can create an obsession with spiritual liberation as a means to overcome suffering that turns into a very personal spiritual path. You may be Fated to go through an intense struggle, illness, or near-death experience and come out the other side with healing powers, visions, or great insight. It may transform you, and you may become a charismatic leader, start a cult or movement, and gain followers. You may form a life from your unique enlightenment or healing experience. This may either liberate your Fate or harden it into a story that you obsess over and tell again and again.

If this is unafflicted by other Ghost Stars, then you will likely succeed due to grit and determination. You will adapt and overcome obstacles and use self-reliance and independence to shape your own destiny. The more this is afflicted, the more difficult your struggle, the more intense your isolation and loneliness, and the more likely you are not to adapt and succeed but to remain your own worst enemy, stuck in a pattern of struggle. You may lash out at others and isolate yourself, growing angrier at the world and more bitter, frustrated, and resentful. You may blame others for your failures. You may go through a huge downfall, loss, or tragedy that becomes central to your Fated lone wolf story. Further affliction here can make you more obsessed and driven to risk-taking or indulgence, and this may burn you out. You may die young, alone, or as a kind of martyr. You may do something courageous and brave and sacrifice yourself for others.

Ancestors Palace

If Tan Lang rules the Ancestors Palace, then you have a strong but potentially difficult Fated connection with your Ancestors, as there is some kind of discontinuity and breaking away from tradition and lineage here. This, again, represents an Ancestor or Ancestors who migrated, immigrated, and broke away from tradition; it represents hard work, isolation, and struggle in a new land. It may be connected to Ancestors who were displaced by war, natural disaster, or ethnic or political strife. An Ancestor or Ancestors had to struggle to survive, and like in the Ming Palace, you inherit their struggle in some way; it shapes you and drives you unconsciously, but in this House it comes specifically through your relationship with your parents or possibly grandparents. One or both of your parents may be ruled by a "loner" Ancestor, and this will shape their experience and the way they treat you. A parent may be a lone wolf who struggles with their own Ancestral inheritance.

You probably come from a long line of tough, self-sufficient, and strong Ancestors, and as such, your parents will be tough and self-sufficient, and so will you. You inherit a strong sense of survival, grit, determination, and "stick-to-itiveness." You Ancestors may be recent immigrants, or you may be a recent implant. Your parents may speak a foreign language or practice a different religion. This may shape your family experience as outsiders, foreigners, or migrants. Your family may be isolated and without resources, or you may be a loner because of your outsider status. This is a common experience in America, and Europe, too, has seen a lot of immigration in the past few decades. The history of the world is one of migration, but eventually, we settle, naturalize, and integrate. This is the pattern of having to struggle and adapt. This Star may also be a direct connection to an Ancestor from up to seven generations back who fled war, famine, or persecution or who got on a boat to the "new world," leaving the "old world" behind. You might be called to reconnect with that story, which may have faded or been forgotten.

You may have an antisocial parent or parents who ignore you or are angry and abusive or discipline you harshly, especially if you stand out or assert yourself. They likely experienced the same kind of treatment and are repeating it. There is likely an Ancestral pattern of isolation and anger here, and one of your Ancestors may have been betrayed, murdered, or cast out, forced into isolation. It is up to you to break this pattern, or you will continue it yourself. This can represent an ongoing pattern of parental abuse or violence, and these Ancestral Ghosts may haunt you; this haunting may shape your life and cause lifelong scars. There may be ongoing strife among your extended family or your parents' siblings, and your parents may be the black sheep or outcasts, or they may have broken away or cut ties with other family members. This may cause your family unit to be isolated, and you grow up without a connection to family or tradition.

You will likely struggle with your parents and your Ancestral inheritance, but you can overcome these differences and difficulties by midlife. Because of your parents' influence, you may struggle with authority until midlife, when you must overcome antisocial patterns from youth. You may reject your parents and leave home early, run away, change your name, and so on. You may strike out on your own, move, learn a new language, practice a new religion, and reinvent yourself. You may cut yourself off from your family in some way: This may be intentional; you may have to break ties to get away from their negativity. Or it may be circumstantial; you may be cut off from them due to war, strife, or natural disaster. Cutting ties may be the key to resolving your Ancestral Fate, and you may need to set strong boundaries and end toxic relationships. Separation may be hard-won, and you may become a recluse or isolated because of it. If you don't heal this, you may resent your family and have ongoing conflicts.

The more Ghosts appear here with Tan Lang, the more likely the conflict becomes dark or abusive, and the more you will likely have to cut ties and become independent from your family. If you resolve this, then it can be a source of creativity, inspiration, and determination. You can benefit from the Ancestral pattern of courage and become strong and independent. Your Ancestors may admire and support your individuality, and you can even start a new tradition.

Youth Palace

If Tan Lang rules the Youth Palace, then your youth and your shared Fate with siblings will likely be tumultuous and shaped by an Ancestral Ghost whose experiences create isolation, struggle, and antisocial behavior. The Greedy Wolf here represents an Ancestral pattern of punishment, escape, cutting ties, and abandonment. Therefore, childhood will probably be rough, and you may be forced to adapt, mature, and grow up early. You may have no childhood as such. If there are no other Ghost Stars here, then you may develop a unique and independent personality early in life, and this can become an advantage to you. You may have few or no siblings, or you may also be Fated to be separated from them or from your family in some way early in life.

The sibling Fate here can go two ways. The first is having few or no siblings. The lone wolf quality of this Star can definitely mean being an only child. You may grow up isolated and cut off from your greater family. You may be home alone a lot, live in your own world, and be forced to adapt and learn things on your own. This can forge a unique and independent personality, or it can create difficulties in life because you will have trouble trusting people, making friends, and asking for help. You may be a loner, outcast, geek, nerd, or weirdo at school and have few friends. You may also bond with a group of outcasts and make friends with the other weirdos in the chess club or theater or with other kids who dress like punks or goths. You may develop a lifelong identity of being a loner due to early experiences of rejection or punishment.

You may also be separated from parents or siblings, and/or you may be adopted, a stepchild, or live in foster care. You may have stepparents, half-siblings, or stepsiblings. You may grow up isolated and alone and bounce around in foster care. You may feel isolated and alone as an orphan, like Oliver Twist. You may be sent to military school or private school. Your childhood may be rough due to these isolating circumstances. If there are no other afflicting Stars, then eventually you may find a good home, and this can turn out well. There are many successful adoption stories, but you may be drawn later in life to meet your birth parents, and you yourself may be drawn to be a stepparent or adopt kids to pay back this Fate. You may even find your true family among strangers.

If there is further affliction from other Ghost Stars here, you may be abused by step-, foster, or adopted parents, as abuse is statistically much higher in these situations. This Greedy Wolf can also represent a gang or group that takes you in like family early in life. You may find family on a sports team with a coach or with other outcasts in your neighborhood who take you under their wing; this is very *West Side Story*. You may become a juvenile delinquent, get in trouble with the law, and go to juvenile hall.

If you have blood siblings, then your Fate with them may be uneven, and you may experience little or no support for them. You may even experience abuse from a sibling, uncle, or older relative here. You may have an older sibling who is rebellious and defiant, which gets you in trouble. They may argue with your parents and run away, and you may be hurt and abandoned by this. You may also be punished unfairly or experience abuse in childhood. All this will cause you to mature fast, and it may create lifelong abandonment issues. You may be alienated from your siblings throughout life, but you can repair these relationships and liberate this Fate. If there are more Ghost Stars in this House, then you may need to cut ties, form strong boundaries, and end toxic relationships. You may feel like you barely survived childhood, and this may create a strong, independent, and self-reliant personality that forms the basis for the rest of your life.

Partners Palace

If Tan Lang rules the Partners Palace, then you inherit an Ancestral Ghost pattern of isolation, independence, and struggle, and you will likely struggle with relationships throughout life. This is the image of a lone wolf, and that doesn't bode well for partnering. Character matters a lot here, for some Characters are more naturally independent and content to be single, and for them this may work out fine. However, Characters who are naturally dependent will struggle more and are also more likely to find a positive adaptation or resolution here. In this House, there is always the question of whether the Greedy Wolf (or any Ghost Star) represents you or your partner, and the answer to that is yes! An Ancestral Ghost in the Partners Palace can possess both you and your partner independently and/or simultaneously.

In the first case, Tan Lang possesses you, and this creates an independent, unconventional, antisocial, and possibly selfish streak in you that makes it difficult to meet people and get into or stay in relationships. Remember, this is called the Greedy Wolf Star. It is an Ancestral Ghost who died alone or was betrayed, possibly cast out or ostracized due to their behavior, and you inherit this behavior pattern. So, self-reflection here is crucial. Something you do keeps you alone—always a bridesmaid, never a bride. You may struggle to find suitable partners due to being too picky, critical, vain, jealous, demanding, high-maintenance, or neurotic. You may always find faults in your partners, and so you find reasons to leave. You may bounce from person to person looking for the perfect match or Prince Charming, but no one is good enough or lives up to your standards. However, it is likely that you are not perfect yourself (just in case you forgot); you may find that all your neuroses and jealousy come out in relationships, and this drives people away.

This placement may also make you driven and independent to a fault. You are always busy, always working, always finding excuses to be alone. You may be married to your job. Or you may just be a loner who finds it difficult to meet people, make friends, and come out of your shell. You may be shy, nervous, or timid. Or you may be the opposite: overbearing, intimidating, or pushy. Either way, you are always alone. You may find it difficult to rely on others, open up, or be vulnerable. You may put up huge walls and barriers so that no one can ever really get to know you. This can put an expiration date on all your relationships: You get to a certain point, but when it is time to let them in, be vulnerable, and actually be in a partnership, then you drive the other person away.

You may have a deep fear of intimacy and/or commitment. You may also just be very unconventional, weird, and unique. You may find it very difficult to meet like-minded people who get you. You may have a quirky, odd, and potentially off-putting personality that makes you unrelatable or even unattractive. You may also be too attractive, to the point that you intimidate people. No one thinks that they have a chance with you, so they don't try. You may be in the top 1 percent of conventional attractiveness, and so dating "up" or "across" is almost impossible. You may have the "tall girl problem" and feel you are only able to date professional basketball players.

The last possibility here is to be a "player." You may be promiscuous and love to play the field. You simply don't want commitment and enjoy casual sex and dating. You may be into hook-up culture or be a pickup artist. You may also be into more unconventional forms of dating, drawn to polyamory, open relationships, or S and M. This may lead to sex work, or you could work in adult films or be an escort. You may be greedy and full of insatiable lust, looking to increase your body count and fulfill all the unmet carnal desires and needs of your Ancestors. This may create the constant desire for more, and no amount or sexual pleasure or partners ever satisfies.

If any of this is the case, the answer is self-reflection and then to grow up and settle. You aren't perfect, and there are no perfect matches. You may need to lower your standards or go to therapy. Or you can be content to be alone. You may be asexual and happy to be by yourself, as you are simply uninterested in sex. You may be self-sufficient, self-nurturing, and self-fulfilling. You may become a monk, nun, or celibate religious figure of some kind. But be careful that you are not deceiving yourself here, for this is the Greedy Wolf, and it often represents patterns based on unmet needs.

The last case is that Tan Lang possesses your partner or the relationship itself. You may be Fated to marry a Greedy Wolf. You may be more or less normal, but you marry someone who turns into Tan Lang. Or you may be attracted to "bad boys" or red flags or have a pattern of choosing abusive partners based on childhood issues. They may be sweet before the wedding but then turn jealous, unfaithful, mean, argumentative, and needy after you get married. They may be demanding, overbearing, and antisocial. They may drive others away from you, and your partnership could isolate you from friends or family.

Or, you may have an unusual and unconventional relationship together that actually works. You finally find another lone wolf like you, and you get to be weird together. You may meet at a convention for other weirdos like you, or you may meet on the internet through a support group for your particular quirk. As this is the image of a dog, you also may substitute a dog or pet for a partner, or have an unusually strong affinity for pets, and many people seem to do this. Dogs are a lot easier than people.

Tan Lang can be resolved, and it usually works itself out by midlife. You may simply marry late, after a long pattern of being single. You finally partner after working out all your issues. You may experience divorce and go through a difficult or nightmarish relationship. If Tan Lang shows up with other Ghost Stars here, then it is more likely that you will be hurt by partners and/or hurt others with your behavior. You may go through a kind of emotional sadomasochism and actually enjoy hurting others as payback for being hurt. You may have a lot of twisted Fate with people you hurt and have to work it all out before becoming content. You may also lose a partner prematurely to death, illness, or an accident. You may become a widow or widower and be alone for the rest of your life, unable to love again.

Offspring Palace

If Tan Lang rules the Offspring Palace, then you will no doubt struggle with being a parent, either due to your own sense of independence and selfishness or due to the discomfort of having a rebellious or antisocial child who is possessed by Tan Lang. This Ghost Star is the Ancestral pattern of isolation and struggle, and an Ancestor likely either died alone, possibly as an orphan, or was abandoned, betrayed, hurt, or unloved. This placement can represent patterns of difficulty around parental circumstances, childhood struggles, single parenting, foster care, orphanages, difficult pregnancies, miscarriages, and so on. One of your Ancestors may have been forced to raise kids alone without help, or they may have lost a child early due to illness, accidents, or war. They also may have been forced to give a child up for adoption. You have a Fated debt with a troubled Ancestor who will create difficult circumstances around being a parent.

If you are possessed by Tan Lang, then you may be a lone wolf who cherishes your independence and freedom and is averse to giving it up. Character matters a lot here as well, as more independent characters will find it harder to give up their freedom, and more domestic characters will be naturally drawn to having children. However, they may still struggle internally as parents, which could be very hard for, say, a Rabbit, whose instincts tell them to be a parent. If you are independent and love being free, then this placement may simply mean you postpone having kids until later in life, or you may be Fated to not have kids and simply embrace that.

Tan Lang here can also create a large sexual appetite, a desire for more and more sex, pleasure, or partners, and your sexuality may be rebellious or even antisocial. All this is the confusion of your Ancestors' "calling for children," which you interpret as horniness. You may also be polyamorous, promiscuous, and unable to be a steady parent. If there is further affliction here, you may commit sexual misconduct or be the victim of it.

If Tan Lang possesses your pregnancy or kids, then you may be Fated to have a troubled, rebellious, or antisocial child. You may struggle to get pregnant in the first place or have miscarriages, a difficult pregnancy, or abortions. You may be a single parent, forced to raise your child alone; this may be from the get-go, or it may happen at any point along the way. You may also struggle to keep guardianship of your kids or to support them. You may be too poor, young, or immature, and you may give up your kids for adoption or foster care. You may leave them with relatives and go off to be independent because you don't want to be a parent. Your kids may also be taken by child services, they may be abducted, or they may run away from home or be lost in public. You may also lose a child in divorce and only get to see them on weekends. They may grow up apart from you, raised by someone else. You may also be a stepparent and/or raise children with different partners. You may volunteer to be a foster parent or adopt kids yourself.

If Tan Lang possesses your child, they may be rambunctious, rebellious, and uncontrollable. They could have boundless energy and bounce off the walls. They may ignore you and their teachers, misbehave, and never do what they are told. You may struggle with teachers, babysitters, and so on, as your child always gets in trouble. They may be sent to the principal's office, expelled, or put in detention. They may be an angel child when young, but then when they hit puberty, they become deeply troubled, rebellious, or antisocial. They may run away from home, join a gang, or get in trouble with the law. You may send them to military school, private school, or religious school. They may grow apart for you as they get older and seem like a stranger. There may not be a strong Fate binding you together, and you may not feel connected to your child. Nonetheless, you can grow together and work it out.

If Tan Lang is afflicted with other Ghost Stars here, then the likelihood of the above possibilities gets stronger, potentially darker, and more full of drama. You may have to go through a lot of struggles to resolve this Fate, or you can mostly avoid it by simply not having kids. You can choose not to have children, but you may then struggle with feelings of loneliness and regret about the family you never had. Still, in the end it may save you a lot of heartache.

It could also be the case that your child is self-sustaining and just does not need parenting. They are here to do their own thing and work out their identity on their own. You just need to get out of the way and let them be. If this is the case, you're not a failure—trying too hard might make things worse.

Wealth Palace

If Tan Lang rules the Wealth Palace, then you are Fated to struggle to earn money independently, possibly through unconventional or entrepreneurial means. This placement represents an Ancestral pattern of struggling with money, resources, and work. Your Ancestors may have been poor, which is most people in history, but here they struggled alone and without support, and you are Fated to continue this pattern to resolve it. This may have been due to immigration, as many people have been forced to start over and make a new life in a new place, and often that meant that they left behind their support networks. The immigrant spirit often has a strong sense of determination and hard work, and it forces people to be resourceful, ingenuitive, and frugal. But again, it also comes with struggle. So, this is a mixed bag. The Greedy Wolf here can also represent patterns of disenfranchisement, oppression, and class struggle, which is usually a part of poverty, as we often structure society to keep people poor and unable to get out of their condition.

If there are no other afflicting Ghost Stars, then you can steadily improve yourself financially with hard work, determination, and frugality. You will likely be underpaid and overworked, and you will struggle a great deal with money. Your lifestyle or expenses could exceed your income, and you may have to be frugal, scrimping and saving. You may have to live in cheaper accommodations, have roommates, eat ramen noodles, and adapt to a low-income life. You may even thrive as a minimalist. Without affliction, this situation can improve, especially if you can find a clever, unconventional, or unusual way to make money. You may have to string together a lot of odd jobs and side jobs and turn this into a hustle. Or, you might just get by doing menial labor, but you save well and are able to make a decent life and retire.

This placement can also indicate making money by utilizing a peculiar skill or unique trait or by becoming an entrepreneur. You may be successful doing an unusual job or a job that no one else wants to do, like sanitation worker, undertaker, embalmer, or something more exciting like an undercover cop, spy, crime scene investigator, or hostage negotiator. This job could be solitary, like being a forest ranger. You may have to invent it. You may come up with a new product, idea, or technique that becomes the key to your success, like inventing the pet rock. Or you could make a new giz-widget that revolutionizes the tech or medical industry. You may invent a longer-lasting light bulb or create a new patent and become very wealthy. This can also indicate a very odd legacy or collection, and you may own a shop that sells antiques, trinkets, or unique handmade goods.

Or Tan Lang here could mean starting your own business. It could be a struggle at first, and you may start with few resources, connections, or clients. But, with persistence, your work can pay off, and you may own a successful self-made business. It could be even wildly successful, and you could be a famous fashion designer or social media influencer. Or this could simply mean owning a string of successful dry-cleaning businesses. The key here is to find a need, gap, or newly emerging demand and fill it; our society is changing all the time, and we must invent new jobs to meet new needs and demands.

If there are more Ghost Stars in this House, then this turns into a darker struggle, and you could have a lot of bad patterns around money. You may be selfish, greedy (as the name Greedy Wolf implies), immature, and impractical. You may overspend, gamble, or take big financial risks. This could lead to debt, addictions, or high costs, fees, or bills that you cannot pay. You may live paycheck to paycheck, blowing your money on partying or expensive handbags and shoes. Or, you could work really hard but get paid very little and struggle with poverty your whole life.

If further afflicted here, you may also just be alone and have very little family support. Your family may be poor and unable to help you. You may also alienate people who try to help you or squander other people's money and resources. You may be a spoiled rich kid who drains the family fortune. You could inherit money or be given everything only to be irresponsible with it and then get cut off. You could be a mooch, con artist, lowlife, or even a criminal whose antisocial behavior makes money a source of disaster and drama. Your greed could be immense and a source of great suffering to yourself and others; you could be ruthless and do anything to get rich, including hurting and taking advantage of others. You may be unable to work with others due to your Character, and this could keep you from connecting with others.

The Greedy Wolf is resolved through generosity and letting go of selfishness, greed, and independence. Learn to connect and work with others. Learn to ask for and receive help. This may take renunciation. You may have to learn to live minimally, with very few possessions. Give things away; give to charity; give for no reason, even if you have very little. The more content you can be, the more you want what you have, the less you will struggle.

Health Palace

If Tan Lang rules the Health Palace, then your health and well-being will be directly tied to an Ancestral Ghost who had to struggle very hard to survive and who likely died sick, alone, and alienated due to their self-centeredness, greed, or dishonesty. They likely fought very hard to survive at all costs, and on your health journey so will you. As an influence on health, this Star is of very mixed auspice, for you will likely have a robust survival instinct, but Fate here is uneven, and you may have to fight for your life to resolve this Ghost. Tan Lang here often creates the image of a "shaman," someone who is brought close to death or put through grievous illness in order to recover and gain insight or power. Disease and death may put you on a spiritual path, and a heroic intervention or cathartic recovery and resolution of this Ghost may create healing abilities, visions, or awakenings.

Tan Lang's strength here is not conventional; you will likely have a weak constitution and possibly be a sickly child and adult, but you will have a strong will to survive and overcome obstacles and can, therefore, have a long life. But you must follow your own path to achieve this. You inherit this will to live from an obstinate Ancestor, and as usual, it can be powerful to do genealogy here to find out who this is. Their story of survival may be resolved through you.

Here, your health is tied to an Ancestor's negative emotions, which become yours. You may have a powerful and unique personality or negative emotions—anger, frustration, fear, compulsion, anxiousness, or defensiveness—and these emotions compromise your immunity and make you susceptible to illness and burnout. Your feelings may alienate you by making you lash out at others. You may be a loner, or life circumstances may force you to be alone and without help or resources, and this either makes you ill or causes your illness to spiral out of control. Isolation can create loneliness in the soul, and your health can deteriorate due to a lack of community, so you may have to fight and struggle to survive without help. This struggle can cause premature aging or even death if it gets too intense.

The more your emotions rule your life, the worse your health will get. You may suffer from many chronic conditions, but you will be hard to diagnose, for there will not be a rational explanation for your symptoms. You may become a hypochondriac as a result, as you may live your whole life with minor chronic illnesses that come and go and change all the time. It will also be quite challenging to be consistent with a health routine when negative emotions get the better of you, and paranoia about your health will make things worse. Therefore, you will have a strange medical history and may not respond to conventional treatment. Conventional medicine may even make your symptoms worse, and you could be the victim of iatrogenic disease. Therapy, self-reflection, character growth, and all that are important to keep all this in check and ultimately resolve this Ghost. It is also essential to let go of self-centeredness, greed, and ego and to ask for help, seek friendship and community, and not struggle alone. You may feel like an outcast and like no one understands you, but don't be a lone wolf; it's terrible for your health.

You will, therefore, require and develop an unconventional and very personal approach to health. This could include unusual food, exercise, or meditation practices that you invent or are given by a teacher or in a dream. You may be put onto a healing journey or spiritual path by an illness or injury that conventional medicine cannot understand, and so it forces you to adapt and find a new path. You may need to seek out alternative or traditional medicine and healers and try many unconventional means to heal. These kinds of alternative treatments and modalities will work better than conventional medicine, allowing for different ways of thinking and knowing.

You may become an alternative healer or shaman after your health journey, which may require that you come close to death through a severe illness, near-death experience, or accident or after a vision quest. If you go out into the wilderness alone, you could return as a healer after meeting your Ancestors. You may also have a relationship with a shaman or spirit who heals you through strange or even violent means; you may be poisoned or take drugs. This healing could involve doing rituals with psychedelics or a sweat lodge or a long ritual dance. You may see spirits and Ghosts and communicate with the dead or other worlds. Your life will be offered as a sacrifice, but you can recover if you give up everything. This creates a debt you must repay by helping and healing others. But this kind of thing is rare, and this process may look more ordinary for you, so think outside the box here.

The more Ghost Stars show up with Tan Lang, the more uncomfortable these minor illnesses get, the worse the negative emotions, isolation, and alienation get, and the more likely this all turns out badly. You may suffer from things like food or skin allergies and sensitivities and inappropriate medical treatments. The more affliction, the more you may lash out and alienate yourself and others, and the more dramatic and cathartic your health experiences can get. The more dramatic things get, the more at risk you are for serious illness, injury, and death. You may also be at risk of being killed, murdered, or dying from medical treatment. You may have scars, missing limbs, disabilities, handicaps, or permanent disorders. You may suffer from infections or sexually transmitted diseases. You may exhaust and burn yourself out in your struggle to survive. But if Tan Lang is resolved, you can be long-lived, though you may carry scars for life.

Career/Travel Palace

If Tan Lang rules the Career/Travel Palace, then you will be possessed by an Ancestral Ghost or a group of Ancestors who struggled very hard to make it in life but died unsuccessful and without fulfillment. This can be the Ancestral pattern of exile, migration, immigration, and struggle in a new land without help or resources. Again, many hundreds of millions of people were uprooted in the past few hundred years due to war, ethnic struggles, persecution, slavery, genocide, and so on. Despite being awful, these are common experiences and nothing special. Many people also immigrated and started over in new lands seeking opportunity and had to work hard to make it without much help.

Some of your Ancestors likely left behind centuries of tradition and got on a boat. Tan Lang here represents that experience, but it is not finished, so you inherit their core struggle in life. While this could go back a few generations, their dream is a continuity that may still be unfulfilled. It may also come to you through a more recent and specific expression of Tan Lang—a Greedy Wolf–like parent or grandparent whom you take after and who pressures you.

Tan Lang here creates a unique and personal struggle to find what you want to do in life and where you want to go. It creates a drive to strike out on your own and find your way due to some pressure, which could be internal or external. "Ordinary" work or life will seem unfulfilling and boring. The more you are stuck at a desk or a nine-to-five job, the more unhappy and resentful you will be. The Ghost of Tan Lang will bite at your heels and tell you to escape and strike out on your own. If there is no further affliction, you can follow your quirkiness and find a unique path in life that suits your odd personality, but it may be hard-won and require a lot of cleverness and ingenuity.

You will likely struggle to succeed at work, and if you lack perseverance, you will fail. You may be driven internally to escape your awful, boring hometown, and you may run away from home early, travel widely, move to a new city, state, or country; you may live life as an outsider, foreigner, expatriate, hermit, or outcast. External pressures like family strife, war, ethnic struggles, persecution, and so on could force you to escape and strike out on your own. Whatever the case, all this will be burdened by a sense of survival at all costs. That fight for survival may be very real, or it may be self-imposed.

If the pressure to succeed is internal or self-imposed, it is due to your own ego, selfishness, and unruly character, which is independent and peculiar. You likely inherited a quirky, strange, or unique personality, set of interests, and eventually life skills from an Ancestor's unresolved struggle or belligerence. You may be a lone wolf, outcast, or strange individual, making it difficult to fit in and figure out what to do with your life. Nothing may feel or seem right. Nothing fits the puzzle that is you. You may have very narrow or specific interests or passions, but no set path appears to you or makes sense. So, you may feel lost, discouraged, unsure, and even suffocated by what is typical, conventional, or expected. You may then struggle to find your way and bounce around, rejecting everything, becoming a jack-of-all-trades and master of none.

You may do odd side jobs and piece together your life. You may also be aggressive, passionate, ambitious, and driven to do anything to succeed, but in the process, you hurt others, alienate yourself, and make a mess of things. You may be driven to succeed where your father failed, only to repeat the same mistakes. If you can manage this, then you may become a success due to your unique personality or skills. You may become an entrepreneur and create your own path or succeed at an unusual, wolf-like job. You may make or invent a job or do something that is all about you and your personality: artist, actor, tattoo artist, travel writer, shaman, or one of the many new digital-nomad jobs on the internet. You could work in new, trendy, or peculiar fields, but they could also burst and leave you unemployed.

If the pressure to succeed is external and due to living in harsh conditions or under social pressure, then you will likely be driven to "escape" and travel widely, move to a new place, and become a foreigner, expat, or outsider. Without further affliction by Ghost Stars here, you may find happiness in a new place, but you will probably always feel like a foreigner. You may be an expat who hangs out in expat bars, never learns the local language, and never truly assimilates. You hold on to your nostalgia but never go home. You may become a nomad, vagabond, or wanderer and change jobs or move every few months or years. The road will be your home. This Ghost will be resolved when you settle down and are done wandering. They say not all who wander are lost, but here you're lost until you stop.

The more other Ghost Stars here, the more endless the sense of struggle. Stability feels suffocating, and the darker sides of the Greedy Wolf come out. Further afflicted, the less likely you are to succeed, and the more likely this placement will manifest as dark, Greedy Wolf jobs. You may be drawn to crime and live on the run or get arrested and become an inmate. You may be a homeless vagabond. You may become injured or die in a war. If you are forced to immigrate or are exiled due to war or strife, the more your life will be in danger, and the harder life will be in the new land. You may be an illegal immigrant, sex worker, migrant laborer, or slave. These Ghosts are unfortunately resolved through wandering and going through all kinds of struggles; they must get burned out. Alternatively, you can commit to letting go of selfishness, dedicate your life to serving others, and resolve all this from the get-go, which is easier said than done.

Assistants Palace

If Tan Lang rules the Assistants Palace, then you will likely struggle with friendship and with your career; however, you may be in a unique place to resolve this Ghost through service to others. Tan Lang represents the Ancestral pattern of alienation and isolation due to selfishness and greed, which does not bode well for friendship. But as the House of Service, the Assistants Palace provides the chance to turn this around and apply your aggression to helping others. The Greedy Wolf here can represent the people, or the conditions in which, you serve. If you don't, this placement will likely turn out poorly and cause a struggle with friends, coworkers, classmates, and career.

The negative side of this placement is that Tan Lang possesses you when you are around others, which can create a harsh, moody, or unpredictable character that undermines you. You may act aggressive, antisocial, belligerent, critical, rude, offensive, or simply like an asshole. You may unintentionally turn others against you and alienate yourself. At best, you are awkward, unusual, weird, different, quirky, shy, and so on. This may make it difficult to find and make friends, and it may undermine your career. People may not like you, may turn against you, and might not want to help or work with you. How you are causing this may be not easy to see, because you may justify your behavior or think you are just being genuine or honest. But rethink that, and take feedback. You may just be an asshole.

You may also suffer from deep resentment or jealousy that obstructs your progress in your career or school, causing self-destructive or limiting patterns. Or, you may be Fated to have a relationship with an unpredictable boss, teacher, or agent who undermines you and your career. Tan Lang may possess other people around you and cause scandal. You may be seduced, blackmailed, or ruined by an assistant or subordinate who is out to get you due to their own greed. If there is further affliction from Ghost Stars, you will more likely encounter scandal and struggle with friends or at work. Further affliction can also mean gang and criminal activity, so watch out.

The way to resolve Tan Lang is to use your aggression or passion to become a champion or warrior for others. This is the recipe for a soldier. You can literally be a soldier and join the military, which is excellent in this case, because you won't have to interact with the people you are protecting and serving, and you can also be with other aggressive people. You could also be a police officer, FBI or CIA agent or spy, bodyguard, prison warden, union organizer, bouncer, firefighter, undertaker, or the like. Or you could be a career fighter, boxer, or martial artist—some way to get the aggression out in service to others, even as entertainment. You can also take your antisocial bent to the bank and make it work. You could be a successful artist, musician, or writer and make a living off your angst and rebellion. The image of Tan Lang as the shaman or alternative healer also works very well here, and you can use your experience of illness or pain to help and heal others.

Other wolf-like careers are anything where you get to direct your anger productively to fight for others. You could be a social worker, lawyer, parole officer, or counselor and work with people who are at-risk, underprivileged, or disadvantaged. You could be a teacher or mentor or work in special education and help young people in need, advocating for them. You could be an activist, social justice warrior, campaigner, promoter, or reformer; you could work in politics and fight to change things for the better.

But be careful not to be possessed by bad ideas here. Many people become activists because they are angry, and various causes get taken up just because people want to fight for something, even if those causes are wrong. Many people want to be freedom fighters and part of the resistance. People want to wear a Che Guevara T-shirt and fight the man, champion the underdog, and stand up for the oppressed. This is all good, but double-check if your cause is worthy or if you're just angry. You may try to start a revolution and fail, or you may end up supporting a bad cause and become the villain, turning into the very thing you oppose.

Superiors Palace

If Tan Lang rules the Superiors Palace, then you are in an advantaged place to make the best of this Ancestral Ghost and resolve it, as this is one of the best placements for the Greedy Wolf. Here, the lone wolf's independent and radical unconventional nature can succeed either through the influence of an unconventional teacher or mentor or through utilizing your own ego to your advantage. If there is no further affliction, you inherit this Ancestral pattern of striking out in search of opportunity, here with the potential for great reward. However, there is a danger of reinforcing the core pattern of greed or selfishness. The Greedy Wolf may want it all here: money, power, fame, status, and so on. You may dream big, and this can be a complete delusion.

You will likely have an unconventional, independent, and unique personality, skill, or attributes, and Tan Lang here is all about embracing and utilizing your ego. You are "one of a kind," and you should embrace this and cultivate your unique skills early, whether artistic, musical, academic, or physical. Without further affliction, you can potentially make a living and gain recognition from these qualities. It may take drive and determination, but this is an Ancestral Ghost hungry to make a name for itself. You may be hardcore and determined to succeed as an artist or athlete (or whatever talent you have), and you will do whatever it takes to make it.

This ego is a mixed bag, for it is the key to your success but also a trap. You may be full of yourself, and you may end up being arrogant, cocky, or pushy. You may act entitled, thinking the world owes you or that you are God's gift to the world. So, use the ego, but keep it in check. You also may not be particularly talented, and your desire to be a rock star or famous actor may be a complete fantasy that you must let go of.

Even if you are not particularly talented, you may be still driven strongly to succeed, and your wolf-like, aggressive personality makes it happen. You revolt against the odds, and you become obsessive or monomaniacal in your goals. This can lead to great innovation, success, and invention. You may become a CEO, manager, boss, or business owner. Tan Lang here thrives in unique and self-made occupations, so you may be an entrepreneur or inventor, start your own business, or be self-employed. Again, this may involve a unique talent, invention, or skill, or it may be because you cannot work for others due to your independent and disagreeable character. You may have a vision early in life that you want to do your own thing, so you make it happen. Like in the Career/Travel Palace, the Greedy Wolf here will make "ordinary" work seem unfulfilling and boring. The more you are stuck at a desk or a nine-to-five job, the more unhappy and resentful you will be. The Ghost of Tan Lang will bite at your heels and tell you to escape and strike out on your own.

Here, Tan Lang wants things bigger and better, and it wants more power. Your rise to success in pursuit of fame, power, wealth, or status may be full of drama, ups and downs, and obstruction. But the Greedy Wolf is determined. Your success story will be unconventional and unexpected, but it will be yours. You can say, "I did it my way," despite what everyone else said. If you do make it, then Tan Lang can be resolved—but only if you can taste a sense of satisfaction and completion that you did it. If not, you will likely never be satisfied, like in the Rolling Stones song; you will always want more money, power, prestige—more everything. If you are not careful, this can become an obstruction and lead to your downfall.

If other Ghost Stars appear with Tan Lang here, you will likely encounter more obstacles to success and/or be filled with many more negative emotions—anger, fear, struggle, and rebellion. You may end up a loser, burnout, or washed-up hack at midlife. You may be forty-five and still think that your band can make it big. Affliction here can cause you to undermine yourself with jealousy, revenge, or immaturity. You may also become more ruthless, violent, or abusive to others on your path to success. Or you may simply work hard and never reach the top, or never even get off the ground. Your radical, rebellious ideas may fizzle out. You may become a sellout or remain utterly average, despite your dreams of glory. In many ways, the Greedy Wolf is the Ghost of failure, and you may be haunted by a parent or grandparent who failed and put that failure on you. You may feel like you let them down or that you were never good enough and did not have what it takes, and that they were right about you all along.

Without further affliction, Tan Lang here can also take the form of an unconventional or radical teacher, parent, or mentor who drives you to succeed. They may be a family member who recognizes your talent early and pushes you, or they could be a coach or agent. Perhaps your father recognizes that you have a talent, so he trains you and forces you to practice after school, and while you may hate or resent him for it, you grow up successful because he pushed you. Many famous people seem to have this kind of story. Tan Lang may also be a radical boss or mentor at work whom you follow, learn from, and take after. You may take their place or do your own unique thing modeled after their example.

You may also encounter a radical teacher or healer with whom you end up apprenticing at some point. This may be a spiritual teacher, shaman, or guru with whom you have a Fated debt. They may teach you in an unconventional way, pushing you to the brink of sanity, challenging your ego, or even poisoning you with drugs so that you break down. They may then try to mold you and guide you to enlightenment. This is the teacher–student model of Chan and Zen Buddhism and the guru–disciple relationship of Tantra and the Mahasiddha traditions in India and Tibet. Shamanic traditions also tend to follow this model, and here you may become an enigmatic teacher or healer yourself. Chögyam Trungpa called this "crazy wisdom." If other Ghost Stars are present, then this teacher–student or parental relationship may be abusive and traumatic. It may also turn out that you are unteachable, and this may end in failure, with you resenting the teacher and being hurt and traumatized by the relationship.

Property Palace

If Tan Lang rules the Property Palace, you will be possessed by a restless Ancestral Ghost who will make it difficult to ever feel at home or settled or to own property. You will likely be nomadic, and your sense of home will be unsettled throughout life until this Ghost is resolved. Again, this is often related to Ancestral patterns or immigration, migration, exile, persecution, war, and so on; it is the desire to escape a place either to survive immediate danger or to escape famine, disease, poverty, religious persecution, or ethnic strife.

More immediately, the Ghost of an Ancestor became a lone wolf and struggled alone and without much help or support, possibly due to their own fault. You inherit this struggle here, which may be a long Ancestral pattern or more recent. Tan Lang here can also be a pattern of greed, and you may inherit the desire to acquire more and more property for selfish reasons, but it is unlikely that you will succeed, and it is still likely that you will not "settle down" until much later in life.

If Tan Lang represents a more recent pattern, your family may come from torn and dire conditions. You may be a refugee or a recent immigrant, or you may in some way reject or conflict with your birthplace, heritage, culture, language, religion, or inheritance. This could be due to strife or simply that you find it boring or suffocating. There may be unsafe, unsettled, or simply mobile circumstances at home. You or your family may be forced to leave home and start over, and you may have to live in a trailer, hotel, tent, or car or be homeless at some point as you transition and try to start over. You or your family may lose property at some point due to the above conflicts, or you may lose property due to poverty, job loss, eviction, or a hostile lawsuit. This pattern may afflict your childhood and be difficult to escape, or it may befall you later in life during a period of hardship. If it does, then it is likely due to an ongoing pattern of negative behavior on your part. It may also be due to being attacked or persecuted by others as part of Ancestral debt.

You may be cursed with a restless, nomadic spirit that never feels safe or at home anywhere. You always want to be on the move. You may again reject your family, culture, or hometown and want to escape. You may grow up in the boondocks, a trailer park, or in the middle of nowhere and want to escape to the big city. Or you may grow up in a crowded urban environment or slum and want to escape that and move to the countryside. Your living situation may have been abusive, traumatic, or isolating. You may have been poor, neglected, or hungry. Whatever the case, you want to escape and don't feel safe or settled, which becomes a pattern throughout life. You may bounce from place to place, town to town, always renting or mooching, and every few years, you get the itch to leave. You are a wanderer, nomad, vagabond, or prodigal child. You may have grown up in a good environment, but you inherit the Ghosts of Ancestors who are restless, so feeling unsafe or wanting to escape may feel inexplicable. Genealogy is essential here to discover what pattern you may be playing out.

It may be the rejection and abandonment of home that sets you free. You may need to escape a bad environment and cut ties to thrive and heal. The more Ghost Stars appear here, the more likely this situation is haunted, abusive, or traumatic, and the more restless or dire the need is to escape. The Greedy Wolf will do anything to survive, and here it can be very adaptable, resourceful, and clever. You may become a survivalist and learn to hunt, build a fire from scratch, and make your own shelter. You may plan for the apocalypse and build bomb shelters, hoard supplies, and amass weapons and ammo for the coming darkness. This may be completely unfounded, but it will feel necessary. If this is you, watch out for paranoia, conspiracy theories, and catastrophizing; there's no secret cabal out there ruling the world or engineering its end. Also, watch out for isolation and alienation. Tan Lang is a lone wolf, so you may struggle to find your home, people, tribe, or place. You may both enjoy and hate solitude, as it is both natural and an escape strategy or coping mechanism.

Resolution of Tan Lang's influence is possible when you settle and put down roots and the need to escape or survive no longer haunts you. Resolution can also come when you return home after the exile, like the prodigal son, and finally confront your past as a new person. You may die far from where you were born, successfully reinvent yourself once or many times, or even go to prison and be reformed to then help others escape dire circumstances. If this Ghost gets resolved, you can own property, but this may not happen until later in life. If you try earlier, it may be very difficult and unsuccessful. You may struggle to acquire wealth or even lose property due to financial issues or "acts of god," floods, fires, earthquakes, theft, and so on. Gain and loss will likely alternate, and your relationship with owning property will be uneven and erratic. You also may thrive as a minimalist and do well with nothing but what you can carry on your back.

Pleasure Palace

If Tan Lang rules the Pleasure Palace, then your sense of enjoyment and pleasure in life will be haunted by an Ancestor who struggled a lot and was likely unhappy. Tan Lang here can make you a bit of an Ebenezer Scrooge—a misanthrope or miser. You may be all work and no play, or the Greedy Wolf may torment you with an uncontrollable and problematic sense of pleasure. This Star is the Ancestral pattern of isolation, struggle, alienation, and being alone and without help, but here you are enjoying it.

This Ghost probably did not have much fun in life, so you may be born with a serious, stern, or intense disposition that has no explanation in this lifetime. You may be a serious child who rejects childlike games and silly fun. You may be a very serious person until later in life when you become like a child. People find you intense, but you like this. You may be austere and critical of frivolous things, which works well if you become a monk, nun, or priest. You may actually enjoy austerity, discipline, and struggle.

Tan Lang here enjoys the struggle and enjoys being uncomfortable, and this can be a difficult pattern to get out of. It can also turn into sadomasochism. If you want to stop suffering, you have to stop enjoying it, which is a lesson many people need to learn. Or, you can embrace it and get into bondage. You may be austere, controlled, disciplined, and serious at work, and then all bets are off at night or on the weekend. You may be a dentist or lawyer in the day and retire to your pleasure dungeon full of whips and chains at night.

It can be powerful to do genealogy here, as this pattern may relate to a specific Ancestor who either died having too much fun or never had fun. This may give insight into your own pattern, which might be very specific, like you hate Christmas and must confront the "Ghost of Christmas Past."

Tan Lang can also represent bottomless greed and desire that comes from unmet needs, which can be insatiable here. Your Ancestors may have been poor or toiled in labor their whole lives, never having any luxuries, and now you have uncontrollable and insatiable desires and addictive tendencies that can never be satisfied. The more Ghost Stars here, the more likely this will turn to addiction and self-destructive behaviors.

In general, you will likely have and form a unique and strong sense of personal enjoyment and pleasure that is different, odd, uncommon, quirky, or weird. Ordinary or popular pleasure may bewilder you. You may reject the entertainment of the "unwashed masses" and become a snob. If there are no other afflicting Stars here, this may work out just fine. You should embrace your own weirdness in your own way. These may become particular hobbies and interests you are drawn to and may even become obsessed with. They are likely individual and deeply personal. This is all about authenticity. You may reject collective enjoyment or team sports. You would rather do things alone and enjoy solitary pursuits. Independence may be your greatest pleasure, and others will likely not understand you. You may never fit in, but you may also find community among other lone wolves. This sense of solitude could turn to alienation, but this may also become a kind of path.

The Greedy Wolf is resolved when you relax and become a kid again or when you learn to stop enjoying the pain. Tan Lang can also be very lonely and isolated here; you may eternally feel alone, like no one gets you. In that case, this is resolved when you learn to enjoy being with others and you rejoin the wolf pack. So, go to parties and clubs and play on the team occasionally. The more affliction here, the more challenging it will be for you to accept and enjoy pleasure. You may have a lot of fear, anxiety, guilt, or shame around pleasure.

When you release this Ghost, you will lighten up and be less serious. Life will be more fun and less of a struggle. You may have to learn to let go and have fun, or if you have insatiable needs and desires, you must learn to feel satisfied and say no. Resolving Tan Lang here can be cathartic and lead to big releases of pent-up or frustrated emotions. You may also need to learn to stop gnawing at wounds that are long closed. Again, the key to stop suffering is to stop enjoying it.

PO JUN (破軍)—THE REBEL OR BREAKING RANK STAR

NAME AND TRANSLATIONS:
Po Jun (破軍), the Rebel Star, the Breaking Rank Star

Po, 破—to break, strike against mightily, smite; lay into, lay on. a) crush, smash, mammock; overthrow utterly; destroy, demolish, ruin; lay waste; ravage. b) assail; bring down, confute, disprove (a proposition or interpretation). 2 squander, waste; expand recklessly. 3 (med.) concluding section of musical performance, finale.[11]

Jun, 軍—army, the collective name for the largest military unit, usu. prefixed with identifying designation. a) army-group, traditionally numbering 12,500 men; because the Son of Heaven in Zhou times supposedly had a sixfold army, while feudal lords were allowed only a threefold army, the phrase 六軍 liujun, "6 armies," was commonly used later to ref. the emperor's army, not meaning 6 different armies. b) troops, soldiers. 2 encamp(ment); bivouac. 3 (med.) in Tang times, frontier garrison.[12]

The word Po (破) means "to break," and Jun (軍) refers to the military, explicitly to one's rank, group, platoon, or garrison. It is the image of a military officer who rebels against the chain of command and "breaks rank," so we call this the Rebel or Breaking Rank Star.

ELEMENT: Yin Water

TRADITIONAL IMAGE: A low-ranking military officer, standing proud and defiant or obstinate, holding a blade or staff[13]

GHOST PROFILE: An Ancestral Ghost who died on the battlefield, who was lost or killed in action and did not receive proper burial; represents all the war dead in our family, as well as those who died accidentally or due to their own actions; an Ancestor who rebelled and struggled unsuccessfully and hurt or harmed others

RESOLUTION/EXORCISM: Resolved through self-sacrifice, self-reflection, accountability, responsibility, and discipline when we stop rebelling, follow the wisdom and advice of others, apologize, and get out of self-destructive loops; resolved through clarity, maturity, and seeing through delusions and illusions

LUMINOUS PLACEMENT: Horse and Dog Palaces

DIMINISHED PLACEMENT: Tiger, Rabbit, Monkey, and Rooster Palaces

AFFILIATIONS: Southern Array—affiliated with the General, Emperor, or Vassal but in defiance of the Chain of Command

We now move on to the last of the Four Major Ghosts (which are the most afflicting Stars of Polestar Astrology): Po Jun, the Rebel or Breaking Rank Star. As an afflicting Star, Po Jun is considered second only to Qi Sha, the Seven Killings Star. Lian Zhen and Tan Lang can also be afflictions, but they tend to have a more positive path to resolution in the form of other Stars or creative adaptations. But like Qi Sha, Po Jun is a trickster and challenging to resolve, for it represents a blind spot, difficult-to-learn lesson that perpetuates a pattern until we finally break free.

The tricky part about the Rebel Star is that it is a *pattern of* breaking patterns; it is all about defiance. It is where we think we are doing something that is good for ourselves or others, but we are totally delusional. The Rebel is not evil, hateful, or vengeful like Qi Sha, however, and it does not turn Demonic. It's just stupid. The Rebel is naive and foolish. It has good intentions, but as they say, the road to hell is paved with good intentions. Po Jun tends to be a more subtle self-undermining pattern that can be frustrating and ongoing. It is also eclipsed and lessened in severity by stronger Stars, but it also afflicts them with loss and reversals of power.

Po Jun, the Rebel or Breaking Rank Star, represents Ancestral patterns of defiance, revolt, and revolution; it represents patterns of self-inflicted negativity born from delusions, tantrums, misunderstandings, and confusions. It is the image of a military officer who is ordered to charge into battle with his platoon to distract the enemy, knowing he and his troops will likely die in the process. He realizes he is being sacrificed as "cannon fodder," so he "breaks rank," the meaning of the characters Po Jun (破軍), defying the general's orders in order to save himself and his platoon. To do this, he kills his commanding officer, and his troops escape. His rebellion disrupts the general's larger plan, and thousands get killed as a result. The officer's platoon was supposed to sacrifice themselves so that thousands of others could escape.

As an Ancestral energy, this Star represents an Ancestor who died doing something they thought was good, right, righteous, or moral, and perhaps it was from their point of view; however, they were wrong or at least failed to understand the greater context and consequences of their actions. They were delusional and pigheaded; what they thought was the right thing was an illusion or misunderstanding of reality. This may be because doing the right thing required sacrifice, like in the traditional example, and they were too afraid to step up and do it. In that case, this can represent Ancestral patterns of fear and cowardice in the face of difficulty or danger; it can represent an Ancestor who did what they had to do to save their skin. It can also represent ongoing negative behavior patterns of self-preservation or pride, including lying, cheating, stealing, deception, brashness, improper rebellion, defiance, or improvisation. It can also include idealism or moralizing used to rationalize bad behavior, whether religious or secular. It represents an Ancestor who was too proud to admit their mistakes or too stupid to see their delusions, and so you inherit this pattern in whatever House the Ghost rules.

Po Jun can also be more benign, as it may also represent those who died suddenly and unexpectedly while in the middle of doing something positive but with a conflicted mind. As this is a military image, it can often represent war dead; you may have an Ancestor who died while protecting others in battle but was full of guilt about the other soldiers, family, wife, or child they left behind and could not protect. They may have died far from home and are now trying to find their way home through you. Or, they may have been an ordinary civilian who died in a car crash on the way to the store after getting into an argument at home, and in that moment their mind was stuck on how they were right. Or, they may have died trying to save themselves from a burning building feeling full of guilt about leaving their mother behind to die due to their own panic and terror. Now, you are reliving their death experience in a loop. They may have also died as a negative consequence of their actions, from the vengeance of others, or because of a series of mistakes and miscalculations. These kinds of deaths can all create Po Jun. As usual with Ghost Stars, it is essential to do genealogy and find out what pattern you inherited here. Do you have any Ancestors who died in an act of rebellion, heroism, or stupidity?

In general, the Rebel represents patterns of behavior in which we think we are doing something good or heroic for ourselves or others but then accidentally incur negative or even disastrous consequences. We may do this kind of thing over and over until we learn the lesson. In this sense, it is like Qi Sha: We say, "I can't believe I did that again!" or, "I can't believe this is happening to me again . . . why me!?" We do not see that we are causing these things with our actions, choices, stupidity, or small-mindedness. We are blind to our faults or do not want to take responsibility for our actions. We defy, rebel, and remain stuck in the same childish patterns. The Rebel can represent irrational fears and catastrophizing that have no basis in this lifetime, for they come from the death of an Ancestor.

If Po Jun rules a House or is combined with other Ghost Stars, it becomes a powerful Ghost, and we are charged with resolving this troubled Ancestor. Whatever House it rules becomes a dark, frustrating, or destructive loop where we constantly make the same mistakes over and over, sometimes with disastrous consequences, or constantly but unknowingly find ourselves in the same negative situation. We may curse Fate, blame others, blame God, blame the devil, and do anything but look in the mirror and take responsibility. We think we are doing good; we believe we are in the right; we think we are doing this to survive or because we are helping others. But we are only making things worse.

Po Jun is liberated when we fall in line and stop whatever pattern it represents. It is resolved when we take responsibility for our actions, apologize, and stop blaming others. We must self-reflect, look in the mirror, and be able to recognize whatever pattern we are playing out in a loop, repeatedly, expecting different results—a common definition of insanity. When we finally break the loop, we are free of Po Jun. This could involve self-sacrifice or finally doing what everyone tells you to but you've been resisting. Maybe your parents and friends have told you about the thing for years, but you're always defiant. Perhaps you need to face your fear and do that thing. Grow up. Stop rebelling. Hold yourself accountable. Apologize. Learn the lesson. Eat humble pie. Eat bitter, or Chi Ku (吃苦), as the Chinese say. You may also need to go through an accident, illness, loss, sudden reversal, or trauma in which you relive Po Jun's death and finally complete their death experience. This act may release them, which could be painful but cathartic. There is a traditional idea that if you do not resolve Po Jun before death, it will consume you in the moment of death and create a negative rebirth. So you better work this out!

Let's walk the Rebel through the Twelve Houses.

Ming Palace

If Po Jun rules the Ming Palace, then you are possessed by a rebellious and defiant Ancestral Ghost whose incomplete death haunts you; your life and Fate will be uneven and characterized by escape, rejection, defiance, and rebellion. If you resolve this Ghost, you can experience great renewal, catharsis, and reinvention. Here, the central theme of your life will revolve around that unlearned lesson or incomplete death, so as always, it is important to do genealogy when a Ghost rules a House. Here, an Ancestor's rebellion failed, and they died with "unfinished business." You are here to finish it and to learn the lesson, so it can be powerful to find out what Ancestor you are burdened with. You are looking for stories of rebellion, defiance, righteousness, and so on.

Po Jun may also be linked with an Ancestor who died on the battlefield or who died suddenly or unexpectedly in an accident. In some way, you will have to atone for their unfinished business. You will be driven by this Ancestral pattern, and it can manifest in many ways, but the core pattern is this: You feel righteous and think you are doing good—you think you are justified—but you are delusional or mistaken.

You must first look in the mirror. You will likely find a rebellious, immodest, immature, or antisocial streak accompanied by a great deal of irrational angst. You may have deep feelings of conviction or a set of beliefs and stories about your life that have no rational basis. This can be subtle, and you may simply have a lot of charged, negative emotions that run your life and create negative behavior patterns that hold you back; they may affect your relationships and/or define your personal narrative as a story of suffering or victimhood in which you think you are the hero and in the right. Your nihilism or pessimism—your negative assessment of the world or yourself—may eat you up inside, creating anxiety and angst. You may be a Rebel without a cause.

You may also have a very strong sense of idealism, justice, moral righteousness, victimhood, or delusional fantasy. These feelings may revolve around escape, revolt, battle, danger, or subversion. You may feel strongly about social justice or a personal or universal cause and want to change the world. You may hate authority or some kind of out-group or "other." You may fancy yourself Robin Hood, wanting to steal from the rich and give to the poor. These kinds of patterns can be very convincing and powerful. We can form very strong narratives about how we or others have been wronged or about how we are victims. And we can rebel, fight, and struggle in the name of that righteous victimhood. Sometimes it is justified, but sometimes it is a self-created delusion. If the Rebel shows up with the Emperor or another strong Star, then sometimes this is a righteous fight, justified and necessary to resolve Fate, but if the Rebel is alone, then it is likely a fantasy that hardens Fate instead. So, be sure to double-check.

Po Jun will keep you in a loop, repeating the same negative pattern of breaking away, rebelling, escaping, or fighting in life, and as a result, your Fate will be very uneven; you will probably experience many ups and downs. You will think you are doing good, but then you will harm yourself or others. You may have great purpose, enthusiasm, and conviction, and you may experience life as a battle, revolution, or revolt.

If the Rebel shows up with positive Stars, then you may be creative, intelligent, inventive, and even a trendsetter. There are many ways that a Rebel can succeed. Again, with strong Stars, the revolution may be just, and you may meet other rebels and actually take part in history fighting for a just cause. But if Po Jun is alone or shows up with other Ghosts, then you will likely experience catastrophe, betrayal, disaster, and failure due to your own actions.

And you will likely have no clue why everything has gone wrong, which is why the pattern keeps repeating. You may be stuck in a loop of negativity, repeating the same pattern in life, addicted to rebellion and unable to break out of it. There is a central lesson of Fate that you must recognize and learn to resolve and liberate Po Jun. At the base, this will involve healing the core negative emotions that lead to angst, defiance, rebellion, and so on, and then you must get out of the loop and stop repeating it. This may involve letting go of whatever story you are holding on to that keeps driving you, or it may mean hitting rock bottom and going through a dramatic disaster or failure to finally let go. It may also involve an accident, illness, or dramatic reversal in life in which you resolve Po Jun. This experience may be cathartic; afterward, you may be renewed, rehabilitated, and reinvented.

Ancestors Palace

If Po Jun rules the Ancestors Palace, then you are possessed by an Ancestral Ghost who has been isolated, orphaned, or rejected by their own family for many generations. They likely died a long time ago, possibly in battle, and this Ancestor may have been betrayed, hurt, or forgotten. Perhaps they were not properly buried, honored, or remembered, or may have even been intentionally forgotten because of their actions. There could be family shame or regret here. This causes a rift in you, and you may be driven to rebel against your own Ancestors and to reject your heritage. This House is one of the most inauspicious placements for Po Jun, and here you are charged with resolving this Ancestral Ghost and honoring or repairing relations with your Ancestors. If you do not, then the Ghost can turn Demonic and cause negative after-death experiences and rebirth.

This placement means your Ancestral Qi is afflicted, and you will likely have a negative experience of family, including your parents and grandparents. You may reject your heritage, ethnicity, traditions, religion, or immediate family and rebel against their authority. You may want to change your name, drop your accent, move, run away from home, and so on. You may even hate and resent your ancestry and the values of the culture you were born in. This will cause a rift with your parents, and you will likely have a lot of arguments, disagreements, and bad feelings. Your relationship may even be abusive in both directions. You will probably be stuck in a pattern of rebelling against them, only to be punished repeatedly. If the Rebel shows up with stronger Stars like the Emperor, this placement can be benign and simply create some teenage angst. But, if it shows up with more Ghost Stars, it can turn very dark.

Underneath this pattern is a Ghost that makes you want to escape and reject; it will make you feel suffocated by your family. At worst, it can cause nervousness, angst, paranoia, or anger, and if it shows up with other Ghost Stars, it can cause serious mental health problems and even madness. Here, Po Jun can also cause health problems: chronic illness, accidents, or impotence or infertility. This can be a sign your Ancestors do not want you to reproduce and want to push you out of the family. This is all your Ancestral Ghost playing out the unresolved death experience that has turned them angry at those who rejected them. This placement can cause untimely death or death on the battlefield, where Po Jun compels you to join the military or seek danger and put your life at risk to relieve your Ancestor's incomplete death experience. The more this is afflicted, the more your life is at risk in this case, but surviving war or something like a car accident may release Po Jun.

This pattern of Ancestral negativity and rejection can cause many problems and disadvantages throughout life. You may intentionally disadvantage yourself and undermine your success in life by having to work hard outside of standard social conventions. On the one hand, you will inherit many unresolved family issues, but you will also be without their support if you reject your immediate family. Your self-centeredness and the denial of your roots can cause you to be alone and without support in life, but you may also be the victim of abuse and violence at home. You may also hurt your parents very deeply. Your Fate may involve cutting ties and breaking away; you may immigrate, learn a new language, or convert to a new religion. But if you do not heal this Ghost, you will be haunted by it, and it will consume you in death.

So, the key to resolving Po Jun is to repair ties. As always, you should do genealogy and try to find this Ancestor and their unresolved story. You may need to tell their story, heal their shame, or give them a proper funeral or ritual, even if it is only symbolic. You may need to "clean their grave," which could mean washing literal tombstones, or it could mean repairing ties with people in the family and resolving old blood feuds. You may need to work things out with your parents and other family members, and you may need to honor, accept, and take care of them. This won't be easy, but it will cause great catharsis and healing. Again, if you do not do this, then you will be alone in death, literally and in the after-death states. Your Beneficial Ancestors will not appear at your death, and you will be consumed by Po Jun. Remember, this may involve healing things from generations back. Perhaps you need to learn a lost Ancestral language or tradition; this kind of action honors your Ancestors and can heal old wounds. You may also need to start a new family and reestablish tradition or start an unconventional family.

Youth Palace

If Po Jun rules the Youth Palace, then your childhood or sibling relationships will be haunted by a rebellious, orphaned Ancestral Ghost. This Ancestor may have died in childhood, or they may have been orphaned, hurt, neglected, or forgotten in such a way that caused them to become full of anger, angst, and rebellion. As such, your childhood may be full of drama or sudden reversals of Fate. The Rebel in this House is usually about you as a child, as often, the sibling Fate here is weak. The Rebel here can also represent divorce and broken family struggles that cause isolation or rifts between siblings and family members and inspire negativity that causes rebellion and angst.

You may be an only child or adopted or only have step-siblings. If you do have siblings, the connection will be weak, and you will likely struggle to relate to each other. They may not be supportive, and if there is a further affliction, the siblings' Fate may be harsh and full of difficulties, arguments, and negative emotions. This can also be a rebellious older or younger sibling whose actions cause you harm. They may rebel or run away and cause you solitude, isolation, or loss. If there are more supportive Stars here, you may have siblings who encourage and support your independence or support you within a broken family. Stronger Stars can represent supportive strangers or adopted families.

If Po Jun represents you, then you will likely be a rebellious child. You may be possessed by Po Jun as a child and full of inexplicable anger and angst, and you may spend your childhood bucking against authority. You may be a rebel without a cause. You may defy your parents' authority, argue with them, and run away from home. You may rebel against authority at school or in society, becoming a juvenile delinquent. You may become an at-risk youth and get involved in crime or gang activity early in life.

Rebellion may start early, and you may throw temper tantrums as a young child. You may always argue, disobey, and get into trouble. You may bully or hurt other kids, or you may be bullied and then turn angry and defiant. Or later, in puberty, you may suddenly lash out and turn angry. You may run away from home, leave home early, or be sent away to military school or private school. This is the kind of behavior that could baffle child therapists, and you could be put on medications young for bad behavior.

If there is a further affliction here, then Po Jun can also represent childhood trauma and abuse from parents, siblings, or authority figures. It can represent ongoing patterns of negativity that you get stuck in early in life and have difficulty escaping. You may have to run away from all this, and you could barely survive childhood. Things may only be resolved with time and distance. You may carry these scars with you throughout life, and if you do not resolve them, then they will stay with you and can haunt you even in death. It is important to resolve Po Jun, but here, it may not be able to find resolution until adulthood. You may need to repair things with siblings or do therapy work to resolve childhood trauma. Patterns of rebellion can continue into adulthood and undermine your success later in life as patterns of immaturity, defensiveness, and anger. The Rebel will be resolved when you feel like childhood happened to someone else and when you no longer play out the patterns of escape, rebellion, or anger of your youth.

Partners Palace

If Po Jun rules the Partners Palace, then you or your chosen partner will be possessed or haunted by an Ancestral Ghost, who died alone, unloved, rejected, betrayed, or abandoned by someone they loved. They may have died full of longing and loneliness, never having partnered; they may have been widowed, or they may have died with bitterness, anger, or resentment about a divorce. Po Jun here can also represent patterns of spousal abuse that you inherit and that cause you to run away from relationships. Either way, this Star here will create a pattern of rebellion in some way against the idea of partnership altogether, which will undermine relationships and create negative behavior patterns that make it difficult to meet people and get into or stay in relationships. Your Ancestor died with negativity around partnership, which makes you unsure about the whole thing: You're not sure who or what you want, and you may also be filled with deep longings, fantasies, and desires as well as fears, uncertainties, immaturities, and confusion.

You may be perfectly reasonable and rational, but you get possessed in relationships, which bring out all kinds of immature, selfish, or negative patterns. These can vary, but the core is that these immature patterns of rebellion and rejection undermine your getting into or staying in relationships. More important, these are unconscious patterns within yourself: You think you are doing good things, but you are actually your own worst enemy. You can always rationalize your behavior, why you reject people, why it didn't work out, or why you fell in love with the wrong person, but it always seems to turn out badly. And you probably always make things worse when you are trying to help.

When you get close to people, Po Jun possesses either you or them and makes a mess. You may be irrationally picky and quickly find fault in your partners, so you always have a reason to reject others, move on, or leave. You may misjudge people and project fears or fantasies onto them that cause you to either run away or become intensely clingy. You may become obsessive, lustful, or attached, which drives people away and causes rejection. You may have deep, irrational desires for "the one"—the perfect match, Prince Charming, and so on. No one ever lives up to your standards, so you are always alone, moving on to the next person, who then fails to meet your expectations. You may be immature and terrible at communication with poor relationships skills.

You may fall in love with the wrong people and constantly choose poor partners, attracted to all the red flags. You may always fall for people who are unavailable, literally or emotionally, and so you have a reason to get rejected. You may also be attracted to rebels, bad boys, starving artists, or tattooed biker ex-cons. You could partner with people against the advice of parents, family, friends, and so on as an act of rebellion. This could include marrying a boss or assistant, someone half your age, someone from a different class, religion, or culture, and so on. Po Jun can also create fear of intimacy or of being in a partnership. You may run away as soon as you get close to someone or drift from partner to partner, easily distracted or fearful.

You may also have a rebellious or unconventional approach to relationships altogether. You may be promiscuous and rebel against the idea of monogamy or traditional marriage. You may live with a lover and never get married. You may adopt alternative forms of relating like polyamory, open relationships, polygamy, polyandry, and so on. This can also represent the struggle of being in relationships that are rejected by society, so homosexuality can fall under this, as it can be a rebellion against tradition, family, or religion. You may also have a strange, quirky, or weird marriage ceremony that rebels against all conventions.

If there is further affliction by Ghost Stars here, then you may experience a nightmare relationship, abuse, rejection, or divorce. You may also be widowed or lose a partner early. The way to resolve Po Jun here is not to avoid relationships but to dive in and make a mess. Qi Sha may require avoiding them, but Po Jun is made worse this way, because you never get to work out its delusions. You need to put yourself out there, get into relationships, get rejected, and so on, and then grow up, do the work, and learn to be a good partner—so self-reflect, take responsibility, hold yourself accountable, heal your trauma, apologize for hurting yourself and others, learn how to communicate your needs, listen to the advice of others, take feedback from partners, family, and friends, and ultimately work to change this pattern.

The Rebel here will cause you to repeat the same negative pattern repeatedly until you grow up. This may involve settling down and letting go of fears and fantasies; there's no perfect person or relationship. If you can resolve this Ghost, you can have a successful partnership and learn much from past mistakes. But if you do not, then you will likely never settle down, and you will have a long string of bad experiences that haunt and consume you in death. You could die alone, having been abandoned by and abandoning others. Character matters a lot here.

Offspring Palace

If Po Jun rules the Offspring Palace, then your Fate as a parent is haunted by an Ancestral Ghost who could have died as an orphan, died in childbirth (either the child or parent), or died unloved, unprotected, and resentful. They died with negativity toward their parents in some way, and their experience is caught in a state of rebellion or anger against you as a parent. This can manifest as a rebellious child or as difficulties in your experience of being a parent or conceiving. This Ancestral Ghost may also have died never having had a child, and so you want one badly but can't, and you get stuck in a loop of trying and trying but being unable to conceive or find a partner.

Anytime a Ghost Star rules the Offspring Palace, it can create fear, doubt, or uncertainty about being a parent, especially if an Ancestor died in childbirth or died due to the circumstances of being a parent. If this is the case, you may fear and rebel against being a parent. You may have a host of fears that you project onto parenthood: fear of giving birth, fear of dying in childbirth, fear of losing a child, fear of your child getting sick, fear of losing your freedom, fear of being a bad parent, fear of parental expenses, and so on. These fears may possess you and cause you to avoid being parenting altogether. These fears may cause you to postpone parenthood, or they can be resolved by simply choosing not to have children. However, you may wait too long and then be unable to have children, and this could send you into a negative spiral or cause you to spend a fortune on fertility medicine.

Po Jun here can cause infertility and difficulties in conceiving. It can cause difficult pregnancies as well as miscarriages, stillbirths, and abortions. It can cause health problems to arise during pregnancy or after birth, like postpartum depression. Childbirth itself may be difficult, complicated, or dangerous. You may need an emergency C-section or hysterectomy, or the baby could need surgery. If there is further affliction by other Ghost Stars, this complicates things and makes the possibilities worse. It can also increase the possibility that the child will be born with health problems, handicaps, or other medical concerns that will require lifelong care.

Po Jun in this House can create irreconcilable differences between you and your children and create difficult circumstances around being a parent. You may have a rebellious, disagreeable child who constantly defies your authority. The Rebel possesses them and seeks to play out its unresolved anger against you. You may develop adversarial lifestyles and views or hurt each other in a way that causes a rift. Your child may reject your parenting and run away, disobey, and leave home early. This may hurt and confuse you. There may also be difficulties that cause you to be an absentee parent, such as divorce, financial, or legal difficulties. If this manifests as neglect or abuse, then your child may be taken from you. You may also be a harsh and angry parent, and this could cause your child trauma and lifelong anger or resentment toward you. You may also be a stepparent or adopt and have trouble raising someone else's children. They do not accept you as a parent and, again, rebel against you.

If there are other positive Stars here, then this pattern can be resolved by separation and time. Your child may leave early or leave on bad terms, but they will eventually return and repair things. Even if further afflicted by other Ghosts, Po Jun can be resolved in time once it has worked out its anger at you. Your children may return as adults, having realized that you did your best and were a great parent, despite the challenges or difficulties of their childhood. Resolution here is difficult, and it is a question of whether to avoid being a parent altogether or to jump in and work it out. Either can work, and unless Fate decides for you, it is up to you which way you resolve this Ghost. As always, you should do genealogy and find out what Ancestor is afflicting you here; this could give you a lot of insight into the nature of this Fate and whether the Rebel is about you and your fear or about the child.

Wealth Palace

If Po Jun rules the Wealth Palace, then you will likely struggle with finances throughout life, but this can be resolved by establishing financial security and legacy. An Ancestral Ghost may have died broke or been murdered over money. They may have been involved in crime, gambling, or other illegal activities, and you inherit their curse. They may have been a rebel, wildly irresponsible with finances, and they could even have made and lost a fortune. Ghost Stars can always turn a profit from high-risk activities like speculation, investment, or gambling; they may be resolved through a high-risk gamble or come to you as a cursed windfall or blood money. Again, it is important to do genealogy and find out the nature of the Ancestral pattern here.

If there is no further affliction, you will likely be rebellious, irresponsible, or widely ambitious when it comes to money. You are possessed by Po Jun and have something to prove or accomplish to resolve it. You may hate and resent money altogether and rebel against having a normal job or against any obligation or responsibility. As a result, you may be a bum, mooch, or loser. You may be broke or, at best, a minimalist who gets by with very little. You may rebel against expectations and find a way around financial responsibilities, either by working the system or by fulfilling financial obligations through various unconventional means. You could work many odd jobs or in strange, unusual settings. You may do rebellious, eccentric, or socially disagreeable work, or you may find a way to profit off being a rebel.

Either way, your finances will likely fluctuate wildly throughout your life. If there is further affliction, you may go bankrupt, lose everything, and leave nothing behind. You may lose a business, have things repossessed, and even become homeless or in serious debt. You may gamble, steal, profit by illegal schemes, or be duped by them. You may be possessed and driven to earn great wealth and do anything, including hurt others, to make it happen. This may cause you to sell out, become corrupt, or lose your soul. You may drive yourself to physical and mental exhaustion in pursuit of wealth, and succeed and fail with great drama. You may also have an obsession but lack the skills, stamina, or intelligence to be successful; failure may cause you to die broke, feeling humiliated.

If there is no further affliction, or if the Rebel shows up with more positive Stars, then you can eventually achieve financial security and success and create a legacy, but it will likely be hard-won and involve a lot of ups and downs. Achieving this success may resolve Po Jun, but Po Jun may also be resolved by letting go of your obsessions and ambitions and settling with "good enough." Modesty and generosity can always resolve Ghost Stars in this House. You may also have to let go of resentment or hatred toward the rich, capitalism, competition, or whatever, as these kinds of negative emotions may also possess you. Resolution could be a rags-to-riches story, but it is in vain if you do not create a legacy and turn it into generosity, charity, or altruism. You may also need to grow out of teenage rebellion and hold down a good job as a responsible adult. This might be all you need to do to resolve Po Jun.

Health Palace

If Po Jun rules the Health Palace, then you are possessed by an Ancestral Ghost who is coming for your life. Po Jun is like Qi Sha here, but while Qi Sha, the Seven Killings Star, does not respond to treatment, Po Jun does, and it can be more easily resolved. Qi Sha can turn Demonic because it does not want to be resolved, but Po Jun does. It may put you through some serious health challenges, but healing is possible and could be cathartic, heroic, or intense. Ultimately, you can be free of Po Jun, which could turn into a kind of power. This Ancestral Ghost likely died due to a challenging injury, illness, or disease they were unable to heal; they tried but failed. Now, you are here to finish their experience and liberate them from their painful death. This can be a kind of shamanic initiation that transforms you as a person.

As always, it is important to do genealogy and look for Ancestors who died from intense accidents, illness, injuries, diseases, and so on or who had long, protracted, or difficult deaths where they fought and underwent treatments that ultimately failed. This loop of treatment, pain, and recovery is where this Ghost is stuck and looking to complete its experience and find resolution. This can manifest in several ways. If you have Po Jun here, you tend to respond better to traditional and alternative medicines with alternative ways of viewing illness. Conventional or allopathic medicine tends to make things worse and lead to more addictions, overtreatment, misdiagnosis, and iatrogenic disease. You may need a rebel doctor, shaman, or priest to recover, and you could become one of these in the process.

If an Ancestor died in an accident or from an injury, then you may be Fated to have a similar accident or injury. You may be in a car crash or fight, have a fall, and so on and sustain bad injuries. You may undergo heroic treatment and recover, left with a scar, limp, or tick, but Po Jun will be resolved in this process. If there is no further affliction in this House, you may respond well to treatment or surgery, and that is that. If there are other Ghost Stars here, then it may be a fight. There may be complications, infections, or multiple failed surgeries. Or, you may have a long battle to be able to walk again or to return to full function. Po Jun will be resolved in this battle.

If the Ancestral Ghost died because of an illness or disease, then either you will suffer from several chronic conditions that are an echo of that disease, or you may be Fated to get seriously ill or diagnosed with a serious disease yourself. If their condition was chronic, then you may be a sickly child and have a weak constitution as an adult, you may be haunted by fear and hypochondria, and you may suffer from many subclinical chronic medical problems, such as low-grade infections. Or, you may become obsessed with healing and doctors and addicted to medical treatment. You could be possessed of Po Jun's desire to be healed, so you become a professional patient and carry around huge notebooks full of blood-work results, diagnoses, and medical scans. You could become addicted to medications, pain pills, supplements, or getting treatments. You could be addicted to binging and purging. You may have a host of allergies, sensitivities, and negative emotions that are inexplicable.

Po Jun here can cause digestive weakness and chronic constipation or diarrhea to the point that you are unable to absorb nutrients. It can cause skin problems and consumptive lung disorders. There are many ways that Ghosts can cause health problems, and so it is important to look to your Ancestors, as they will likely be genetic. Symptoms are also likely to be psychosomatic and characterized by wind, always changing with the emotions.

You may be so exhausted by all this obsession with treatment that you cause things to get worse, and you are then unable to recover from anything. The Rebel can spiral out of control here and get caught in a loop of illness caused by medicine. You will likely develop a very personal path of illness, recovery, and health. This Ghost can be resolved, and it can respond to treatment, but the key is to break out of whatever pattern is keeping you ill or in pain. You may experience sudden reversals of health when Po Jun possesses you and when you resolve it. You may become sick suddenly through invasion by external forces or get into a sudden accident, and you may make a dramatic or miraculous recovery when Po Jun is resolved.

The Rebel here can also cause you to be a rebellious and undisciplined patient. Attempts to heal are undermined by inconsistency and lack of personal discipline. It is essential, then, to develop strong habits, routines, and health practices. It is also important to comply with doctor's orders and directions. Many symptoms are also made worse or even caused by negative emotions, and so anger, worry, fear, and so on all need to be worked with, as you may be your own worst enemy in this case. These kinds of health problems will likely manifest early in life, so you should start good health practices early.

If you do not resolve Po Jun, your health will continue to decline as you age. If there are additional Ghost Stars here, you may have a short life or severe illness that challenges you earlier in life. That being said, it is important not to get obsessed with illness and treatment, as this feeds the very nature of Po Jun here. You need to strike a balance between creating strong personal discipline and health practices and not overdoing it or becoming professionally ill.

The resolution of Po Jun here can be cathartic, heroic, and transformative, and you could become a healer or shaman in this process. Resolving Po Jun can become a power to heal others, which you learn through your own dramatic recovery.

Career/Travel Palace

If Po Jun rules the Career/Travel Palace, then you will likely struggle with career and purpose—the question of what to do or be in life—as well as where to live. You will be possessed by an Ancestral Ghost who died lost, far from home, or unfulfilled due to failure or hardship or because of their own mistakes or misconduct. This gives you a rebellious and irrational need to wander, abandon opportunities, quit jobs, and move from place to place looking for fulfillment. You may be possessed by angst, fear, anger, or defiance, so you are unsuited to "regular work."

Due to your character, you may find it difficult or even impossible to hold down a regular, nine-to-five job. You may also hold powerful views that turn you toward alternative careers like political activism, alternative medicine, art, music, investigative reporting, or independent entrepreneurial work based on your unique personality or interests. You may have a strong need to do things your own way and be your own boss. You may resent others' success and consider it "selling out." Po Jun here may also make you an obsessed and aggressively competitive workaholic.

If there is no further affliction, this placement can work out well, and although you will likely wander, change jobs many times, and travel a great deal, you will eventually settle down and stop drifting. The Rebel may just need to wander and work things out. You may try out many jobs, wear many different hats, and abandon many possibilities, but eventually, you can figure things out. Po Jun is resolved when you settle down, choose a path, and make an honest go of it. This may be a process of growing up and out of youthful and rebellious angst.

You may be a punk rocker and eventually find yourself wearing a suit and tie. You may be an activist and march in the streets, but eventually, you will find yourself as an environmental lawyer fighting a just cause in the courtroom. You may be a wild yogi type or hippie who wanders between full moon festivals and Burning Man but eventually settles down as an alternative doctor or healer. There are many ways this can turn out well. The Rebel's best career expression may be as an artist or musician: Put an instrument or paintbrush in front of your rebellion, and you may turn out like Bob Marley or Banksy.

However, if there are other Ghost Stars with Po Jun here, then you will likely struggle and live a very unsettled life. You may do all of the above but fail to gain skills or mature. You may detest the notion of a career and be stuck in a rebellious phase, still a punk rocker at forty-five with no prospects, still working a menial job while partying on the weekends with teenagers. You may continuously quit jobs or get fired due to your rebellious and disagreeable character. You may tell off your boss and constantly get in trouble because you hate taking orders or are lazy and hate working. You may be constantly underpaid and underappreciated and become more and more resentful and frustrated. You may settle into unpleasant work, like being a sanitation worker or janitor, and feel like a second-class citizen.

More Ghost Stars here can also push the rebellious streak further and get you into trouble. You may get involved with crime or gangs, or you could push your activism into dangerous territory, setting fire to buildings, breaking windows, or spray-painting graffiti on public property as an act of rebellion. You may think you are fighting a just cause and that violence is the only way to resist, even leading to acts of terrorism. This could be disastrous, but the intense negativity here could burn out Po Jun in the process.

Po Jun in this House can also cause you to reject your home, nationality, culture, language, or religion due to an unsettled Ancestral Ghost. This may be resolved by moving to a new place and adopting a new culture, language, and so on. But this involves an escape, which may be due to violence, war, oppression, persecution, famine, strife, and so on in your country of origin. You may be forced to flee or be exiled as a refugee, or your Ancestors may have been forced to do so. You may be part of a resistance movement, go to war, and die on the battlefield far from home.

As usual, here the Rebel is stuck in a loop of frustration and failure due to their own acts of rebellion and defiance. You think you are making good choices; you think you are in the right or standing up for justice. You may believe wholeheartedly that you are making the right decisions, but you may throw the baby out with the bathwater. You are probably unconscious of how you get in your own way, undermining your success and happiness with bad choices.

To resolve Po Jun, you may need to eat bitter, grow up, seek and listen to the advice of others, and make the hard choice to settle down, going against your beliefs. You may need to sell out and take a corporate job. Or you may need to take your art or activism seriously and turn it into a real job. Embrace the strange and the progressive, and turn it into something good.

Assistants Palace

If Po Jun rules the Friends/Assistants Palace, then you will be haunted by an Ancestral Ghost who was likely hurt, tortured, betrayed, or even murdered by someone close to them, either a friend or confidant. This is an inauspicious placement for Po Jun, as it creates paranoia and suspicion, making it difficult for you to maintain relationships with friends, co-workers, assistants, and schoolmates. It can cause you to suspect others, and it can also possess others, inviting them to abandon or betray you. This makes your Fate with friends and helpers very uneven; it will likely be a roller coaster—lots of ups and downs and drama.

Character matters a lot here, for more independent Characters can resolve this by simply choosing to work alone, but the more domestic and relationship-oriented Characters will likely struggle and may make this pattern worse by indulging in feelings of paranoia, betrayal, or victimhood. Further affliction can create intense emotions and experiences of victimhood, abuse, and persecution that profoundly undermine both your progress in your career and your friendships. As an influence on career, the Rebel can steer you toward an alternative and activist orientation, which can be resolved through service work.

If there is no further affliction, then this House can become an auspicious but challenging place to have Po Jun. You can resolve this Ancestral Ghost by practicing kindness, generosity, forgiveness, and patience. You will likely experience many challenges with other people, and they may even be disastrous, but you are working out an Ancestral Ghost, and to some degree, you must accept this and the consequences. Whatever happens, accept it, have patience, and forgive others within reason. There is no reason to be a doormat or accept bad behavior toward you, but fighting against it or indulging feelings of victimhood or persecution will only worsen things. You may have to take the "slings and arrows of outrageous fortune," but the more you accept things and the less you struggle against them, the more you liberate Po Jun. We may be tempted here to seek justice or even vengeance, but this only creates more victimhood. You may experience betrayal and be undermined by vicious or conniving people at work or in social circles, but you must turn the other cheek. Easier said than done, but with patience the truth will come out.

If Po Jun shows up without further affliction and with stronger Stars, then the possibility of turning this into something positive is strong. You can work in alternative education or medicine. You can be an activist or public servant who works for social justice and equality. You may also possess an unusual skill and be capable of great innovation or invention. You can succeed in "rebel work," and you may be Fated to meet and follow a rebel teacher or mentor. You may meet an innovator or inventor and help them as their assistant. This placement can also translate into working with or living in alternative communities. You may be involved with a group of like-minded rebels who work toward a common goal or cause. However, these situations can easily turn dark and invite all of the above negativity. Like in any career House, the Rebel here can make it difficult to accept and do "ordinary" work; you will inherit a rebellious or defiant bent, and you will want to be different and do things differently.

If there are additional Ghost Stars here, then the possibilities of betrayal, drama, abuse, and persecution get darker and potentially more violent. You may be possessed by terrible ideas and crippled by idealism, fantasy, or even religious or cultlike behavior that never comes to fruition or that turns violent. You can get involved with fanatics or even become one. Look out for fanatical, antisocial, or cultlike behavior and psychology, which can be subtle and cunning at manipulating you or others. Or, this behavior can be overt, and you may be drawn to things like martyrdom, jihad, or any number of the enormous sacrifices that appear justified or righteous but are really just awful. Getting involved with these kinds of people will not turn out well.

This may sound dramatic, and it is, but the Rebel's influence can also be totally banal. You may be haunted by certain idealisms, fantasies, and dreams that never come true. You may fancy yourself a rebel, revolutionary, or rock star but never amount to anything. As always, it is essential to do genealogy and discover your Ancestral Ghost's story. If they died due to betrayal or because of the malice of others, then it is good to know that you are here to work out this betrayal; it does not belong to you, and your feelings of victimhood or persecution may be a projection.

You may need to do everything alone and work this out through solitude, or you may need to jump into the mix, make a mess, and practice generosity and patience with others. You may need to dedicate yourself to service and take the slings and arrows in good faith. If you do not resolve this Ghost, then feelings of betrayal or regret will haunt you in death. Remember, the Rebel always thinks they are doing good, but they often make things worse when trying to help. In this House, this comes into play with friends and at work, so watch out for it. There may be some kind of lesson here about holding back, biting your tongue, apologizing, and turning the other cheek to avoid creating more drama.

Superiors Palace

If Po Jun rules the Superiors Palace, you are in an excellent position to resolve an Ancestral Ghost who likely died as a rebel attempting to do something courageous, change the world, or better their community. They may have been killed in battle or during an act of defiance or rebellion against authority. They may have been a leader or innovator who tried to change things but perhaps failed. You inherit this mission and are driven to succeed where they failed. This is one of the only places where Po Jun's rebellion can turn out well; if there is no further affliction, then this Ancestor may have been a Robin Hood–like figure whose spirit can be honored, and their rebellious streak continued. If there is further affliction, they may have gone too far, incurred a lot of negative results, or hurt many people with their actions; now, you must resolve this Fate through discipline and by making amends.

Resolving the Rebel in this House is traditionally associated with the military, martial arts, and monasticism. This Ghost can be resolved by living or working in an environment where discipline, authority, and self-cultivation are strong. Here, you are in an excellent position to flourish with the help of strict or stern teachers or drill sergeants or through a radical shaman, guru, mentor, or spiritual teacher who whips you into shape and turns you into a warrior; they essentially take care of the Ghost for you this way.

Warriorship is one of the best ways to resolve the Rebel here, either literally through the military or martial arts or through any disciplined behavior that toughens you up and turns rebellion into a source of strength. Routines, schedules, exercises, practices, and so on all create a powerful container to work out this Ghost and turn it into something positive. Monasticism is also a powerful way to resolve this, but the Rebel will struggle hard against the rules. You can also succeed in physical or protective work as a police officer, firefighter, bodyguard, bouncer, security officer, or anything where you protect others and are willing to sacrifice yourself for them.

You may also be drawn to work out this Fate in the community with like-minded rebels, but here, you are more likely to be their leader or to start your own alternative community. You may also have a Fated connection with the leader of an alternative community, but watch out for cults, false gurus, and abusive teachers. And watch out for becoming one yourself. In this House, the Rebel here may be drawn to power, and abuse their position to gain advantage, especially if they feel justified in a cause or mission to change the world. You may turn into the very thing you are fighting and live long enough to see yourself become the victim.

In the Superiors Palace, the Rebel's sphere of influence grows, and your rebellion can gain an audience and reach more people. Again, you may meet an influential rebel teacher, mentor, or boss who influences your career and shows you the way, or you may invent your career yourself through your life path, which could "radicalize" you. You will likely have strong ideals and be driven toward "rebel work." You may work in alternative education or medicine or become an activist or advocate. You may be an innovator, inventor, or influencer.

You will likely have a rebellious streak and want to do things differently. You will struggle with authority and want to be your own boss and do things your way. You may be drawn to champion your ideals through your work and change the world. Entrepreneurial work can succeed here, as you can create a unique image and brand that sells defiance. Here, anything can succeed if you have strong will and discipline, which is both the challenge of this Ghost and the way to resolve it.

You may even be Fated to work in a field that is challenging or even disgusting to others but that needs to be done. You may be willing to roll up your sleeves and do the difficult things; this may require sacrifice and hard work, but you may feel born to do it or called to the challenge. Po Jun can be resolved here through a significant sacrifice, but as in the previous House, watch out for cult behavior, fanaticism, and martyrdom, which can be appealing to people who want to be freedom fighters.

This can also be very dark. You may be killed in the line of duty, die on the battlefield, or incur public consequences for your rebellion. This may inspire others, and you could go down in history as a famous rebel, activist, and revolutionary, like Martin Luther King Jr., Rosa Parks, Mahatma Gandhi, Nelson Mandela, William Wallace, and so on. If there is no further affliction here, then you may be remembered and honored after death, like these people.

If there is further affliction, then your revolution may fail. You may go down as a failed rebel or villain. You may be burdened by your excessive idealism, fantasies, or desire for justice that never comes to fruition. You may fight and struggle and never amount to anything. You may have to sell out, get a "real" job, and let go of your dreams of being a rock star. With additional Ghost Stars, the consequences of Po Jun going bad here are higher, but most people's rebellions are pretty banal. You will likely just be "alternative," weird, and so on. You may identify as a punk or metalhead, or you may be a bleeding-heart liberal who goes to marches. As always, do genealogy and find your Rebel Ancestor; your fight may be theirs. If you do not resolve this, then you may be haunted by regret in death—either that you did not stand up and fight or that you did not fight hard enough. This desire to fight may be Po Jun itself; watch how it drives your mission and purpose in life.

Property Palace

If Po Jun rules the Property Palace, then you will be haunted by an Ancestral Ghost who likely died either at home, unable to escape, or far away from home, also unable to escape. They may have been killed on the battlefield, or they may have died at home due to war, political strife, or a natural disaster like an earthquake or fire, or they could have been attacked, assaulted, or murdered at home. If they died on the battlefield, it may have been due to friendly fire, an accident or mistake, or by bombing, where they died in a structure. Either way, they died feeling unsafe. This will create the feeling of never being safe at home or of being trapped and unable to escape. You may have claustrophobia or agoraphobia. This Ancestor may also have died homeless, or they were simply a vagabond, poor, or unable to maintain a safe home. Po Jun is like Qi Sha here, but less intense and more manageable. Here, Po Jun is caught in the loop, trying to get safe or escape.

You will likely have a rebellious streak when it comes to staying put and settling down. You may travel a great deal with a restless spirit or be a wanderer, vagabond, nomad, and so on. If there is no further affliction, then this can turn out okay. You may enjoy life on the road in your youth and simply wander from place to place and consider it an adventure. You may also be called to join the military, to escape and protect your homeland. But look out for that deeper feeling of needing to escape, feeling unsafe, or feeling trapped. You may feel like you are "on the run." This can be worked out by midlife, and here you can resolve the Rebel by settling down, buying property, and putting down roots.

If there are additional Ghost Stars here, then this can create an irrational fear of stability, and you may generate a lot of drama in your wandering. You may also have an unstable living situation due to circumstances that are self-created or inflicted on you, such as unemployment, weak economy, high rent, divorce, crime, fires, earthquakes, floods, and so on. You may be unable to hold on to property because of your own instability, or you may lack any sense of responsibility due to your own rebellion and defiance.

The Rebel here may reject their original identity or identify with a noble minority or as an outcast. You could rebel against your country, culture, or religion of origin, and this may drive you to leave home, move, or strike out in search of a new home. You may then feel at home in a foreign land and live as an expat. If there is further affliction, this may be a mistake, and you may face discrimination or difficulties in the new place. Po Jun may also represent an Ancestor who died or was persecuted because of being a minority, and this could make being in that minority feel unsafe to you. So, you reject it, change your name, or hide your accent. You may also identify more strongly with that minority and become a rebel fighting for their rights.

You may become a kind of working-class hero or rebel who fights issues of class, status, and social structure that keep people disadvantaged or poor. You may identify with the poor and hate the rich. This is very Robin Hood, but here, the Rebel may cause you to actually steal property or work to redistribute property. You may live or work in community housing or help homeless people get on their feet and get access to shelter. You could work at a homeless shelter, or you may, at some point, live in one.

You may also have a Fated connection to a haunted, ruined, or run-down piece of property. Your family's resources may be diminished, and you may have to get rid of things you inherit or sell them at a loss. You may acquire property that was damaged in an accident or natural disaster or that someone died in. You may also purchase property that is haunted and becomes a money pit. You may acquire property only to have it burn down due to bad wiring, collapse in an earthquake, or get washed away in a flood. You may spend a fortune on a property and then the market collapses and so you must sell it very low, losing a lot of money.

The Rebel here can also create a haunted shared space, and you may be involved with a rebel community, cult, or intentional community of outcasts who get together to live off the grid or by socialist or communist ideals. Watch out for cult brainwashing or negative communities that take things from people. Intentional communities or collectives are a disaster if they are filled with individualists or people looking to abuse or take advantage of others.

Po Jun is resolved here by settling down. You need to self-reflect and confront that feeling of never being safe. Po Jun always thinks it is doing the right thing, and here it is running away. It is likely that you are running away from nothing, from a Ghost. It can be powerful to do genealogy and find out if an Ancestor died at home or on the battlefield. They may require a proper burial or death ritual, or you may need to tell their story or clean their grave. You may need to confront the fear and stay put. Or you may need to work hard to become stable and responsible enough to own and create a stable home. You may need to create a legacy and resolve the Ancestral pattern of wandering or being on the run by creating safety for you and your family. You may also need to embrace your homeland and return.

Pleasure Palace

If Po Jun rules the Pleasure Palace, then you will be haunted by an Ancestral Ghost who died accidentally while enjoying themselves or with a very conflicted or rebellious relationship to pleasure. They may have died due to addiction or substance abuse, or they may have been the victim of sexual abuse or violence. This may also have been a very serious, stern, or even masochistic Ancestor who never had any fun or who actually enjoyed hurting others. They may have been "all work and no play" or possessed of religious ideals that considered all pleasure the work of the devil while they secretly enjoyed punishing people for their sins.

It is important to self-reflect here and also to do genealogy. If there is further affliction by Ghost Stars, then this can go very dark, so it is important to identify the Ancestral pattern you have inherited. If this Po Jun is not resolved, then life can be very miserable, and you may feel sad, desolate, and isolated; you can be swallowed up by negative emotions and eventually become a Ghost. You may also be caught up in patterns of addiction or even a masochist sense of seriousness and struggle.

It is likely that you will struggle a great deal with pleasure, happiness, and enjoyment. You may be a stern, serious, all-work-and-no-play individual who never has fun or enjoys anything. You may be anhedonic, actually unable to feel pleasure or take satisfaction in anything. This may drive you to work yourself to the bone, and paradoxically, you may enjoy the suffering. The positive side of this is that you can enjoy discipline and excel at things like martial arts, strength training, and military-like disciplines. But you can take this too far and become like a drill sergeant. You may also push this into sadomasochism and enjoy taking or inflicting pain, which can go down some dark roads. This is Po Jun being confused about pleasure, which, for this Ghost, is all mixed up with pain and death.

If there is no further affliction or if Po Jun shows up with positive Stars, you may take pleasure in more rebellious, antisocial activities, which can go okay. You may enjoy being a rebel or marginalized and create an identity out of it. You may enjoy communal disobedience and join a militia or gang or go to political demonstrations, march in solidarity, and protest things. You may love and identify with rebellious music like punk, reggae, metal, or hip-hop and turn your defiance into an art form. You may also enjoy and use art itself as a form of protest. You could get into graffiti, vandalism, or public art that makes statements about environmental justice, human or animal rights, or political ideologies.

With positive Stars here as well, you can turn your own sense of struggle or your own irresponsible behaviors or acts of defiance into life lessons and a source of growth. You can learn from them and turn them into art, poetry, music, and so on, so that others can identify with your pain and struggle. Without further affliction, this pattern can be transformed, and you can have a bittersweet relationship with pleasure that has a hard and soft edge. You may have a lot of regrets and reservations around pleasure, a lot of "should haves" and "could have beens." You may grow up and have mixed memories of your rebellious and crazy youth.

If there is further affliction from Ghost Stars, then the Rebel's sense of struggle and suffering can become difficult. You may distrust or fear pleasure, causing you to abandon people, places, or situations to be sure that you never have any fun. You rebel and run away when having fun to remove yourself from danger. You may fear crowds, parties, concerts, drugs, dancing, and so on because letting go and having fun feel unsafe and dangerous. And it may be dangerous: You may be at risk when having fun or letting go of your inhibitions; if you do indulge, then you may go too far, and this can spin out into addiction and abuse. You could love the feeling of being drunk or high so much that you kill yourself in the process. You may die searching for an external form of pleasure, seeking to fill an inner void that can never be filled or satisfied.

Further affliction here can also turn the sadomasochism darker and more abusive and violent, both to yourself and others, and you are at further risk of being abused or becoming an abuser. More Ghosts here make Po Jun more and more confused and more likely to miscalculate pleasure and generate a lot of negative emotions in the process. You may be clueless, out of sync, and make many mistakes when trying to have fun, relate to others, and so on.

Po Jun is resolved here by self-reflection and discipline. You are at risk when enjoying yourself and need to find a balance between being too harsh and too indulgent. If you are on the "all work and no play," sadomasochist side, then you may need to learn to lighten up and have some silly fun; you may need to let go a little and realize that it is safe to have a bit of fun. If you are on the indulgent, rebel side, then you may need to maintain strong discipline through something like martial arts or gym training. Either way, this placement is challenging, and if you do not resolve this Ghost, it can put you in danger in this life and in the after-death states.

THE FOUR MINOR GHOSTS

NOW THAT WE HAVE FINISHED OUR DISCUSSION of the Four Major Ghosts, we can move on to the Four Minor Ghosts. These are Huo Xing (火星), the Fire Star; Ling Xing (鈴星), the Water or Ringing Star; Qing Yang (擎羊) or Yang Ren (羊刃)—hence referred to as just Yang Ren—the Goat Blade or Sacrificial Star; and Tuo Luo (駝羅), the Humpback or Rejection Star. These four Stars, and all the remaining Stars, warrant a different discussion, for none of these Stars are strong enough to "rule" a House. In other words, if they show up alone without stronger Stars, that House is technically a Kong Gong (空宮), an Empty Court, and because of this, they do not create significant patterns of Fate. So, we will not walk them through the Twelve Houses, but instead, we will discuss how they can generally be interpreted in whatever House they appear in.

The Four Major Ghosts, on the other hand, are strong enough to rule a House if they show up in that House alone. They are potentially the darkest, most afflicting forces in Polestar Astrology, capable of creating some of the darkest human scenarios, although sometimes they are eclipsed and mostly harmless. So, it was necessary to walk them through each House and discuss the various possibilities. The Four Minor Ghosts are more like flavors: They add a particular dimension of negative emotion to each House, except for Yang Ren, which is more likely to be "incidental," as it represents a significant sacrifice and is resolved once that sacrifice is made. The other three—the Fire Star, Water Star, and Humpback Star—all represent more classic Ghosts in the Chinese sense: They are weak but subtle and persistent in the way they breed false views and negative emotions. Again, they are like cigarettes: One is not particularly harmful, but over time they become destructive.

The Four Minor Ghosts are minor Ancestors who died in a very particular way and who were consumed with a particular negative emotion at the moment of death. You then inherit that emotion as a subtle pattern of internalized anger (the Fire Star), fear or hopelessness (the Water Star), or rejection or self-loathing (the Humpback Star). Whatever House they show up in is flavored by that negative emotion, and these patterns can occur repeatedly, create loss, and undermine the Fate in that House. They are much more subtle than the Four Major Ghosts and do not constitute the kind of "haunting" that causes major Fate patterns. They are internal and can be very minor, but sometimes they can flare up and cause intense emotions.

As usual, the particular emotion is directly related to the Ancestor in question, so these vary from person to person and may be stronger or weaker due to various factors. If the death was more recent, then the emotion is likely to be stronger. If the Star shows up alone, then it can be stronger, though never strong enough to actually drive Fate. If a Minor Ghost shows up with a stronger Star, it tends to undermine and afflict that Star with anger, fear, doubt, and so on, but Minor Ghosts do not hinder the overall resolution of Fate. Rather, they slow it down or make it more of a struggle, and they can add a dimension of catharsis when that Ancestor is released and resolved.

Stronger Stars act as exorcists for these Stars, so if a Minor Ghost shows up with the Emperor, Empress, Tutor, Oracle, General, or the like, then this means that your Beneficial

Ancestors are acting as guardians and working through you to resolve Minor Ghosts in the family. Stronger Stars make the Ghost more likely to resolve quickly and have a beneficial outcome. If you see strong Stars, especially if they or the House is exalted, with a lot of Minor Ghosts, then that is an Ancestral "setup." Your Beneficial Ancestors are using your strength to resolve a lot of Ghosts in the family.

If the Minor Ghosts show up with Major Ghosts, and the Major Ghosts rule the House, then the Minor Ghosts tend to compound the negativity and make the Major Ghosts more afflicting in nature. They gang up and cause further affliction. This is the worst scenario in Polestar Astrology, as it sort of adds gasoline to the flame. It adds deeper dimensions of negative emotion to the already empowered Ghost, which makes it stronger. That being said, it is important that we don't get too dramatic about Ghost affliction, as Ghosts are weak in nature. "Strong Ghost" is an oxymoron. But they can be persistent, like cigarettes, and these kinds of Ghosts thrive and feed off negative emotions. They are their food. The more you indulge anger, fear, self-doubt, and so on, the "stronger" Ghosts get, meaning the more they get entrenched in their pattern.

We will now discuss the Minor Ghost Stars in general, but again, we will not walk them through the Twelve Houses because they do not cause major patterns of Fate. Think of them like flavors or subtle dimensions of negative emotion. As such, they are really quite simple in their interpretation and should not be overthought.

HUO XING (火星)—THE FIRE STAR

NAME AND TRANSLATION:
Huo Xing (火星), the Fire Star

Huo, 火—fire; fiery, ablaze. a) start a fire, set fire to, enkindle. b) torch, brand, firebrand. 2 one of the 5 "agents" or "phases" in wuxing theory, having symbolic correlations with the direction south, the season summer, the color red, planet Mars, etc. 3 or 火星 huoxing, fire-star, Antares; also, alt. name for xin 心, "Heart," constellation, one of the 28 lunar lodgings, comprised of 3 stars, α (Antares), σ, τ Scorpii, in the eastern quadrant (Qinglong 青龍 orcanglong 蒼龍) of the sky. In early texts and through med. times 火星 huoxing does not ref. Mars (which is Ying huo 熒惑). a) 大火 dahuo, Grand Fire, same as preceding, and also the name of one of the 12 Jupiter stations, comprising the lunar lodgings di 氐, fang 房, and xin 心.[1]

Xing, 星—star; astral, sidereal, star-like; e.g., 星漢 xinghan, "the Han River in the stars, the starry Han," i.e., the Milky Way. 2 silver-speckles of hair partly gray. 3 one of the 28 lunar lodgings, comprised of stars in Hydra and Leo, in the southern quadrant (chiniao 赤鳥) of the sky. a) 星紀 xingji, one of the 12 Jupiter stations, comprising the lunar lodgings dou 斗 and niu 牛.[2]

The translation here is literal, and we call this the Fire Star. However, it is also an astronomical term that refers to the planet Mars. So, although it has the same name in Chinese, and we can translate it as Mars, in Polestar Astrology, this Star does not refer to Mars and should not be confused with the planet. It is a Minor Ghost, and so we translate it as the Fire Star, as it represents fiery, negative emotions.

ELEMENT: Yang Fire

TRADITIONAL IMAGE: A young, brash military officer with glaring eyes, unsheathing a weapon in an attacking stance[3]

GHOST PROFILE: An Ancestral Ghost that possibly died in a fire, explosion, accident, gunfight, or the like, who died angry and frustrated, with hatred and blame

RESOLUTION/EXORCISM: Resolved when we release and are no longer controlled by anger, frustration, or angst; this Star turns to clarity, bravery, and decisive action

LUMINOUS PLACEMENT: Tiger, Horse, and Dog Palaces

DIMINISHED PLACEMENT: None

AFFILIATIONS: None

As just mentioned, Huo Xing, literally "Fire Star," is also the Chinese term for the planet Mars, but in Polestar Astrology, this does not refer to Mars and should not be confused with the planet or any of its Western or Indian astrological interpretations. We call Huo Xing the Fire Star, and it is often understood as a Yinyang pair with Ling Xing, the Water or Ringing Star. Again, as a Minor Ghost it does not represent major patterns of Fate but rather more subtle patterns of negative emotion inherited from a troubled Ancestor. It is always generally inauspicious, but its resolution can become wisdom if properly worked with.

The Fire Star is an Ancestral Ghost who lived a fiery life or died a fiery death, and this death may have been sudden. The literal interpretation is that they died in a fire, explosion, accident, or gunfight—a situation in which they may have burned up, hurt violently, or been attacked by an outside force. This death may have been an accident, but it also may have been caused by compulsive, impulsive, impatient, or fiery action that was taken without careful thought and with total disregard. It is also assumed that this Ancestor died with a mind full of anger, frustration, hatred, or blame. If no Ancestor died in such a violent way, then it is likely that this Star represents a more or less normal Ancestor who lived an ordinary life but was consumed by fiery emotions in such a way that they died with unresolved anger or blame, which you now inherit.

These emotions are incomplete and without memory, so they do not cause reliable or predictable Fate patterns; rather, they add a dimension of immaturity, impatience, restlessness, impulsiveness, and mishaps from rash behavior, outbursts, or poor judgment. The Fire Star causes fiery emotions in whatever House it shows up in. It is, therefore, pretty easy to interpret. Wherever it shows up, you get frustrated, angry, and struggle against obstacles. Wherever it is, it creates instability and anxiety. The key here is that you blame others for those obstacles and perceive them as coming from outside yourself. The Fire and Water Stars are both "blame" Stars: One is inward, and one is outward. The Fire Star is outward, and it causes you to point the finger and blame others, life, the world, Fate, and so on, for your struggles. You may feel persecuted, attacked, or judged, and therefore, you get defensive.

If the Fire Star shows up in the Ming Palace, then this blame and these emotions can become a central theme in your life, and this House is probably the most significant placement for Huo Xing. If it shows up in the Ancestors Palace, you will struggle with anger and resentment and blame your parents or family. In the Youth Palace, you will struggle and get frustrated with your siblings; in the Partners Palace, with your partner; in the Offspring Palace, with your kids; and so on. You can interpret the rest.

The Fire Star is like a fire: When it burns, it can get out of control. When you get possessed by Huo Xing, you may lash out and yell, start an argument or fight, or punch a wall for seemingly no reason. These kinds of outbursts tend to pass, but if they are continually indulged, it can lead to anger issues. Getting angry and lashing out can also lead to serious consequences. This Star can also undermine your resolution of Fate due to blaming others and not taking responsibility.

When it shows up with other Ghosts, Huo Xing tends to burn harder and faster and cause more damage. It easily gangs up with other Ghosts to create affliction, more tantrums, more intensity, and possibly more violence and destruction. It can be meteoritic and short-lived, or it can smolder for a long time without self-reflection. If it shows up with stronger Stars, it is easily eclipsed in severity, but it tends to make them moody and adds a subtle dimension of frustration to them. It can simply cause impetuousness, youthful folly, arrogance, and ineptitude.

The Fire Star is resolved when we stop getting angry, stop blaming others, and take responsibility for our actions. When we can control our anger with mindfulness and become aware of whatever patterns of blame are undermining us, this Ghost is on its way to being resolved. It can sometimes be resolved quickly, through a big dramatic event and a single incident, but sometimes it takes time to work out a pattern of conduct. When Huo Xing is resolved, anger and blame turn to clarity, decisiveness, courage, bravery, and confidence.

LING XING (鈴星)—THE WATER OR RINGING STAR

NAME AND TRANSLATIONS:

Ling Xing (鈴星), the Water Star, the Siren Star, the Ringing Star

> *Ling,* 鈴—grelot, folly-bell, croatal, jingler, small clapper-bells used on horses or carriages. a) onom. [onomatopoeia] of preceding sound. 2 (med.) 鈴鼻 lingbi, grommet, eyehole, for attaching an object with string.[4]
>
> *Xing,* 星—star; astral, sidereal, star-like.[5]

The first Chinese character here refers to a bell, so the more literal translation is Ringing Star or Bell Star. Ling Xing is sometimes translated as the Siren Star, as it implies a kind of alluring or eerie music. However, here we understand it to be in a Yinyang pair with the Fire Star, so we call it the Water Star, and it represents the "waterier" negative emotions.

ELEMENT: Yin Water, Yin Fire

TRADITIONAL IMAGE: A young military officer disarmed, shackled, and imprisoned, in a cowering, frightened stance[6]

GHOST PROFILE: An Ancestral Ghost that possibly died of drowning, from being crushed in an accident, in a coma or from protracted terminal illness, or who died in fear, with hopelessness, terror, anxiety, and self-blame

RESOLUTION/EXORCISM: Resolved when we let go of attachments, conquer our fear and anxiety, and stop blaming ourselves for our mistakes; fear then turns to wisdom

LUMINOUS PLACEMENT: Tiger, Horse, and Dog Palaces

DIMINISHED PLACEMENT: None

AFFILIATIONS: None

Ling Xing, the Water or Ringing Star, is in many ways the opposite of the Fire Star, which is why it is in a Yinyang pair with it. They are both "blame" Stars, and while the Fire Star is Yang and causes us to look outward and blame others, the Water Star is Yin and causes us to turn inward and blame ourselves. Traditionally, these are seen to be related to two different kinds of death. The Fire Star is about being burned, so you die feeling attacked by an outside force that is burning you, and this causes you to struggle against it. The Water Star is about being "drowned," dying in water, which may not be that painful at first, but it is cold, surrounds you, crushes you, and invades you on the inside as opposed to from the outside. You die feeling helpless. You may thrash and try to swim, but you can't. You try to breathe but can't. You panic, but the nature of drowning is slow and offers a lot of time to think, blame yourself, and die with inward terror, hopelessness, and anxiety. This kind of death is said to create a different kind of Ghost, a Water Ghost.

So, if you have an Ancestor who drowned, then this Ghost is pretty straightforward. If not, then we understand this as an Ancestor who died with a lot of unresolved, watery conflicting emotions, feeling helpless or hopeless. They may have also died in an accident in which they were crushed or died slowly, blaming themselves for what happened. They may have died slowly from a long, protracted terminal illness or disease. They may have died in a coma, drug overdose, or during surgery. The key is that they died slowly, painfully, internalized, and most important, blaming themselves, wondering what they did wrong and what they could have done better or differently, or full of guilt or shame. If you do not have an Ancestor who died in such a dramatic way, then it is likely that this Star simply represents a more or less normal Ancestor who lived an ordinary life but was consumed by these kinds of watery emotions in such a way that they died with unresolved fear, hopelessness, or self-blame issues, which you now inherit.

Like the emotions linked to the Fire Star, these watery emotions are incomplete and without memory, so they do not cause reliable or predictable Fate patterns; rather, they add a dimension of inexplicable or irrational fear, anxiety, trauma, and emotional turmoil to whatever House Ling Xing shows up in. The Water Star creates dramatic, overemotional, and clingy attachment. It is whiny, fearful, self-centered, and complaining. It exaggerates emotions and creates sentimentality, separation, and disappointment.

Again, the big difference from the Fire Star is that, here, you turn inward and blame yourself for your troubles. This creates low self-esteem, self-doubt, self-loathing, and even self-hatred, which are still forms of self-cherishing. The Water Star causes you to abandon hope, give up, stay home, not try, and then hate yourself for it. It can cause you to project irrational fears, catastrophize, and imagine the worst possible scenario. It can create nihilism and pessimism. The Water Star causes these kinds of watery emotions in whatever House it appears in.

So, if Ling Xing shows up in the Ming Palace, these emotions can become a central theme in life, and this House is Ling Xing's most significant placement. If it shows up in the Offspring Palace, then you will have anxiety, fear, and hopelessness around being a parent; in the Pleasure Palace, you will be shy, afraid, and timid about enjoying yourself, and you may even fear having fun. If it shows up in the career Houses, then self-doubt, anxiety, and attachment can undermine your career. And so on—you can interpret the rest.

Wherever the Water Star appears, you become a whiny victim—fearful, inflexible, and so on. If it shows up with other Ghost Stars, it tends to get more dramatic, and the watery quality can make the affliction seem interminable. This creates a more intense inner experience of negative emotions rather than an outer drama like the Fire Star does. Here, further affliction just makes the internalized experience of suffering more intense. If this Minor Ghost shows up with stronger Stars, it, again, just makes them moody. The Royal Court mostly eclipses it, but it can add subtle dimensions of self-doubt, fears, anxieties, and so on that slow down the process of resolving Fate and make it more protracted and drawn out.

The Water Star is resolved when we let go of attachments and conquer our fears. We may have to do exposure therapy or force ourselves to do things that scare us: Speak in public, apply for the job, ask them out on a date, go to the party, and so on. Get out of your comfort zone and break out of your shell, and fear can turn to cautious confidence. We must also stop blaming ourselves, falling on our swords, and realize that the world doesn't revolve around us. We may always want to take responsibility and the blame for everything, but this is selfish. No one cares. As this Ghost resolves, hopelessness, pessimism, and paranoia can turn to hard-boiled realism and wisdom. It turns to healthy self-knowledge. Resolving this Star tends to be longer and more drawn out, but it can be a cathartic release when you confront a big fear.

QING YANG (擎羊) OR YANG REN (羊刃)—THE GOAT BLADE OR SACRIFICIAL STAR

NAME AND TRANSLATIONS:

Qing Yang (擎羊) or Yang Ren (羊刃), the Goat Blade Star, Sacrificial Star

Qing, 擎—lift up, raise; hold up, hold toward. 2 (med.) take away, remove.[7]

Yang, 羊—sheep, goat; ovine.[8]

Ren, 刃—blade; sword-blade, knife-edge. a) by synecdoche, gen. term for swords, halberds, other bladed weapons. 2 to run through (with a blade), dispatch.[9]

This Star has two common names—Qing Yang and Yang Ren—but we will refer to it as Yang Ren for simplicity. Both names contain the character Yang (羊), "goat," and refer to the tradition of ritually sacrificing a goat to Ancestors, Spirits, or Gods. The name Yang Ren contains the character for "knife," Ren (刃), and is an image of the specific blade used to kill goats in ritual, so we call this the Goat Blade Star or Sacrificial Star.

ELEMENT: Yang Metal, Yang Fire

TRADITIONAL IMAGE: An ageless, genderless shaman or priest, wearing a cap and vest of the sacrificial rites, holding the sacrificial knife in one hand and saluting with the other[10]

GHOST PROFILE: An Ancestor who sacrificed their life so that others could live or survive; an Ancestral Ghost who was murdered, executed, or died on the battlefield or during medical treatment with a sense of loss, pain, and self-sacrifice for others, the greater good, and so on

RESOLUTION/EXORCISM: Resolved through a significant act of sacrifice or loss that turns into something positive or just

LUMINOUS PLACEMENT: Ox, Dragon, Goat, and Dog Palaces

DIMINISHED PLACEMENT: None

AFFILIATIONS: None

For simplicity's sake, we will call this Yang Ren, the Goat Blade Star, as it is the more common name. It is possible that "Goat Blade" refers to the constellation this Star is in, and that the constellation looks like the traditional blade used to sacrifice goats in religious rituals. In traditional Buddhist iconography, dakinis and other deities are often depicted holding a sacred blades, swords, or knives called ***kartikas*** or ***kilas*** in Sanskrit and ***drigugs*** or ***phurbas*** in Tibetan. There are similar terms in Chinese, but here we call it Yang Ren, the Goat Blade, as these blades were often hooked in such a way as to cut the throat of a goat and drain them of blood very quickly.

The energy of the Goat Blade Star is fierce, wrathful, and transfixing, as this tool was used in rituals for exorcism, weather manipulation, meditation, and blessings. Here, it refers to the exorcism of an Ancestral Ghost through your act of sacrifice or loss. This sacrifice may be traumatic and painful, but it is done with wrathful wisdom that turns into something positive, liberating, or just.

Yang Ren represents an Ancestor, sometimes beneficent, who died in the act of making a sacrifice so that others could live, escape, or gain benefit in some way. It can also refer to an Ancestor who was unjustly murdered or executed or who died on the battlefield or during medical treatment with a sense of loss, pain, and self-sacrifice—trying to help others, serve the greater good, and so on. Their act was possibly noble or at least well-meaning, but it was incomplete, as they died in the process. Yang Ren comes to you to complete this sacrifice and free it. As this is an image of a knife, it also represents everything associated with knives, blades, or weapons, which in the Health or Offspring Palace can represent surgery.

Just about every culture on Earth sacrificed goats or other animals during religious rituals. It was prevalent, although today, many probably consider it barbaric. The idea of sacrificing an animal is simple: You perform a rite or ritual and invoke a connection to the dead, the Ancestors, the Spirit World, the Underworlds, Heaven, or wherever you want to communicate. You then kill the animal, and as it is "crossing over" to the other side, you shout your prayers, offerings, blessings, requests, and so on across, and their dying spirit carries it over to the land of the dead. The animal is treated very well until the end; they are honored, and it is considered a blessing for the animal to die in such a way. They are often eaten, and every piece of the animal is used so as not to be wasted.

The Goat Blade Star means we are put on the altar as the sacrificial lamb to our Ancestors. We must make some kind of sacrifice in life or experience some type of significant loss in whatever

House it shows up in. This is usually a form of self-sacrifice and may involve stepping up in a big way. If Yang Ren shows up with stronger Stars, especially the Emperor, then that self-sacrifice may be crucial to resolving our Fate. If it shows up with more Ghosts instead, then this Star often represents some form of loss, trauma, upheaval, or hero's trial in life, where we go through a period of hardship and suffering and come out on the other side a better person. So, although this is considered inauspicious in the short term, it is generally regarded as positive in the long run. No matter what, this has the potential to be the kind of sacrifice or hardship that turns you into a better person. With Yang Ren, you will say, *Even though that was difficult, I would not be the person I am today had I not gone through that—had I not lost that person, that job, all my money*, and so on.

So, this Star is easy to interpret in each House. In the Ming Palace, self-sacrifice or loss will be central to your whole Fate. In the Ancestors Palace, you may be Fated to lose a parent early or sacrifice something to repair the relationship or for them to heal. In the Wealth Palace, you may be Fated to lose or offer money, give it away to someone in need, or sacrifice something important to attain it. In the Health or Offspring Palace, the Goat Blade Star can indicate a surgery or medical procedure you must undergo in order to heal or to procreate. In the Partners Palace, you may divorce or lose someone only to meet your life's love sometime later. You can interpret the rest.

Remember, the sacrifice will likely be hard or painful, but it will have a beneficial outcome in the long run. And you must first make the sacrifice to receive the benefit. It is up to you to determine what this sacrifice is. However, it may not be apparent until long after; you will look back and see that you had to go through a sacrifice or hardship to become a better person. Hindsight, as they say, is twenty-twenty. Whatever it is, it may suck when you are going through it. It may include painful generosity, losing inessentials, giving up needless luxury, spiritual austerity, and renunciation, and it may feel like a "dark night of the soul," a hero's trial, or a long journey home after defeat. All this may not feel optimistic, but it is.

TUO LUO (駝羅)—THE HUMPBACK OR REJECTION STAR

NAME AND TRANSLATIONS: Tuo Luo (駝羅), the Humpback Star, the Rejection Star

Tuo, 駝—camel (*Camelus bactrianus*), the 2-humped bactrian camel. a) hump-backed. 2 Use a pack animal to carry a burden on its back.[11]
Luo, 羅—bird-net, bird-snare; web, mesh, retiary. a) ensnare(d), net(ted), enmesh(ed); catch, capture. 2 silk-gauze or chiffon in net weave; gossamer. a) veil(ed); filmy; finely stretched; e.g., a) set around, lie around; envelop.[12]

The character Tuo (駝) means "hump" or "humpback" and is also the Chinese word for camel. Luo (羅) refers to a trap used to ensure birds. In Polestar Astrology, these characters refer to an evil nature spirit caught in such a trap by a witch and deformed as punishment for its wrongdoings. So, we translate this as the Humpback Star in the image of a hunchback demon.

ELEMENT: Yin Metal

TRADITIONAL IMAGE: A hunchback demon, naked, skinny, greenish sickly body and deformed face with bulging eyes, wheezing breath, cowering in a frightened posture[13]

GHOST PROFILE: An Ancestral Ghost who died in an accident or from injuries, who had a slow, agonizing, and painful death and was possibly disfigured, mutilated, or dismembered; an Ancestor who was vicious, petty, unrepentant, vengeful, and full of deceit and trickery

RESOLUTION/EXORCISM: Resolved through repentance, apology, taking responsibility, forgiveness, and self-reflection; resolved when we let go of revenge and hatred

LUMINOUS PLACEMENT: Ox, Dragon, Goat, and Dog Palaces

DIMINISHED PLACEMENT: None

AFFILIATIONS: None

Tuo Luo is probably the darkest of the Four Minor Ghosts. The Chinese characters used for this Star vary, including 陀羅, 陀螺, and 駝羅, which are all pronounced Tuo Luo and have several meanings, but the characters 駝羅 most capture the image of this Star, which we translate as the Humpback Star. These characters imply both the image of a humpback but also a trap used to ensnare, which captures the story behind the Humpback Ghost.

This is the image of an ancient nature spirit who enjoyed hurting and toying with others with petty deceit and trickery. Tuo Luo was unrepentant and vicious. The story goes that a witch, shaman, or probably Daoist priest captured this evil spirit in a trap and used magic to punish it for its wrongdoings. In the process, Tuo Luo became twisted and deformed. Tuo Luo is described as a hunchback demon: naked, skinny, with a greenish, sickly body and deformed face and bulging eyes, wheezing breath, cowering in a frightened posture. The image is exactly like the character Gollum as depicted in the *Lord of the Rings* trilogy, both physically and in personality. If you want to understand this Star, watch those movies, read the books, and study Gollum. Gollum is the Humpback Ghost—deeply rotten to the core and full of revenge and hatred but, beneath, weak and rejected.

As an Ancestral Ghost, this Star refers to an Ancestor who possibly died from injuries from an accident and who may have had an arduous and agonizing death. They may have even been disfigured, mutilated, maimed, or tortured. Their death was traumatic, and they had a long time to suffer. Others may have inflicted their death, but ultimately it was self-caused, and they likely died full of feelings of repulsion, hatred, rejection, and wanting revenge on the people who did this to them. It is also likely that they lived this way, as most people die the way they lived. They may have been sneaky, suspicious, petty, resentful, and deceitful in life. They may have experienced a great deal of trauma themselves, which they never healed, and so they let it twist them into a bad person. Tuo Luo is a generational trauma that not only failed to be resolved but got worse and turned into something deformed and dark. If you have no such Ancestor who died horrifically, they may still have lived in such a way and died alone, rejected, bitter, and with a mind full of resentment and anger for their self-imposed suffering.

As such, Tuo Luo is always an inauspicious Star, and whatever House it appears in creates feelings of loathing, rejection, and pain. It creates suffering, adversity, selfishness, isolation, confusion, and excessive thinking and feeling that bends us toward bitterness, revenge, and hate. It turns us into Gollum. This Ancestral Ghost is not "strong" like Qi Sha, but it is similar in its trickery and difficulty to resolve, for it will fight to survive. Like Gollum, Tuo Luo is bitter to the end, will do anything to survive, and avoids taking responsibility. It will especially create feelings of self-loathing and rejection that it will cover up by lashing out at others, lying, or gas-lighting; it will always tangle things, muddy the waters, and avoid criticism. But the Humpback Star is not strong; it is weak, cowardly, and in pain. So, wherever it appears, we must self-reflect and acknowledge this ugly part of ourselves. This Star asks us, ***Can we eat bitter? Can we accept rejection, adversity, and criticism without lashing out, deceiving, or taking revenge?***

If it shows up with stronger Stars, then Tuo Luo is eclipsed in its overt negativity, but it still adds subtle dimensions of all the above characteristics. It will add complex negativity to the process of resolving Fate. If it shows up alone or with more Ghost Stars—especially with Qi Sha, as they feed off each other—then it tends to compound the negativity and create drama and bitter tangles of Fate. The Humpback Star is especially devious alone and with other Ghosts, but even with stronger Stars, it can create hardship, as it always feels like a victim and wants to take revenge or get back at people.

If Tuo Luo shows up in the Ming Palace, then this bitterness and revenge becomes a central pattern of Fate, and it may become an intricate part of your Character that you must resolve. In the Youth Palace, Tuo Luo essentially creates a traumatic, harsh, and emotionally uneven childhood or sibling relations. In the Partners Palace, it will cause patterns of argument, abuse, and revenge, ending relationships or tangling them in bitter deceit. In the Health Palace, it can cause injuries, chronic illness, and complex mental and emotional problems. And so on—by now you can interpret the rest.

How is this Ghost resolved? With kindness and self-reflection. Wherever the Humpback Star appears, we must eat bitter, take responsibility, hold our tongue, and check our actions and reactions. We must not blame others or seek revenge. We must be honest with ourselves and others. Most important, we must repent and be remorseful, confess our wrongdoings, and seek forgiveness.

THE FOUR INCIDENTALS

THE NEXT CATEGORY OF MINOR STARS is called the Four Incidentals, and it includes You Bi (右弼), the Right Assistant Star; Zuo Fu (左輔), the Left Assistant Star; Lu Cun (祿存), the Storehouse Star, and Tian Yao (天姚), the Beauty Star. While all the Lesser Stars are considered "Ghosts," these four Stars are more like gentle guardian spirits. So far, all the Ghosts have been quite negative, but these four Stars are all generally positive and auspicious in whatever House they appear in. These Stars are minor Beneficial Ancestors who hang around after having resolved their human Fate, acting as protectors and benevolent spirits to bestow minor boons, blessings, and support to all their living Ancestors, appearing from time to time to help you and the rest of the family. These are not "strong" Beneficial Ancestors like the Royal Court and do not represent significant patterns of Fate. So, if they show up alone in a House, then that House is still an Empty Court.

The Four Incidentals are weak in nature and may be, as the name suggests, "incidental," meaning they can represent a single instance of good Fate or temporary condition rather than an ongoing pattern. That being said, they can represent multiple instances, meaning they may show up a handful of times throughout your life before they are finished with you; still, that is what they are: incidents, not patterns. These incidents can come and go and can often be found through Progression Charts rather than in the Natal Chart, but we will get to that later.

These Stars are like fairy godparents or guardian angels or spirits who watch over you and show up at opportune moments to grant a small blessing or helpful nudge or to offer a path out of a tangled pattern of Fate through a small opportunity. They open doors, send signs, whisper wisdom, and grant boons to help gently nudge the resolution of Fate along in whatever House they appear in, as well as in the Houses that are proximal and opposite to that House.

The Four Incidentals also work as servants to the Royal Court and are more auspicious when they show up with the Emperor or any of the Four Rulers. Wherever they appear, they link that House to the Stars of the Royal Court, especially the Emperor and Empress, and act as messengers to create a network of help and communication throughout the chart.

YOU BI (右弼)—THE RIGHT ASSISTANT STAR

NAME AND TRANSLATIONS: You Bi (右弼), the Right Assistant, Female Helper Star

> *You*, 右—right (hand, side, etc.). a) traditionally, the side of honor, to which priority is given. b) the side where a warrior places himself in a war-chariot. 2 equivalent to west, deriving from the viewpoint of the ruler who sits facing south. 3 ⊙ 佑 you, aid, assist.[1]
>
> *Bi*, 弼—frame used for maintaining a bow's shape when it is unstrung. a) to correct; keep right, maintain. 2 assist(ant), aid(e). a) sustain; uphold, assist. 3 "Straightener," name of one of the 2 supplementary or "hidden" stars of the Northern Dipper (the other is → 輔 fu), being an invisible star located amid the Dipper's bowl.[2]

This translation is straightforward: You (右) means "right," Bi (弼) means to uphold or assist, and the right side is traditionally considered Yin or female, so we translate this as Right Assistant or Female Helper Star.

ELEMENT: Yin Water

ZUO FU (左輔)—THE LEFT ASSISTANT STAR

NAME AND TRANSLATIONS: Zuo Fu (左輔), the Left Assistant, Male Helper Star

> *Zuo*, 左—left side, ant. 右 you, right side. The relative values of left and right depended on context. Anciently, the master stood on the left side of the chariot. For the ruler, who ceremonially faced south, left was east, the direction of the rising sun and more auspicious than west. In office titles prefaced with "left" and "right," the occupant of the "left" appointment usu. took precedence. But left was often the inferior side, → 3 below. 2 cmpd., 左右 zuoyou, left and right, to the left and right, esp. those to the left and right of the ruler, close advisers, attendants and acolytes; also, all around; also, when used with number, approximately; also, aid and assist, be at one's elbow; also, control, command; also, indirect term (hence honorific) for addressee of a letter.[3]
>
> *Fu*, 輔—side-supports, props, bulwark of cart. 2 buttress, prop, stabilize, sustain; assist, aide, second. a) euph. [euphemism] for loyal ministers and

dedicated vassals. 3 near vicinity or near suburbs of capital city; vicinage, adjunct region. 4. "Sustainer," name of one of the 2 supplementary or "hidden" stars of the Northern Dipper (the other is → 弼 bi), identified with Alcor in Western astronomy, being a companion star to Mizar which is the penultimate star of the Dipper's handle.[4]

This translation is also straightforward: Zuo (左) means "left," Fu (輔) is another character that means to uphold or assist, also referring to loyal ministers of the Emperor, and the left side is traditionally considered Yang or male, so we translate this as Left Assistant or Male Helper Star.

ELEMENT: Yang Earth

You Bi, the Right Assistant Star, and Zuo Fu, the Left Assistant Star, are a Yinyang pair (with the Right Assistant being Yin and the Left Assistant being Yang), and so we will discuss them together. These Stars are minor Beneficial Ancestors and act like guardian spirits, heralds, or messengers. They have resolved their human Fate, and they hang around to finish up and help the Ancestral line as we all move on together. They are not headed toward Great Completion like the Royal Court, but instead, they are headed toward the Spirit World as something more like fairies.

The two Assistants work together, creating connections and helping wherever they appear, especially if they arrive in the same House together. If they are in different Houses, then those two Houses will also become linked. These Stars are like the servants you see trailing behind the Emperor, taking orders and doing their bidding. They act as ministers, messengers, and helpers. They are associated with transitory good Fate, and they show up in subtle and unexpected ways in life, sometimes by temporarily possessing people you know or interjecting in situations to create opportunities. They are also especially helpful to Stars in the Houses that they are proximal or next to, both before and after, and to the Houses at 120 and 180 degrees (in a trine and opposite). These Houses also become linked and support each other in the resolution of Fate.

You Bi, the Right Assistant Star, is the Yin or Female Helper, and it is associated with the Empress. It tends to be the stronger, more worldly and grounded Assistant. Its nature is optimistic, and it brings about surprising good fortune, luck, and opportunity. It possesses people in your life, acting as a guide to encourage timely help and show you the way out of afflicting Fate. This may manifest as opportunities, advice, connections, and so on. This help is subtle and gentle, but it can be powerful and well timed when it shows up to the rescue. However, you must always activate these opportunities by recognizing and acting upon them. Otherwise, they pass. We must listen to advice and trust our gut when good opportunities arrive. We only get so many chances to resolve Fate.

So, if You Bi appears in the Ming Palace, you will have a significant opportunity to shape and resolve Fate through a given juncture, and you will generally have a beneficial spirit looking out for you in resolving Fate. The junctures will be subtle but powerful in the overall big picture of your Fate. If You Bi shows up in the Youth Palace, you will have a guardian spirit helping you as a child; they may be an "imaginary friend" or spirit only children can see. If it appears in the Wealth or Property Palace, it may offer some subtle financial opportunities or connections that help secure a home. In the career Houses, it can help arrange meetings, interviews, and make connections that help you progress. And so on.

Zuo Fu, the Left Assistant Star, is the Yang or Male Helper, and it is associated with the Emperor. It tends to be the more otherworldly, modest, and subtle influence of the two. While the Right Assistant tends to show up in real life, the Left Assistant shows up more in dreams and in the subconscious as intuition, gut feelings, instinct, and whispers telling you where to go. It can manifest as signs and omens and serendipitous synchronicity. It works through more spiritual and energetic means rather than worldly ones. Its nature is more generous but also more cryptic, as Zuo Fu works through symbols in the imaginal world, whereas You Bi shows up in the "real" world.

If Zuo Fu arrives in the Ming or Ancestors Palace, you may receive many messages, symbols, visions, and gut feelings that help guide you; this guardian spirit may be a significant but subtle companion in the resolution of Fate. In the Partners Palace, it may be a "rescue" telling you to choose a certain person or when to leave the wrong person. In the career Houses, it may manifest as instinct about taking a job, connecting with a certain person, or studying with a particular teacher. In the Wealth or Property Palace, it can be advantageous instincts to buy or sell or to move or stay put. And so on—you can figure out the rest.

These Stars cannot be made more powerful, but they also are not easily eclipsed. The negative Ghosts can afflict them, but these two tend to be clever and work around them to offer a way out of affliction. So, even if the Assistants show up with Ghosts, they will open doors and offer a path out, if you have the sensitivity to listen. However, Ghosts by nature make it hard to take good advice or make good choices. Therefore, if you lack subtlety, these Stars are easily missed.

LU CUN (祿存)—THE STOREHOUSE STAR

NAME AND TRANSLATION: Lu Cun (祿存), the Storehouse Star

Lu, 祿—favor(able), good fortune; benefice(nt). 2 official salary, emolument.[5]

Cun, 存—to exist, to deposit, to store, to keep, to survive. 1 exist materially, be present, survive, remain (ant. 亡 wang, defunct, perish, gone). a) keep safe, preserve. 2 keep in one's mind, preserve the thought of. 3 (Dao.) visualization technique of focused intention by which particular energies or deities are made sensibly present and actualized to a practitioner. 4 look for, seek; inquire after. a) do the same with the intention of providing aid or comfort, usu. from superior to inferior.[6]

This translation is also straightforward: It means wealth storage, to deposit or store good fortune, or literally to deposit your salary or paycheck in the bank. It refers to the royal storehouse, where the royal court would store gifts bestowed upon the emperor, so we call it the Storehouse Star.

ELEMENT: Yang Earth

The Lu Cun, or the Storehouse Star, is the image of a warehouse or depository of gifts; it is something like a bank, vault, or safe deposit box. In ancient China, it was part of the ritual of court to bring and present a gift to the emperor and empress before being allowed to speak. Anyone who came to the royal court had to make an offering, and all the offerings were then stored in the Lu Cun, the storehouse. So, this Star represents a repository of gifts understood to be the result of your past-life generosity or the generosity of your Ancestors, coming back to you in this lifetime at an opportune moment.

Traditionally, Lu Cun is also said to be related to your past life's generosity to monks and nuns. In short, this is a debt repayment, which will vary from person to person. It may be significant or minuscule, depending on your past-life generosity. Also, the more generous you are in this lifetime, the more you will pay it forward to your future Ancestors; this is just something to consider. If we are greedy and do not pay it forward, these gifts are squandered and can turn into negative Fate that hurts future generations.

The Storehouse Star often manifests as material or financial gains but can also come as a physical gift, act of service, or giving that comes without cost or as a transaction. It is just a payback, and as such, it is like a bag of gold coins going around the chart. This payback may be one-and-done, coming at a significant or opportune moment, or it can be a reservoir that comes back repeatedly to help you out. This is again based on your specific Ancestors or past-life generosity.

This Star is an Ancestral spirit who successfully resolved Fate through the wise management of resources and so is charged to remain around long enough to deliver this payback; once they provide it, they are resolved. It may take them a few deliveries if the payback is significant. The sense of this Star is that it is a gift and not directly linked to your hard work; it comes as a surprise or boon, seemingly without cause. It can be indirectly related to your hard work, as it may come along with a job, child, marriage, and so on, but it will seem like a gift or good fortune.

When it is enhanced with stronger Stars, Lu Cun is more associated with a timely incident, and it can manifest as a unique doorway out of affliction. This Ancestor will bring you a powerful, timeless moment of clarity, freedom, or enlightenment that creates a temporary junction in the cosmos you must step through. It may feel like déjà vu, serendipity, or what Chan/Zen calls *kensho* or *satori*. Once the moment passes, the Ancestor is resolved, and the opportunity passes too. So, recognize and make use of it, as it may only happen once. This is especially true when this Star appears in the Ming, Ancestors, Pleasure, or Career/Travel Palace.

In its more ordinary manifestation, the Storehouse Star arrives as gifts, money, opportunity, job offerings, and so on. It can be straight-up cash or property if it shows up in the Wealth or Property Palace. This can mean a promotion, bonus, inheritance, or settlement. If Lu Cun is in the Ancestors Palace, this gift may be given to you by a parent or grandparent. In the Partners Palace, it can come from or even be bestowed upon a partner. In the Offspring Palace, it may arrive with the birth of a child to help you out as a parent, or it may help your child in the form of a college or trust fund. In the career Houses, it can come as promotions or bonuses, gifts from friends or teachers, or as job opportunities and fortuitous connections. And so on.

Stronger Stars can enhance these benefits and may connect the gifts to the specific Ancestors associated with that Star. If Ghost Stars accompany Lu Cun, it is eclipsed and has almost no influence—the positive benefit is wasted—and it can even represent the greed, trickery, and stinginess of our Ancestors or of us during past lives. Again, it is essential not to be greedy with whatever this Star brings, as that will stop the benefit and possibly create negative patterns. So, watch out for entitlement, selfishness, stinginess, and so on. Enjoy the gift and take advantage of any benefits, but pay it forward. The more you give away, the more you get.

TIAN YAO (天姚)—THE BEAUTY STAR

NAME AND TRANSLATION: Tian Yao (天姚), the Beauty Star

> *Tian*, 天—refers to the sky or heavens; the highest cosmic principle or force.[7]
>
> *Yao*, 姚—handsome, beautiful, good-looking; feateous, featly; graceful, fine and featly, graceful and seemly.[8]

This translation is also straightforward: "heavenly beauty" or "heaven's grace." Heavenly Beauty sounds a little too significant, as it is a very weak Star, so we call it the Beauty Star.

ELEMENT: Yin Water

Finally, we arrive at Tian Yao, the Beauty Star. This is the most insignificant and "weak" of these Minor Stars, so there is little to say about it. It should not be emphasized, but it can represent a temporary and delicate moment or windfall in life, and it is the only one of these Minor Stars that can come with a sense of haunting or negative consequences. It represents beauty, romance, and vanity, and it can be associated with instances of Fate where our physical appearance can shape or alter our path in life, for better or worse. It is also the most likely to involve a single incident bestowed at the moment when this Ancestor resolves.

This Ancestor died young and potentially with unresolved romantic longings. It suggests that they were elegant, handsome, beautiful, or graceful and died with a sense of immature vanity or regret that they never married or never used their beauty to their advantage. It is a delicate and fleeting spirit that lingers and can either offer a moment of good Fate or transform into promiscuity, lewdness, or depravity. They come to you to provide a moment of release that works out this lingering Fate.

If it is unafflicted by other Ghost Stars or enhanced with Stronger Stars, Tian Yao can create a beautiful or inspired spiritual moment when this Ancestral Ghost is resolved. It can create a fleeting experience of elegance, awe, inspiration, and freedom. This can be a compelling experience and offer bittersweet wisdom about the ephemeral nature of beauty, impermanence, and life itself. It can also attract others to you in a positive way, and it can offer moments of passion, romance, or intense love. These are fleeting, however, and indulging them can be short-lived but meteoric. Tian Yao can also represent a fleeting moment in which your appearance becomes a boon: You may get a job, meet a partner, make a friend, or receive an opportunity because of your perceived physical beauty, regardless of your actual looks—the Beauty Star possesses your beholder to your advantage.

If it is afflicted by other Ghost Stars, the Beauty Star can be eclipsed so entirely as to have no effect, or affliction can twist this delicate Star into a short-lived possession that fills you with lust and leads to a whirlwind of licentiousness. In this case, it can represent the negative consequences of physical beauty and can lead to a problematic instance of harassment, assault, or pursuit that is unwanted. You may also misuse your physical beauty to take advantage of others or manipulate people. This can also simply manifest as superficial immaturity and indulgence. Either way, this is a temporary, fragile, and fleeting influence and will not likely create a lasting impact. Again, this is a weak Star and likely to be a single incident that passes once this Ancestor is resolved.

THE ORPHAN SPIRITS

NOW THAT WE HAVE FINISHED DISCUSSING THE FOUR INCIDENTALS, we can discuss the Orphan Spirits. These are Tian Kui (天魁), the Leader Star; Tian Xi (天喜), the Happiness Star; Tian Yue (天鉞), the Halberd Star; De Jie (地劫), the Loss Star; Di Kong (地空), the Void or Empty Earth Star; Tian Xing (天刑), the Punishment Star; Tian Ma (天馬), the Travel or Heavenly Horse Star; and Hong Luan (紅鸞), the Red Bird Star.

These Stars are even weaker than the Four Incidentals, and as influences, they are broader and less specifically connected to your personal Ancestors. In a way, these are related to distant heavenly forces that govern everyone's lost Ancestors. So, these are "lost" or "orphaned" Ghosts drifting about, unable to move on. They may be connected to your personal Ancestors but are lost, abandoned, and struggling to resolve. As such, they are of a mixed auspice and generally negative. A few of these stars can have a beneficial influence, but it is minor, fleeting, and incidental.

Again, it is important to emphasize that these are weak Stars, and they cannot rule a House. If they show up alone in a House, that House is an Empty Court. Most of these Stars are incidentals, manifesting as a single incidence as the Ghost resolves through you. Again, they are a "one and done"—once they are resolved, you are finished with that Fate. That incident may be powerful and cathartic, but when it is over, it's over.

The Orphan Spirits do not represent patterns of Fate, and the Royal Court very easily eclipses them. In fact, if they show up with stronger Stars, they can almost be ignored. These can represent such minor incidents that you will hardly remember them. So, while it may be interesting to consider these Stars, it is imperative not to focus on them or exalt their importance. They are more like mosquitoes than anything else. This is because these Stars are far away, outside the sphere of direct Ancestral influence. They Stars are a cleanup crew, resolving wayward and lost spirits that linger. We all act to resolve lost Ghosts all the time through our ordinary human conduct, and often it takes little else to work these out.

A few of these Stars, specifically De Jie, the Loss Star, and Di Kong, the Void or Empty Earth Star, are considered ongoing patterns rather than incidents and can be difficult to resolve. These are the most pernicious of the Orphan Spirits, and it is because they are the weakest. Weaknesses are more challenging to resolve because they are hard to notice and grasp, and they can be so subtle and minor that we easily brush them off and ignore them. These are, again, like cigarettes: One is harmless, but over time, they undermine our health. However, if these two Stars show up with any of the Royal Court, especially the Four Rulers, they are eclipsed and become so minor it is safe to ignore them.

All these Stars are generally easy to resolve, so they can mostly be ignored, in fact. Occasionally, they can manifest as significant cathartic resolutions or subtle undermining patterns, but there is no secret to resolving them. Just be a kind and well-balanced human, and these influences will settle and likely resolve early in life. Any adult with a modicum of self-reflection who reads their Natal Chart will have resolved these long ago. Sometimes, these Stars can be significant in the Progressed Chart, but again, it is crucial not to exalt their importance.

These Stars can be said to be in a bardo or purgatory, waiting to be released.

TIAN KUI (天魁)—THE LEADER STAR

NAME AND TRANSLATION: Tian Kui (天魁), the Leader Star

Tian, 天—refers to the sky or heavens; the highest cosmic principle or force.[1]

Kui, 魁—ladle, dipper, scoop. a) the 4 stars making up the bowl of the Northern Dipper; also, ref. specifically to the 1st star, Dubhe. 2 leader, foremost, chief; principal. a) prominent, remarkable; outstanding; imposing. 3 mound, monticule.[2]

This translation is straightforward: "Heaven" simply indicates that this is a Star, and Kui refers to the Big Dipper, which here means leader, so we translate this as Leader Star.

ELEMENT: Yang Fire

Tian Kui, or the Leader Star, is the first and most beneficial of the Orphan Spirits. This is the distant, lingering echo of a steady and beneficial Patriarchal Ancestor who was a leader who successfully resolved their Fate. Here, they are stuck in the Bardo because they are looking for one last chance to help. They feel like they could have done a bit more, something extra, or made one final gesture to finish what they started.

Tian Kui manifests as an instance of courage, leadership, bravery, promotion, or opportunity to take charge, command respect, or stand up for yourself or others in a pivotal or beneficial moment that quickly resolves Fate. This may also be an act of "rescue," which could rescue you from bad habits or negative Fate, or it could be a Ghost possessing you to rescue someone and resolve themselves in the process. It can add a dimension of leadership or authority to a stronger Star and potentially boost you to leadership roles in your career. Look to the House in which this arrives to determine where this opportunity occurs.

TIAN XI (天喜)—THE HAPPINESS STAR

NAME AND TRANSLATION: Tian Xi (天喜), the Happiness Star

Tian, 天—refers to the sky or heavens; the highest cosmic principle or force.[3]

Xi, 喜—delight in, joy(ful), happiness usu. of a temporary nature; light-hearted(ness), glad(ness), mirth(ful). 2 felicitous, well-suited. 3 嬉 xi, diverting 熙 xi, shine brightly, glory in.[4]

Again, this translation is simple "heaven" here refers to this as a Star, and Xi simply means happiness, so we translate this as Happiness Star.

ELEMENT: Yang Water

Tian Xi, or the Happiness Star, is the second of the Orphan Spirits. This Star is also the most positive but fleeting of the Orphan Spirits, and it is auspicious wherever it arrives. This is the distant, lingering, remnant happiness of a fairylike Minor Ancestor who sticks around in the Bardo looking for one last experience of joy, enjoyment, humor, laughter, and so on. They want to experience one more laugh, so they will possess you at some point in life and "haunt" you with enjoyment, humor, or joy. This can manifest as an inexplicable moment of getting the giggles, or it can manifest as a peak moment of pleasure followed by an experience of release. It can linger for a while and create a "perfect day," in which you have a fantastic day full of fun and happiness.

This Ancestor may possess you to relive its most significant experience of joy in a parallel moment, like a wedding, party, vacation, adventure, or sexual experience. It fills you with happiness and joy and then releases you, leaving you with the memory of the high. This can come out of nowhere and feel unrelated to anything happening in life, or it can coincide with a happy period in which the Ghost "rides" that experience vicariously with you. This is a single incident, and once it is gone, it is gone, which does not mean that you will not experience happiness again; it simply means that the Ancestor is finished. This Star is not strongly affected by surrounding Stars, so stronger Stars or further affliction makes little difference. Look to the House that this arrives in as a clue to where this possession will happen.

TIAN YUE (天鉞)—THE HALBERD STAR

NAME AND TRANSLATION: Tian Yue (天鉞), the Halberd Star

> *Tian*, 天—refers to the sky or heavens; the highest cosmic principle or force.[5]
>
> *Yue*, 鉞—battle ax, halberd, large ax with crescent-shaped blade that was attached to a long staff, used for beheadings and as object of authority wielded by honor guard of ruler, rarely in battle. 2 name of the star Propus (η Geminorum), in the lunar lodging "Well" (jing 井).[6]

Again, this translation is simple: "Heaven" refers to this as a Star, and Yue means battle ax or halberd, referring to a ceremonial ax attached to a long staff that is used in ritual.

ELEMENT: Yin Water

The next of the Orphan Spirits is Tian Yue, the Halberd or Heavenly Ax Star. As the name suggests, this is the image of the long ceremonial ax used in China for both beheadings and ceremonial rituals. It was wielded by the emperor's guards who stood watch over the royal court. It was heavy, clumsy, and rarely used in battle. It is associated with the military and martial arts, as well as the blind faith and militant discipline exhibited by servants of the emperor. As an Ancestral Ghost, this represents an Orphan Spirit who died on the battlefield long ago. They were probably just a young kid following orders. This Star means a pattern of struggle that temporarily haunts us, looking for a fight.

This Ghost is looking to finish its unresolved final moments on the battlefield. It manifests as an incident of heroism or as getting into a fight or into trouble. We get possessed and may dive into an act of heroism or belligerence, stand up for a friend or stranger as a protector in a dangerous situation, or take a blind leap of faith at the behest of another person. Once we have completed that act, this Ghost is resolved and moves on.

As a subtle influence, Tian Yue can add a dimension of militant discipline, fighting spirit, or focus to the House it arrives in. However, this is a very minor influence and more likely to be an incident. Look to the House it shows up in to see where this fighting spirit may occur: If it shows up in the Offspring Palace, you will do it for your kids, and so on.

DI JIE (地劫)—THE LOSS STAR

NAME AND TRANSLATION: Di Jie (地劫), the Loss Star

> *Di*, 地—earth, as paired with "heaven" (tian 天). a) (Budd.) 地獄 diyu, "earth-prison," hell; 地黃 dihuang, "yellow of earth" or 地髓 disui, "marrow of earth," foxglove (*Rehmannia glutinosa*), medicinal herb, the roots a dye-source for "imperial yellow" in med. times; 地節 dijie, "nodes of earth," alternate name for 萎蕤 weirui, sealwort (*Polygonatum odoratum*), medicinal herb; (Dao.) 地關 diguan, "earthly barrier," Dao. esoteric term for feet; (Dao.) 地戶 dihu, "earthly door," Dao. esoteric term for nose. 2 earth, as land, soil. a) territory. b) place, locality, site. c) terrain, topography. 3 floor; e.g., 地衣 diyi, "floor-clothing," i.e., carpet. 4 position, state or stage (of being), condition, situation.[7]
>
> *Jie*, 劫—pillage, plunder, despoil; rob; take by force; e.g., 劫略 jielüe, annex, appropriate. 2 imperil, menace, threaten; assault, raid; beset.[8]

This translation is not as straightforward: Literally, it means "to pillage the Earth," or "Earthly Loss," as this is the image of someone who died while being robbed and assaulted. Their Ghost wanders the earth, Di (地), looking for what was taken from them. So, we translate this as the Loss Star.

ELEMENT: Yang Fire

De Jie is in a Yinyang pair with Di Kong, the Void Star, as they both represent "Lost Ghosts," so we will discuss them together.

DI KONG (地空)—THE VOID OR EMPTY EARTH STAR

NAME AND TRANSLATIONS: Di Kong (地空), the Void Star, Empty Earth Star

> *Di*, 地—earth, as paired with "heaven" (tian 天).[9]
>
> *Kong*, 空—empty, void; vacant, unoccupied. a) hiatus, blank; gap. b) uninhabited area, wilderness; e.g., 空閑 kongxian, wasteland, desert. 2 space; the sky, the air; e.g., 碧空 bikong, the cyan void, elegant variation for 青天 qingtian, blue sky; (Dao.) 太空 taikong, Grand Emptiness, locus of Dao. stellar mansions. a)空同 or 空洞 kongtong (MC [Middle Chinese] khuwng-duwng), the hollow (of) space, hollow and cavernous. 3 hollow; insubstantial, immaterial; e.g., (Budd.) trns. of Skt. śunya, śunyata, the essential insubstantiality and illusoriness of all phenomena; 空無 kongwu, emptiness and nothingness. 4 vapid(ly), in vain, to no avail, pointless(ly). 5 (med.) (ADV) [adverb] do no more than VB, to VB and nothing else; e.g., 空飲 kongyin, just drink; drink it straight. a) (med.) sgl. or 空自 kongzi, personally, by oneself; alone. b) (med.) simple, plain, with nothing added; e.g., 空飯 kongfan, a plain meal. 6 transparent (of water).[10]

This translation is more straightforward: It means "empty earth" and refers to an empty grave. So, we translate this as the Empty Earth or Void Star.

ELEMENT: Yin Fire

Di Kong, the Void Star, is in a Yinyang pair with the De Jie, the Loss Star, so we will discuss them together. These Stars represent the "Lost Ghosts," Ghosts that are so long dead that they have forgotten being human as well as why they are stuck as Ghosts. This makes them particularly tricky to resolve, setting these two Stars apart from the rest of the Orphan Spirits, which are looking to resolve quickly through a single incident and act of possession. Most of the Orphan Spirits are lingering in the Bardo to finish one last piece of unfinished business, but the Loss and Void Star are lost and have forgotten what that business was. They, therefore, represent very subtle and weak patterns of haunting that can linger for a long time if they are not addressed. Once they are addressed, they resolve quickly, for they are simple in nature. The trick is that they are subtle, and these subtle negative emotions can be potent in the way that they can control our lives and cause misfortune.

De Jie, the Loss Star, is Yang and more active in the image of someone who was killed while being robbed a long time ago. Their Ghost is lost and wandering, looking for what was taken from it, possessed by the feeling of loss and wanting something back. But it cannot remember what, so it is just a hungry Ghost, full of wanting. It is not evil or aggressive, just consumed by loss, lack, and deprivation. It is the feeling of scarcity itself. So, this Ghost expends and wastes our energy, makes us sloppy and lazy, and wherever it shows up, it creates subtle feelings of melancholy, misplacement, and loss. It creates a phantom "want."

In the Wealth or Property Palace, De Jie can create ongoing patterns of scarcity and a poverty mindset. In the Health Palace, it can exhaust our Qi and cause us to waste away, longing for fulfillment and healing that don't come. In the Partners Palace, it can create an insatiable need for something no partner can fulfill. And so on—you can figure out the rest.

When it gangs up with other Ghosts, the Loss Star feeds on their negativity, and vice versa, which makes the feelings of loss and longing more intense and more challenging to resolve. If it shows up with the Royal Court, it is mostly eclipsed, nothing other than an occasional sense of melancholy for no reason. This is resolved when we feel fulfilled, complete, and satisfied, no longer wanting what we cannot have—and wanting what we do have.

Di Kong, the Void Star, is Yin and more passive and tends more toward feelings of groundlessness, hopelessness, and despair. It is the image of an empty grave, a long-dead Ghost that was unearthed and is wandering in a wasteland. This Ghost is consumed by wanting to get home and rest, but it is lost and doesn't know how to get home or even who and where it is. It is the feeling of hopelessness and despair. Wherever it shows up, we get feelings of being ungrounded and lost in an empty void; it creates nihilism and the feeling that life is meaningless. It creates inexplicable anxiety and feelings of grief. It brings about a lack of spirit or enthusiasm and creates resignation and feelings of futility.

So, Di Kong undermines whatever House it shows up in with all these negative emotions. And these emotions are compounded if it shows up with other Ghost Stars, as they all feed off each other's negativity. This Ghost can become a subtle theme of life in the Ming Palace. In the career Houses, it can make finding a path, friends, or success seem meaningless and futile. In the Pleasure Palace, it can cause you to abandon the hope of being happy or having fun. And so on. If the Void Star shows up with the Royal Court, it too is mostly eclipsed but can still undermine the stronger Stars with occasional hopelessness. This is resolved when we find true meaning and purpose, and we let go of that ungrounded hopelessness.

TIAN XING (天刑)—THE PUNISHMENT STAR

NAME AND TRANSLATION: Tian Xing (天刑), the Punishment Star

Tian, 天—refers to the sky or heavens; the highest cosmic principle or force.[11]

Xing, 刑—punish by mutilation, corporal disfiguring, "deform"; punish(ment); cf. 罰 fa, lighter punishment incl. fines. a) chastise physically; torture, cause to suffer. 2 mold; model; bring to proper form. a) correct formally; discipline by law.[12]

This translation is straightforward: "Heaven" refers to this as a Star, and Xing means "punishment," so we translate this as Punishment Star or Heaven's Punishment.

ELEMENT: Yang Fire

The next of the Orphan Spirits is Tian Xing, the Punishment Star. This is a dual image: It can be an Ancestor who was punished for their wrongdoings and is lingering out of a sense of guilt, looking to punish themselves to seek retribution. Or it can be an Ancestor who was unjustly punished for something they were innocent of; they linger, seeking justice and absolution of the crime. Either way, this Orphan Spirit haunts us with a sense of foreboding and impending doom.

Wherever Tian Xing shows up, we expect the worst and fear retribution. It can also create feelings of guilt and shame for no reason. This Ghost seeks to possess us to relieve its punishment or even to inflict punishment. This can manifest as an incident of hardship, punishment, retribution, justice, or comeuppance in whatever House it appears in. Once this experience has occurred, this Ghost resolves and moves on, and you are free. This is an experience of paying for the sins of our Ancestors.

The Punishment Star can also be a mandate to absolve an Ancestor of false charges. So, if you have an Ancestor who was unjustly accused and punished for a crime they did not commit, this Star can haunt you and charge you with a detective case to prove their innocence, especially if it is in the Ancestors Palace. If this is the case, then the Ghost will linger until this task is completed and be resolved when you clear their name. More often, though, this is an afflicting Star that brings about a punishment.

If Tian Xing shows up in the Youth Palace, this incident of punishment will happen in childhood. If it shows up in the Wealth Palace, you may experience lawsuits, bankruptcy, financial disaster, and so on. If it shows up in the Partners Palace, it can cause a period of relationship turmoil. In the Assistants Palace, you may be punished by a co-worker or friends. And so on. Wherever this Star appears, you can be temporarily possessed and make a bad decision that you then get punished for. Or you may be unjustly accused of doing something and experience unjust persecution. This experience then resolves the Ghost.

It is best to accept this to some degree. If you are unjustly accused, stand up for yourself and clear your name, as the truth will come out, but think of this as resolving Ancestral Fate and that something good will come to you in the wake of this punishment. If Tian Xing shows up with more Ghosts, this punishment can be calamitous or painful. With stronger Stars, it is generally eclipsed. Still, it can add a significant experience of punishment to your process of resolving Fate.

TIAN MA (天馬)—THE TRAVEL OR HEAVENLY HORSE STAR

NAME AND TRANSLATIONS: Tian Ma (天馬), the Travel Star, the Heavenly Horse Star

Tian, 天—refers to the sky or heavens; the highest cosmic principle or force.[13]

Ma, 馬—horse (*Equus caballus*); equine, e.g., 兵馬 bingma, war-horse, a blonk.[14]

This translation is very straightforward: We simply translate it as the Heavenly Horse or Travel Star, as it represents traveling on horseback.

ELEMENT: Yang Fire

The next of the Orphan Spirits is Tian Ma, the Heavenly Horse or Travel Star. This is the image of the winged horse, or Pegasus. In Tibetan, this is called the Lungta or Wind Horse. As an astronomical symbol, it is a powerful image, but as an influence in our chart, it is weak. This minor Ancestor successfully used immigration, innovation, or travel to resolve their Fate. This Ghost creates feelings of restlessness but also of whimsical freedom.

The Heavenly Horse Star relates to foreign travel, moving house, immigration, and so on. Wherever it shows up, we are Fated for an incident of travel and possibly to cut our losses and run. This is especially true in the Career/Travel Palace or Pleasure Palace. This Star can initiate change, activities, and movements. Wherever it appears, there will be much change until it is resolved. This Ghost is generally resolved when we make a big change, move, travel, and so on. It does not usually represent ongoing patterns but rather a single incident.

This Ancestor is looking to live out one last change or move to help us initiate a vital aspect of Fate resolution, so often this move is essential and a catalyst for important things in life. If Tian Ma shows up with other Ghost Stars, then it becomes the Crippled Horse, and it can signify that a move, trip, or change will bring about failure or struggle. Affliction can also indicate car accidents and injuries when traveling. If Tian Ma shows up with any of the Royal Court, then it can indicate the opposite: Travel will bring about important resolutions of Fate and may be a crucial aspect of that House. If it appears in the Youth Palace, this travel may occur in childhood. In any career House, it can be a trip or a move for a job that may bring about success. In the Pleasure Palace, it may be purely for fun. And so on—you can interpret the rest.

HONG LUAN (紅鸞)—THE RED BIRD OR PHOENIX STAR

NAME AND TRANSLATIONS: Hong Luan (紅鸞), the Red Bird Star, the Phoenix Star

> *Hong*, 紅—gen. term for light to medium-deep red, usu. lustrous, not dark reds; esp. (increasing in deepness) pink, cerise, rose, crimson; e.g., 紅粉 hongfen, pink powder (of women's makeup); 紅顏 hongyan, rosy-faced, i.e., young and healthy; 紅淚 honglei, tears of blood-red, normal tears all cried out and now weeping blood; 紅塵 hongchen, red dust, of the tumultuous mortal world. 2 紅藍 honglan, "pink indigo," safflower (*Carthamus tinctorius*); 紅花 honghua, safflower flowers, used medicinally. 3 紅嘴烏 hongzuiwu, red-billed daw, red-billed chough.[15]

> *Luan*, 鸞—fabulous bird similar to the "phoenix" (fenghuang 鳳凰) in occupying a position of high status and dignity among feathered creatures, though traditionally considered of somewhat less charisma; often symbolic of cultural elegance, literary talent, conjugal harmony; sometimes associated with feminine beauty and grace; e.g., 鸞鳳 luanfeng, simurgh and phoenix, men of comparably high worth and capacity, well-matched husband and wife; 鸞鏡 luanjing, simurgh mirror, i.e., mirror of lovely lady. 2 鑾 luan, harness-bells, esp. simurgh(-shaped)-bells, croatals; ruler's carriage.[16]

This translation is straightforward. We simply translate it as the Red Bird or Phoenix Star, as it is the image of the phoenix rising from the ashes.

ELEMENT: Yin Water

The last of the Orphan Spirits is Hong Luan, the Red Bird or Phoenix Star. This is one of the weakest Stars in Polestar Astrology, and it is rarely significant in the Natal Chart. In the Progression Chart, it becomes significant in the Ming, Travel, and Health Palaces, but otherwise, it is insignificant. This is the image of a phoenix rising from the ashes. As an Ancestral influence, this represents a Beneficial Ancestor who is lingering and waiting for one last opportunity to give an offering of rebirth before resolving for good.

This Star manifests as an incident of starting over, redefining or reinventing yourself, or recovering from an illness or injury. This may come at a low point in life, so an experience of rebirth or rising from the ashes can be compelling. Here, an Ancestor comes to save you and gives you a boost of Qi in an auspicious moment that catalyzes an experience of rebirth for you. That Ancestor is then resolved, and this influence is done.

You may experience this boost as auspicious good fortune that helps you in a rebirth or recovery, which can come in many forms. It is a gift and should be appreciated. It may be subtle, minor, or significant, but it arrives precisely when you need. This only happens once, so it is hard to find when this will occur in a chart and often easier to recognize in hindsight, as we never know when we will have to start over. If Hong Luan shows up in the Ming Palace, it may be significant and represent a big rebirth experience in life. In the Health Palace, it represents recovery from an illness or accident. In the Travel Palace, you may start over and reinvent yourself in a new place or job. In any other House, this Star is likely insignificant.

THE FOUR TRANSFORMERS

NOW THAT WE HAVE DISCUSSED THE ORPHAN SPIRITS, we can finish our exploration of Fate with the final four Stars we will discuss in this book: the Four Transformers. These are Hua Lu (化祿), the Salary or Prosperity Star; Hua Quan (化權), the Authority Star; Hua Ke (化科), the Examination Star; and Hua Ji (化忌), the Jealousy or Scandal Star. These Stars are unique and in a category of their own, as they are different from all the other Stars we have discussed. These Stars are somewhat mysterious, and it is not always straightforward to interpret them or predict their influence, which is twofold: in the Natal Chart and in Progressions, which is actually their primary interpretation and application.

These Stars are not considered Ancestors or Ghosts; they are cosmic forces that initiate change at specific periods in life. They are related to the concept of Hua (化), or transformation; they are step-up/step-down "transformers." They are connected to the Royal Court and indicate conditions and catalysts for change. In the Natal Chart, whatever House these Stars appear in represents an area of life that catalyzes change and transformation in general. In other words, if one or more of these Stars shows up in the Property Palace, you will experience many transformations and changes in relation to where you live or the property you own. This change will come in the form of a specific Star; for example, Hua Lu (化祿), the Salary or Prosperity Star, may initiate the sale of a particular property, and that becomes the catalyst for the next major phase of your life. We can look to the Progressed Chart to see when this might happen.

We will discuss Progression more thoroughly later in the book, but in Progression, these Stars can potentially initiate or catalyze periods of change related to the original position of the Star when they show up in certain Houses. For example, when a Hua Star shows up in the Career/Travel Palace, it may initiate a trip. So, if you have the Hua Quan, the Authority Star, in the Superiors Palace in your Natal Chart, then in a year when it progresses into the Travel Palace, you may take a trip for work that lands you a promotion and helps establish you as an authority in your given field. If you have Hua Ji, the Jealousy or Scandal Star, in your Friends/Assistants Palace in your Natal Chart, and it progresses into the Wealth Palace, then in that year, you may lose money and end up in a scandal due to one of your co-workers. And so on.

It is also the case that one of these Stars may catalyze a significant Fated event when it progresses into its Natal position. These kinds of events are not necessarily predictable, but we can say that the potential is there during these years. If something does happen, then it may be apparent in hindsight, but not always. These Stars are mysterious; while they can have predictive power, I would not rely on them. However, we can take precautions if we see negativity coming or attempt to activate it if we see a positive opportunity in the future.

Hua Lu, the Salary or Prosperity Star; Hua Quan, the Authority Star; and Hua Ke, the Examination Star, are all considered positive, and they initiate positive change and transformation. They can, however, be afflicted by Ghosts, which can turn them into sources of negative change related to the original image. Hua Ji, the Jealousy or Scandal Star, is always negative, and it is one of the more feared Stars in Polestar Astrology, as it can bring scandal, misfortune, and jealousy.

HUA LU (化祿)—THE SALARY OR PROSPERITY STAR

NAME AND TRANSLATION: Hua Lu (化祿), the Salary Star, the Prosperity Star

> *Hua*, 化—transform(ation), change, transmute, permutate; e.g., 造化 zaohua, Fashioner of Change, Shaper of Mutations, the selecting and synthesizing principle of Nature. a) provide the trigger or reason for change, catalyze; persuade, suasive. 2 bring round to new perspective or understanding, convert[1]

> *Lu*, 祿—favor(able), good fortune; benefice(nt). 2 official salary, emolument.[2]

All these Star names contain the character Hua (化), which means "transformation," and Lu means "salary" or "good fortune," so we call this the Salary or Prosperity Star, but we can also translate it as Transforming Fortune or Transmuting Prosperity.

ELEMENT: Yin Earth

Hua Lu is known as the Salary or Prosperity Star, and it brings about financial gain and prosperity through progress, expansion, growth, development, and amplification. This Star is generally positive, and whatever House it arrives in will be an area of change that brings about increased prosperity. It is related to fortune, money, and wealth, and so it is exalted in the Wealth and Property Palaces, but it is not always related directly to money, and it can initiate change that helps you to earn money through other avenues.

For example, if Hua Lu shows up in the Partners Palace, you may get better at earning money after you marry or with the help of your partner. If it shows up in the Pleasure Palace, you may become adept at earning money through a hobby, like becoming a professional chess player. If it shows up in the Ming Palace, you may be adept at earning money because of your charisma, social skills, and character. If it shows up with any of the Royal Court, that Star gets a boost and can become a source of prosperity. If it shows up with Ghost Stars, you may experience financial challenges and losses.

As stated in the introduction, these Stars can initiate change in Progression. So, if you have Hua Lu in the Wealth Palace in the Natal Chart, then in a year when it progresses into the Travel Palace, you may take a trip that ends up becoming very lucrative. If you have it in the Offspring Palace, and it progresses into the Property Palace, then in that year, you may buy a new house after having a second child. And so on; you can interpret the rest, as there are many possibilities.

HUA QUAN (化權)—THE AUTHORITY STAR

NAME AND TRANSLATION: Hua Quan (化權), the Authority Star

Hua, 化—transform(ation), change, transmute, permutate; e.g., 造化 zaohua, Fashioner of Change, Shaper of Mutations, the selecting and synthesizing principle of Nature. a) provide the trigger or reason for change, catalyze; persuade, suasive. 2 bring round to new perspective or understanding, convert[3]

Quan, 權—have the balance of power, carry weight; authority; privilege, prestige; e.g., 當權 dangquan, to hold sway; 權門 quanmen, gates of the powerful, families of influence. a) influence, advantage(ous); compel(ling), effect(ive); dominant. 3 flexible, adapt(ive), responsive to circumstances. a) expedient, opportune; contingent, relative, conditional; circumstantial, impermanent, provisional.[4]

Again, all these Star names contain the character Hua (化), which means "transformation," and Quan means "authority, privilege, and prestige," so we call this the Authority Star, but we can also translate it as Transforming Power or Transmuting Authority.

ELEMENT: Yang Wood

Hua Quan is known as the Authority Star, and it brings about mastery, authority, and capability through progressions and dynamics of power, competition, desire, and aspiration. It is connected to the Four Rulers and more authoritative Stars and empowers them if they arrive together. It is mostly at home in the career Houses and Wealth and Property Palaces and can be out of place in the more relationship-oriented Houses.

Whatever House Hua Quan arrives in becomes driven by aspiration and the desire to work toward mastery, power, and authority. If it is in the Ming Palace, this can become a central aspect of Fate. If it arrives in the Wealth or Property Palace, you may be driven to earn and own more and more. In the career Houses, you will likely seek positions of leadership and power, and you may even become bossy and aggressive in this pursuit. The Authority Star is out of place in relationship Houses, so if it shows up in the Partners Palace, you may become competitive in relationships and lord things over your partner.

As stated in the introduction, these Stars can initiate change in Progression. So, if you have Hua Quan in the Health Palace in the Natal Chart, then in a year when it progresses into the Ming Palace, you may initiate a process of personal mastery that gives you the power to overcome an illness. If you have it in the Superiors Palace, and it progresses into the Assistants Palace, then in that year, you may get a promotion due to the help of an assistant or co-worker. And so on—you can interpret the rest, as there are many possibilities.

HUA KE (化科)—THE EXAMINATION STAR

NAME AND TRANSLATION: Hua Ke (化科), the Examination Star

> ***Hua***, 化—transform(ation), change, transmute, permutate; e.g., 造化 zaohua, Fashioner of Change, Shaper of Mutations, the selecting and synthesizing principle of Nature. a) provide the trigger or reason for change, catalyze; persuade, suasive. 2 bring round to new perspective or understanding, convert[5]
>
> *Ke*, 科—class(ification), category; section, division; type. a) classify; assess; esp. for taxation. 2 article in legal code; ordinance; e.g., 科律 kelǜ, regulations. a) judge, pass judgment in accordance with law; adjudicate. 3 protocol; behavioral framework or organizational structure; rules, regulations. 4 (med.) examination, esp. exam-type, usu. appended to exam-name, such asjinshike 進士科, boxuehongcike 博學鴻辭科. a) (med.) sit for exam. b) (med.) course of study. 5 (med.) requisition, levy; e.g., 科取 kequ, appropriate by command or law.[6]

Hua (化) means "transformation," and Ke (科) means "examination" and is related to classifying, studying, and organizing, so we call this the Examination Star, but we can also translate it as Transforming Study or Transmuting Assessment.

ELEMENT: Yang Water

Hua Ke is known as the Examination Star, and it helps us progress in life through study, training, examination, and scholarship in the pursuit of knowledge, wisdom, and intelligence, and it can initiate periods of testing, assessment, and promotion. It is related to status, honor, fame, and reputation and can help to manifest and maximize our innate talent. Its nature is joyous and optimistic, and whatever House it shows up in becomes a source of transformation toward greater intelligence through growth.

If it appears in the Ming or Health Palace, then we tend toward pursuing knowledge and personal growth through study and scholarship. In the Youth Palace, we may be precocious and have an active academic career early in life. In career Houses, you may find and progress your career through academics and examinations. In the Pleasure Palace, you can constantly train and progress your talents through testing and competition. If Hua Ke shows up with any of the Royal Court, it adds a dimension of examination and academics and especially empowers the Tutor, Magistrate, and Priest.

As stated in the introduction, these Star can initiate change in Progression. So, if you have Hua Ke in the Superiors Palace in the Natal Chart, then in a year when it progresses into the Travel Palace, you may have to travel for an exam that becomes crucial to your career success. If you have it in the Ancestors Palace and it progresses into the Youth Palace, then in that year, you may work with your brother to study and understand your great-grandfather's legacy. And so on—there are many possibilities.

HUA JI (化忌)—THE JEALOUSY OR SCANDAL STAR

NAME AND TRANSLATION: Hua Ji (化忌), the Jealousy Star, the Scandal Star

> *Hua*, 化—transform(ation), change, transmute, permutate; e.g., 造化 zaohua, Fashioner of Change, Shaper of Mutations, the selecting and synthesizing principle of Nature. a) provide the trigger or reason for change, catalyze; persuade, suasive. 2 bring round to new perspective or understanding, convert[7]

> *Ji*, 忌—antipathy, aversion. a) averse to, antagonistic, hostile; spite(ful), hate(ful). 2 eschew, shrink from, dread(ful), be on guard against; abstain from, shun; e.g., 忌日 jiri, "dread day," day on which one's parent(s) died; any inauspicious day. 3 taboo; proscribe, prohibit(ion); interdict(ion).[8]

Hua (化) means "transformation," and Ji (忌) means "to shun or hate" and is related to jealousy and being eschewed, so we call this the Jealousy or Scandal Star, but we can also translate it as Transforming Hate or Transmuting Hostility.

ELEMENT: Yang Water

Hua Ji is known as the Jealousy Star or Scandal Star, and it is the most negative of the Hua Stars. It is feared as the bringer of scandal, worry, anxiety, misfortune, and jealousy. It tends to do the opposite of the other Hua Stars in that it creates change and transformation by creating hindrances, obstacles, and roadblocks that we are forced to work to transform and overcome. Whatever House it shows up in comes with significant concerns that can turn into frustration, as it can bring scandal that arises from jealousy, arguments, and misunderstanding. That House can then become a source of dynamic changes in the negative sense, and in Progression, Hua Ji can catalyze periods of upheaval and drama. Ghost Stars and further affliction exacerbate this drama. If this Star shows up with stronger Stars, it can be eclipsed, but it can also make dealing with scandal a significant part of resolving your Fate.

If you have the Jealousy Star in the Partners Palace, you may experience jealousy, misunderstandings, and infidelity in relationships. In the Wealth Palace, you may experience a scandal over money, which could involve theft, embezzlement, or misappropriating funds; this can be something that you do or that happens against you. In the career Houses, you may experience a scandal at work involving a co-worker or subordinate. In the Pleasure Palace, this scandal may be sexual or licentious in nature. And so on.

As mentioned earlier, these Stars have the power to bring about significant changes in Progression. For instance, if Hua Ji is in the Property Palace in your Natal Chart, and it progresses into the Partners Palace in a given year, it could lead to a negative shift in your living situation or relationship dynamics that causes scandal, discord, or jealousy. Similarly, if it's in the Superiors Palace in the Natal Chart and progresses into the Assistants Palace, it could signify a year where collaborating with an assistant or subordinate goes wrong and undermines your position as a leader; they may be jealous and want your job, and so they accuse you of incompetence or wrongdoing. And so on—there are many possibilities.

EXALTED HOUSES, LUMINOUS STAR PLACEMENTS, AND LUMINOUS STAR PAIRS

NOW THAT WE HAVE GONE THROUGH EACH OF THE INDIVIDUAL STARS, we can discuss luminous or exalted placements and Star pairs. The terms *luminous* and *exalted* here mean the same thing and are interchangeable, but exalted tends to be more commonly used in Western and Indian astrology. Luminous is more common in Polestar Astrology, as it refers to the brightness of the Stars. An exalted or luminous Star exalts the House it is in, so having an exalted Star or an exalted House also means the same thing.

Stars and Houses can be normal, luminous/exalted, afflicted, or eclipsed, which has a lot to do with their placement and proximity to other Stars. If a Star is well placed or arrives in combination with other strong and supporting Stars, this exalts the House and increases the luminosity or power of the ruling Star, which is always the strongest Star in the House.

An exalted House increases the potency of Fate and the capacity or likelihood of resolving the Fate in that House. An afflicted House has diminished potency and reduces the capacity to resolve Fate, increasing the chance for negativity and obstruction. Stars that are eclipsed become neutral or inactive, which is often the case with weaker Stars that show up with stronger Stars. Again, the Stars have been listed and described in the order of their potency. The strongest Star in a House rules that the House, and each other Star is subordinate to that central image.

A Star is well placed if it shows up in a House that is similar thematically to that Star, and it is also luminous/exalted in Houses that certain Zodiac Animals rule. For example, the Emperor is exalted in Dragon and Horse Palaces, as the Emperor is very Dragon- and Horse-like. The Emperor is also exalted in the Superiors Palace, as this is the natural House of leadership. The Emperor is diminished in Rooster and Rabbit Palaces, for the Emperor is not Rabbit- or Rooster-like, as these Characters tend to overthink things and go haywire when they are in charge. These luminous and diminished placements are listed in the discussion of each individual Star. Diminished placements are a kind of affliction to that Star, and the Fate of a diminished Star is often weaker, stranger, or unusual in some way that makes it more difficult to interpret. Diminished placement may postpone Fate resolution or put some kind of constraint on relationships in the Ancestors, Youth, Offspring, Partners, Assistants, or Superiors Palace.

A Star can also be diminished in placement but placed well in a House. For example, the Tutor can be exalted in the Superiors Palace, but if the Superiors Palace is also the Rooster Palace in a particular chart, then it is diminished. In this case, they cancel each other out, and the Star is then standard in its interpretation. Sometimes, this means the Star is strong in capacity but weaker in opportunity, meaning you may be a very skilled employee but have few job options.

Stars commonly show up with other Stars. They can arrive alone, but this is rare. Remember, these Stars are in fixed constellations and belong to the Northern or Southern Array in fixed positions following the Emperor and Empress, respectively. Therefore, Stars in the Northern Array cannot arrive with other Stars from the Northern Array, and the same goes for Stars in the Southern Array. Thus, there is a limited number of Star combinations, but they also tend to show up in fixed patterns called Geju (格局).

Any combination of Stars in the Royal Court, especially of the Four Rulers, is auspicious and can exalt the House and increase the potency of both Stars. Still, not all combinations are necessarily exalted, for we must activate that power and engage with it by actively stepping up to the challenges and opportunities in our life. If we fail to do so, the exalted influence may pass us by.

Ghost Stars afflict or diminish a House, but stronger Stars can eclipse that affliction. When a Ghost Star rules a House, that House is afflicted, but strong Stars like the Emperor or Tutor can eclipse a lot of a Ghost's negativity.

Here are some of the most exalted Star pairs to play with. This does not cover all the Star combinations or their interpretations but the ones that are the most potent and always exalt the House. If you understand how these Stars act individually and in pairs, you can then walk them through the Twelve Houses and interpret them accordingly. As always, this is an exercise in synthesizing symbols, which is the heart of Polestar interpretation.

ZI WEI WITH TIAN FU

The Emperor with the Empress

This is the most exalted and potent combination in Polestar Astrology. If the Emperor and Empress show up together, it is called the Royal Procession, which highly exalts any House it arrives in. Zi Wei and Tian Fu are the primary Yinyang polar counterpoints of Fate and represent the best of all your Patriarchal and Matriarchal Ancestors, united in your benefit for the resolution of your Ancestral Fate. This combination unites all the best aspects of Yin Fate resolution and Yang Fate resolution, meaning everything you are Fated to do (Yang) and everything you are Fated to receive (Yin) are in the same House working together. This makes the resolution of Fate smooth and, in a way, easy (although nothing in life is easy).

The Royal Procession exalts the meaning of the House into a spiritual dimension and guarantees that you will resolve your Fate in this lifetime and go beyond it to experience wisdom. You will experience Human Freedom; this is your best chance to go beyond Fate and experience your inner or original nature. If you have this arrangement, the rest of the Chart is moot. Just focus on this House, and the rest will fall into place; your Ancestors have arranged everything. If you have this, consider yourself blessed.

ZI WEI WITH TIAN XIANG

The Emperor with the Tutor

Zi Wei, the Emperor, and Tian Xiang, the Tutor, are the most potent Yang Stars, and the Tutor is the most loyal and influential supporter of the Emperor. Tian Xiang is the Tutor of the Emperor, his teacher, and most trusted adviser, the power behind the throne. The imperial tutor met with the generals and vassals; he read and communicated all the reports to the emperor. Here the Tutor adds a dimension of scholarship, professionalism, and academic integrity to the Emperor's Fate.

When they show up together, this combination exalts the House into a decisive threshold to resolve Yang Fate and achieve great success in the world. This pair is very much about your work in the world, and it helps you to become a contributor to or expert in your field. It means your greatest intelligence and intellectual capacity unite with everything you are here to do, which increases the likelihood that you will do it. When these Stars are together in a House, your Yang Fate communicates and cooperates, which makes that House the most functional, focused, and productive in the chart. This combination can also indicate an exalted teacher or mentor relationship that helps you to resolve Fate.

ZI WEI WITH JU MEN

The Emperor with the Great Gate

If Zi Wei, the Emperor, arrives with Ju Men, the Great Gate, it exalts the House and increases the magnitude of the Emperor's power and scope of influence. Ju Men increases the scope of Fate and opportunity, and it combines with Zi Wei to create an enormous threshold of freedom. The Great Gate makes everything bigger and more universal. This combination is almost too big and can even distract the Emperor, as the possibilities and influence here can be endless. You may struggle with too many opportunities and choices in whatever House this pair arrives in.

When these Stars come together, you have tremendous freedom to choose in that House, and you can resolve Fate in many ways, as it becomes open-ended and unrestricted. You can also influence many people, and the potential to reach the world at large is increased. In a way, the openness the Great Gate creates here means that it doesn't matter what you do—whatever you do can powerfully resolve Fate—but you must choose something and focus on it. Otherwise, you will be distracted, with unlimited potential.

ZI WEI WITH WEN CHANG OR WEN QU

The Emperor with the Magistrate or the Priest

If Zi Wei, the Emperor, arrives with Wen Chang, the Magistrate, or Wen Qu, the Priest, or with both, then this exalts the House and adds a dimension of Wen—scholarship, learning, and self-cultivation—to the image of the Emperor and to the central resolution of Fate. Your capacity to resolve Fate will increase with and include self-cultivation.

With one of these combinations in a House, learning, self-cultivation, and teaching will become a pivotal part of the resolution of Fate in that House and of the whole chart. It even becomes a mandate. The Wen Stars, especially if they arrive together with the Emperor, mean that you can go beyond ordinary worldly Fate to experience wisdom, and you can communicate and teach that wisdom to others to become of great benefit in the world. This is likely to weave self-cultivation into worldly success and progress.

TIAN FU WITH WU QU

The Empress with the General

This is a very potent Yin pair, combining the most accomplished female Yin Star, the Empress, with the wisest and most experienced of the male Yin Stars, the General. The Empress represents all our most potent and innate gifts and talents, and she brings to any House all the best circumstances to resolve Fate naturally and with ease. The Empress represents what we are Fated to receive, and the General is retired and has finished all the hard work. He now advises the Emperor and represents the strategy and wisdom that come from direct experience and the inevitable rewards of hard work.

Together, then, these Stars represent patience and Yin Power. As a pair, they create a powerful threshold to resolve Fate through the combination of precise strategy and resources. In other words, the General gives you a critical temperament and wisdom, and the Empress is powerfully networked and offers power with elegance, persuasion, and effective work in the shadows. This combination often delays success and creates late-blooming rewards, but it also increases the potency of those rewards later in life. The General also connects the Empress to your oldest original Matriarchal Ancestors, and it draws wisdom and strategy through your whole Ancestral line.

TIAN FU WITH WEN CHANG OR WEN QU

The Empress with the Magistrate or the Priest

If the Empress arrives with either of the Wen Stars or both, then this exalts the House and adds a dimension of Wen—scholarship, learning, and self-cultivation—to the image of the Yin Fate of the Empress and to the central spiritual resolution of Fate. The House becomes a deep pool of inner reflection and cultivation, adding depth and refinement to the Empress. She can contribute to the world and offer great wisdom and insight from a natural and effortless place. This House will include great cultivation and reflection for its own sake, not for any practical or professional success.

Here, you cultivate yourself purely for wisdom, and self-cultivation becomes a way to unravel Yin Fate and benefit others through your countenance and deportment. Art, literature, music, and so on are exalted to become truly meaningful and transformational—again, not for "success" but for fun, play, and pleasure. If the Wen Stars arrive with the Empress, this House becomes a threshold for enlightenment and liberation.

TIAN JI WITH TAI YIN

The Oracle with the Moon Lady or Princess

This is one of the most potent but difficult-to-understand spiritual combinations, combining the two most mysterious Yin Stars. This combination exalts the House but puts the image of Fate's resolution into deep, murky waters that, although you will likely never get to understand them, will nonetheless be embodied as a potent Lunar Oracle. Fate in this House will unfold through a complex inner process that may seem irrational, otherworldly, and dreamlike. This pair makes the House where they appear into a threshold for inner experience and spiritual transformation. It unites all the Matriarchal Ancestors in their wisdom, empathy, sensitivity, and intuition, creating a powerhouse for things like meditation, yoga, medicine, and any inner work in Fate's resolution. This combination creates an army of "fairy godmothers" who work behind the scenes on your behalf. Nothing here will make any sense, but everything will work out perfectly.

TIAN JI WITH JU MEN

The Oracle with the Great Gate

The Great Gate exalts the influence of the Oracle and expands her intuition, sensitivity, and empathy. The Oracle is already working in a spiritual dimension, but here, the Great Gate blasts the Oracle into the stratosphere and connects it to the Heavens. The Fate in the House where they appear will be visionary, and you will have countless opportunities brought to you by mysterious means. You will also have great freedom and choice with strong spiritual aspirations in this House. You will be gifted and talented, which will be enhanced by premonitions, lucid dreams, and omens that are hard to interpret and take you beyond the ordinary. The Great Gate is too open, big, and unrestricted, so the danger of going off the rails here is intense. This pair can turn you into a prophet who gets detached from the world; it makes it hard to stay grounded and puts you at risk of becoming dissociated from reality. Wherever these Stars show up together, staying focused and grounded—directing the vast spiritual benefit toward tangible or realistic goals—is essential.

TIAN JI WITH TIAN LIANG

The Oracle with the Roof Beam

The Roof Beam grounds the Oracle and makes its spiritual Fate solid and practical. It was traditionally associated with the mantic arts and connects the Oracle to skills and trades. This pair can connect you to things like astrology, spirituality, and medicine, but it can also turn carpentry into a spiritual experience. Work, labor, service, and skill can become a spiritual path that resolves Fate.

The Roof Beam can also connect the spiritual Fate of the Oracle to a particular place, and you may have strong spiritual ties with people in specific places that you must find and travel to in order to fulfill. You may be Fated to work as an Oracle in a particular community with people with whom you have a Fated debt. This work may not start until you are in the right place, which can be called a Fated "power spot" that becomes central to the resolution of your Fate. This combination of Stars also makes the premonitions and lucid dreams of the Oracle practical and straightforward; you will be able to translate them into tangible skills and prescriptions.

TAI YANG WITH TAI YIN

The Sun or Prince with the Moon Lady or Princess

This is a powerful Yin Yang combination; these Stars exalt each other and the House where they show up together. They are a less potent but more practical form of the Emperor and Empress. The Prince and Princess represent a union of your more worldly, practical, and transformational Yin and Yang Fate. Both effort and ease will characterize the Fate in this House; you will have to work hard and prove yourself, but you will also receive many opportunities, help, and support. You will be able to move forward, advance, and progress, but you will also know when to wait, when to hold back, and when to strategize, and this combination will make for a very smooth and potent resolution of Fate. The Fate in this House is secondary and in service of the Emperor and Empress, but it can be potent. It will likely be more worldly and related to the process of "becoming," as the Prince and Princess must prove their right to ascend the throne.

TIAN XIANG WITH WU QU

The Tutor with the General

This is one of the most potent combinations for the resolution of Fate through strategy and hard work, for it combines the professional, hardworking, and refined Yang image of the Tutor with the strategic, wise, and experienced Yin image of the General. This duo can work very efficiently together, exalting the House where they appear into a threshold for success by any metric. This is a powerful indicator of successful work in the world, especially in career Houses. The General may delay the success, but the Tutor's professionalism and attention to detail make it inevitable. There will be progress, promotion, and in-depth experience wherever this pair shows up.

TIAN TONG WITH TAI YIN

The Vassal with the Moon Lady or Princess

If the Vassal arrives with the Moon, this exalts the House and combines many beneficial aspects of Yin and Yang Fate resolution. The Vassal is hardworking, loyal, and service oriented, and it is given an added dimension of depth through the Moon, which adds feeling, sensitivity, and favorable opportunity or circumstance to the Vassal's dedication. This pair unites commitment and discipline with the lunar cultivation of art, music, and dance. This combination is powerful for allowing Yin things to find practical Yang success and application. It is also great for self-cultivation through disciplined and refined means. Success here is modest and often sought in support of something greater or in service to others.

WEN CHANG WITH WEN QU

The Magistrate with the Priest

When the Wen Stars arrive together, they are very powerful, and special attention should be paid to that House, as it becomes very exalted and represents a kind of Fate Threshold through which all a person's spiritual and worldly Fate can be transcended through the application of spiritual means or technologies. This pair combines all the most beneficial aspects of Wen through spiritual and worldly knowledge and cultivation. This threshold does not apply to worldly Fate in the ordinary sense of success, but rather, it creates a kind of doorway to go off the chart. If you have this combination, then that House is where you should apply great spiritual focus, which can lead to enlightenment, liberation, and transcendent wisdom.

These are just a few examples of Star pairs. There are, of course, many more, but these are among the most potent, and these pairs always exalt the House they are in to create a powerful Fate Threshold, which means that you can resolve Fate very strongly here. As a practice, you should play at combining and synthesizing these symbols with Star pairs from real-life examples, using your own chart and the charts of friends and family.

BORROWED AND OPPOSITE INFLUENCE

NONE OF THE STARS IN POLESTAR ASTROLOGY EXIST IN ISOLATION. They are all in a relationship with each other, and ideally they should all communicate and work together in the resolution of Fate. So, whenever we look at a particular House to interpret its meaning, we must also look at other Houses to see if other Stars will support the Stars in that House. The most important influences or "aspects" are in the opposite House (the Stars of which can be borrowed in the case of an Empty House), in the Stars in a trine (at 120 degrees), and in the proximal Houses.

The first of these is the borrowed and/or opposite influence. These are the Stars in the opposite House, or, in other words, in the Houses at 180 degrees to each other. This orientation is the most direct and potent aspect, or influence. The Stars that are opposite to each other are mirrors, and they communicate back and forth. The Houses opposite each other in the natural Twelve Houses already share relationships. For example, the Pleasure and Wealth Palaces are opposite and naturally related, as the more wealth you have, the more freedom you have to enjoy your life. The Ancestors Palace is across from the Health Palace, as your health is partly inherited from your Ancestors (i.e., as your body). And so on—I suggest that you study the opposite Houses and contemplate how they are all related.

Stars in the opposite Houses can powerfully support each other; this is called Gong Zhao (拱照), and it means "to shine at each other." For example, if you have the Emperor in the Pleasure Palace and the Empress in the Wealth Palace, the wealth gifted to you in this life will directly fund your Fated pursuit of pleasure. Also, you can look at the Stars themselves and contemplate their relationships. For example, if the Magistrate shows up in the House opposite the Emperor, you may look to the opposite House for a teacher or education to support the Emperor's path. Strong stars can also eclipse or diminish Ghost Stars in the opposite House. For example, if the Emperor and Empress appear in the House across from the Seven Killings Star, its potency diminishes greatly.

Some Stars are always across from one another due to their fixed placement in the Northern and Southern Array. For example, the Empress is always across from the Seven Killings Star, and the Tutor is always across from the Rebel Star, which suggests that these two potent Stars from the Four Rulers in some way work to resolve these particular Ghost Stars. These two relationships can be very revealing as patterns for working out our afflicted Fate.

The next related influence is that of borrowed Stars. If a House has no ruling Star, it is an Empty Court, a Kong Gong (空宫). As the chapter on the Twelve Houses states, an Empty Court has no significant Fate in this lifetime. In this case, it is traditional to "borrow" the Stars from the opposite House. So, if the Offspring Palace is empty, you can borrow the Stars from the Property Palace and read them as if they were in the original House. But you read them at half strength, as borrowed Stars are not as potent, and any Fate they represent is much weaker.

However, in my experience, the image of the Empty House having no significant Fate is a much more important message than that of the borrowed Stars. So, when I do readings, I tell the client that their House is empty and that they have the freedom to choose in that House. I do not generally read borrowed Stars. To me, the message of freedom is more important. However, there are a few exceptions. For example, I tend to read the borrowed Stars for parents with an empty Offspring Palace, as they have already activated their parental Fate, and the borrowed Stars can be helpful. I also tend to read borrowed Stars for people with health problems but an empty Health Palace, as here the Stars are borrowed from the Ancestors Palace and often reveal patterns of Ancestral illness.

If someone feels they have a strong Fate in an Empty House and insists, only then do I read the borrowed Stars. First, though, I state that, if the feeling of Fate is strong in an Empty House, it may also be generated by freedom. If you have an empty Offspring Palace, then you may be meeting your kids for the first time in this lifetime, as you were not strongly Fated to be a parent. This does not mean that you love them any less; it means you are choosing to generate that love out of freedom rather than an obligation of Fate, which can be just as powerful, if not more so.

PROXIMAL INFLUENCE

THE NEXT INFLUENCE IS THAT OF PROXIMAL STARS. These are influences from the Stars in the adjoining two Houses; this is called Xiang Jia (相夹), and it means "to flank." For example, the Emperor in the Ming Palace is strongly supported by Stars in the Ancestors and Youth Palaces. If a Star has strong Stars on both sides, then it increases in strength and potency, as it has close allies. If a Star is alone on both sides, it is naturally weaker, as it is more isolated and has less support. If it is empty on one side, then it can still be supported by a preceding or following Star.

Here, we look to the relationship between the Stars, and we also look for special pairs. The Assistant Stars, for example, exalt the Emperor if they show up in either of the proximal Houses. Many Stars also naturally fall next to each other in the fixed positions of the Northern and Southern Array. For example, the Oracle is always to the right of the Emperor, the Sun is always to the left of the General, and the Moon is always to the left of the Empress. These Stars are natural supporters and allies to each other.

The Oracle is the voice of the Ancestors guiding the Emperor. The Sun trains with and is guided by the General. And the Moon is daughter of the Empress and must train in Yin Power. This creates predictable Fate patterns in that everyone who has the Emperor in the Partners Palace will always have the Oracle in the Offspring Palace, which suggests that significant Fate to partner will also come with significant Fate to be a parent and give birth to an Oracle nonetheless!

As an exercise, I suggest you study and look for these patterns and contemplate what they mean, using your own chart and the charts of family and friends as examples.

120-DEGREE STAR INFLUENCE AND STAR FORMATIONS

THE LAST SIGNIFICANT INFLUENCE is that of Star Formations and the Stars in a "trine" with a Star—meaning in the two Houses at 120 degrees to it; this is called Hui Zhao (会照). You find this by counting four Houses in both directions and drawing a triangle connecting the three Houses. These Houses and the Stars in them vary in influence based on Star placement and potency, and they often fall into predictable patterns, as these Stars are fixed in their relationship to other Stars based on their order in each constellation of the Northern and Southern Array. As two constellations circle each other, they form various patterns; some of these patterns form trines, and some form unique relationships and combinations that tradition has deemed important.

All these patterns are called Star Formations, or Geju, and they are a unique and powerful aspect of Polestar Astrology. Altogether, about fifty-two major Star Formations are made with the various Stars. Sometimes, these are formed in trines called San He (三合); some are formed with single Stars, and some are formed with double Star pairs. Some Star Formations are traditionally considered auspicious, and others are considered malicious. They are generally used to determine the relationships between Stars and Houses.

In Progression, they are used to assess the auspices of different periods in the Yearly and Decade Cycles. This is a more advanced subject in Polestar Astrology, but in my experience, Star Formations are not very important. We will touch on a few things in the Progressed Charts chapter; otherwise, these Star Formations do not mean much in the Natal Chart when it comes to the basic and most important story of Fate.

In the Natal Chart, they are more an exercise in studying the symbolic relationships between the Stars. For example, suppose the Rebel, Emperor, and General appear in a trine in the Partners, Career/Travel, and Pleasure Palaces, respectively. In that case, these three Houses will relate in that our rebellious nature will affect our relationships, which will afflict our primary Fate in our career, which our strict and disciplined approach to pleasure will rein in. And so on.

You should draw triangles between all the Stars at 120 degrees, look at each individual Star and each House, and consider their symbolism and nature. Contemplate the relationship between the Stars and Houses and ask how they could relate and inform each other through your lived experience. If you do this, you will discover deeper connections and meaning in the relationship between the Stars and Houses, for they are all interrelated and arrive in various patterns as determined by your Fate. The patterns revealed by these Star Formations are subtle and require deep study and self-reflection.

PUTTING IT TOGETHER: INTERPRETATION AND SYNTHESIS

NOW WE GET TO THE HEART OF POLESTAR ASTROLOGY: How do we read and interpret a Natal Chart? How do we synthesize all these complex details and make this information useful, accessible, and personally meaningful? How do we use this information to resolve our Fate and discover our Original Nature? And how do we communicate this information to others in astrology readings?

So far, I have attempted to give you the complete basic vocabulary of Polestar Astrology. We have reviewed the individual details of each symbol of Character and Fate. We have attempted to understand each of these symbols alone, for you must first understand them as individuals before understanding how they synthesize and interact with other symbols.

Now, we must put them together, for none of these individual factors ever shows up alone. While some Stars do show up alone in a House, they often show up in combination with other Stars, and each solo Star or Star combination must be considered in relation to each person's individual Character, which is a combination of their birth year and hour. Every situation requires synthesis, and this is the true art of Polestar Astrology. We must be able to merge all the separate factors and discuss all the possibilities that can arise from their interactions.

We will now walk through all the steps I recommend you take when reviewing and reading a Natal Chart for yourself or a client. These steps are based on the main sections of this book: understanding the View Teachings and then reviewing how the Character, Fate, and Inner Nature play out in your life or your client's life.

I recommend that you first take these steps when reviewing your own chart, and if you ever do readings for other people, I suggest you take the same steps each time. This gives you a basic template for composing an astrology reading. Once you are experienced, you can change these steps and devise your own method, or you can shorten specific preparations, if you have internalized the information to the degree that it becomes second nature. I have done hundreds of readings, and I still take these same steps each time.

Let's go through each step as if you are doing a reading for a client, and then we can review some example charts. These steps combine the study of a chart and preparation of notes for a Natal reading, as these steps should happen with both.

HOW TO REVIEW AND READ A NATAL CHART: TAKE THESE STEPS EACH TIME

STEP I

Calculate the Birth Chart, including the Character, Fate, and Inner Nature

FIRST, YOU MUST CREATE A NATAL CHART. It is essential that you get the correct birth information so that you can generate a proper chart. Double-check the birth date and time; it is best if you can find a birth certificate and eyewitness. Double-check A.M. versus P.M. (I can't tell you how many people make this mistake.) And double-check whether you (or your client) were born during Daylight Savings Time (DST). Daylight Savings Time is an issue if you were born in the first half of a Chinese Hour, which is two hours total, as the adjustment puts you back into the preceding Chinese Hour. If you (or your client) were born in the second half, then it does not matter. If DST changes the chart, then adjust the chart.

Common sense suggests that changing the clocks does not alter nature or the cycles of time. However, it is a social convention that does change our society. In my experience, the chart adjusted for DST is the correct chart. If the clock says it is 2 P.M., then it is 2 P.M., because we all agree to participate in this convention. Chinese Tradition suggests that this is also part of your Fate. You can, therefore, make two charts and review or at least consider both. However, I have done enough Natal readings to see that the chart adjusted for DST is always more accurate.

Once you have the correct time, generate a Natal Chart. You can use a computer program or do it by hand. The example charts in the following chapter show how I choose to format a chart, but you can format it however you like. My formatting was chosen to emphasize Star potency and highlight the most important information.

Make sure that the chart includes the person's Character in the form of their Four Pillars: the Zodiac Animal and Element of the Year, Month, Day, and Hour in which they were born. I make the Year and Hour font bigger, as these are the primary images of a person's Qi Character, which is their basic capacity to resolve Fate, and this is what we review in the second part of the reading, after discussing the View Teachings.

Then, make sure that the chart contains all Twelve Houses properly arranged, with each of the Stars in their proper Houses, as this provides an image of the person's Fate or opportunities in life. Like the Year and Hour, I format the Stars of the Royal Court with a bigger font to emphasize their importance. This information will be reviewed in the third part of the reading as a discussion of Fate.

Finally, ensure that the Inner Nature is placed in the chart. This will be reviewed as the final part of the reading, as it provides an image of the spiritual Fruition of Polestar Astrology.

Once you have the correct chart, you can begin the reading, provided you have prepared using the following steps.

STEP 2

Introduce or Review the View Teachings

A Natal Reading should review the three main subjects of Zi Wei Dou Shu—Character, Inner Nature, and Fate—but before doing this, you should first introduce or review the View Teachings of Polestar Astrology. If you are studying your own chart, I encourage you to constantly go back to the View Teachings discussed in the first part of this book and review them repeatedly. We must not forget why we study this information and what we are doing here. If we ignore the View Teachings, we will inevitably misunderstand and even abuse the information in our chart or from our reading. We will turn them into fortune-telling or into another set of false views used to solidify a separation between self and world.

If you are reviewing this information with a client, then before you start the reading, you should introduce the subject and review the View Teachings before you proceed. Like, what the hell are we even talking about here? What is Polestar Astrology? What is Character? What is Fate? What does it mean to resolve Fate and experience your Inner Nature? If you are not both on the same page, then it is likely that the reading will go over their head and not be helpful. They will be entertained but forget everything you tell them.

You can choose how you would like to introduce the material. Still, I suggest that you offer a basic introduction to and summary of the main ideas of Character, Inner Nature, and Fate, as well as some pith form of the View Teachings on the resolution of Fate and the experience of our Original Nature/Human Freedom. I also recommend including something about Ancestors and Ancestral Qi, as this is the primary language we use to discuss the origins of Fate. Most people get this idea quickly and can at least accept it on the level of genetics.

After discussing the basic View Teachings, I generally tell people that the reading will have three parts, emphasizing Character and Fate and finishing with a brief discussion of Inner Nature. I tell people that the goal is to go through each section individually but ultimately to understand how these three factors interact and inform each other. I tell people that human life is a dance between these three factors—Character, Inner Nature, and Fate—and that the goal of the reading is to discover how these factors manifest in their life.

It is essential to communicate to people that astrology readings are a dialogue. The point is to discuss and find out how these symbols manifest in one's real-life, lived experience; this is not theoretical. Using the symbols, we reverse-engineer the meaning of the chart from their life. It is not the job of an astrologer to tell people about themselves or predict anything by projecting things onto the client. The astrologer's job is to communicate the nature of the symbols and help the person make connections to their real life to discover their Fate for themselves and then work toward a resolution of Fate on their own. To do this, you must talk to them and ask them questions. You must check in with them to see if the symbols resonate, and if they do not, then you must clarify their meaning and offer further interpretations until it all makes sense.

In the case of Fate, you should study a chart and come up with as many interpretations for a House as possible. You should then present as many different options as possible to the client, emphasizing and communicating the Qi of the symbols so that they can understand their essence and then make connections to their real life. They will then choose the interpretation or interpretations that resonate with them. If none of your interpretations make sense, they will often be able give you the correct interpretation, if you have adequately communicated the essence, or Qi, of the symbols.

In turn, you should devise as many interpretations for your own chart as possible and hold them lightly. Do not lock into a single interpretation or explanation—keep asking questions, keep exploring, and let the symbols unfold for you slowly. These symbols may take years to reveal their true depth, and if you come to understand them deeply, they will continue to speak to you.

After twelve-plus years with these symbols, I continue to have revelations about them and rethink my understanding. I also have clients return to me years later to tell me that they finally understand what I told them in their Natal reading.

Remember, these influences change over time; they may mean different things in different years and decades of your life or in your client's life. So, have patience, and do not rush to understand.

Once you feel that you have a basic mutual understanding, you can review the Natal Chart, starting with Qi Character. Again, I suggest you take notes on this beforehand.

STEP 3

Review the Qi Character by Combining the Stem and Branch of the Year and Hour

After introducing the subject matter, reviewing the View Teachings, and ensuring you are on the same page, you can review the person's Qi Character in the second part of the reading. This is an image of the person's fundamental capacity to resolve Fate. I tell people that Qi Character is something like personality but more profound, as not everyone born in the Year of the Dragon has the same personality. But we can say that everyone born in the Year of the Dragon has the same basic Qi Character, which can manifest as many different and diverse personalities, each with something in common.

It is also important to emphasize that a person's Qi Character is somewhat immutable and does not change. The client must understand that they will be a Yang Fire Tiger, Yang Earth Horse, Yin Water Pig, and so on until they die. Qi Character can soften, it can become transparent, and we can learn to accept and liberate our Qi Character, but we cannot get rid of or change it. It does not resolve until death.

The following is detailed earlier in the chapter "Synthesizing the Qi Character of the Year and Hour," and this step should follow the same steps outlined in that chapter, which I will review now.

Here, I introduce the idea that a person's Qi Character is a synthesis of the Stem and Branch of the year and hour in which they were born. I tell them that the year is the primary image, like a noun, and that the hour is secondary and like an adjective, modifying the primary image. I then go through each image separately, discussing the primary symbol of the Zodiac Animal of the year and how it is modified by the Character's Inner and Outer Element or Heavenly Stem. For example, for a Water Snake, first I talk about the Snake, then the Snake's Inner Element of Yin Fire, then the Outer Element of Yin Water, and then how they interact and modify the Snake image. I then do the same thing for the hour. Next, I synthesize the two Characters, discussing the dynamics of the various Zodiac Animals and Elements and how they interact. I then summarize this synthesis as a basic image of their Qi Character, addressing both its strengths and weaknesses. It is essential to blend the year and the hour for the client, but it is also necessary to explain them separately so that the client can synthesize for themselves and see how these two factors interact within their experience.

I finish by telling the client that our Qi Character is our capacity to resolve Fate, which we will discuss in the third part of the reading. Our Qi Character gives "auspice" to the Fate in the Twelve Houses. It is important to emphasize that each Qi Character will react to, work with, and resolve Fate differently. What is auspicious for a Monkey may be an affliction for a Tiger. Here, it is essential to communicate that Fate will manifest differently for each Character, so we must always be mindful of Character when discussing Fate.

Once the client has a strong connection with their Qi Character, we can then discuss the Twelve Houses of the Natal Chart and the symbols of Fate contained within.

STEP 4

Discuss the Twelve Houses of the Natal Chart, and the Symbols of Fate Contained Within—Principles of Preparation and Interpretation

Once the client has a strong connection with their Qi Character, we can then discuss the Twelve Houses of the Natal Chart, and the symbols of Fate contained within. It's important to be mindful of Character and study each of the Twelve Houses, one by one, by determining the ruling Star in each House by rank. Consider the influence of the ruling Star as if it were alone. Then, add and synthesize that influence with each subsequent Star in that House in order of rank, considering the relationships between each Star's image and strength. Consider the relationship between the Stars in all the affiliated Houses, considering the opposite, proximal, and 120-degree influences. This process of interpretation is a form of self-reflection or a tool that you can use to present interpretations to the client, allowing them to choose the one that resonates with them.

Before you review each of the Twelve Houses with your client, I highly suggest you study the Natal Chart extensively beforehand and take copious notes. I generally spend about two to three hours reviewing a client's Natal Chart before doing a reading, and I come up with as many different interpretations as possible, being mindful of their Character and how best to communicate the information.

For example, if I am doing a reading for a Rabbit, I will emphasize the Houses that pertain to relationships, and I will assume that they will be less likely to take risks and more opt to seek safety. Therefore, the Emperor is more auspicious for a Rabbit if it is in the Partners or Offspring Palace. If it is in the career Houses, this is somewhat inauspicious and more likely to cause anxiety and struggle. The more you understand the person's Character, the more insight you will have into the different factors of Fate presented in the Twelve Houses. In turn, the more you understand your Character, the more you will realize how Fate manifests in your own life, which is the foundation that we must have to understand the Fate of others.

So, when reviewing the Twelve Houses and making self-reflection notes or presenting information to your client, take the following steps.

Again, first, make sure the chart is correct by double-checking the birth time. Once you are sure you have the chart, look at the chart as a whole and examine the placement of the Emperor and Empress and the Ming Palace, as these are the two most important Stars that determine our major Fate and the most significant House. Notice what Houses the Emperor and Empress are in and their relationship: Are they in the same House? Opposite Houses? Are they in a 120-degree relationship? Are they afflicted? What is the ruling Star in the Ming Palace? Is it afflicted? Is the Fate in the Ming Palace Yin or Yang, based on the ruling Star?

Again, think of all this in terms of the person's Character: Are these significant patterns well matched with the Character? In other words, are they a Yin Character with a Yang Fate? This will give you the big picture of Fate and the main story. This should be the focus of the reading. If you can communicate essential themes related to the Emperor's placement and Fate's main image in the Ming Palace, you will be doing yourself or your client a big service.

Next, determine the "ruling" Star in each House and consider it as if it were alone. This will provide the main image of Fate in that House, which will then be modified by other Stars if it is not actually alone. The ruling Star is always the most potent Star in that House; any other Stars that show up are subordinate to that main image and can modify or alter it but not change the primary story. Note each Star's order in each House in terms of potency, from most to least potent, as this will determine the influence of the Stars.

The more potent Stars will dominate and can diminish and even eclipse weaker Stars. This is important because it tells you what to focus on. Focus on the big Stars, and pay less attention to the weaker ones, especially if they show up with stronger ones. Notice if there are any Empty Houses, and note them in relation to the other Houses, as these Houses are free of any significant Fate. You can borrow Stars into these Houses from their opposite House, or leave them empty and consider those Houses free. This is important, because a person may have little or no Fate in their career Houses and a lot of Fate in the Partners and Offspring Palace. If they are spending a lot of energy on their career and are unhappy, then you can tell them that their Fate is in the family and that this should be their focus. This does not mean they cannot have a career; it simply means they are working opposite the Qi of their chart, and it will likely be a struggle. You can advise them to get married, have kids, and then do the work for them; it will be much more rewarding.

Also, take note here of any Houses that are ruled by the Four Ghosts and if they have further affliction. These Houses will likely be a focus of negativity, and it can be tempting to obsess over these and how to "fix" them. You should acknowledge these Houses—having someone recognize and validate your struggle can be liberating—but you should downplay them and focus on the Four Rulers. The Major Ghosts are resolved by focusing on the positive Qi in the chart, not by obsessing over the negative Stars.

Now, go through each House one by one, and synthesize all the Stars in each House, making as many interpretations and notes as possible, always keeping the person's Qi Character in mind. Again, please start with the ruling Star, consider it the main story, and then add and synthesize each successive Star into that story. Consider the relationship between the ruling Star and all the other Stars based on their symbolism in the Royal Court.

For example, the Empress and the Concubine are a potent Yin pair that can create powerful alliances or generate gossip and drama. Consider any Ghost Stars or afflictions in the House with them, as these can complicate the story. Again, do not overvalue the Ghosts Stars or Minor Stars, but consider them modifiers. Always come back to the Royal Court as the main images. Even if the affliction is strong in the client's experience, the Royal Court provides the image of resolution; hence, these Stars should be the focus.

Consider whether each Star is luminous/exalted or diminished, either due to placement or to being in an exalted pair. Then, consider the opposite and proximal Houses and the Stars at 120 degrees, and evaluate their influence. In preparation, go through each House individually, study each in-depth, and make as many interpretations as possible. Take copious notes.

If I am giving a reading, I go through the Houses one by one, first introducing and summarizing the House itself, starting with the Ming Palace. I then go back to the Ancestors Palace, move forward to the Youth Palace, and continue forward from there.

Once I summarize a House, I introduce the ruling Star and successively go through each of the Stars in order of potency with the client, explaining the nature of each of them as a symbol. I try to communicate and transmit the "pith," or Qi, of each so that they understand it enough to think about it for themselves. If the client understands the nature of the House and the Qi of each Star, they will essentially be able to self-reflect, and they can give you the interpretation!

I then give the client all the interpretations I came up with when I studied their chart. I will try to provide at least five interpretations, if not more, and let them choose and tell me which ones resonate. I tell them it could be like this, this, or that. I remind them that it is up to them to discover how these symbols manifest themselves in their lives. It is essential to have a discussion and dialogue about each House until you come up with a satisfactory interpretation together. If you can't, then it is imperative that they at least understand the symbol enough to reflect on it for themselves in the future. They may come back to you months or years later, finally understanding what they could not grasp in the reading.

STEP 5

Summarize the Twelve Houses and the Play Between Character and Fate

Once you have gone through each of the Twelve Houses, it is time to take a step back and summarize. Take a step back and consider the chart as a whole. Look at the big picture and the dynamics at play between all the Houses, again with Character always in mind. Consider how all the Houses interact. Are the Partners and Offspring Palaces harmonious? Are the Career Palaces working together? Is the Health Palace afflicted? Do Wealth and Property align? Is there Ancestral affliction or blessing? Find the overarching theme or get a sense of the chart's flavor. Is it rough, smooth, dramatic, dull? Where is the affliction, and where is the favorable Fate? Return to the Emperor, Empress, and Ming Palace: What is the big picture, and does the rest of the chart support it? These questions are essential to review for yourself or your client, as these will be the big takeaways. Return to the client's Qi Character and reemphasize the importance of Character and the relationship between Character and Fate. Offer them all the different insights and dynamics you discovered when studying the big picture of their chart, and offer them a path toward resolution. Again, take lots of notes and think about how to summarize this for your client. Hopefully, you found this path together through dialogue, remembering that the client must choose; you are here to provide insight and guide them toward the positive Qi in the chart.

STEP 6:

Consider and Review the Ancestor and Ghost Profile of the Chart and the Inner Nature as the Fruition of Polestar Astrology

Finally, review the chart's spiritual nature as it relates to your or your client's Ancestor and Ghost profile and their Inner Nature as one of the Five Elements. This is about the very nature and resolution of Fate itself. We will discuss Inner Nature in the final section of this book. We have already discussed Ancestral Fate and how we resolve it by understanding the symbols of Polestar Astrology. The final part summarizes this and brings people to an understanding of the Fruition of Polestar Astrology itself, which is to resolve our Ancestral Fate and then experience our Inner or Original Nature.

If you are studying your own chart, this comes in time, after deep self-reflection and coming to understand the nature of your unique Ancestral inheritance. Your client must do the same and find this out for themselves. Your job is to communicate the nature of the symbols the best you can and offer them a path toward resolution through dialogue and discussion.

In the last part of the reading, I offer a summary of the spiritual nature of their Inner Element, which we will discuss in greater depth in the final section of this book. This is the deepest part of the chart and the "goal" of Polestar Astrology, if there is such a thing. I tell people that this is not something they really know about themselves until they do a lot of deep spiritual work, but it can peek through in "spiritual experiences." It begins to become more apparent as they resolve their Fate.

Here, I offer the client a positive and hopeful view of Inner Nature. I try to communicate and transmit the "pith," or Qi, of their Inner Nature in the hope that they can hold this and return to it throughout life. See the final section for a more in-depth discussion of the Five Inner Natures.

EXAMPLE CHARTS

EXAMPLE CHART I

THIS IS OBVIOUSLY MY NATAL CHART. I can think of no better example than walking through my own chart, as this is the first and most crucial step in studying Polestar Astrology. You must understand your own chart before interpreting charts for others. I have also included the charts of my parents, as they are my most immediate Ancestors, and this is a book about Ancestral Fate.

As I said in the beginning, this is to be a personal journey through Polestar Astrology, and it seems fitting to me to use real-life examples that I am close to and that have been insightful in resolving my own Fate. It is also valuable to see how these patterns play across the generations. I highly suggest that you do the same. With permission, get your family members' charts, examine them all in relation to each other, and look at the patterns of Fate that emerge.

When you look at my chart, you will notice that each box, or "House," contains a list of the Stars in that House, followed by an age range in parentheses. These numbers aren't relevant to interpreting the Natal Chart itself, but they can be used to create Progressed Charts, which will be explained in another chapter later.

For this and example charts to follow, I will write some abbreviated notes in the section labeled General Image as if I were preparing them for a client. This is the gist of what I might say after describing the nature of each House and each Star. I will include a general overview of the Stars and analyze how the Qi Character will digest this. Then, I will include my own synthesis, reflection, and interpretation based on my lived experience of these symbols. If I were giving a reading, the reflection piece would be blank, as it would be the client's response to what I have said.

The following notes follow steps 3 and 4 outlined in the previous chapter, and step 3 follows the steps outlined in the chapter "Synthesizing the Qi Character of the Year and Hour." Steps 1, 2, and 6 from the previous chapter are left out of these examples, as they are not relevant to our review—creating the Natal Chart, reviewing the View Teachings, and discussing Inner Nature.

My goal is to provide a pith summary of each House along with reflections based on understanding each Star's full potential. Remember, your goal as an astrologer is to transmit the Qi of each symbol by communicating their essence as concisely as possible, which is what I will try to offer in these examples. I suggest you standardize your preparation, doing it the same every time, starting with your own chart.

Here is my interpretation of my chart. I will write it in the second person as if I were giving myself a reading, but I will answer in the first person in my reflections.

<table>
<tr>
<td>MING
TIAN FU (EMPRESS)
Lu Cun (Storehouse)
Huo Xing (Fire)

(2–11) Snake Palace</td>
<td>ANCESTORS
TIAN TONG (VASSAL)
TAI YIN (MOON)
WEN CHANG (MAGISTRATE)
Yang Ren (Goat Blade)
Hua Lu (Salary)
Hua Quan (Authority)
(12–21) Horse Palace</td>
<td>PLEASURE
WU QU (GENERAL)
Tan Lang (Greedy Wolf)
Ling Xing (Water)
Di Kong (Void)
Tian Xi (Happiness)

(22–31) Goat Palace</td>
<td>PROPERTY
TAI YANG (SUN)
JU MEN (GREAT GATE)
Hua Ji (Jealousy)
WEN QU (PRIEST)
Tian Yao (Beauty)

(32–41) Monkey Palace</td>
</tr>
<tr>
<td>YOUTH
Tuo Luo (Humpback)
Tian Xing (Punishment)

(112–121) Dragon Palace</td>
<td colspan="2" rowspan="2">GREGORY DAVID DONE
Zi Wei Dou Shu Chart
FOUR PILLARS:
YEAR: Yang Fire Tiger
MONTH: Yin Fire Rooster
DAY: Yang Metal Horse
HOUR: Yang Metal Dragon

SOLAR BIRTH INFORMATION
1986/9/23 7:00am to 8:59am (DST)

LUNAR BIRTH INFORMATION:
Bing Yin /8/20
Chen

Tiger, Yang Male

INNER NATURE: Water</td>
<td>SUPERIORS
TIAN XIANG (TUTOR)
Tian Yue (Halberd)

(42–51) Rooster Palace</td>
</tr>
<tr>
<td>PARTNERS
Lian Zhen (Concubine)
Po Jun (Rebel)
You Bi (Right Assistant)
De Jie (Loss)

(102–111) Rabbit Palace</td>
<td>ASSISTANTS
TIAN JI (ORACLE)
TIAN LIANG (ROOF BEAM)
Hua Ke (Examination)

(52–61) Dog Palace</td>
</tr>
<tr>
<td>OFFSPRING

(92–101) Tiger Palace</td>
<td>WEALTH
Hong Luan (Red Bird)

(82–91) Ox Palace</td>
<td>HEALTH

(72–81) Rat Palace</td>
<td>CAREER/TRAVEL
ZI WEI (EMPEROR)
Qi Sha (7 Killings)
Zuo Fu (Left Assistant)
Tian Kui (Leader)
Tian Ma (Travel)

(62–71) Pig Palace</td>
</tr>
</table>

Example Chart 1

Qi Character

YEAR: Yang Fire Tiger

HOUR: Yang Metal Dragon

STEP 1

Consider the Earthly Branch, or Zodiac Animal, of the Year

The Tiger is daring, willful, impulsive, and characterized by their stripes. In other words, the Tiger has a dual nature that alternates between action and stillness. They are immensely strong, but this requires solitude and personal downtime to restore energy. They are courageous, energetic, dedicated, competitive, strong-willed, enthusiastic, unconventional, imaginative, dignified, honest, and generous when charged. When depleted, they are restless, impulsive, rebellious, indecisive, inconsiderate, morose, egotistical, stubborn, overly sensitive, prideful, and vain.

STEP 2

Consider the Influence of the Heavenly Stem, or Element, on the Earthly Branch of the Year

The Native Element of the Tiger is Yang Wood—the forceful, emerging energy of spring, of the sprout bursting out of the seed or the chick breaking its shell. The Outer Element, or Heavenly Stem, here is Yang Fire, and Wood is the mother of Fire, which means that the Native Element of the Tiger generates and empowers the Heavenly Stem of the Fire Tiger. Yang Fire adds force, vigor, sensuality, and intensity to the already forceful image of the Tiger. Fire Tigers are more active, aggressive, and engaged than other Tigers, and they are land mines of passion and emotion but also natural leaders. They find it difficult to see, accept, and stay within boundaries. Their power is found when they turn their power inward to devour their egotism, which turns to unlimited energy and capacity.

STEP 3

Consider the Earthly Branch, or Zodiac Animal, of the Hour

The Dragon is the symbol of the Emperor and the mystical synthesis of all the Twelve Animals; it represents unlimited Yang Power and the creativity of Heaven and is characterized by being ineffable and undefinable. This unlimited capacity of the Dragon must find a path and learn to self-reflect. When it does, there is nothing that the Dragon cannot do. When charged, the Dragon is strong, willful, grand, adventurous, outgoing, assertive, ambitious, charismatic, confident, flamboyant, demanding, and generous. When depleted, they are stubborn, aloof, insensitive, dramatic, sarcastic, compulsive, egotistical, overconfident, garish, attention-hungry, blunt, selfish, and unrealistic.

STEP 4

Consider the Influence of the Heavenly Stem, or Element, on the Earthly Branch of the Hour

The Native Element of the Dragon is Yang Earth—the ruling power of the dynamic center. The Outer Element, or Heavenly Stem, here is Yang Metal. Earth is the mother of Metal, which means that the Native Element of the Dragon generates and empowers the Heavenly Stem of the Metal Dragon. Yang Metal adds refinement, restraint, and discretion to the image of the Dragon. Metal Dragons are more withdrawn, fastidious, and self-reflective than other Dragons. Spiritual, political, and intellectual matters are enhanced, which lends the Metal Dragon to a natural transcendence and mysticism. Metal Dragons are the most articulate, knowledgeable, and moral of the Dragons.

STEP 5

Synthesize and Summarize the Earthly Branch and Heavenly Stem of the Year and Hour

First, we notice that these are powerful Yang Characters, so together, this Character is very Yang, which means very active, dynamic, and restless. In this case all the Yang characteristics of each Character will be empowered and strengthened, for better or worse. This Character is like Wile E. Coyote strapping himself to the Acme Rocket. The Tiger and Dragon are very similar, and we can say that the Tiger is like a terrestrial Dragon. They are often depicted in Chinese art fighting over a ring, so we can say that they are competitive but aligned in their nature.

However, the Heavenly Stems of Yang Fire and Yang Metal are in discord, as Fire controls or melts Metal. In other words, they blend well as symbols but not elementally, so this Character will be at odds with itself, creating a lot of mental and emotional turmoil. It will battle between the forceful enthusiasm, angst, and boundless energy of the Fire Tiger and the Metal Dragon's restrained, pensive, and withdrawn power. Elementally, this is like trying to sit down and stand up simultaneously; they will always be looking to move forward while simultaneously holding back, which often means they get stuck in the in-between and internalize this Yang energy. This can create a pressure cooker of frustration. The Fire Tiger is an eternally angsty teenager, and the Metal Dragon is a wise old man. This Character will then be a conundrum—immature and compulsive yet discriminating and controlled.

Both Tiger and Dragon are very capable and almost unlimited in capacity, so if this elemental discord can be resolved, then this Character can accomplish anything. However, it must rein itself in and apply itself diligently to a path; otherwise, its unlimited energy will become self-destructive and burn out quickly. This Character requires a challenging Yang Fate and many obstacles to overcome. Without challenges and obstacles, this Character will create them just to demonstrate their power and will be their own worst enemy. This Character is very independent and self-reliant and will have difficulty forming relationships, so we must pay special attention to the relationship and career Houses to see where there is support and where there are challenges to overcome.

REFLECTION

So, this is me. I have always been described as "intense," and this is indeed an intense Character. Understanding this dynamic between the Tiger and Dragon, between Fire and Metal, has been one of the most transformative aspects of studying astrology for me. I am constantly amazed at how accurately these Character dynamics describe me.

In short, I am all of the above. I embody the intense withdrawn impulsive and moody nature of the striped Tiger, frustrated and yet boundlessly energized by the Fire Element, empowered yet restrained by the profoundly pensive and yet expansive Metal Dragon. There's not much else to say. Every Character will probably think they have it the worst, but I must say, it is not easy being a Fire Tiger, and the Metal Dragon only makes it more challenging. Very often, things that I perceive as Fate are just my intense Yang Character acting out in relation to the Fire–Metal dynamic, which creates a lot of inner turmoil and restlessness. I am indeed my own worst enemy, and many of the challenges in my life are self-created, especially due to the mismatch between my Character and Fate, which I'll examine in the next section.

It took me a long time to accept my Character, but in the end, I am grateful to have such a "strong" one, as it has gotten me through a lot of challenges and allowed me to accomplish a lot so far. I know that I have a tremendous capacity and can accomplish anything I set my mind to, which includes writing this book in under a year.

In the end, the deepest challenges of this Character are its immaturity, restlessness, independence, and lofty idealism. I am too Yang for my own good and cannot rest to save myself, but often I find that I don't need to and can work far beyond what seems normal. I am deeply self-reliant, so relationships, whether with friends, family, or others, have been challenging to find and just as difficult to maintain. And my aspirations are often too big to be realistic, but this has also driven me to much deeper and more meaningful pursuits. It's enlightenment or bust.

I have therefore also learned that with great power comes great responsibility, and that I must reconcile the difficult aspects of my Character so that I can use my strength and vision for the benefit of others as a protector, healer, and teacher. I must turn this Yang energy toward the spiritual path for the benefit of all beings. However, as we will see in the reading of my Fate, this is not always so easy, as my Fate is decidedly Yin.

Fate in the Twelve Houses

MING PALACE

RULING STAR: Tian Fu, the Empress

SUBORDINATE/MODIFYING STAR: Huo Xing, the Fire Star

INCIDENTAL STAR: Lu Cun, the Storehouse

SYNTHESIS AND INTERPRETATION

GENERAL IMAGE: First, we acknowledge that the ruling Star of this House, and therefore the primary image of Fate in the whole chart, is the Empress, which is to say that Fate in this chart is very Yin, or mysterious and resultant. The Empress is a beneficial Fate with a strong connection to the Matriarchal Ancestors. Before going further, we must synthesize this with the Fire Star, which is mostly eclipsed by the strength of the Empress but is important here nonetheless, precisely because it is in the Ming Palace, which makes it somewhat central to life.

The Fire Star adds a strong dimension of anger, frustration, immaturity, and negative "fiery" emotion, making this a "moody" Empress. There will be a central theme of frustration and perceived outer obstacles that are mostly self-created. In other words, the Empress represents our powerful and guaranteed Yin Fate. As one of the Four Rulers and as the Yin counterpart to the Emperor, the Empress here means that the resolution of your Fate is guaranteed, but the unraveling of Fate is out of control; it happens by itself, and there is no clarity, certainty, or obvious direction available in life. What to do, where to go, what to be, and so on, will never be obvious, and you will never get to understand the mechanisms of Fate, but you will also be driven to pursue these questions because the Emperor is in the Career/Travel Palace.

However, the knots of Fate will unravel naturally, and life is more about learning to wait, listen, and receive. It is more about being than doing, and cultivation, deportment, and spirituality are essential. If you trust in the process and let go, it will happen. The Empress alone will naturally feel blessed, lucky, and confident, but the Fire Star is a Ghost that undermines this and creates doubt, frustration, and self-undermining through negative emotions, which means that you are your own worst enemy and can easily mess up your positive circumstances and Fate.

The Storehouse Star is auspicious but weak here. It does not influence the central image of Fate but essentially means that you or your Ancestors were very generous in past lives and that you will receive some payback for this generosity in this lifetime. When we look across to the Career/Travel Palace, we see that the Emperor is there with the Seven Killings Star, which means that there will be tremendous adventure, adversity, and challenges to unravel this Yin Fate, and this axis of the Ming and Travel Palaces is the most important in the chart. Looking at the Ancestors Palace, we see strong support and a lot of Ancestral Fate to overcome. All the Fate is piled up in this chart in the career Houses, so this is where the main story will occur.

CHARACTER: At first glance, this situation is inauspiciously matched with the Character, which is very Yang. In other words, the central image of Fate is very Yin, so the Yang nature of the Fire Tiger/Metal Dragon will likely struggle and create many obstacles where there are none, for it is very challenging for this Character to wait and do nothing. We can, therefore, say that the mismatch between Character and Fate makes this chart generally inauspicious, but this is not a detriment. It simply means that this Character must learn to be more Yin, and in fact, having a strong Yin Star here offers a counterbalance to the Character, as the Ming Palace offers hints of Character. You must learn to cultivate and carry yourself with the Awesome Deportment of the Empress, and you must learn the art of Wuwei, or non-striving. If this mismatch between Yin and Yang can be resolved, then this makes the resolution of Fate and the capacity to go beyond Fate to spiritual Fruition very likely in this lifetime.

REFLECTION: The central or ruling Star in the Ming Palace is the most important image to reflect on in a chart, and the Empress has been a powerful guiding force in my life. As I already mentioned, my Qi Character is very Yang, which is to say restless. With the Emperor and Seven Killings Star in the Career/Travel Palace, it is hard for me to stay put, wait, relax, receive, and be, at least when it comes to the outer circumstances of my life. However, my life has always been driven by a deep spiritual longing and sense of things. My life has felt like following the "breadcrumbs" and reconnecting with many past-life spiritual threads and deeply worn Yin Fate grooves. I have always felt that I have been here before and like I was "old."

I have been asking deep spiritual questions since I was a young child. I was introduced to Eastern spirituality and meditation at a young age and have pursued it since. Therefore, I could always "just be" in the spiritual sense despite the outer circumstances of my life changing all the time. Paradoxically, I also have always been like the Empress—restrained, patient, and cultivated—despite my brash Yang character, which is profoundly restless and frustrated. The sense of frustration and struggle created by the Fire Star has been subtle but powerful force in my life as well, and so often, I am my own worst enemy. I often make things worse with my own immaturity and moodiness. The Fire Star here is then worse because this is a central challenge for the Fire Tiger.

When I look at my life objectively, I see no substantial obstacles other than some pretty significant childhood trauma, but I have always been deeply frustrated by a sense of being unable to find my way and achieve what I want, which I have worked very hard to overcome. This sense of frustration lessens as I age, but in my early twenties, it was very strong. When I look at the Empress Star, I see that I have always felt compelled to follow my own path, and that at every given juncture in life, I have chosen what I felt was the best option based on my gut instinct. Each of these choices has led me down a different path.

I have never had a clear sense of what I am supposed to "do" with my life in the worldly sense, and no preexisting path, job, or career has ever made sense to me. I have, however, always had deep spiritual aspirations and an evident sense that I am here to "be" or "express" these aspirations rather than "do" something. I have had many passions, hobbies, and inspirations; the problem is that none of these things are "jobs." I have many talents, and my capacity is quite intellectually, physically, and creatively strong. However, again, I could never conceive of a clear path or career, which is still true today, despite having chosen one.

My life has been a frustrating, circuitous route of following my spiritual aspirations and intellectual interests, hoping it will somehow work out, which it did after many years of being somewhat lost. This led me to get four college degrees, travel to over twenty-five countries, live abroad, and eventually discover Chinese astrology and medicine as a profession, which is suitable but not my "calling." The Empress says that Fate is mysterious and nonlinear and that you never get to understand it. But, if you go with the flow, things will work out, and this has been true for me; I find myself now with a fortunate life, and it is a mystery as to how I got here.

I have accepted that life will never make sense or be straightforward, but I must keep moving forward while trusting the Empress. As for the Storehouse Star, I have been blessed to have support at opportune moments in life, and I surely would have failed to thrive without them. This support has always come from women and mother figures, although not from my birth mother, which aligns with the image of the Empress. This support has never been numerically significant, but it has been timely, and for this I am grateful. I do my best to develop gratitude and generosity and dedicate my life to the self-cultivation of the Empress, with service to others as my guiding force.

ANCESTORS PALACE

RULING STAR:

Tai Yin, the Moon Lady or Princess (diminished placement)

SUBORDINATE/MODIFYING STARS: Tian Tong, the Vassal; Wen Chang, the Magistrate; and Yang Ren, the Goat Blade or Sacrifice Star

INCIDENTAL STARS: Hua Lu, the Salary or Prosperity Star, and Hua Quan, the Authority Star

SYNTHESIS AND INTERPRETATION

GENERAL IMAGE: Here, the ruling Star of the Ancestors Palace is Tai Yin, the Moon Lady or Princess, in a diminished placement in the Horse Palace. This means that, especially with the Empress ruling the Ming Palace, the chart is deeply Yin and deeply connected to the Fate of your Matriarchal Ancestors, especially with that of your mother, as indicated by the Moon. However, the diminished placement of the Moon suggests that this relationship is challenged and weak, which is made worse by the presence of the Goat Blade Star.

In general, we can see that there are six Stars here, which is a lot for one House. This means there is a lot of Ancestral Fate and a strong connection in general to the Ancestors and parents. Ancestors rain blessings on this chart but also fill it with Fated obligations to resolve Ancestral patterns. The Vassal and Magistrate here are Yang and represent the Patriarchal and Matriarchal Ancestors. This means that the chart is strongly connected to both sides of the family, but the Fate being worked out is stronger on your mother's side. It is likely here that the Moon represents your mother, the Vassal represents your father, and the Magistrate likely represents a grandfather or intellectual lineage in the family.

The diminished Moon means that your mother will likely struggle, and challenges between you will strain the relationship. The Vassal and Moon together are an exalted pair and further exalted by the Magistrate, which means you are a "precious Ancestor" and that the Ancestors are working strongly on your behalf to resolve Fate. The Vassal implies that your father is very hardworking and will likely be very loyal and disciplined in the service of raising you. This pattern will be inherited, and you will also be hardworking, loyal, and disciplined.

The Magistrate implies an intellectual connection, and through the Ancestral line you inherit and are connected to the tradition of Wen, or cultivation. The Goat Blade Star here can indicate that you may be severed from your Ancestors and may grow up separate from them, or you may cut ties with them at some point. It can also suggest that you may lose a parent early, likely your mother, as the Moon is the ruling Star here.

The two Hua Stars indicate that this House will be the source of a lot of change and transformation, particularly around money and the success of your parents regarding work and authority.

CHARACTER: This Character will likely be very independent, and you rely very little on your parents or family for anything other than material support. The Tiger/Dragon will likely rebel against the authority of parents and want to reject any demands put on it. This Character will also be extremely capable of resolving Ancestral patterns, but you will do so in your own way by striking out on your own. The likelihood that you will cut ties and resolve things by creating distance is very strong.

REFLECTION: This House is quite profound for me, and despite being a Minor Star, the Goat Blade Star is crucial in understanding how it has manifested in my life. I can say that I have a powerful spiritual connection to my Ancestors, but I was mostly severed from them, physically speaking, as I grew up completely isolated from my extended family. My family consisted of just me and my parents, who moved to California to escape their respective families. They were "black sheep" of sorts. Both of their families were very religious—Mormon on my father's side and Christian on my mother's—and neither of them wanted to live out or give me that religious upbringing. So, I have a lot of aunts, uncles, cousins, and so on, but I barely know them, having met only a few of them a few times.

Therefore, my childhood was very isolated, reflected further in my empty Youth Palace, and I had very little connection to the tradition of my Ancestors, as I was not raised with any Western religion. Yet, I felt a strong spiritual connection to them, primarily through my father and grandfather, which the Vassal and Magistrate here represent to me. My dad was definitely a Vassal growing up, as he worked very hard, often two jobs, to support us. The Goat Blade represents sacrifice, and he certainly sacrificed a lot for our family.

To me, the Magistrate here is his father, my grandfather, and the continuity of intellectual and spiritual tradition is through them both to me. My grandfather was an astrologer and was very interested in Eastern spirituality and Western mysticism, which he passed on to my father and then to me. I feel a strong sense of lineage here, and I continue this through my practice of astrology and pursuit of spirituality and mysticism.

The Moon, which is the ruling Star here and which is diminished, is most certainly my mother. She had a tough life in many ways, which I will get to when we examine her chart, and our relationship was challenged, as the chart suggests. She was quite physically abuse to me when I was very young. She drank heavily and was also emotionally distant and unavailable through most of my childhood. The Goat Blade Star suggests losing a parent early, and indeed, my mother passed away when I was twenty-six. She struggled her whole life with mental health challenges from a very traumatic childhood, which resulted in many health problems that included alcohol and substance abuse. She died from hospital complications due to alcohol. While she loved me very much, and I her, the Fate here through the Moon was challenging, and I feel most of the negative Ancestral Fate I have in this lifetime comes through her side of the family, which the chart affirms.

The Vassal and Magistrate here are more positive, and I feel these offer a path toward resolution through hard work and self-cultivation.

YOUTH PALACE

RULING STAR:

None—this House is an Empty Court, or Kong Gong

SUBORDINATE/MODIFYING STAR:

Tuo Luo, the Humpback Star (luminous placement)

INCIDENTAL STAR: Tian Xing, the Punishment Star

SYNTHESIS AND INTERPRETATION

GENERAL IMAGE: First, we must acknowledge that no Star here is strong enough to rule a House, so this is considered an Empty Court. The Minor Stars will add a flavor of experience but no significant patterns of Fate. It is important to emphasize, then, that despite any difficulties in childhood or with siblings, no significant Fate will be resolved through these challenges. This does not mean that youth will be uneventful, but it means that nothing is finished or resolved by these events, and in childhood you are sort of at the mercy of the Fate of others.

Youth for you is sort of a vacuum, waiting period, or holding pattern. You will likely feel lost, despondent, alone, and like you are waiting to become an adult, waiting for your Fate to kick in. This is made worse by the presence of two Ghost Stars, the Humpback, which is luminous here and much stronger, and the Punishment Star, which likely represents a single incident but could also act to strengthen the harshness of the Humpback.

The Humpback Star here will add dimensions of trauma, struggle, rejection, isolation, and bitterness, which will likely manifest at home or through sibling relations. The Punishment Star can manifest as an incident or potentially as a pattern of violence, punishment, or trauma, and it can create a sense of foreboding. You will probably not have any siblings, but if you do, the relationship will likely be challenged in some way, or you may be distant from one another.

The empty nature of this House also means a lack of protectors or mentors, which can mean that you are alone in facing challenges and will have to develop self-reliance. It also means that there is no mitigating force eclipsing the Humpback, so youth will be rough, traumatic, and haunted by this Ancestral Ghost.

CHARACTER: Thankfully, the Qi Character here is already strong, resilient, independent, and capable of digesting just about anything. So, this Character will be a boon, because this is a rough childhood, which will likely push an independent Character to be more isolated and self-reliant. It will also make it difficult for you to develop relationships or rely on others. Tigers are very vulnerable when young, so this Character will likely bear the scars of childhood deeply, and trauma here can affect this Character for the worse. This Character will find solace alone in imagination, by having adventures, and by looking to the future, as the sense of emptiness here due to the lack of Fate will feel unbearable. You will also likely be a moody, serious, and intense child.

REFLECTION: This is a powerful House to reflect on, for despite my childhood being very intense, in many ways, it feels like not much really happened, like I was in a holding pattern, waiting to escape into adulthood. So, it makes sense that this House is empty and that no major Fate was resolved in my Youth, despite it being intense. In the absence of any stronger Stars to eclipse it, the Humpback Star dominated my youth.

It will suffice to say that my childhood was mostly blessed in the sense that I always had food, went to good schools, and had a roof over my head, but a lot of darkness plagued it. My father lost his business when I was five, which we'll discuss when we examine his chart, and this led to a lot of financial struggles in my family. My parents both drank heavily, were verbally abusive to each other, and fought violently for most of my childhood, and they both continued to have many problems until my mother's passing in my mid-twenties. Without going into too many details, the atmosphere this created was emotionally harsh a lot of the time, as my mother was very physically abusive early on, and many would say that it was traumatic. I don't dwell on these things, but it was rough for sure.

I have a half-sister, but we grew up separately, and I was raised as an only child, isolated from most of my extended family. So, I went through all these struggles alone and with very little support. I had two close friends through most of my youth, but otherwise, I lived in my own world, waiting to get out on my own, which I did as soon as I graduated high school.

Otherwise, there is not much to say, as this is an Empty House. Youth was harsh and showed me early the reality of human suffering, but I made it through. I do feel that I had significant Fate connections to Eastern spirituality in my youth, but most of these did not gain momentum until adulthood. I feel like these are connected to the Empress and are part of me picking up the threads of past lives through deeply Fated grooves.

PARTNERS PALACE

RULING STAR/S: Lian Zhen, the Concubine (diminished placement), and Po Jun, the Rebel or Breaking Rank Star (diminished placement)

SUBORDINATE/MODIFYING STAR:
You Bi, the Right Assistant

INCIDENTAL STAR: De Jie, the Loss Star

SYNTHESIS AND INTERPRETATION

GENERAL IMAGE: Unfortunately, this is a very afflicted House, as it is ruled in conjunction by two Ghost Stars, the Rebel and the Concubine, accompanied by the Loss Star, which is another Ghost. Thankfully, they are in a diminished placement, which makes them weaker and not as severe, but which also makes them more challenging to resolve, as they will be less obvious and play out through subtle emotional patterns of immaturity and rebellion. These Stars represent the Ghosts of Ancestors who died with unresolved negative relationship patterns, possibly from abuse, abandonment, arguments, or betrayal.

The Right Assistant offers a light, and potentially a way out, through help and self-reflection. However, you will likely struggle with romantic relationships and be possessed by Ancestral Ghosts who died with unresolved negativity around partnership. The Concubine will make you vulnerable and clueless, but it will also make relationships an obsession that you constantly look to for resolution, for the Concubine is dependent on partners for her livelihood.

The Rebel will create repeated, self-undermining patterns that you play out over and over, thinking that you are doing the right thing but that, in fact, are making things worse. This Ghost Star will cause you to rebel against everything as you cling to fantasy and personal beliefs. The Loss Star will create anxiety and fear of loss, which will likely result in more loss. Overall, this is a pretty dark picture that will require a lot of self-reflection, maturity, and unfortunately negative experiences to resolve.

Thankfully, the Right Assistant will offer help, which may come from other people, but you must recognize and act on this positive Fate. For even when you are surrounded by good people, you will continue to repeat these harmful patterns until you take ownership of them. It is your responsibility to actively break this cycle, rather than allowing your personal growth to happen at the expense of others. You will likely experience several challenging relationships, as these Stars will possess others around you. This can be resolved later in life, and you can become free of this negative pattern, but it will probably be a long and painful road. Thankfully, the Ghosts are diminished, so it may not be too dramatic or risk abuse, but again, seeing the subtlety of these immature patterns will also be more challenging. Character matters a lot here.

CHARACTER: The Qi Character here is both a blessing and a curse with these Stars. The blessing is that you are independent and don't need much from others, which is not to say that you do not benefit from them. This Character can be alone and make it work, and part of the resolution here as a Tiger will be alternating between being alone and putting yourself out there. The curse is the same thing: By using your independence and moodiness as a shield, you choose to avoid the very relationships that would challenge your behavior. Unless you take responsibility for staying through the discomfort, you remain your own worst enemy here, prolonging a cycle that only breaks when you decide to stop running.

REFLECTION: This is the most challenging House in my chart and has historically been a source of deep pain and confusion in my life. I have worked hard to resolve these afflicted Ghost patterns, and while it remains an ongoing journey of growth, I remain vigilant against the self-delusion these patterns could create for me. I recognize these Ancestral Ghosts stem from trauma in my family lineage, rooted in my grandfather's abuse of my mother, the unresolved trauma passed down through my mother to me, and my parents' conflicted relationship, which was the most significant source of trauma in my early childhood. Their relationship significantly impacted my early perception of relationships and led to years of struggling with romantic projection, immature fantasies, and unhealthy coping mechanisms.

For a long time, I lived in the shadow of the Concubine Star, lost in immature fantasies and projecting my unmet needs for safety and approval onto others, often viewing them as savior figures rather than real people. This was mirrored by the Rebel Star, which kept me caught in a self-created loop of struggle. I repeated patterns of unrequited love and emotional immaturity, falling for those who were emotionally unavailable until the pain of rejection finally forced me to look honestly at these Ghosts, which my previous spiritual work had failed to do. I had to grow up and do the character growth necessary to become a good partner.

The Right Assistant Star is the clear, positive light in this part of my chart. The Right Assistant Star is an Ancestral guardian spirit that works in the world in tangible ways to facilitate the resolution of Fate by creating a "butterfly effect," subtle opportunities for growth, change, or progress. But it is up to each of us to recognize those opportunities, step up, take responsibility, and do the work ourselves. You must "activate" the Fate resolution through choice and action, or it will pass you by. I believe the Right Assistant has helped me along the way, creating subtle opportunities for growth by leading me to the experiences I needed to resolve these afflicted Ghost patterns. All the challenging experiences I had in this House were a mirror reflecting these Ghosts, and although I used to view them as negative, I eventually learned to reframe them as gifts. All along, they were prompting me to grow emotionally and become more stable and successful in the world. That inner and outer work made me a more complete person and opened the door to meet the love of my life, get married, and move past old patterns into the beauty of a real, committed partnership.

OFFSPRING PALACE

RULING STAR:
None—this House is an Empty Court, or Kong Gong

SUBORDINATE/MODIFYING STARS: None

INCIDENTAL STARS: None

SYNTHESIS AND INTERPRETATION

GENERAL IMAGE: This House is straightforward, as there is no ruling Star, no Minor Stars, and no Incidentals. This is truly an Empty Court. The simple interpretation is that you are not Fated to be a parent. Done. This does not mean that you cannot have children. It simply means that doing so would express freedom rather than Fate. You would meet your children "for the first time" and create Fate with them in the process.

If you choose to have kids, then in this case, you can borrow the Stars from the opposite House (the Property Palace), which would be the Sun, Great Gate, and Priest. Having an empty Offspring Palace likely means you will not feel strongly called to have kids and could be ambivalent about it. Character matters here, as more domestic signs are more inclined to have children. The Empty Court here also means that your Fate is freed up to be directed elsewhere, which in this chart is in the career Houses. The fact that the Partners Palace is afflicted in this chart also makes children less likely.

CHARACTER: Your Qi Character is very independent and not as inclined to have kids as other signs, so having an Empty House here makes children even more unlikely but not inauspicious. If you have kids, you will be a strong, responsible, hardworking parent and role model.

REFLECTION: This has always made perfect sense to me, as I have never felt strongly called to be a parent and have indeed been ambivalent about it until getting married. I have always been open to the idea, but I prioritized finding the right partner first, and since my Partners Palace has been a challenge, having children has not felt possible until recently. As of now, I do not currently have children, but this could still change. If I do, then being a parent would be an expression of my freedom that I would embrace wholeheartedly, and I would endeavor to step up to the challenge and be the best father that I could be.

WEALTH PALACE

RULING STAR:
None—this House is an Empty Court, or Kong Gong

SUBORDINATE/MODIFYING STARS: None

INCIDENTAL STAR: Hong Luan, the Red Bird

SYNTHESIS AND INTERPRETATION

GENERAL IMAGE: This House is also straightforward, as there is no ruling Star nor Minor Stars, and the Incidental Star here, the Red Bird, is almost meaningless in this case and can be basically thrown out. This is an Empty Court, meaning you do not have Fate when it comes to generating wealth. You are sort of on your own in this regard. This does not mean you cannot make money or become wealthy; it simply means that it does not come easily, and you must use your freedom and work hard to generate it. You will not have much help or support, so it could be slow, but there is also nothing difficult standing in your way.

There is no mandate to earn, be generous, or create resources, but there are also no Ghost patterns that will make these things hard or cause you to lose money. We see significant Fate in the career Houses in this chart, so having an empty Wealth Palace means that you will work hard and resolve a lot of Fate through your work in the world, but this is not likely to be particularly lucrative. It's up to you. It also means that you may not be interested in earning money, and worldly wealth is not your main concern but more of an afterthought. You may wake up in midlife and realize that you should probably save money to retire. The Red Bird, again, means almost nothing, but it can mean that you experience a kind of financial renewal or rebirth at some point, perhaps resolving a debt.

CHARACTER: This Qi Character is naturally very hard-working and determined if it can focus, but it is also compulsive and prone to inconsistency and idealism. The Tiger and Dragon can achieve anything if they can focus and decide what they want, which is the hard part. This Character will also struggle with being both in the world and out of it, so staying dedicated to worldly goals of earning money will feel meaningless if it is not aimed at a higher purpose.

REFLECTION: This House always makes perfect sense to me in that I have never had a strong desire to earn money for money's sake, and earning has never been easy. I do not come from money—as my father would say, I was not born with a silver spoon in my mouth. As a kid, I never thought about earning money, and it was never a consideration or motivating factor in my life.

However, growing up lower-middle class in a house where money was always a contentious issue created a "scarcity mindset" in me. I, therefore, became minimalist and learned to be happy with very little. Buddhism, too, inspired me from an early age to appreciate renunciation and minimalism and to give things away. I have always had high, lofty ideals and a Buddhist sense of spiritual purpose, so I never took earning money seriously until much later in my adulthood. I have also been a career student for most of my life, always working in menial retail jobs while I went to school, so I never earned much. But I always got by.

I have always had to work hard for little money, and it was not until my mid-thirties that I woke up and realized that I needed to take creating wealth seriously if I wanted the second half of my life to be comfortable (and I do). Earning is still not easy and comes very slowly. I also chose a profession (Classical Chinese Medicine) that is perhaps noble but very inconsistent in income and generally does not pay well. Having an empty Wealth Palace is both a blessing and a curse, as I don't suffer much over it, but it is also hard to gain financial momentum. I am still waiting for that Red Bird Star to kick in and help me resolve my student loan debt!

HEALTH PALACE

RULING STAR:

None—this House is an Empty Court, or Kong Gong

SUBORDINATE/MODIFYING STARS: None

INCIDENTAL STARS: None

SYNTHESIS AND INTERPRETATION

GENERAL IMAGE: This House is also an Empty Court. There is no ruling Star, no Minor Stars, and no Incidentals, meaning this House has no significant Fate. This is also straightforward: You have no Fate to work out through illness, injury, disease, healing, or recovery or in the practice of medicine. This does not mean that you can't experience any of the above. It means that, if you do, it is the result of your freedom or conduct or simply a random act of nature.

Sometimes, people get sick and die through no means of Fate. However, many illnesses are Ancestral, and we can see this through the Health and Ancestors Palaces. If there were strong Ghosts in the Ancestors Palace, then we could infer Fated Ancestral illness in an empty Health Palace, but since the Ancestors Palace here is positive, we can say that its influence will more likely be strength, health, and resilience. Having an empty Health Palace means that your freedom, conduct, and personal choice are essential, as they are the primary factors that determine illness, health, and recovery. Character becomes very important, as it will create the main behavior patterns around health cultivation.

CHARACTER: This Qi Character is very Yang, active, and strong. This is both a blessing and curse, for you may be too strong. Without a strong Fate, this Character will still find it easy to be proactive, busy, physical, embodied, and full of Yang energy. You will find it easy to work out and cultivate routine. Resting will be the problem; you will find it difficult to stop, hold back, restrain, and rest. Burnout is more likely, but there are no Ghost Stars here to make it worse. Your health is purely a matter of Character, which in your case is strong and resilient. Learning to rest is critical, for you are like a rocket ship: If you do not refuel, you will crash and burn.

REFLECTION: Having an Empty House here has always made perfect sense to me. I feel that I have been blessed with generally good health for most of my life, and it is clear to me that health concerns are not a central part of my Fate. I have never had any significant illness, accidents, injuries, or health challenges to speak of. I do not take any medications or prescriptions. I have never had surgery. I take a few supplements, but otherwise, I am very minimalist in my health practice and focus on health cultivation through diet, exercise, and various "yoga" practices from multiple traditions.

Oddly, I work in healthcare, but this House suggests it is unrelated to my Fate, which frees me to practice medicine without deep concern for my own healing journey. As my Character suggests, I am very active, and most of my health challenges are constitutional and related to my Character rather than Fate. I am more prone to overdoing it, and I find resting difficult. At the same time, I generally have boundless energy and physical capacity that I am grateful for, as it allows me to be very capable. This will end someday, but this House suggests that any future challenges will not be due to Fate but rather freedom.

CAREER/TRAVEL PALACE

RULING STAR: Zi Wei, the Emperor Star

SUBORDINATE/MODIFYING STARS:
Qi Sha, the Seven Killings or Executioner Star,
and Zuo Fu, the Left Assistant Star

INCIDENTAL STAR/S: Tian Ma, the Travel or Heavenly Horse Star, and Tian Kui, the Leader Star

SYNTHESIS AND INTERPRETATION

GENERAL IMAGE: In this House, we find the Emperor Star, the central and ruling Star of Fate, which makes this the center of the chart, the pivot point around which all the other Stars revolve and resolve. Essentially, this means that your primary Fate in this lifetime is with your "work in the world," and it means that where you do this is important. You were possibly born in the wrong place to resolve your Fate and will likely need to travel a great deal, and perhaps relocate, in search of it.

The Emperor here is directly across from the Empress in the Ming Palace, and this dynamic is powerful, for the overarching Fate of the chart is Yin and uncertain. The Emperor suggests you were born in the wrong place, and this compels you to strike out in search of meaning, purpose, and adventure, to travel and to find your Fate far from where you were born. Your Fate will not manifest until you travel and move away from home. The Emperor mostly eclipses the Ancestral negativity of the Seven Killings Star here as a Patriarchal Ancestral protector, but the Emperor is afflicted by Qi Sha, which will create doubt and fear and a myriad of negative emotions and obstacles that make it more challenging to resolve your Fate.

The Emperor will push you to travel and find your Fate out in the world, but Qi Sha will undermine you and make it a bumpy and unexpected road; this makes the Yin Fate of the Empress even more uncertain, as you will experience a lot of challenges and obstacles and be haunted by the negativity of the Seven Killings Star. You will never be sure where to go, what to do, or what you are supposed to be, but you will be driven to find out, and this process of searching will resolve Fate. The struggle and conflict of Qi Sha and the Emperor together will grind away negative Ancestral Fate and give way to eventually finding purpose and meaning, but this will be a long process full of hard work, challenges, and trials.

What you do and where you do it are essential, as three of the Four Rulers are in the career Houses, including the Emperor in the Travel/Career Palace. The presence of the Travel Star in the Travel Palace suggests that travel will be more significant than otherwise. The Left Assistant offers spiritual and otherworldly support to the Emperor and creates opportunities, connections, signs, omens, and dreams that will point the way. The Leader Star here is minor, but it supports the Emperor and Left Assistant and suggests that you must step into a leadership role to resolve your Fate. The Seven Killings Star suggests that you will travel, move, and even try to immigrate, but you may fail several times (up to seven, perhaps) before you settle down. Once this process of doubt and searching is over and you dedicate yourself to your work and purpose in life, your Fate will be resolved.

CHARACTER: The Yang nature of this Character makes it restless, impulsive, and far too active to stay put for too long, so you would be likely travel and do all the above regardless of what is in this House. This Character will make it challenging to settle for anything normal or to stick with something you deem unworthy, which is both a blessing and a curse, for you are suited to this Fate but will also make it worse and more dramatic by being impulsive. This Character will be its own worst enemy in this regard and must learn patience and perseverance so as not to abandon ship too soon. However, this Character is so strong that it can handle all the challenges that the Emperor and Qi Sha provide, which is auspicious. More timid Characters would find this a curse, but the Tiger and Dragon will step up to the challenge and devour it.

REFLECTION: This is the most important House in my chart, and I have felt this as the deep feeling of being called to a spiritual purpose or mission in life, paired with a deep sense of doubt and uncertainty as to what this looks like in the real world. I knew early on that I would travel a great deal and move far away from home. I moved out of my parents' house at the age of seventeen, as soon as I graduated high school, and this catalyzed my ongoing journey, as I have been on my own since then and have had to work to find my way.

Since I left home, I have moved house well over twenty-five times, traveled in over twenty-five countries, and lived abroad twice. Both times, I attempted to immigrate but failed and had to return to the United States and start over. I have lived in four different states and moved many times for school or work. Many times, I have had to start my life over again in a new place, making new friends, finding a new community, and so on.

I have never had a clue about what to do with my life regarding a "career," so I just kept going to school, where I accumulated four seemingly unrelated college degrees. I have changed the direction of my life many times, hoping each time that I would find my purpose and what I was meant to do. I have pursued endless interests, skills, hobbies, and so on, becoming a jack-of-all-trades and master of none. Whenever I choose something and get good at it, I discover it is not "the one." Everything I do feels "off." Nothing I have done has ever felt like my true purpose, including what I do now.

I did eventually choose Chinese astrology and medicine. I obtained a doctorate and have been in practice full-time for years now, and again, while I am very good at it, I do not feel like it is my calling or purpose. This, to me, is the doubt created by Qi Sha. I do know my purpose is to serve people as selflessly as possible, and this is a beautiful way to do so, so I accept this.

Qi Sha has also made it a long, circuitous, and bumpy road for sure, full of many challenges, uncertainties, and obstacles, but I do not doubt that this journey has been the central pivot of my Fate in this lifetime. Therefore, this is a powerful example of the Emperor Star, and it has helped me understand the Emperor as central to Fate. I have also been called to travel and live abroad my whole life, and I will continue to do so for as long as I live. My wife and I aspire to live in Europe and travel widely, and deep down, I feel that my Fate will not be complete until I immigrate for good. Despite the uncertainty, I also feel like I have received a lot of signs, omens, and dreams that have guided me, and this is a manifestation of both the Left Assistant Star and the Empress working together to support the Emperor. The following two Houses are where I find my sense of purpose and meaning, as the Oracle and Tutor work together vigorously in my chart in service of the Emperor.

ASSISTANTS PALACE

RULING STAR: Tian Ji, the Oracle Star

SUBORDINATE/MODIFYING STAR:
Tian Liang, the Roof Beam Star

INCIDENTAL STAR: Hua Ke, the Examination Star

SYNTHESIS AND INTERPRETATION

GENERAL IMAGE: To the right of the Emperor, we find the Oracle, which arrives here with the Roof Beam Star, which together are an exalted pair and exalt the House. The Oracle makes this the central place in the chart where your spiritual path and abilities will manifest, and the exalted nature of this pair suggests that your spirituality will be central to your life and work in the world, and it will be oriented through service. This is where the spiritual sensitivity of your Ancestors and their spiritual or religious heritage will manifest the strongest and speak.

The Examination Star suggests that a lot of transformation will occur here through education and examination. This House is both exalted and unafflicted, and that makes this the strongest Fate Threshold in the chart and, therefore, where you will resolve Fate the strongest. The Roof Beam grounds and makes the spiritual Fate of the Oracle solid and practical, and it connects the Oracle to skills and trades traditionally associated with religion and the mantic arts, like astrology, spirituality, and medicine, which you are Fated to discover and study.

You will also be Fated to study with and serve many teachers on this path. As this is the House of career through service, your work can become a spiritual path that resolves Fate. The Roof Beam can also connect the spiritual Fate of the Oracle to a particular place, and you may have strong spiritual ties with people, teachers, and communities in specific places that you must travel to and find to fulfill, which is reinforced by the Emperor in the Career/Travel Palace.

You may be Fated to work as an Oracle in a particular community with people with whom you have a Fated debt. This work may not start until you are in the right place, or it may be in multiple places and challenging, as the Emperor with Qi Sha suggests. You may work as a traveling, barefoot doctor or nomad looking for Fated "power spots" that become central to your Fate's resolution. This combination also makes the premonitions and lucid dreams of the Oracle practical and straightforward. You can translate them into tangible skills and prescriptions, which exalts practices like astrology and medicine. As the Friends Palace, you will also find deeply Fated spiritual connections to people, communities, and traditions in different places, and these will tie into and be a central part of your work in the world. However, the Oracle can be shaky and inconsistent when it comes to friendship, so you will likely find friendship and community difficult to maintain as you move from place to place resolving your Fate.

CHARACTER: This Character is by nature very independent and not as domestic or people-oriented as other signs, so you will likely be more of a loner by nature. You will find it challenging to connect with people and maintain long-term relationships, but you will find it easy to work hard to serve others, if you have a clear purpose and mission. You will make friends and find work through your magnetism, charisma, and extraordinary capacity. You will naturally be adept at learning skills and overcoming challenges and obstacles. You will find the sensitivity of the Oracle challenging and unnatural, but the Roof Beam will make this easier.

REFLECTION: Along with the Career/Travel Palace, this is my most important House, as I have always felt that my purpose is to be an Oracle in the service of others. This Star has been the guiding force in my life, and it has led me to study many different spiritual traditions worldwide in search of my path. The Oracle has been a beacon or divining rod, and I have followed it for as long as I can remember. I have dedicated my life to embodying and expressing the wisdom and wellness traditions of India, China, and Tibet.

I have studied with many teachers and learned countless practices, teachings, and skills, and I now manifest all of these through the study and work of Chinese Polestar Astrology and Classical Chinese Medicine. Most of the places I have moved to in search of Fate have been about finding different spiritual teachers and communities, and I have been connected to many different lineages over the years. I moved to Colorado to attend Naropa; I moved to Thailand to study with my primary spiritual teacher; and I moved to Portland to study Chinese Medicine. I have now moved three times to serve as a doctor to different communities, and I will likely do this again at some point. This combination is probably what explains this book and my connection to astrology and medicine, as well as to Buddhism and many other important traditions. As this House is unafflicted, I consider it my guiding force, making my expression of these traditions feel "pure" and without baggage.

SUPERIORS PALACE

RULING STAR:
Tian Xiang, the Tutor Star (diminished placement)

SUBORDINATE/MODIFYING STARS: None

INCIDENTAL STAR/S: Tian Yue, the Halberd Star

SYNTHESIS AND INTERPRETATION

GENERAL IMAGE: Here, we find the Tutor Star in a diminished position, but we also see it in the Superiors Palace, which is an exalted placement. This balances out to make this Star diminished in potency and effectiveness but also strong in purpose, which makes it modest and delayed in its success. The Halberd Star is not a strong affliction and adds a dimension of discipline and militant hard work.

The Tutor is at home here in the House of leadership, teaching, and career, so you will be hardworking and find success, but the diminished placement suggests that this success will be modest and come later in life. Your true success will come in your fifties and beyond. You will be studious and find success and achievement through academics and learning, and you will be adept at leadership and management as a public servant. You will resolve a great deal of Fate through your job or career, and you will be dedicated and resourceful and eventually receive rewards and honors for your work.

You also have a strong Fate with a leader, wisdom holder, or spiritual teacher and will be a successor or heir to their tradition. You are Fated to have strong connections with teachers and to eventually teach. You may teach at a university or advise, train, and tutor successful people. Eventually, you will have students who will bring you further success.

This Star aligns strongly with the previous two Houses, and here it serves both the Emperor and Oracle, making career strong in this chart and the primary way you resolve your Fate. This House is also opposite an afflicted Partners Palace and so acts as a counterbalance. By focusing here, you will work out the afflicted Fate with partners.

CHARACTER: This Character is an adept leader and can be very diligent, capable, and hardworking. This further exalts this House and makes it an auspicious match with no notable mismatch. The capacities of the Tiger and Dragon match well with the Tutor, who will work hard for academic, spiritual, and worldly success.

REFLECTION: For me, this manifests in my life as being a career student with four college degrees and many academic and literary achievements. I have always read voraciously, and I have written poetry and prose since I was a child. So far, I have written five books of poetry and three nonfiction books, including this book. I have had many great teachers, including academic and spiritual teachers, and I have been a teacher myself. I aspire to be a teacher of Classical Chinese Medicine and hope to one day teach at a university.

I have studied under many spiritual teachers and have been authorized to teach in a lineage through Dharma Bodhi. This House also reinforces the reality that my Fate is in my career, as this is where all my energy has gone so far in life, and it has been through school and study that I have made this happen. As the Halberd Star suggests, I have strong, even militant discipline and am incredibly hardworking, diligent, and persevering. I have taken these three career Houses seriously since I started studying astrology as the primary way to resolve Fate. I trust that everything else will fall into place if I focus here.

PROPERTY PALACE

RULING STAR: Tai Yang, the Sun or Prince Star

SUBORDINATE/MODIFYING STARS:
Ju Men, the Great Gate Star, and Wen Qu, the Priest Star

INCIDENTAL STAR/S: Tian Yao, the Beauty Star, and Hua Ji, the Jealousy or Scandal Star

SYNTHESIS AND INTERPRETATION

GENERAL IMAGE: Here, we find an exalted combination of the Sun, Great Gate, and Priest. This is a very Yang and open House with a lot of freedom and opportunity, but it is mismatched with the concept of ownership. You will not feel at home anywhere, but this is a source of freedom. The Sun is modest here and suggests that you have a lot of active and dynamic Fate involving property, but the Great Gate makes this open and unfixed. So, you will move a lot and have good luck and access to a lot of property, but this will be conflicted in terms of ownership and make you somewhat of a nomad, drifter, or ronin until midlife or after you resolve your Yang Fate.

You will drift from place to place renting as you work out your Yang Fate, never feeling at home anywhere, but this can be sorted out if and when you settle down and purchase property. This matches with the Emperor in the Travel Palace and reinforces Fate's open, unfixed, and travel-oriented nature in this chart, as the Sun or Prince serves the Emperor and Four Rulers in the Career and Ming Palaces.

The Priest here makes you sensitive to Fengshui and talented at design and the auspice of placement. The Priest also manifests as a spiritual Fate connected to places, temples, pagodas, churches, and so on. It offers Fate resolution through meditation retreat, hermitage, renunciation, minimalism, pilgrimage, and spiritual practice in community and in wilderness and nature. You may live in a spiritual community in partnership with others or own property in conjunction with others. The Jealousy or Scandal Star and the Beauty Star are inauspicious and suggest that you will incur some scandal where you live.

CHARACTER: As suggested in other Houses, the Yang nature of this Character is active, restless, and impulsive, and you are likely to move a lot regardless of what is in this House. This is, therefore, a mixed auspice, as it is natural for your Character, and can also make it harder to settle down. The Character here will exacerbate the negative aspects of Fate, but it will also embrace the challenges and make the best out of them without suffering over it. You will embrace being a nomad or hermit and be adept at travel and retreat. The danger is staying still.

REFLECTION: This matches my life until now, as I have been a nomad all my adult life. I have moved repeatedly, always renting, and started my life over many times. I have always had decent homes and good luck finding apartments, but I have never owned property until now and have always been a minimalist. I have often sold all my possessions and reduced my life to a backpack and a suitcase. I have lived abroad twice, once in an intentional spiritual community on a permaculture farm in the middle of the jungle.

I have also spent about a year of my life in meditation retreats and done many months of solitary meditation retreats, and I want to do much more of this later in life, which the Priest Star reflects. And, without going into too much detail, as the Scandal and Beauty Star suggest, I indeed had a traumatic experience of misunderstanding with a roommate that became a source of suffering and strife between us, which was never resolved.

As of now, I have put down roots, started a family, and made my home. I have been able to share in the ownership of my house, and I feel that the positive Fate of the Sun here is finally starting to manifest for me. However, the Great Gate always lends to the feeling of adventure and openness, and my wife and I aspire to move to Europe, travel widely, and continue to grow our prosperity through the ownership of property.

PLEASURE PALACE

RULING STAR: Wu Qu, the General Star

SUBORDINATE/MODIFYING STARS:
Tan Lang, the Greedy Wolf; Ling Xing, the Water or Ringing Star; and Di Kong, the Void or Empty Earth Star

INCIDENTAL STAR/S: Tian Xi, the Happiness Star

SYNTHESIS AND INTERPRETATION

GENERAL IMAGE: This is certainly an odd and inauspicious placement in the Pleasure Palace, as we have the image of a grumpy old man in the form of the General with a lone wolf in the form of Tan Lang, the Greedy Wolf. We also have two inauspicious Ghost Stars: the Water or Ringing Star and the Void or Empty Earth Star. Together, they afflict the House and do not match its theme. The General is the most potent exorcist, so it will resolve their negativity, but it is not much fun.

The General makes you stern, serious, and disciplined. Here, it makes you enjoy discipline and hard work, which is a boon, but it makes you unlikely to enjoy yourself, leaning into an all-work-and-no-play person. However, you will enjoy working hard for the benefit of others. You will be critical of artifice and popular entertainment and find ordinary forms of enjoyment difficult.

The Greedy Wolf will make you a loner and stranger by the usual standards, and it will make you even more of a Scrooge—more austere, more all-work-and-no-play. You will be unique and very personal in what you enjoy; others will find you intense, but you will like that. You will enjoy solitude and independence and be adept at hard work, training, sports, martial arts, and so on.

The Water and Void Star will add dimensions of anxiety, attachment, fear, and emotionality to your sense of pleasure, also making enjoyment in life difficult. The General will resolve all this later in life, and you will enjoy yourself more as you get older and become more like a child as you age, experiencing a second childhood. The Happiness Star is well placed here but very minor; it will manifest as a compelling but incidental experience of happiness at some point in life as this Ancestor resolves.

CHARACTER: This is yet another House where the Character matches the Fate but also can make it worse. The Tiger and Dragon are prone to being very intense and different, and the Tiger is by nature moody and morose, which will make the General and Wolf even more intense. This will diminish this Character's gregarious and fun-loving aspects and bring out your moody and dramatic tendencies, making the General and Wolf grumpier and lonelier. The key here is to focus on the Yang discipline and pour enjoyment into things like training, sports, and martial arts.

REFLECTION: This is me, especially when I was younger. I have always been very intense and more of a loner. I find it challenging to enjoy ordinary or popular things; for example, I wouldn't say I like dancing to popular music, but I love death metal and mosh pits. I enjoy solitary sports like pool, chess, bodybuilding, powerlifting, and so on, which require tremendous discipline. I enjoy training, discipline, working out, and studying, and I enjoy hardship and challenges.

I used to suffer from a lot of anxiety and fear when it came to having fun, but this has gotten better as I age. I am much sillier now, but in my childhood up to my early twenties, I was deadly serious and found it hard to enjoy myself. I can point to a few times in my life that may have been the Happiness Star, but the most profound was in Thailand when I experienced an entire day of euphoria and happiness while staying in a beach bungalow; it definitely felt like something was passing through me.

<table>
<tr>
<td>CAREER/TRAVEL
WU QU (GENERAL)
Po Jun (Rebel)
You Bi (Right Assistant)
Tian Ma (Travel)

(66–75) Snake Palace</td>
<td>HEALTH
TAI YANG (SUN)
Tian Yao (Beauty)
Hua Quan (Authority)

(56–65) Horse Palace</td>
<td>WEALTH
TIAN FU (EMPRESS)
De Jie (Loss)
Tian Yue (Halberd)

(22–31) Goat Palace</td>
<td>OFFSPRING
TIAN JI (ORACLE)
TAI YIN (MOON)

(36–45) Monkey Palace</td>
</tr>
<tr>
<td>ASSISTANTS
TIAN TONG (VASSAL)

(76–85) Dragon Palace</td>
<td colspan="2" rowspan="2">MOM
Zi Wei Dou Shu Chart
FOUR PILLARS:
YEAR: Yang Wood Horse
MONTH: Yin Metal Goat
DAY: Yang Fire Rat
HOUR: Yang Fire Monkey

SOLAR BIRTH INFORMATION
1954/7/19 3:00pm to 4:59pm
LUNAR BIRTH INFORMATION:
Jia Wu /6/20
Shen

Horse, Yang Female

INNER NATURE: Fire</td>
<td>PARTNERS
ZI WEI (EMPEROR)
Tan Lang (Greedy Wolf)
Zuo Fu (Left Assistant)
Huo Xing (Fire)
Hong Luan (Red Bird)

(26–35) Rooster Palace</td>
</tr>
<tr>
<td>SUPERIORS
Yang Ren (Goat Blade)
Di Kong (Void)
Tian Xi (Happiness)

(86–95) Rabbit Palace</td>
<td>YOUTH
JU MEN (GREAT GATE)
Hua Lu (Salary)

(52–61) Dog Palace</td>
</tr>
<tr>
<td>PROPERTY
Lu Cun (Storehouse)
WEN CHANG (MAGISTRATE)
Tian Xing (Punishment)
Hua Ji (Jealousy)

(96-105) Tiger Palace</td>
<td>PLEASURE
Lian Zhen (Concubine)
Qi Sha (7 Killings)
Tuo Luo (Humpback)
Tian Kui (Leader)

(106–115) Ox Palace</td>
<td>ANCESTORS
TIAN LIANG (ROOF BEAM)
WEN QU (PRIEST)
Hua Ke (Examination)

(116–125) Rat Palace</td>
<td>MING
TIAN XIANG (TUTOR)
Ling Xing (Water)

(6–15) Pig Palace</td>
</tr>
</table>

Example Chart 2

EXAMPLE CHART 2

I will now examine my mother's chart. She passed away in 2012, and I will do my best to honor her through this reading while reviewing the most relevant examples from her life that will hopefully elucidate the connections here to myself, our shared Ancestors, and my father's chart, which we will discuss last. My mother's life was difficult, and she suffered a great deal, but it was also full of a great many beautiful things. Although she is gone, I believe she would appreciate some of her story being told here. Out of privacy, I will, of course, not share everything, but I will also be honest about her challenges, as her chart contains one of the darkest and most afflicting arrangements in Polestar Astrology, and it highlights just how dark things can get.

Qi Character

YEAR: Yang Wood Horse

HOUR: Yang Fire Monkey

STEP 1

Consider the Earthly Branch, or Zodiac Animal, of the Year

The Horse is energetic with a strong and independent nature, characterized by an edgy balance between being wild and being trained. The Horse is an unsuccessful plow animal, but it thrives in battle as a warhorse, meaning it needs to have a "battle" to fight. It needs things to do, and it is very successful when its energy is set to tasks and challenges. It goes haywire without struggle and will create challenges just to give itself work. Horses are strong, independent, fast, industrious, clever, magnetic, physical, consistent, outdoorsy, social, honest, gregarious, eloquent, and funny when charged. When depleted, they are restless, thoughtless, stubborn, hot-tempered, wild, accident-prone, violent, antisocial, and criminal.

STEP 2

Consider the Influence of the Heavenly Stem, or Element, on the Earthly Branch of the Year

The Native Element of the Horse is Yang Fire, and the Outer Element, or Heavenly Stem, here is Yang Wood. Wood is the mother of Fire, so the Outer Element here generates the Native Element, which empowers the Wood Horse to be inwardly impulsive and short-tempered. The Wood Horse is the baby horse, which makes it somewhat of an untrained bucking bronco. Wood adds an element of youthful responsiveness, ambition, and enhanced imagination and creativity to the Horse image. Wood Horses have an appetite for knowledge that can be applied to their constant and endless youthful activity and industriousness. They have trouble with too much wind, leading to difficulty with concentration and focus, and they tend to be more uneven and have difficulty expressing emotion due to immaturity.

STEP 3

Consider the Earthly Branch, or Zodiac Animal, of the Hour

The Monkey image is the closest to that of human beings and, therefore, represents our most fatal flaw: imagination driven by desire. The Monkey actively swings from branch to branch in search of fruit, and it actively scans the jungle to avoid danger. It represents the perilous balancing act of climbing to the top of the highest tree, which gives it broad awareness and vision and allows it to see far and imagine what lies beyond the jungle.

The Monkey represents "monkey mind" and fluctuates between wisdom or vision and selfish fantasy as fundamental impulses to push boundaries, test limits, explore, play, manipulate, imagine, imitate, and take risks. Monkey represents a kind of responsive, vigilant, alert, pervasive "scanning" that seeks to recognize threats and to adapt, play, poke, and test, ultimately to avoid danger. When charged, Monkeys are imaginative, intelligent, investigative, curious, resourceful, capable, adaptable, innovative, imitative, responsive, funny, and resilient. When depleted, they are frantic, nervous, erratic, crafty, cunning, manipulative, deceptive, unfocused, anxious, compulsive, and criminal.

STEP 4

Consider the Influence of the Heavenly Stem, or Element, on the Earthly Branch of the Hour

The Native Element of the Monkey is Yang Metal, and the Outer Element, or Heavenly Stem, here is Yang Fire. Fire controls, destroys, or melts Metal, so the Fire Monkey is at odds with itself. Yang Fire represents a kind of energetic consuming quality, and it adds vigor, vitality, passion, and even aggression to the image of the Monkey. Although we say that "Fire melts Metal," this does not necessarily mean conflict. Fire represents a kind of warmth or friction that softens the razor's edge of the Monkey's analytical imagination. While it can make reason and logic a bit blurry for the Fire Monkey, it can also help them not to get too fanatical with their imagination. The Fire Monkey is intense but organized, industrious, and frank.

STEP 5

Synthesize and Summarize the Earthly Branch and Heavenly Stem of the Year and Hour

First, we notice that these are both very active and physical Yang Characters, so together, this Character is very Yang, which means very active, dynamic, and restless, and all the Yang characteristics of each Character will be empowered and strengthened for better or worse. Next, we can say that the Outer Elements of Yang Wood and Yang Fire are generative, and the Year generates the Hour, so these Characters are elementally well matched and will blend well into one image. In many ways, the two Characters are very similar in that they are both very physical and need to be busy doing things. The Horse needs to be busy doing physical things, and the Monkey needs to be busy using its imagination, which is a double whammy when it comes to being active. This Character is active inside and out, and as such, it will have a lot of difficulty controlling itself. It needs to direct all this energy somewhere, or it will self-destruct.

This Character will have a powerful imagination and a very short temper, so they will be a handful, and they are unfortunately prone to anxiety and mania. If this Character is not given ways to utilize their energy, they will direct it both inward and outward in a destructive way. If it is well managed, then this Character is competent and productive both physically and mentally, and there is nothing that it cannot accomplish.

REFLECTION

This pair characterizes my mother very well, as she was indeed a very active, intelligent, and productive person with a lot of physical and mental energy that unfortunately did not find proper channels later in life and, therefore, often became self-destructive. Until midlife, she was very physically active and fit and embodied the Yang energy of the Horse and Monkey. She was sharp and quick, read voraciously, and loved science fiction, fantasy, and adventure books. As we will see in her chart, she had a tough childhood and experienced a lot of abuse; she was also born four months prematurely and spent the first four months of her life in an incubator. As a result, she struggled with a lot of mental illness in the form of severe anxiety and an obsessive-compulsive disorder, which went undiagnosed until her late forties.

My mother suffered from panic attacks, was constantly worried and fearful, and often catastrophized, which is characteristic of the depleted Monkey. She was also very self-conscious and obsessive about other people. She had difficulty controlling and expressing her emotions; she had a short temper and was prone to anger and violent outbursts, which is characteristic of the depleted Horse. I feel that this was made worse through the overly Yang strength of the Horse and Monkey combined with the combustible force of the Wood and Fire Elements. Although she was very physically active in her youth, later in life, she would ultimately succumb to her mental health challenges and develop substance abuse problems that evolved into many physical challenges.

Ultimately, my mother was unable to work and was put on disability. She took a lot of anxiety medication and dealt with an ongoing alcohol addiction. She also developed a lot of physical pain and became physically inactive. As a result, I feel that her incredible Yang energy, active mind, and imagination turned self-destructive, and this eventually contributed to her getting worse.

My mother's life had many ups and downs, and toward the end, she had a few years of recovery. It was physical activity that helped her to heal and get back on track, but ultimately, her anxiety during a difficult period caused her to drink again, which spiraled out of control and contributed to her death. Despite all these challenges, my mother was a very loving person, and I loved her very much. I always did my best to help her, but I regret that she could not get the help she needed. I was grateful that she had some resolution toward the end of her life, even if it was incomplete.

Fate in the Twelve Houses

MING PALACE

RULING STAR: Tian Xiang, the Tutor

SUBORDINATE/MODIFYING STAR:
Ling Xing, the Water or Ringing Star

INCIDENTAL STARS: None

SYNTHESIS AND INTERPRETATION

GENERAL IMAGE: Here, we see that the ruling Star of Fate in this chart is the Tutor, which is one of the Four Rulers, and it shows up here afflicted by an Ancestral Ghost in the form of the Water Star. The Tutor is Yang, so the overall nature of Fate in this chart is Yang, which is to say it is active, dynamic, clear, and characterized by things to do and connections to be made, and Fate will require that you engage with it to make it happen. However, the chart will be afflicted by an underlying trauma, anxiety, and emotional turmoil that must be overcome; otherwise, it will undermine the resolution of Fate.

Fate here comes in the image of the Tutor, which is all about achievement in career and education through perseverance, hard work, self-reflection, and proper judgment. The resolution of Fate is about learning central lessons and then demonstrating that through deportment. It is dignified and noble and represents the highest Confucian ideals of self-cultivation and character. In the Ming Palace, it asks you to maximize your most noble innate abilities and utilize your capacity toward leadership, knowledge, and wisdom for the benefit of others.

The Tutor serves the Emperor and is intrinsically connected to whatever House the Emperor arrives in, which is the Partners Palace, where it is afflicted. The Tutor is a powerful Ancestral guardian, and often this means being born in a stream of helpful family and friends, as well as quickly finding your role in life. However, as it shows up here with an Ancestral Ghost in the form of the Water Star, trauma will challenge your family relationships.

You will be intelligent and studious and work hard to develop the skills you need to resolve Fate. It is highly possible that you can resolve your Fate in this lifetime and then influence other people. You will likely have good relationships with teachers and may end up in a leadership role as a teacher or authority figure. You may also work in politics, government, or bureaucracy.

However, the Water Star may haunt you with fear, anxiety, self-doubt, emotional entanglements, and trauma, which could hold you back, limit your success, and make your Fate late-blooming if it is not resolved. Overall, this image is auspicious, but the Water Star, the afflicted Emperor, and heavy affliction in the Pleasure Palace strain this auspice and make Fate's resolution difficult.

CHARACTER: The overall Yang image of Fate here is an auspicious match with the double Yang Character in the form of the Horse and Monkey. This Character is very capable of resolving this Fate, but the struggle here will be focus and immaturity. The Tutor is a disciplined, mature, and studious image, but this Character is restless, distracted, and prone to erratic eruptions. The Tutor will add a dimension of studious intelligence, but you will struggle to stay on track. The Water Star will also underline the inherent flaws of the Monkey and plague you with anxiety. If this can be overcome, then you can manage this Fate and will likely activate it physically, mentally, and creatively.

REFLECTION: In many ways, my mother reflected the image of the Tutor, but she was unable to maximize it, and I feel the affliction in her chart got the better of her. She was very studious and intelligent, and when she was working, she was responsible, hardworking, and had moderate success. She mostly worked bureaucratic office jobs for insurance companies, which is an underwhelming, banal, but fitting manifestation of the Tutor.

She never went to college, but she was well read and proper and appreciated learning, which she passed on to me. She learned the piano and would make me rewrite all my homework in cursive handwriting, reflecting a sense of the Tutor's cultivation. She had a sense of dignity and presented herself well to the world. I think she struggled with work and wanted to do well, but she had too much self-consciousness and anxiety. Eventually, for several reasons, she could not continue to work, and I think she felt unfulfilled after this.

The Water Star here, which is not always strong, seemed quite strong for her, as it is tied to another affliction in the chart, making it more powerful. She had a central experience of trauma and anxiety, and this trauma came from her father and family, which we will get to in another House. She suffered from Water Star–type afflictions—stress, worry, fear, depression, weak self-esteem, and self-blame—for her entire life. This is an example of how Fate can be strong and show high potential but be undermined by negative emotions and trauma; we can fail to live up to our potential. I believe that my mother ultimately worked through a lot of difficulties and learned some powerful lessons that helped her find some peace in life, which was unfortunately lost at the end.

ANCESTORS PALACE

RULING STAR:
Tian Liang, the Roof Beam (luminous placement)

SUBORDINATE/MODIFYING STAR:
Wen Qu, the Priest (luminous placement)

INCIDENTAL STAR: Hua Ke, the Examination Star

SYNTHESIS AND INTERPRETATION

GENERAL IMAGE: Here, we see an exalted combination of the Roof Beam Star with the Priest, and both are in a luminous placement in the Rat Palace, so this House is exalted and therefore becomes a Fate Threshold. The Roof Beam represents the central pillar, or Roof Beam, of the Ancestral Home, and it connects you to place, tradition, and language. Here, it directly connects to your Ancestral homeland and its culture and heritage. It makes living in this place important, and if you do not, then pilgrimage to this place becomes an integral part of the resolution of your Fate.

You may also travel and live in different places because of your Ancestral Fate. The Priest here connects you very strongly to the religion of your Ancestors, and it is an auspicious connection and blessing to the Ancestors in general. The Examination Star suggests a lot of transformation in this House centered around school and learning, and this combination suggests a very strong sense of religious clan in the family, with a deep connection to place, ethnicity, geography, and heritage. It makes the Ancestors' home very important and makes returning home necessary.

Religion will be a strong influence, and a sense of lineage, inheritance, and power is associated with spirituality. As an exalted House, this becomes a Fate Threshold, which means that you can resolve Fate very strongly here, and this House becomes a doorway to transformation. It can alter your path in life, and here it comes through land, pilgrimage, and returning to your place of Ancestral Origin. If you do not make the pilgrimage, then Fate will be stunted.

This combination also creates prophetic dreams; you can connect to previous generations through dreams. You should learn the language of the Ancestors, read their stories, eat their food, and so on. You will be a source of pride for your Ancestors, and they will rain blessings on you and be the way to spiritual fulfillment and happiness.

CHARACTER: This Character is youthful and rebellious, and you will likely revolt against the authority of parents and Ancestors. You will struggle with the demands of religion and tradition, as you will want to be independent, creative, and free. Although this House is exalted, the match is a bit inauspicious. The influence of the House will be a powerful, but it may not be easy to manage or take advantage of, especially in youth.

REFLECTION: This house is somewhat of a conundrum in my mother's chart, but it does make sense, as she had a solid connection to her Ancestral origins in many ways. The conundrum comes from the fact that her father was an abusive monster, which we might expect to see here, but instead, that appears in the Pleasure Palace, which we will examine later. As I mentioned earlier, she was born four months prematurely and lived in an incubator, and I believe this powerfully contributed to her anxiety in life.

My mother was born in Würzburg, Germany, as her father and grandfather were soldiers, and her father was stationed there. My understanding is that her father, my grandfather, met my grandmother there; they married, and they traveled back and forth between there and the United States often during the early years of their marriage. My mother was one of four sisters, and one other sister was born in Germany. The rest were born in the United States in Georgia, which is where my grandfather's family has been since the 1700s. They were among the original American settlers who came from Scotland and settled in the Southern Appalachian Mountains there.

My grandfather also traveled a lot in the military when my mother was young, and she went with him on a few occasions, including living in Ethiopia for a period, which she spoke very highly of, as it strongly influenced her. Her family was very religious, and the Christianity of the American South was a strong influence on her life. However, she rebelled against this somewhat.

My mother had a baby, my half-sister, when she was sixteen, and she left home and left my sister in Georgia. She left for many reasons, but in part, it was due to religious guilt from the family for having a baby "in sin." She always wanted to be a good Christian due to her upbringing, but she could never fully accept it, perhaps because it condemned her, and so I was not raised with any connection to Christianity. My mother left Georgia and moved to California, where she eventually met my father.

In her heart, I think she was always conflicted about the Christian God and religion. She returned home a few times to Georgia but never to her birthplace in Germany. Her return home was an act of pilgrimage, and in one case, it helped her to heal for a brief period. I believe she resolved some of her Fated Ancestral affliction there, at least in part. Her father's side of the family had a long history in America, as they were here with some of the first Chesapeake settlers, and this connection was essential. I also believe she could have resolved a lot of Fate by returning to Germany as an adult and reconnecting with that culture.

YOUTH PALACE

RULING STAR: Ju Men, the Great Gate (diminished placement)

SUBORDINATE/MODIFYING STARS: None

INCIDENTAL STAR: Hua Lu, the Salary or Prosperity Star

SYNTHESIS AND INTERPRETATION

GENERAL IMAGE: The ruling Star of this House is the Great Gate, which is in a diminished placement, making this a somewhat afflicted and inauspicious House. The Great Gate is not an afflicting Star, but when it is alone and diminished, it can act as an affliction, as it means that Fate is open and uneven, and no resolution is really possible. It is not a Ghost Star, but its openness can make you and the House vulnerable, attract Ghosts, and create a haunting. So, you will likely have a very uneven and rough childhood, during which no Fate is resolved.

You will have little connection to your siblings, and even if you do well in school, it will amount to little in terms of resolving Fate. You may be slow to mature and be a late bloomer. You may have a vivid imagination and be very open, but this can make you vulnerable. You will probably not be close to your siblings, and it will be hard to maintain any connection to them or home. The lack of connection will make it easy to leave home. The Salary Star here means that you will experience many transformations and changes in the family around money and finances. Overall, this is inauspicious.

CHARACTER: This Character is very Yang and, by nature, rebellious and slow to mature, and it will have a hard time sitting still and obeying rules as a child; this will make school and home life challenging. The independent nature of the Character will also make it difficult to maintain relationships with siblings. This Character will find solace in imagination and activity as a child. The open nature of this House, then, will make this a struggle, and the wild Yang here will likely get out of control, leading to chaos and rebellion.

REFLECTION: I don't know much about my mother's childhood, but I do know that she had three siblings, and this House suggests that they were not close by Fate, which makes sense, as my mother left home before graduating high school and moved to California to escape her family situation. I know that she loved her sisters, but she always felt judged and betrayed by them and did not maintain much of a relationship with them as she got older. I only met them a few times, and there was little connection in my life to my relatives in Georgia.

I'll discuss it more later, but my mother had a very traumatic childhood. In short, she was sexually abused by her father, and the family did not believe her and called her crazy. This is why she felt abandoned and betrayed by her sisters, family, and religion, as they all condemned her rather than her abuser. This abuse was likely the source of a lot of my mother's mental health challenges, as it was rejected and unacknowledged by the family, and she repressed it for many years.

The difficulties this abuse caused went undiagnosed in my mother for many years, and she never fully healed. Her sisters did not show up to help her when she was dying, and I imagine that they blamed and judged her for this, too; at least, this is the feeling I got when I spoke with them while she was on her deathbed. Although the Great Gate here is not a Ghost, its openness makes the House vulnerable, and so the affliction in the Pleasure Palace manifests here.

PARTNERS PALACE

RULING STAR: Zi Wei, the Emperor (diminished placement)

SUBORDINATE/MODIFYING STARS: Tan Lang, the Greedy Wolf; Huo Xing, the Fire Star; and Zuo Fu, the Left Assistant

INCIDENTAL STAR: Hong Luan, the Red Bird

SYNTHESIS AND INTERPRETATION

GENERAL IMAGE: Here, we find the Emperor in the Partners Palace, which makes partnership and marriage the central way of resolving Fate in this chart. The Emperor is diminished in the Rooster Palace and afflicted by the Greedy Wolf and Fire Stars, however, which makes the central image of Fate resolution afflicted and reduces your capacity to resolve this Fate. The Left Assistant Star offers some positive support, and the Red Bird Star is almost completely insignificant here and does not need to be addressed.

The Emperor here means that you have a very strong Fated connection with a partner and to marry. The marriage ceremony is essential, and the marriage itself will be the crucible for resolving Fate in this lifetime. However, this partnership will be afflicted and likely full of arguments and struggles. The Greedy Wolf Star creates an unconventional and selfish approach to partnerships, and you may be alone until you resolve this, then you will find it easier to meet someone and partner. Once you do, the partnership, too, will be challenged by the Greedy Wolf and create isolation, selfishness, and arguments. The partnership itself may be antisocial.

The Fire Star is all about anger, frustration, and blame, creating fiery, explosive arguments and conflict here. Despite the affliction, you are Fated to work things out and resolve things in partnership, and this process will grind away Fate, as this is a debt you have with someone and need to fulfill. The Left Assistant offers some windows of positivity and the possibility of working through things, but overall, this is a very challenging House, and it will take work. But the work is unavoidable and necessary. This Fate can end and be resolved in a divorce, or it can play out as an endless, repeated pattern of argument, emotional abuse, and struggle.

CHARACTER: Again, this Character is very independent and strong-willed and will likely be challenged by partnership; the restlessness here means that you can only partner with other strong Characters who do not need you, as you will find it challenging to keep up with the demands of partnership. The strong Fate of the Emperor, Fire, and Wolf Star here will make this very difficult, for you will be forced into a demanding and challenging situation that is not natural for you, and the affliction will bring out your short temper and make the arguments worse. This Character finds it challenging to focus on others, but they can make things work if they turn partnership into a job or training.

REFLECTION: This is a tough one, for I was witness to my parents' marriage firsthand, and it was challenging, to say the least. I know that my mother dated a lot before marriage and played out her unconventional, Greedy Wolf Fate in her twenties, as she did not get married to my father until thirty, which was late in life for that time. As they remained married until she died, it was clear that they had a very strong Fate together. Given that my mom stopped working, it is also clear that her marriage was central to her Fate, especially given the intensity of the relationship.

Without divulging too much, it will suffice to say that the reading of this House is apt and that my parents' marriage was plagued with many challenges. They fought and argued for my entire childhood, and their relationship was often emotionally abusive both ways. There was physical violence, but only from my mother directed at my father. He was never physically abusive to her, but he would defend himself, and things would get very heated. My mother had an extremely short temper and was also very critical and demanding. As she got older and drank more, she did less and less to help around the house, and my father did everything for our family, which also led to conflict.

Their marriage was also antisocial and isolating for both, which had a lot to do with my mother's mental health problems. But they stuck it out until the end. There were a lot of ups and downs, good and bad periods, and it was clear that they loved each other very much, despite how dysfunctional their marriage was. The Left Assistant Star here may have helped in that regard. Although she had a very independent Character, she eventually became dependent on my father for everything and could not function alone. My parents were married until my mom died in 2012, and it was clear that their partnership was a grinding away of Fate for her that was unavoidable.

OFFSPRING PALACE

RULING STAR: Tian Ji, the Oracle

SUBORDINATE/MODIFYING STAR:
Tai Yin, the Moon Lady or Princess

INCIDENTAL STARS: None

SYNTHESIS AND INTERPRETATION

GENERAL IMAGE: Here, as always, we find the Oracle, one of the Four Rulers of Fate to the Emperor's right hand. She shows up with the Moon, and there are no other afflicting Stars, which makes this combination an exalted pair that exalts the House. This is the strongest and most positive House in this chart, which suggests that being a parent is a clear, Fated mandate from the Ancestors, who speak here through the Oracle. For you, being a parent is a powerful way to resolve Ancestral Fate and invoke a spiritual path of transformation.

The combination of the Oracle and Moon is very Yin and very potent. This combination is one of the most mysterious and otherworldly, for it combines the work of the spirit medium in a trance with the misty, lunar strangeness of the Moon, invoking visions, spirits, and intuition that will awaken upon having kids. This suggests that having children will become a source of spiritual growth and resolve your main spiritual Fate; it may even open latent psychic and spiritual abilities.

The presence of the Moon also suggests that Fate in this House will wax and wane and go through many chapters—some bright, some dark. This can refer to your relationship with your children and to your experience of being a parent. As there are two Stars here, it suggests having two children, one an Oracle and one like the Moon. As they are both Yin, this suggests having daughters or very "sensitive" children. Tradition says they will be capable and attractive and that your closeness with them will grow over time as the Moon waxes and wanes.

The children, especially the Oracle, will be a returning Ancestor who will act as a voice for the Ancestors and their collective spiritual Fate. Both Stars also suggest that sex itself is a mystical experience and spiritual path for you and that your desire for sexual union is very powerful. You may also use seduction and Yin Power very strongly to your advantage. As this House is without affliction, the Fate here is clear and positive, and as such, it should be one of your main focuses in the chart.

CHARACTER: This Character is not naturally inclined to be a parent and may even rebel against it, as it is independent, wild, and not very touchy-feely. The Horse, by nature, has difficulty showing love through words but rather expresses it through doing and action. You will work very hard for your kids, but you may need to improve at communicating feelings and emotions. The Monkey will make you a fun and playful parent, but the strong spiritual energy of the Oracle and Moon may also make this Character more anxious and nervous, so you go haywire and find it difficult to understand and enforce rules and boundaries, as you will have difficulty with these yourself.

REFLECTION: As this is my mother's chart, I am obviously represented here, as is my half-sister. My mom did have two children, so that aligns nicely. The Oracle and the Moon apply to my mother as a parent as well as to both of us as children. However, given my overt spiritual nature, I will go out on a limb and say that I am more the Oracle, and given my sister's waxing and waning relationship with my mom, she is more the Moon.

Again, my mom got pregnant in high school and had my sister when she was sixteen. From what I know, there was much contention about this in the family, so she left Georgia and ran away to California, which was a decisive act of the Horse and Monkey Character. She likely rebelled against the responsibility of being a parent and against the family's religious disapproval. She left my sister with her parents, including her father, whom she knew to be abusive people. From what I know, my sister's biological father was not involved much in raising her.

My mother had me fourteen years later, after meeting my father. She said she felt guilty about abandoning my sister and wanted to do things over again and do them right with me, so I was very much wanted and loved. Over the years, my mother tried to repair things with my sister, and they had some success, but I think my sister was always angry with my mother for leaving her, and for leaving her with abusive people. They did not speak for long periods and came in and out of each other's lives, which is very lunar—waxing and waning.

I was a different story, as I was planned for, though it was very difficult for my mom to conceive, and it took a few years. It was also a complicated birth, as I was placenta previa with the placenta blocking the birth canal. It was, therefore, an emergency C-section, and my mother almost died giving birth to me, losing her uterus in the process.

I think coming close to death while giving birth may have opened some latent spiritual gifts in my mom. My mother had a lot of anxiety, and she worried a lot as a parent and was probably overprotective of me. Again, as I have been overtly spiritual since birth, the connection between me and the Oracle seems clear enough, and here, this is a mandate from the Ancestors to birth an Oracle for the resolution of Ancestral Fate.

WEALTH PALACE

RULING STAR: Tian Fu, the Empress (luminous placement)

SUBORDINATE/MODIFYING STARS: None

INCIDENTAL STARS:
Tian Yue, the Halberd Star, and De Jie, the Loss Star

SYNTHESIS AND INTERPRETATION

GENERAL IMAGE: Here we have the Empress, the Yin counterpart to the Emperor, and the second most important ruling Star of Fate. The is the ruler of Yin, or resultant, Fate, which here means that your Fate with money is very Yin, indirect; you do not have direct control of your finances. The Empress is in a luminous placement here in the Goat Palace, so it is very strong, and it is flanking the Oracle and Moon with the Emperor in the Partners Palace, which makes these three Houses very strong and connected.

Money will likely be intimately tied to partnership, and you may marry for money. The Empress shows up with the Halberd Star and the Loss Star, which are weak afflictions, but nonetheless, there is the possibility that you may live in luxury but also meet financial ruin. Essentially, the Empress doesn't work—she is cared for by others—but she can manage and manipulate wealth, which makes this placement potent for speculation and investment but makes you unsuitable for ordinary hard work, as you may feel entitled and above labor.

This represents a powerful resultant good Fate and a payback in this lifetime, as money will never be a concern; you will be taken care of and supported financially by others. Again, you may marry a wealthy person or be taken care of by family. You have Yin Power here and can use it to your advantage to acquire wealth. Again, the afflicting Stars are weak, but they may cause you to mismanage and lose wealth and be forced to live more modestly.

CHARACTER: This Character is resourceful, adaptable, and hardworking, so you will naturally find it more challenging to rely on others, making you more capable of providing for yourself but also more likely to squander money irresponsibly, especially when you are younger. This Character is also likely to resist the nature of the Empress, which is to lay back and receive, but Fate here will push this Character in that direction, toward wanting to manage and manipulate money rather than work.

REFLECTION: This House makes sense, as although my mother was hardworking and responsible with money later in life, she did eventually stop working. I believe that she somewhat resented having to work in the first place, as she complained about it often and resisted it more and more as she got older. As far as I know, my mother often relied on men for money in her twenties, and I got the impression that she used them for this purpose, which was much more common and expected in the seventies and earlier, as women had much less financial mobility then.

My mother had a job when she met my father, but he was successful and owned his own business, so she stopped working. When I was young, we lived an upper-middle-class life and had a decent house. From what I know, my mother spent a lot of money frivolously at that time and resisted helping with financial responsibilities. My father then lost his business (which we'll get to in his chart), and as a result, we plummeted into a lower-middle-class life. My mother had to return to work, which I feel she resented. I think she hoped to be taken care of forever.

After that, my mother always kept a neatly organized checkbook and was responsible with money, but I do not believe she wanted to work. Because of her health problems, she would eventually get on disability and stop working, and everything was essentially provided for her, which is very Empress. She did not really work for the last fifteen years of her life, and she died at fifty-seven.

HEALTH PALACE

RULING STAR:
Tai Yang, the Sun or Prince (luminous placement)

SUBORDINATE/MODIFYING STARS: None

INCIDENTAL STAR/S:
Hua Quan, the Authority Star, and Tian Yao, the Beauty Star

SYNTHESIS AND INTERPRETATION

GENERAL IMAGE: Here we see the Sun, the Prince of the Royal Court and a potent Yang Star with a powerful capacity to resolve Fate through action. The Sun is luminous in the Horse Palace, and it shows up with the Authority Star and Beauty Star, which do not afflict by nature. So, overall, this is a very positive and strong House, but there are still dangers here. The presence of the Authority Star suggests a lot of transformation and authority in health matters, which is a boon, and the Beauty Star is mostly inconsequential but suggests incidents of Fate surrounding physical beauty.

The Sun provides a strong Yang constitution from the Patriarchal Ancestors, giving strong immunity and physical strength. It means that you are very physical and more prone to accidents and injury rather than illness. You can respond quickly to medical treatment and heal through tonification, routine exercise, and disciplined self-care. You are more likely to overextend and burn out young if you do not cultivate Yin and learn to hold back. You will seldom be ill, but you may be too strong for your own good, and overindulgence may be your downfall and catch up to you by midlife. If you do not channel your strength, it will be a handicap and lead to injury. If you can channel it, it can lead to longevity and robust health. You heal the best in summer. Traditionally, the Sun is associated with poor eyesight.

CHARACTER: This is a very Yang character, especially with the combination of Wood Horse and Fire Monkey. This is a match, but this also makes this placement much more dangerous, as it heightens the likelihood that you are too strong for your own good and that you will burn out and injure yourself. This Character must find ways to channel their Yang energy properly, or they will overdo it and self-destruct. If you can manage this intensity, you can be a physical powerhouse and make an excellent athlete.

REFLECTION: This is a paradoxical House for my mom, but it does make sense, for although she had many health problems and died young, this was the result of having too much energy rather than too little. It was a case of self-destruction from overdoing it and not having proper channels for all that Yang energy. The health affliction in this chart comes from the Pleasure Palace, which we will get to later.

When she was young, my mother was physically fit and active. At the beginning of my childhood, she would exercise a lot and often went to the gym. However, after my father lost his business and my family began to face many difficulties, she exercised less and less and started drinking more and more. My father drank a lot, but he was much more functional. The more my mother drank, the less functional she would become, and she started getting more and more health problems as a result. She became more physically inactive, and all her Yang energy was directed inward. It became more and more destructive, and eventually led to her burning out and developing many challenging health problems.

I'll discuss this more in the Pleasure Palace, but here we see how positive Yang energy can become destructive with a strong Yang character if they do not adequately channel the Yang. My mother died young and because of overindulgence and burnout. Her death was complicated, and while there were many factors, alcohol was underlying all of them. I believe that, if she never drank and maintained her early exercise routines, she could have lived a very long life. As it was, she had too much Yang and too much Wood and Fire Element.

CAREER/TRAVEL PALACE

RULING STAR: Wu Qu, the General (diminished placement)

SUBORDINATE/MODIFYING STARS: Po Jun, the Rebel or Breaking Rank Star, and You Bi, the Right Assistant

INCIDENTAL STAR:
Tian Ma, the Travel or Heavenly Horse Star

SYNTHESIS AND INTERPRETATION

GENERAL IMAGE: Here, we see the General Star in a diminished placement, showing up with the Rebel, Right Assistant, and Travel Stars. Although the General is a powerful exorcist, it is diminished here, so the Rebel Star creates more affliction, making this a complex and challenging House. The Rebel Star causes rebellion, or to "break rank," and often this means that you are forced to leave home due to difficult circumstances and that you leave as an act of rebellion, possibly against authority and elders, as represented by the General. You are then forced to struggle and work hard to resolve this with late-blooming success, as the General always postpones success until later in life. The Travel Star makes it more likely that you will travel and leave home, and there will be an element of wandering and self-sacrifice that you must overcome.

Your success will be gradual, and discipline, perseverance, and adaptability are crucial, but these will be undermined by the Rebel, which is an Ancestral Ghost that likely died far from home, possibly on the battlefield. This Ghost makes you act out and rebel, but it will be in contention with the General, who pushes you toward responsible, hard work. There will be a push and pull between these, and although the General will win out, it will be a struggle because the General is diminished. The Right Assistant will provide guidance, teachers, opportunities, and career help.

You will likely settle into a standard job, possibly one that no one else wants to do, and be hardworking and succeed in management and strategizing. However, you will take your accomplishments lightly, and your contributions will not be recognized. This House is somewhat dark and may be a struggle and not a lot of fun. Your Fate with work and travel in the world outside the family is not the main event in this chart, as none of the career Houses are very strong. Overall, the Fate is much more modest here; family is where all the Fate is in your chart, so this House becomes more of an obligation.

CHARACTER: As already mentioned, the Yang nature of this Character is active, restless, and rebellious, so you will have a hard time staying put and being responsible. But the Horse can be very productive if it is set to a task; for the Horse, life is work, and it needs stuff to do. The Monkey will be easily distracted and will rebel at the drop of a hat. This makes the House more dramatic, and it is likely that a significant act of rebellion will initiate the Fate here and make the General less potent.

REFLECTION: As far as I can tell, the Fate in this House was initiated by my mother leaving or running away from home as an act of rebellion against the judgment and authority of parents, family, and religion, which is represented here by the General Star. As I already mentioned, she had a baby, my half-sister, when she was very young, and she ran away from home to California to escape her family and the responsibility of being a parent. Until she met my dad, she had a life of wandering, and she was more of a rebel in her twenties.

Ultimately, my mother settled down, but she never had much of a career; she did more midlevel strategic work in insurance, which is more reflected in the next House. She worked but never saw any real career success. Her success was much more moderate, and high level success would have been possible but late-blooming if she had stuck with it. As this combination's diminished and afflicted nature was lackluster in terms of work, I think the dynamic between the General and Rebel more strongly represents her striking out on her own, rebelling against tradition, and moving away from home and to California. In other words, it is related more to this being the Travel Palace than the Career Palace.

This House is a mixed image, for it was rebellious and irresponsible to leave her child, but it was also understandable, as she was escaping an abusive and judgmental environment that was probably very unhealthy and not likely to get any better. Her Character made this rebellion much easier and more predictable; there are many Characters that probably would have stayed, but a Wood Horse born in Fire Monkey Hour is primed to rebel and lash out very easily. We can see here a Fated choice between staying and being responsible but having a very hard time (the General) versus rebelling and striking out on her own (the Rebel). The diminished General and restless Yang character make it easy to see how my mom chose to run away from home.

ASSISTANTS PALACE

RULING STAR: Tian Tong, the Vassal

SUBORDINATE/MODIFYING STARS: None

INCIDENTAL STARS: None

SYNTHESIS AND INTERPRETATION

GENERAL IMAGE: Here, we see the Vassal Star alone and unafflicted, which makes this an easy House to interpret and understand. We only have to understand the single image of the Vassal with no other modifying Stars. The Vassal is very well placed in the Assistants Palace, and alone, it makes for a modest, service-oriented career as a subordinate or assistant. You will make a sterling assistant and excel as a Vassal in service of something greater. You will be generous, hardworking, and loyal and enjoy being second in command.

The Vassal here enjoys working behind the scenes, being part of a team, and following orders. It is not trying to be the Emperor or compete with the Prince. Here, it really is a samurai who will work hard and die in battle with their platoon. You will have a favorable Fate with friends, helpers, and co-workers, and you will both give and receive a lot of help with good outcomes. This House is unafflicted, but the afflicted Career/Travel Palace and empty Superiors Palace make the overall image of Fate in a career quite modest, ordinary, and banal.

CHARACTER: With maturity, this Character can succeed in this setup, but it is by nature more rebellious and immature, so success is challenging. This Character will find mundane work boring and a chore, so the more creative, engaging, and active the work, the more likely you will be to succeed at work. This Character can be gregarious, playful, and fun, so this House is great for making friends.

REFLECTION: This House is easy to interpret, and I think it applies primarily to my mother's career, which, as the Vassal suggests, was modest and mostly successful. As far as I know, she worked simple, service-oriented jobs before working in risk management for insurance companies. She worked midlevel desk jobs, and as far as I know, she had an ordinary work life, not much to write home about.

My mother had a lot of social anxiety, and she was quite antisocial, which is a depleted expression of her Character. But she got along well with her co-workers and, at times in her early life, was more social and had friends. The Fate in her chart is not strong in the career Houses, so there is little to say here. As I already mentioned, she was on disability and stopped working in her forties, as she was in a lot of pain.

SUPERIORS PALACE

RULING STAR:

None—this House is an Empty Court, or Kong Gong

SUBORDINATE/MODIFYING STAR:

Yang Ren, the Goat Blade or Sacrifice Star

INCIDENTAL STARS: Tian Xi, the Happiness Star, and Di Kong, the Void or Empty Earth Star

SYNTHESIS AND INTERPRETATION

GENERAL IMAGE: This is an Empty House, meaning you do not have Fate here. It has a few Ghost Stars: the Happiness Star, the Void or Empty Earth Star, and the Goat Blade or Sacrifice Star, which is the strongest; so this House has an element of haunting. In general, an empty Superiors Palace suggests that you do not have Fate for significant success in your career or as a leader or teacher. This does not mean that you cannot achieve success; it simply means that Fate does not support it, and it will be harder to achieve. The Fate is elsewhere in this chart.

The Goat Blade suggests that you may lose or quit a job, lose a leadership position, or have a falling out with a teacher, boss, or mentor. This may be negative, but it will have a positive outcome in the long run. The Void Star makes it much harder to utilize the freedom here due to feeling lost, and it can create minor misfortune. The Happiness Star is almost entirely inconsequential and can be ignored. It may be as minor as feeling happy when you get a promotion.

CHARACTER: This Character is not suited to leadership and is more of a creative, independent type who wants to do its own thing. You will naturally need help with maturity and discipline, so much so that a standard career path would be challenging. An Empty House here is not an affliction, but it makes sense of direction and purpose more open-ended and unclear, as there will not be a direct path in life regarding work. This can undermine your focus and make it more challenging to follow a path.

REFLECTION: This House is easy to understand, as my mother did not have much of a career and eventually stopped working. It was not a significant mandate of her Fate, so there is little to say. As far as I know, she had little aspirations for a career nor a strong sense of purpose or mission in life outside of motherhood. Her major Fate is in the Partners, Offspring, and Wealth Palaces; it was at home with family, which is how her life played out.

PROPERTY PALACE

RULING STAR: Wen Chang, the Magistrate

SUBORDINATE/MODIFYING STARS: None

INCIDENTAL STARS: Lu Cun, the Storehouse; Tian Xing, the Punishment Star; and Hua Ji, the Jealousy or Scandal Star

SYNTHESIS AND INTERPRETATION

GENERAL IMAGE: The strongest Star in this House is the Magistrate, and it shows up with the Storehouse Star, the Punishment Star, and the Jealousy or Scandal Star. Overall, this House is modest, as the Magistrate is one of the weaker Stars of the Royal Court. The Magistrate offers a modest Fate with owning property, but it also suggests that the Magistrate is more focused on other things. The Magistrate will be more interested in owning things representing Wen: learning, culture, art, music, literature, and so on. This placement says that you can do well and that your Fate with property can increase in value as you age. You can also be rewarded with property as a gift or inheritance.

The Magistrate goes where they must for their work, and property is a sidenote, so you may move often due to Fated circumstances around work. The Punishment and Jealousy Stars suggest a lot of transformation and strife at home and with the property you own or receive. The Storehouse Star suggests you will receive some payback through gifts or inheritance. Overall, this is a modest, slightly afflicted, and weak Fate for significant property ownership, and it suggests your connection to property is stronger as a connection to the legacy and tradition of your Ancestors through art, music, literature, and so on.

CHARACTER: As already mentioned, this Character is quite restless and prone to agitation if it sits still for too long. The Wood Horse and Fire Monkey will not have a strong need for or interest in owning property, but they will be naturally attracted to things that represent creativity, so you will want to own things related to Wen, which is an auspicious match.

REFLECTION: The strongest connection here is to my mother's love of Wen, as she was an avid reader and loved music. When I was growing up, we had two upright pianos, and our house was full of books. It was basically a library, with at least two full-sized bookshelves in every room. We had thousands of books, which made moving difficult, and we moved many times. My father has this Star in the Pleasure Palace, so there was an affinity between them for books and learning. My mother had a sense of culture and refinement, although her social anxiety made it difficult for her to go out and enjoy these things, so she enjoyed them at home.

Her Fate here, and my father's, was modest, for we always had to rent after my father lost his business. We lived in nice houses, but they were modest, and we had to move a lot over the years due to different circumstances regarding work, money, and landlords. There was a lot of arguing, strife, and difficulties at home for my mother, both in her childhood home and at our house, so the Punishment and Jealousy Stars make sense here, as home for her always seemed to be afflicted. The Storehouse also makes sense, for she was mostly gifted property and provided for by others.

PLEASURE PALACE

RULING STARS: Lian Zhen, the Concubine, and Qi Sha, the Seven Killings or Executioner Star

SUBORDINATE/MODIFYING STAR: Tuo Luo, the Humpback or Rejection Star (luminous placement)

INCIDENTAL STAR: Tian Kui, the Leader

SYNTHESIS AND INTERPRETATION

GENERAL IMAGE: We now get to what is, unfortunately, the central House in this chart, as it is the most afflicted and represents one of the darkest possible combinations in Polestar Astrology. This House is so strong in its affliction that it undermines the rest of the Houses and creates the potential to distort the overall picture of Fate.

This House contains the Concubine and Seven Killings or Executioner Star, which, when combined, are the most potent afflicting force in Polestar Astrology and can create some of the darkest possible stories. This is made worse by the presence of the Humpback or Rejection Star, which is in a luminous placement, making it even stronger. Combined, we can say that this is potentially an Ancestral Demonic possession and that Qi Sha, the Seven Killings Star, is coming for your life, especially in the Pleasure Palace, which is arguably the worst place to have this combination.

When Qi Sha shows up with the Concubine Star, it gets very dark, and it essentially means that you will have a short life and that pleasure and enjoyment in life will always be a dark struggle. You will suffer from challenging mental health problems due to the promptings and obstructions of the unsettled dead. You will likely die in a tangle of negative emotions and be devoured by this Demon in death. In the Pleasure Palace, this means that pleasure, sex, drugs, and so on are all very problematic, and there will be trauma, addiction, abuse, and possibly an untimely, confusing, and tragic death.

The Leader Star here suggests that there will be trauma associated with an authority figure. Unfortunately, this is all very difficult to overcome; it is not impossible, but the likelihood is high that this will manifest as a very dark story. It is very important to study your genealogy here and discover the source of this Ancestral Demon, as there is likely a dark generational trauma in your family that has been passed down, unresolved, through the generations and is getting worse and worse.

CHARACTER: Unfortunately, this Character is prone to immaturity and is so Yang that it makes self-discipline very challenging and addictive behavior patterns more likely. This makes the darkness in this House even more difficult to overcome, so this is a very inauspicious match.

REFLECTION: This House is difficult to talk about, but in honor of my mother's struggles in life, it should be discussed plainly and with honesty, as it is a powerful example of how dark this combination can get. In hindsight, it is powerful to see my mother's challenges—and in many ways, my own challenges—reflected here, as our Fate was intertwined. The challenges here reverberate in my own life, as they affected my mother deeply and, therefore, affected me and my father.

The first part of this story, I believe, starts with my mother's birth. She was born in Germany on an army base four months premature. This was in 1954, so the medical technology was not great. She spent the first four months of her life in an incubator without any human contact or touch. Her whole life, she suffered from severe anxiety, claustrophobia, and paranoia; she always felt like people were watching her. She had panic attacks and could not ride in elevators. I believe the incubator contributed to this, but I suppose that is hearsay.

The next part of the story is the worst. Without going into detail, it will suffice to say that her father was a monster. He repeatedly sexually abused my mother as a young child, and from what I know, he singled her out, although it is possible that he abused all of them. It is also possible that he was a serial rapist and even a murderer, although he was never charged as such. I was also told that he invited other men to abuse her. Because she was singled out, her sisters and mother did not believe her, and the family was in denial about the situation. She was called crazy and a liar. I believe this was part of the reason she moved to California: to escape.

The rest of the story is summarized by the fact that my mother suffered a lot of mental health problems because of this trauma, and they went undiagnosed, unrecognized, and untreated. She was eventually diagnosed with OCD and severe anxiety, depression, and bipolar disorder. The final part of the story was slow and took place over most of my life. When I was young, my mother was much healthier and more positive, but her mental health challenges created many problems in my parents' relationship, and these were brought out during the challenges that my family faced.

My father lost the international business that he had spent twelve years building, and after that, we faced significant challenges. In short, both my parents drank to cope, and they became alcoholics. My father remained functional, but my mother did not. She drank more and more over the years, which led to her many health challenges that she almost died from many times.

My mother had periods when she drank less and recovered, but she could not overcome the use of alcohol as a coping mechanism, and the last time she started drinking again, it led to her death, which was complicated: In short, she mixed alcohol with anxiety medications, and this caused her to lose consciousness. She was taken to the hospital, and the doctors were not told that she was an alcoholic. This caused them to misdiagnose her and prescribe medications that have deleterious effects when mixed with alcohol. She then went into a drug-induced coma, which she never came out of. She was put on life support, but eventually, her liver and kidneys shut down; the official cause of her death was hepatorenal failure. I was told that she could not live if taken off life support, so I decided to take her off it, as I did not want her to live in a vegetative state. She died within a few hours.

From the perspective of Polestar Astrology, this was an Ancestral Demon that came for my mother's life. Qi Sha wants to cause pain, slow suffering, and death, and this was the case with my mother. I have done genealogy, but I still do not know the exact origin of this darkness on her side of the family. It came through her father and went after her.

I loved my mother very much, and although her life was difficult and tragic in many ways, it also contained a lot of joy and happiness. I believe that she was happiest when she was with me and that I was the most important thing she was proud of creating in her life. I have personally done a lot of work spiritually with my mother to resolve her death and to resolve this Ancestral Demon, and I believe that I have done this and that she is at peace.

It took many years for me to feel that my mother is at peace, but I have had visions of her taking a good rebirth, and now I know that she is resolved. My father also has the combination of the Concubine and Qi Sha, the Seven Killings Star, in his chart, which we will examine next, and his life has been very tough in many ways as well. Both of my parents' charts have Demonic possession in them, but my chart does not. Essentially, they dealt with this so I did not have to. Here, we can see how this Ancestral Fate is reflected across generations and across charts. I highly suggest that you look at your parents' charts and examine these kinds of patterns.

<table>
<tr>
<td>SUPERIORS
WU QU (GENERAL)
Po Jun (Rebel)
Ling Xing (Water)
Tuo Luo (Humpback)
Hua Ji (Jealousy)

(82–91) Snake Palace</td>
<td>ASSISTANTS
TAI YANG (SUN)
Lu Cun (Storehouse)
De Jie (Loss)

(72–81) Horse Palace</td>
<td>CAREER/TRAVEL
TIAN FU (EMPRESS)
Yang Ren (Goat Blade)
Tian Yao (Beauty)
Hua Ke (Examination)

(62–71) Goat Palace</td>
<td>HEALTH
TIAN JI (ORACLE)
TAI YIN (MOON)
Tian Kui (Leader)
Tian Xi (Happy)

(52–61) Monkey Palace</td>
</tr>
<tr>
<td>PROPERTY
TIAN TONG (VASSAL)
You Bi (Right Assistant)
Di Kong (Void)

(92–101) Dragon Palace</td>
<td colspan="2" rowspan="2">DAD
Zi Wei Dou Shu Chart
FOUR PILLARS:
YEAR: Yin Earth Ox
MONTH: Yang Water Monkey
DAY: Yin Water Rooster
HOUR: Yin Earth Goat

SOLAR BIRTH INFORMATION
1949/8/11 1:00pm to 2:59pm

LUNAR BIRTH INFORMATION:
Ji Chou /7/17
Wei
Ox, Yin Male
INNER NATURE: Water</td>
<td>WEALTH
ZI WEI (EMPEROR)
Tan Lang (Greedy Wolf)
Hua Quan (Authority)

(42–51) Rooster Palace</td>
</tr>
<tr>
<td>PLEASURE
WEN CHANG (MAGISTRATE)
Tian Xing (Punishment)

(102–111) Rabbit Palace</td>
<td>OFFSPRING
JU MEN (GREAT GATE)
Zuo Fu (Left Assistant)
Huo Xing (Fire)

(32–41) Dog Palace</td>
</tr>
<tr>
<td>ANCESTORS
Hong Luan (Red Bird)
Tian Ma (Travel)

(112–121) Tiger Palace</td>
<td>MING
Lian Zhen (Concubine)
Qi Sha (7 Killings)

(2–11) Ox Palace</td>
<td>YOUTH
TIAN LIANG (ROOF BEAM)
Hua Lu (Salary)
Tian Yue (Halberd)

(12–21) Rat Palace</td>
<td>PARTNERS
TIAN XIANG (TUTOR)
WEN QU (PRIEST)

(22–31) Pig Palace</td>
</tr>
</table>

Example Chart 3

EXAMPLE CHART 3

I will now examine my father's chart. He is alive and doing well. He has certainly faced many challenges in his life, but he has made the best out of it, and I believe that he has resolved a lot of the Fate represented in this chart. Out of respect for him and his and our privacy, I will not share everything, but I am including the most relevant and demonstrative examples with his permission. As I did with my mother's chart, I will draw as many connections as possible between his chart, my mother's chart, and my own. Again, the purpose is to show real-life examples and connections between charts as an expression of Ancestral Fate. I suggest you do the same with your own chart and your family members' charts.

Qi Character

YEAR: Yin Earth Ox

HOUR: Yin Earth Goat

STEP 1

Consider the Earthly Branch, or Zodiac Animal, of the Year

The Ox is the image of the sturdy plow animal, and it is connected to the profits of consistent hard work and the Confucian value of perseverance in what is right and just; it is deeply connected to the continuity of tradition, convention, and culture. Oxen are naturally strong, but their strength is Yin and comes from their steady and unwavering ability to keep plowing forward. When charged, they are calm, conscientious, dignified, sincere, uncompromising, dependable, quiet, independent, punctual, tenacious, loyal, and supportive. When depleted, they are insensitive, humorless, sullen, aloof, dull, slavish to convention, and ruthless if crossed.

STEP 2

Consider the Influence of the Heavenly Stem, or Element, on the Earthly Branch of the Year

The Native Element of the Ox is Yin Earth, so this is the natural Ox, as the Outer Element matches. So, there are no other elemental influences to consider. Yin Earth represents the damp soil ready to be plowed, making the Ox very stable, calm, and steady, adding a stronger sense of conventionality and maturity to the Ox image. Earth Oxen are the most grounded, solid, and strong, and the Earth Ox is, therefore, the most characteristic Ox.

Because of the abundance of Earth, all the above qualities can seem exaggerated in the Earth Ox. The capacity of Earth Oxen to work, remain unflappable, and keep plowing forward in life is very strong, and they make excellent leaders and caretakers. They are independent and do not need the help of others; instead, they need to have others to help. Otherwise, they feel useless. The Earth Ox is at its best when it is constantly challenged and given fields to plow. If the Earth Ox does not have work, routine, and convention, it will create it, no matter the circumstances. Earth Oxen often struggle to make sense of the nonsense in the world, and their strength can create more problems than it solves.

STEP 3

Consider the Earthly Branch, or Zodiac Animal, of the Hour

The Goat is the image of the egalitarian herd animal; traditionally, they were sacrificed to honor the Ancestors for the good of the collective. The mountain goat is sure-footed, adaptable, and capable of scaling any terrain. By nature, they are collectivists interested in the welfare of others, the community, and the world at large. They thrive in groups, family, and community and seek to compromise, cooperate, and negotiate. They are naturally artistic and represent the interconnectedness of all things, which they experience directly. They live to communicate, express the inexpressible, and organize the human world to reflect their idealistic values. When charged, they are aesthetic, artistic, persuasive, charming, cooperative, compromising, easygoing, kind, generous, encouraging, and supportive. When depleted, they are impatient, nervous, anxious, worrisome, perfectionist, fussy, intolerant, cranky, stubborn, and incommunicative when flustered.

STEP 4

Consider the influence of the Heavenly Stem, or Element, on the Earthly Branch of the Hour

The Native Element of the Goat is also Yin Earth, so this is the natural Goat, and there are no other elemental influences here to consider. The Yin Earth Goat, therefore, expresses the above Goat qualities most strongly. Here, Yin Earth represents adaptation, accommodation, and alliance. The Earth Goat is the most stable and sure-footed of the Goats, and it can adapt to anything. Earth Goats are the most confident, grounded, and least flustered of the Goats, but they can also be the most stubborn. They are very inclusive and consider anyone who shares their idealism and ideology to be family. They are natural politicians and treaty makers but are also very critical, proud, and obstinate and can, therefore, make many enemies. They will defend their honor and ideology and headbutt others if necessary. They are supportive, nourishing, motherly, and care deeply about others. They are natural artists but also have an interest in materiality.

STEP 5

Synthesize and Summarize the Earthly Branch and Heavenly Stem of the Year and Hour

First, we see that these are both Yin Characters, so together, this Character is very Yin, which is to say gathered, reserved, patient, and so on. We can also see that these two Characters are diametric opposites, which means they are in a mirror relationship and represent the opposites of each other. This does not mean they are enemies or necessarily incompatible, but it does mean that they do not blend, and this Character will be two-sided and have a kind of split personality. Their sides will alternate rather than blend, which means that, in certain situations, the Ox will come forward and dominate, and in other situations, the Goat will become dominant.

However, these Characters are both Yin Earth and are both at home in their Native Element, so they are stable, and the oppositions will not likely be problematic. Opposite relationships can sometimes cause strife, leading to mental health challenges, but here, this is not the case, especially given the nature of the Ox and Goat. They differ in that the Goat is the most compromising and accommodating, while the Ox is often the least compromising. The Goat is very dependent and relies on the Herd, while the Ox is entirely independent and needs no one. The Goat wants to refine, edit, and alter tradition to suit the needs of the people, while the Ox seeks to preserve, standardize, and maintain tradition unchanged and wants people to follow suit. The Goat is very attuned to the environment and unseen forces, and the Ox is oblivious. The Ox is unflustered, and the Goat is easily flustered.

These may seem like opposing dynamics, but since the elemental Earth makeup is so harmonious, they will make this Character more well-rounded and able to hold both realities simultaneously. Again, they will not likely blend, however, and this Character may alternate between the two at different times; at times, this may seem at cross-purposes. This Character may have an internal struggle with this, but it is not like the Ox to struggle over such things, so it is no big deal.

The Ox here is the primary image, so it will act as the main Character. The Goat will likely come out in downtime, in relationships, and in time with family, and also through hobbies and artistic aspirations; it will also be available in practical situations when negotiations and compromise are needed. If this opposition can be well managed, then this is a very powerful capacity and can resolve any challenges that Fate presents.

REFLECTION: My dad is, in many ways, the definitive Earth Ox, as he is one of the most hardworking, reliable, and stubborn people I have ever met. Yet, he has another side that is very characteristic of the Goat, so this Character fits him well. My dad has faced many challenges in his life, but he has been able to overcome them all, and I think this is in part due to the capacity of the Earth Ox to keep plowing forward and remain unflustered. Any other Character likely would have been destroyed by some of the challenges my dad has faced, but he keeps going, unphased.

My father has always worked very hard, and at times, he worked multiple jobs to keep our family afloat. He started and built a multinational business from the ground up and naturally expresses the leadership qualities present in the Ox. He is sturdy, grounded, and can be uncompromising to a fault. He is a person of routine and thrives when he does the same thing repeatedly; he can very easily get into a rut, and in my observation, he finds it difficult to change, especially his core beliefs. He is the same person I have always known, as his core personality has remained the same despite all the challenges.

But he has another side that does feel like a separate personality. As I suggested in the reading, in him it does not seem opposed, but more like another dimension of his Character. My father is very artistic, sophisticated, and spiritual and is also a people person who does very well in groups, all of which are uncharacteristic of the Ox. He has been a writer his whole life and has written many books, including poetry, short stories, plays, and fiction. We even published a book of family poetry together.[1] He also draws, paints, and enjoys acting in plays. However, these things were always put aside because the Ox had to work, and this dimension only came out a little once he retired. The Goat comes out more when the Ox is at rest, so he has made this dynamic work.

Fate in the Twelve Houses

MING PALACE

RULING STARS: Lian Zhen, the Concubine, and Qi Sha, the Seven Killings or Executioner Star

SUBORDINATE/MODIFYING STARS: None

INCIDENTAL STARS: None

SYNTHESIS AND INTERPRETATION

GENERAL IMAGE: Here, we see right off the bat the most afflicting and challenging combination in Polestar Astrology: the Concubine Star and Qi Sha, the Seven Killings or Executioner Star, together in the Ming Palace as the central ruling image of Fate. Thankfully, they do not arrive with any other Ghost Stars, so this is not as tangled as it could be, but it is, no doubt, very tough. It means that you are born with an Ancestral Demon who is coming for your life. This Demon will make your life very difficult, which is the worst possible situation for resolving Fate.

This Demon must be exorcised, but this can only be done if your life is in danger. There is an unresolved generational trauma in the family here that has been passed down through the generations, and it has fallen on you to resolve it. When we look over at the Ancestors Palace, we can see that it is empty, which is very inauspicious, as it means that your Ancestors do not support you and may even abandon you. This combination can manifest in many ways, but essentially, you may have to go through a near-death experience—or many—and if you survive, it will be by the skin of your teeth.

Your life story may be harsh and full of many life-threatening, dangerous, or disastrous challenges. You are at risk. Your family and friends may even be a hazard to you, and you to them. You could be born into, or find yourself in, very inhospitable circumstances with limited resources to escape. Character is essential here, and weaker Characters with this combination of Stars here may have a short life. You will need heroic survival skills; if you survive, it can give you further skills so that you make it in life and overcome anything.

This Demon will come after you until it is finished, and it can cause dark mental health challenges, drug problems and addiction, illnesses, accidents, injuries, or lawsuits, and even get you caught up in illegal activities and prison. You may spend time in the hospital and undergo lifesaving surgeries. If you survive all this, you can exorcise this Demon, and it will not be passed down to future generations. If you fail to resolve this, it will take your life. It is also important to note that every House in the chart is affected by this affliction in the Ming Palace, as it is the overall ruling image of Fate. Every House will take on an element of the struggle represented here, and until it is resolved, it will cast a shadow on the Emperor and the Royal Court.

CHARACTER: Thankfully, the Earth Ox is one of the best Characters to handle such a challenge, as it has the profound capacity to work and overcome obstacles and remain undamaged. You can, of course, be hurt, but Oxen are the least likely to be severely traumatized; they are unflappable. This Character can meet the challenge but get stuck repeating the same negative patterns repeatedly. The Earth Ox will have difficulty seeing the problems and will stay in difficult situations for years and years, unwilling to change or quit. The Goat here, though, can learn to navigate challenges and compromise, negotiate, and have finesse, so together, they are a good combination. This is an auspicious match for an inauspicious House, and the likelihood of survival is much higher for you than otherwise.

REFLECTION: First, I must reflect on the fact that both my parents had the Concubine and Seven Killings Stars ruling a House, which means that Ancestral Demons were coming down both of my Ancestral lines, and my parents took the brunt of them so I did not have to. I experienced many secondary effects, as many of their challenges became my challenges growing up, but my life was made easier through their sacrifices and struggles. I am grateful for this, and especially for my father, as his life was tough, as this House suggests. We'll get into some of his stories as we go through the Houses, but it is clear that this Ancestral Demon was coming after my father's life, as he has almost died many times, and it is a miracle that he is still alive.

My dad's life is a dramatic example of having the Concubine and Seven Killings Star ruling your Fate. He had a very unusual childhood, was abandoned by his father due to extraordinary circumstances at an early age, and had to go to work early to support his family. Throughout his life, he has been in many life-threatening and dangerous situations. He has had many bad accidents and suffered severe injuries, including breaking over fifty bones after being hit by a truck and thrown off the San Francisco Bay Bridge!

He has been in the hospital many times on the verge of death, sometimes with strange, inexplicable illnesses, and he miraculously pulled through. He has dealt with alcoholism, been to prison, and recovered to become a better person; this was undoubtedly a Demon he had to slay. He has worked hard to build a huge, multinational business only to be betrayed by employees and lose that business in a series of controversial financial battles that put him in tremendous debt.

He has had to work multiple jobs, day and night, to survive, pay off debt, and support his family. He has dealt with many challenges, to say the least. I have researched our family history, but I have no idea what the origin of this Demon is. I feel it has something to do with our Mormon Ancestors, who were intimately tied to the founding of Mormonism and the settling of the Salt Lake Valley in Utah, which we will discuss in the Ancestors Palace. There was a lot of strangeness in my dad's early life and on his side of the family, and it started a long series of challenges that he had to overcome. I feel that he has overcome them and resolved this Ancestral Demon. Although it almost took his life many times, miraculously, he is alive.

ANCESTORS PALACE

RULING STAR:
None—this House is an Empty Court, or Kong Gong

SUBORDINATE/MODIFYING STARS: None

INCIDENTAL STARS: Hong Luan, the Red Bird, and Tian Ma, the Travel or Heavenly Horse Star

SYNTHESIS AND INTERPRETATION

GENERAL IMAGE: Here, we can see that this House is empty and contains no ruling Star. The Red Bird Star and the Travel or Heavenly Horse Star mean almost nothing here. You are free of Fate in this House, meaning you have no Fated relationship with your Ancestors or parents and no obligation to resolve Fate with or for them. This means that you are free in many ways to pursue your Fate outside the family, but it also means that you do not have their support, and the affliction in the Ming Palace is, therefore, much more challenging.

You do not have Ancestral guardians to help you resolve the Demon in the Ming Palace. You may not feel connected to your Ancestors and may feel out of place, like a stranger in your own family. You may feel disconnected from your tradition, language, place, or religion of origin. You may grow apart from your family and must work to stay connected with them, as there is no Fate here. The Red Bird and Travel Star imply that you may leave home, break ties, and start over again away from your family and parents.

CHARACTER: This Character is very independent but also loyal and dependable. So, it makes sense that, although there is no Fate here, this Character will stick with family and work very hard to support them no matter what, even if they do not serve or support them back. However, this Character is also not sentimental, so it will not be too tragic when they ultimately drift away and split from their family. They will always take responsibility for any problems and take it upon themselves to uphold tradition and convention.

REFLECTION: My dad's side of the family is Mormon, and they were all from Denmark and the United Kingdom. In the same generation, they came to America to cross the country and help settle Salt Lake City with Brigham Young. That side of my family is enormous, and I have many cousins, but my grandfather and father essentially rejected and left this environment, so I grew up separate from Mormonism, and it had no influence on me.

My grandfather, Clark, was an astrologer who was interested in Eastern and Western mysticism, and then so was my father, and so am I. Due to unusual circumstances that we will discuss in a moment, my grandparents divorced, and Clark left my father and disappeared from his life at an early age. This is a fascinating story that is far too complex to tell here fully, and we can see elements of this story in the Ming and Youth Palaces as well.

In short, Clark was an oil scientist who worked for Shell and traveled all over the country. His half-brother, Bob, was an eccentric man who studied psychology and was also interested in astrology and mysticism. Clark discovered a large oil field in Colorado on Hopi Indian land, and out of respect, he went to them to ask their permission, but mainly to tell them that the government would take the land. They appreciated this from him and initiated him into the peyote ritual of their tribe. This changed his life, and he then introduced peyote to his brother.

After this, Clark and Bob started growing peyote and gave psychedelic trips to many people. Eventually, they began performing psychological experiments on people during these trips, regressing them into past and future lives with hypnosis and recording them. The word spread about this, and several people, including some famous people and even a few government officials came to their house, and the FBI started to watch them.

Long story short, this caused a lot of drama, and my grandparents divorced over the issue, and that's when my grandfather disappeared. My dad did not see him again for over ten years. After Clark left, my dad had to go to work to support the family as the "man of the house" and eldest sibling, which was natural for an Ox anyway. We see this in the Youth Palace with the Roof Beam Star. This may sound like a strong Fate, but this House shows that my dad's connection with his father and Ancestors was weak.

I believe this strange story is reflected in the Ming and Youth Palaces and through the Concubine and Seven Killings Star. With this Empty House, we see that, Fate-wise, my dad was actually abandoned by his Ancestors, and he was open to disconnecting and drifting away from them, which he eventually did. My dad broke from the Mormon tradition like his father, and eventually, he drifted from the extended family and moved away, which we see also in the Youth Palace.

He raised me separately from the family and from Western religion. My dad has not remained close to his extended family over the years, so the Empty House here makes sense, as he was not Fated to stay close to them. The Oracle and Moon can also be borrowed into this House, reflecting this strange story. Still, the main image here is the freedom to break away and the fact that my dad does not have Ancestral support, which makes the Ming Palace much more challenging to resolve, as it was all put on him, spiritually and practically.

YOUTH PALACE

RULING STAR:

Tian Liang, the Roof Beam Star (luminous placement)

SUBORDINATE/MODIFYING STARS: None

INCIDENTAL STARS: Tian Yue, the Halberd Star, and Hua Lu, the Salary or Prosperity Star

SYNTHESIS AND INTERPRETATION

GENERAL IMAGE: Here, we see the Roof Beam Star in a luminous placement without any strong afflicting Stars, so this is a modest but exalted House. The Fate here is strongly connected to Fengshui and the auspice of placement, land, and geography and potentially to culture, tradition, language, and so on of childhood. Home is essential in the resolution of Fate in this House. The Halberd Star here can create a sense of discipline and struggle that eventually leads to a cutting of ties, as this is the image of a blade. The Salary Star implies a lot of transformation and Fate around money, so that you may work a lot as a child.

As this is the image of the central Roof Beam, it creates the image of support and structure. You may give and receive a lot of support from your family and siblings, and you are Fated to be the backbone of the family. This Star implies being a well-behaved and responsible child and implies working for the family or in a family business and potentially carrying on a tradition. The Roof Beam means that your placement is essential, so the house, town, and community you are in may be very important in youth, as will be the geography and nature of where you grow up—the mountains, forests, rivers, and so on of childhood will be an important part of your Fate.

You will find solace in nature and your imagination. You will also be sturdy, athletic, and have a strong body, playing an important role in youth, so sports, teams, and competition may define you here. You may also travel and move a lot, as the Roof Beam pushes you to find the proper place to unravel your Fate, which is here tied to family and siblings. Youth will be active and dynamic, and you will work hard and move a lot to resolve Fate. Eventually, you will leave home early and cut ties but continue looking for a new home. If you leave home, it will be hard to resolve Fate with siblings.

CHARACTER: This is an auspicious match for this Character, so they will naturally be hardworking, and the Ox is the image of support and structure, which matches the Roof Beam. This Character will naturally become the backbone of the family and work hard to support their family and siblings. They will easily take on the challenges of working, moving, and carrying on tradition.

REFLECTION: Here, we see a continuation and further expansion of the story I told in the Ancestors Palace. As I mentioned, my grandfather was an oil scientist who worked for Shell, so my dad had to move around a lot as a child. They went to different places for Clark's work, looking for oil, including Colorado, as mentioned in the story, but eventually, they settled in Los Angeles, California. We see here that placement and Fengshui were very important, as my father moved a lot growing up, and my father told me that geography and nature played an important role for him early in life, especially in Colorado.

Home was also very significant for him, as this is where the strange story of the peyote and the ensuing drama with the FBI took place, eventually leading to my grandfather leaving and my dad having to go to work to support the family. So, he did indeed become a pillar of support for his mother and siblings. He has two siblings, a brother and a sister, whom he has struggled to keep in touch with over the years, as he did leave home and cut ties as the Halberd Star implies.

My dad also worked many odd and side jobs as a child, as the Salary Star implies. He was also very athletic and played many sports. There was also a sense that Fate really started to unravel for him once they arrived in Los Angeles, which is often the case with the Roof Beam once you find the important place. Although my grandfather had disappeared, he and my father eventually reconnected, and Clark explained where he went and why he left.

Many traditions were passed down to my father as a child. He told me that his father and his uncle Bob imparted a lot of esoteric knowledge and tradition around the dinner table about astrology, mythology, history, and spirituality, which they reconnected about later when Clark returned. Clark remarried, and his new wife forbade him from much communication with the family, so I met him only once, and I always had the sense that he and my dad could never fully resolve their issues around his childhood.

PARTNERS PALACE

RULING STAR: Tian Xiang, the Tutor

SUBORDINATE/MODIFYING STAR:
Wen Qu, the Priest (luminous placement)

INCIDENTAL STARS: None

SYNTHESIS AND INTERPRETATION

GENERAL IMAGE: Here we see that the Tutor is the ruling Star, and it is augmented by the Priest, which is in a luminous placement, so this is in an exalted pair, which exalts the House, making this a powerful place to resolve Fate. However, the Tutor Star is misplaced here, as it is not a very romantic Star; it is associated with work and success. The Tutor here often implies significant discrepancies between partners in age, status, education, or identity. The Priest implies a strong spiritual connection, so you may share a spiritual path or religious connection with your partner. You can grow together spiritually and mature, both spiritually and practically, through partnership.

The Tutor can mean that you partner with a colleague, co-worker, or person with like-minded interests and values, especially spiritual values, as the Priest suggests. You may marry someone who works a lot or is a successful professional or student; you may also work a lot and be "married to the job," and your Fate with work may be part of your marriage or even interfere with it. You may have to work hard in your marriage and be very hardworking, responsible, and supportive of your partner. You may also be their teacher, or they are yours.

You will be a model partner and have strong values and a sense of tradition when it comes to marriage. You will likely have to "work" on your partnership, but you will resolve a lot of Fate through this process. You may be very close, but this relationship is not very romantic and more about responsibility, obligation, and work. As there are two Stars here, this may imply two different Fated partnerships, or it may apply to all of them.

CHARACTER: As in all the relationship Houses, the Ox and Goat in this House are very hardworking and responsible, and here they match the image of the Tutor, which is very Ox-like. This Character is a loyal, hardworking, and supportive partner, but the Ox is not very sentimental or romantic, so it is likely that marriage turns into a job or something that the Ox keeps plowing forward with. The Ox is not likely to make a big deal out of the spiritual nature of the partnership represented by the Priest, but it will be modest, traditional, and respectful in relationships.

REFLECTION: Many aspects of this reading match up with my dad's life, as he has been married three times. His first wife was a student working on her PhD, and my dad worked to support her in this process. So, this matches both sides, as she was a Tutor-like, but he also worked to support her as a Tutor and an Ox would do.

His second wife was my mother, and he was definitely the Tutor in that partnership, as he was the hardworking, responsible one who did everything. My dad did almost everything in our house, including cooking, cleaning, and shopping, and he worked hard to support my mom at work and at home. He was in many ways married to work, as he spent more time there than at home.

While I am sure there was romance at the start of their relationship, my parents' marriage was not what I would call romantic, and it was plagued with difficulties, arguments, and disagreements. When we looked at my mom's chart, we saw that her primary Fate with the Emperor was through partnership with my father, but her Partners Palace was afflicted, and we see that my father's is not. While they were both responsible for their actions, from this perspective, we see that a lot of the conflicted Fate was on my mom's side, which makes sense to me. My dad played his part, but I always got the feeling that my mom's mental health challenges and struggles in life were at the root of their marital problems. My mom was often the aggressor and the one who initiated arguments. She would also refuse to work and help out a lot of the time, and put everything on my father. She was violent and would yell and lash out. My dad would take everything, keep working, and plow forward like an Ox. Despite their challenges, my dad stuck it out, and they were together until my mom died.

My dad remarried, and I feel that this is represented by the Priest Star here, for they have a stronger spiritual connection and are more compatible. She also has the Priest Star in her Partners Palace, which is auspicious. They are happily married, and I think my dad has grown spiritually through this, as the Priest Star implies.

OFFSPRING PALACE

RULING STAR: Ju Men, the Great Gate (diminished placement)

SUBORDINATE/MODIFYING STARS:
Huo Xing, the Fire Star, and Zuo Fu, the Left Assistant

INCIDENTAL STARS: None

SYNTHESIS AND INTERPRETATION

GENERAL IMAGE: Here we have the Great Gate Star in a diminished placement, afflicted by an Ancestral Ghost in the Fire Star but supported by the Left Assistant. Overall, this is an afflicted House, and the Fate here is open, unfixed, and challenging. It is characterized by ambivalence and complacency, and your Fate to be a parent is unclear, uncertain, and muddled. You may be unsure about being a parent, or your sexuality may be rebellious and antisocial.

If you want children, you are Fated to have many challenges and obstructions, such as difficulty conceiving, and you may be haunted by unborn children or incomplete pregnancies, or your children may have medical problems or bring stress and hardship into your life. They may reject you, and you may feel distant and not close. You may be a distant parent, and you may not spend much time with your children or not be careful or watch them closely.

Your children may have very different sensibilities and argue with you. They may be troublesome, reject your authority, and leave home early. The Left Assistant offers some positive support through this, which can temper some of the negativity here, so despite all this, you can have a good relationship with time.

CHARACTER: The Ox is a responsible and conventional parent and not overly sentimental or touchy-feely. Oxen love their children and work hard to support and provide for them, but they will have trouble expressing feelings. The Goat will do much better at this, so this Character will have a mixed relationship with children. They will struggle but be able to stick with the challenges; the Ox is tenacious and will keep going, and they also will not be too broken up about the challenges, as they are not overly sensitive to begin with. So, although the house is afflicted, it is not as challenging for this Character as it would be for many others, and they will make the best of it.

REFLECTION: It is interesting to see how you are reflected in your parent's chart, but from what I know of my dad, this is quite accurate. He always wanted children, but it took quite a long time to make this happen, and there were a lot of challenges along the way, which we see here through the uncertain and afflicted nature of the Great Gate and Fire Star. Here, we can also see how difficulty conceiving can be Fated for men, despite being fertile; this Fate is not always on the woman's side.

My dad's first marriage ended, in part, because he wanted children and she did not. She aborted a few children without consulting or telling him, so we see the idea of being haunted by unborn children reflected clearly. My mother wanted another child badly, as she felt that she had messed up with her first child, my sister, and tried to do it better with me. However, despite wanting me, they had difficulty conceiving, and it took medical intervention and a few years of trying, and then I was a difficult birth. So, it took a long time, and there were a lot of challenges along the way. I was not born until my dad was thirty-seven. And since my mother lost her womb in giving birth to me, he could only have one child.

Although I know my dad loves me very much, and he was a very good father, he worked a lot and was absent for a lot of my childhood, which the Great Gate also implies. I was alone and unsupervised often, which was fine, as I am a Tiger. We have always had a good relationship but are not close in the touchy-feely sense, and I moved out early, at seventeen. I think I am the Left Assistant Star here, as my dad went through many challenges, but something positive came through, and I can see a more positive Fate in my mother's chart in the form of the Oracle and the Moon.

WEALTH PALACE

RULING STAR: Zi Wei, the Emperor (diminished placement)

SUBORDINATE/MODIFYING STAR:
Tan Lang, the Greedy Wolf

INCIDENTAL STAR: Hua Quan, the Authority Star

SYNTHESIS AND INTERPRETATION

GENERAL IMAGE: Here we see the central ruling Star of Fate, the Emperor, in a diminished placement in the Rooster Palace, afflicted by the Greedy Wolf Star. This is a challenging image, and we can say the Emperor and, therefore, the central image of Fate in this chart is afflicted and will be resolved through some hardship and difficulty, which is made worse by the fact that the Ming Palace is afflicted. Your central Fate is with money, wealth, and resources, but it is characterized by the struggle of a lone wolf. Whether you like it or not, much in life will revolve around your relationship with work and money, mainly because we see the Empress in the Career/Travel Palace and many other Stars in the other career Houses.

So, work is important, but the strongest aspect of that Fate and the story of life will unravel around money and wealth. The diminished placement implies that this will not be easy and that resolving Fate here may be a struggle, especially with the Greedy Wolf, which implies that you are haunted by an Ancestral Ghost that creates isolation and struggle. You will struggle with money and finances, often alone and without help, but with the strength of the Emperor, this can eventually be overcome, and you will resolve all your most important Fate through this grind and struggle with finances.

You may squander, lose, or mismanage finances, and this may be due to others who leave or betray you, causing you to do everything alone. You may work very hard to create and generate wealth and even be skilled and resourceful, but this may never amount to much, and you may be dissatisfied and resentful about money. The Authority Star implies a lot of transformation regarding money and positions of authority, so you may make and lose a lot of money as a manager, business owner, or authority figure.

CHARACTER: This Character has the fortitude and stick-to-itiveness to endure the potential challenges here. The Ox will keep plowing forward through all the vicissitudes, and the Goat will likely "work smart" to adapt. The Ox will be baffled at the incompetence and mismanagement of others, and it will naturally take on everything itself, so being a lone wolf will feel normal to you. This is an auspicious match for this combination, as both are Earth Element Characters, and Earth is the Element of wealth, stability, and abundance.

REFLECTION: This certainly makes sense given my dad's life, and money may well have been the central theme for him throughout his challenges. As we'll get to later, he also has the Empress, Sun, and General spread throughout the career Houses, so work is a big part of his Fate, but money is the driving factor.

As the Empress in the Career/Travel Palace implies, my dad naturally fell into a career working in import-export, but he has had over fifty different jobs in his life. The theme of having to struggle alone without support started early, when he had to go to work as a teenager to help support the family after his father left. As I understand it, this theme would continue throughout his life.

In his first marriage, my dad had to work to support his wife as she went to school, so he had all the responsibility. In his late twenties, he started his own import-export business called Atlantis Lines and spent twelve years building it up from nothing. At the peak of its success, it had offices in over twenty countries and hundreds of employees. For a while, he was quite successful, and our family did well. Long story short, some angry rival competitors intentionally sabotaged my dad's business and spread false rumors that caused clients to leave, eventually leading to the business's collapse.

After this, my dad got caught up in several contentious financial battles that resulted in his losing a tremendous amount of money and getting into deep debt with the IRS. After this, my dad had to go to work for other import-export companies as an employee, and the IRS garnished most of his salary to pay the debt. This led to our having to sell our house and downgrade to renting a smaller one. My dad often had to work two jobs to keep us afloat. He would spend his nights waiting tables, so he would get home late most nights, often working over twelve hours a day.

My mom worked but did not make much, and eventually, she went on disability, so all the financial burden was on my dad. She would also actively refuse to help, and she seemed resentful and often blamed my dad for our troubles. He very much had to struggle as a lone wolf, and the process of getting out of debt was a very slow grind that took many years and a lot of hard work. This work was an obligation, as my dad had no other choice, which makes it feel clearly Fated. Seeing as how this was the central grind of his life for such an extended period, it makes sense that the Emperor Star represents this. It is auspicious that my dad is an Ox, for I am not sure another Character would have been able to do this. He has since retired and achieved financial stability, so I would say that he successfully resolved his Fate.

HEALTH PALACE

RULING STAR: Tian Ji, the Oracle

SUBORDINATE/MODIFYING STAR:
Tai Yin, the Moon Lady or Princess

INCIDENTAL STARS:
Tian Kui, the Leader, and Tian Xi, the Happiness Star

SYNTHESIS AND INTERPRETATION

GENERAL IMAGE: Here we see the Oracle, one of the Four Rulers of Fate, at the Emperor's right hand, modified by the Moon or Princess of the Royal Court. This combination is very Yin and mysterious; together, they are an exalted pair. There are no afflicting Stars, and the Leader and Happiness Stars are very minor and mean almost nothing here. This is undoubtedly auspicious, especially with the afflicted Ming Palace and the empty Ancestors Palace, which suggests that an Ancestral Demon is coming after your life and you do not have much backup from the Ancestors.

Here is where the Ancestors show up as protectors, as the Oracle is the leading voice of the Ancestors, and here it speaks through your health. It arrives with the Moon, which is connected to the Matriarchal Ancestors, and together, they provide a very powerful Yin spiritual sensitivity and capacity to heal. This is a powerful, even miraculous, capacity to recover, but it is not easy to understand, and it does not mean that you won't face health challenges.

This combination means you are very sensitive and are basically a shaman of sorts; you may be brought close to death to find magical and miraculous healing abilities. You have a deep sensitivity and emotionality, and you are open to possession and nervous disorders. Illness, injury, and recovery are basically a spiritual path. There is nothing concrete that can be said about this combination, other than that you will have many strange, inexplicable injuries and illnesses that you will miraculously recover from through strange, otherworldly forces.

Your health will wax and wane and go through many changes, many ups and downs, periods of wellness and illness, and onset and recovery will seem uncontrollable. You will develop a deeply personal and intuitive practice of health cultivation, and you can heal others. You can go beyond health practice to develop wisdom and express the cultivation of your Ancestors.

CHARACTER: This is an odd match for the Earth Ox, but it goes well with the Earth Goat. Oxen are naturally strong and sturdy, but they are not sensitive by nature. So, this more emotional, sensitive, and otherworldly nature will be muted, but it will express a profound capacity to heal and work through possession without even noticing. The Goat will express and articulate the more sophisticated Yin aspects of health, and the Ox will be able to form consistent health practices and routines.

REFLECTION: As I mentioned earlier, my dad has almost died many times, and he has always miraculously pulled through. So, despite not having a strong backup in the Ancestors Palace, I feel that the Oracle in his chart has been watching over him. He has dealt with a lot of strange health challenges, of which there are far too many to list. One of the most profound examples happened before I was born.

My dad was driving on the San Francisco Bay Bridge late at night in the rain, and there was an accident in front of him. He got out of his car to help, and in doing so, he was struck by a large truck. The Bay Bridge has two levels: an upper deck going into San Franciso from Oakland and a lower deck returning. He flew off the top level and landed on an I-beam sticking out of the lower level, which was a miraculous, one-in-a-million chance. No one saw this happen, so no one knew he was there. He was stranded there for hours, yelling for help, with nearly every bone in his body broken. Eventually, he was discovered and taken to the hospital. He broke over fifty bones, but he made a full recovery. If he had missed the I-beam by an inch, he would have flown into the bay and died, and I would have never been born. This is just one example of the Oracle and Moon strangeness.

Once, in my early twenties, a hospital called me telling me that my dad was there and that he would likely die from multiple strange ulcers eroding his digestive tract that they had no explanation for. He later recovered without any medical explanation from the doctors. Just recently, he went to the hospital and was in a coma for a week with a strange kidney infection; he recovered and is doing well. He also had a stroke but has since made a full recovery with no sequelae. He has also been robbed at knife- and gunpoint and survived, multiple times.

Again, there are many stories like this from my father's life. Furthermore, he is somewhat of a shaman regarding health, as he has always read widely about herbs, natural healing, and supplements, and he has experimented with many different herb concoctions over the years. He has always taken large handfuls of supplements and has a very personal approach to health. But he does this all in a very Ox-like way, as he is very routine and disciplined regarding health.

CAREER/TRAVEL PALACE

RULING STAR: Tian Fu, the Empress (luminous placement)

SUBORDINATE/MODIFYING STAR: Yang Ren, the Goat Blade or Sacrifice Star (luminous placement)

INCIDENTAL STARS:

Tian Yao, the Beauty Star, and Hua Ke, the Examination Star

SYNTHESIS AND INTERPRETATION

GENERAL IMAGE: Here, we see the Empress, the second most powerful Star and the ruler of Yin Fate, in a luminous placement in the Goat Palace, which means work and travel are very important. It is powerfully modified by the Goat Blade Star, which is also in a luminous placement here. The Beauty Star is minor and means almost nothing. The Examination Star is the great transformer of reputation, and it brings academic success as well as status, honor, and promotion. This is the House of Yin Fate, which means it happens by itself, and you are Fated to find your way here by following the signs, receiving gifts, and experiencing the positive results of your Ancestors' and your own past lives.

As the Career Palace, this means you will find a career naturally, or more likely, it will find you. It will be an expression of your innate talents and gifts. It will just happen, or you may fall into it and find great success. The Empress falls naturally into the role of leader, and you may serve as a manager, boss, president, or owner who delegates work to others. You will succeed at advising, counseling, or contract work. Your success may be brought to you by others, and you may be a successor; you may apprentice with a person of great power and replace them or follow in their footsteps; this person may be female.

As the Empress is luminous, this success may be significant, and you may become a person of great power. However, we can see that the afflicted Superiors Palace suggests that success is hard-won, and it may be fraught with challenges, hard work, and late-blooming success. As the Travel Palace, you will have to leave home to find work and success, you may travel widely throughout life, and travel may unite you with previous life or Ancestral connections.

You may even emigrate or live abroad, and you will likely find a new life far from home. Your work may also involve travel or foreign countries. The Goat Blade Star suggests that you are Fated here for a significant loss, sacrifice, or cutting of ties. You may lose a job, business, or leadership role, and with the Emperor afflicted in the Wealth Palace and the General afflicted in the Superiors Palace, this suggests that you may lose money and experience financial and job hardship as a result. There will be a lot of transformation here regarding reputation and success, but you will also have great academic achievement.

CHARACTER: The Ox is the definition of Yin work, so to have the ruler of Yin Fate in the Career/Travel Palace is very auspicious. The Ox will be very interested in work and will naturally step up to leadership roles. The Goat will do well to delegate, make connections, and bring people together, so together, this is a powerful pair to find success and handle all the potential challenges. As always, the Ox will keep plowing forward and doing the work.

REFLECTION: As I have already mentioned, my dad has worked a lot, over fifty different jobs, so he is a jack-of-all-trades. Here, combined with the Emperor in the Wealth Palace and the General in the Superiors Palace, which we'll get to later, we see a powerful image of my dad's business and its downfall. From what I was told, in his twenties he met an older woman, which is the Empress here, who worked in the import-export business, and she was a role model and set him on the path to working in this industry. He eventually started his own import-export business and naturally stepped up to the role of leader, boss, and owner, which fits well with the Empress image.

He was quite successful for a while, as I already mentioned, with offices in over twenty countries and hundreds of employees. He also traveled a lot for this business and lived in other countries, including England, Australia, and New Zealand, which fits well with this being the Travel Palace. As the Empress and Goat Blade Star are both luminous, it makes sense that both the success and the loss here would be dramatic.

It is clear that the Goat Blade or Sacrificial Star here represents the loss of my father's business, which also pairs with the afflicted image of the Emperor and General, who are also in leadership roles in the chart. Since losing the business, my dad has had good success, found work, and had leadership roles. He has since retired. The Examination Star fits well, too, as my dad has always been literary; he is very widely read and has written many books, short stories, poetry, and plays.

ASSISTANTS PALACE

RULING STAR:
Tai Yang, the Sun or Prince (luminous placement)

SUBORDINATE/MODIFYING STARS: None

INCIDENTAL STARS:
Lu Cun, the Storehouse, and De Jie, the Loss Star

SYNTHESIS AND INTERPRETATION

GENERAL IMAGE: Here we see the Sun, the Prince of the Royal Court, in a luminous placement in the Horse Palace. The Loss Star modestly afflicts it, and this loss here may also be related to money as represented by the Storehouse Star, which a subordinate may bring about. The Sun is a potent Yang Star, so this House is active and dynamic, and there is much work to do in career in service or as a subordinate. The Sun must prove his right to ascend the throne. The Sun belongs here, as he is the Prince and second-in-command; he also gets all the help and support that he needs, so success here is supported but sometimes a mixed bag, as people are jealous of the throne. Some assistants will be helpful, but some will not.

This means you will make an excellent assistant and work in a service-oriented profession or have many service-oriented jobs; you will also receive outstanding help and support, both at work and through friends. Older and wiser people may help and support you. You will excel at teamwork, and because this is the House of friendship, you will also have a vibrant and bright social life with many friends and co-workers. The Storehouse Star suggests that resources here may come through others and be a boon in your career, and you may receive gifts and opportunities from helpers that enhance your career. The Loss Star, however, suggests that you may also struggle with helpers who will be disobedient and turn against you. You may mismanage people and resources, and others may abandon you, leading to a loss of resources.

CHARACTER: The Ox is a leader, not a follower or subordinate, but it is also a very strong supporter of others; the Ox carries people and burdens itself with responsibility. The Ox here will be more drawn to leadership, but there is also a strong Fate here to serve others, and the Goat will be more beneficial in this regard. The dual nature of this Character serves this House well, as there is Fate to lead and to serve. The Goat is more suited to this House, and overall, this is an auspicious match.

REFLECTION: As I already mentioned, my dad has worked a lot in his life and had over fifty jobs. We can see that most of the strong Stars in my dad's chart are in the Career and Wealth Palaces, so this is where most of his fate lies. The Sun here no doubt played a role in his business, as he did act in the role of leader, but he also had a lot of employees, subordinates, and helpers along the way. Some of them were helpful, but some were not, and a few contributed to his business's downfall, which we can see in the Loss Star here. But before and after losing his business, he was an employee and often in a subordinate role.

He also worked in many service-oriented jobs, including waiting tables for many years. My dad has always been very sociable, and when he was younger, he had a vibrant social life, which we can see here. He has always had many friends and a large social circle, but this was hindered when he was married to my mother and worked so much.

SUPERIORS PALACE

RULING STAR: Wu Qu, the General (diminished placement)

SUBORDINATE/MODIFYING STARS: Po Jun, the Rebel or Breaking Rank Star; Ling Xing, the Water or Ringing Star; and Tuo Luo, the Humpback or Rejection Star

INCIDENTAL STAR: Hua Ji, the Jealousy or Scandal Star

SYNTHESIS AND INTERPRETATION

GENERAL IMAGE: Here, we see the General in a diminished position in the Snake Palace, and the Water, Humpback, and Jealousy Stars heavily afflict him. So, overall, despite the General's being the strongest exorcist, we can say that he is weakened here, and this House is afflicted by Ghosts and characterized by struggle. The General is a leader and belongs in this House, so you can lead generously and effectively and make many difficult decisions. However, this ability and the reality of the Fate in this House are bogged down in difficulties and struggles, and you will have to work very hard in this life to achieve success. The Rebel is the antithesis of the General, for he rebels against the military chain of command, and this will create strife in your work life.

You may have people rebel against your leadership and undermine you, or you may work for an incompetent leader, struggle under their leadership, and rebel against them yourself. This is the image of being at war in a career, and there are internal struggles in the chain of command, making it hard to carry out missions. So, life may feel like a battle, and the Humpback Star suggests a pattern of bitter self-loathing, excessive negative emotions, selfishness, and feelings of isolation. At the same time, the Water Star adds a dimension of fear, anxiety, and hopelessness.

Internally, this creates many struggles as you strive to work and achieve success in life, and externally, this can create a lot of obstacles, challenges, and setbacks. The Jealousy Star will create a lot of dynamic transformations that create scandal from jealousy, frustrations, arguments, and misunderstandings, and you may be Fated for a consequential, even cataclysmic scandal. No matter what, the General is strong enough to overcome all these, but he is weakened and, therefore, will struggle, and the resolution of Fate here will be late blooming. Ultimately, you will work through all these challenges, but your work life will be a long, hard-fought battle, and you will resolve many Ghosts and mature in the process.

CHARACTER: Thankfully, the Earth Ox is one of the strongest Characters and is most capable of handling a challenging House like this. The Earth Ox would take all the responsibility and hard work on its shoulders, even if this House were wholly positive. It is its nature to lead, and the Ox is very much like the General, so this is an auspicious match for an afflicted House. The Goat will also do well here to negotiate, sign treaties, and compromise, making the Ox a more effective leader, but the combination may also make you a leader who is at crossed purposes with yourself.

REFLECTION: Here, we can see many elements of the story of my father's work life and business. As an Ox, my dad was already like the General, and I always felt that his work life was a battlefield. He has had to work very hard; it has never been easy, and there have been many challenges, setbacks, and scandals. We can see my dad rising to the top of the chain of command as a leader and General of his company, only to have a Rebel go against him, leading to a breakdown and scandal that ended his business. That is all shown here in this House, but we see it double in the Wealth Palace with the afflicted Emperor, and triple in the Career/Travel Palace with the Goat Blade Star.

Here, we have a big stack of Ghosts, and the General is fighting against all those hardships to keep moving forward. I think this characterizes my dad's work life, and with the Tutor Star in the Partners Palace, he had to work hard at home, too. As an Ox, he was able to step up to these challenges, and I think many others would have cracked under all the pressure. As my dad was able to get out of debt and retire comfortably enough, I would say that he resolved the Fate here.

PROPERTY PALACE

RULING STAR: Tian Tong, the Vassal

SUBORDINATE/MODIFYING STAR:
You Bi, the Right Assistant

INCIDENTAL STAR/S: Di Kong, the Void or Empty Earth Star

SYNTHESIS AND INTERPRETATION

GENERAL IMAGE: Here, we see the Vassal Star supported by the Right Assistant and moderately afflicted by the Void Star. The Vassal Star is modest here and has a weak affinity with owning property. This is a military image, like the General, and it goes wherever it is commanded. The Vassal lives and moves where Fate requires it to move, and it does not settle down until Fate is finished. So, often, this means that you move a lot, rent, and generally have less interest in ownership and material possessions so that you can be unattached and ready to move on to the next mission. The Void Star suggests some misfortune and loss, but this is minor overall. The Right Assistant does well to support the Vassal, so you will have good opportunities with property, but you will probably rent for quite a while and only own property much later in life. You are generally not concerned with local identity, but after you retire, you can own property, put down roots, and develop a sense of home. You may return to your birth home many times in life, but you will die far from where you were born.

CHARACTER: Oxen, by nature, have a sense of duty and purpose and a strong sense of tradition and values, so they will do their duty here and take pride in where they live. The Ox, as always, will plow forward and not be too broken up about having to move on constantly to the next place where it is demanded to go, so this is not a mismatch. However, the Ox likes routine, and so moving a lot will be disorienting. You will create routine and structure wherever they go. The Goat here will do well in making friends and alliances, creating community and herd wherever you go, which is a boon for this House. The double Earth Element is also auspicious, as it helps to stabilize a mobile image.

REFLECTION: This House also makes a lot of sense and goes well with the rest of the chart, as it thematically matches the Youth House and career Houses. My dad has moved a lot over his life and has never been strongly attached to local identity or place. He moved many times for work and, due to the other important factors of Fate, always went where life demanded. He moved many times in his youth to different states; he lived in other counties for work, and when I was growing up, we moved house over five times.

After I moved out, my parents moved many more times. They ultimately relocated from California to Washington, but they continued to move, going back to California, where my mother passed away, and then my dad relocated back to Washington. He has since retired, bought property, and settled down, but he was always very mobile before that. We owned a house for a brief period when my dad's business was successful, but we had to sell it when he lost the company. This is a modest and straightforward image, and that is how it manifested.

PLEASURE PALACE

RULING STAR:
Wen Chang, the Magistrate (luminous placement)

SUBORDINATE/MODIFYING STARS: None

INCIDENTAL STAR: Tian Xing, the Punishment Star

SYNTHESIS AND INTERPRETATION

GENERAL IMAGE: Here, we see the Magistrate Star in a luminous placement in the Rabbit Palace, slightly afflicted by the Punishment Star, but this is a minor affliction. Overall, this is a simple and modest image, suggesting that you are a Magistrate regarding your sense of pleasure and enjoyment in life. In short, you enjoy Wen: culture, art, literature, education, history, and so on.

You are a lifelong learner, and you enjoy self-cultivation, which revolves around learning, self-reflection, and art. You will enjoy the public and social manifestations of Wen, including libraries, museums, concert halls, and theaters. You will enjoy watching and participating in public events, and even contributing to or performing at them. Your sense of enjoyment is social and connected to the well-being of others and society, so you will enjoy seeing others succeed. You will be mindful of social welfare and work for the betterment of humanity with a sense of pleasure.

CHARACTER: The Ox is not artistic in nature, but it does have a strong sense of tradition, culture, and continuity, so the Ox will be connected to the more historical and conventional expressions of Wen. The Goat, however, is a natural artist and is much more likely to produce art. Seeing as these two are opposites, this Character will probably alternate between the two, and the Goat may come out in times of peace, when the Ox is not hard at work. So, you will probably have two sides: one that is social and responsible and one that is artistic and flowery.

REFLECTION: This definitely characterizes my dad, as he has always had two sides, which we see in his diametric Character. My dad had to work too much for most of my life to express his artistic side, but it was always there. He grew up appreciating art, music, history, and literature, and he studied English literature and poetry in college. Our house growing up was essentially a library, and my dad's bookshelves were full of books on history, philosophy, poetry, and religion. He instilled these values in me growing up, and we often had many discussions about various subjects. He wrote a lot in his youth but had to put these aspirations aside to work and raise a family. Since he has retired, these aspirations have returned, and he has written many books, he draws and paints regularly, and he has returned to acting in local plays. He has also always been social, and his sense of enjoyment is connected to others while also being personal and private.

PROGRESSED CHARTS: TEN-YEAR AND YEARLY PERIODS

NOW THAT WE HAVE EXAMINED THE PRACTICE OF STUDYING THE NATAL CHART, we can move on to discuss Progressed Charts. This is a complex subject, and while it is powerful and much can be learned from it, it is not the main subject of this book. I will, therefore, introduce the idea and cover the basic practice with an emphasis on what is most important, but we will not go into it in much depth. The Natal Chart is the primary image of our Character and Fate and the most important subject to study. It is important to avoid getting fixated on small details or obsessing about trying to predict the future, which often happens when progressing charts.

Chart Progression is more "predictive" in nature, and although many fortune tellers will try to sell you on this idea, as far as I am concerned, prediction cannot really be done with any confidence. The practice of Polestar Astrology is one of self-reflection and cultivation, and as I said at the beginning of the book, Polestar Astrology is not fortune-telling. However, this idea is how it survived, and it is often how it is sold in East Asia. The purpose of this book is to try to inject some spiritual depth back into the subject and move away from fortune-telling practice. So, while this subject can be studied in a lot of detail, I believe it can become a distraction and sidebar that will lead you astray if you misuse it.

So, let's simplify Chart Progression, as the idea is quite simple. The idea is that we can "progress" the time of birth represented in the Natal Chart into the future to see how the original image presented in the Natal Chart might unfold throughout the years and decades. At birth, the Stars are fixed in their position, and in Progression, they remain fixed; it is the Houses that "progress" and move in a circle around them. They progress in yearly periods totaling a twelve-year cycle in accordance with the zodiac and Twelve Houses of our chart, each of which is ruled by one of the Twelve Animals, and in twelve periods of ten years, each of which is also ascribed to one of the Twelve Houses, which becomes the Ming Palace in that respective cycle. The Houses, each of which is ruled by one of the Twelve Animals, progress yearly for twelve years in accordance with the zodiac, and they progress every ten years twelve times total, in accordance with one's time of life.

These yearly and decade periods can give us clues and indications as to when certain things might manifest or when certain opportunities and Fate Thresholds may arise. However, the influence of Stars in Progression always refers to the Fate in the Natal Chart, and the influence of the Stars gets weaker as we get older, provided we are resolving our Fate. It is very important to emphasize that the Stars in Progressed Charts, especially the Ghost Stars, are weaker and should not be held in the same regard as in the Natal Chart, which is why we will not dwell on them. In order of power, the Natal Chart is first, followed by the Decade Chart and the Yearly Chart.

In Progression, the positive Stars of the Royal Court become more like protective deities, but they back off and move on to help other Ancestors once they see that we have resolved our Fate and released our Ancestral Ghosts. They give us more and more freedom and influence us less and less, but they are still there and can be worked with and called upon through spiritual practice.

The Ghost Stars get weaker, and as they are resolved, they cease to represent affliction, and instead, they remain vigilant forces of wisdom, making sure we do not repeat the same mistakes. This is because the Stars themselves are not Ghosts but more like step-down transformers that hold Ghosts in a transitory state and reduce their negativity slowly until they are dissipated.

In other words, the influence of Fate in the Twelve Houses of the Natal Chart is total and applies throughout life until Fate is resolved. So, even if we have an auspicious year in Progression for career, if the Fate for career is afflicted in the Natal Chart, this does not undo that affliction. However, it offers a good year for working with and overcoming that affliction, and we can use that information strategically.

Suppose we have an afflicted Partners Palace, and we go through a decade cycle in which our Partners Palace is auspicious or contains a powerful Fate-resolving Star. In that case, it is possible that we will resolve that affliction in that decade. It does not mean that the decade will be easy—it may be very challenging—but we may be able to work through things productively rather than make things worse. In turn, if we have affliction in the Natal Chart and go through a year or decade with further affliction, things may get worse during that time if we are not careful. More on this to come.

Let's go through the basics.

In Polestar Astrology, there are actually three types of charts: Heaven, Earth, and Human. The Heavenly Chart, or Tian Pan (天盘)—also called the Ming Pan (命盘)—is the original Natal Chart determined at birth, which is used to determine one's overall Character and Fate. This chart fixes the position of the Stars in their constellations. The Stars here remain fixed, and the Houses revolve around them. This is the most important chart, and it is the main subject of this book. It should determine the main course of study and self-reflection used to follow Polestar Astrology as a path. However, from the Natal Chart, we get two types of Progressed Charts that can be useful for self-reflection and determining when and how certain aspects of Fate may unravel. These are as follows:

- Earth Chart, or Di Pan (地盘)—used to determine a decade's luck
- Human Chart, or Ren Pan (人盘)—used to determine a year's luck

EARTH CHART (地盘)

The Earth Chart, or Di Pan (地盘), is also called the Decade Chart, or Daxian Liu Pan (大限流盘). Daxian (大限) means "within the boundary of ten years." As you will see in the example charts, each House contains an age range of ten years at the bottom. The person's sex and the Element of their birth year determine this age range. The first decade period will start somewhere between ages two and six, and they will progress forward in periods of ten years, starting from the Ming Palace. You will see an age range at the bottom of each House, beginning at the Ming Palace, with the following age range appearing in the next House, and so on. So, your first decade period could start from age 2 to 11, then progress to 12 to 21, then 22 to 31, and so on, for twelve cycles covering the Twelve Houses, adding up to 120 years.

In Polestar Astrology, it is said that we are each allotted 120 years to live, and if we are lucky to live this long, then we have "lived out our allotted years." Few make it this far, but it is still considered the default amount of time we should each aspire to. If you reach 120 years old, you will have gone through your entire chart and all the possible Progressions. You will achieve a kind of natural enlightenment if you live this long, merely from having gone through so much.

The idea is here simple: During each of the allotted ten-year periods, the House with that age range in it becomes the Ming Palace, and all the other Houses are adjusted accordingly from there in the same direction that they flow in the Natal Chart, which is either forward in the natural order or backward against the flow. So, when creating a progressed Decade Chart, you shift the Ming Palace to the House with the corresponding age range you are in, and you then shift the rest of the Houses to follow. All the Stars remain fixed as they are in the Natal Chart and do not move. Only the Houses shift, and the same goes for the Yearly Progressions.

The Twelve Houses may again flow forward in the natural order from Ming to Youth to Partners and so on, or they may flow backward, going from the Ming to the Ancestors Palace. This flow is also determined by the person's sex and the Element of their birth year. Make sure to double-check which direction the Houses flow in.

If the Houses flow forward, then life is more straightforward, as each House represents a natural stage in life as the Chinese see it. First, you are born, then you experience Youth, then you get married, then you have kids, then you make money, then you progress in your career, then you own property and retire, then you have fun and live for pleasure, then you become an Ancestor. It is suggested that each decade cycle is when you are supposed to fulfill those life stages, and the Decade Chart represents the Fated opportunity in that regard. However, the main image of Fate is still the Natal Chart, so each of the decade periods refers to that original image and does not replace it.

If the decade periods flow backward from Ming to Ancestors to Pleasure, then life is a bit more interesting. It is my experience that charts with this setup are a little more "spiritual," for lack of a better word, and their lives flow in a less predictable fashion, which does not necessarily mean that they cannot live an ordinary life.

So, how do we interpret the decade cycle? The idea is simple: We interpret it more or less the same as the Natal Chart, but we shift our emphasis. In other words, the principle of interpreting the Stars is identical, but we must remember that the Natal Chart determines their auspice and refers to the Fate depicted there. The key to all Polestar interpretations is understanding each Star as a symbol and how it operates. Once you understand that, you can interpret how it might act in any scenario. This is why we spent so much time going through each of the Stars in all twelve of the Houses. Hopefully, this gave you an in-depth understanding of how each Star might operate, so now you can apply the same wisdom here.

Here, we are looking at a period of ten years, so the Star now represents opportunity and affliction during that time, but it again refers to the Natal Chart. So, if you have an auspicious Career/Travel Palace in your Natal Chart, in a decade in which your other career Houses are also auspicious, that will be a good time for success. If the House is afflicted in the Decade Chart, then expect setbacks and challenges, but since it is auspicious in the Natal Chart, success is inevitable but may be postponed during that period. If a House is afflicted in the Natal Chart, but it is auspicious in a Decade Chart, then that again may be an excellent time to resolve that Ghostly Fate. We look to the strong Stars, especially the Emperor and Empress, for clues as to where the opportunities are, and we look to the Ghost Stars to see where the challenges may arise.

The Ming Palace always determines the main image of Fate, so the decades during which Ghosts afflict the Ming Palace will be challenging, but this is also a time when the Ghost Star will likely be resolved. The decades in which the Emperor or Empress appears in the Ming Palace will be blessed and among the most transformative and progressive.

HUMAN CHART (人盘)

Now we can examine the Human Chart, or Ren Pan (人盘), also called Current Year or Yearly Chart. In order of strength, this is the weakest Progressed Chart, behind the Decade Chart. The Yearly Chart is precisely what it sounds like: It is the influence of Fate on the current year following the twelve-year cycle of the Chinese zodiac. However, this influence is couched within the influence of the Decade Chart, which is then couched within the overall influence of the Natal Chart. So, you may have an auspicious year for having kids within an afflicted Decade Cycle, but the Fate in the original Natal Chart may be auspicious. So, we must interpret this on a scale: Overall, it is auspicious, but you may have challenges and setbacks in a specific decade, and within that, a year may come along where things work out nicely, and so on.

The idea here is similar to the Decade Chart. In this case, a House becomes the Ming Palace during the corresponding Year of that Animal, and all the Houses shift accordingly.

We, therefore, have twelve Yearly Charts, and every twelve years the rotation begins again. (We have twelve Decade Charts, too, but we only experience each one once, if we live that long.) In this sense, we go through each influence multiple times, and our lives are sort of in a loop, repeating the same pattern every twelve years. Each year, we should look back twelve years and ask, where was I *last* Snake Year? This is not easy when we are young, but as we get older and have lived through multiple twelve-year cycles, we can start to look back and notice patterns.

The only difference between each Year of the same Animal is the Element, and otherwise, every Yearly Chart matches the one twelve years earlier or later—so each Dragon Year chart looks the same, with the only difference being that this may be a Wood Dragon Year while the last one was a Water Dragon Year. And now, twelve years later, we are a very different person, and we may be in a whole new place with a whole new group of people. So, although the chart is the same and we are repeating the same patterns, they may feel very new and different. But we can still ask, *What is the same or similar? How am I playing out the same patterns that I did twelve years ago?*

Yearly Cycles, then, must be read more strongly against the auspice of the Qi Character, for the influence of each year will strongly affect how your Character digests each year. In other words, you may have an auspicious match in terms of Character, like a Tiger in Pig Year, but then that Yearly Chart may have an afflicted Ming Palace, suggesting that it may be a tough year. However, because the Qi Character of the year is an auspicious match, your Character may step up to the challenge more easily. And vice versa, you may struggle more to appreciate an auspicious Yearly Chart in a zodiac year that conflicts with your Character, like a Tiger in Monkey Year.

The principle of interpretation is again the same as in the Decade and Natal Charts. First, understand how each Star operates; then, you can interpret it anywhere. Here, they are weaker, and Yearly Charts get weaker and weaker, less and less meaningful, as we get older, because we should be working through our Fate. However, Fated issues may return twelve years later if we still need to address something. Or we could work through something in a different way the next time around, or see a challenge coming and avoid it.

Here is an example of how to shift the Houses for the Decade and Yearly Cycles using my chart. The original Natal Chart is first, followed by the Decade Chart progressed to my current age of thirty-nine, which falls into the decade of "32–41," followed by the Yearly Chart for this year I am writing this book, which is the Year of the Dragon.

MING

TIAN FU (EMPRESS)

Lu Cun (Storehouse)

Huo Xing (Fire)

(2–11) Snake Palace

ANCESTORS

TIAN TONG (VASSAL)

TAI YIN (MOON)

WEN CHANG (MAGISTRATE)

Yang Ren (Goat Blade)

Hua Lu (Salary)

Hua Quan (Authority)

(12–21) Horse Palace

PLEASURE

WU QU (GENERAL)

Tan Lang (Greedy Wolf)

Ling Xing (Water)

Di Kong (Void)

Tian Xi (Happiness)

(22–31) Goat Palace

PROPERTY

TAI YANG (SUN)

JU MEN (GREAT GATE)

Hua Ji (Jealousy)

WEN QU (PRIEST)

Tian Yao (Beauty)

(32–41) Monkey Palace

YOUTH

Tuo Luo (Humpback)

Tian Xing (Punishment)

(112–121) Dragon Palace

GREGORY DAVID DONE

Zi Wei Dou Shu Chart

FOUR PILLARS:

YEAR: Yang Fire Tiger

MONTH: Yin Fire Rooster

DAY: Yang Metal Horse

HOUR: Yang Metal Dragon

SOLAR BIRTH INFORMATION

1986/9/23 7:00am to 8:59am (DST)

LUNAR BIRTH INFORMATION:

Bing Yin /8/20

Chen

Tiger, Yang Male

INNER NATURE: Water

SUPERIORS

TIAN XIANG (TUTOR)

Tian Yue (Halberd)

(42–51) Rooster Palace

PARTNERS

Lian Zhen (Concubine)

Po Jun (Rebel)

You Bi (Right Assistant)

De Jie (Loss)

(102–111) Rabbit Palace

ASSISTANTS

TIAN JI (ORACLE)

TIAN LIANG (ROOF BEAM)

Hua Ke (Examination)

(52–61) Dog Palace

OFFSPRING

(92–101) Tiger Palace

WEALTH

Hong Luan (Red Bird)

(82–91) Ox Palace

HEALTH

(72–81) Rat Palace

CAREER/TRAVEL

ZI WEI (EMPEROR)

Qi Sha (7 Killings)

Zuo Fu (Left Assistant)

Tian Kui (Leader)

Tian Ma (Travel)

(62–71) Pig Palace

<table>
<tr>
<td>OFFSPRING
TIAN FU (EMPRESS)
Lu Cun (Storehouse)
Huo Xing (Fire)

(2–11) Snake Palace</td>
<td>PARTNERS
TIAN TONG (VASSAL)
TAI YIN (MOON)
WEN CHANG (MAGISTRATE)
Yang Ren (Goat Blade)
Hua Lu (Salary)
Hua Quan (Authority)
(12–21) Horse Palace</td>
<td>YOUTH
WU QU (GENERAL)
Tan Lang (Greedy Wolf)
Ling Xing (Water)
Di Kong (Void)
Tian Xi (Happiness)

(22–31) Goat Palace</td>
<td>MING
TAI YANG (SUN)
JU MEN (GREAT GATE)
Hua Ji (Jealousy)
WEN QU (PRIEST)
Tian Yao (Beauty)

(32–41) Monkey Palace</td>
</tr>
<tr>
<td>WEALTH
Tuo Luo (Humpback)
Tian Xing (Punishment)

(112–121) Dragon Palace</td>
<td colspan="2" rowspan="2">GREGORY DAVID DONE
Progressed Decade Chart, Age 32–41
FOUR PILLARS:
YEAR: Yang Fire Tiger
MONTH: Yin Fire Rooster
DAY: Yang Metal Horse
HOUR: Yang Metal Dragon

SOLAR BIRTH INFORMATION
1986/9/23 7:00am to 8:59am (DST)

LUNAR BIRTH INFORMATION:
Bing Yin /8/20
Chen

Tiger, Yang Male

INNER NATURE: Water</td>
<td>ANCESTORS
TIAN XIANG (TUTOR)
Tian Yue (Halberd)

(42–51) Rooster Palace</td>
</tr>
<tr>
<td>HEALTH
Lian Zhen (Concubine)
Po Jun (Rebel)
You Bi (Right Assistant)
De Jie (Loss)

(102–111) Rabbit Palace</td>
<td>PLEASURE
TIAN JI (ORACLE)
TIAN LIANG (ROOF BEAM)
Hua Ke (Examination)

(52–61) Dog Palace</td>
</tr>
<tr>
<td>CAREER/TRAVEL

(92–101) Tiger Palace</td>
<td>ASSISTANTS
Hong Luan (Red Bird)

(82–91) Ox Palace</td>
<td>SUPERIORS

(72–81) Rat Palace</td>
<td>PROPERTY
ZI WEI (EMPEROR)
Qi Sha (7 Killings)
Zuo Fu (Left Assistant)
Tian Kui (Leader)
Tian Ma (Travel)

(62–71) Pig Palace</td>
</tr>
</table>

<table>
<tr>
<td>ANCESTORS
TIAN FU (EMPRESS)
Lu Cun (Storehouse)
Huo Xing (Fire)

(2–11) Snake Palace</td>
<td>PLEASURE
TIAN TONG (VASSAL)
TAI YIN (MOON)
WEN CHANG (MAGISTRATE)
Yang Ren (Goat Blade)
Hua Lu (Salary)
Hua Quan (Authority)
(12–21) Horse Palace</td>
<td>PROPERTY
WU QU (GENERAL)
Tan Lang (Greedy Wolf)
Ling Xing (Water)
Di Kong (Void)
Tian Xi (Happiness)

(22–31) Goat Palace</td>
<td>SUPERIORS
TAI YANG (SUN)
JU MEN (GREAT GATE)
Hua Ji (Jealousy)
WEN QU (PRIEST)
Tian Yao (Beauty)

(32–41) Monkey Palace</td>
</tr>
<tr>
<td>MING
Tuo Luo (Humpback)
Tian Xing (Punishment)

(112–121) Dragon Palace</td>
<td colspan="2" rowspan="2">GREGORY DAVID DONE
Yearly Chart, Dragon Year
FOUR PILLARS:
YEAR: Yang Fire Tiger
MONTH: Yin Fire Rooster
DAY: Yang Metal Horse
HOUR: Yang Metal Dragon

SOLAR BIRTH INFORMATION
1986/9/23 7:00am to 8:59am (DST)

LUNAR BIRTH INFORMATION:
Bing Yin /8/20
Chen

Tiger, Yang Male

INNER NATURE: Water</td>
<td>ASSISTANTS
TIAN XIANG (TUTOR)
Tian Yue (Halberd)

(42–51) Rooster Palace</td>
</tr>
<tr>
<td>YOUTH
Lian Zhen (Concubine)
Po Jun (Rebel)
You Bi (Right Assistant)
De Jie (Loss)

(102–111) Rabbit Palace</td>
<td>CAREER/TRAVEL
TIAN JI (ORACLE)
TIAN LIANG (ROOF BEAM)
Hua Ke (Examination)

(52–61) Dog Palace</td>
</tr>
<tr>
<td>PARTNERS

(92–101) Tiger Palace</td>
<td>OFFSPRING
Hong Luan (Red Bird)

(82–91) Ox Palace</td>
<td>WEALTH

(72–81) Rat Palace</td>
<td>HEALTH
ZI WEI (EMPEROR)
Qi Sha (7 Killings)
Zuo Fu (Left Assistant)
Tian Kui (Leader)
Tian Ma (Travel)

(62–71) Pig Palace</td>
</tr>
</table>

MAJOR STARS IN PROGRESSION

We can now discuss the nature of Stars in Progression, starting with the Major Stars. For the most part, the Stars can be interpreted symbolically in the same way as they are in the Natal Chart, if you understand the basic ideas explored above. Remember that the Progressed Charts are weaker and more temporary in their influence and always relate to the Natal Chart. The Stars remain fixed on their mandate of Fate from the Natal Chart, and in Progression they move around the chart, working out that mandate in different Houses. As we resolve our Fate, the Ghosts Stars weaken and become sources of wisdom, and the Major Stars become a source of spiritual connection. We look to the Stars in Progression for where opportunities and challenges may arise regarding the original image of Fate as it is represented in the Natal Chart, and for when and how we can utilize them as spiritual forces.

Zi Wei, the Emperor

The Emperor is the most important influence in Progression, as it is the ruler of Yang Fate in the Natal Chart, and we should follow it as it goes through the Houses decade after decade and year after year. We look to the Emperor for our most potent opportunities and where we can most effectively resolve Fate. Wherever the Emperor appears in Progression, this period is optimal for the resolution of Fate, for making deep and powerful connections, for advancement in career, and for celebrating life in whatever House it arrives in.

The resolution of Fate in that House will happen naturally, and the struggle there may be relinquished with the proper application of Yang effort. And we must remember that the Emperor is Yang, and we must step up and activate the potential that it brings us. This is a period when you can unravel the bitterness of Fate with the support of your Beneficial Ancestors. You can access your innate majesty, dignity, and generosity during this period.

Prepare for this transit influence with introspection, self-reflection, and planning. For example, a Yearly Chart with the Emperor in the Offspring Palace is a great year to have a baby, so you can plan accordingly. If it arrives in the Career/Travel Palace, that is a great year to move, change careers, or make a journey. If it rules the Superiors Palace during a Decade Cycle, then expect that to be a period where you make the most fruitful advancement in your career. When free of affliction, the Houses ruled by the Emperor are the best years of your life regarding that House, so utilize this powerful force to resolve your Yang Fate. Be magnanimous and regal, and share the power with generosity and grace.

Tian Fu, the Empress

The Empress, the second most important Star in Progression, guides the resolution of Yin Fate in the Natal Chart. Where the Empress appears in Progression, it signifies a period of effortless progress, serendipitous opportunities, natural connections, and receiving gifts in both the personal and professional aspects of your life. During this period, things flow and unfold naturally, and you need to relax and follow the flow, even when there are challenges, for what may seem like losses, compromises, or setbacks could end up placing you in an advantageous position.

The years that the Empress rules are full of surprise gifts, belated rewards, personal and professional recognition, and gratitude from others. You are also more able to be of great help in advising and educating those around you. Prepare for this transit by solidifying your family ties and social contracts and conserving your financial assets. To make the best use of the Empress, you must reduce goals and expectations and excessive ambition, and go from being Yang to Yin in whatever House she arrives in, which may require a change of direction.

For example, during a year when the Empress arrives in the Assistants Palace, you should be less proactive at work and instead initiate teamwork, support others, and lift them up to shine; this may create belated rewards that come back to help you later. In a year when she arrives in the Offspring Palace, you may unexpectedly get pregnant with joyous results. A decade when she rules the Pleasure Palace may be more carefree, easeful, and full of social connection and fun. Free of affliction, the Houses ruled by the Empress are the most gracious and profitable years of your life regarding that House, and they naturally unravel your Yin Fate, so be generous and regal, and spread the love.

Tian Xiang, the Tutor

Wherever the Tutor appears in Progression, it creates a very powerful and productive period for the resolution of Yang Fate regarding your profession, work in the world, and contribution to society. You will feel inspired and called to a greater purpose, mission, or view, and this Star can bring out your best qualities and innate talents and bring about rewards, recognition, and promotions. You can work more intelligently and more accurately apply your learned wisdom, for which you may receive acknowledgment and be able to help others. You can learn a great deal in this period and make progress that will seem irreversible. These are years of success. Prepare for this transit with careful planning, education, and networking.

For example, in a Yearly Chart where this arrives in any career House, you may see promotion, job offers, raises, work productivity, and success. A decade during which it rules the Pleasure Palace may be optimal for turning a talent, hobby, or personal pleasure into a profession. Free of affliction, the Houses ruled by the Tutor are years of solid maturation, helpful education, and practical acquisition. Used properly, this may be the most practical accomplishment Star.

Tian Ji, the Oracle

In Progression, the Oracle acts as the Ancestors' divining rod and voice, telling us where and how to unravel our more intuitive and spiritual Fate. This period is optimal for introspection, meditation, and research, and the Oracle can help to produce revelation and insight in whatever House it arrives in. The messages of your Ancestral Qi, both of affliction and blessing, will be heightened in this House during this period, so look to signs, omens, and dreams for guidance and visitation. If there is an affliction, you may feel a heightened sense of vulnerability and sensitivity in that House. Still, you can also work through deep negative emotions and liberate Ancestral Ghosts.

This represents a period of inaction, planning, and inspiration, and it is not suited to aggressive productivity. Instead, this is a period of mysticism, spiritual growth, and renunciation. Prepare for this transit by solidifying your resources and organizing your support systems so that you can receive spiritual gifts and messages that may come forward.

For example, when the Oracle appears in the Youth Palace in your Yearly Chart, you may have a heightened emotional connection to your siblings and be able to heal old wounds with them. In a year when it appears in the Property Palace, you may go on a spiritual pilgrimage or meditation retreat. During a Decade Cycle where it appears in the Wealth Palace, you may spend that time using your intuition and foresight to earn money through speculative means. When free of affliction, the Houses ruled by the Oracle are the most insightful and spiritually transformative of your life regarding that House, so utilize these periods to grow.

Tai Yang, the Sun or Prince

Wherever the Sun appears in Progression, this is an optimal period for industry and productivity. The Sun pushes us forward in the resolution of our Yang Fate, especially with worldly ambitions, so you will be more active and busier, and things will move fast during this period. You will feel a heightened sense of power, purpose, and clarity in whatever House this arrives in, and you may feel pushed to prove yourself and achieve. These are the years of action, adventure, travel, and progress, and they are not suited to introspection, laziness, or indecision.

The Yang Fate associated with the Sun is obvious and reliable, like the Sun, so there is no need to overthink or question opportunities here. Prepare for this transit by solidifying your alliances and making practical plans that can be implemented. The Sun helps us to be consistent and reliable, rising and setting like the Sun, so it can help establish routine disciplines, health practices, and structures in our lives and relationships.

For example, during a year when it arrives in the Wealth Palace in your Yearly Chart, you may get a promotion or raise and be able to generate wealth effectively. When it arrives in the Assistants Palace, you may receive generous and practical help and support from older mentors. In a decade where the Sun rules the Partners Palace, expect to meet many suitable partners and have many relationship opportunities. Free of affliction, the Houses ruled by the Sun are the most constructive of your life regarding that House. Be active and ambitious, and work diligently!

Wu Qu, the General

Wherever the General appears in Progression, this is an optimal period for strategy, leadership, career development, acquiring property, saving money, and retirement. The messages of realism, hardship, responsibility, and hindsight from the Ancestors will be strong in this House during this period. You may feel a heightened sense of isolation, social responsibility, and duty, and life may call you to battle—to work hard, make tough decisions, and lead. It may postpone success and Fate resolution in the House during this period as well.

These are periods of battle action, attrition, and treaty making, and they are not suited to selfishness, fantasy, and frivolous romance. These are years of ordinary wisdom, practical tactics, and strategy. Prepare for this transit with sober assessment; expect things to be challenging but rewarding, so strategize and solidify a chain of command.

For example, a year when the General appears in the Offspring Palace in your Yearly Chart may bring a lot of hard work, sobriety, and disciplined action to care for a child. A year when it appears in the Superiors Palace may see you taking charge as a manager or leader, forcing you to make tough decisions—or it could indicate a good year to retire! Life during a decade when the General rules the Ming Palace may feel like a battle, and you may have a long period of challenge that is ultimately productive in life. Free of affliction, the Houses ruled by the General are the most responsible years of your life regarding that House, so look to these for maturity, wisdom, and retirement.

Tai Yin, the Moon Lady or Princess

Wherever the Moon appears in Progression, this is a period of natural ease, introspection, and spiritual awakening. The Moon brings forward hidden aspects of our mysterious Yin Fate, and the messages of the Matriarchal Ancestors will be strong during this time, maybe inspiring a sense of gratitude and grace. The years ruled by the Moon are not characterized by certainty and solidity; things wax and wane, sometimes hidden, sometimes bright. However, these are the years of wisdom gathering, where we can recognize a broader and more interconnected view of life. This period is not about what to do or acquire but rather about what to become and what to be. These are periods of being rather than doing, and they bring spiritual maturity and expand our experience to include a sense of the numinous and sacred along with compassion. Prepare for this transit by reducing worldly ambitions, relaxing, and gathering information and resources for the long run.

For example, a year when the Moon appears in the Health Palace in your Yearly Chart may be profoundly transformative through addressing health concerns with self-care practices like yoga and meditation. When it appears in the Wealth Palace, that year may see generous support come forward, allowing you not to worry as much about finances. A decade when it rules the Ming Palace may be full of many mysterious chapters, with things progressing in a way that seems beyond your grasp and out of your control. Free of affliction, the Houses ruled by the Moon may be the most illuminating and spiritually rewarding years of your life regarding that House.

Ju Men, the Great Gate

Wherever the Great Gate appears in Progression, this becomes a period of being spaced out and unfocused, where we may be faced with openness, lack of direction, and even too many possibilities that create "paralysis by analysis." Opportunities may abound, but this can make decisions, change, and commitment more difficult or even impossible. As we mature, this Star becomes more of an opportunity, and it can expand our scope of influence and contacts. The more selfish, uninformed, and ignorant we are, the more this opportunity will seem overwhelming and unclear. The more we know ourselves, the more we can navigate and use the open possibilities. Prepare for this transit by taking stock of your life and committing to a clear direction; establish healthy and disciplined habits, which will eclipse the Great Gate's worst effects.

For example, in a year when the Great Gate appears in the Partners Palace in your yearly Chart, it may inspire promiscuity or make you look for more options. A year when it appears in the Career/Travel Palace may cause you to feel uncertain about what to do with your life or where to go. A decade when it rules the Wealth Palace may be a challenging time for generating and maintaining wealth, but it may also greatly expand your opportunities. Free of affliction, these Houses are the most unfocused of our lives, so lock things down and stay the course regarding that House.

Tian Tong, the Vassal

Wherever the Vassal appears in Progression, this is a modest but productive period for career development, alliance making, education, and marriage. This Star pushes Yang Fate's resolution through tribal alliance and service to the greater good. It is not as strong as the Emperor or Sun, but it strives to be like them and serve them. During this period, you will likely make modest worldly progress, receive promotions, find a partner, move into a new home, and so on. During this period, you may feel a heightened sense of loyalty, competence, and pride in whatever House this arrives in, and you will be more conscious of working hard, like a samurai who is ready to serve. Prepare for this transit with education. Cultivate self-discipline and humility, and things will go smoothly. Be prepared to take orders, follow instructions, work with others, and serve the greater good.

For example, a year the Vassal arrives in the Career/Travel Palace in your Yearly Chart may be an active year when you receive a promotion and travel widely for work at the behest of a new boss. A year when it arrives in the Health Palace may be great for establishing solid health routines and getting in shape. A decade when the Vassal rules the Ancestors Palace may be full of heightened familial obligations, serving and caring for your parents. Free of affliction, the Houses ruled by the Vassal are ones of steady and modest progress in service of your greater goals and ambitions.

Tian Liang, the Roof Beam

Wherever the Roof Beam appears in Progression, it denotes a period of calm stability and even material progress. It brings up issues of Fengshui and can indicate optimal periods for making Fengshui adjustments, moving House, or going on pilgrimage, or it may indicate when place, land, architecture, or material act in a significant way to unravel our Fate. It calls us to connect with the people, place, language, and traditions of our Ancestors. The Roof Beam pushes us to persevere in what is right and stabilize our connections.

This is a period that may include land or wealth acquisition, property building or maintenance, or inheritance. It is a time for alliances, business mergers, treaty making, friendship making, partnering, and the renewal of old relationships and enhanced bonds with family members. You may enjoy the support, encouragement, and investment of others during this period. Prepare for this transit with practical concerns for property and by practicing generosity and inclusion.

For example, a year when the Roof Beam appears in the Property Palace in your Yearly Chart is optimal for buying, selling, remodeling, or building property. A year when it appears in the Ancestors Palace is a great year to make Ancestral Pilgrimage. A decade when it rules the Career/Travel Palace may be optimal for moving and finding your true home and tribe. Free of affliction, Houses ruled by the Roof Beam are rewarding and help us to establish stability and security through the tangible.

Wen Chang, the Magistrate

Wherever the Magistrate appears in Progression, this is a period of education, self-cultivation, and slow and steady career development. It is an ideal time to be in school and advance your education, training, or retraining for professional reasons. It is a time for deep learning, consideration of others and your place in society, group efforts, and making and appreciating art and culture.

For example, a year when the Magistrate appears in the Assistants Palace in your Yearly Chart may be an excellent year to go to school, learn a new skill, or take a class or for teamwork at your job. A year when it appears in the Health Palace may be a great time to actively learn about and utilize medicine to help yourself or your family members. A decade when it appears in the Superiors Palace may see you earning a higher degree and actively using it to get a job. Free of affliction, these Houses are characterized by learning, self-cultivation, perseverance, and steady progress.

Wen Qu, the Priest

Wherever the Priest appears in Progression, this is a period of self-cultivation, education, spiritual practice, development, and experimentation. It is a time for retreat, renunciation, isolation, and inner reflection. It is also a time for creating or connecting with a spiritual community. Prepare for this influence by minimizing worldly responsibility and renewing or deepening spiritual practice.

For example, when the Priest arrives in the Career/Travel or Property Palace, it may be a great year to go on a meditation retreat. A year when it appears in the Ming Palace may be full of spiritual growth and revelation. Free of affliction, these Houses are full of insight, transformation, and enlightenment.

Lian Zhen, the Concubine

Wherever the Concubine appears in Progression, it denotes a period when you are in flux and when Fate feels out of your hands. You may feel more vulnerable and easily influenced in whatever House this arrives in, which may make you more open to affliction, victimhood, and difficulty here. You may feel lost and clueless and be taken advantage of. It is important to remember that the auspice of this Star depends on the influence of the other Stars that accompany it.

The affliction of this Ghost Star will be stronger when we are younger and we have not yet resolved this Ancestral Ghost; until it is resolved, it may inspire periods of loss and a lack of safety. As we mature and resolve this Ghost, this same image may soften and become a period of editing, discipline, and developing self-confidence. Though the years that the Concubine rules are often harsh and open to trauma, they also expose what might otherwise be our hidden capacity to survive and recover. Prepare for this transit by working on self-possession and self-confidence.

For example, a year when the Concubine arrives in the Partners Palace in your Yearly Chart may see you being taken advantage of and used by a partner. A year when it arrives in the Wealth Palace may see you following someone into a financial venture only to have it go poorly. A decade when it rules the Career/Travel Palace may be a period of wandering when you feel lost and vulnerable but slowly progress and stand up for yourself.

Qi Sha, the Seven Killings or Executioner

Wherever the Seven Killings Star appears in Progression, this Ancestral Ghost creates a period of heightened struggle and anxiety. It is the most afflicting force in the Natal Chart and in Progressions. Simply put, until it is resolved, it can possess us and create distrust, fear, paranoia, and any host of negative emotions as it goes around the chart. It creates affliction, struggle, conflicts, accidents, arguments, and challenges wherever it goes. As we mature and resolve this Star, the anxiety and struggle should fade, and this becomes a cautious force that becomes resolved, never to enact the same negativity and struggle ever again. Prepare for this transit by becoming self-reliant and working to resolve this negativity in your chart. Do not be naive and think this is resolved. Be cautious, and prepare for challenges here; do not expect it to be easy. Eat bitter, as the Chinese say.

For example, a year when the Seven Killings Star appears in the Ancestors Palace in your Yearly Chart may be full of inexplicable anxiety and mental health challenges. A year when it appears in the Health Palace may incur an accident, injury, or strange illness, or it may bring forward unresolved trauma or mental health issues. A decade when the Seven Killings rules any of the career Houses may be full of challenges and setbacks and see little progress.

Tan Lang, the Greedy Wolf

Wherever the Greedy Wolf appears in Progression, this Ancestral Ghost creates a period rife with strain, isolation, and nervousness. The Greedy Wolf may push you into a period of survival, and you may give in to manipulation and selfish, seductive conduct. It is a time for many challenging personal tests caused by our own misconduct, and you may be cast out of the wolf pack for your behavior, forced to struggle alone and without help. You may work hard on your career with little results. You may lose yourself in twisted, predatory relationships. As we mature, the darkness of the Greedy Wolf should fade, which can be transformed into independence, empowerment, and the expression of unique talents and skills. Prepare for this transit with self-reflection and taking personal responsibility. Establish healthy humility, good relationships, and disciplined habits to mitigate the Greedy Wolf's worst effects.

For example, a year when the Greedy Wolf shows up in the Youth Palace in your Yearly Chart may see you breaking off contact with a sibling due to a selfish argument. In a year when it arrives in the Superiors Palace, you may follow a charismatic leader, teacher, or boss. A decade when it rules the Offspring Palace may be a period of struggling as a single parent.

Po Jun, the Rebel or Breaking Rank

Wherever the Rebel appears in Progression, this Ancestral Ghost creates a period of self-created struggle and compulsive judgment. The Rebel can possess you and create distrust, rebelliousness, and criticism. Self-reflection may be forgotten, and you can become your own worst enemy here. As we mature and resolve this Ghost, the struggle aspect of this star should fade and soften into wisdom. Until this is resolved, it will continue to perpetuate self-created struggle and immaturity. Prepare with disciplined self-reflection and by renouncing self-centeredness.

For example, a year when this appears in the Assistants Palace in your Yearly Chart may see you losing a job due to rebelling against your boss. A year when it appears in the Property Palace may see you struggling to find a new apartment due to being critical, confrontational, and distrustful. In a decade when it rules the Partners Palace, you may be constantly ending relationships due to immaturity and lack of commitment.

MINOR STARS IN PROGRESSION

Huo Xing, the Fire Star, and Ling Xing, the Water or Ringing Star

Wherever the Fire or Water Star appears in Progression, these Ancestral Ghosts can create incidents of confusion, false views, and negative emotions, but they are incidental in Progression. In the Natal Chart, they can represent Fated patterns, but in Progression, they merely lead to incidents of negativity.

The Fire Star creates impatience, restlessness, impulsiveness, and rash behavior. It creates incidents of anger and frustration that undermine us. The Water Star creates fear, anxiety, trauma, and emotional turmoil. It makes us overly emotional, attached, and dramatic. As we mature and resolve these Ghosts, the struggle of these stars should fade, and the roller coaster may soften into adaptable wisdom. The anger of the Fire Star turns into clarity, and the fear of the Water Star turns to compassion. Prepare through meditation and self-reflection.

Yang Ren, the Goat Blade or Sacrifice Star, and Tuo Luo, the Humpback or Rejection Star

Wherever the Goat Blade or Humpback Stars appear in Progression, these Ancestral Ghosts create incidents of hardship and loss. The Goat Blade acts like a knife, and in Progression, it has an editing and cutting-out effect. It sheds inessentials, edits luxury, and creates spiritual austerity and renunciation. If it is further afflicted, it can result in accident and injury.

Until it is resolved, the Humpback creates excessive emotions and thinking and feelings of isolation, selfishness, and confusion; it creates rejection and revenge and is petty, vicious, and deceitful. While the Goat Blade can become a force of wisdom and cutting clarity, the Humpback is generally inauspicious wherever it appears.

You Bi, the Right Assistant, and Zuo Fu, the Left Assistant

In Progression, the Right and Left Assistants work together to help the Emperor and Empress to create timely good fortune and help. These Stars become more potent in Progression, acting like guardian angels or fairy godparents who sneak around the chart doing subtle good deeds.

The Left Assistant is the master of altruism; it is Yang and more ephemeral and therefore subtler and gentler in the way that it creates support, and it does so through more otherworldly means by making signs, omens, and premonitions through dreams, intuitions, and the subconscious.

The Right Assistant Star is "harder," and it works to manifest support and opportunities in the "real world," as it is Yin and more manifest and solid. It works to possess people and create help, opportunity, guidance, leadership, and good fortune.

Lu Cun, the Storehouse

In Progression, the Storehouse Star acts like a gold coin, moving around the chart and bestowing blessings. It manifests as tangible wealth and resources, and it is exalted and most beneficial when it arrives in the Ming, Wealth, and Property Palaces. Look for gifts, windfalls, raises, loans, and so on wherever it shows up.

Tian Yao, the Beauty Star

The Beauty Star is weak in Progression. At best, it can create temporary and fleeting moments of beauty, elegance, and freedom. It may act as an indicator of how your physical appearance influences your Fate.

Tian Kui, the Leader

In Progression, the Leader gets empowered as a benefactor to curb misfortune and bring about timely good luck in a House. It may act through a leader, mentor, or older person to provide guidance or support.

Tian Xi, the Happiness Star

The Happiness Star is very weak in Progression, but it can indicate marriage or partnership when it enters the Ming, Wealth, or Partners Palace. Otherwise, it can create brief moments of whimsy and delight; it can cause giggles, but it is fleeting and almost meaningless in both the Natal Chart and Progression.

Tian Yue, the Halberd Star

Like the Goat Blade, this Star can have a cutting and editing effect in Progression, but it is much weaker. It can help to assist other Stars with discipline and to curb misfortune.

De Jie, the Loss Star, and Di Kong, the Void or Empty Earth Star

The Loss and Void Stars get somewhat magnified in Progression, but they are still overall weak. They are generally Stars of misfortune and inauspicious wherever they show up.

The Loss Star can create loss and deprivation, and it is most inauspicious in the Wealth and Property Palaces, as it can lead to material losses. In the Ming Palace, it can create instability, uncertainty, and failure. It is not malicious but afflicts by creating a sense of hopelessness and weakness.

The Void Star afflicts by creating a sense of nihilism, pessimism, and negativity. Progression can create a lack of spirit and enthusiasm, resignation, and feelings of futility in whatever House it arrives in. This Star is more afflicted in the relationship Houses, as it affects our mental state, so it is more inauspicious in the Ancestors, Youth, Offspring, Partners, Assistants, and Pleasure Palaces.

Tian Xing, the Punishment Star

In Progression, the Punishment Star can create incidents of "punishment," but it is overall weak and not to be overestimated if you are a good person. However, it can potentially create detachment and isolation and engender libel, lawsuits, and punishment for wrongdoings if you have it coming. It can bring about retribution, payback, revenge, and the results of previous bad actions. It is transactional in nature, and it calls in debts wherever it arrives.

Tian Ma, the Travel or Heavenly Horse Star

In Progression, the Travel Star catalyzes movement and travel. It is generally weak, but it can inspire travel, movement, change, and restless activity in whatever House it arrives in. It is most potent in the Ming and Travel/Career Palace and can inspire big life changes or journeys. Most of the time, it indicates more subtle change, movement, and locomotion; when it is afflicted, it can indicate things like car accidents or similar types of misfortune.

Hong Luan, the Red Bird

The Red Bird or Phoenix is generally weak, but when it arrives in the Ming Palace or Health Palace, it can indicate periods of rebirth and starting over. When it arrives in the Partners Palace, it can also indicate marriage or partnership.

The Four Transformers

The Four Transformers, which are Hua Lu, the Salary or Prosperity Star; Hua Quan, the Authority Star; Hua Ke, the Examination Star; and Hua Ji, the Jealousy or Scandal Star, are to be understood primarily as Progression Stars, and their central interpretation is in Progression. They also influence the Natal Chart, but otherwise, they act as catalysts for change in Progression. Please refer to chapter on the Four Transformers for a more thorough discussion of their influence.

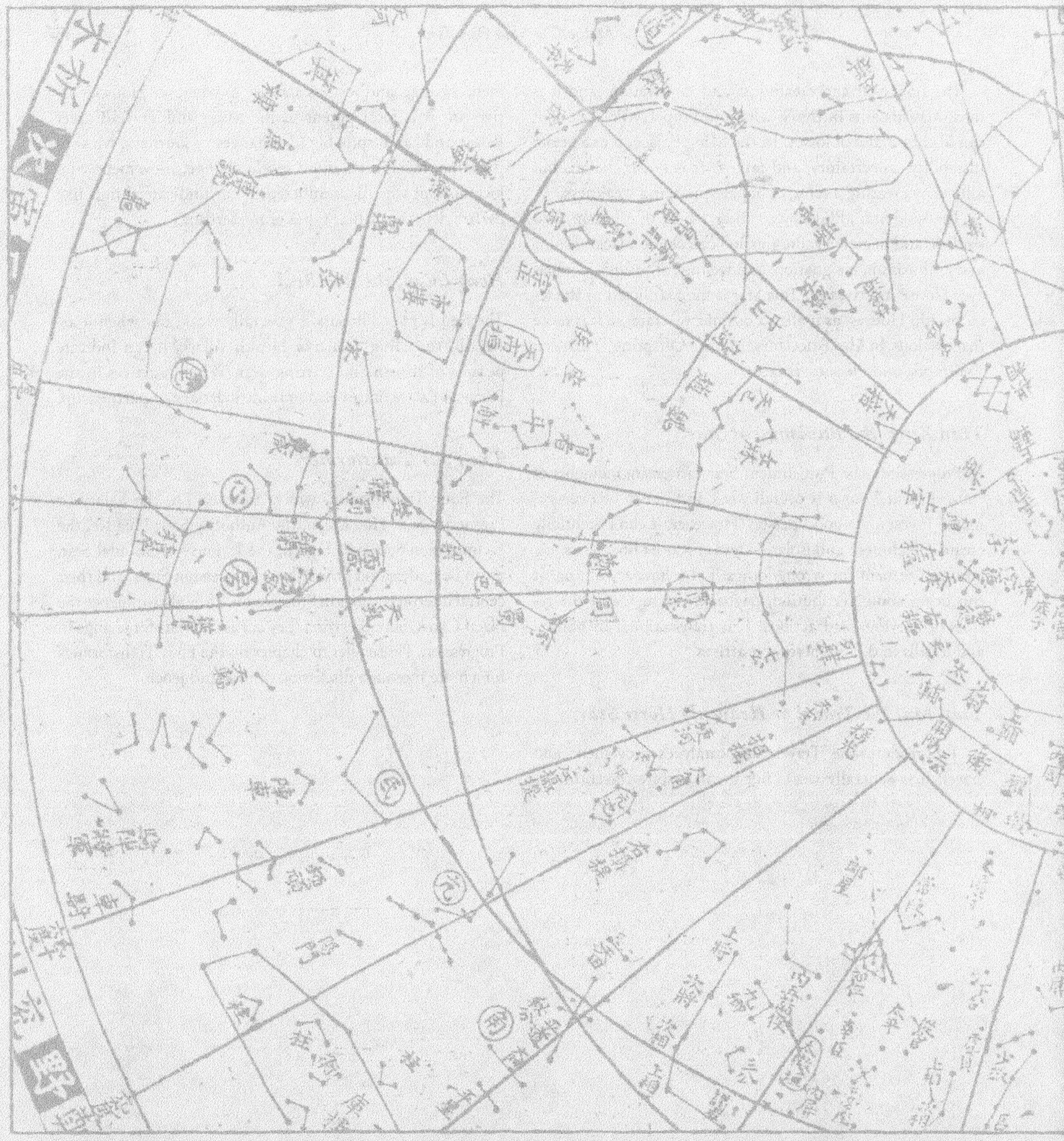

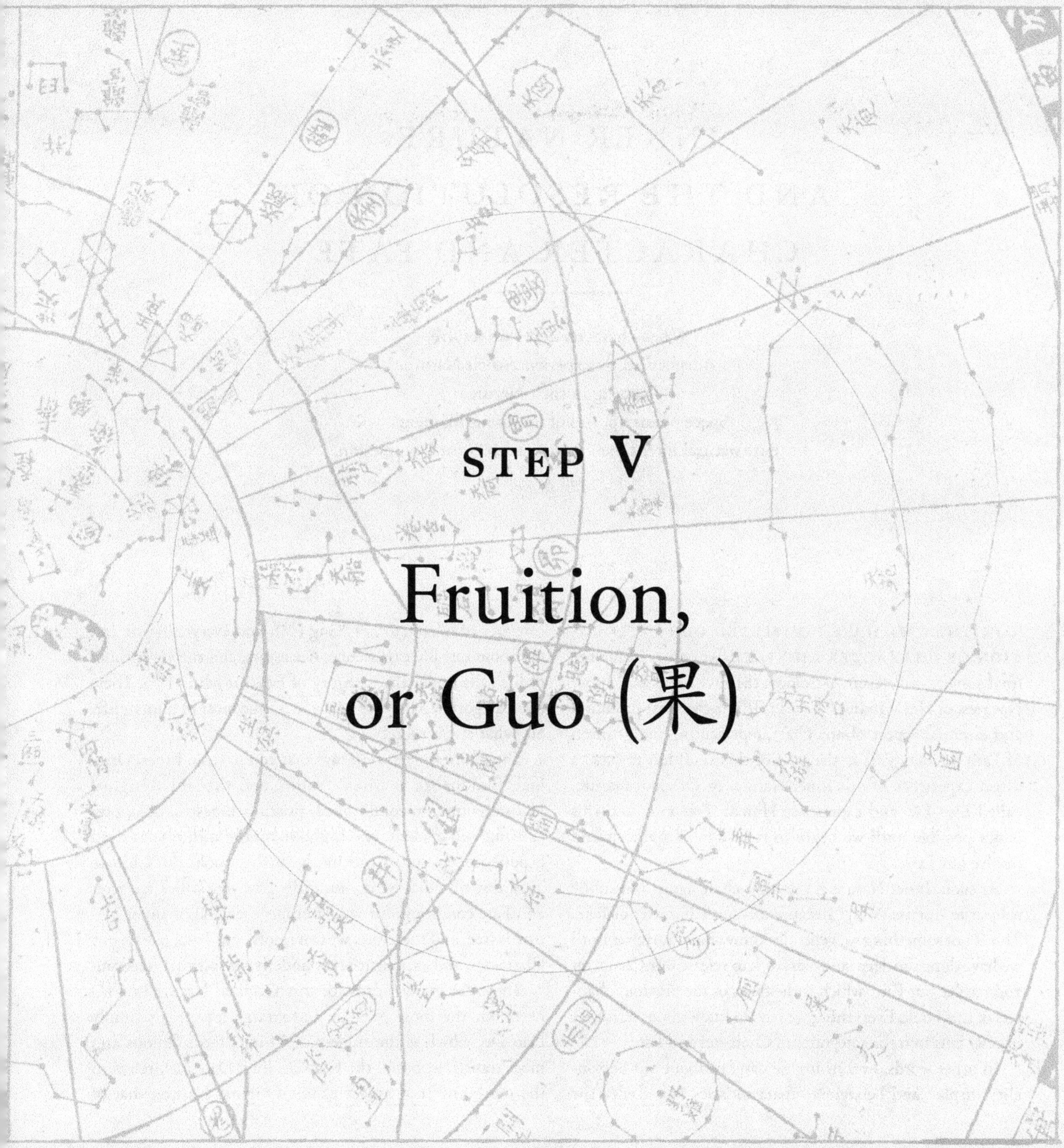

STEP V

Fruition, or Guo (果)

INNER NATURE AND THE RESOLUTION OF CHARACTER AND FATE

When character and Fate resolve,
Adepts directly experience their Nature.
Resting in their Nature,
Space opens up, full of luminous filaments.
Pure natural intent then manifests as Great Completion.

—*Liu Ming*[1]

NOW THAT WE HAVE COMPLETED OUR EXPLORATION OF CHARACTER AND FATE, we can examine the final subject of Polestar Astrology: the Five Elemental Inner Natures, or Nei Wuxing (内五行). This is the most profound and essential aspect of any chart, representing the Fruition of Path Astrology. It is the goal of this tradition to have a direct experience of our Inner Nature, or Original Nature, called Dao De, and experience Human Freedom, and this is not possible until we begin to release our Character and resolve our Fate.

As such, Inner Nature is the most challenging and subtle subject to discuss. Why? Because it is not Character or Fate. This is not something we generally know about ourselves until we have done the deep spiritual work to release our Character and resolve our Fate, which is the focus of the previous chapters of this book. Everything we tend to know about ourselves usually falls into the categories of Character and Fate.

In other words, everything we can say about our personality display and behavioral characteristics falls under the category of Character, or Xing (性), and everything we can say about our life experience, Ancestors, and the vicissitudes of life falls under the category of Fate, or Ming (命). These two categories, Xing and Ming, describe most of human life. So, what else is there?

The Chinese Tradition says that you have an Inner, Original, Buddha, or Spiritual Nature and that this Original Nature is free, unconditioned, pristine, indestructible, preexisting, self-evident, and found naturally within your lived experience. As stated previously in this book, the Chinese Tradition says that we do not really have free will; Character and Fate condition our will. But our Original or Inner Nature is free, and therefore, we can resolve our Fate, release our Character, and experience this underlying spiritual freedom.

There are many words for this Original Nature in Chinese, but the most popular and straightforward is simply Dao De, which is the subject of China's most famous and most translated book, the Dao De Jing. Dao (道), refers to the more universal aspect of our Original Nature, that of

Heaven. De (德), often translated as Virtue, refers to the more personal or individualized aspect of that Universal Nature as it is found in human beings. Jing, (經) here simply means the "classic of" or text.

Everyone should read the Dao De Jing to understand more about what the Chinese mean when referring to our Original Nature. The Dao De Jing is also a manual for the main form of meditation practice recommended in this book: Zuo Wang, or Sitting and Forgetting. Zuo Wang is central to the path of Polestar Astrology and the basis for resolving Character and Fate, in conjunction with studying your Natal Chart and working with the patterns found there.

This tradition, however, goes a step further and says that we are each predisposed to experience our Original Nature through one of the Five Elements, that this predisposition is determined astrologically by our birth, and that we can just look this up, which is pretty amazing. This calculation can be made for anyone, and we include it in each Natal Chart. I often discuss it at the end of a Natal reading and offer it as a positive conclusion to the subjects of Character and Fate.

Each of the Five Elements is a flavor of Dao, and Dao is essentially light—the Original Light. Everything is a phantasm of light. The Original Light is pristine, still, and aware of itself, or Zhidao (知道), which we can translate as a "naked knowing" of Dao. When the Original Light moves, it creates a spectrum or rainbow of infinite diversity, and we categorize this spectrum of light into Wu Xing (五行), or the Five Elemental Movements.

We can call these the Five Lights of Creation or, simply, the Five Elements that make up everything. The infinite spectrum of light can be categorized into these Five Movements. The nature of these Five Movements is also Zhidao (知道), meaning they are an expression of Pristine Awareness leading back to the pristine, unmoving Dao, and they are not separate or distinct from each other. They exist on an ever-flowing spectrum. Everything is a complex permutation of the Five Movements/Lights, and the Five Movements exist at every level of existence.

This tradition states that, behind the cycles of Time, these Five Movements are always turning and that everything in astrology falls into one of these categories. We each emerge as an individual embodied expression of the time and place of our birth. This determines our Character and Fate, but it also determines a resonance with one of the Five Elemental Movements, which we call our Inner Nature. Each of us is and contains all Five Elemental Movements within, as they are not separate from each other, but we each resonate with one in particular. And it is through one of these that we each find our way back to the Pristine Original Dao. In Buddhism, these are called the Wu Fang Fo (五方佛), or the Five Buddha Families.

These determine the nature of our "spiritual experience" and the kind of spiritual practice we should pursue. In other words, as we resolve our Fate and release our Character, our inner spiritual nature starts to shine through, and we have "spiritual experiences." This tradition suggests that each spiritual experience, and the following realizations and insights, aligns with and expresses one of these Five Elemental Flavors of Dao. Therefore, it behooves us to pursue spiritual practices that align with our Inner Elemental Nature, as this will make that practice more natural and easeful, for we will be going with our own nature.

Again, our Inner Nature is not something we know about ourselves until we start to do spiritual practice or release our Character and resolve a lot of our Fate. It is common that when people have a profound and life-changing experience of resolving Fate, when they finally let go or release an ongoing pattern or resolve an Ancestral Ghost, they experience catharsis, and it is in those moments that people often experience something divine, transcendent, or spiritual. In those moments, people see beyond their limited sense of a self and world and experience something bigger, deeper, or more essential. Spiritual practice catalyzes and speeds up this process, and people often experience catharsis and have spiritual experiences through meditation practice and self-reflection.

Again, the Five Inner Natures are difficult to describe because they are not Character or Fate. In other words, we are not talking about "what Inner Wood people are like," per se. Everyone wants to turn this into Character, but it is much deeper and more essential than that. These represent the spiritual impulse at the center of our being, and this impulse underlies all the motives and movements present in the Natal Chart.

So, in some ways, Inner Nature can come out or express in behavior, if we are strongly spiritually motivated, but otherwise, most people are dominated by their Character and Fate and generally do not experience their Inner Nature. It is essential, then, not to say too much about it, for the more we describe it, the more we are likely to misunderstand it and turn it into a form of Character. If you find yourself saying, "Oh, I'm Inner Fire, so I am really intense," then you have turned it into Character and misunderstood.

We will, therefore, talk around the subject and keep it simple. We will also focus on the kind of spiritual practice you should pursue, as this is the best way to use this information. I generally recommend nonconceptual meditation—Zuo Wang, Sitting and Forgetting—for everyone, but beyond that, your Inner Nature should inform your practice. Let it be a guide that points the direction of your practice and orients you on the path.

Hold your Inner Nature lightly, and remember that it is the most profound thing about you, so it is not easily understood. We aspire to experience this, and as such, it can be a central Icon of Essence in your spiritual path. What you should do after you experience your Original Nature is not for me to tell you; you'll have to wait and see.

ON DIRECTIONALITY

Another essential aspect of your spiritual journey is understanding the Generative and Destructive Cycles of the Five Elements. This principle, discussed briefly in the earlier chapter titled Non-Theism, Non-Materialism, and the Five Elements, helps you evaluate the relationship between your Inner and Outer Nature. Your Outer Nature is the Element of your birth year. For example, suppose your Inner Element is Water and your Outer Element is Fire, like mine. In that case, your Outer Element has the potential to either destroy or control your Inner Element, creating a unique dynamic.

The primary dynamics are that your Inner and Outer Elements are either Same; Generative, as mother or child; or Destructive. Let's discuss these briefly.

- Same—If they are the same, then your Inner Element and Outer Element match, and therefore, life is smooth; there is a harmonious resonance between your spiritual Inner Nature and your Outer Character expression.
- Generative—If your Inner and Outer Nature are in a mother–child relationship, determine the direction. If the Inner generates the Outer, then your Inner Nature will support, bolster, and express naturally in your life, and you will be more outwardly oriented in your spirituality. If the Outer generates the Inner, then you will be more inwardly oriented in your spirituality, and your outer life will naturally flow inwards and inform your deeper spiritual experiences.
- Destructive—If the relationship is Destructive, then again check the direction. The Destructive Cycle tends to create more conflict but also more dramatic spiritual experience and suffering that leads to awakening. If the Outer destroys the Inner, then your outer life will conflict with your inner spiritual life and make it more difficult to pursue spiritual life. If the Inner destroys the Outer, then your inner spiritual nature will dampen your outer life and make it more difficult to pursue worldly goals in lieu of your spirituality.

These dynamics can teach us a lot, and we should study and contemplate them before contemplating Inner Nature alone.

Let's go through each of the Five Inner Natures. The names of these were given by Liu Ming.[2] To understand these, we must return to each Element's fundamental essence, directionality, and symbolism. We must realize that Inner Nature is not produced by anything; it does not come from anywhere. It is not connected to Character or Fate, but it is something we naturally discover as self-existing and within. We express it through our very being. Each connects us directly to all the Five Elements and represents how Dao returns to itself.

NEI MU (内木), INNER WOOD—THE VIRTUOUS BEGINNER

We call Nei Mu the Virtuous Beginner, as Wood is pure creativity and expansion. It is the "start" of the cycle and represents birth and the moment of "creation" and renewal. Wood Inner Nature is all about the simplicity and purity of the Eternal Now. When spiritual teachers wax philosophical about "presence" and the "now," they are talking about the Wood Inner Nature experience, which is available to everyone, of course.

The spiritual essence of the person with Wood Inner Nature is constantly poised on the razor's edge between being and pure perception where all experience and thought bubbles up from "don't know"—from the death and darkness of its mother, the Water Element. The moment of cognition that is present before the mind perceives thought, sensation, or experience is Wood; it is the eternal state of spontaneous, natural, effortless cognition and perception that happens all by itself, or Ziran (自然). As such, the Wood Inner Nature person directly experiences the emptiness, openness, and fresh spontaneity of Presence as their natural state. They easily see and express egolessness and gentleness.

The deep inner experience of the person with a Wood Inner Nature is very similar to what Shunryu Suzuki called "beginner's mind." Spiritually, they are in a constant state of "start" that does not evolve but stays in a fluid state of "beginning" and renewal that is flexible, spontaneous, innocent, and fresh.

Wood is unformed, invisible, and constantly generating all things. However, if we look, we cannot find where things come from, where they abide, or where they go when they pass away. As such, Inner Wood stays in the "don't know" mind.

Practice

People with Wood Inner Nature are, therefore, adept at nonconceptual practices and traditions based on such practices. Zuo Wang, Sitting and Forgetting, is the true Wood (and Water) Element practice; people with Wood and Water Inner Natures can practice Sitting and Forgetting as their main path, and they need not go beyond this if they do not wish. Traditions like Wuwei Daoism, Caodong Chan and Soto Zen Buddhism, Dzogchen, Shambavopaya and Anupaya Shaivism, and apophatic prayer in Western mysticism are all very Inner Wood.

Spiritually, Inner Wood people respond to and thrive in nature and the wilderness, untouched by human conceptual projections, as it is through simplicity, nakedness, and innocence that they find their path. Mountains, trees, rivers, and so on are their shrines, and the open sky, their temples. They should seek vision in the wilderness and solitude. By extension, nature-based practices like shamanism, Shintoism, paganism, and so on can all be profound for the Inner Wood person.

Art, spontaneity, music, dance, and all acts of creativity too are expressions of Wood Inner Nature, provided that the act of creation is the point, rather than to construct artifacts of the mind. First thought, best thought, as Chögyam Trungpa used to say, is the realm of Inner Wood. Whatever bubbles up from "don't know" mind is perfect as it is.

Spiritually, the person with a Wood Inner Nature must stay on the brink of creativity in the Eternal Now, fresh and pliant, always the Virtuous Beginner.

NEI HUO (内火), INNER FIRE—THE COURAGEOUS WARRIOR

We call Nei Huo the Courageous Warrior, as Fire is the warmth, friction, and generative momentum of creation, charging forward and upward into being. Like Wood, Fire is still invisible and unmanifest, but it represents the burning desire and longing for light to appear and stabilize through Earth. After Wood bursts forth spontaneously from "don't know"—the darkness of the Water Element—it generates momentum and movement, a spark that creates the warmth, friction, and direction that we call the Fire Element. If Wood represents the Eternal Now, Fire then represents the generative flow and direction of Time moving forward. It creates energy, power, and transformation. Fire Inner Nature, then, is all about the burning drive to overcome duality, and it presents as inner valor, intensity, and courage.

The spiritual essence of the person with a Fire Inner Nature is driven, and they are all about risk, struggle, and overcoming. Their consciousness is on fire, and the spiritual path is an imperative. They must confront obstacles, and it is through daring discovery, victory, and breakthrough that they find release. The realization of Inner Fire is a revelation of light, and it is sudden. They find it by hurling themselves forward into the unknown as if driven by a mad longing to see the face of the divine and unite with Dao. Fire illuminates, consumes, and transforms.

The deep inner experience of the Inner Fire person is a fearless confrontation with life and death, seeking life, light, and illumination, seeking to manifest fully into the Earth Element. While Wood is poised in equanimity in the freshness of the Now, Fire is rebellious, destructive, surprising, overcoming, energizing, and exciting. It catalyzes, stimulates, and activates. It consumes the Inner Fire person with love and longing and pushes them to the brink in search of revelation.

Practice

As such, the Inner Fire person is adept at warriorship and yoga. They must find presence in movement and in an inner battle to strike to the heart of things with precision. They thrive in martial arts practices and are like samurai, willing to die in battle to achieve enlightenment. They define traditions of sudden enlightenment, like Linji Chan or Rinzai Zen Buddhism, as opposed to Soto Zen, which is more Wood. They can excel as tantrikas in the practice of Kundalini, Hatha, and Tibetan Tummo, or Inner Fire, Yoga and as chodpas, Aghoris, shamans, exorcists, and as intense devotees and selfless servants. Embodied practices of yoga with breathwork, channels, chakras, and bindus as well as practices of visualization, ritual, chanting, and offering are profound for the Inner Fire person, especially those involving fire and light. Their practice should burn with passion, longing, and the desire to awaken.

When fully awake, the Inner Fire person will throw themselves off a cliff if it means attaining enlightenment. They do not need an organized path, religious precepts, or progressive stages of practice. They need only to confront their deepest fears and blockages and consume their ego in deep self-reflection, focused meditation, and unrelenting discipline. They will stop at nothing to wake up, and they will do anything if it means finding true freedom. Spiritually, the Inner Fire person must stay focused and find their devotion and longing. Inner Fire is all about momentum and fearlessness. They are Courageous Warriors, fearless and determined, ready to overcome all obstacles and consume duality.

NEI DI (内地), INNER EARTH—THE DYNASTIC RULER

We call Nei Di the Dynastic Ruler, as Earth is the stable, manifest center around which all the other Elements move. It rules as the central pivot point and represents the continuity of time and tradition. Wood and Fire are invisible. Wood is birth and creation, and Fire generates warmth through movement in the direction of manifestation into form. Earth is the appearance and stabilization of light as apparent form. It is the still center, representing abundance, form, and wealth.

The spiritual essence of the person with Earth Inner Nature is all about tradition, memory, and Ancestors; it is about connecting to the greatness and continuity of what has been established and affirmed, what is tried and true. The nature of their consciousness is stable, still, and deeply connected to the memory of their past lives and Ancestors. It is connected to the history of their people and land. Earth Inner Nature is not pushed or pulled inwardly, but rather their essence is stable, supportive, nourishing, solid, and grounded.

The person with Earth Inner Nature will seek to follow tradition and connect with the stream of the past and express it forward into the future. They respond to traditional iconography and confident, secure visions of the divine. Spiritually, they want to connect to the tradition of people and place through established religion and rituals. They will feel deeply connected to human expression of the sacred through temples, monuments, sacred texts, chants, prayers, and rituals as old as humanity itself. When they step into places where humans have prayed for generations or chant a prayer that has been spoken for millennia, their hearts open and they can feel one with that continuity.

Practice

As such, the person with Earth Inner Nature should seek tradition and to connect to their Ancestors—everyone should, of course, but for the Earth Inner Nature, it is an imperative. Voices and hearts will speak through the past and call toward leadership and to hold and preserve knowledge and wisdom for future generations.

Any established religion or tradition will do, but especially if it is connected to Ancestors. People with Earth Inner Nature are the most adept at becoming lineage holders: monks, nuns, priests, saints, prophets, gurus, lamas, rabbis, ministers, mullahs, and imams. If they are not called to leadership, they may become temple or library builders, ritualists, community organizers, sponsors, donors, and maintainers of tradition. They are a bridge between tradition and the rest of the world.

They should study classical language and text and memorize and preserve oral teachings. And they should respect, honor, and follow tradition and teachers. Inner Earth people do their best to follow a teacher, guru, lama, or the like with love and devotion, as they make excellent devotees and disciples. They thrive with a clear, established path with steps, stages, and rites of passage. They need clear instructions and prescriptions given with authority, and they should develop devotion, trust, and faith in their teachers and traditions.

Of course, today, teachers need to be well vetted, but Earth Inner Nature needs this guidance because it responds to tradition rather than invention, intellect, or rhetoric. Spiritually, the person with an Earth Inner Nature should open their hearts, resonate, and merge with the collective experience of the past, the Ancestors, and the enlightened teachers who came before them.

NEI JIN (内金), INNER METAL—THE SCHOLAR OR ALCHEMIST

We call Nei Jin the Scholar or Alchemist, as Metal is the refinement, distillation, and stripping away of things to their essence. Wood is birth and creation, and Fire is the warmth and movement of manifestation seeking form. Earth is the appearance and stabilization of light as apparent form, and then Metal is the crystallization of that form into separate and distinct entities. It refines apparent form into what the Chinese call the Myriad or Ten Thousand Things. Metal, then, defines the intellect, imagination, and mental precision.

The spiritual essence of the person with a Metal Inner Nature is all about what the Chinese call Nei Dan (内丹), or Inner Alchemy. It is about refinement, esoterica, and the inward withdrawal from the outer world into the active inner world of intellect and imagination. By nature, the Inner Metal person's consciousness is cutting, piercing, and precise. They must use their minds and intellect and should not shun or avoid their mental faculties.

The conceptual mind is a powerful tool for the Inner Metal person, but it is also their greatest enemy, for the conceptual mind and imagination can be like the sword of Mañjuśri (the bodhisattva who represents prajna, "penetrating insight")—that is, they can be used like a knife or scalpel to cut out our delusional thoughts—or instead, they can bind us and create delusion by hardening our concepts. Ultimately, a person with a Metal Inner Nature experiences the emptiness of all beings and things after taking them apart and discovering that all things are "composite," composed of small and smaller things with no ultimate undividable essence that can be found.

The deep inner experience and awakening of the Inner Metal person is a distillation, a stripping away of things to reveal their essence: Emptiness indivisible from Awareness. They are spiritual scientists seeking truth, discovering and refining the interconnectedness of all beings and things. Alchemy is the opposite of chemistry. If chemistry is how things interact, combine, and change to form new things, then alchemy is the process of unwinding those things back to their original components. Spiritually, this involves the practice of meditation, insight, and deep self-reflection and study.

Practice

People with a Metal Inner Nature are, therefore, adept at mentally precise practices rather than general doctrine, universal teachings, and ethical or moral precepts. They will always question, poke, and prod at general doctrine and seek to get to the essence of things. Therefore, they do not respond well to faith- or belief-based traditions. Within these traditions, they will seek apophatic transcendence and to become hermits or monks. They will reform, redefine, and edit wherever they are. They will seek esoteric, inner, and secret knowledge to go beyond symbols to essential truth and direct experience.

Spiritually, Inner Metal people respond to and thrive in traditions with academic and intellectual rigor. They respond well to logic, debate, and traditions like the Madhyamaka school of Buddhist philosophy. They excel at meditation practices like Vipassana, which means "clear seeing."

They are adept at Nei Dan, or Inner Alchemy, as well as visualization practice and yoga that involves channels, chakras, and bindus. Inner Fire does this through burning devotion, but Inner Metal does well with these practices as a cold scientist, refining the channels and bindus into the elixir of immortality. Inner Metal people should study, debate, and refine their ideas with precise clarity and rigor and use ritual as a precise tool.

NEI SHUI (内水), INNER WATER—THE MERCURIAL WIZARD

We call Nei Shui the Mercurial Wizard, as Water is the complete dissolution, return, and resolution of all things into fluidity and death. Again, Wood is birth and creation; Fire is the warmth and movement of manifestation seeking form; Earth is the appearance and stabilization of light as apparent form; and Metal is the crystallization of that form into separate and distinct entities. Water is then the completion and release of that distinction back to death and darkness. It completes the cycle from "don't know" to the known and back again. The Mercurial Wizard is all about feeling and death; Water Inner Nature is a magical river that overflows the brink of conceptuality and returns to the indivisible and inexpressible fluidity and interconnectedness of all beings and things.

The spiritual essence of the person with Water Inner Nature is chaos and catharsis. Their consciousness is close to death and "don't know"; the Great Mother; and Xuan Zhi You Xuan (玄之又玄), the darkness that is darker than darkness, the mystery of mysteries, as expressed in the Dao De Jing. It is from this darkness that the Wood Element is born, and the cycle starts again. Water Inner Nature is the most mysterious, emotional, and tumultuous, for inwardly, the Inner Water person must accept the reckoning of time—that all things eventually die, come apart, and collapse.

The deep inner experience of the person with a Water Inner Nature is found in the inclination to release and return to "don't know." Their consciousness cannot maintain or hold on to definitions, borders, boundaries, identities, or even memories. They find their path through letting go, releasing trapped emotion, and relaxing. They need only to ride the current and follow the river back to the ocean. The Inner Water person finds their path through expansive universality and profound oceanic feelings.

Practice

Like Inner Wood people, people with a Water Inner Nature are adept at "nonconceptual" practices and traditions based on such practices, but for a different reason. People with Inner Wood are poised in the freshness of the Now before a thought is formed, while Inner Water people cannot hold on to anything and naturally relax and release things without effort. Zuo Wang, Sitting and Forgetting, then, is an excellent Inner Water practice, and people with a Water Inner Nature can practice Sitting and Forgetting as their primary path, and need not go beyond this if they do not wish.

Traditions like Wuwei Daoism, Caodong Chan and Soto Zen Buddhism, Dzogchen, Shambavopaya and Anupaya

Shaivism, and apophatic prayer in Western mysticism are also very Inner Water. People with Inner Water should practice the yogas of sleep, dream, and death as a path, for these are all in the realm of Water. Sleep and Dream Yoga and contemplations of impermanence and death should be central.

Spiritually, Inner Water people respond to profound universal teachings and a loving community yet thrive in chaos, mystery, and darkness. They can try to follow tradition and well-established paths, but these are futile in the long run, for they need only to relax and release into death before they die. They do not respond to esoteric knowledge or doctrinal specificity but are naturally eclectic and fluid synthesizers. They can connect with and express the ineffable mysteries and become inspired teachers and healers. They experience awakening through cathartic release and are poised to experience liberation at the time of death.

CONCLUSION

Great Completion and the Dao of Astrology

It is important to understand that participation in any of the Asian contemplative traditions is not simply a means to achieve expertise—it is committing to a lifelong path of self-cultivation. In Asian traditions, education is not only a method of gaining knowledge, but also of developing empathy and a way to artfully express that empathy in the world. Empathy develops when we abandon the notion that expertise is a kind of perfection. In fact, recognizing that we are irreversibly the way we are is a truly great accomplishment. As it turns out, great accomplishment does not offer certainty.

—*Liu Ming*[1]

POLESTAR ASTROLOGY IS A PROFOUND AND UNIQUE TRADITION. If you have made it this far, I hope you have begun to taste some of the wisdom this path has to offer, and I suppose it is time to review and leave you with some parting words. What I have given you here only skims the surface of this tradition, and interestingly, what you find here may resemble little to nothing of the Zi Wei Dou Shu you find elsewhere. As I stated in the beginning, this book was inspired by the unique but often enigmatic teachings of the late Liu Ming. However, as I also stated in the beginning, I do not officially represent Liu Ming or his school. I am just an avid student of his work. So, this book is a synthesis of the public teachings he left behind mixed with the experience and insights I have developed from grappling with these teachings over the past decade as an active Polestar Astrologer.

This book is not meant to be a comprehensive guide, for that would be impossible to create. Instead, it is intended to be a practical overview of what is most important, a basis for astrological interpretation and self-reflection, and an outline of how to use this tradition as part of a spiritual path. I have done my best to honor and synthesize the legacy teachings of Liu Ming as well as the cultural and religious origins of this tradition from ancient China while at the same time bringing these teachings into more modern parlance. I have also done my best to write this book from my perspective by offering examples from my life and family. So, of course, Liu Ming's influence can be felt on every page, but I also hope that my voice and understanding have shined through. As I said in the beginning, the style of this book is called Fu (賦) in Chinese literature, which means "to compose or rhapsodize," and it came from rhapsody with great enthusiasm and delight.

So, what is important? Let's review. As the quote from Liu Ming says, this practice "is not simply a means to achieve expertise—it is committing to a lifelong path of self-cultivation." The education here is "not only a method of gaining knowledge, but also of developing empathy and a way to artfully express that empathy in the world." In other words, the details and "information" presented in this book are not what is important. Details are easy enough to learn, and there are a lot of them. It is also easy to get overwhelmed and miss the point. The point is to commit to a lifelong path of self-cultivation and to stick to it within a consistent framework. This tradition is potentially a complete spiritual path if you follow it correctly, but to practice it requires a solid outline of the path, a framework, which I have tried to give you in this book.

To create a complete path, we must develop a meditation practice and continue to study and self-reflect on the teachings in an ongoing feedback loop that propels us toward our intended Fruition. This is what Buddhism calls the Three Trainings of learning, contemplation, and meditation, which must be applied to the View, which gives us eyes to see the path, the Method, which provides us with the feet to walk it, and the Fruition, which gives us a destination. This is how we eventually discover the Dao of Astrology, develop wisdom and empathy, and begin to artfully express this empathy in the world, as Ming puts it. But what does this mean?

It means that human beings and human life are incredibly complex and subtle. We cannot hope to understand life by dissecting it into a billion details, like taking a watch apart to find the time. A scalpel can remove suffering, but it can also inflict pain without anesthetic. The many details of Chinese astrology can become sharp edges, and we can use them to hurt ourselves and others if we misuse them. If we rush to become "expert" astrologers and amass sharp details, we may begin cutting and inflicting wounds. We may get overwhelmed, confused, and miss the forest for the trees. We may even become judgmental maniacs and use astrology to exalt ourselves or put down others. The anesthetic here is the wisdom of associative symbolic thinking, and in the case of the mantic artist, it is to express that wisdom with empathy and compassion with just a bit of reluctance.

In other words, don't be afraid to get out there and use this tradition, but hold back just a bit. As Ming's teacher might say, practice with enthusiasm . . . but not that much. Strike a curious balance between inspiration and caution. Play with astrology, but know that you will make some mistakes. You may confuse yourself and others, but you will also have great insights and discoveries. Approach this with curiosity, humility, and a healthy amount of doubt. Don't be a true believer, but don't be a needlessly cynical skeptic. Use it to find its value. As the Buddha once said, "Just as a goldsmith tests gold by rubbing, burning, and cutting before buying it, so too, you should examine my words before accepting them, and not just out of respect for me."[2] So, test the ideas and symbols here, and if you find them powerful, as I do, come back to them and go a bit deeper. With every insight, come back and then go a bit deeper still.

And remember, this is not fortune-telling. Be careful with what you say to people and what you tell yourself. Astrology has the power to awaken and mislead. Be cautious about giving advice or predictions. An astrology reading can change someone's life and have profound consequences. I have had people quit their jobs, move, and end relationships after a reading. So, don't be a fortune teller; give people as many options and interpretations as possible. Let them choose, and remember we are not trying to predict but rather see the world through a different lens, through a dialogue with symbols. To do this, we must change our way of thinking and perceiving. We must reorient ourselves to think like the ancient Chinese masters.

The wisdom of the ancient Chinese masters comes from associative thinking and through the understanding of symbols, which form the big categories and ideas, for it is in these categories that we pile the details and begin to make sense of them. As I have stated throughout this book, the wisdom of the Chinese Tradition and Polestar Astrology comes through the study of heavenly symbols, Tian Xiang (天象), for symbols are the first manifestation into duality from the non-dual Dao, and everything that we can perceive flows from 天 (Heaven) through 象 (symbols).

The most important symbols presented in this book are Dao; Huntun; Yinyang; the Five Elements; Ancestors or Ancestral Qi; the Ten Heavenly Stems and Twelve Earthly Branches or Animals of the Zodiac, representing Character;

the Twelve Houses and Thirty-Six Stars of the Polestar System, representing Fate; and the Five Inner Natures. My heartfelt advice is to study these symbols deeply, contemplate them, and apply them to your life; learn to play with them, but please hold them lightly, for they are not rigid boxes but flowing rivers. These are 象 that form principles through which the laws of the universe manifest the mess we call human life. We know human nature is good, but good luck seeing this in our recorded history. We know nature is ordered, but good luck finding straight lines out there. We can only make sense of the mess through association based on philosophical principles.

Associative thinking with a light touch softens our minds and hearts by softening our hardened concepts about reality. The more we perceive everything as a play of symbols, the less rigid we are and the more creative and dynamic our minds become. We then develop empathy and compassion, because we understand that nothing is established in the way it appears; everything is impermanent and in flux, in the process of changing into something else. All our suffering is created by trying to maintain rigid concepts about a separate self and world. We can let go, forgive, and empathize with others who make the same mistakes, because we are all human and bound by the same principles of Character and Fate. The more you see the symbols of Character and Fate come to life through the study and practice of Polestar Astrology, the more we see that our so-called unique experiences of self and suffering are as common as dirt. Knowing this, we can become artful.

I will leave you with some words from Liu Ming:

> When we see how to disentangle our Qi from our Fated debts and patterns of aggression, we can taste the freedom of our true nature. This nature is Freedom with a hue or flavor [one of the Five Elements] but no predetermined agenda. This nature relates openly with its so-called environment—clients, calendars, and lineage. Our vision of a "self in a world" changes if we have truly resolved Fate and ended the patterns of creating new Fate. If Fate is not resolved, we visit this vision but cannot open it and "stay." If we study hard and use our knowledge to help others, our intent (found in our deep nature) becomes clearer and stronger. This is the Dao of mantic arts/science. If we cling to the intent to benefit self, we remain theorists—visitors to freedom. From consistent application of study and practice, Freedom becomes the base. This base is envisioned as open space full of dancing light filaments. When our Fate vision (a world) is gone, this is what is "seen." When Freedom is stabilized, natural and relative visions do not seem like TWO. Great Completion is finding our being perfectly situated in the magnificent network of Dao itself. Path changes from formative/relative to art (a truth complete with expression). Great Completion is Great Freedom—devoid of self/other, Character, Fate, Nature, Intent, or View—and at the same time freely generating all Characters, Fates, Nature, Intent, and View.[3]

Great Completion, or Da Yuan (大圓), is the highest expression of enlightenment and Human Freedom. It is said to happen in Four Visions, the final of which is called "crossing over," which culminates in the Rainbow Body, Hong Shen (虹身), as demonstrated by Liu Ming's teacher, in which our identity with the nameless Dao is so seamless that all sense of individuation is released in light. These visions are expressed all over the world as "sacred geometry," as mandalas, yantras, and visions of deities. The experience of Great Completion is irreversible, and it is the Ocean of Wisdom to which we all return.

BIBLIOGRAPHY

Belyea, Charles, and Steven Tainer. *Dragon's Play: A New Daoist Transmission of the Complete Experience of Human Life.* Great Circle Lifeworks, 1991.

Da Yuan Circle. "Polestar Astrology," www.dayuancircle.org/collections/polestar-astrology.

Done, Gregory, David Done, and Robert Churchill. *The Great Equinox: Three Generations, Four Voices.* Albion-Andalus Books, 2015.

Dzogchen Ponlop. "The Three Trainings." In *Rebel Buddha: On the Road to Freedom.* Boston: Shambhala, 2010.

Gibbs, Darren. *Class Text/Notes.* Da Yuan Circle, 2017–2021. PDF. Accessed December 7, 2025. PDF. www.dayuancircle.org and in DYC app.

Hammond, Holly. "Being Human Is Nothing Extraordinary: An Interview with Liu Ming." *Yoga Journal* (May/June 1995): 72–75, 143–145. www.biroco.com/yijing/liu_ming_yoga_journal_interview.pdf.

Knechtges, David R. "From the Eastern Han through the Western Jin (AD 25–317)." In *The Cambridge History of Chinese Literature, Volume 1: To 1375*, edited by Stephen Owen. Cambridge University Press, 2010. pp. 116–198.

Komjathy, Louis. "Tracing the Contours of Daoism in North America." *Nova Religio* 8, no. 2 (2004): 5–27. https://doi.org/10.1525/nr.2004.8.2.5.

Kroll, Paul W. *A Student's Dictionary of Classical and Medieval Chinese.* Rev. ed. Brill, 2012–17.

Lim, Y. M. *The Empyrean Matrix: A Guide to Purple Star Astrology (Zi Wei Dou Shu).* CreateSpace, 2013.

Man-Ho, Kwok. *The Complete Book of Chinese Horoscopes.* Sunburst Books, 1995.

Ming, Liu. *Changing: Zhouyi: The Heart of the Yijing.* Da Yuan Circle, 2005.

Ming, Liu. *Class Notes.* Chinese Polestar Astrology: Recorded Lectures (Da Yuan Circle, 2012), PDF. Accessed December 7, 2025. www.dayuancircle.org.

Ming, Liu. *Class Notes.* Healing Apprenticeship Possession: Recorded Lectures (Da Yuan Circle, 2011), PDF. Accessed December 7, 2025. www.dayuancircle.org.

Ming, Liu. *Class Notes.* Sleep, Dream, and the Dao of the Night: Recorded Lectures (Da Yuan Circle, 2007–08), PDF. Accessed December 7, 2025. www.dayuancircle.org.

Ming, Liu. *Facets: An Inner Journey Through Asia.* Da Yuan Circle, 2016.

Ming, Liu. *Yin Metal Rabbit New Year's Program Notes.* Da Yuan Circle, 2011.

Ming, Liu, trans. *Observing: Wuwei: The Heart of the Daodejing.* Edited by Daniel Burgess, Jason Luban, Christine Wallis, Michael Zhai, Da Yuan Circle, and 101 Editions. Da Yuan Circle, 2016.

Phillips, Scott P. "Portrait of an American Daoist: Charles Belyea / Liu Ming." *Journal of Daoist Studies* 1, no. 1 (January 2008): 161–176.

Roberts, Bernadette. *The Experience of No-Self: A Contemplative Journey.* State University of New York, 1993.

Walters, Derek. *The Complete Guide to Chinese Astrology: The Most Comprehensive Study of the Subject Ever Published in the English Language.* Watkins, 2005.

Zhuangzi. *The Complete Works of Zhuangzi.* Translated by Burton Watson. Columbia University Press, 2013.

NOTES

LIU MING AND THE CHINESE TRADITION

1. Liu Ming, *Yin Metal Rabbit New Year's Program Notes* (Da Yuan Circle, 2011).
2. Da Yuan Circle, www.dayuancircle.org.
3. "Liu Ming," Da Yuan Circle, accessed August 21, 2023, www.dayuancircle.org/pages/liu-ming.
4. Scott P. Phillips, "Portrait of an American Daoist: Charles Belyea / Liu Ming," *Journal of Daoist Studies* 1, no. 1 (January 2008): 161–176.
5. "Liu Ming," Da Yuan Circle, accessed August 21, 2023, www.dayuancircle.org/pages/liu-ming.
6. Phillips, "Portrait of an American Daoist," 166.
7. Today, Dharma Bodhi's school is called Trika Mahasiddha Yoga, www.trikapath.com.
8. Liu Ming, *Observing: Wuwei: The Heart of the Daodejing* (Da Yuan Circle, 2016).
9. About, Trika Mahasiddha Yoga, accessed September 15, 2024, www.trikapath.com/about/#dharma.
10. For a more detailed background story, please see *The Great Equinox: Three Generations, Four Voices* (Albion-Andalus Books, 2015).
11. See the works of Alexis Sanderson.
12. Charles Belyea, *Dragon's Play: A New Taoist Transmission of the Complete Experience of Human Life* (Great Circle Lifeworks, 1991).

AN INTRODUCTION TO THE SYSTEM AND PRACTICE OF ZI WEI DOU SHU (紫微斗數), OR POLESTAR ASTROLOGY

1. Destiny and Luck, www.destinyandluck.com.
2. Sunburst Books, 1995.
3. CreateSpace, 2013.

ZI WEI DOU SHU (紫微斗數)

1. Y. M. Lim. *The Empyrean Matrix: A Guide to Purple Star Astrology (Zi Wei Dou Shu)* (CreateSpace, 2013), 3.
2. Paul W. Kroll, "Zǐ , 紫," in *A Student's Dictionary of Classical and Medieval Chinese*, rev. ed. (Brill, 2012–17).
3. Derek Walters, *The Complete Guide to Chinese Astrology: The Most Comprehensive Study of the Subject Ever Published in the English Language* (Watkins, 2005).

THE THREEFOLD TRAINING OR SAN HUI (三慧)

1. *Rebel Buddha: On the Road to Freedom* (Shambhala, 2010), 80.

THE THREE MOTIVES OF THE MANTIC ARTS

1. Liu Ming, *Class Notes: Chinese Polestar Astrology* (Da Yuan Circle, 2012), accessed December 7, 2025, PDF in DYC Polestar app.
2. Liu Ming, *Class Notes: Sleep, Dream, and the Dao of the Night*: Recorded Lectures (Dream Notes 5, Da Yuan Circle, 2012), PDF, accessed December 22, 2025, www.dayuancircle.org, 5.

3. Ming, *Class Notes: Sleep, Dream, and the Dao of the Night.*
4. Ming, *Class Notes: Sleep, Dream, and the Dao of the Night*, 4.
5. Liu Ming, *Class Notes: Healing Apprenticeship Possession* (Da Yuan Circle, 2011), PDF, accessed December 7, 2025, www.dayuancircle.org. This section is adapted from Liu Ming's teachings on possession.
6. "Polestar Astrology," Da Yuan Circle, www.dayuancircle.org/collections/polestar-astrology.
7. "Polestar Astrology," Da Yuan Circle.
8. Liu Ming. *Yin Metal Rabbit New Year's Program Notes* (Da Yuan Circle, 2011), 1.

SITTING AND FORGETTING, ZUO WANG (坐忘)

1. Liu Ming, *Observing: Wuwei: The Heart of the Daodejing* (Da Yuan Circle, 2016), 236.
2. Liu Ming, *Observing: Wuwei*, 239.
3. "Seven-Point Posture of Vairochana - Rigpa Wiki." n.d. www.rigpawiki.org. www.rigpawiki.org/index.php?title=Seven-point_posture_of_Vairochana. These points are listed in different orders in different sources. This follows the order as found in Khenpo Ngakchung's Zindri, page 42.

WHAT IS THE UNIVERSE? THE RESOLUTION OF FATE

1. Bernadette Roberts. *The Experience of No-Self: A Contemplative Journey* (State University of New York, 1993), 108–09.

NON-THEISM, NON-MATERIALISM, AND THE FIVE ELEMENTS

1. *Monty Python's The Meaning of Life*, directed by Terry Jones (Universal Pictures, 1983).

THE TWELVE CHARACTERS OF DESTINY, PART 10: MONKEY QI

1. *The Complete Works of Zhuangzi*, trans. Burton Watson (Columbia University Press, 2013).

THE TWELVE HOUSES OF POLESTAR ASTROLOGY

1. Reproduction of the Suzhou star chart (thirteenth century), BabelStone, www.babelstone.co.uk/China/Images/1247Planisphere.jpg.

THE FOUR RULERS

1. Photo by Patrick McManaman, July 31, 2016, Unsplash, https://unsplash.com/photos/LN_g3qA8ohg?utm_source=unsplash&utm_medium=referral&utm_content=creditShareLink.
2. Paul W. Kroll, "Zǐ, 紫," in *A Student's Dictionary of Classical and Medieval Chinese*, rev. ed. (Brill, 2012–17).
3. Kroll, "Wēi, 微."
4. Liu Ming, *Class Notes: Emperor*, Chinese Polestar Astrology: Recorded Lectures (Da Yuan Circle, 2012), accessed December 7, 2025, PDF in DYC Polestar app.
5. Kroll, "Tiān, 天." This translation applies to all the stars that share this character.
6. Kroll, "Fǔ, 府."
7. Ming, *Class Notes: Empress.*
8. Kroll, "Tiān, 天."
9. Kroll, "Xiàng, 相."
10. Ming, *Class Notes: Tutor.*
11. Kroll, "Tiān, 天."
12. Kroll, "Ji - 機."
13. Ming, *Class Notes: Oracle.*

THE FOUR HONORABLES

1. Paul W. Kroll, "Tài, 太," in *A Student's Dictionary of Classical and Medieval Chinese*, rev. ed. (Brill, 2012–17).
2. Kroll, "Yáng, 陽."
3. Liu Ming, *Class Notes: Sun*, Chinese Polestar Astrology: Recorded Lectures (Da Yuan Circle, 2012), accessed December 7, 2025, PDF in DYC Polestar app.
4. Kroll, "Wǔ, 武."
5. Kroll, "Qū, 曲."
6. Ming, *Class Notes: General.*
7. Kroll, "Tài, 太."
8. Kroll, "Yin, 陰."
9. Ming, *Class Notes*: Moon
10. Kroll, "Jù, 巨."
11. Kroll, "Mén, 門."
12. Ming, *Class Notes: Great Gate.*

THE FOUR HIGH RANKING STARS

1. Paul W. Kroll, "Tiān, 天," in *A Student's Dictionary of Classical and Medieval Chinese*, rev. ed. (Brill, 2012–17).
2. Kroll, "Tóng, 同."
3. Liu Ming, *Class Notes: Vassal*, Chinese Polestar Astrology: Recorded Lectures (Da Yuan Circle, 2012), accessed December 7, 2025, PDF in DYC Polestar app.
4. Kroll, "Tiān, 天."
5. Kroll, "Liáng, 梁."
6. Ming, *Class Notes: Roof Beam.*
7. Kroll, "Wén, 文."
8. Kroll, "Chāng, 昌."
9. Ming, *Class Notes: Magistrate.*
10. Kroll, "Wén, 文."
11. Kroll, "Qū, 曲."
12. Ming, *Class Notes: Priest.*

THE FOUR MAJOR GHOSTS

1. Paul W. Kroll, "Lián, 廉," in *A Student's Dictionary of Classical and Medieval Chinese*, rev. ed. (Brill, 2012–17).
2. Kroll, "Zhēn, 貞."
3. Liu Ming, *Class Notes: Concubine*, Chinese Polestar Astrology: Recorded Lectures (Da Yuan Circle, 2012), accessed December 7, 2025, PDF in DYC Polestar app.
4. "Intimate Partner Violence, Sexual Violence, and Stalking among Men," Centers for Disease Control and Prevention, Centers for Disease Control and Prevention, accessed December 7, 2025, www.cdc.gov/intimate-partner-violence/about/intimate-partner-violence-sexual-violence-and-stalking-among-men.html.
5. Kroll, "Qi, 七."
6. Kroll, "Shā, 殺."
7. Ming, *Class Notes: Seven Killings.*
8. Kroll, "Tān, 貪."
9. Kroll, "Láng, 狼."
10. Ming, *Class Notes: Greedy Wolf.*

11. Kroll, "Pò, 破."
12. Kroll, "Jūn, 軍."
13. Ming, *Class Notes: Rebel.*

THE FOUR MINOR GHOSTS

1. Paul W. Kroll, "Huǒ, 火," in *A Student's Dictionary of Classical and Medieval Chinese*, rev. ed. (Brill, 2012–17).
2. Kroll, "Xing, 星."
3. Liu Ming, *Class Notes: Fire Star*, Chinese Polestar Astrology: Recorded Lectures (Da Yuan Circle, 2012), accessed December 7, 2025, PDF in DYC Polestar app.
4. Kroll, "Líng, 鈴."
5. Kroll, "Xing, 星."
6. Ming, *Class Notes: Water Star.*
7. Kroll, "Qíng, 擎."
8. Kroll, "Yáng, 羊."
9. Kroll, "Rèn, 刃."
10. Ming, *Class Notes: Goat Blade.*
11. Kroll, "Tuó, 駝."
12. Kroll, "Luó, 羅."
13. Ming, *Class Notes: Humpback.*

THE FOUR INCIDENTALS

1. Paul W. Kroll, "Yòu, 右," in *A Student's Dictionary of Classical and Medieval Chinese*, rev. ed. (Brill, 2012–17).
2. Kroll, "Bì, 弼."
3. Kroll, "Zuǒ, 左."
4. Kroll, "Fǔ, 輔."
5. Kroll, "Lù, 祿."
6. Kroll, "Cún, 存."
7. Kroll, "Tiān, 天."
8. Kroll, "Yáo, 姚."

THE ORPHAN SPIRITS

1. Kroll, "Tiān, 天."
2. Kroll, "Kuí, 魁."
3. Kroll, "Tiān, 天."
4. Kroll, "Xǐ, 喜."
5. Kroll, "Tiān, 天."
6. Kroll, "Yuè, 鉞."
7. Kroll, "Di, 地."
8. Kroll, "Jié, 劫."
9. Kroll, "Di, 地."
10. Kroll, "Kōng, 空."
11. Kroll, "Tiān, 天."
12. Kroll, "Xíng, 刑."
13. Kroll, "Tiān, 天."
14. Kroll, "Mǎ, 馬."

15. Kroll, "Hóng, 紅."
16. Kroll, "Luán, 鸞."

THE FOUR TRANSFORMERS

1. Paul W. Kroll, "Huà, 化," in *A Student's Dictionary of Classical and Medieval Chinese*, rev. ed. (Brill, 2012–17).
2. Kroll, "Lù, 祿."
3. Kroll, "Huà, 化."
4. Kroll, "Quán, 權."
5. Kroll, "Huà, 化."
6. Kroll, "Kē, 科."
7. Kroll, "Huà, 化."
8. Kroll, "Jì, 忌."

EXAMPLE CHARTS

1. Gregory Done, David Done, and Robert Churchill, *The Great Equinox: Three Generations, Four Voices* (Albion-Andalus Books, 2015).

INNER NATURE AND THE RESOLUTION OF CHARACTER AND FATE

1. Liu Ming, *Class #13 Notes*, in Chinese Polestar Astrology: Recorded Lectures (Da Yuan Circle, 2012), PDF, accessed December 7, 2025, www.dayuancircle.org.
2. Liu Ming, "Introduction to the Mantic Arts of China: Five Elements and Inner Nature," in *Chinese Polestar Astrology: Recorded Lectures* (Da Yuan Circle, 2012).

CONCLUSION

1. "Liu Ming," Da Yuan Circle, accessed August 21, 2023, www.dayuancircle.org/pages/liu-ming.
2. From Santaraksita's Tattvasamgraha.
3. Liu Ming, "Class #13 Notes," in *Chinese Polestar Astrology: Recorded Lectures* (Da Yuan Circle, 2012), PDF, accessed December 7, 2025, www.dayuancircle.org.